The Economic System
in the U.K.

THE ECONOMIC
SYSTEM
IN THE U.K.

EDITED BY
DEREK MORRIS

OXFORD UNIVERSITY PRESS
1977

Oxford University Press, Walton Street, Oxford OX2 6DP

OXFORD LONDON GLASGOW NEW YORK
TORONTO MELBOURNE WELLINGTON CAPE TOWN
IBADAN NAIROBI DAR ES SALAAM LUSAKA ADDIS ABABA
KUALA LUMPUR SINGAPORE JAKARTA HONG KONG TOKYO
DELHI BOMBAY CALCUTTA MADRAS KARACHI

CASEBOUND ISBN 0 19 877077 4

PAPERBACK ISBN 0 19 877078 2

© Introduction Selection, Chapters 3, 19, 20 and editorial matter Derek Morris
© Chapters 2 and 6 H. G. Jones
© Chapters 4 and 15 M. J. C. Surrey
© Chapters 5 and 11 P. J. N. Sinclair
© Chapters 7 and 9 A. W. M. Graham
© Chapters 8 and 14 C. J. Allsopp
© Chapter 10 D. Robinson
© Chapter 12 R. G. Smethurst
© Chapter 13 P. J. N. Sinclair and R. G. Smethurst
© Chapter 16 C. J. M. Hardie
© Chapter 17 D. K. Stout
© Chapter 18 D. L. Bevan
© 1977

Printed in Great Britain
Typeset by Western Printing Services Ltd, Bristol
Printed by photolithography and bound at
The Pitman Press, Bath

For
Norman, George, and Ray Kidwell Q.C
and in memory of
Neville Ward Perkins

Preface

This book is mainly, though not exclusively, intended for non-specialist and certain specialist students in economics (see p. 5). It attempts to explain the general principles underlying both the working of the U.K. economy and Government economic policy whilst meeting two other objectives. These are, first, that it should be intelligible to the introductory reader who is prepared to study it carefully, whether he or she is a student or a member of the general public, and, second, that at the same time, the book should examine at least some of the complexities which are frequently excluded in introductory texts but which cannot be avoided in the day-to-day management of the economy. (See section 1.2 of Chapter 1 for further discussion of these objectives.)

Some of the chapters are based on pamphlets which have been used for teaching applied economics to students over a number of years. But these pamphlets, and indeed part of the rationale for this book, arose out of a rather unusual and possibly unique form of economics teaching that has been developing in the last two decades.

In 1953 a group of industrialists and academics from Oxford University met with the intention of establishing a permanent vehicle for mutual discussion on the state of the economy, its impact on industry, the development of management techniques, and other related economic matters. A precedent existed for such contact in an earlier series of interviews with businessmen conducted by several economists from the University which had been designed to explore the validity of current economic theory as it applied to the industrial sector.

This meeting resulted in the formation of the Oxford University Business Summer School which has now been held every July for twenty-three years. It is of four weeks' duration and has developed into an intensive course in economics for middle-level managers from the public and private sectors, primarily those who are regarded by their companies or departments as likely to reach board level or its equivalent and who are therefore likely to require a good understanding of how the economy works and how it impinges on companies' behaviour, objectives, and performance.

The school is staffed by a number of academic economists, all of whom are involved in direct application of economic analysis to practical problems either in the private or public sector, and all of whom therefore have an interest in regularly exploring and developing the usefulness of economic theory when applied to the real world. In addition, there are lectures by the tutors and by outside economists, leading industrialists, politicians, and others.

Lack of satisfaction with the economics books available to back up such a course led to the writing of internal pamphlets which subsequently, with some modification, were also found to be useful for certain students. The format and perspective, which were rather different from most textbooks, appeared to have certain advantages but the range and cohesion of the pamphlets taken together were not always adequate or appropriate. This book developed from the attempt to overcome these drawbacks. The range of economic policies discussed was extended, the level of detail increased, and a section added to provide a necessary basic introduction to the operation of the economy. It is hoped that the resulting book provides a series of useful articles on specific issues, but also a coherent introduction to the working of the U.K. economy as a whole.

Most contributors are past or present tutors of the University Business Summer School. Most have written on a topic of particular interest to themselves and in areas where they are heavily committed to extensive advisory work on top of their academic commitments. This naturally leads to difference of viewpoint and emphasis. In certain cases contributors have strong opinions which may or may not concur with the prevailing orthodoxy. A certain amount of editorial licence has therefore been used, not to remove such differences, but to present as far as possible a framework within which different schools of thought can be described, compared, and evaluated. Unnecessary duplication has been avoided where possible, but different chapters have occasionally required re-presentation and development of earlier points to preserve the sense or flow of argument.

Several contributors have offered comments and criticism on other chapters, and the editor is indebted to them for this. Similarly, a number of anonymous reviewers have provided detailed comments and criticisms on early drafts, and suggestions for the final one. This has proved extremely helpful. The assistance of various students in reading and commenting on several chapters has likewise proved invaluable. All remaining errors of fact, argument, or judgement are of course our responsibility alone. The contributors' thanks are also due to those who cheerfully helped to type both early and final drafts: Pip Bevan, Jean Brown, Angela Fossett, Clare Jones, Peggy Smith, Joe Wilkins, and typists at the Oxford Institute of Economics and Statistics.

Finally, because of the very heavy commitments each contributor already faced, both within the University to teaching and research and frequently outside it in an advisory capacity, most of the work of writing this book has had to come out of already greatly squeezed leisure time. We would all like to thank very much those in our personal lives who have borne the brunt of this pressure.

DEREK MORRIS

Oriel College, Oxford
21 March 1976

Contents

PART I

PART II

PART III

PART I

I

Introduction

D. J. MORRIS

1. Background to the Book

1.1. The Performance of the U.K. Economy

The impact of the economy on all aspects of life has never been more evident. Governments, politicians, and civil servants are more preoccupied with economic performance both domestically and internationally than ever before; company sales, costs, and profits are increasingly determined more by the general level of activity in the economy than by the efforts and ability of the companies themselves to improve their performance. At both managerial and shop-floor level the number of jobs available as well as the incomes received are often seen as more dependent on the state of the national economy and nationwide policies on employment and incomes than on the decisions of the particular company concerned. Most important of all, individual living standards are seen as determined by factors which lie far beyond the ability of the individual to influence, and this is true whether the individual is an employer or employee, a housewife, pensioner, student, or child

This impact would have been less worrying and indeed less noticed or emphasized if it had in general been viewed as a beneficial one. In fact, the performance of the U.K. economy has been almost universally regarded as poor, if not disastrous. Three distinct, though not necessarily unrelated, aspects of this performance can be identified. First, in the recent past both unemployment and inflation have hit record levels; the economy has ceased to grow, at least temporarily, and real living standards have on average fallen for the first time since the war; the balance of payments has been in record deficit and the value of the pound internationally has fallen heavily. These have all served to emphasize the dependence of individuals on the performance of the national economy and on the economic actions of other countries, to which this recent performance is partly attributable.

Second, and looking over a somewhat longer period, the U.K. economy has been subject to almost continuous cyclical fluctuations in the general level of activity. These, together with the changes in economic policy associated with it, have created great difficulties for those in the public (government) and private sectors who are attempting to plan for and achieve sustained long-term economic growth and development.

Third, and probably most serious of all, is the poor performance of the U.K. economy over thirty years when compared to nearly all other developed countries in the world. The level of output per man (labour productivity) is relatively low and has increased at a slower rate than in other countries. Living standards have consequently grown at a slower rate than elsewhere. The competitiveness of British goods abroad has been inadequate and has only been sustained through successive depreciations of sterling.

The general result is that while both the causes of, and solutions to, this poor performance are a central topic of discussion and dispute in industrial, academic, and government circles, there is little disagreement with the judgement that the economy has failed to behave as it should. Consumer prices are thought too high, wages too low, production costs too high and profits too low, taxation is frequently regarded as excessive not only by those paying the highest levels, and the provision of goods and services by private companies, nationalized industries, and government agencies is often regarded as inadequate in terms of quantity and quality, or both.

1.2. Purpose of the Book

Two very important repercussions of this situation may be noted. First, there is an increasing need for all those involved in any way in the economic processes of production, distribution, and sales, or in the management of the economy as a whole, to have a good grasp of the fundamentals and some of the complexities involved in the operation of the economy. This includes managers, civil servants, union representatives, and politicians. Many of them feel, in a way which they did not several years ago, that they need the economic training necessary to understand what is happening in the economy, to assess its likely behaviour in the future and to recognize the limitations which interdependence of unions, management, and government places on all three. Their difficulty is the limited time available for this purpose, and it was with this in mind that the Oxford University Business Summer School (despite its somewhat inappropriate title) developed into an intensive one-month course in economics. This book arises out of some of the written material used on the course and therefore retains some of the characteristics of a crash course and, as one objective, the provision of an introduction to economics for those who will have little or no opportunity to pursue an extended course in the subject.

A second repercussion has been a rapidly growing interest in economics on the part of students. This arises partly because it is recognized that the tendency for economic aspects to dominate issues will probably increase, and be reinforced by an ever more rapidly increasing interdependence of the different sectors of the economy on each other in the future economic development of the U.K. This will place ever greater demands on the economic literacy of the future managers, civil servants, and trade unionists which many of today's students will become. In addition, however, it arises from a general and very sensible desire to comprehend the economic issues that constrain and determine so many human activities in all walks of life. An understanding of the very powerful, but often unanalysed, forces at work in society is seen more and more as a central factor in the process of education, and economic forces represent some of the most powerful ones. This book is therefore very much directed at students, and both the original summer school pamphlets and drafts of various chapters have been found useful for student teaching purposes.

As this book is very far from being a conventional introductory textbook it is advisable to be explicit about the two particular types of student for whom it is intended:

First, there is an increasing number of students at universities, polytechnics, business schools, and many other institutions who, though not specializing in economics, nevertheless wish to study it to some extent, so that they will be better informed about their economic environment and better equipped to judge the performance of economists and politicians in the attempts they make to manage the economy. There are all too many cases, however, where the course for such non-specialists has been little more than the introductory work of those doing specialist courses in economics. This is unfortunate as the demands of the two groups are quite different. There are many aspects of economic analysis (often abstract, rigorous, and complex) which are appropriate for a three-year course because there is sufficient time available to reach a relatively high level of sophistication. The introduction to a specialist course therefore rightly emphasizes the tools of analysis, starting with the simplest, most basic ones, and building up gradually. Initially, therefore, it makes sense to abstract from the economic environment and its complexities until the modes of analysis have been grasped. If the non-specialist is provided with only the first part of such a programme he can easily end up with a few pieces of simple deductive theory, little evidence on how to apply them (or even on whether they are applicable at all as they stand), little understanding of the economy, and the misguided belief that economic theory and the real world have little connection.

In fact, the needs of the non-specialist are much closer to those of management, civil servants, etc., namely an introduction to economics which reduces technical analysis to the minimum necessary to understand the systematic forces at work in the economy; which avoids the elaborations required to understand detailed problems that the student will never face, and which are not central to general economic activity; but which nevertheless brings out the complexity of the central issues, permits assessment of the controversies existing in the area of economic policy, and assists the formation of his own judgement on the vast literature on economics poured out each week in newspapers, journals, and all manner of government publications.

Second, some of the later chapters (mainly Parts III and IV) look at difficult, controversial, and often not easily understood areas of economics. These chapters, which are the core of the book, will stretch non-specialists, but should be quite intelligible to them given that they have read the more basic economics in Part II. In addition, however, specialists, for whom Part II would be unnecessary, may well find the later chapters useful material as an introduction to the applied side of their course. These chapters summarize particular areas, identify the main issues and problems, and give some preliminary guidance on their analysis, thus providing a perspective prior to more detailed examination.

There are also, of course, many students not studying economics at all who none the less feel that some understanding of it is essential nowadays. It is hoped that this book will prove useful for them in pursuing this objective.

One other point needs stressing. The content and analysis are almost entirely economic. A number of issues of great interest and concern which have important economic aspects, for example social welfare and housing and environmental policies, are not covered. Many of the economic principles involved are examined, however, so that the text can provide introductory material for those whose course centres on such issues.

To repeat, this is not a textbook of economics in the normal sense. Its aim is to help those without either the time or the inclination to pursue a full economics course to quickly absorb the general principles of economics and economic policy, so that they have a sound basis for critical assessment of the economy, day by day. Neither economic theory, history, nor economic institutions is examined except in so far as it is necessary to this end. The book is elementary in the sense that no previous economics is presumed. It is not elementary, however, in the sense of being highly simplified or very extended in its step-by-step build-up of a picture of the economy. Often a paragraph must suffice where a standard textbook would spend many pages, and from the non-economist it therefore requires careful attention and considerable thought.

Such an approach, dictated by the origin and aim of the book, has evident dangers which must not be conveniently overlooked. Many qualifications and implications can only be hinted at, and much of the argument behind particular conclusions can only be summarized briefly. The most serious problem, however, is that there are still many uncertainties and many controversies (not always in the same areas!) in economics, the reasons for which are discussed below, which complicate the explanation of the corresponding economic phenomena. Every effort has been made, however, to see that the pressures of space have not prevented a statement and some examination of these problems, as they are important elements in the understanding of the current economic situation.

2. Historical Development in Economics

2.1. Pre-Keynesian Economics

It is conventional to define economics as the study of the allocation of scarce resources—in other words the study of who produces which non-freely available goods and services and who receives them. In practice, and in general terms, this means the analysis of the factors, including price, that determine (i) the amount of a product or service which its suppliers wish to supply; (ii) the amount prospective purchasers 'demand', i.e. can and wish to pay for; (iii) the price which then equates the supply and demand; and (iv) the amount of the good or service then exchanged. This approach has been applied to all sorts of 'products' and 'services', including not only tangible goods and intangible services bought and sold, e.g. cars, bread, hair-cuts, insurance, but also different financial assets like company shares, money itself, and also labour services. Each was presumed to have a 'price' deter-mined by supply and demand, though in some cases this 'price' was different from the conventional notion associated with that word. In addition, this approach was applied at various levels; the individual producer, the total market[1] for a product, the economy as a whole.

In each case the same basic market mechanism was presumed to operate unless there was direct interference with it. The essence of this mechanism was, first, that a *market-clearing price* existed in each case, and second, that the market if left to itself would *find* that market-clearing price. If at a going price demand (in the sense given above) exceeded supply then competition amongst potential purchasers to buy would drive the price upward. This would induce suppliers attracted by the higher price to supply more and purchasers discouraged by the higher prices to purchase less. The excess of demand over supply would tend to disappear. This process would continue until the price was reached at which no excess demand existed. This price therefore 'cleared' the market in the sense that supply and demand were now equal, with no supplier left with unwanted stock and no purchaser willing to buy at the prevailing price left unsatisfied.

It was not, of course, suggested that suppliers and customers generally haggle between and amongst themselves to determine the market-clearing price. In most cases it was recognized that suppliers would in the short-term set the prices which any customer had to pay to obtain the product concerned. Rather it was suggested that if manufacturers, wholesalers, and retailers found *over a longer period* that they were unable to meet the demand for a product, then price rises would, if permitted, generally occur. Price reductions would tend to occur if, over a period, suppliers were left holding unsold stock. Given this it appeared reasonable to adopt the market mechanism described above as a simple picture of the long-term tendency inherent in most if not all unrestricted markets.

This essentially very simple and very plausible view of the basic economic force at work in the world has in fact been one of the most controversial ideas propounded this century. Failure to recognize its inappropriateness on the one hand, and persistent refusal to recognize its basic truth on the other, have both been given by different people as reasons for economic and social loss on a vast scale, not least in the U.K. Much of the current contro-versy in economics (which is discussed later) can be traced to disagreement over the extent to which this picture facilitates or distorts analysis of econo-mic problems. In order to explain this it is useful to focus on one particular market to which the analysis has been applied, especially in the early decades of this century, namely the 'market' for labour. The 'price' of labour on which, amongst other things, the supply and demand for labour was supposed to depend was the *real* (as opposed to *money*) wage of that labour. As the

---

[1] By 'market' we simply mean all the suppliers and all the potential customers for a product. No physical maket in a particular location is implied.

distinction between a real and a monetary variable is used repeatedly it will
be useful to emphasize the difference straight away.

A wage of £40 per week is a monetary variable because it is the wage in
terms of *money*. Nothing is said about the wage level in terms of what it could
buy. The latter is known as the *real* wage. For example, if a wage level
doubles from £20 per week to £40 per week, and at the same time the price
of everything available in the shops doubles, it should be clear that in real
terms the wage is unchanged. The recipient can still only buy the same
volume of real goods as before. His money wage has, however, doubled. In
the same way, suppose an individual has an amount of money—£100—in
the bank. This money balance is a monetary variable. If all prices double,
and his money balance stays at £100, his *real* balance is halved—his money
balance will only buy half as much as before. The distinction is important
partly because people may react in different ways to changes in real and
monetary variables, and partly because their impact on people's well-being
will be different.[2]

The supply of labour was argued to be dependent on *real* wages because
over the long term a man deciding whether and how much to work is not
concerned with the number of pounds he earns *per se*, but with what he can
buy with his wage. (This tendency to think in real terms is very much more
obvious since the rate of inflation has become so much higher.) Similarly,
the demand by companies for labour was thought to be dependent on real
wage levels because a higher money wage would be no disincentive to employ
labour if the price of the goods produced by that labour had gone up pro-
portionately. The implication of the market mechanism in this case was that
over the long term all who wished for employment could obtain it, provided
that there was no interference with the ability of the individual firms and
employees to bargain with each other over the latter's real wages.[3] In the
short term there might be unemployment as a result of shifts of demand from
one firm to another, or from one country to another, but in either case if
those without jobs could freely compete for jobs, offering to work for lower
wages if a pool of unemployed existed, but able to obtain higher wages if
there was a shortage of labour, then it was argued that any such unemployed
person could eventually obtain a new job. In general the only unemployment
existing at any point of time would be essentially temporary, except for
voluntary unemployment comprising those who did not wish to work at

[2] Real variables can only be given as index numbers which are related to the value of the
real variable in a 'base' year. Thus the real wage might be said to be 113 in 1974 with
1970 = 100. The 1974 figure is calculated as

$$\frac{W1974}{P1974} \bigg/ \frac{W1970}{P1970} \times 100$$

where W indicates the average wage level in the year specified, and P indicates the average
price level in the year specified. With real variables given by corresponding monetary ones
divided by the price level it is clear that real wages only rise if money wages rise faster than
price and vice versa.

[3] Although bargains will be struck in terms of money wages, any suggested money wage
implies a particular real wage given the price level (or expected changes in it over the period
the wage will be paid).

prevailing wage levels. Long-term involuntary unemployment was not possible on this view, *unless* it was caused by some interference in the free workings of the market, keeping the real wage level above that at which firms would wish to employ all those who wished to work.

2.2. The Keynesian Revolution

In the 1930s a new approach was developed, primarily by John Maynard Keynes, which later completely altered most people's way of thinking about economic problems and which at heart challenged the picture of the market mechanism described.

Keynes's work stemmed from observation of long-term involuntary mass unemployment in the interwar years, despite falls in wages, and his belief that *even if there was no interference in the process of wage setting*, there would not necessarily be a tendency towards full employment. Keynes therefore regarded the then existing economic theory as fundamentally wrong, and so set out to provide a new explanation of how the economic system functioned.

This new approach focused on the *aggregate* demand for goods and services. If this fell in the *short term* for any reason, firms would find themselves over-producing. Stocks of finished goods would accumulate, overtime working would be reduced, and some people would lose their jobs. Keynes accepted that eventually they might take on new jobs at lower wages, but *initially* they would look for new work at a wage roughly comparable to their previous wage. During this period their lack of income would greatly reduce their power to buy goods, and firms would find themselves facing *further* reductions in demand as a result. By the time the unemployed had come round to working for the lower wage at which they could all have been employed, the further reductions in demand could easily mean that this wage was itself too high. There might well therefore still be some unemployment, futher falls in demand for goods, and yet more unemployment. The *long-term* position under which everyone accepted a wage low enough to ensure full employment might, therefore, be delayed for a very long time indeed as unemployment caused lower demand, causing further unemployment. In fact the economy could, as a result of the short-run recession, run into long-run stagnation. Firms would be unwilling to employ more people because there was no increase in demand for their products, but no increase in demand would occur because there was not the necessary increase in employment and wage payments to permit people in aggregate to spend more. Those unemployed would still want to buy goods and services, but they would not be able to back this up with ready money. Without wages their 'demand' would be ineffective and without increased *effective* demand, firms would not employ more people or pay them wages.

Much more will be said about the Keynesian model in later chapters. Several points are of immediate interest, however. First, Keynes saw that when demand fell the initial impact was on the *volume of output* and, therefore, on employment, rather than on *prices*. Although prices and wages might start to fall as firms and employees began to recognize that the fall in demand was not just a temporary fluctuation, the short-term fall in output and employment, and the consequent further falls in both, would *amplify* the initial fall of demand into a major recession of long duration. This was in sharp contrast to the previous view that changes in *prices* (wages) would tend to *reduce* the existing excess demand or supply. Keynes's approach, therefore, heavily emphasized the response of output and employment rather than of prices and wages.

Second, the earlier idea of a supply of labour which, if it exceeded demand for its services, would compete for jobs and reduce wages, largely disappears. There is, of course, a supply of labour, and potentially it might compete for jobs if there is unemployment, but the tendency to search first for another job at the existing wage entails a period of zero or low wage for those unemployed, reduced expenditure, and further falls in employment which undermine the effect of eventually accepting a lower wage. Only the demand for labour is then important, indeed crucial, because only rises in demand can halt the process.

To solve the problem, aggregate demand had to be increased. If the public did not have the income to increase its expenditure, and firms did not have sufficient expectation of future increases in demand to increase expenditure on new factories, machinery, etc., then, Keynes argued, the government would have to intervene to achieve the expenditure increase. Instead of the previous emphasis, therefore, on non-intervention by government in economic behaviour to avoid interference with the automatic equilibrating of supply and demand by the market (i.e. price) mechanism, Keynes laid emphasis on the need for active intervention by government to avoid long periods of high unemployment. Since the war the acceptance of Keynes's views has led to continuous use of government monetary and fiscal policy (both discussed at length later on) to attain and maintain levels of virtually full employment. This intervention into the economic life of the nation, so familiar since the war, stems directly, though not solely, from the Keynesian view that left to itself the economy might well stagnate with high unemployment.

2.3. Macro- and Microeconomics

It may have been noticed that the difference in the pre-Keynesian[4] and Keynesian views does not lie solely in their disagreement about how people respond to situations in which supply and demand are unequal. The Keynesian view crucially focused on a circularity of economic effects. In order to emphasize this let us consider an individual firm employing labour and selling its products. In general, a negligible proportion of its output will be bought by its own employees. If the firm increased production by employing more people, it would simply move into a situation of over-production, for virtually none of the extra wages it paid out would be used to purchase the firm's increased production. For the economy as a whole, however, the amount supplied and the amount demanded were seen to be related in a circular fashion. An increase in *aggregate* production would increase *aggregate* income which in turn would lead to increased *aggregate* demand for products. While it is therefore generally useful to presume that the factors determining how

---

[4] Usually termed 'neo-classical'.

much *one supplier* (or even a group of suppliers, e.g. an industry) wishes to supply and the factors determining how much purchasers wish to buy are separate, it is definitely not legitimate to imagine that these are separate at the level of the *national economy*. In consequence, the methods of analysing the two levels are very different.

Analysis which concerns itself with only a part of the economy, e.g. one consumer, one firm, one industry, such that the circular effects described can be ignored, is termed microeconomic analysis. That which examines the behaviour of the whole economy is termed macroeconomics, and it must explicitly recognize the circularity.

This distinction, which is of considerable important in economics, will be observed in several chapters later on, with microeconomic analysis of individual sectors of the economy subsequently put together into a macroeconomic analysis of the whole. But it is nevertheless appropriate to stress certain features of macroeconomic analysis at this point.

Clearly, it must involve the analysis of aggregates (in fact much of microeconomics does as well), because it examines the aggregate impact of countless millions of decisions and the general trends that result. Four important observations must be made on this, each of them fairly obvious when stated, but often not fully appreciated. First, suggested macroeconomic relationships cannot be shown to be invalid by individual observations at the microeconomic level. If hypotheses concerning the behaviour of aggregate variables are to be tested adequately, the tests must involve the *aggregate* variables concerned. No damage is done to the hypothesis that high wage earners spend more by meeting a man who saves nearly all his £200 per week. Second, and stemming from this, it is frequently very misleading to judge any such hypothesis only by reflection on one's own behaviour or experience. Different individuals may act differently, and different types of institutions may operate in totally different ways. At best such introspection is a fertile source of hypotheses; it is no basis for testing them. Third, much economic analysis must operate at a fairly high degree of abstraction. Most of the myriad influences on any decision are of little concern. It is only the major systematic influences which are important and these may not always be the most obvious.

Fourth, an important feature of the Keynesian approach was the fact that government could intervene at the macroeconomic level, changing taxation, public expenditure, the availability of credit, etc., to ensure full employment, but without intervening at the microeconomic level. No selective interference in specific firms or industries was required, unless they exhibited specific problems. Total employment would be influenced without detailed control of any of the thousands of firms which provided it. This point is taken up below, but one implication should be singled out. The fact that particular cases will arise where a macroeconomic policy is counterproductive cannot be taken by itself as evidence that the policy is unsuccessful *per se*, hard as this may sound to the particular individual concerned. Only widespread examples based on a wide survey can give some indication of the success or otherwise of a macroeconomic policy.

The macro/micro distinction is by no means a rigid one, as will be seen. In addition, it is increasingly argued that this classification fails to recognize the giant companies now in existence which, though being individual firms, are so large that they can frequently influence the performance of the whole economy. These firms generally operate in several different countries, and this multinational aspect creates new opportunities and new problems for both the firm itself at the microeconomic level, and for the countries they operate in at the macroeconomic level: the framework of economic analysis may therefore need to develop in order to cope with this phenomenon.

2.4. Post-Keynesian Developments

Three important distinctions have been introduced above: Supply and demand; micro- and macroeconomics; the short term and the long term. This would suggest that both supply and demand factors could be analysed at both the micro- and macroeconomic levels over both the short term and the long term. However, while each category can easily be identified at the microeconomic level, the interrelation of supply and demand frequently makes for complications at the macroeconomic level. Some approaches emphasize the demand aspect, some the supply side, while others focus specifically on the interrelationship between them. In particular, short-term macroeconomic analysis has been primarily one of demand factors. This emphasis arises mainly from the fact that demand conditions appear much more flexible than supply ones in the short term. The goods and services which an economy can supply will primarily depend on the labour force available, the capital equipment in existence, the quality of each, the efficiency with which they operate, and the technology they embody. None of these can change very much in the short term. Furthermore, evidence appears to suggest that the total amount the U.K. economy can supply increases at a fairly stable rate of perhaps 3 per cent or so each year, though a number of the contributory factors may themselves depend on the particular demand conditions that have existed, suggesting that a significant change in demand might radically change this situation.

Aggregate demand, on the other hand, is much less stable. It has grown at up to 6 per cent in some years, and fallen in others. As a result, demand tends to determine what proportion of the existing labour force and capital stock available is actually employed over the short term, and short-term macroeconomic policy has therefore heavily concentrated on influencing demand.

Over the longer term, economic forces and government policy may both be expected to bring the growth of demand into line with the growth of the capacity of the economy to supply. With regard to the long term, therefore, the focus of attention has shifted to the supply side—in particular the supply of factors listed above such as capital, labour, their quality, etc. which together determine or influence the economy's over-all supply capacity. Demand factors cannot, for the reason given, be ignored in this. For example, the growth of the capital stock will depend partly on the demand industrialists expect for their products; and another supply factor, labour efficiency, as measured by average output per man (labour productivity) appears to be dependent on changes in the level of demand. None the less, the long-term focus has been on the determinants of the *supply of inputs* as opposed to the short-term focus on the determinants of *demand for output*.

Keynes himself had much to say on these longer-term issues, and many economists have used a Keynesian framework to analyse supply and demand relationships over the longer term. It is nevertheless true that in the hands of some commentators the term 'Keynesian' has not unnaturally become more specifically associated with the short-term management of aggregate demand that has been so all-pervasive in the last thirty years or so. This short-term Keynesian macroeconomic analysis and policy has recently come under considerable attack for a number of reasons. At a superficial level this could be explained by the fact that unemployment has recently climbed to historically very high levels again, but at a deeper level lie several more fundamental explanations.

Firstly, Keynes was concerned to solve the immediate and pressing problem in the 1930s of unemployment. Since then new problems have arisen besides this one, in particular inflation. The Keynesian model was little concerned with the problem of persistently rising prices, primarily because the 1930s were years of relatively little movement in the average level of prices. In the 1950s, and even more in the 1960s and 1970s, the existence of gradual and then accelerating inflation has changed this. The Keynesian model, like pre-Keynesian ones, accepted that if demand rose above the capacity of the economy to supply, i.e. if either full employment of labour and/or capital was reached, then because the volume of output could no longer rise, shortages would occur and prices would start to rise. Keynes himself argued that even at somewhat below full employment of labour there would be a tendency to inflation, a prediction which experience after the Second World War appears to have confirmed. But the appearance of very rapid inflation despite considerable unemployment is apparently a different phenomenon which requires different analysis and new solutions. This had led to suggestions that the Keynesian framework is inappropriate for the task of developing anti-inflationary policies, and indeed many Keynesians favour direct control to prevent excessive rises in prices and incomes.

More seriously, the late 1950s and 1960s have seen the development of economic theory which implies serious faults in the Keynesian analysis, and as a result an inevitable lack of success in the application of policies based on it. Much of this theory stems initially from work by Professor Milton Friedman, and in several central areas of concern—fiscal policy, monetary policy, inflation—this school has done much to expose problems of Keynesian analysis. Lying behind much of it is the pre-Keynesian view that over the long term it is the response of price to excess demand or supply that dominates, and that many of our difficulties, not least that of inflation, are due to the preoccupation there has been with short-term output-manipulating policy to the exclusion of the long-term price repercussions they generate. In later chapters, therefore, we shall be concerned to present a picture of the economy in terms of which both approaches (and others where relevant) can be understood and compared.

Inflation, however, is not the only new problem to have arisen in the U.K. since the war. Another is the slow rate of economic growth and advance in real living standards. While this has been rapid in comparison with the inter-war period, it has been significantly slower than in nearly all the other industrialized countries of the world. Here again many have thought the Keynesian framework inappropriate. The problem seems inherently long term and to a considerable extent one which arises from the unwillingness or inability of firms to expand their supply potential because inputs to the productive process are inadequate, unreliable, inefficient, or too expensive. Intervention on the supply side is therefore likely to be required and quite possibly on a more microeconomic basis if particular industries or even particular firms can be identified as sources of poor performance. This raises the need for new analysis and reappraisal of the desirability and efficiency of government economic policy.

Furthermore, it may be that poor economic growth generates further poor economic growth. A number of ways in which this might occur are discussed later. If this is so then the problems facing the economy might be very deep-seated and the measures needed to get out of such a vicious circle might well be both quantitatively and qualitatively different from those thought appropriate if the economy was in a more healthy position. Here again the basic Keynesian analysis could be inadequate for the purpose of creating useful economic policies.

Finally, in recent years increasing attention has been paid to the relative rate of increase of demand of different sectors of the economy over the *medium term* of four or five years. This has focused on whether consumer expenditure and government expenditure are growing too fast, thus pre-empting resources that are not then available to produce the capital goods and exports necessary for future growth and a healthy balance of payments. This inevitably raises political as well as economic problems, but the longer-term background to demand analysis has raised new issues the implications of which are far from clear at the present time.

Economics is therefore at an interesting and crucial stage in its development. The relative stability of the post-war period has been severely shaken. inflation and growth problems have arisen which appear difficult to analyse or influence, and the prevailing economic orthodoxy has been challenged at both theoretical and policy levels.

3. Conflict and Methodology in Economics

3.1. *Disagreement in Economics*

It is perhaps not surprising in the circumstances that economics should itself be under attack. Certainly politicians, industrialists, the media, and the public generally have all in differing degrees been critical, in part because economists have appeared unable to provide answers to the many problems besetting the U.K. economy already referred to. Like most blanket criticism there is some truth and some inaccuracy in this view. For example, a valid criticism is that despite many microeconomic investigations by economists and others, including various government agencies (the Monopolies Commission, the National Board for Prices and Incomes, etc.), relatively little work has been done at that level to compare different firms, especially in different countries, in order to identify some of the factors lying behind the U.K.'s poor economic performance. To some extent this may be because companies are reluctant to allow outside investigation and comparison of their operations, but economists also have been less ready to examine at the microeconomic level such factors as the comparative efficiency of management and work force in terms of their education, skills and training, union organization, industrial relations and management techniques, company financing, research, innovation and development, etc., despite their obvious economic impact.

Criticism is less obviously valid with regard to the difficulties experienced in controlling the economy in order to avoid excessive instability. It is undoubtedly true that lack of complete understanding of the economic forces at work has exacerbated the inherent problems. In particular, policies have been less successful than they would otherwise have been because the speed with which certain economic phenomena operate was misjudged. Yet against this it must be said that very little previous evidence existed to indicate how quickly demand might respond to government policy, nor could it be ignored that the existence of a new situation in the economy—active intervention, near-full employment, more rapid growth and inflation—might well itself render previous evidence irrelevant. In fact, considerable progress has been made even in the last ten years in developing a picture of the economy in terms of which many of the earlier difficulties can be understood, and avoided in future. The shocks to which the economic system has been subject have, however, increased, tending to obscure the advances that have been made.

There is relatively little validity in the view that the recent crisis, which resulted in virtually none of the country's economic objectives being achieved, represented a major failure of economic analysis. Not only was the crisis of 1973–5 initially caused by factors largely out of control of the U.K., but economic analysis was in fact rather successful in predicting the likely course of the crisis and in indicating the severity of the different policy options needed to deal with it. Such successes and failures in economics could each be illustrated many times over.

Lying behind all this is a rather more complex criticism—that economists disagree amongst themselves. This has already been implied in the description of the Keynesian approach and some of the reactions to it. It is disturbing, and confusing, when, in receiving professional economic advice, one is aware that a different opinion would be given by another economist, and so it is important to ask why this should happen. There are two factors, each of which generates controversy wherever it occurs in the field of human study, but which only come together in the social sciences. First, there is the impossibility of doing laboratory tests. Many scientific controversies can be settled by testing in specially designed laboratory conditions with all distorting influences removed. Wherever this is not possible, for example in many areas of medical science, astronomy, and archaeology, controversy is always present. The same is true of economics. In a situation in which a vast range of forces is at work, but where no possibility exists for temporarily removing some or holding them constant, the question of how to test, and indeed what constitutes a good test, becomes extremely complex and controversial, as is discussed below.

Second, economics cannot be divorced from politics, and whenever the latter appears, for example in history, sociology, some literature, and in the study of politics itself, controversy is widespread. If the development of an economy over time were completely determined independent of any action by any person in society, then even though economic conditions affected people greatly, the study of it would be as non-political as meteorology. The economic environment would be given and unchangeable. Given that this is not so, and that people's actions can and do partly determine others' well-being through their influence on economic conditions, economics is inevitably partly political. In the areas economists study, the assumptions they use, the constraints they recognize, and the policies they suggest, they cannot completely remove their own social and political standpoint. It is not surprising, therefore, that some important economic controversies closely parallel some political ones.

In practice there is far less disagreement than there appears to be, but faced with these two serious causes of controversy economists have had to examine their approach and methods of analysis very closely, developing certain ground rules and reasonable means of testing the hypotheses they construct.

3.2. Positive and Normative Economics

An important distinction frequently made in economic analysis, therefore, is one between *positive* and *normative* economics. In essence the difference between them is very straightforward. Normative economics includes statements about what *ought or ought not* to occur in economic affairs, e.g. inflation ought to be reduced. Positive economics includes statements about what *does or does not* occur in economic affairs, e.g. inflation will be reduced if taxes are increased. The latter, it is argued, can be assessed by reference to empirical data, whereas the former is based on the personal value-judgements of the speaker. Thus argument over whether higher unemployment would reduce inflation are potentially capable of being settled by analysis of the facts. Argument over whether it is more important to reduce inflation or reduce unemployment is *per se* not capable of being so resolved, as the argument hinges on the value the two sides place on the different hardships the two phenomena occasion. The fact that differences of view based on different value-judgements may be unresolvable creates obvious difficulties if economic judgements depend on them.

It may be thought, and is often argued, that given this distinction, provided economists stick to positive economics, no value-judgements will be involved and no 'political' controversy can creep in. Indeed, economists have examined in considerable detail how far they can go in making recommendations divorced from value-judgements. As will be seen, the answer in both theory and practice is that they cannot go all that far. This is not always sufficiently emphasized, but is particularly important in the present context where much of what follows is devoted to understanding government economic policy, with its explicit blend of economics and politics. These issues are therefore considered in more detail prior to the chapters on policy.

3.3. Testing Economic Hypotheses

Even within the framework of positive economics there still is the second cause of disagreement in economics—the difficulty of testing hypotheses. Economic analysis essentially consists of constructing *models* and testing them. A model comprises three elements: a set of simplifying *assumptions*; a set of *deductions* from them; and a resulting *prediction* which then represents a hypothesis which can be tested empirically. The purpose of the assumptions is to simplify the process of investigation, e.g. many considerations will operate in the determination of the expenditure by consumers in Britain this year, but in analysing consumer expenditure we assume away or abstract from those which are thought to be of relatively minor importance, and concentrate on a few key factors which appear important at the aggregate level.

It may be immediately obvious what follows from these assumptions, e.g. if we assume all influences other than incomes to be unimportant in determining expenditure, then it follows immediately that we are predicting that expenditure will be determined by income. In other cases it will not be obvious, and a series of logical deductions will have to be made, e.g. if we assume that a firm (i) tries always to maximize its profits, and (ii) is a monopolist, we can deduce (given several other assumptions in addition) with the use of a model what would happen to its price if profits tax was increased. Here the prediction to be made is much less obvious, but can be deduced dependent on the assumptions made.

Given the assumptions and the deductions we end up with predictions which we can then go on to test. If the prediction is not borne out it could be because of faulty deductions, but in general will be because the simplifying assumptions have removed from consideration one or more factors that are significant influences on the matter under examination. In general, attempts will be made to reformulate the model if its predictions are not borne out by empirical observation.

Clearly, the testing of models or hypotheses is an important part of this whole process. In fact, a very large amount of testing now goes on in economics, and the literature abounds with the results of this testing. For many introductory readers this generates what might be termed the 'magic wand' effect. A piece of perhaps very simple theory is explained, data relevant to it are (sometimes) presented, and then some results are presented which claim to validate the theoretical analysis. It is clear what has been done and why, but it is not clear *how* it has been done, rather as if a magic wand had been waved to achieve the result.

Many quite difficult issues are involved in testing hypotheses in economics, and it is necessary to say a little about this, not because the reader is likely to do any testing himself, but because it is important that as much as possible of the mystery surrounding the principles involved can be removed so that he will have a better idea of the proper weight to be attached to the results of tests which he encounters.

It is best to take a very simple example. Suppose it is hypothesized that the level of firms' aggregate investment expenditure on new factories, plant, and machinery depends on the profits that firms in aggregate earn. If this is so one would expect some correlation between aggregate investment expenditure and firms' aggregate profits. The first and most major difficulty is in finding out whether this supposed correlation exists.

In principle nothing would seem simpler, provided the information on aggregate investment and aggregate profits is available. A graph could be plotted, as shown in Figure 1.1, with the investment expenditure measured

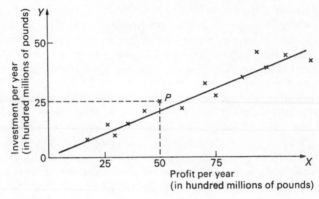

FIG. 1.1

vertically along the axis OY and profits measured horizontally along the axis OX. Each piece of information, which includes one level of profit (for example, £5,000 million per year) and the corresponding level of investment (for example; £2,500 million per year) could be represented on the diagram by a point (in this case the point labelled P). This is found by moving to the right from o a distance corresponding to £5,000 million per year and then upwards a distance corresponding to £2,500 million per year. The same could then be done for each piece of information, giving a scatter of points in the figure. If these lie roughly in a line, as shown, then it does appear that as profits get higher so investment does; otherwise not.

Now let us consider the problems. These can be split into two groups, the first of which concerns the difficulty of correctly specifying the relationship to be tested. Six separate though related points are involved.

(i) Which measure of investment and profits do we use? In the former, for example, we may or may not include the replacement investment that occurs when existing machinery becomes obsolete. We may or may not include along with the investment of manufacturing industries investment in agriculture, mining, and retail trades, etc. Perhaps factories should be treated separately from machinery, and similarly for transport equipment, etc. In the profit figures we may use pre-tax profits, post-tax profits, profits before payment of company interest payments on loans, or profits after payment of this, etc.

(ii) Next it has to be checked whether we are dealing with *stocks* or *flows* or a mixture. A stock variable is one like employment, or job vacancies, for example, which has a particular value at a particular point in time. The total amount of money in an economy and the total amount of capital—plant and machinery, etc.—are two other very important ones. All have the characteristic that we can at least in theory specify the level or amount at the point of time chosen, e.g. at the end of each month, the middle of each year, etc. A flow, on the other hand, is a variable the value of which cannot be specified unless a *period of time* is defined. An individual's spending can be so much per day or per week, etc., but a figure for spending has no meaning unless the period is stated or implied. A wage of £600 means nothing unless we know if it is per week, per month, or per year.

In our example both investment expenditure and profits are flows. If we have a stock and a flow—for example, if we want to correlate investment expenditure and the total stock of capital—then there is the problem of deciding which *period* for the flow variable to put with which *date* for the stock variable.

(iii) Next it has to be decided whether to use a *cross-sectional* or a *time-series* approach. In the first we look across firms, industries, or countries for a particular period, i.e. each piece of information in the diagram includes the investment done and profits made for example in a particular country during 1975. The correlation, if it exists, suggests that countries with higher profits carried out higher investment, at least in 1975. This cross-sectional result could be checked by repeating the analysis for 1974, 1973, etc. Problems begin to arise of course if the cross-sectional correlation works for some years, but not for others.

In the time-series approach we take one particular firm, industry, or country and look at it over a number of months or years. In this case each unit of information is the investment and profits of, e.g., the chosen country for each of a number of years past. If the correlation exists it suggests that when profits rise investment rises, and vice versa, at least for the country examined. Difficulties arise here if the correlation appears to exist for some periods, but not others, or if, as can happen, the correlation exists over a long period but not over shorter ones contained in the longer one, or vice versa. Such difficulties are further compounded if the evidence from cross-sectional and time-series studies do not agree.

(iv) In both cross-sectional and time-series studies there is a problem in deciding what *time lags* are involved. In either approach, does one hypothesize that investment in 1975 depends on profits in 1975, or on profits in 1974, 1973, etc., or partly on each of them? If the latter, how far back should one go, and what importance should be attached to each year relative to the other?

The argument over whether the fall in investment in 1970–1 was the fault
of the Conservative Government in power at the time, or the previous Labour
Government is a good example of the difficulty.

(v) Worse still, what if the main influence on investment is *expected* profits?
No solid evidence is available on the latter, and researchers may be forced
to use data from questionnaires about business expectations or to attempt to
identify the current factors that determine expectations about the future.

(vi) To say that investment depends on profits says nothing about the form
of the relationship. Investment might be proportional to profits, might
comprise one part independent of profits and another part dependent on it,
could rise progressively faster the higher profits become, and so on. A particular form has to be specified for any actual test (though several different
ones may be tried).

The next set of problems are statistical. There will almost certainly be a
whole range of other influences on investment expenditure, and the probability is therefore that the data points will look as shown in Figure 1.2,

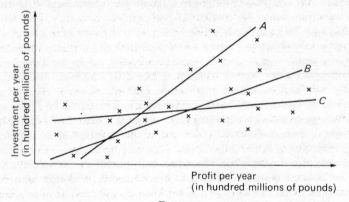

Fɪɢ. 1.2

rather than as in Figure 1.1. Ignoring the lines A, B, and C for the moment,
the points do indicate in a very vague and rough way a correlation between
investment and profits, but how do we decide if the correlation is a good
enough one on which to base analysis and policy? This leads to a further
set of problems in trying to decide whether the data justify the hypothesis
that the two are related in the way specified.

Two main problems arise. First, it does not help much just to look at
Figure 1.2. Any of a number of lines (A, B, and C are but three examples)
could be the line that best fits the points shown. *Econometric* analysis provides
ways of finding out which line is the 'best fit'. This generally means finding
the line such that if one calculates how far each point is vertically off the line,
squares this amount, and adds up the total for all the points, the figure is
less than it would be for any other possible line. A main argument for squaring
the deviations between the points and the line is that large deviations count
very heavily indeed against a line.

The second problem is to decide whether the line found is 'good enough'. Suppose line B in Figure 1.2 were found to be the best fit. Our belief in the hypothesized correlation will be much weaker than if the situation represented in Figure 1.1 had been the result of the empirical work (even if the line shown there was identical to line B), because the points are much more widely dispersed in Figure 1.2. A measure is therefore established (called a squared correlation coefficient) which measures how well the best-fit line fits the data points. If all the points lie exactly on the line it will have a value of 1. If at the other extreme the points are completely random it will have a value of 0. The line in Figure 1.1. would therefore have a correlation coefficient much nearer to 1 than line B in Figure 1.2.

In rough terms we can say that if the squared correlation coefficient is 0·7 then 70 per cent of the observed variation in investment is associated with variations in profits. When is such a coefficient high enough? The answer is that it all depends. At one extreme so little is known about some economic phenomena and they are so unpredictable that a value of 0·5 or 0·6 is quite useful. At the other extreme it may be disastrous if a major economic variable cannot be predicted to 98 per cent accuracy. In addition, the variable may be sufficiently stable that just using last year's figures will regularly give at least 95 per cent accuracy. Clearly here explanatory hypotheses require much higher correlation coefficients than in the first case.

The above points are largely technical. There is, however, another type of difficulty involved in testing hypotheses, that of inference. This is more philosophical in nature and more fundamental. To start with, it is often the case that one can find a correlation for the past which does not continue into the future, thus undermining the use of the correlation as a basis for accurate prediction of future behaviour. This may be because of other influences, because the relationship identified was partly or completely coincidental, or because people's behaviour has changed, probably as a result of new circumstances. For example, if working people tend to save a higher proportion of their income when unemployment becomes very high, because of the fear of further unemployment it induces, then this will invalidate any stable relationship which explains savings if that relationship was identified previously at a time when unemployment was never high enough to have this effect. Such an effect could, of course, have been hypothesized before, but would have been impossible to test.

A more serious version of this occurs if phenomena which hitherto appeared to have little economic effect and could be ignored by economic analysis start to have an effect. An increased awareness of income inequalities, or a changed political climate in which previous income differentials are no longer passively accepted, may both have powerful effects on inflation, productivity, and growth, but require extensive research, new modes of thinking, and new tools of analysis before these effects can be properly integrated into the mainstream of economics. In an extreme case the whole of our previous observations may become suspect. In the meantime existing analysis is inadequate. It could even be that people change their behaviour because they come to recognize that policy will radically alter the progress of the economy, thus invalidating the relationships on which economic analysis and the policy itself were initially based.

The most fundamental problem, however, is that even if a correlation is good and does continue to hold over time, it says nothing about the *direction of causality*. Suppose that it is found cross-sectionally that countries with high rates of economic growth generally have high levels of investment expenditure, and vice versa. Do we conclude (a) that higher investment causes faster growth by expanding an economy's capacity to produce faster, (b) that faster growth leads to higher investment expenditure by creating more profitable opportunities to invest, (c) that both faster growth *and* higher investment are caused by some third factor, for example a high level of managerial efficiency? The simple correlation throws no light on this, yet the implications for policy are very different in the three cases.

Several of these difficulties have indicated the possible significance of other variables besides the two mentioned. In fact it is an ever-present problem that any one economic variable tends to depend on quite a number of others. Econometric techniques have been developed to deal with this. (Conceptually the approach is as before, though it is difficult to portray diagramatically because the value of one variable is now explained by two or more others.) In such cases, fortunately, we can in principle not only find out econometrically how much of the variability of the former is 'explained' by variations in all the others, but also how important each separate variable is.

This, however, raises a new problem in deducing a causal relation from a statistical one. Suppose investment, profits, and total expenditure on all goods and services in the U.K. all rise and fall together. It may be that rises in total expenditure raise profits and also raise investment *directly*, the latter effect being because of shortages of the industrial capacity required to produce the goods demanded. Alternatively, it may be *only when profits rise* in response to the rise in total expediture that investment rises. Again it is hard to tell simply from the data which hypothesis is correct, and again the policy implications of the two interpretations can be quite different.

Many other difficulties exist. It may be that the relationship examined is not linear, i.e. the best-fit line on the diagram is not a straight line at all, but a flattening or rising curve. There may be two or three separate causal links between two variables, one suggesting they rise and fall together, another suggesting the reverse. Worse still, a great number of variables may all be interrelated in a large number of relationships, making analysis of any part of the system inadequate, but making analysis of the whole system highly complex.

In this case it may be necessary to identify each separate relationship, formulate it as an equation, put all the equations together simultaneously, and mathematically deduce the over-all relationship between two or more variables. This can then be tested, but it is often very difficult to know which *individual* relationship hypothesized is incorrect if the *over-all* prediction is not borne out.

Some cases are so complex that the above method is inappropriate. At this stage the model frequently has to be programmed into a computer and a battery of further techniques used to identify the predictions that arise from combining a large number of separate hypothesized relationships. Enough has been said though to illustrate the potential problems.

In many important cases the complexities are sufficiently great that it has been questioned whether testing of the type described is appropriate at all. The game of chess has been used here as a useful analogy. In chess all the relationships of the pieces to each other are known completely, as is the over-all objective. In both ways the situation is much simpler than that which exists in the economy yet one would have great difficulty in empirically testing the hypothesis that a particular move was more likely to achieve checkmate than another. Rather it is argued one would seek the views of an expert chess player. Similarly for the solution of economic problems it may, in some cases at least, be impossible to do reliable testing and be more important to obtain the judgement of those who have had success in making economic judgements previously. One important role of the study of economic history is to help provide the perspective, insight, and experience which such judgement requires. In practice some combination of prediction based on correlation and judgement based on experience is likely to be better than emphasis on either one alone.

4. Outline of the book

Against this brief background it is possible to describe the structure and content of the book. The rest of it is split into three parts. Part II summarizes in fairly condensed form the basic economic forces at work in the economy. In five chapters it covers macro- and microeconomic behaviour, domestic and international aspects, mainly within a 'positive' framework but also looking briefly at more normative aspects. As in the other sections, each chapter draws on concepts and arguments presented earlier in the book, but is otherwise as self-contained as possible.

Chapter 2 includes a simple introduction to consumer theory at the microeconomic level and includes some elementary tools of analysis used widely in economics. The analysis is then placed in a macroeconomic context. While the framework is essentially Keynesian in that it focuses on volume rather than price adjustment mechanisms, post-Keynesian developments which introduce longer-term considerations ignored by Keynes are also discussed.

Chapter 3 examines the behaviour of firms in some detail, reflecting the origins of the book in the teaching of managers. Nothing emphasized more strongly the gap between the theory of the firm taught to most economics students and the behaviour of actual companies than the attempt to teach the former to businessmen at the Oxford University Business Summer School. This is due partly to differences of purpose and partly to the different levels of abstraction involved but it also derives from the largely static equilibrium-based analysis used in economics as compared to the dynamic disequilibrium situation which most real world firms face. None the less there are significant links between the two approaches, each of which has much to gain from the other, and Chapter 3 attempts to present a picture of firms' behaviour which can act as a basis for linking the two. The first part focuses on company decisions and accounts. Industrial economic analysis and the basis of the theory of the firm are developed as abstractions from this and focus on those particular economic forces likely to be most important in the long-term economic development of firms.

Chapter 4 then places the behaviour of both consumers and firms in a macroeconomic context; introduces the monetary sector of the economy into the picture; briefly introduces international trade and government economic behaviour, and looks at several of the approaches developed to explain the behaviour of the economy as a whole. The framework is again primarily Keynesian in that it is largely short run and demand-orientated. Interpretations of the role of the money supply which conflict with the Keynesian view, and over which considerable controversy exists, are also introduced. Chapter 5 then develops the international aspect in view of its vital importance, not only to the U.K. economy. International accounts, trade, payments, and the world monetary system are all discussed briefly so that some appreciation of these rather complex matters can be gained.

Although much of the book is macroeconomic it will be necessary at several points to examine certain microeconomic considerations. The role of competition, state and private monopolies, and the need for taxation are all examples, and need some background analysis regarding the way in which resource allocation mechanisms can be evaluated. Chapter 6 looks at the economic analysis of this and focuses on the great difficulties inherent in it. The chapter is overtly more theoretical than most, presenting the standard approach by economists to more normative questions, and emphasizing the restrictive nature of this approach.

It was stated earlier that in recent times two problems have come to dominate the U.K. economy which had neither been seen before nor analysed in any depth in the basic Keynesian analysis. Part III deals with these two problems, inflation and growth. Both are controversial matters in economics and the different viewpoints are in each case examined, though as with several other chapters the approach will inevitably to some extent reflect the views of the author concerned.

Having described the working of the economy and the major problems it generates, Part IV looks at the range of economic policies designed to overcome them. Chapter 9 commences by looking in general terms at the issues involved in identifying objectives and selecting economic instruments to pursue them in an overtly political framework and discusses the frequently ignored complexities of policy formation in an industrially developed democracy such as the U.K. This is followed by three chapters dealing in turn with incomes policy, fiscal policy, and monetary policy. Chapter 13 focuses on the interrelationships between fiscal and monetary policy and looks at some of the different views that have been adopted with regard to the stabilization of the economy both internally and externally. This is then followed by two chapters concerned with two factors that have been increasingly recognized as major constraints on the ability of policy-makers to control the course of the U.K. economy. One deals with the growing dependence of the U.K. economy on the fluctuations in demand at the international level, the impact of the oil crisis, and the attempts by governments to deal with the problems such matters raise. The other deals with the technical aspects involved in forecasting the behaviour of the economy which can easily undermine the success of active intervention in the economy.

All of this is again predominantly short term and demand-orientated. Longer-term considerations on the supply side concerned with industrial structure, conduct, and performance are discussed in the next four chapters. Four main areas are covered; the promotion of competition or measures designed to obtain the benefits competition confers; medium-term planning; public ownership as it operates in the nationalized industries; and a brief mention of the more recent developments in Government Industrial policy outside the traditional areas of government control. A final chapter emphasizes certain strands of analysis presented in the book and speculates on the way forward for the economy of the U.K.

PART II

2

Consumer Behaviour

H. G. JONES

1. Introduction

Any modern developed economy typically includes millions of individuals who spend their different incomes on literally thousands of different goods and services. In the United Kingdom the *Family Expenditure Survey*[1] provides a wealth of detailed information on the pattern of expenditure of U.K. households at a particular point in time. Although, like all useful statistical compilations, it represents a necessary compromise between detail and clarity, it does reveal the bewildering *complexity* and *diversity* of household expenditure. The factors influencing the behaviour of households, both individually and considered together, in determining the pattern of expenditure, constitute the subject-matter of this chapter. Although it is convenient if, as in the *Family Expenditure Survey*, attention is concentrated on natural groups of individual consumers—the 'household' or the 'income unit'—almost all of the discussion and analysis does apply to the individual as much as to the household.

It is appropriate that our survey of the workings of the economy should begin with a discussion of the economic behaviour of households, for they constitute one of the principal groups of actors on the economic stage. In an economy such as the United Kingdom's, a typical household sells, or attempts to sell, its labour services to employers and receives, as proceeds of the sale, labour income. Moreover, the household may own financial assets (such as savings certificates, shares, etc.) and non-financial assets (such as property) from which it also derives income. The household's income may also include payments from the government in the form of social security payments, old age pensions, etc. With its income the household purchases goods and services, pays taxes, and, perhaps, saves. Although much of this book is concerned with macroeconomic policies and problems, it is important to remember that beneath many important macroeconomic aggregates—e.g. the level of unemployment or the flow of aggregate consumption expenditure —lie the individual households whose independent decisions and responses have generated, or contributed to, the macroeconomic phenomenon in question.

In this chapter we concentrate on the economic behaviour of the household

[1] Dept. of Employment, Government Statistical Office.

as a *buyer* of commodities rather than as a seller of labour, although the framework of thought, centred upon household *choice*, can easily be applied to these other economic activities. Our emphasis is on the simple analysis of general tendencies. We cannot, and probably should not, hope to adequately *describe* the economic behaviour of all households in their role as buyers. Even the *Family Expenditure Survey*, for all its wealth of detail, cannot mirror reality, and our objective will be to adequately represent and summarize the major characteristics of household economic behaviour.

One final introductory point should be made. For at least two centuries successive generations of economists have attempted to analyse the economic behaviour of the household. Countless textbooks and monographs have been written on even small parts of the subject. It should be clear that a brief chapter cannot hope to encapsulate all the rich variety of results, hypotheses, and conclusions that have been arrived at in that period. This chapter, in keeping with the over-all purpose of the book, aims to provide only the basic framework of thought and the main points required for an understanding of Parts III and IV. Consequently, we rely heavily on assertion, and many important topics have to be ignored or merely alluded to.

2. Household Demand for Goods and Services

2.1. The Law of Demand

Consider an individual household (or, indeed, an individual consumer). In any time period (e.g. week, month, or year) its pattern of expenditure will, in general, depend upon the *households' preferences or tastes*, the *prices* of goods and services, and the household's *income*. The basic problem for the household is to *choose* a collection of products or 'shopping list' which is feasible in the sense that it can be paid for given the household's income and the prices of goods and services. The chosen set of products should, moreover, be considered by the household as preferable to (or at least as good as) any other feasible set. Thus the preferences and choices of all households are, in general, constrained by available income and the prices of goods and services. Now, some discussion is required to elucidate and elaborate the precise meaning of the foregoing remarks. In the present section we assume that the concept of household income-per-period is unambiguous and, in particular, that household income is constant or fixed. Thus we discuss here the influences upon the demand for goods and services of preferences and prices *given a fixed income*. The variety of ways of conceiving of household income are discussed in the next section.

We have already stated that the object of choice for a particular household in any period is a list of the quantities of each product and each service that the household purchases. It is convenient, at this point, to draw a distinction between *durable* and *non-durable* goods. Some goods (non-durables) are, by their very nature, purchased so as to be immediately consumed, e.g. food and drink. But one can easily think of other goods (durables) whose purchase is, in general, based on the assumption that the goods can be expected to provide services over a relatively long period of time, e.g. a washing machine or a car. (It is, of course, possible to purchase a bottle of good wine as an investment rather than for consumption, and such an example illustrates the fact that the distinction between durable and non-durable goods does not really stem from an intrinsic property of the goods but from the motivation for purchase, and planned use.) We draw the distinction because the factors influencing the demand for durables are quite likely to be rather different from the factors determining the demand for non-durables. We return to these considerations in the next section.

In analysing the economic behaviour of the household as a purchaser, the economist often assumes that every individual consumer and every individual household has a complete set of preferences which do not change and which determine his choice of goods in any buying situation. Thus it is as though each household simply observes a whole series of possible shopping lists and simply chooses the one that is 'best' on the basis of the household's given preferences.[2]

The treatment of household preferences as *data*—in the sense that they are simply assumed to be given and unchanging—removes from the analysis a large variety of influences which may affect preferences. They may simply change with the passage of time—because, for example, of a desire for change *per se* or because the average age of a household is changing such that children's toys and perambulators no longer appear so desirable. Household preferences will be influenced by the current state of knowledge concerning the available goods and services, and are likely to change as more information becomes available as a result of experience or deliberate search. In particular, it is worth noticing that many consumers, in the absence of more 'objective' information (such as *Which* magazine reports) as to the quality of goods, habitually use the *price* of a good as a rough index of its quality. Advertising expenditures of all kinds are likely to alter household preferences—both between different brands of similar products and, possibly, between different products. Preferences may be moulded by all manner of psychological and sociological influences. Thus, for example, the pattern of household expenditure may be influenced by a desire to 'keep up with the Joneses' or by a desire to be different from other families in the neighbourhood. Changing views of the future may markedly alter current preferences.

It seems clear, therefore, that in attempting to analyse the economic behaviour of the household, the assumption of a given set of preferences is very powerful and must be handled with care. Its usefulness lies in the fact that the influences discussed above do not, in general, vary much in intensity and, as a consequence, people's preferences between the major goods and services that are available tend to remain fairly stable. Thus the assumption of given preferences may not, in fact, constitute a particularly serious distortion of reality—and it certainly provides a simple framework for much useful analysis.

Accepting the foregoing difficulties, imagine a household with a fixed set of preferences that is considering how much to buy of a certain commodity

[2] These preferences are usually assumed to satisfy a series of axioms or assumptions from which behavioural predictions can be derived.

(which is considered desirable by the household) given its income and *given that the prices of all other goods and services are known and fixed.* Introspection and observation reveal[3] one of the best known of all economic propositions—sometimes known as the Law of Demand. The quantity of any commodity—say, beer—that a household plans to buy will, in general, be inversely related to the price of that commodity.[4] Thus the demand for beer can be said to be a 'function' of (i.e. depend upon) the price of beer and this idea can be succinctly summarized by writing $D_B = f(p_B)$ where D_B represents the demand for beer, p_B represents the price of beer, and the expression $f(p_B)$ represents the functional relationship namely that the former depends on the latter.

The so-called Law of Demand is illustrated in Figure 2.1. The curve DD

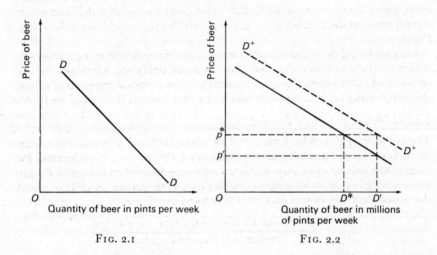

FIG. 2.1   FIG. 2.2

indicates the quantities of beer that a particular household will, given its preferences and income, plan to buy at different prices. This 'demand curve' or 'demand function' is drawn as downward sloping, reflecting our statement of the Law of Demand. Different households will, depending upon their relative liking for beer, have different demand curves but, given the Law of Demand, all the curves will be downward sloping.

If, for each possible price of beer, the quantities that *all* households would buy at that price are added together horizontally we *obtain the market demand curve* illustrated in Figure 2.2. The market demand curve, which shows the total demand for beer at each price, is again downward sloping and is, in fact, conceptually very similar to the individual demand curve—apart from the change in the scale of the horizontal axis from 'pints per week' to 'millions

---

[3] This proposition, together with possible exceptions, can be rigorously derived on the basis of a small set of assumptions concerning household preferences. Section 4 of this chapter briefly illustrates the method. For more detail see Green [3], Chs. 2–4.

[4] The principal source of possible exceptions to the Law is briefly outlined in section 4.

of pints per week'. At the price p^* households as a whole plan to buy a quantity OD^* of beer whereas at the lower price, p' households would like to buy the larger quantity OD'.

Market demand curves for particular commodities can be estimated by statistical means and used as practical tools for government and business. In this book, however, we are more concerned with the *concept* of the market demand for any commodity being, in general, inversely related to the price of that commodity.

It is important to distinguish between movements *along* any given market demand curve and *shifts* in the whole demand curve. An increase in the desired quantity of beer from OD^* to OD' may come about as a result of a fall in the price of beer as discussed above. The same change could, however, arise as a result of changes in the preferences of households such that, at every price, they are prepared to buy more beer. The market demand curve consequently shifts to the right—as illustrated by the dotted curve D+D+ in Figure 2.2.

In considering the effect of a change in price on the demand for a product, it is important to recognize that there may be delays or 'time-lags' in the response of consumers. Thus, for example, quite a considerable time might elapse following an increase in the price of petrol before the demand for it fell.

2.2. *The Price Elasticity of Demand*

The fall in the price of beer from p^* to p' illustrated in Figure 2.2. generated an increase in the quantity demanded from OD^* to OD'. The demand for some goods will be more responsive to changes in price than others. A simple measure of the relative responsiveness of demand to changes in price is called the 'price elasticity of demand' and is defined as follows:

$$E_p = \frac{\text{Percentage change in quantity demanded}}{\text{Percentage change in price}}$$

where E_p signifies the price elasticity of demand for a commodity. Thus if a 1 per cent fall in *price* generates a 1 per cent increase in *quantity demanded* then the *price* elasticity of demand is said to be 1.[5] If, on the other hand, a 1 per cent fall in price generates a 2 per cent increase in quantity demanded then the price elasticity of demand is 2 and demand is described as *relatively elastic* (i.e. the elasticity is above 1). If, finally, a 1 per cent decrease in price generates a $\frac{1}{2}$ per cent increase in demand then the elasticity of demand is $\frac{1}{2}$ and demand is described as *relatively inelastic* (less than 1). The definitions can, of course, be symmetrically stated for an increase in price. Two extreme cases can be defined. If demand is totally unresponsive to a change in price (in which case the demand curve is a vertical straight line) then the elasticity of demand is zero and demand is said to be perfectly inelastic. If, at the other extreme, demand is *so* responsive to price that the slightest fall in price would induce households to attempt to buy infinite quantities of the good (in which

[5] Since a *fall* in price generates an *increase* in demand (i.e. price and demand move in opposite directions) the elasticity of demand is inherently negative. In practice, the sign is ignored so that this elasticity is said to be 1 rather than −1.

case the demand curve would be a horizontal straight line) then E_p would be infinite and demand 'perfectly elastic'.

It is easy to think of the demand for necessities as being rather inelastic while the demand for luxuries might be expected to be rather elastic—but the ambiguity in the definition of the terms 'luxury' and 'necessity' means that it is rather difficult to make statements of this kind, and possibly quite misleading.

It is important to note that the elasticity of demand[6] for a commodity might well change through time so that the measured elasticity might be very different depending upon the time period over which the change in demand was measured. Consider, for example, the effect of a large increase in the price of electricity. Some considerable time might elapse before any significant change in the quantity of electricity used occurred, for households would already be committed to the use of electricity because of previous purchases of electrical equipment. Thus in the short run the demand for electricity might appear highly inelastic. As time elapsed, however, a higher proportion of households might avoid electrical equipment in favour of, for example, gas central heating, with the result that the long-run elasticity of demand for electricity might be considerably higher. This distinction is of considerable importance in some later chapters.

The elasticity of demand for a commodity may be very important for policy purposes. Consider a commodity whose elasticity is 1. We know, therefore, that a 1 per cent increase in price will generate a 1 per cent fall in demand and it should be clear that, in this case, there will be *no change in total expenditure* on the commodity—the loss of sales being just balanced by the increased price. If, on the other hand, the demand for some commodity is relatively elastic—say, 2—then a 1 per cent increase in price will generate a 2 per cent fall in demand, and total expenditure on that commodity will consequently *fall*. Finally, it should now be clear that if demand is relatively inelastic a 1 per cent increase in price will generate a less than proportionate fall in demand, and total expenditure on that commodity will increase.

Thus decisions concerning prices, whether they be made by private companies or nationalized enterprises, will be much influenced by the elasticity of demand of the product concerned. (See Chapter 3.)

2.3. Complements and Substitutes

Thus far we have discussed the demand for an individual commodity on the assumption that prices of other goods and services are constant, and we have concluded that the demand for any commodity is usually inversely related to its own price. If we relax this assumption, it is immediately clear that the demand for any commodity will no longer depend simply on its own price but also on the prices of other goods. The demand for beer will depend in part on the prices of whisky and cider, etc., and the demand for cars will, in part, depend upon the price of petrol. Any economy is very interdependent in the sense that changes in any one part of the system may affect all other

---

[6] Although there are other types of elasticity of demand beside the price elasticity of demand, the latter is so frequently used that it is often simply called 'the elasticity of demand'.

parts of the system. Thus, in principle, the demand for any commodity will not only depend upon its own price but also on its price relative to the prices of *all* other commodities. In practice, of course, we would expect the prices of only some other commodities to be particularly quantitatively significant. In the above examples, whisky can be seen to be a partial *substitute* for beer in the sense of being an alternative alcholic drink, and there can be little doubt that a halving of the price of whisky in the United Kingdom would reduce the demand for beer. On the other hand, petrol and cars are *complementary* and a large increase in the price of petrol might be expected to reduce the demand for cars.[7] Thus, it is clear that our demand function should, at a minimum, include some other prices—i.e. $D_B = f(p_B, \bar{p})$ where D_B again represents the demand for beer, p_B the price of beer and $\bar{p}$ represents a list of the prices of other goods which are relevant to the demand for beer.

Before proceeding to the next section, it is worth noticing that the demand for any commodity might be influenced not only by its own price and the prices of other goods but also by its *expected price* and the expected prices of other goods. If households believe that the price of a washing machine is going to rise then they may bring forward in time the planned purchase of the commodity so as to avoid the effects of the price increase. Furthermore one might generally expect the effect of expected future prices to be much more significant for the demand for durable goods—for the exact timing of the purchase is probably more open to choice. We return to this subject in the next section.

3. Household Income

3.1. The Concept of Income

In section 2 we concentrated on the effects of prices upon the demand for commodities, on the assumption of a fixed and unambiguous idea of household income. In the present section we elaborate on the idea of income as a fundamental constraint preventing the unfettered expression of household preferences *given* the prices of commodities.

Consider, once again, an individual household facing fixed and known prices for all commodities. Given its income, its problem is to allocate that income amongst the available goods so as to purchase the consumption bundle or shopping list that it likes best. But what precisely is meant by 'household income'? In any period a typical household will receive a measurable income from a variety of sources and depending upon a variety of factors. Firstly, this 'measured income' will typically include a large component of labour income in the form of wages or salaries and this labour income will in turn depend upon wage rates, salary scales, the amount of overtime or short-time workings, etc. Moreover, the typical household's labour income will be paid net of various taxes, social security contributions, and pension contributions that are deductable at source. Thus it is clear that the measured disposable labour income depends upon a large variety of

---

[7] The concept of a substitute or a complement is more complicated than it appears here. See Green [3], Ch. 5 for further detail.

factors many of which are effectively outside the household's control. On the other hand, it is clear that *some* of the factors determining income, and, in particular, the amount of overtime worked and the wage demands made by labour representatives, *are* partially under the control of the household. Thus the response of households to either decreases in their incomes (as a result, say, of income tax increases) or to increases in the prices of goods may be to work more overtime, or demand that their unions apply for wage increases, thus attempting to maintain the previous income level.

Secondly, the measured income of a typical household in any period may include sums accruing from the ownership of various forms of wealth. Thus interest may be paid on building society or bank savings, dividends may be paid as a result of the ownership of shares, or rents paid as a result of the ownership of property. Furthermore, the typical household may receive a variety of payments from the state in the form of pensions, unemployment pay, or various forms of subsidy. Finally, the measured income of a typical household may, in any period, include a variety of transitory components of the 'windfall' variety—e.g. unexpected gifts, gambling winnings, or tax repayments.

Now, the measured income of a household clearly forms part of the constraint on its expenditure in any period of time but, equally clearly, that is not the whole story. Many items in any household's shopping list, and in particular durable goods such as cars and washing machines, simply could not be financed out of the measured income of any individual period. Such purchases are typically financed by various forms of borrowing—consumer credit, hire purchase, bank overdrafts, bank loans, or, in the case of house purchase, mortgage loans. Whether an individual household can, in any period, contract for such items will depend, *inter alia*, on availability of finance, the cost of finance in terms of the rate of interest charged on the loan, and, in general terms, the ability of the household to make the appropriate repayments. It is clear that we are moving away from the idea that current measured income is invariably the decisive constraint upon household expenditure. What may be more germane, particularly in terms of determining the demand for durable goods, in some concept of long-term, 'normal' or 'permanent' income[8] based upon the household's past income experience and its reasonable *expectations* of future income. For example, if a household has every reason to believe that its measured income will steadily increase through time (consider a young couple in which the income earner is on a rising salary scale in a secure job), then one might expect that the pattern of borrowing and expenditure will vary in a systematic way through the lifetime of the household with expenditure exceeding measured income in the early years. The amount by which expenditure could be allowed to exceed income would stem from the household's own prudence and the lender's desire to minimize the possibility of default—but ultimately the *expection of measured income* over time would constitute the decisive constraint. These expectations will, of course, be determined by a very large variety of factors—

---

[8] These ideas were principally derived in the context of the theory of the aggregate consumption function (see below) in macroeconomics. See, for example, Friedman [11].

the ability of the income earner, the probability of continuous employment, the probability of promotion, the expectation of wage increases, etc. It follows that, although the Law of Demand may be expected to hold in general, the demand for particular commodities may be much more sensitive to such factors as incomes, prevailing consumer credit regulations, rates of interest, the general availability of credit, etc. than to their prices.

3.2. A Household's Total Consumption Demand

Our discussion has indicated that a household's income and the relative price of a good are two major determinants of its demand for the good. When we come to examine the household's *total* demand for all goods, then real income, i.e. effective purchasing power, becomes the main determinant, with relative prices determining the *composition* of consumption rather than the total. A change in the relative price of one good may change the household's total demand, but this effect arises because the price change results in a new real income—the household's money income can buy more of all goods if the price of one good falls. Current and expected income are therefore the main determinants of a household's *total* demand for goods.

As a matter of common observation, however, not all income is consumed. The remainder represents saving, and we need to examine what might determine a household's desire to save before we can fully specify the relationship between income and consumption.

The going level of interest rates that can be earned on savings will usually be one determinant of the proportion of income that a household is prepared to save. But the relationship between aggregate saving and interest rates is difficult to generalize about because two different factors are involved. First, the higher the interest rate available the more incentive there is to save, tending to increase saving out of a given income. Second, if the purpose of saving is to provide a given benefit, e.g. a fixed income in retirement, then a higher rate of interest will provide this income from a *smaller* capital sum, and the incentive to save is thus reduced.

A second, and probably much more important, determinant of the proportion of a household's income which is saved is the level of income itself. Low-income households which have greater difficulty in meeting their basic needs—for housing, food, clothing, and so on—will probably be unable to save more than a very small fraction of income, if that, while relatively well-off households, facing a choice at the margin whether to buy (relative) luxury goods and services, can ordinarily be expected to save a significant proportion of income.

Another factor influencing saving is the variability of income over time. Since an important motive for saving is as a precaution against the uncertainty of the future, it is likely that people with fluctuating incomes—for example, farmers—are more likely to save a relatively high proportion of their incomes than people with secure and steady incomes, for example, many white-collar workers.

In fact, this conclusion follows directly from our previous discussion of the income constraint. If measured income is classified partly as 'permanent' income, i.e. that part regarded as secure and likely to persist, and partly as transitory, i.e insecure, variable, or largely random (either positive or negative), and consumption is regarded as a function of permanent income, then two households with the same average measured income, one of which is stable, the other less so, will have different saving propensities. The household with the more fluctuating income will have the lower 'permanent' income and hence will consume less and save more of the measured or actual current income.

Finally, the amount of wealth owned by a household is also likely to affect saving behaviour. Generally speaking, a household which has a substantial amount of assets which could, if necessary, be realized in order to meet unforeseen contingencies will have less need to save out of current income.

All these factors, by influencing decisions to save, will influence a household's final decisions on how much to spend.

4. Theoretical Demand Analysis

4.1. Indifference Curves

Most of the discussion of the previous section has been heuristic and intuitive. In the present section we re-examine the behaviour of consumers in a slightly more theoretical manner which can be utilized in a whole range of 'choice' situations. For simplicity, we consider the case of a household (or individual consumer) that must choose how to allocate its fixed income between two goods, bread and ale, that are on sale at fixed and known prices. Although we conduct the analysis in terms of only two goods, all of the ideas outlined below will, in fact, apply however many goods can be purchased.

Our primary requirement for any theoretical analysis of the choice behaviour of a household is some means of representing its preferences. The *object of choice* for the household is a 'bundle' of certain quantities of bread and certain quantities of ale. Consider any two bundles of bread and ale—say, x and x'.[9] An elemental requirement for household choice is that it knows either that it prefers x to x' or that it prefers x' to x or that it is indifferent between the two bundles. We also assume that 'goods are good' in the sense that (a) if a bundle x includes more of *both* bread and ale than a bundle x', then x must be preferred to x', and (b) if a bundle x includes *at least as much* of *either* bread or ale and *more* of the other good than another bundle x' then x must be preferred to x'.

Given these preliminaries, we can introduce the idea of an *indifference curve* and an *indifference map* as a means of simply representing household preference, as is shown in Figure 2.3. The vertical axis of the diagram is measured in terms of quantities of bread and the horizontal axis is measured in terms of quantities of ale. Each point in the figure therefore represents a bundle of bread and ale—e.g. the point x represents a bundle of 3 loaves of bread and 4 pints of ale. The curve I–I, which is called an 'indifference curve', is a line joining all bundles of bread and ale that are considered

---

[9] Thus, for example, the 'bundle' x might contain three loaves of bread and four pints of beer, while x' might contain two loaves and five pints.

equivalent or 'indifferent' by the household under consideration. Thus, for example, the curve shows us that the household is indifferent between the bundles x, x', and x''. Given our assumptions, the indifference curve must slope downwards to the right. Consider the bundle x on the indifference curve I–I. All bundles to the north-east of x (in the area marked P for preferred) must be preferred to x, for they contain more ale *and* bread. Moreover, all bundles lying on the vertical line above x and the horizontal line to the

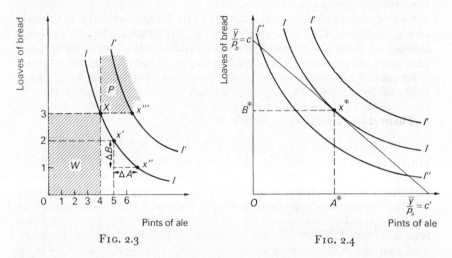

FIG. 2.3   FIG. 2.4

right of x must be preferred to x, for they contain the same amount of ale and more bread or the same amount of bread and more ale. Similarly, all bundles to the south-west of x (in the area marked W for 'worse') must be considered inferior to x, for they contain less bread *and* ale. Finally, all bundles lying on the vertical line below x and the horizontal line to the left of x must be considered inferior, for they either contain the same amount of ale and less bread or the same amount of bread and less ale. Thus all bundles that are indifferent to x *must* lie to the north-west or the south-east of x—and the indifference curves are therefore downward sloping.

The slope of an indifference curve has an important economic meaning. Consider a small move along an indifference curve—from x' to x'' in Figure 2.3. Such a move involves a reduction, ΔB, in the quantity of bread (the symbol Δ simply means 'a change in') and an increase, ΔA, in the quantity of ale which, given the household's particular preferences, *just compensates* the household for the loss of bread, such that bundle x'' is indifferent to bundle x'. Now, by analogy to the conventional idea of the slope of a hill (the distance 'up' divided by the distance along), the slope of the indifference curve between x' and x'' is approximately $\Delta B/\Delta A$—i.e. the ratio of the loss of bread to the quantity of ale that just compensates for the loss. This slope is called the household's *marginal rate of substitution* of ale for bread (MRS_b^a).[10]

[10] Another way of looking at the slope of the indifference curve is as follows. Assume for the sake of argument (see p. 152 below) that a person can measure the 'utility' that he derives

The curve I–I is simply a typical curve of a household's *indifference map* which consists of a large set of indifference curves which fill up the whole diagram. Thus I'–I' is another typical indifference curve, but it is crucial that the reader should note that *every* bundle on this curve is preferred to every point on the lower indifference curve I–I—the consumer is indifferent between all points on I–I, and indifferent between all points on I'I' but point x''' on the latter is preferred to point x' on the former, since x''' contains more bread *and* ale. Therefore any point on I'–I' is preferred to any point on I–I. Thus a move to a higher indifference curve (i.e. in a north-easterly direction) implies improvement for the household. The complete indifference map is a relatively simple theoretical way of summarizing the preferences of a household. The objective of any household will be to attain a bundle of bread and ale on the *highest possible* indifference curve. The word 'possible' in the previous sentence leads us automatically to examine the constraint of the household's income.

4.2. The Budget Line

Considering Figure 2.4, if a household has a fixed income. $£\bar{y}$, and spends all of it on bread at a price of p_B it will obtain a quantity $£\bar{y}/p_B$ of bread and we assume that this quantity equals OC for the household under considera-tion. Similarly, if the household spends all of the fixed income, $£\bar{y}$, on ale at a price p_a it will obtain a quantity, $£\bar{y}/p_a$, of ale, and this quantity equals OC' in Figure 2.4. The line joining the point C to the C', is known as the *budget* line. It represents all the different *combinations* of bread and ale that the house-hold can obtain by spending its fixed income on mixtures of bread and ale at the prices p_b and p_a. As more ale is bought, so less bread can be bought. The slope of the budget line will equal the distance OC divided by the distance OC'—i.e.

$$\frac{£\bar{y}}{p_b} \div \frac{£\bar{y}}{p_a} = \frac{p_a}{p_b}$$

Thus the slope of the budget line equals the ratio of the prices of the com-modities.

4.3. The Analysis of Decisions

We are now in a position to analyse the household's allocation of income between bread and ale. It is clear that, given the fixed income of the house-hold, it can only buy bundles in the triangle OCC' of Figure 2.4 or bundles

from consuming a particular good. We define *marginal utility* as the additional utility or satisfaction that a person obtains from having one more unit of a good. In general, we presume that this will decline the more units one has (the third bar of chocolate gives less additional utility than the second, the second less than the first). If the marginal utilities of two goods, for an individual, given he has a certain amount of each, are six and three respectively, then the individual could exchange one unit of the former for two of the latter and be no better or worse off. This would be a shift along the indifference curve with a marginal rate of substitu-tion of $2/1$, i.e. 2. This of course was found from the ratio of the marginal utilities hence

$$\frac{MU_1}{MU_2} = MRS_1^2$$

actually on the budget line. But we have already stated that the household's objective is to attain the highest indifference curve, so, on our assumptions, the household will buy the bundle x^* (consisting of OB^* of bread and OA^* of ale) at the point where the budget line is tangential to the indifference curve I–I. All higher indifference curves, like I'–I', are outside the triangle OCC' and all lower ones, like I''–I'', represent less preferred positions. At the point x^* the slope of the indifference curve, the household's marginal rate of substitution of ale for bread, is equal to the slope of the budget line, the ratio of the prices of ale and bread.

The indifference curve apparatus can be used to analyse the effects of the change in price of one of the commodities with the household's income remaining constant. Assume that the price of ale falls. If the household spent all of its fixed income, $£\bar{y}$, on ale then it could, after the price fall, buy more ale. The budget line will consequently move as shown in Figure 2.5. The original budget line is CC'. After the fall in the price of ale the new budget line is CD. Originally, the household purchased the bundle of bread and ale represented by the point x on the indifference curve I–I. After the price fall the household purchases the new bundle, x', including more ale and more bread, and is, given its own preferences, better off—for the new bundle is on the higher indifference curve I'–I'. Thus Figure 2.5 provides an indifference curve representation of our heuristic law of demand—the fall in the price of ale has increased the household's demand for ale. This is known as

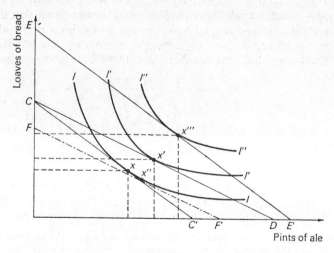

FIG. 2.5

the price effect. The demand for bread has also increased even though the absolute price of bread has remained unchanged, because the price of another good—ale—has changed.

4.4. Income and Substitution Effects

The same apparatus can be used to show the effect of a change in the other major determinant of consumer expenditure by a household, namely income. Imagine that, starting with budget line CC', there is an increase in the income of the household, but no change in the relative prices of the two products. Instead of OC being the maximum amount of bread that could be bought it is now OE, and instead of OC' being the maximum amount of ale that could be bought it is now OE'. The budget line moves outwards from the origin (point O), indicating that more can now be bought. The slope of the new budget line EE' will be the same as that of CC'. This follows from the fact that the relative prices of the two products have not changed, but can be seen diagramatically from the fact that if income increased z per cent then *both* the maximum amount of bread and the maximum amount of ale able to be bought must have increased by z per cent.

The new consumption bundle will be x''', comprising more bread and ale. The change in the demand for a product as a result of a change in income is sometimes known simply as the 'income effect'.[11]

It should be noticed that the income effect may, for certain products over certain income ranges, be negative. A traditional textbook example often cited is margarine, which many consumers consider inferior to butter. Thus an increase in income could lead consumers to switch to butter, reducing the demand for margarine.[12] This is shown diagrammatically in Figure 2.6.

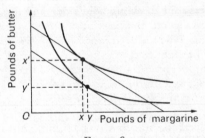

FIG. 2.6

The distance xy represents the *fall* in demand for margarine resulting from the rise in income.

Having examined the income effect, the change in the household's demand for bread and ale following a fall in the price of ale can be analysed a little more thoroughly. We saw in Figure 2.5 that, following the fall in the price of ale, the household was 'better off' in the sense of attaining a higher indifference curve. Assume now that the household is made such that it is no better or worse off than prior to the price change, i.e. income is reduced so that the household can only just attain the original indifference curve I–I. The dotted line FF' in Figure 2.5 represents such a reduction in income in that it is

---

[11] The income effect can be measured by the *income* elasticity of demand, i.e. percentage change is the quantity of a good demanded, divided by the percentage change in income.

[12] The current emphasis on the possible health advantages of margarine has, in fact, meant that this product is frequently no longer regarded as inferior, especially by high-income groups concerned with the possibility of heart disease.

parallel to the new budget line CD. Its slope represents the new price ratio following the fall in the price of ale. It is now possible to decompose the whole move from the bundle x to the bundle x' (as a result of the fall in p_a), i.e. the price effect, into two separate components or 'effects'. In Figure 2.5 the move from x to x'' is called the *substitution effect* of the price fall—for it represents the tendency for the household to substitute towards the relatively cheaper good (ale) *even though* its income has been reduced so that it remains on the same indifference curve. Given our assumptions on the shape of the household's indifference curves, the substitution effect invariably implies that more will be demanded of the good whose price has fallen. The move from x'' to x' in Figure 2.5 is the *income effect* of the price change, for it represents that part of the change in the demand for commodities that stems from the fact that the fall in the price of ale has increased the real income or effective purchasing power of the household. Although this may seem rather complicated, the intuition is fairly simple. If the price of ale falls, the household will normally buy more ale for *two* reasons. Firstly, ale is relatively cheaper *vis-à-vis* bread and there is an automatic tendency to buy more of the relatively cheaper good —i.e. the substitution effect. Secondly, the fall in the price of ale means that the household's fixed income, $£\bar{y}$, has increased in the sense that it will now buy more goods—this is the income effect.

In general, as shown in Figure 2.5, both the income and substitution effects tend to increase the demand for a product whose price has fallen. In the case of an 'inferior good' the income effect will be negative and tend to offset the substitution effect. If it is sufficiently strong to completely offset it, then we would have a case in which a fall in price actually led to a reduction in demand. This should not be confused with the case where, because price is taken as a guide to quality, consumers buy less of a product when its price falls in the belief that it is a lower-quality (i.e. different) product.

We have introduced the ideas of income and substitution effects in the context of changes in the prices of goods. It is important to note that the ideas are, in fact, remarkably general.

We can, for example, analyse the effect of interest rates on consumption with the same theoretical apparatus. To simplify, let us ignore future income and see how much of a household's current income it consumes in the current time period and how much in a future time period. The situation is portrayed in Figure 2.7. Current consumption, C_t, is plotted on the vertical axis and future consumption, C_{t+}, on the horizontal one. If all the income were spent today C_t^* could be purchased. If all of it were spent tomorrow $C_t^*_+$ could be purchased. This will be higher than C_t^* because interest could be earnt on the income in the intervening period. The budget line is the line C^*_t–C^*_{t+}. Given the indifference curves shown, which indicate the household's preferences as between current and future consumption, C_t' will be spent today and $C_t'_+$ tomorrow. If the interest rate were to rise, then maximum future consumption could be higher and the budget constraint would shift to C^*_t – C^{**}_{t+}. Now current consumption would be C_t'' and future consumption C''_{t+}.

Any income saved for the future will earn a higher interest rate, so over-all income will have increased. There is, therefore, an over-all income effect tending to increase both current and future consumption. There is also a substitution effect as the household substitutes relatively cheaper future consumption for relatively expensive current consumption. This tends to increase future consumption and to reduce current consumption. Adding the two effects together, future consumption will increase for both reasons, but current consumption may rise or fall, dependent on whether the income

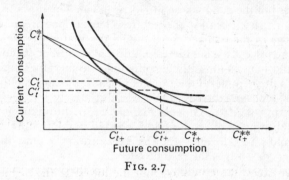

FIG. 2.7

or substitution effect is stronger (in the diagram we have current consumption falling—a stronger substitution effect). Thus the response of current consumption to interest rates can be interpreted in terms of the substitution and income effects.

Secondly, consider the reaction of a worker to an decrease in income tax rates. Such a decrease *increases* the net wage earned per hour and, by implication, increases the 'price' (i.e. the amount of income foregone) of leisure. Conventional demand analysis would imply that the worker would consequently consume less leisure and do more work—for leisure is now 'more expensive'. If, however, the income effect is very strong, then it is quite possible that the worker will, in fact, increase the amount of leisure taken and work less, being still able to preserve his consumptions standards, i.e. the tendency to substitute more work is offset by the increase in leisure as a result of the higher real income obtainable. The concepts of income and substitution effects are very widely applicable in economics.

5. The Consumption Function

5.1. The Cross-Sectional Consumption Function

A household's *total* demand for goods and services can be illustrated in simplified form by plotting *a consumption function*, i.e. the relationship between household expenditure and its main determinants. We simplify here by assuming that only income is important, and ignore the other influences, e.g. interest rates, that were previously discussed.[13] Following the previous

---

[13] The rationale for this is that it allows us to further analyse consumer behaviour while not precluding a discussion of the other influences when examining real world situations.

chapter, there are two different ways of examining consumer behaviour graphically. First, a *cross-sectional*[14] consumption function may be plotted as in Figure 2.8. This shows permanent income on the horizontal axis and consumption on the vertical axis. The consumption function CC indicates that, at a certain time, a household with permanent income Y_1 has consumption of C_1.

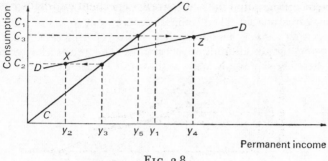

FIG. 2.8

As we move across the economy from the lowest to the highest permanent income households (i.e. rightwards) so consumption increases. In practice there are serious difficulties in plotting this consumption function because we cannot directly measure households' permanent income, but only their *actual* income. Plotting consumption against actual income tends to give a much flatter consumption function, e.g. like DD in Figure 2.8. To see why, consider households with a very low actual income, e.g. Y_2. Although some households on this actual income will be receiving higher income than their (*very* low) permanent incomes, the majority will be temporarily on incomes significantly lower than their permanent incomes which might be at a point like Y_3. It is this income level which determines their consumption spending shown by C_2, and plotting this against actual income gives the point X.

Similarly, households with very higher actual incomes (Y_4) will tend to contain a large proportion who temporarily are receiving more than their permanent income (Y_5) with the result that consumption is at C_3 and the point plotted emperically will be Z. This the consumption function *appears* as the flatter line DD when we plot consumption against actual income cross-sectionally.[15]

5.2. The Time-Series Consumption Function

We can also plot a household's expenditure over time. A *time-series* consumption function is shown in Figure 2.9. This looks very similar to the consumption function in Figure 2.8, but it is significantly different because we are now plotting the consumption behaviour of *one household* through

[14] See Ch. 1, p. 19.
[15] It may be noted that the line DD is consistent with the argument above that low-income groups will tend to save a smaller proportion of their incomes than high-income groups.

time and against measured income, e.g. in 1971 the household's income was Y_1, Consumption C_1. In 1972 they were Y_2 and C_2 respectively, and so on. If all a household's future income were known with certainty and were all included as permanent income, then the household could adjust its consumption immediately to that level and maintain a constant level of consumption throughout a lifetime of changing (generally rising) income. This would give a very flat time-series consumption function. In practice, of course, income over only a relatively short period of time, e.g. three or four years can be reasonably relied upon as secure, and so households are continually revising (usually upwards) their notion of their permanent income, and changing their consumption over time. The time-series consumption function therefore slopes upwards, as shown in Figure 2.9.

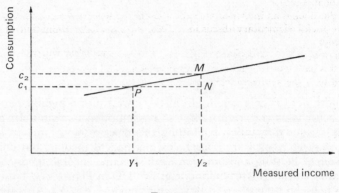

FIG. 2.9

5.3. The Marginal Propensity to Consume

The slope of the consumption function is of particular importance, and is known as the *marginal propensity to consume*. Suppose income rises from Y_1 to Y_2. Consumption rises from C_1 to C_2. Out of the additional or 'marginal' income of $Y_2 - Y_1$ the household has a propensity to consume $C_2 - C_1$ extra. The marginal propensity to consume is simply the additional consumption as a proportion of the additional income, i.e. $C_2 - C_1 / (Y_2 - Y_1)$. But $C_2 - C_1$ equals the distance MN, and $Y_2 - Y_1$ equals the distance NP, so that the marginal propensity to consume equals MN/NP, which is the slope of consumption function.[16] The importance of this measure will be seen later.

6. Conclusion

In this chapter we have outlined some of the principal factors influencing the demand for commodities. We have seen the importance of preferences, relative prices, and incomes in the demand for a commodity, and the central importance of income in the determination of a household's total demand for commodities. We have introduced the concepts of elasticity, the consumption

[16] By analogy, once again, with the gradient of a hill.

function, and various different ideas of income. We have also referred to the role of wealth, interest rates, and expectations. Each of these factors will be seen to be important in the analysis of the working of the economic system.

Bibliography

The subject matter of this chapter is discussed in any orthodox economics text. Section A of the following list outlines some of the textbook expositions that are available. Section B constitutes a selective list of more detailed and, in some cases, more advanced readings.

SECTION A

[1] BAUMOL, W. J. *Economic Theory and Operations Analysis*, 3rd edn. (Prentice-Hall International, 1972).
Ch. 9 of this book is an intermediate exposition of the theory of demand. Ch. 10 is an extremely useful elementary discussion of the empirical determination of demand relationships.
[2] BROOMAN, F. S. *Macroeconomics*, 4th edn. (George Allen and Unwin, 1970).
Ch. 5 of this basic macroeconomics text provides a useful exposition of the basic ideas associated with the aggregate consumption function.
[3] GREEN, H. A. J. *Consumer Theory* (Penguin, 1971).
This book provides an excellent exposition and survey of all the principal ideas associated with the microeconomic theory of consumer behaviour. Although more advanced than some of the texts listed, it can be followed by anyone who is prepared to read patiently.
[4] JOHNSON, M. B. *Household Behaviour: Consumption Income and Wealth* (Penguin, 1971).
A useful survey of the principal ideas of aggregate consumption behaviour.
[5] LIPSEY, R. G. *An Introduction to Positive Economics*, 4th edn. (Weidenfeld and Nicolson, 1975).
Chs. 5–7, 10, and 14–16 of this well-known textbook provide an elementary account of the theory of demand. Ch. 37 is an exposition of the consumption function.
[6] SAMUELSON, P. A. *Economics*, 9th edn. (McGraw-Hill, 1973).
Chs. 4, 20–2 of this justly famous introductory textbook provide a simple exposition of basic ideas of demand theory. Ch. 11 is a simple introduction to the idea of the consumption function.
[7] SCITOVSKY, T. *Welfare and Competition* (George Allen and Unwin, 1971).
Chs. 3 and 4 constitute a neat and clear exposition of the theory of consumer choice. Ch. 5 provides a useful discussion of the worker's choice between work and leisure.

SECTION B

[8] DUESENBERRY, J. S. *Income, Saving and the Theory of Consumer Behaviour* (Oxford University Press, 1967).
[9] EVANS, M. K. *Macroeconomic Activity: Theory, Forecasting and Control*, Chs. 2 and 3 (Harper and Row, 1969).
[10] FARRELL, M. J. 'The New Theories of the Consumption Function', *Economic Journal* (Dec. 1959).
[11] FRIEDMAN, M. *A Theory of the Consumption Function* (N.B.E.R. Princeton University Press, 1957).
[12] GHEZ, G. R. and BECKER, G. S. *The allocation of time and goods over the life-cycle* (Columbia University Press, 1975).

[13] KEYNES, J. M. *The General Theory of Employment, Interest and Money*, Chs. 9 and 10 (Macmillan, 1936).

[14] LANCASTER, K. *Consumer Demand: A New Approach* (Columbia University Press, 1971).

[15] MAYER, T. *Permanent Income, Wealth and Consumption* (University of California Press, 1972).

[16] PYATT, G. *Priority Patterns and the Demand for Household Durable Goods* (Cambridge University Press, 1964).

[17] WORKING, E. J. 'What do Statistical "Demand Curves" show?', *Quarterly Journal of Economics* (1927).

3
The Behaviour of Firms

D. J. MORRIS

1. Central Elements in Firms' Behaviour

1.1. A Basic Framework

There now exist many thousands of business enterprises of one form or another in the United Kingdom concerned with the production, transport, and trading of goods and services. They range from very small one-man private companies to giant firms whose annual turnover is larger than the gross national product of some European countries. They differ in their legal constitution and regulation, their financing, organization and decision procedures, their types of ownership, the number of production stages they cover, the competition they face, and many other characteristics. As a consequence, many differences may be seen in the impact on them of both the prevailing economic conditions and government economic policy.

Despite this, there are a number of similarities in their economic behaviour, which are considerably more important than the differences. All need to obtain finance, all need some inputs of labour and materials, and all have to determine a selling price for their products or services. It is with these sorts of common activities that we will be concerned in examining the behaviour of the private sector.

The purpose is, first, to provide a framework in terms of which the activities and performance of any particular business enterprise can be understood and interpreted, and, second, to provide a further step in the analysis of the economic system in the U.K. as a whole.

Figure 3.1 summarizes the framework, giving an outline of the 'typical' company. With only unimportant exceptions almost all businesses engage in the activities it depicts. It highlights the firm's internal operations and the external influences on them. The diagram is a circular one, each of the anti-clockwise arrows indicating a relationship to be mentioned. We start with the boxes marked 'demand conditions' and 'supply conditions'.

1.2. Demand Conditions

The previous chapter explained the derivation of the market demand curve for a product, showing the total demand for a product at each possible price, given the prices of other goods, consumers' preferences, and incomes (see p. 32). If any of these latter three change, the demand curve will shift its position.

If a firm were a monopolist (sole supplier) in the production of a good, then the market demand curve would also be the demand curve facing the firm, and would tell us the demand which the firm would receive for each possible price. In general, however, there will be other firms producing

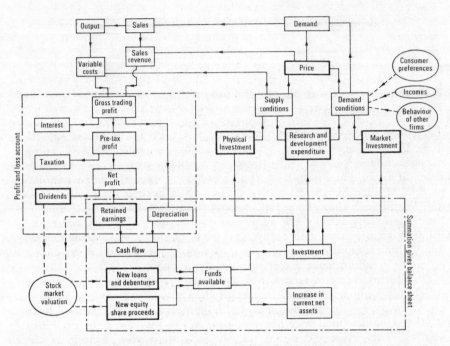

FIG. 3.1   (The author is indebted to Donald Hay of Jesus College, Oxford, for the idea behind this presentation.)

either identical or similar products, and the demand curve facing the firm will depend on these other firms. In particular, it will depend on (a) the number of such firms and their size, (b) the degree of similarity of the products they produce, and (c) the type of competitive behaviour they exhibit, e.g. the prices they set, their sales policy, etc. The possibility that new firms might start to compete by introducing similar products may also be important. Figure 3.1 shows these, i.e. consumer preferences, incomes, and the behaviour of other firms as external influences (dotted lines) on the demand conditions facing the firm. The other determinants we examine below.

1.3. Supply Conditions

To meet demand, finished goods must be produced from the firm's input of materials. It will need factors of production to do this, premises, employees, capital equipment.[1] Some of these inputs, particularly premises and equipment, are fixed in the short term; it may take several years for a firm to expand them. *Fixed costs* are the overhead costs associated with such inputs; they are independent of the firm's current rate of production. Other costs associated with factors of production which are flexible in supply at short notice are termed *variable costs*, and these are affected by the current production rate. At a given time, therefore, a firm will be incurring some fixed costs which it cannot avoid, e.g. rental on land, depreciation[2] on capital equipment; and some variable costs, the level of which depends on its decision on how much output currently to produce, e.g. raw materials, wages.

Paradoxically, part of a company's profits, as measured in its financial accounts, should be regarded as a cost, like wages for example. Just as wages are what the company has to pay to obtain the services of its labour force, without which the company could not continue, so there is some (perhaps ill-defined) minimal level of profits which has to be received over a period by the owners, if the company is to retain their services as providers of finance for business operations entailing financial risks, again without which the company could not continue. Hence, one 'cost' to the firm is this required level of profit, usually termed 'normal profit'. It may be a fixed or variable cost, dependent on whether it varies with the level of output in the short term or not. These cost factors represent the supply conditions of the firm.

1.4. Pricing

Given these demand and supply conditions, a firm must decide upon its selling prices. How this is done is examined in detail later, but, as Figure 3.1 indicates (given the firm's demand curve), the price set will determine the actual demand for the product and hence the sales made by the firm. Assuming for the moment no change in the level of finished product inventory (unsold stock) held by the firm, output must adjust to this level of sales. As described above, the employment of some factors of production can be adjusted to this level of output, but not others. Once this adjustment has occurred, both fixed and variable costs are determined for the firm. The difference between the revenue from the sales made (i.e. price × quantity sold) and the variable costs incurred corresponds approximately to the firm's gross trading profit (or loss).

1.5. The Profit and Loss Account

Out of these gross trading profits various fixed costs will have to be met. First,

---

[1] 'Capital' can refer either to physical capital—factories, machinery, etc.—or to financial capital—the funds available for projects. The term will be qualified if the context does not indicate which is meant.

[2] i.e. the proportion of previous capital expenditure attributable to the current time period. In fact, the wear and tear of a machine in a particular year is partly due to the passage of time (and hence is an unavoidable fixed cost) and partly due to usage (and hence is an unavoidable variable cost). In general, however, firms make a series of annual fixed notional depreciation allowances independent of production levels, the final total of which equals the initial capital cost of the equipment. If two or more products use the same equipment, serious problems arise in deciding how much of the depreciation cost is attributable to each product.

interest charges on funds borrowed (and trade debts) will have to be paid. A firm may borrow either by negotiating a specific loan, usually from a bank of one sort or another, or by issuing debentures (i.e. certificates entitling the holder to a specified amount of interest) to individuals or financial institutions.[3] With either type of borrowing the interest payable is a first charge on the firm's gross trading profits.

Second, the firm will deduct a sum for depreciation. This operation is an accounting one, and does not involve any flow of funds from the firm. In order to calculate the 'true' accounting profit of the company, i.e. the excess of revenue over *all* costs, this deduction has to be made from gross trading profits to allow for the cost of the machinery used in the current year, even though it was purchased in previous years. In other words, although the expenditure on a piece of capital equipment may occur at a single point of time, and out of the company's retained profits, the cost of this to the company is represented in its accounts as a series of annual deductions from gross trading profit prior to the calculation of 'profit before taxation'. The total of these depreciation charges for any piece of equipment may sum to the original cost, known as the 'historic' cost, of the equipment to the company, or to the company's estimate of how much it will cost to replace the equipment when it wears out or becomes obsolete, dependent on the depreciation method used.[4] (But for tax purposes a standard method must be used.)

Only that part of gross trading profit left after deduction of interest and allowance for depreciation is liable to tax, payment of which leaves the company's net profit. This belongs to the owners of the firm who may remove all or some of it from the firm for their own purposes as dividends, or they may leave it in the firm for future use. In the case of firms owned by the shareholders, but run by salaried managers, the latter usually decide what dividend the shareholders may receive, and what proportion of net profit will be retained by the firm. It is always legally possible for the shareholders to appoint new managers, however, if they are unsatisfied with the dividends received, and they are always free to sell their shares.

A statement known as the Profit and Loss Account is usually published annually by firms as part of its published accounts (and in most cases is legally required), showing the amount and breakdown of gross trading profit into interest, depreciation, taxation, dividends, and retained earnings. These items are, therefore, boxed together in Figure 3.1 under the heading 'Profit & Loss Account'.

1.6. The Balance Sheet

The funds available to the firm for expenditure on new capital equipment, research, etc., indeed on anything not already covered under expenditure on variable costs, comes from three main sources:

(a) The gross trading profit, minus the funds that have flowed out of the firm in the form of interest, tax, and dividends. This, however, as Figure 3.1

---

[3] These may generally, like shares, be bought and sold in the stock market.

[4] Practice also differs on the methods used to allocate the total cost across the expected life of the equipment.

shows, is equal to the depreciation charge set aside at the beginning, plus the retained earnings left after the various cash outflows. The sum of retained earnings and depreciation is usually known by the rather misleading term 'cash flow'. The fact that depreciation is a source of cash should not lead one to conclude that an increased depreciation charge would necessarily increase the cash flow. An *increased* depreciation charge would *reduce* profit before taxation by a similar amount, and if the tax bill and dividends paid were the same as before, retained earnings would be lower by exactly the amount that depreciation had increased. If, however, the reduced profit before taxation led to a lower tax bill and lower dividends, both of which are very likely, then cash flow would be higher than before. But it is only by causing a change in one or both of taxation and dividends that a change in the depreciation charge can alter the firm's cash flow, even though it is often referred to as a source of cash.

(b) New funds may be raised by issuing new debentures, and raising new loans.

(c) Alternatively, or in addition, the firm may issue new equity shares to new or existing shareholders. The extent to which these can be carried out will partly depend on the valuation the stock market places on the company, which in turn will be heavily influenced by the dividends paid and/or expected, and the prospects for future growth of the company as a result of its retained earnings.

These funds may be spent on various types of long-term investment projects. If not, they may be used to pay off current liabilities (i.e. debts the company must stand ready to pay off at short notice), or used to build up stocks and work-in-progress, increase holdings of short-term financial assets (e.g. government securities), or left in current or deposit accounts with a bank. These would occur either because the firm regarded the current level of these assets as too low in the light of possible demands upon them, or because cash flow exceeded the sums required to finance current investment plans. Stocks, financial assets, cash, and short-term debts owed to the company are termed 'current assets' as either they are cash, or can be turned into cash very quickly. *Net* current assets, equal to current assets minus current liabilities, will therefore rise by the amount of funds available which are not used for long-term investment.

Clearly, what flows into the 'funds available' box must equal what flows out in any time period,[5] i.e.

$$\left.\begin{array}{l}\text{Retained Earnings} + \text{Depreciation} \\ + \text{ Net New Loans and Debentures} \\ + \text{ New Equity Issue}\end{array}\right\} = \left\{\begin{array}{l}\text{Investment} \\ + \text{ Increase in Net Current} \\ \quad \text{Assets}\end{array}\right.$$

Therefore, the sum of the amounts on the left-hand side for all previous time periods equals the sum of those on the right for all previous time periods. The sum of all previous retained earnings is termed the 'reserves' of the firm, but it should be stressed that they do not constitute any reserve of funds in

[5] Bearing in mind that money retained, e.g. in a current account, counts as an increase in current assets.

the normal sense, all of it having flowed already into investment, or increases in current net assets. The sum of all equity issues is usually split up into two parts, (i) the funds that would have been raised if all shares had been bought by investors at their nominal face value (known as par value), and (ii) the difference between this and the amount actually received. The latter would be higher or lower, depending on the demand for the shares in the stock market when they were issued. In general this share 'premium' is positive.

Summing over all previous periods, and subtracting total depreciation from both sides, we get

$$
\left. \begin{array}{l} \text{Shares at Par Value} \\ + \text{ Share Premium} \\ + \text{ Reserves} \\ + \text{ Debentures} \\ + \text{ Loans (long-term)} \end{array} \right\} = \left\{ \begin{array}{l} \text{Total Capital Expenditure} \\ - \text{ Total Depreciation} \\ + \text{ Net Current Assets} \end{array} \right.
$$

It should be noted that only *long-term* loans are included on the left. Short-term ones which might have to be paid soon are current liabilities and are subtracted from the right-hand side in claculating current net assets. Total capital expenditure minus total depreciation to date is the current value of the firm's fixed assets according to its books—and is known as the 'written-down' value of its fixed assets.

This table is a simplified presentation of the firm's Balance Sheet which is also usually published once a year.[6] The total of either column is generally known as the Capital Employed, and it is a measure of the capital available to the firm over the medium term. It can be calculated either from the sources of funds (left-hand), or from the uses (right-hand). The ratio of net profit to capital employed is often taken as a major indicator of a firm's economic performance.[7]

1.7. The Medium and the Long Term

It was stated earlier that in the short term the demand and supply (or cost) conditions facing a firm are more or less fixed. Over a somewhat longer period —the *medium term*—the demand curve facing the firm may to some extent be controlled by the firm through market investment, i.e. advertising, promotional schemes, etc.[8] In the long term, as defined above, the cost conditions will be changed by the capital investment which the firm carries out. A third

[6] The items are boxed together in Figure 3.1 under the heading 'Summation gives Balance Sheet'. An older alternative form arises if current liabilities are added to both sides. The right-hand side is then the company's total *assets* (capital and current). The left-hand side is its total liabilities (debentures, loans, and current liabilities owed to people other than the owners of the company; shares at par value, share premium, and reserves 'owed' by the company as a legal entity to its owners).

[7] Very serious problems arise in company accounts under inflationary conditions, e.g. the depreciation allowances may sum to far less than the cost of replacing a machine when it is scrapped; assets and liabilities fixed in monetary terms will have declining real values; a large part of accounted profit may be used up simply in maintaining constant stock levels at higher prices, etc. See P. Kirkman: *Inflation Accounting* (Assoc. Business Programmes, 1975). Also Report of Sandilands Committee of Enquiry into Inflation Accounting.

[8] In practice, much market investment expenditure is regarded as a recurrent cost and,

use of the funds available is research and development. This may be directed towards the production process, thus again changing the cost conditions of the firm over the long term, or may be in the form of product development which will change the demand conditions over the long term by changing the products available.

These three uses of funds shown in the Figure 3.1 will, of course, have to be co-ordinated—process research to improve production performance and reduce costs; capital investment which embodies the new process; capital investment for the production of new products, and marketing and advertising to establish or improve the demand for the product. By means of these expenditure decisions the cost and demand conditions which constrain the firm in the short run can to some extent be manipulated over the medium and long term, provided the funds can be made available. This to a great extent depends on the firm's profits, not only because they are a major source of funds, but also because they are a main determinant of whether new funds will be made available in the form of loans, debenture stock, and equity shares. Hence there is a circularity. The firm can only actively influence its cost and demand conditions in the long term if it can generate adequate funds from the current cost and demand situation, or if this is poor, attract support from creditors convinced of its future improvement.

1.8. The Firm's Decisions and the Firm's Accounts

Eight of the boxes in Figure 3.1 are in heavier surround. These, out of the many decisions taken in firms, indicate the seven[9] main ones with which we shall be concerned. Three are financial, namely:

(i) The division of net profit between dividends and retained earnings;
(ii) The funds to be raised through new borrowing;
(iii) The funds to be raised through new equity issue.

The results of these decisions will appear directly in the firm's financial statements.

The other four decisions are also vital in determining the firm's performance and profitability. The expenditure decisions (market investment, research and development, and physical investment) are major elements in determining the cost and demand conditions, which, together with the pricing decision, determine profitability. Although, therefore, the main statements of a firm's position are given in its Balance Sheet and Profit and Loss Account, economists have generally been more concerned with the pricing and investment decisions, because these are the main determinants of the firm's performance as a user of scarce resources. The financial statements primarily describe this performance, rather than analyse the behaviour that has led to it.

---

therefore, deducted from sales revenue along with other variable costs in calculating gross trading profit. In this case the expenditure is financed directly out of sales revenue, without becoming part of 'trading profit' and 'cash available'.

[9] Two boxes refer to what is essentially one decision—the division of net profit *between* dividends and retained earnings.

1.9. The Firm's Objectives

One thing is missing from the figure. Each type of decision is taken on the basis of certain criteria, and these will be chosen in the light of the firm's objectives. There is much controversy over what these are, and we will here simply note four main ones:

(i) Profit. Maintaining or increasing the level of profits is a central objective. Firstly, in smaller firms the profits earned may represent the main or only source of income for the directors, while in firms with shareholders, profits are necessary to pay the dividends which ultimately justify the holding of the shares.[10]

Secondly, profits are essential if funds are to be available for the various types of investment described. Thirdly, the rate of return on capital employed (i.e. ratio of net profit to capital employed) is often regarded as an indicator of how successful a firm has been. Both the firm's pricing and various investment decisions will be designed at least to maintain current profit levels, and more generally, over the longer term, to increase them as much as possible, subject to any constraining effects that result from pursuit of other objectives.

(ii) Size. Most business decision-takers are partly concerned to increase the size of their firm, be this measured in terms of assets, sales, or turnover. Partly, large size may help to maintain profits through its effect in allowing greater specialization; in allowing lower average costs per unit of output to be obtained from larger plant; and through economizing in such things as purchasing, advertising, training, etc. It may also lead to an element of market domination by the firm, with consequent gains in its competitive position. Thirdly, managers in large firms generally control more resources, have larger staffs and higher salaries, all of which contribute to their satisfaction. Finally, a certain amount of prestige attaches to the managers of large firms, which again is a reason for them attempting to increase the size of their firms.

(iii) Growth. Consequent upon this desire for size, managers may well want their companies to grow as fast as possible. This requires that firms tie their different decisions together effectively, e.g. lower prices and more advertising may ensure faster growth of demand for their products, but both these things reduce the margin of profit and perhaps the supply of funds for future investment. Thus the pricing, finance, and expenditure decisions have to be properly co-ordinated if the funds available are going to grow as fast as the demand for the firm's products.

(iv) Security. Pursuit of any objective clearly requires that the firm be financially viable, which implies maintaining sufficient net current assets and adequate cash flow to be secure against bad trading conditions. In addition, the directors of publicly quoted companies will be concerned to ensure dividend payments and stock market valuation adequate to satisfy share-

---

[10] Alternatively, it may be argued that the managers attempt to increase the value of their shareholders' equity as much as possible, but this will depend principally on profits and the firm's financial decisions.

holders, and to thus secure themselves against the possibility of replacement or take-over.

Many other influences will be present, but these four, specified in broad terms, are reasonably comprehensive, well attested to by firms' executives and well supported by various empirical studies of firms' behaviour.

Having looked at the flow of funds, the financial statements of firms, and the objectives of firms, we now go on to look at the decisions which are central—pricing, investment, and finance.

2. Pricing

2.1. Introduction

Firms use a very large number of procedures for setting prices, dependent on their objectives, their products, their organizational characteristics, and the competitive pressures they face. Here we identify only the major methods of pricing, but this will be enough for us to later identify both the response of firms to their external situation—the behaviour of the economy and government economic policy—and their role in the allocation of resources in an economy with a large private sector. We follow the framework of Figure 3.1 by examining first the dependence of price on cost and demand conditions, and then the impact of income, consumer preferences, and other firms on price behaviour.

2.2. Average Cost Pricing

By far the most prevalent form of price behaviour is to calculate the variable costs incurred per unit of production in a specified period, and to add percentages to this figure to arrive at a price. The first percentage is to allow for the fixed costs attributable to the production being priced—and the second is to provide a margin of profit. As the amount sold partly depends on price, this procedure only makes sense if (as quite often happens) average variable costs per unit do not vary much with the level of production (at least for a 'normal' range of output levels) and so can be calculated independent of the demand that results from the price set. If demand turned out to be particularly high or low, however, then actual average costs might differ from the 'standard' ones on which the price was based, and the price set would probably be reconsidered.

The main problem is to identify the factors which determine the size of the two percentages added. The first will depend on the ratio of the firm's fixed costs to its variable costs, but will only be a rough approximation to this ratio because it changes somewhat every time output—and, therefore, variable cost—changes. More important is the second percentage, for in choosing this the firm, given the first addition to cost, determines its over-all gross 'mark-up' on average variable cost. The main factors influencing the size of this gross mark-up are examined in the next five sections.

2.3. Profit Maximizing in the Short Term

One possible objective, given the cost and demand conditions, will be to set price exclusively to maximize current profits. Given the level of average costs, a high gross mark-up will give a high profit per unit sold, but will result in a high price and a lower number of units sold, while a low mark-up will give high demand, but a low profit per unit sold. In general, therefore, there will be an intermediate price which maximizes profit. This profit-maximizing price will depend on the price elasticity of demand (described in the last chapter). If this is low, then a high gross mark-up will be required to maximize profit because demand is reduced very little by the high profit per unit. If this elasticity is high, a lower mark-up will be required because a relatively very large increase in demand can be obtained in return for the lower profit per unit. In fact, it can be shown that the gross mark-up on average variable cost, expressed as a percentage *of the price*, must equal $1/E$, where E is the price elasticity of demand,[11] if short-run profits are to be maximized, and this shows clearly that the higher the elasticity of demand the lower the profit-maximizing mark-up. Much market research is designed to discover the sensitivity of demand to price (and by implication the elasticity of demand) in order to determine a profit-maximizing price.

Frequently, no actual calculation of the elasticity of demand will be made, however, because changes in demand will be indicated by decreased stocks of finished goods, higher utilization of capacity, and lengthening order books, and executives will be able, on the basis of past experience, to judge approximately the magnitude of the mark-up required to establish or re-establish more or less maximum profits, if they are required. Potentially very costly market research is therefore avoided.[12] Figure 3.2 explains the price set.

The vertical axis measures various cost and revenue characteristics of the firm, each as a function of the level of output in the short term. As fixed costs are a given fixed sum, the average fixed cost per unit of output will be lower the higher the level of output, and this is shown by the average fixed cost curve which falls continuously as output increases. The average variable cost curve shows average variable cost falling at first, as a result of economies of bulk buying, better use of labour, savings on fuel, maintenance, etc., becoming constant over a range, and then eventually rising as overtime becomes more prevalent, machine utilization becomes excessive, etc. Adding the two curves together vertically gives the total cost of production per unit of output, termed the average total cost curve. There will, of course, be a different average total cost curve for each possible size of plant.

Constant returns of scale are said to exist if an X per cent increase in all factors of production increases output by X per cent. If the cost of all factors of production are unchanging, constant returns to scale imply that the average total cost curve for larger-scale operations will have the same minimum level. *Economies of scale* imply a larger than X per cent increase in output, with lower minimum average total cost therefore (again assuming the cost of all factors of production fixed) for larger scale. The opposite case is known as *diseconomies of scale*.

---

[11] Assuming average variable costs are constant, no matter what the output level. See Appendix 1 for a proof of this.

[12] Charging 'what the market will bear' is generally an intuitive attempt to find the price which gives the best trade-off between profit margin and demand.

Superimposed on these curves, we put the demand curve for the product, from Chapter 2. This is labelled the average revenue curve, because average revenue equals total revenue/output which equals price × output/output which equals price. Hence the average revenue curve relating average revenue to output sold is the same as the demand curve which relates price to output sold.

To discover the price which maximizes current profits, we introduce the *marginal cost* and *marginal revenue* curves shown in Figure 3.2. Marginal

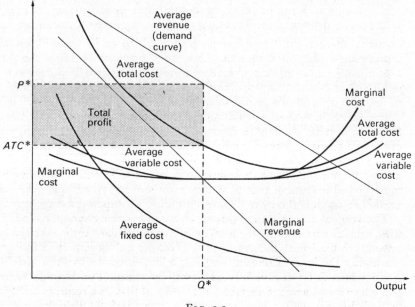

FIG. 3.2

cost is defined as the change in total cost which occurs when output is in-creased by one unit, and marginal revenue as the change in total revenue. The curves show marginal cost and marginal revenue for different output levels.[13] The concept of marginal cost is of central importance in many re-source allocation issues, as will be seen. Here it is crucial because a firm only maximizes current profits if it produces a level of output at which marginal cost equals marginal revenue (Q^* in Figure 3.2). If output is at a lower level than this, generally meaning marginal revenue is above marginal cost (see Figure 3.2), then production of one more unit of output will add more to revenue than to cost, and therefore increase total profit. If output is at a higher level, generally meaning marginal cost is above marginal revenue, then the last unit of output produced has added more to cost than revenue, thus

[13] Note that the marginal cost curve coincides with the average variable cost curve when the latter is horizontal. With variable cost per unit constant (and fixed costs fixed) the addition to total cost from one extra unit (marginal cost) equals the additional variable cost per unit.

reducing profits, and production should be cut back to increase profits. Only at an output level, where marginal cost equals marginal revenue (Q^*), can profits not be increased by reducing or increasing output. To generate demand at this level requires a price of P^*, as shown by the demand (average revenue) curve. The profit-maximizing gross mark-up as a percentage of price is $1/E$ (see p. 58), because this is the margin which logically ensures that marginal cost equals marginal revenue. Average total cost is ATC^* and total profit equals the profit per unit ($P^* - ATC^*$) multiplied by the number of units sold (Q^*).

This analysis allows us to examine the implications of the other main influences on demand (see Figure 3.1). Income, preferences, and other firms all affect the profit-maximizing price by influencing the elasticity of demand.

2.4. Impact of Income

As the last chapter indicated, increases in income will generally increase the level of demand facing a firm.[14] This may or may not lower the price elasticity of demand, dependent on the specific form of the relationship between price, income, and demand. Thus the mark-up of a profit maximizer might rise, but not necessarily. His price would rise if the increase in output raised average variable costs, for example through paying more for raw materials, now in short supply, or higher wages to retain the labour force. Net profit would then rise disproportionately fast because the fixed cost element to be deducted from the higher gross profit would not have changed.

2.5. Impact of Consumer Preference

The price elasticity of demand may be expected to be partly determined by the tastes or preferences of consumers. An individual is less likely to reduce consumption in response to a price rise if he regards the product as a necessity (resulting in a low price elasticity of demand) than if he regards it as inessential. This would suggest a high profit-maximizing mark-up on necessities, but this may not be observed in practice either because of the impact of other influences on the price elasticity of demand (see below) or because high-income consumers regard as essential products which low-income consumers have to regard as luxuries.

2.6. The Existence of Close Substitutes

With regard to the impact of other firms, three central aspects can be identified. First, the degree of similarity (in the consumer's view) between the firm's product and that of one or more other firms, i.e. the extent to which these are close substitutes for each other. If one or more firms do produce a close substitute, then purchasers will be very ready to switch to a competitor if the first firm raises its price. This means that the elasticity of demand is high and the profit-maximizing price low.

In the extreme case in which one or more other independent firms produce a product which consumers regard as identical, then, in the absence of

[14] Even if a product is 'inferior' for some consumers, the firm's demand will only fall if this is true for a sufficiently large number of consumers.

transport costs, the elasticity of demand would tend to become infinite and the gross mark-up zero.

In interpreting this theoretical extreme, two points must be stressed. (a) No contribution will be made towards covering fixed costs, implying losses. If this situation continued, the firm would eventually leave the industry. In the long term *all* costs are variable, however, and long-run considerations would lead the firm to base price on long-run average *total* costs, thus avoiding these losses. (b) Normal profit is part of cost. A zero gross mark-up does not, therefore, imply zero profit as conventionally defined in company accounts, but only that no profit in excess of the amount required by the firm to continue operating will be made.[15]

2.7. The Number of Close Substitutes

Second, irrespective of the number of firms producing close substitutes, if the profit margin or demand for the product is inadequate, then the firm will have either to improve its efficiency and therefore lower its average costs, switch to other products, advertise more, or begin to go out of business. In this way the prices other firms set exert a competitive pressure on the firm.

If, however, there are very few firms—an industrial structure known as oligopoly—an additional and quite direct pressure may be exerted on the price policy of any one of them. A price change by one firm will tend to have a marked affect on the demand facing the others.[16] Retaliation of some sort is therefore likely, making it difficult or impossible for the first firm to know the full affect of its new price policy. More specifically, if a firm thinks that a price rise will result in a large loss of demand because it expects none of its competitors to follow, and if it thinks that a reduction in price will gain it little extra demand because the competitors will be forced to follow, then any change or price may lead to lower profits, resulting in considerable price rigidities over a period, despite changes in cost and/or demand conditions.[17]

This will generally only be a temporary phenomenon, however, because

(a) firms may collude or develop a price 'leader';
(b) frequently one firm will eventually take the chance of a price rise, and others may then in fact take the opportunity to follow;[18]
(c) boom conditions may easily make one or more firms prepared to raise

---

[15] 'Perfect competition' is said to prevail if the product is homogeneous and divisible, if there are many quite independent buyers and sellers, if there are no transport costs, barriers to entry by new firms, rigidities in the movement of factors of production, or limitations on people's information about the market. These rigorous conditions ensure a horizontal demand curve. Few examples, if any, actually exist, but the model provides a useful bench mark for comparison and over the long term may give valid predictions of economic behaviour. This is developed in Chapter 6, p. 160.

[16] Giving a high *cross* elasticity of demand, defined as the ratio of proportionate change in the quantity of one firm's demand to the proportionate change in the price set by *another* firm.

[17] This is known as a kinked demand curve situation, because of the shape of the demand curve that portrays it. It should be noted that many other types of expectations may exist, giving different implications for price policy.

[18] It is frequently profit maximizing for a second firm to follow, *given* that the first raises prices, and knowledge of this may itself lead to the first firm raising price.

prices in the expectation that other firms, faced with rising costs, are anxious to do the same, and in the knowledge that demand is running at a relatively high level anyway.

Oligopolistic firms will ideally need to estimate all the different possible results of each possible new price, and develop some criterion for selecting the 'best' strategy —an approach known as game theory. In practice the number of alternatives and uncertainty about both the economic environment and other firms' reactions may lead to adoption of simple, well-tried, and well-known rules of thumb.

2.8. Barriers to New Entry

The third factor is the possibility that *new* firms will compete by commencing production of a close substitute. In some cases strong forces will operate to prevent this, e.g. if a firm has established a dominant market position through brand advertising; if particular scarce skills, technical know-how, etc. are necessary in the product line; if the processes used are patented; if a very large initial outlay is required to commence production; if competitive production can only be carried out on the very large scale necessary to generate very low average costs. To the extent that such barriers do *not* exist, the threat of new competition can usually only be thwarted by a deliberate policy of keeping profits sufficiently low, so that there will be no inducement for new firms to come into the market, or inducement sufficiently low to substantially reduce the rate of new entry.

Thus even a relatively simple analysis of firms' pricing behaviour must take account of the impact of income, preferences, the existence and number of close substitutes, and the threat of new competition. But this still ignores at least five further elements which complicate the situation. These are the existence of objectives other than profit maximization; the interdependence of pricing and other decisions in determining the firm's over-all performance; the use of advertising as an additional determinant of demand; the fact that all the elements mentioned may be expected to vary over time; and the possibility of a firm foresaking a purely independent approach to its price policy. These we now consider.

2.9. Target Return Pricing

Firms frequently select a margin in order to obtain a previously specified target level of profits, or to allow a required return to be obtained from a specific capital project. This can arise for two reasons:

(1) Objectives such as the maximization of the firm's growth rate require, as we have seen, a particular level of profits in relation to capital employed. Too high a level makes more funds available, but tends to reduce the growth of demand; too low a level leads to an inadequate supply of funds. By experience managers will come to know the sort of profit levels required to ensure that the firm's development is not hindered by inadequate supply of funds or inadequate demand for goods. Their price decisions may then be seen as attempts to generate approximately this target level of profits, or target return on capital employed.

(2) Even if profit maximization is their only objective, firms generally will not know if they are achieving it. A useful way of proceeding, therefore, is to try new products as they are developed, retaining only those which give reasonable profits, and rejecting the others. Firms may, therefore, apply a given profit margin to all products, continuing production over the long term with only those products which can be successful with this target margin. This provides another reason why firms often take price decisions systematically on the basis of required target profits.

2.10. The Product Package

For many consumer products, firms attempt to provide an over-all 'package' —a particular product of particular specification aimed at a particular type of consumer in a specified income bracket with advertising, packaging, and presentation designed specifically for him, and at a price that attracts him. This attraction is based partly on the price relative to his income, partly on what he deduces from the price about the supposed quality of the product, and partly on the implications for status and social position of being the type of person who pays that sort of price for such a product. The emphasis put on this approach by marketing executives, plus the many instances where demand has been higher despite higher prices, both indicate the extent to which it is the *combination* of price and other features which determine the demand for the product. In this situation, firms faced with inadequate margins may attempt to reduce costs, even at the expense of some change in product specification, rather than change the price and the associated attraction of the product. Again it is the interrelation of price decisions with others—this time product specification and marketing—which leads to a different approach than that implied by simple short-run profit maximizing.

2.11. Life Cycle Pricing

The relative importance of the different factors influencing price policy may well alter over the life of a product, and this can lead to the forward planning of price variation over the life of the product to take account of the change. There are a number of forms of this, but a typical one involves a high initial price when the product is launched, as a result of the high average costs of small-scale production and the high mark-up obtainable in the absence of close substitutes. If the product is successful, price is reduced significantly (in real terms) as large-scale production reduces average costs, mark-ups are reduced to deter at least some potential entrants, and as the introduction of new close substitutes begins to raise the price elasticity of demand. The main pressure may well be to expand production as rapidly as possible to obtain the potential economies of scale first, and achieve a dominant market position. Finally, the market stabilizes, often dominated by a small number of firms, with a fairly stable price and margin, and strong competitive pressures not to vary them independently of competitors' reactions.

2.12. Restrictions on Price Competition

In situations of acute price competition, particularly those where high fixed costs mean that even a relatively small reduction of demand results in losses, firms frequently wish to resort to some form of agreement to regulate prices. There is a whole spectrum of possible types of regulation, running from explicit co-ordination of prices, discounts, quantities, etc. at one extreme, to the most vague and purely implicit understanding, based only on experience of past price behaviour. In general, however, we may distinguish three main types:

(i) Collusion, where firms secretly, or occasionally openly, agree on a price for their product which they will all maintain, thus preventing competitive price-cutting which might be harmful to them in the long run.

(ii) Price Leadership. In some cases, particularly where a dominant firm exists, there may be a specific agreement or a tacit understanding that all firms will set a price equal to (or related in some determined manner to) the price set by the price leader. His price changes are a signal for the others to follow suit.

(iii) Information agreements, in which firms simply supply information on their price changes and related aspects, e.g. quality specifications, either prior to the actual change or after it. There is therefore no actual agreement on price levels, but the information supplied can serve as a vehicle for obtaining greater uniformity of prices, if this is desired.

In conclusion, there are a large number of factors to be taken into consideration when pricing behaviour is examined. To draw out the implications of such behaviour for efficiency and resource allocation is very difficult. Chapter 6 presents a much more abstract approach to provide a starting-point for this, which in turn is a basis for investigating the desirability or otherwise of various policies designed to alter industrial structure, firms' behaviour, their performance, and allocative function (see Chapter 16). The effectiveness of policy none the less crucially depends on the details of actual price formation reviewed above.

3. Financial Decisions

3.1. The Cost of Finance

The firm's financial decisions are important because they help to determine the amount of funds available, and the cost to the firm of obtaining those funds. Section I identified four main sources, namely depreciation provision, retained earnings, short-, medium-, and long-term borrowing, and equity issue. We therefore look at what determines the cost and availability of each.

It might be thought that there is no cost to the firms of depreciation provision and retained earnings, because no interest has to be paid to obtain them. This is incorrect. There is what is known as an *opportunity cost* to the owners of the firm. By utilizing the funds, the firm deprives the owners (shareholders) of the opportunity of receiving the funds in the form of dividends.[19] If they were fully paid out the owners could invest the funds else-where and earn a return. Foregoing this return is a cost to them, and it will only be in the owners' interest for the firm to retain the funds if it can use them more profitably.

The situation is complicated by the tax position. Corporation tax is levied on taxable company profits. Two items are generally deducted from gross profits to arrive at taxable profits; the depreciation allowance allowed by the Inland Revenue (which will generally depend on existing law on investment incentives and bear no relation to a 'normal' wear and tear provision) and interest charges on the company's financial obligations (bank overdraft, trade debt, loans, and debentures). The company then splits the post-tax profits between dividends and retained earnings. If dividends are liable to *further* tax—the shareholder's income tax for example—the tax system is said to have a pro-retention bias, which will reduce the cost of internal funds relative to new equity financing. This is because if funds are retained, all of them can be used to earn a return for the shareholder, but if paid out only that part left after payment of the additional taxation is available to earn more in the same (or another) company. The tax system can be designed to have a neutral, pro-, or anti-retentions bias.

Borrowing over whatever period in general involves a fixed interest cost over the life of the loan, though many loans, e.g. overdraft facilities, mort-gages, involve an interest rate that can be altered at the discretion of the lender. Again, taxation reduces the effective cost of these capital funds because interest charges are a tax-deductible cost, i.e. if the loan had not been incurred, profits would have been higher because of the absence of interest charges. However, taxation would also have been higher as a result of the higher profits, and the firm's net profit position would have been improved by only the post-tax amount. It is this amount foregone because of the inter-est charges which is the *effective cost* therefore. If the interest rate is 12 per cent and the company tax rate is 40 per cent, the effective cost is

$$(1 - 0.4) \times 0.12 = 0.072 = 7.2 \text{ per cent}$$

The cost of new equity funds is more complicated to determine in practice. It depends on the yield that potential shareholders require to be prepared to buy shares, and thereby provide funds. The yield comes partly through dividends, and partly through appreciation in share prices. The latter will depend heavily on the firm's continuing ability to earn higher profits in the future, and this will require retained earnings. Therefore while too high a level of retained earnings can cause people to sell shares because the current dividend is inadequate, too low a level can also cause them to sell shares be-cause there is too little prospect of future earnings increase. In both cases share prices fall, and the firm's decision on how to split net profits between dividends and retained earnings must partly be an attempt to find the intermediate level of retained earnings that keeps the share price as high as possible.[20]

[19] Using depreciation provision to pay dividends may, however, change the tax position and hence the funds available, besides being subject to various constraints.
[20] Some economists have shown that under certain assumptions the share valuation will be

Maximization of the firm's share valuation may be an objective in itself, but in addition it will reduce the cost of equity finance. If in a given economic situation with a known stream of dividends share prices fall, it means that current or prospective shareholders will pay less for a claim on the future stream of dividends, implying that they require a higher return on their out-lay than previously. New equity funds will only be forthcoming if this higher return can be earned, and so the cost of new equity finance will be higher. To the extent that managers are more concerned that their firm grows fast, they will tend to retain more earnings for growth than if they were only concerned to increase the value of the firm's equity.

3.2. Gearing

A firm is legally required to pay loan interest, which is therefore a first charge on its trading profit, but only subsequently pays dividends if it can and so chooses. Except in bankruptcy, therefore, the return to the *lender*, unlike the return to a *shareholder*, is known and certain. The higher variability of dividend payments means that the average return required by debenture holders is often less than that required by shareholders.[21] Given this, and the greater tax advantage with loans, the effective cost of borrowing is frequently less than the effective cost of new equity finance, and often less than that of internal cash flow. Considerable cost savings arise therefore from increasing the proportion of a firm's total finance which is provided by loans (i.e. debt finance). On this basis the over-all (weighted) average cost of capital funds will be lower, the higher the proportion of debt finance. There will, however, be a limit to the extent of this effect. If debt finance becomes a high proportion of total finance, interest charges will be high relative to dividends. If trading profits fall, dividends can always be cancelled, but interest must be paid, and so the existence of a high proportion of interest charges increases the prob-ability that a fall in gross trading profits will bankrupt the firm. In addition, the percentage reduction in dividends consequent upon a fall in gross trading profits will be greater the higher the ratio of debt to equity finance, unless firms act to stabilize their dividend payments over time. Both equity holders and lenders will therefore be at a greater risk. The former will sell shares, reducing the price and increasing the cost of equity finance. The latter will ask for higher interest to offset the risk (or sell debentures, depressing the price and giving the same effect), and the cost of all types of finance will therefore rise. After a point, therefore, more debt finance can only be raised if the firm will accept a higher cost of capital.

The ratio of debt finance to total finance is known as the gearing ratio, and

dependent on earnings, but independent of the proportion retained. The assumptions are, however, very restrictive, e.g. a perfect market for financial capital, no tax effects, etc.

[21] Two things may offset this: (a) the prospect of capital gains for the shareholder; (b) inflation will cut the real value of interest received, but may not cut the real value of dividends or capital gains received if these keep pace with inflation. A 'reverse yield gap' can then appear between interest rates and equity yields, and this is not uncommon. Equity finance is none the less quite expensive for the company in this situation because it is one which will only continue as long as equities really *are* a 'hedge' against inflation, i.e. as long as the company can maintain earnings in line with inflation.

it follows from the above that there will be an optimal gearing ratio which minimizes the cost of capital (though in practice there may be quite a range of gearing ratios that give approximately minimum cost of capital).[22]

3.3. The Availability of Finance

We may summarize by saying that firms either attempt to retain that proportion of earnings which maximizes share value, or the maximum proportion consistent with maintaining acceptable share values and equity yields. They raise funds externally if required, but the declining profitability of the uses to which more and more funds may be put will eventually lead to a reduction in share valuation again, putting a limit on the total external finance that can be raised. The proportion of the external finance borrowed will be increased until it no longer makes a significant difference to the firm's cost of capital, unless halted by consideration of the borrower's risk. A typical firm might finance approximately two-thirds of its investment by retaining half its earnings, a sixth by new debt finance, and a sixth by new equity finance, giving an average value of rather less than 20 per cent for the gearing ratio.

Given these decisions, both the amount of funds available and the average cost of them are given. There will be little further scope to increase the amount (except by drastically increasing the cost) or to decrease the cost (except by cutting back on the amount raised). The cost and availability of funds for investment will then largely depend on the net profits earned, the level of interest rates on borrowing, and the yield required by shareholders. The last in turn depends partly on the interest that can be earned by lending rather than holding shares, partly on the level of profits being made, and, more importantly, on the likelihood or otherwise that the firm will continue to make profits in the future to finance further dividends, investment, and growth. The two central determinants, therefore, of a firm's ability to finance its investment expenditure are the current and expected level of net profits, and the level of interest rates.

---

[22] Two factors may interfere with this: (i) If the borrowing firm assesses the possibility of its not being able to maintain interest payments as more serious than does the lender of the funds, then the firm may deliberately choose to keep its gearing ratio below the level which minimises the weighted cost of capital. (ii) An investor holding shares in a highly geared company may find it more profitable to borrow funds himself and invest them, together with his own funds, in a low-geared company. This allows him to increase his over-all return while facing the same proportionate interest charges as before. (The difference being that it is the investor who pays them out of his dividends, rather than the company paying them before giving the investor his dividend). This type of behaviour is not widespread, but the consequent switch from geared to ungeared company shares depresses the price of the former relative to the latter, and hence raises the former's weighted cost of capital. This could then, to some extent, offset the lower cost of finance that moderate gearing normally brings. See F. Modigliani and M. Miller: The Cost of Capital, Corporation Finance and the Theory of Investment. American Economic Review 1958 for the original (and difficult) statement of this view.

4. Investment Expenditure

4.1. Investment Objectives and Investment Planning

It was stated earlier that, in general terms, companies are primarily concerned with the profitability, size or rate of growth, and security of their
operations. At any one time, however, it may be very difficult, particularly in
a large company, for its managers to identify those business opportunities
the pursuit of which will most aid these objectives. This arises partly because
of uncertainties as to the future course of economic events, and the impact of
different possible strategies on the company's objectives; partly because of the
complexity of the repercussions which occur as a result of the decisions
taken at board level concerning major company developments, and finally
because of the interdependence of the objectives specified.

Much effort is often spent, therefore, in establishing formal or informal
means of making major business decisions amenable to careful and rational
analysis and decision-taking. Three mechanisms in particular are important:

(i) Company planning. Long-range planning will frequently be carried out
as a means of establishing a coherent picture of how the company may attain
its objectives, within which the rationale for, and consistency of, individual
decisions can be evaluated. This first requires identifying a consistent set
of objectives, which itself is far from easy. On the financial side, a company
can generally increase its finance over time: (a) by increasing its return on
capital employed. This directly increases the funds available internally
and generally makes it easier to raise new loans and new equity finance
externally; (b) by reducing its net current assets or by raising new loans in
the absence of an improvement in profitability. Both these latter two tend to
increase the financial risks facing the firm, however, with the possible consequence that shareholders will sell their shares, depressing the share price
on the stock market. Thus the growth of supply of funds tends to be directly
related to profitability and inversely related to security.

Growth of demand for a firm's product will depend partly on the state of the
market and the nature of the product. If these are conducive to commercial
success then higher growth and higher profitability will generally result.
Given the particular rate of growth and profitability determined by the
market, a firm will generally only be able to obtain faster growth if it is
prepared to sacrifice some of its profitability (and vice versa), e.g. growth of
demand can generally be increased by lowering prices to encourage new
customers; by increased advertising and promotional expenditure for the
same reason; by developing new markets geographically; and by developing
new products as a means of expanding its operations faster than might be
possible within the confines of the existing product range. Each of these will
frequently reduce profitability, however, unless the new markets are notably
more profitable than existing ones; and so faster growth of demand will be
attainable only at the expense of lower profitability.

Even in this very simple example, therefore, there are several relationships
between different objectives which will limit the ability of the company to

identify a plan that will ensure that the growth of demand for company products is matched by growth in its supply of funds. This can be illustrated, as in Figure 3.3 (based on an approach by Marris [34]).

The line DD indicates the inverse relation between profitability and growth of demand. S_1S_1 shows the direct relation between profitability and growth of supply of funds, for a given level of security. If a lower level of security can be risked then the line shifts rightwards, e.g. to S_2S_2, indicating a faster growth of supply of funds at any given level of profitability. The construction of a plan that ensures consistency between finance and production growth

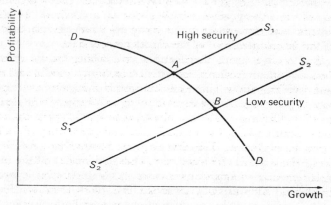

FIG. 3.3

can be thought of as attempts, within this stylized approach, to identify points like A and B, and to select one which gives adequate security (i.e. an SS curve not too far to the right), and the preferred balance of profitability and growth. The selecting of objectives, construction of corporate plans, and identification of the corresponding financial plans are therefore three major functions of the senior levels within many companies' managements.

(ii) Decentralization. Once the over-all plan is clear, the next step involves working out its implications for different parts of the company, and indicating the sort of decisions that it entails. The degree of diversification, the average profit margins, and the major capital projects required can be estimated and analysed. In addition, those lower down the company responsible for this aspect of operations will need to be constantly looking for and investigating the business opportunities likely to improve the company's performance as measured by its objectives. In particular, this requires the search for investment opportunities within one or more of various categories of expenditure, each of which can be interpreted as a type of investment likely to further the objectives stated. In a comprehensive classification this would include; (a) replacement of obsolete or unworkable equipment; (b) reduction of unit costs through modification and improvement of production processes; (c) expansion of plant to meet expected demand increases; (d) plant and machinery for the production of new models or new products; (e) the production of a previously purchased input (sourcing); (f) provision of distribution facilities; (g) offices, canteen, and recreational facilities; (h) equipment necessary for research and development prior to full commercial production.[23]

These reasons for investment, derived from the high-level objectives, may themselves be broken down further and converted into more specific form. Particular cost levels, capacity utilization levels, market shares, etc. will be watched, extrapolated in various ways, and used to indicate exactly when investment in different categories becomes potentially desirable. Thus not only are the general requirements of the over-all plan filtered downwards, but opportunities to pursue company objectives are monitored and information on them filtered upwards, both to allow revision of plans in the light of changes in the economic environment, and for the purpose of final selection of projects considered necessary or desirable in the light of the company's current situation and future plans.

4.2. Investment Criteria

The third mechanism is to utilize specific investment criteria. As a result of the company's over-all plans it will have a fairly good indication of the return on capital (and cash flow) required, the funds available, and the minimum cost of obtaining those funds (see previous section). As specific investment projects are formulated, they will in general be evaluated, not only in relation to the over-all strategy, but also in the light of specific profit or cash flow criteria, to ensure that the targets envisaged are being met, that the return is greater than the cost of obtaining the funds to be used, and that there are not other projects which might offer a higher return if the funds were to be directed to them instead.

The three most widespread types of criteria are:

(i) Payback. From the estimated cost of the project, forecast running costs and revenue it is calculated how many years must elapse before the project has paid for itself, i.e. before the total accumulated revenue, net of running costs, exceeds the initial capital cost.[24] Only if the figure is below the maximum acceptable or 'cut-off' number of years is the project itself acceptable.

(ii) Accounting Rate of Return. The average annual profit (net or gross of tax) is calculated and expressed as a percentage of the initial capital cost. This must then exceed the chosen minimum satisfactory cut-off level.

Both of these suffer from some fairly obvious deficiencies. The former takes no account of revenue earned after the payback period, while the latter does not allow for the fact that revenue earned today is worth more than the same nominal amount of revenue in the future. This is because the revenue

---

[23] In principle, almost all of these might be carried through by acquisition of another company's existing assets, as well as by the construction of new plant, etc.

[24] In practice, many complications arise in the use of this, and the other criteria. Here only the general nature of the criteria is outlined.

received earlier can be used to earn interest or a return of some form during the intervening period. For these reasons there is increasing and already widespread use of more sophisticated criteria which allow for these elements.

(iii) Discounted Cash Flow (DCF). Suppose a firm spends £100 now on a project which will result in £110 accruing to the firm in one year, and nothing more. The rate of return of 10 per cent is found by expressing the net gain (110 − 100 = 10) as a fraction of the initial sum, i.e.

$$r = \frac{110 - 100}{100} = \frac{1}{10} \text{ (i.e. 10 per cent)}$$

where r is the rate of return.

This equation may be rewritten[25] as

$$100 = \frac{110}{1 + r} \qquad (1)$$

and the rate of return is the value of r which satisfies this equation. If the £110 were reinvested, to obtain £121 in two years' time, then for the second year

$$r = \frac{121 - 110}{110} = \frac{1}{10}$$

again, and this may similarly be rewritten

$$110 = \frac{121}{1 + r}$$

Putting $121/(1 + r)$ instead of 110, therefore, in equation (1) gives

$$100 = \frac{121}{(1 + r)^2} \qquad (2)$$

Thus £100 invested now to generate £121 in two years' time would represent a return of 10 per cent per annum, and this would be found by solving equation (2). More generally, if the initial investment outlay is C, and the sum expected back is A, after t years, the rate of return, r, is found by solving the equation

$$C = \frac{A}{(1 + r)^t}$$

and equations (1) and (2) are just specific examples of this. Typically, firms receive varying cash inflows over a period of years. If we call these A_1 in year 1, A_2 in year 2, etc. up to A_n in year n, the last year of the project, then the formula becomes

$$C = \frac{A_1}{1 + r} + \frac{A_2}{(1 + r)^2} + \frac{A_3}{(1 + r)^3} + \cdots + \frac{A_n}{(1 + r)^n} \qquad (3)$$

[25] Multiplying both sides by 100, adding 100 to each side, and dividing both sides by $(1 + r)$.

This is the basis of the discounted cash flow methods. The company can estimate the future net cash flows expected from an investment project (the A's), estimate the initial capital cost (C), and then find the value of r that solves the equation. The variable r is called the internal rate of return of the project (IRR), and can be compared with either the cost of obtaining the funds, the internal rate of return on alternative uses of the funds, or a cut-off rate which may itself reflect these.

The advantage of this approach is that it takes into account *all* the cash flows associated with the project, but discounts them (i.e. reduces them in value in the calculation) by a larger amount the further they are in the future. Each term in the formula represents not the actual cash inflow for the year concerned, but the value of it to someone *now* who could earn the internal rate of return on it if he had it now, i.e. the *present value* of the future cash flow.[26]

4.3. The Optimal Capital Stock

Simplifying somewhat, we can envisage a company identifying the internal rate of return on a whole range of capital projects (existing and potential) and ranking them from left to right in descending order of their IRR. This is shown in Figure 3.4 by the line AA. The position of this line will reflect all the relevant cost and revenue factors influencing the desired capital stock, e.g. a higher level of wage cost could shift the line, with those projects involving little employment moving nearer the vertical axis relative to those involving high employment levels. The company also selects a cut-off point (10 per cent in Figure 3.4) as described above. The optimal situation for the company will be to have in operation all those projects for which the internal rate of return supersedes the cut-off rate, i.e. projects up to point K^*. This will maximize profits if the cut-off rate reflects the cost of raising funds, and will maximize management utility generally if the cut-off rate is that rate consistent with the company's plans derived from its growth, profit, and security objectives. (Note that in this situation the cut-off rate will partly be chosen in the light of the capital stock desired.) If the actual capital stock existing is equal to K^*, then no further investment in plant and machinery would be necessary.

4.4. The Determinants of Investment Expenditure

If now the cost of raising funds were to fall, such that the company's cut-off rate fell to 8 per cent, the optimal capital stock would rise to $K^{*'}$, and further capital to the value of $K^{*'} - K^*$ would be desired. The rate of investment, i.e. the capital expenditure per year, per month, etc. is a flow variable and depends not only on the fall in the cost of borrowing (which determines how

---

[26] An alternative method—the Net Present Value method—utilizes the same formula, but substitutes the cut-off rate for r, and solves the right-hand side (the A's and r being then known) to obtain the Present Value of the future stream of cash flows. The present cost of obtaining them, namely C, is then subtracted to find the Net Present Value. The project is then acceptable if this figure is positive. The two methods have different advantages and disadvantages, and in certain situations can give conflicting answers. See Baumol [5], Ch. 19.

much new capital stock is required) but also on how rapidly the expenditure can be carried out. This in turn is a function of a number of factors—the extent to which the funds are immediately available, the degree of spare capacity in the capital goods industry, the time involved in planning expansion, placing orders, and carrying out construction, being the main ones. However, the *total* investment to be carried out will largely depend on the change in borrowing costs. As has been seen, the general level of interest rates will be a major factor in determining the cost to a company of obtaining funds and so interest rates changes may be expected to bear an inverse

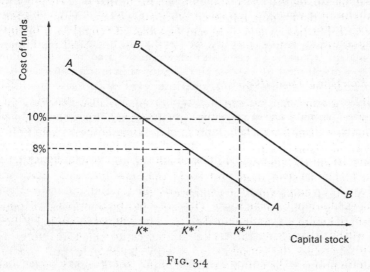

FIG. 3.4

relationship to investment expenditure (having allowed for other determinants to be discussed below).

This is but one factor, however. If a company expects an increase in demand for its products, this will usually lead to an increase in the future expected cash flows associated with its capital projects. The value of A_1, A_2, etc. in the DCF formula will be higher even though C, the initial capital cost, is the same. In solving equation (3), therefore, r will be higher for each project. In Figure 3.4 the line AA, known as the marginal-efficiency-of-capital schedule, will be higher, e.g. at BB, indicating the higher internal rate of return than before that can be obtained for each unit of capital. Such a change in expected demand will, as before, raise the desired capital stock, in this case to $K*''$, and tend to bring about investment expenditure at a rate determined as described above. Thus indications that demand is going to rise to a level where the desired capital stock is above the currently existing one, e.g. rising levels of income, are likely to bring about increased investment expenditure. This relationship, known as the 'accelerator', appears to be a particularly powerful one in the determination of investment expenditure. It should be noted that both influences on investment will tend to work in reverse as well, with falling income levels and rising interest rates tending to inhibit investment.

We have so far assumed a single cut-off rate, dependent on the cost of obtaining funds, but the section on finance decisions indicated that the different sources of funds will have different costs. Typically, a company will generate some internal finance from depreciation and retained earnings (see p. 64), which have an opportunity cost, and raise some external finance from further bank borrowing, further issue of fixed interest debenture stock, and issue of new equity shares. The cut-off rate might then be the cost of obtaining the most expensive funds that the company typically uses; or it might be some weighted average of the costs of the different sources of funds; or the company could construct different cut-off rates dependent on the type of finance that was to be raised for the investment expenditure being contemplated. In nearly all cases an increase in the amount of funds internally generated will tend to increase the amount of investment carried out. This is because in all cases the marginal projects that, prior to the increase in cash flow, were just not worth carrying out, will now become attractive, i.e. the internal rate of return was actually not high enough to make it profitable to raise funds externally for the projects, but will be comfortably above the relatively low cost of internal funds, if they can be generated in greater quantity. This can be shown diagramatically as in Figure 3.5.

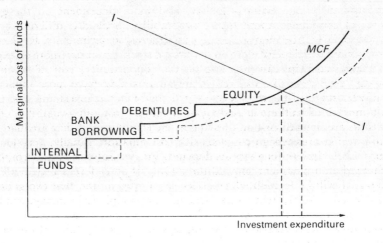

Fig. 3.5

The *MCF* curve shows the marginal cost of funds as the company moves from the cheapest to the most expensive sources. The line *II* indicates for the particular situation the amount of new investment which would be profitable at different levels of the cost of funds. The increase in cash flow pushes the curve outwards to the right, also pushing the intersection with the *II* curve to the right. Thus internal cash flow is another important determinant of investment. This, it will be remembered, is comprised of depreciation allowance and retained earnings, both of which are individually important. The depreciation charge will reflect (abstracting from various investment incentive allowances) the size of the existing capital stock, which, by determining the likely replacement requirements, will have a bearing on the investment carried out. Retained earnings will primarily depend on the net profit earned, particularly if firms attempts to stabilize their dividend payments over time, and these earnings will also be significant as a guide to the prospective profitability of future investment. Thus the capital stock, profitability, and cash flow all help to explain the over-all level of fixed investment, in addition to changes in interest rates and market demand levels. Finally, and implied by the above, movements in stock market prices, by changing the effective cost of raising new equity finance, may also play an important role in determining how much equity financed investment will occur. Furthermore, if a fall in share prices scares some creditors, it can raise the cost of new debentures and even bank borrowing as well.

Four other factors must also be stressed. Firstly, investment expenditure must be planned long in advance, and also earn profits well into the future. *Expectation* of demand levels, interest rates, etc. are therefore vital, and expectations are much more volatile and rapidly changing in the light of economic events, than the events themselves. This adds a strong element of unpredictability to investment expenditure, making it more difficult to manipulate by government policy, and more dependent on the general level of confidence about future profitability. Secondly, different types of investment will be more responsive to different determinants. Replacement investment will depend more on the capital stock, expansion more on expected demand, stock investment more on the (opportunity) cost of holding the stocks, etc.[27] Thirdly, different determinants may have more influence at different stages of the trade-cycle, e.g. demand factors in a slump where funds are available but there is inadequate demand; cost and availability of funds if these are short during an upswing in the economy of if they are inadequate in a period of recession coupled with cost inflation. Finally, very long lags may exist between changes in demand, interest rates, etc. and consequent changes in investment expenditure. Only if it is forecast that all spare capacity will be eliminated, stock levels run down, and that excess demand will not be purely temporary, will investment plans be made, funds earmarked, etc. All this takes considerable time prior to a decision to invest, which itself will precede by months, or even years, the full utilization of the plant concerned.

4.5. Research and Development

Investment in research and development can in theory be dealt with by the DCF approach, but in practice it is usually almost impossible to make any reliable estimate of the expected future cash flows. It cannot be known

[27] Housing investment will depend to a great extent on interest rates, because of the significance of mortgage interest relative to incomes in determining how many houses the public can afford.

whether research and development will lead to a saleable product or usable process, not what they might be, or entail. Firms therefore frequently have a constant research and development budget per year, or one which represents a specified proportion of total sales revenue. For specific research and development projects a higher cost of capital figure is frequently utilized to allow for the greater risk of failure with an unknown venture. In addition, firms have to ensure that such high-risk projects are generally not financed by borrowing on a large scale, but by the safer method of provision of new equity finance or retained earnings. Otherwise failure of the project will not be able to be accommodated by a reduction or cancellation of dividends, and the requirement to pay interest may result in bankruptcy. In practice, people would be very unwilling to lend at fixed rates of interest for a high-risk project, thus making this form of finance either very expensive or unavailable for such projects.

Research and development investment, if successful, results in the firm possessing valuable information rather than a productive process itself. Unlike most valuable assets, however, no ordinary market could develop for it, because no one would pay very much for plans, designs, formulae, etc. unless they had a good ideas as to their content and use. But if these are known then there is no point in paying for them. This situation is dealt with by the patent system under which a firm, by registering a patent on its findings, can ensure either that someone else must pay the firm to use the information, even though anyone can see the information, or that it can develop its research commercially, safe in the knowledge that it will have a monopoly on the design, etc. for a certain period (though others may attempt to develop very similar processes which do not flout the patent act).

Patents restrict the diffusion of new products and processes through an industry, but there are also other obstacles to this. The need for new finance for the physical investment which embodies the new advances may hamper their application; it may be more profitable to use a new design rather than an older one if one has a choice of either, but often more profitable to continue with the older design if the firm already has equipment embodying it rather than to scrap it and replace it with the newer design. For the DCF calculation the net cash flows appropriate to the capital outlay on the new equipment (minus any scrap value of the old) should *not* be the cash flows that will result from the operation of the new plant, but only the *additional* ones on top of those accruing to the existing equipment as a result of the lower costs. For all these reasons, research and development expenditure may not only be relatively insensitive to all factors except availability of funds but also slow in its impact on the existing cost conditions.

4.6. Market Investment

This may be in the form of advertising, but often involves promotional campaigns, bonus payments (or discounts) dependent on sales, stock displayed, etc. It has partly an informative function, but also a persuasive one. It is debatable whether total demand is influenced greatly by the persuasive aspect, but market shares are strongly influenced by it. It will tend to proliferate where the gross profit impact of £X of advertising is greater than £X; where oligopolistic structure makes price-cutting an unprofitable means of competition; and where the image of the product is an important element in the over-all package being offered. In some cases an industrial equilibrium can be reached where an imbalance of market investment between firms is roughly matched, in profit terms, by an imbalance on price. In others the effectiveness of advertising ensures that all firms engage in similar amounts of advertising, which may then simply counter each other. The impact of this on the efficiency with which resources are being used is an element in public policy to be examined later.

5. Conclusion

This chapter has looked at the main decisions which firms take and the major considerations involved in taking those decisions. It has indicated that companies potentially have some control over their profitability, growth, and security, but that their pricing, finance, and investment decisions which promote these ends are all to a greater or lesser extent constrained—by consumers, the actions of other companies, and by a range of economic factors largely beyond their control, including market demand, interest rates, input costs, equity values, availability of loanable funds, to name only the more important. The chapter provides a basis for understanding and predicting the impact on companies of such factors. But in addition it provides an explanation of the main determinants of company pricing and expenditure decisions which together are two vital elements in the explanation of the general price level, inflation, and employment. This chapter is therefore one more component in the general picture of how the economy works.

Appendix 1

Marginal Revenue (MR) is the first derivative of total revenue (TR) (i.e. the rate of change of total revenue with respect to changes in output). If P is price, Q is output

$$\text{Then } MR = \frac{d(TR)}{dQ} = \frac{d(PQ)}{dQ} = \frac{QdP}{dQ} + P = \left(P \frac{QdP}{PdQ} + 1 \right)$$

$$\text{The Price Elasticity of Demand equals } - \frac{dQ}{Q} \bigg/ \frac{dP}{P} = - \frac{PdQ}{QdP}$$

$$\text{Therefore } MR = P \left(-\frac{1}{E} + 1 \right) = P \left(1 - \frac{1}{E} \right)$$

$$\text{and } \frac{P - MR}{P} = 1 - \frac{MR}{P} = 1 - \left(1 - \frac{1}{E} \right) = \frac{1}{E}$$

Profit Maximization requires $MR = MC$ (marginal cost) and therefore requires $\frac{P - MC}{P} = \frac{1}{E}$. If Average Variable Cost (AVC) is constant $MC = AVC$ and Profit

Maximization requires that the profit margin as a fraction of the price $\frac{P - AVC}{P} = \frac{1}{E}$.

Bibliography

SECTION A

A number of good introductory textbooks exist which cover the basic theory of Supply and Demand, Perfect Competition, Monopoly, Oligopoly, and Monopolistic Competition. The best-known British one is:
[1] LIPSEY, R. *Introduction to Positive Economics*, 4th edn. (Weidenfeld and Nicolson, 1975).

A good American alternative is:
[2] SAMUELSON, P. *Economics*, 9th edn. (McGraw-Hill, 1973).

More concise is:
[3] BRAFF, A. *Microeconomic Analysis* (Wiley, 1969), esp. Chs. 1–10.

Those who prefer a more mathematical approach should read:
[4] COHEN, K. and CYERT, P. *Theory of the Firm*, 2nd edn. (Prentice-Hall, 1975), esp. Chs. 1–2.
or
[5] BAUMOL, W. *Economic Theory and Operations Analysis*, 2nd edn. (Prentice-Hall, 1965).

These are very largely theoretical. More empirically orientated work on Industrial Economics covering firms' objectives, costs and pricing, market structure, etc. includes:
[6] NEEDHAM, D. *Economic Analysis & Industrial Structure* (Holt, Rinehart, and Winston, 1969).
[7] DEVINE, P. *et al. Introduction to Industrial Economics* (George Allen and Unwin, 1974).
[8] PICKERING, J. *Industrial Structure and Market Conduct* (Martin Robertson, 1974).

For a very thorough American view see:
[9] SCHERER, F. *Industrial Market Structure and Economic Performance* (Rand McNally, 1970).

For a text which is more orientated to business decisions see:
[10] LIVESEY, F. *Economics* (Polytech, 1972).

A very different picture of industrial behaviour is provided in:
[11] GALBRAITH, K. *The New Industrial State* (Hamilton, 1967).

For an introduction to Company Accounts and Accounting see one of:
[12] BULL, R. *Accounting in Business* (Butterworth, 1972).
[13] HENDRIKSEN, E. *Accounting Theory* (Irwin, 1970).
[14] BAXTER, W. and DAVIDSON, S. *Studies in Accounting Theory* (Sweet and Maxwell, 1962).
[15] TRICKER, R. *The Accountant in Management* (Batsford, 1967).

Introductory texts on managerial theories of the firm and managerial economics include:
[16] WILDSMITH, J. *Managerial Theories of the Firm* (Martin Robertson, 1973).
[17] SAVAGE, C. and SMALL, J. *Introduction to Managerial Economics* (Hutchinson, 1967).

[18] HAGUE, D. *Managerial Economics* (Longmans, 1969).
[19] CURWEN, P. *Managerial Economics* (Macmillan, 1974).
[20] PAISH, F. *Business Finance*, 4th edn. (Pitman, 1968).
[21] MIDGLEY, K. and BURNS, R. *Business Finance and the Capital Market* (Macmillan, 1969).

SECTION B

More advanced reading under various headings is as follows:

Collected articles

[22] NEEDHAM, D. (ed.). *Readings in the Economics of Industrial Organisation* (Holt, Rinehart, and Winston, 1971).
[23] ARCHIBALD, G. (ed.). *Readings in the Theory of the Firm* (Penguin, 1971).
[24] YAMEY, B. (ed.). *The Economics of Industrial Structure* (Penguin, 1973).
[25] ROWLEY, C. (ed.). *Readings in Industrial Economics* (Macmillan, 1972), 2 vols.
[26] COWLING, K. (ed.). *Market Structure and Corporate Behaviour* (Gray-Mills, 1972).

Pricing and Markets

[27] HAWKINS, C. *Theory of the Firm* (Macmillan, 1973).
[28] UTTON, M. *Industrial Concentration* (Penguin, 1970).
[29] SILBERSTON, A. 'Price Behaviour of Firms', *Economic Journal*, lxxx, 1970.

Cost Structure

[30] SILBERSTON, A. 'Economics of Scale in Theory and Practice', *Economic Journal*, lxxxii (Special Issue, 1972).
[31] PRATTEN, C. 'Economics of Scale in Manufacturing Industries', Department of Applied Economics Occasional Paper, No. 28 (Cambridge University Press, 1971).
[32] HALDI, J. and WHITCOMB, D. 'Economics of Scale in Industrial Plants', *Journal of Political Economy*, Aug. 1967.
[33] LEIBENSTEIN, H. 'Allocative Efficiency versus X-Efficiency', *American Economic Review*, June 1966.

Development of Firms

[34] MARRIS, R. *The Economic Theory of Managerial Capitalism* (Macmillan, 1966).
[35] PENROSE, E. *Theory of the Growth of the Firm* (Blackwell, 1959).
[36] McKINTOSH, A. *The Development of Firms* (Cambridge University Press, 1963).
[37] CYERT, R. and MARCH, J. *Behavioural Theory of the Firm* (Prentice-Hall, 1963).

Investment and Finance

[38] BIERMAN, H. and SMIDT, S. *The Capital Budgeting Decision* (Collier-Macmillan, 1966).
[39] HAWKINS, C. and PEARCE, I. *Capital Investment Appraisal* (Macmillan, 1971).
[40] WRIGHT, R. *The Investment Decision in Industry* (Chapman and Hall, 1964).
[41] BARNAR, T. 'Investment and Growth Policies in British Industrial Firms, NIESR Occasional Paper, No. 20 (Cambridge University Press, 1962).
[42] BAUMOL, W. *The Stock Exchange and Economic Efficiency* (Fordham University Press, 1965).
[43] MERRETT, A. and SYKES, A. *The Finance and Analysis of Capital Projects* (Longmans, 1963).
[44] —— —— *Capital Budgeting and Company Finance*, 2nd edn. (Longmans, 1973).
[45] KIRKMAN, P. *Inflation Accounting* (Assoc. Business Programmes, 1975).

Advertising

[46] Schmalensee, R. *The Economics of Advertising* (North-Holland, 1972).
[47] Backman, J. *Advertising and Competition* (University of London Press, 1968).
[48] Cowling, K. *et al. Advertising and Economic Behaviour* (Macmillan, 1975).

Research and Development

[49] Freeman, C. *The Economics of Industrial Innovation* (Penguin, 1974).
[50] Mansfield, E. *The Economics of Technical Change* (Longmans, 1969).
[51] Salter, W. *Productivity and Technical Change* (Cambridge University Press, 1960).
[52] Rosenberg, N. (ed.). *Economics of Technical Change* (Penguin, 1971).
[53] Schmookler, J. *Invention and Economic Growth* (Harvard University Press, 1966).

4
The Domestic Economy

M. J. C. SURREY

1. An Outline of the Economy

1.1. The Circular Flow of Income

In any economy, at any time, an enormous number of economic transactions are taking place. Goods and services are being sold, wages and salaries are being paid, taxes are being collected, and so on. The first stage in macroeconomic analysis is to classify these activities in such a way as to group together sets of transactions which have something in common. Exactly how this is to be done will depend on the kind of analysis which is to be pursued. For example, if we are interested in the volume of production, we shall wish to group together all transactions which involve newly produced goods, but we shall not be interested in the transfer of second-hand goods since no new production is involved.

More generally, there are two fundamental broad classifications which are of the utmost importance. These are, first, classification into Income, Expenditure, and Production Accounts, and second, into sectoral accounts, according to whether households, firms, the government, or overseas buyers and sellers are involved. The second of these distinctions is the more readily appreciated. In general, one would expect different economic agents to act in different ways: as we have seen households receive incomes from various sources which they spend in ways which are presumably intended to maximize the satisfaction which they can obtain; firms employ labour and capital to produce goods and services in pursuit of profits, growth, etc.; governments raise revenue and undertake expenditure in order to maximize the general welfare; overseas transactions involve agents outside the domestic economy altogether. Different sectors will thus behave in economic ways which will reflect their different economic motivations.

The major relationships between these sectors can be summarized as in Figure 4.1.

This shows the various flows of funds that occur as a result of the production and sale of goods and services. Out of the gross revenue that a firm receives, it pays out funds: (1) to other firms for all sorts of semi-finished parts, transport facilities, insurance, etc. These are termed 'intermediate' goods and services as the funds paid return to (in fact effectively never leave) the productive

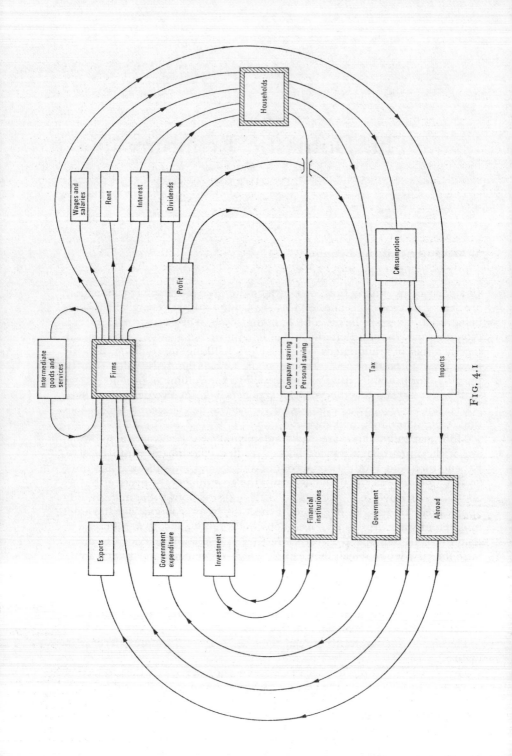

Fig. 4.1

sector; (2) usually in payment for some imported goods, in particular various raw materials; (3) as wages and salaries; (4) rent on property paid to individuals (rent paid to another firm will come under item 1 above); (5) interest on loans from individuals, e.g. the debentures held by households (interest paid to other firms, financial institution, etc. will again come under item 1 as they are payments to other organizations for the productive service they provide).[1] Anything not paid out in one of these forms is by definition pre-tax profit, part of which goes in dividends, part in taxation, and the rest as retained earnings, i.e. company saving. (See Chapter 3, p. 52 for details of this.)

Household income (wages and salaries, rent, interest and dividends paid to households) either goes in income tax, or on consumption expenditure, or is saved (personal saving). Consumption expenditure will be partly taxation, e.g. excise duty on cigarettes, Value Added Tax (V.A.T.), etc. The non-tax element may be spent on imported goods or domestically produced goods, and in the latter case the funds flow back to the productive sector. Thus all the funds paid out have either 'leaked' into saving, taxation, or imports, or have come back again to the productive sector.

We can now imagine a new round of expenditure decisions. Foreigners decide to buy our exports, the government to purchase all sorts of goods and services (e.g. roads, defence, the police force), and firms and financial institutions use funds for expenditure on plant and equipment. These demands for goods and services can be added to the consumption demand coming from households to give the total expenditure on goods and services in this new time period. This becomes revenue for the productive sector, the progress of which through the system could be followed as described above.

1.2. The National Accounts

We are now in a position to explain the first classification mentioned above. Expenditure, Product, and Income Accounts attempt to measure respectively, and in general terms, the total expenditure occurring in an economy, the total value of production, and the total income received in return for contributing towards production. These three totals should be *equal*. This can be seen intuitively from the fact, (i) that the value of a product is regarded as equal to the expenditure required to purchase it, and (ii) that all revenue received is paid out as income to someone or is retained as profit, which also counts as income. The real world situation is more complex, and for that we need to refer to Figure 4.1. again.

If we were to add up the total value of all the goods and services produced by all firms in the economy (or other productive units) there would be a large amount of *double counting*. For example, one firm would value its output of gear wheels and another would value its output of cars, part of which would be the value of the gear wheels it contains. The same would apply for the glass, tyres, indeed for all intermediate goods and services purchased from

---

[1] Financial institutions are separately identified elsewhere in the figure (see later), but they are, of course, one type of producer of services.

other firms for inclusion in the final product. It is only the total of final goods and services, i.e. those sold for final use, that we should include.

Ignoring therefore the 'intermediate goods and services' box, we see from the figure that the total expenditure (Y) in the economy equals Exports (X), Government Expenditure (G), Investment Expenditure (I), and that part of Consumption Expenditure (C) not going on imported final goods (M_F). However, part of this is not attributable to domestic production, namely that part imported by firms for inclusion in final production (i.e. imported intermediate goods, M_I). Thus total expenditure on final goods produced in this country is, using the above notation,

$$X + G + I + (C - M_F) - M_I$$

Rearranging these we get

$$Y = C + I + G + X - M$$

where M is total imports, i.e. $M_I + M_F$.

This is known as Gross National Income at Market Prices. Part of it is not in fact a payment to the productive sector, namely 'indirect' taxes on expenditure, as this accrues to the government. The amount received by the productive sector is known as Gross National Income at Factor Cost (Y_{FC}) and is arrived by deducting indirect taxes (net) from Gross National Income at Market Prices. Therefore

$$Y_{FC} = C + I + C + X - M - T_I$$

In general, we simply use the term Y for this.

The figure indicated what happens to these funds thus expended. Bearing in mind that we are excluding intermediate goods to avoid double counting, and that imports by firms have been allowed for, the funds go either in wages and salaries, rent, interest, or profit. But this is the total of all factor incomes,[2] confirming that total income and total expenditure will be equal.

Clearly, the total value of domestically produced final goods will equal the expenditure on them (and hence total factor income), but in practice the former amount is found by adding up each firm's *value-added*.[3] This is the difference between the value of its output *minus* the value of its inputs from other firms. If one firm's only input is imported steel costing £1 m. and it makes gear wheels, which it sells to another firm for £3 m., its value-added is £2 m. If the second firm makes gear boxes costing £5 m. in total, and has no other inputs, its value-added is £2 m. If these are sold to the public the value of final domestic production is £5 m.–£1 m. imports, which equals £4 m. However, this is also found by summing the value-added of the two firms. More generally, any firm's output is either final output and is valued in the total of all firms' value-added, or it is intermediate, and though added in as part of value-added by the firm producing it, is subtracted out again by the purchasing firm for which it was an input.

---

[2] i.e. income received by factors of (contributors to) production for their contributions.

[3] This method is used because firms can easily identify their value-added, but frequently cannot say whether their output is final or intermediate, since this depends on the use made of it.

Thus total value-added, total factor income, and total domestic expenditure (i.e. expenditure on domestically produced goods and services) are alternative ways of looking at the total—the value of production in the economy. After allowing for production abroad by British residents (i.e. adding 'net income from abroad') and several other minor complications[4] the total is known as Gross National Product (GNP), Gross National Expenditure, or Gross National Income, and the symbol Y can be used for any of them. This is often known simply as 'national income' and it is the determination of the level of national income which is at the centre of macroeconomic analysis, for it is the simplest measure of how well-off on average the people in an economy are.[5] It is also the primary determinant of the level of employment. Table 4.1 shows the breakdown of Gross National Expenditure into the components described, and also the breakdown of Gross National Income.

2. The Components of National Expenditure

2.1. Consumption

In order to begin to explore the way in which the level of national income is determined, we need to examine the determinants of each type or component of expenditure. We can simplify initially by ignoring the foreign trade sector (and therefore exports and imports) and the government sector (and therefore government expenditure and taxation). These will be added back shortly. In this simplified model, national income has only two components, consumption and investment, i.e. $Y = C + I$. Thus in order to explain changes in the level of national income, we need initially to explain changes in the aggregate expenditures by households on consumption and by firms on investment. To do this we can draw heavily on the analysis of the behaviour of households and firms of the two previous chapters.

The relevant part of Chapter 2 may be summarized by stating that a household's total demand for consumption goods is primarily determined by the level of the household's measured income (over several time periods), the variability of its income, its wealth, the availability of credit, the rate of interest, and expectations (in particular those concerning future income and the prices of potential purchases).

In moving to the determination of the level of consumption for the economy as a whole, all households are lumped together, and we consider the behaviour of aggregate consumption over time. It is then necessary to consider how many of the factors summarized above remain significant. The most important change is in the role played by the level of income.[6] In considering individual households, it was suggested that relatively poor households are likely to save little or nothing since expenditure on 'necessities' will all but

[4] See any basic macroeconomics text for discussion of the further complications, e.g. Brooman [2].

[5] It is more reliable for this purpose if it is calculated per head, and it must of course be expressed in real terms if changes in it are not to reflect merely inflation of prices. Even if it ignores many things which affect average living standards—pollution, congestion, the distribution of expenditure—which are not reflected in the GNP figure itself.

[6] In general, it will be 'disposable income', i.e. income after tax, that will be the main determinant of expenditure, as it is this that poses the effective constraint on spending.

TABLE 4.1. *National Income and Expenditure, 1973*

in £ millions

Expenditure		Income	
Consumers' expenditure	44855	Income from employment	42890
Private fixed investment	8314	Income from self-employment	6244
Investment in stocks	574	Gross trading profits of companies	8476
Public expenditure	18827	Gross trading surpluses of public enterprises	2194
Exports of goods and services	16494	Rent	4894
Total final expenditure	89064	*less* stock appreciation	−3111
less Imports of goods and services	−18338	residual error	589
less Net indirect taxes	−8550	Gross Domestic Product	62176
Gross Domestic Product	62176		
Net property income from abroad	1095		
Gross National Product	63271		

Notes

(i) Gross Domestic Product (GDP) is often used instead of GNP because it refers to production of goods *in this country* as opposed to production by U.K. nationals.

(ii) Gross trading profit and surpluses include both interest payments and profits.

(iii) Stock appreciation refers to the increase in stock investment included in GNP which corresponds not to any physical increase in stocks over the year but only a revaluation of them due to inflation. This is subtracted so that only physical increases are included. The figure for stock investment in the Expenditure column already allows for this adjustment.

(iv) If (as always) the columns do not give the same total, the Expenditure column is presumed correct and a residual error added/subtracted from the Income column.

exhaust their incomes. It follows from this that if such a household suddenly found its income increased substantially, other households remaining as before, then in all probability the proportion of income saved would increase sharply. But suppose that, over a period of time, *all* households' incomes increase substantially. Our household remains where it is *relative* to other households. There are strong grounds for believing that in this case the household will continue to save roughly the same proportion of its income as before. This is because the concept of 'necessities' is highly relative: as a community grows richer, more and more goods formerly regarded as luxuries become, conventionally, necessities—television sets, acceptable levels of food consumption, better standards of housing, and so on. It is still true that in passing at *a given time* from poor to rich households, not only will absolute savings increase, but the *proportion* of income saved will increase. *Over time* however, as the whole community grows richer with the household's relative income position unchanged, its concept of 'necessities' will change and it will not greatly increase the proportion of its income saved. Saving will still increase in absolute terms, but the proportion of its income saved will not. Similarly, although differences in the variability of income between households at a given time are an important factor in determining their relative propensities to save, the degree of variability in the economy as a whole is not likely to change much over time and it ceases to be important in determining changes in the aggregate amount of saving.

The response of consumers' expenditure to income changes at the aggregate level will none the less tend to be delayed, reflecting the lag in the consumer behaviour of individuals already described. This may be attributed to inertia or habit—people grow used to a certain level of consumption which it may be difficult to cut quickly if income falls, or which may not immediately be raised when income rises—or to caution about responding fully to income changes which may be reversed. In other words, the change in income may be initially regarded as transitory and have little effect on consumption. As the new income level appears more permanent so it induces a rise in consumption. Over all, the result is the same: relatively rapid income growth, with consumption lagging behind, will tend to raise the ratio of saving to income, while falling income with consumption slow to be reduced will reduce the saving ratio.

Special mention must be made of the factors governing the aggregate level of spending on durable consumer goods—cars, radio and electrical equipment, etc. In the first place, the demand for these goods is a demand for a *stock* of them, i.e. one washing machine per family, etc. (To be distinguished from the demand for a flow of non-durable consumer goods, i.e. so much food *per week*, for example.) This tends to mean that if the desired *stock* of durables depends on the level of income, actual expenditure, which results from the desire to *change* the stock, will depend on the *change* and not the *level* of income. Secondly, since a high proportion of purchases of such goods involves the use of credit—personal bank advances or consumer credit arrangements—the terms on which credit is available will have a powerful influence on the level of spending. This involves the availability of credit, its interest-cost, and (especially in the case of H.P.) formal or informal regulation of minimum deposits and maximum repayment periods.

In addition to all these quantifiable influences on aggregate consumption, a variety of more nebulous considerations are likely to be important. For example, buoyant expectations about future economic growth may encourage consumption now while gloomy expectations may depress it. Expectations of inflation, and of the dwindling real value of saving, may similarly encourage present consumption as opposed to saving. Finally, as mentioned earlier, specific expectations may play an important role from time to time; for example, the expectations of a 'tough' budget which might involve increases in indirect taxes will encourage the purchase of goods prior to the budget which would otherwise have been bought subsequently.

In summary, major determinants of the consumption component of national income are the level of national income itself, changes in it, expectations based on it, and the tax on incomes. As with the household, so for the whole economy we may plot time-series consumption functions of national consumption expenditure against national income, with the gradient of the line representing the nation's marginal propensity to consume.

The marginal propensity to consume may well be different for different types of income, e.g. wages compared with rent, dividends, etc. but for much analytical work we may imagine an average value of the marginal propensity to consume for the whole economy which will indicate what proportion of an increase in national income we can expect to be spent on consumption goods. For reasons given earlier (p. 87) this will probably change little over time, except for the effect of time-lags discussed on p. 87. Nevertheless, wealth, interest rates, the availability and cost of credit, and expectations will all be additional important determinants.

2.2. *Investment*

Turning to investment, it was suggested in Chapter 3 (pp. 70–5) that for a given firm an investment project would be worth undertaking if, in very general terms, it was expected to be profitable. Profitability was described in terms of the internal rate at which the future net cash flows which the investment is expected to earn must be discounted to make their present value equal to the initial capital cost. If this internal rate of return was greater than the rate at which the firm could obtain funds (either internally or externally), the project would be undertaken. It is thus evident that, other things being equal, firms as a whole will invest more the higher and the more certain are expectations about future returns and the cheaper is finance.

Estimates of future returns were found to depend primarily on expected future demand and on existing supply capacity. Higher demand, reflected in higher output, would raise net cash flows unless rising costs, e.g. wages, raw materials, etc. offset the increases. Higher future net cash flows will tend to stimulate investment, unless there is an existing degree of spare capacity which can be employed to meet the expected demand without further capital investment.

The cost of finance was found to depend on a variety of factors. If finance is to be found internally, then a rise in cash flow (itself likely to reflect higher demand) will increase the availability of relatively low-cost funds. If the investment is to be financed by bank borrowing or fixed-interest stock issues, the rate of interest will be crucial, while equity financing will be cheaper the higher is the general level of stock market prices.

Over the longer term, investment may also be expected to be influenced by the relative costs of labour and capital. This follows from the fact that it is often possible to choose different techniques of production characterized by different ratios of labour to capital equipment. This choice will clearly be influenced by the relative costs of the two factors. Thus it has been argued that the higher capital intensity of manufacturing production in the U.S. reflects the fact that during American industrialization, labour had to be attracted away from agricultural production in which, owing to the abundance of land, labour productivity and real wages were high relative to those in, for example, Britain. There was consequently a strong incentive to choose relatively capital-intensive methods of production.

At an aggregate level, therefore, investment might be expected to depend on factors similar to those which determine it at the level of the firm, i.e. expected future demand, the degree of spare capacity, wage and material costs, and financial factors reflected, for example, in the levels of interest rates and profits.

Similarly, as at the level of the firm, so at the aggregate level we can identify two stages in the determination of fixed investment. The first is to decide what the optimum level of capital capacity is, in the light of demand and financial considerations; the second is to decide at what rate investment will be undertaken in order to close the gap between desired and existing capacity. The second decision will be influenced partly by technical considerations— the speed with which production processes can be reorganized, and so on— and partly by financial considerations; other things being equal, a rapid rate of investment is more likely to need recourse to high-cost external finance than a slower rate even though the ultimate desired total addition to capacity is the same.

2.3. The Government Sector

So far, we have considered only a very stylized economy consisting solely of households and firms. In any real economy—especially that of the U.K.— such a simplification, which ignores the roles of the government and the balance of payments, is too far from reality to be of much use except as a starting-point.[7] We therefore next consider the economic significance of the public sector.

The public sector includes central and local government, and also public corporations (the nationalized industries), but the latter play a special role in the economy which will be discussed in Chapter 18. The remainder of the public sector raises tax revenue by means of direct taxes (taxes on income, including profits), indirect taxes (taxes on expenditure), and taxes on capital.[8] Expenditure by public authorities is broadly of three kinds: capital expenditure (on roads, hospitals, schools, and so on), current expenditure on goods and services (largely payment of wages and salaries to public employees), and payment of grants to persons, or 'transfer payments' (social security benefits, student grants, and so on). Tax revenue and expenditure need not balance, given that a deficit can be met by borrowing, for example, from the private sector (primarily through the issue of 'gilt-edged', i.e. government bonds or

[7] Both are the subject of separate chapters, and are reviewed only briefly here.

[8] Other sources of revenue—for example, social security payments or rates—can be regarded as similar to one or other of these kinds of taxation.

securities; see below). A surplus could be used for the repayment of past debt.

Thus, total demand in the economy is increased by public expenditure, either directly through current and capital spending or indirectly through transfer payments to private individuals which raise private consumption. Total demand is similarly reduced by taxation, which either reduces private incomes (direct taxation) or, by raising prices, reduces the real value of incomes (indirect taxation). Decisions on all these are entirely matters of government policy. Discussion of them is left to the policy section of the book, where the types of further expenditure and taxation, the reasons for them, and the policy matters that lie behind them are discussed in detail.

2.4. The Overseas Sector

The overseas sector affects the domestic economy by purchasing goods and services produced at home (exports) and by supplying goods and services to meet domestic demand (imports). Thus, other things being equal, an increase in exports will raise domestic output while an increase in imports, which reflects a switch from domestically produced goods to foreign goods, will lower it.

The demands for exports and imports will, following the analysis of the demand for goods in Chapter 2, be dependent on purchasers' preferences, on income, and on relative prices. Taking preferences as given, it follows that the demand for U.K. exports will depend on the general level of world demand and on the prices of U.K. goods relative to those of our competitors, while the demand for imports will depend on the level of domestic demand and on the prices of imported goods relative to those competing with goods produced at home. While the influence of demand is clear, the question of relative prices is complicated by the fact that exchange rates can be, and nowadays often are, altered. If exchange rates were completely fixed, then changes in relative prices of goods in world markets would depend mainly on differences in rates of inflation between different countries. But a good costing a certain amount at home can be made to sell at a variety of different prices overseas if the exchange rate can be altered. The question of the responsiveness of imports and exports to changes in relative prices—whether caused by differences in rates of inflation or by changes in exchange rates—is a complex one. Imports of raw materials, for example, which cannot be replaced by domestic alternatives, may be fairly insensitive to even very large changes in price, as the oil price rise has shown. On the other hand, imports of manufactured goods, for example, cars will probably be quite sensitive to changes in relative prices. Similar considerations operate on the export side, though since the U.K. largely exports goods which are also produced by other industrial countries, it is to be expected that our exports will be more sensitive to changes in relative prices, however caused, than our imports. These questions will be discussed in more detail on later chapters; for the purpose of our present simple model, we may assume that relative prices are more or less unchanging. We may also assume that world demand is little affected by developments in the domestic economy. This means that imports can be taken as depending simply on the level of domestic demand, while the level of exports can be taken as autonomously determined—that is, determined independently of changes in the domestic economy.

2.5. Injections and Leakages

We can now begin to put the various parts of the economy together. With the public and overseas sections added in, the equation for national expenditure or income was (see p. 84)

$$Y = C + I + G + X - M - T_I \tag{1}$$

where Y is national income or output, C is private consumption, I is private investment, G is public expenditure on current and capital account (i.e. both its 'consumption' and investment expenditure), X is exports, M imports, and T_I indirect taxes.

Next we add a very simple consumption function in algebraic form. The main determinant of consumption is income, but as it is income after payment of income tax ('disposable income'), which will be available for consumption or saving, we write

$$C = b (Y - T_D)$$

where T_D is direct taxation and b is the proportion of disposable income spent on consumption goods. Before proceeding it is useful to note algebraically that total income is therefore either paid in taxes, consumed, or saved. Thus

$$Y = T_D + C + S$$

where S is saving. Combining this with the earlier national income equation:

$$T_D + C + S = C + I + G + X - T_I$$

or, rearranging

$$I + G + X = S + T + M$$

where T is total taxation, $T_I + T_D$. The point to note about this equality is that the quantities on the right-hand side represent the *leakages* from demand (see p. 83), an increase in any of them depressing domestic demand. The quantities on the left-hand side are components of demand which are largely independent of the current level of income (X depends on overseas demand, G on government policy, I on longer-term expected changes in demand, etc.) and are called *injections*. Why the totals should be equal is examined below.

2.6. The Multiplier

Before pursuing the significance of this algebra, it is important to try to explain the distinction, which is crucial for modern economic analysis, between kinds of demand (or expenditure) which are determined *independently* of the current level of income and those which are *consequences* of the level of income. Assume that a certain amount of the first kind of expenditure occurs—say, for simplicity, investment—which is determined by a variety of factors (financial, expectational, and so on) which can be assumed to be largely independent of the *current* level of total income. The factors of production employed in the production of the investment goods will be paid factor incomes (wages, profits, etc.), some of which will be spent on consumptions goods, some saved. To the extent that the consumption goods are produced domestically, this will produce a further rise in income (of those who produced the consumption goods), of which again some will be spent and some saved . . . and so on. The crucial question is, where does this process end? The answer depends on the proportions in which income is spent rather than saved. To take two extreme cases, if all income were spent, the process would continue indefinitely: £100 of income produced by expenditure on investment would lead to £100 of consumption, to a further £100 of income, and so on without limit. On the other hand, if all the income at the first round were saved, the process would terminate there and then. In practice, the proportion of income consumed at each round is neither unity nor zero: the level of income associated with a given level of investment will be some *multiple* of the original level of investment, but this multiple will be finite.

This last statement can only be given more precision if it is expressed in formal terms. Suppose that the initial investment is I, and that a proportion a of income is devoted to consumption. Then the first-round increase in consumption is bI, and this results in a second-round increase of $b(bI)$, or b^2I . . . and so on. Taking a highly simplified model for the moment, with no foreign trade (exports and imports) and no Government (Expenditure or Taxation) total national income is then equal to the sum of investment and consumption expenditures only, and the final level of income will be given by

$$Y = I + bI + b^2I + b^3I + \cdots$$

or

$$Y = I(I + b + b^2 + b^3 + \cdots)$$

Now the bracketed term is a geometric progression whose sum is $1/(1-b)$ (see Appendix for formal proof), so that the final, or 'equilibrium', level of income is

$$Y = \left(\frac{1}{1-b}\right) I$$

The factor $1/(1-b)$ by which the level of investment is 'multiplied up' to give the final level of income is known as the *multiplier*. As would be espested from the earlier informal analysis, the greater the proportion of income, b, spent at each round on consumption, the greater is the value of the multiplier.

A second way of looking at the multiplier follows from the observation that from the expenditure side, income is equal to consumption plus investment, while from the income side income must be equal to consumption plus saving (i.e. ignoring taxation, all income is either spent or saved). Thus

$$Y = C + I = C + S \tag{2}$$

and

$$I = S$$

i.e. it follows that investment must, in the final equilibrium, be equal to saving. But this is, in fact, saying the same thing as the multiplier expression above. That expression may be written

$$I = (1 - b)Y = Y - bY$$

But bY is simply consumption, and thus $Y - bY$ is saving.

This very simple form of the multiplier generalizes very easily to the more complex model of the economy which we considered earlier. Here, exports and government expenditure are additional kinds of demand which we also assume, like investment, to be broadly independent of current income. On the other hand, in addition to consumption, we may assume that both direct taxes and imports increase as income rises. We now have three kinds of expenditure to 'multiply', I, X, and G, and three 'leakages' from income (that is, parts of income *not* devoted to consumption) S, T, and M. Thus consumption is income *less* saving *less* direct tax *less* imports, and instead of equation (2) above we can write

$$Y = C + I + G + X = C + S + T + M$$

or

$$I + G + X = S + T + M$$

This indicates the equality of 'injections' with 'leakages', and, as with the simple model described above, it represents the final equilibrium of the multiplier process.

It is important to stress the direction of causality of the multiplier process. It is the injections which are the prime movers in the determination of income: all that the final equilibrium condition—the equality of injections and leakages—tells us is that when injections increase, income will increase via the multiplier process up to the level at which leakages are equal to the new level of injections.

A rise in planned investment means planned injections exceed leakages. (In the simple model planned investment exceeds planned saving.) This gives the multiplier boost to expenditure in the economy—a process which only ends when the higher level of national income results in a higher level of planned leakages equal to the higher level of injections.

Conversely, a fall in an injection, giving an excess of planned leakages, will deflate the economy, reducing leakages down to the new lower level of injections.

None of this contradicts the fact that *actual* injections and leakages will always be equal. This is a matter of accounting. If actual saving rises despite unchanged investment plans, *actual* investment will still rise because the stocks of finished products which consumers refrained from buying count as 'unplanned' investment. Similarly, during the multiplier process the increase in investment will result in 'unplanned' saving until income rises sufficiently to raise planned saving.

Formally, if we go on to assume that both taxation and imports are likely to rise with income, we can assume simple tax and import functions:

$$T_D = t_d Y$$
$$M = mY$$

As a matter of algebra, by substituting these functions for M and T, and recalling that $C = b(Y - T_D)$, we can obtain an expression which relates national income to the injections (investment, public expenditure, and exports) in terms of the parameters G, t_d, and m; equation (1) becomes

$$Y = b(Y - t_d Y) + I + G + X - mY$$

from which

$$Y = \frac{I + G + X}{1 - b(1 - t_d) + m}$$

$$= (I + G + X) \left(\frac{1}{1 - b(1 - t_d) + m}\right)$$

This useful expression is known as the *multiplier* relationship, since it shows how the injections are 'multiplied up' by the ratio $1/[1 - b(1 - t) + m]$—the 'multiplier'—to obtain national income. Thus for the British economy plausible values for the parameters are approximately 0·9 for a, 0·25 for t, and 0·25 for m, giving a multiplier of about 1·75. So an increase in, say, public expenditure of £100 m. will probably raise national income ultimately by about £175 m.

This is, as we have said, simply a matter of mathematical substitution, and something more needs to be said about the economics, as opposed to the algebra, of the multiplier expression. Suppose that public expenditure, G, is increased by the government. From the national income identity, it immediately follows that total income increases—this simply reflects the income paid to, for example, newly employed teachers or construction workers. These extra incomes, as the consumption function indicates and Figure 4.1 shows, will raise consumption, though not by the full amount of the extra income, since some will be saved and some paid in extra taxes. Thus the output of consumption goods increases, in turn increasing incomes of those involved in their production . . . and so on. At the same time, the increased demand and output will raise imports. Thus an increase in public expenditure will raise national income both directly and through further induced rounds of expenditure, but because of the 'leakages' into savings, taxation, and imports each successive round of induced consumption expenditure will be smaller than the last: when this process finally dies out, the total increase in income can be found from the multiplier expression given above. Assuming investment and exports unchanged,

$$\Delta Y = \Delta G \times \left[\frac{1}{1 - b(1 - t) + m}\right]$$

(where the symbol Δ means 'the change in').

Changes in the level of investment or in exports (the latter reflecting the level of world trade) have effects which may be traced in the same way as for a change in public expenditure.

The effect of a change in taxation can similarly be explored. A rise in tax rates will be reflected in a rise in t. This increases the degree of leakage at each round of the multiplier process, so diminishing the extent to which a given level of 'injections'—G, I, and X—is multiplied up, and thus reducing national income.

The value of the multiplier will be higher the higher is the propensity to consume (since this strengthens successive rounds of the process) and the lower are the tax and import propensities t and m (since these leakages weaken successive rounds), and this can be seen from the mathematical expression for the multiplier.

The multiplier expression can be put in a slightly different form and this then modified to provide results that will be used in subsequent chapters. The first stage is as follows.

Let s be the marginal propensity to save out of *pre-tax* income, and t the marginal propensity to pay tax of both direct and indirect kinds out of income.

Therefore Saving $S = sY$
Taxation $T = tY$
and Consumption (after payment of indirect tax)
$$= Y - sY - tY = Y(1 - s - t)$$
Therefore the basic identity becomes
$$Y = Y(1 - s - t) + I + G + X - mY$$
Therefore $\quad Y + mY - Y(1 - s - t) = I + G + X$
and $\qquad Y = \dfrac{I + G + X}{m + s + t}$

The multiplier is then $\dfrac{1}{m + s + t}$

The model developed, like all economic models, depends on its assumptions. For different purposes, we may make different assumptions. One alternative considered later is to suppose that investment, instead of being autonomous, is a function of income. A simple equation would be

$$I = iY$$
In this case $\quad Y = Y(1 - s - t) + iY + G + X - mY$
and $\qquad Y = \dfrac{G + X}{m + s + t - i}$

The multiplier is then $\dfrac{1}{m + s + t - i}$

This result, based on an extension of the variables assumed dependent on current income in the model, will be seen to be of significance later on.

3. Money in the Economy

3.1. The Functions of Money

This account of the broad structure of the economy is, of course, highly schematic. It is also incomplete in one crucial respect—it entirely ignores the influence of the supply of money on the economy. At this point, it is important to distinguish carefully between *money* and *income*. Income is a flow reflecting the rate at which production is taking place and income paid for it (so much

per month, per year, etc.), while the amount of money—notes and coins,
for example, or more generally 'means of payment'—is a stock, i.e. a given
amount at a particular time. The same stock of money can be used to finance
any rate of production, provided that the rate at which it is passed on, known
as its 'velocity of circulation', is sufficiently variable. In other words, if a
particular stock of money $£X$ goes in a year from person A to B to C, at each
point, in payment for a productive service, each has received an income of
$£X$, and total income is $£3X$. If the stock of money moved twice as fast so that
in a year it went from A to B, etc., right through to person F, then total
income would be $£6X$ even though the stock of money was the same as before.
In each case total income equals the stock of money times the number of
times it is passed on (the income velocity of circulation) in the year, in
transactions which generate factor income.[9]

In general, money can be regarded as serving three purposes. (i) Its
most obvious use is as a means of payment. Individuals and firms need to
hold money balances in order to meet payments for goods and services
purchases, wages paid, and so on. But (ii) Money can also serve as the unit
of account in terms of which the value of assets and transactions are measured.
(iii) Thirdly, money can serve as a 'store of value'—money may be held
not to finance current outgoings, but as an alternative to a deposit in a building society, a national savings certificate, company debentures or shares,
and so on. Money so held represents simply one kind of *asset*. Seen in this way,
money has two important characteristics: it is non-yielding (this statement
is qualified later), and it is totally liquid, i.e. unlike say equities, it is immediately available in the form of cash without risk of loss should the need arise.
(see next paragraph). Since there is no financial return to holding money
as an asset, such holdings will only exist if great importance is attached to
liquidity and/or if the alternatives are thought to be very risky—for example,
if prices of shares on the stock exchange are expected to fall. As we shall see,
there is substantial disagreement amongst economists as to whether the holding of money as an asset is or is not an important feature of economic behaviour.

The concept of 'liquidity' needs a word of explanation. Although cash
is the obvious way of holding reserves, it has a clear disadvantage *vis-à-vis*
holding the reserves in, for example, an interest-bearing account at a bank
or building society, or in fixed-term loans to local authorities or the government, or in other assets of various kinds which offer a financial reward.
The problem is that the assets offering the greatest rewards tend to be those
which are most risky and most difficult and costly to turn into money if the
need arises. Thus withdrawals from bank deposit accounts on which interest
is earned require (at least formally) seven days' notice, while the realization
of other assets may involve not only a waiting period but also dealing costs
and possibly a risk of capital loss. Thus by 'liquidity' is meant the ease, speed,
and safety with which assets can be turned into cash. There is thus a whole
spectrum of financial assets of varying degrees of liquidity.

---

[9] If transactions for intermediate products, second-hand goods and other existing assets
are included the number of times the money is passed on is known as the *transactions* velocity
of circulation.

3.2. *The Supply of Money*

The economics of money, like other goods, can, in principle, be examined in terms of its supply and the demand for it. We start on the supply side by inquiring what constitutes the stock of money and what governs its supply. Taking its 'means of payment' function as a criterion, it is evident that the sum total of notes and coin in circulation is part of the money supply. So too is the total of current accounts with commercial banks, since these, which change hands when a bank honours cheques drawn on such accounts, are fully accepted means of payment. But should deposit accounts with the commercial banks, or share accounts in building societies, also be included? Such accounts differ from 'pure' money in bearing interest and sometimes in being subject to restrictions (in the form of the requirement to give notice of withdrawal) which mean they are not completely liquid. On the other hand, these accounts can be in practice be drawn upon, at least up to a point, quite freely and can thus effectively serve as a means of payment. In Britain, therefore, two concepts are often used. The narrowly defined one, M_1, includes only notes and coin and current sterling accounts with banks, while the more broadly defined one, M_3, adds in all other bank accounts (deposit accounts, accounts in foreign currency, and public sector, i.e. government-owned, deposits). The advantage of M_3 is that it is close to the aggregate of all bank accounts. Its disadvantage is that it still excludes accounts with non-bank institutions such as building societies, and thus goes only part of the way towards aggregating all highly liquid assets in the economy.

Generally speaking, the supply of money—however defined—is at least to some extent under the control of the authorities. This is obviously true of notes and coin, but it is also true of the deposits of the commercial banks. This is a rather complex matter, however, and we start by first examining how commercial banks behave.

At the heart of all banking is the fact that a financial institution's assets equal its liabilities. It was seen how this resulted from standard accounting techniques for a firm in Chapter 3, but the same is no less true for banks. To take the simplest case, if a person pays cash into his bank the bank has both a new asset—the notes and coins paid in—and a new liability—it owes the customer that amount of money and has to stand ready to pay it on demand. The customer no longer has the cash asset but he does have the equivalent amount in his bank account, which is just another form in which he can hold his asset. This bank deposit is his asset, but the bank's liability. In fact, all the different types of bank deposit which have been mentioned above are the customer's asset but a liability of the financial institution concerned. Thus the major form of money in the economy is debt—the liabilities of the institutions concerned.

In the transaction described above no new money came into the hands of the public. The gain in terms of the bank deposit was exactly balanced by the loss from the public's hands of the cash. Similarly, if one person pays a cheque to another. In this case the recipient of the cheque pays it into his bank, which sends it to the bank of the man who wrote (or 'drew') the cheque.

In honouring this cheque this bank will transfer the equivalent amount from its own account at the Bank of England to that of the recipient's bank there. At the same time the account of the drawer of the cheque is reduced at his bank and that of the recipient rises at his. The increased liability of this latter bank to its customer is exactly matched by the increased asset it holds, namely its increased account at the Bank of England (known as Bankers' Deposits). Total liabilities of the banking system have not changed, however, and nor has the money supply. (In practice there will be many transactions between the banks occurring in both directions and only the net amount one way or the other need be 'cleared' in the way described.)

If, however, a customer obtains a bank loan the situation is different. This *creates* deposits at the bank, and this represents an increase in the money supply. This can be most easily seen if we imagine the customer drawing a cheque on the loan facility. The deposit moves to the bank of the recipient of the cheque; for *him* it represents an asset, and for *his bank* a liability. It is part of the money supply. But no reduction in deposits has occurred at the first bank. The customer stands liable to pay back the loan, but the recipient of the cheque now has a bank deposit (which can go from bank to bank in payment for transactions) which did not exist before the loan was given. In this way banks can create deposits and hence increase the money supply.

The mere creation of a loan or overdraft facility does nothing directly to change the bank's assets or liabilities. But when the customer writes a cheque on the overdraft, the bank gains one asset and loses another. It loses some of its Bankers' Deposits as described above in honouring the transaction. It gains an asset in that the customer now has a debt or liability to the bank. More than this, though, it is an interest-earning asset, and this is the way in which banks earn their profits. Nearly all a bank's assets are in the form of loans of one form or another on which they earn interest.

If this were the only consideration banks would lend in order to earn the highest return possible on all their assets, subject to considerations of default by the borrower. But they must also retain the confidence of their customers, who may wish to withdraw their deposits at any time in the form of cash. In general, therefore, the banks will hold some of their assets in cash, some in very liquid assets so that although a return is earned on them they can very readily be turned into cash, some less liquid with a higher return, and so on. In this way they will attempt to make prudent provision for possible withdrawals, but not forego any profit opportunity consistent with this.

Listed below is a simplified version of a bank's asset structure:

Notes and coins in the tills
Bankers' Deposits
Money at call (money lent to Discount Houses and returnable on demand. Discount Houses primarily act as financial intermediaries, borrowing funds from lenders and lending them on to those wishing to borrow.)
Money at short notice (similar, except repayment may be over a longer period, e.g. up to 14 days)
Treasury bills (government debt or I.O.U.s issued by the Treasury through

the Bank of England regularly, interest-earning and repayable by the Bank of England as the government's banker 3 months from the date of issue)

Government Bonds (like Treasury bills, these are obligations of the government but they have longer lives, and the 'maturity' date at which they are redeemed may be many years in the future)

Loans (with fixed or variable interest charges, often for a fixed period to finance a particular investment project or major purchase by a consumer)

Advances (overdrafts to customers, repayable on demand in theory but often very illiquid since they cannot be traded and could not be repaid by the customer if the attempt was made to call them in; these generally earn the highest rate of interest of any of the bank's assets)

Since banks can grant overdraft facilities and thereby create accounts on which customers can write cheques it is within the banks' power to create money. On the face of things, there need be no limit to this power. But in practice, prudence requires that each bank should keep a minimum reserve of cash in order to meet the demand for withdrawals. If this minimum reserve were, say, 10 per cent of total deposits, then the bank would be limited to a maximum volume of deposits equal to ten times the amount of cash actually held. If the amount of cash held by the banks is under the control of the authorities, official control of the money supply is possible if banks always do the maximum amount of business consistent with the reserve ratio being maintained.

In practice, the operation of the banking sector and government control of the money supply are quite complicated. We start by looking at the three ways in which the government affects the total of deposits held by the commercial banks. Firstly, there are payments made to the public—wages and salaries for public sector employees, pensions, social security benefits, and so on. Against this must be set direct payments by the private sector to the public sector—taxes, for instance. When public sector payments exceed receipts, other things being equal, the total of bank deposits (and currency) rises. Secondly, there are net borrowings or repayments of government debt. These generally only affect bank deposits when the payments involve banks' customers. The banks themselves can also buy or sell government debt, but this just involves a switch for them between government securities and cash among their total assets and will only affect the creation of deposits if this switch imposes or relieves the banks' cash reserve constraint. Finally, the Bank of England can buy or sell government securities independently of any change in the volume of total debt. This is known as 'open market operations'. A purchase of securities by the Bank of England is paid for by a cheque drawn on the Bank of England itself and this cheque, when deposited with a commercial bank, increases the total amount of deposits held in banks. (And conversely for sales of government securities.) Again, if such transactions are conducted with the commercial banks themselves, rather than with banks' customers, the volume of deposits will be affected only indirectly through the banks' asset structure.[10]

[10] In practice, the banks buy Treasury Bills indirectly through the discount houses, but this makes no difference to the mechanism described.

Open market operations can, in principle, be used to control the money supply, provided the government stipulates, and the commercial banks observe, a certain ratio of cash, as a reserve asset, to total assets. This is illustrated below, but it should first be stressed that generally since the war other liquid assets besides cash have been allowed to count as reserve assets, and since 1971 in the U.K. they have comprised: Bankers' Deposits, at the Bank of England; *all* government debt with less than a year to maturity, funds lodged at call or short notice with the discount houses and the stock exchange; short-term local authority bills; and (subject to an upper limit of 2 per cent of total assets) very safe commercial bills. The required reserve asset ratio is $12\frac{1}{2}$ per cent.

Suppose now that the government sells £1m. of bonds to a large company. The latter pays by a cheque drawn on its commercial bank, transferring deposits to the government. When cleared, this results in a transfer from Bankers' Deposits to Public Deposits (the government's account at the Bank of England). The commercial banks' total assets and liabilities have fallen by the same amount, as have reserve assets. The $12\frac{1}{2}$ per cent ratio is no longer maintained. The commercial banks must now reduce their non-reserve assets. If we assume there is no way that the banks can collectively augment their reserves this will in fact lead to a *multiple* contraction of non-reserve assets. With a $12\frac{1}{2}$ per cent ratio, a reduction of £1 of reserve assets necessitates a reduction of £8 of bank deposits over all. A single commercial bank could replenish its reserve assets but only at the expense of those of another bank. Only if there is a change in the holdings of these assets by institutions other than banks could the banks collectively augment their reserves.

Chapter 12 examines in more detail this and many other ways in which the authorities have attempted to control the money supply, but it must be pointed out at the outset that there are a number of doubts about the extent to which the authorities can in practice control the money supply in the rather mechanical way described earlier. Firstly, if, because of lack of demand for loans, banks are operating with total deposits less than the permitted multiple of their specified reserves, attempts by the authorities to restrict the money supply by reducing the reserve base may not lead to any contraction of the volume of deposits. Conversely, if the demand for loans is very high, banks may still find it profitable to expand lending (at high rates of interest) even though they must replenish their reserves by themselves borrowing at high rates from institutions other than commercial banks. Secondly, official influence on financial institutions other than the commercial banks—often referred to as 'non-bank financial intermediaries'—is much weaker than that which can be exerted on the banks. Control of their deposits outside even the broad definition of the money supply is thus much weaker than control of the money supply as defined. Thirdly, the existence in banks' portfolios of relatively illiquid assets which although at a loss can nevertheless be fairly quickly and easily converted into liquid assets may, if the loss is outweighed by the gains from continuing to lend on overdrafts, reduce the extent to which the authorities can in fact control the banks' specified reserve assets.

In what follows, therefore, although we refer to changes in the money supply brought about by the authorities, it remains as yet unanalysed exactly how powerful that control is in practice.

3.3. The Impact of Money

Given this qualification, we can now turn to the question of how changes in the money supply might affect the economy. This is the subject of much controversy.

One account of the influence of money on the economy is provided by the orthodox theory which prevailed before the Keynesian revolution, known as the Quantity Theory of Money. This focused on money as a means of payment. In any given period the stock of money multiplied by the number of times it changes hands on average (its transactions velocity of circulation) must be identically equal to the total value of all the transactions taking place in the period which that money stock permits. Symbolically,

$$M.V' = P.T$$

where M is the stock of money, V' its transactions velocity of circulation, T the number of transactions, and P the average level of prices.

V cannot of course be observed directly. It is found from the fact that

$$V' = \frac{P.T}{M}$$

and so can be found by dividing the total value of all transactions by the money stock. Frequently the rather different figure—the *income* velocity of circulation (V)—is estimated. This is given by

$$V = \frac{P.Y}{M}$$

where Y is Gross National Income, and P is the price level for final income-generating transactions. The income velocity of circulation is then the average number of times that the money stock changes hands in generating final income. All transactions in intermediate and second-hand goods are therefore excluded.

As an identity, this equation of course explains nothing. In particular, given any three of the terms, the fourth is determined. Quantity theorists, however, focused on the role of money as a means of financing transactions, and therefore assumed no significant hoarding of money in 'idle' balances. They further assumed that M was exogenously given, i.e. set by the authorities, and that V was highly stable, being given by customary modes and institutions of payment. A rise in M would therefore *cause* an increase in P or Y or both. In fact, most quantity theorists assumed that the number of transactions, which would reflect the level of economic activity in the economy, would be determined by 'real' economic forces, in particular the available labour force and its productivity, so that the Quantity Theory became a simple theory of the determination of the price level.

The Quantity Theory thus depended crucially on the assumption of a stable velocity of circulation. This has some plausibility so long as the only function of money is to finance transactions, for V then depends only on the time pattern of receipts and payments, and this pattern is likely to be fairly stable. Keynes, however, argued that money could also be regarded as an asset. Thus a *variable* amount of money might be held over and above the balances held to finance transactions, with the result that the observed ratio of the total money stock to the value of transactions would no longer be stable. Keynesian monetary theory thus distinguishes two components of the *demand* by private individuals, firms, and institutions for money balances— the demands for 'active' and for 'passive' or 'idle' balances.

Active balances are held, as their description suggests, for the positive purposes of facilitating the current rate of transactions (the transactions demand) and also in order to be in a liquid state in case of unexpected contingencies (the precautionary demand). Other things being equal, the demand for active balances will tend to rise as income rises, since a rise in income will generally entail a rise in the total value of all transactions, and an increase in the scope for unexpected calls on liquidity. (Since interest is foregone on active balances, changes in the interest rate, and thus in the opportunity cost of holding money, will also have some effect, but this is likely to be small in relation to the effect of changes in income.)

'Idle' balances, by contrast, are held for an essentially negative reason, namely the risks attached, in varying degrees, to holding wealth in the form of other assets, such as government securities, equities, and so on. This risk is not so much of possible default, but of capital loss, which is intimately connected with changes in the rate of interest. To take a simple example, consider a government security with no fixed redemption date, such as $2\frac{1}{2}$ per cent Consols. This means that each nominal £100 unit yields a fixed 'coupon', i.e. interest payment of £$2\frac{1}{2}$ per annum. Clearly, if the general level of long-run interest rates were at, say, 10 per cent per annum, no one would buy Consols at £100 to yield only $2\frac{1}{2}$ per cent. There would be a tendency for the price of Consols to fall to £25, so that the £$2\frac{1}{2}$ coupon represented the 'market' rate of return of 10 per cent per annum. Now, suppose that a holder of these bonds expects interest rates to rise to $12\frac{1}{2}$ per cent over the next year. At that rate of interest, $2\frac{1}{2}$ per cent Consols would sell at £20 (£$2\frac{1}{2}$ is $12\frac{1}{2}$ per cent of £20). By retaining his holding, the investor would make an interest gain over the year of £$2\frac{1}{2}$ (the coupon), but this would be more than offset by the capital loss of £5 in the value of his asset as its market price fell from £25 to £20. He will thus prefer to hold idle cash rather than the bond. Expectations of a rise in interest rates will thus tend to increase idle (or 'speculative') money balances, and expectations of a fall, conversely, to diminish them.

Most bonds do have a redemption date, which means that the amount obtainable for the bond if held until then is known with certainty (the nominal or 'face' value). But it is still the case that a rise in market interest rates means bond prices are lower, and vice versa, and bond holding will still depend on expected interest rate movements. The demand for money is then said to be 'interest-elastic' (i.e. sensitive to interest rates). The extent of the effect is measured by the interest elasticity of the demand for money—

the proportionate change in the demand for money divided by the proportionate change in interest rates that caused it.

The general level of interest rates will be determined by several factors. (1) If firms have buoyant profit expectations, then their demand for funds to carry out investment will tend to rise, exerting an upward pressure on interest rates. Thus anything that tends to improve these expectations, for example rising demand, will exert this upward pressure while a fall in demand will exert the opposite effect. (2) If an excess of government expenditure over tax revenue is financed by borrowing from the public this increased demand for funds will again push interest rates up. (3) An increase in the supply of funds from whatever source will depress interest rates as finance becomes more easily available.

Not only will these factors determine the general level of interest rates, but people's expectations of how they are likely to vary will determine the level of interest rates thought appropriate or 'normal' for the current state of the economy. Given that people do have some such notion of a 'normal' rate of interest over a particular (often rather short) period, then it is clear that, in general, rates of interest higher than the normal rate will lead to expectations of a fall in interest rates and lower rates than normal to expectation of a rise. Very loosely, then, 'high' interest rates, leading to expectations of a fall and thus to a rise in the price of bonds and thus to capital gains, will encourage the holding of bonds rather than idle cash, while low interest rates and thus the expectation of future rises and capital losses will increase idle cash balances. There will thus tend to be a negative relationship between the demand for idle balances and the rate of interest.[11]

The precise shape of this inverse relationship needs further analysis. As set out above, the argument implies an 'all or nothing' decision by each investor —all cash if interest rates are expected to rise, and all bonds if they are expected to fall. A smooth inverse relationship for the economy as a whole will result only if (a) different investors' notions of the 'normal' rate of interest (and hence expectations about future movements of the actual rate) differ, or (b) each investor recognizes the uncertainty of the future, and thus hedges his bets by holding both cash and bonds (though in differing proportions

[11] The distinction may be drawn between 'nominal' and 'real' rates of interest. Suppose that prices are rising at a rate of 10 per cent per annum. Then at a nominal rate of interest of 12 per cent, £100 invested now will produce £112 after a year—but this sum will only be worth, in real terms, £102 since prices have risen in the interim by 10 per cent. Thus the 'real' rate of interest is equal to the nominal rate *less* the expected rate of price inflation. The question then arises whether the 'normal' rate of interest does or does not take account of price inflation. There are good reasons for believing that it will. In a situation in which inflation is expected to persist, it becomes expensive (in real terms) to hold cash. But, equally, there is no point in switching into bonds, since these are denominated in money terms. There will then be a preference for holding reserves in other financial assets (frequently equities) whose value is expected, broadly speaking, to keep up more with inflation. The demand for bonds, and hence their price, will fall, and yields—nominal interest rates—will rise. Some economists—though not all—would argue that this process will continue until nominal interest rates have risen to the level at which the 'real' rate reaches its 'normal' level—of 2-3 per cent per annum perhaps. It has been argued that this normal real rate is set by the long-term rate of growth of the economy.

according to his expectations). These two possibilities are not, of course, mutually exclusive. Finally, there may be some lower limit to the rate of interest at which expectations of a rise (and thus of capital losses) are virtually unanimous, and the desire to hold bonds is negligible;[12] and an upper limit at which unanimity of expectations of a fall (and thus of capital gains) reduce idle balances to zero.

To summarize, the demand for active money balances will depend positively on the level of income, the demand for idle balances negatively on the rate of interest. This has two crucial consequences. First, unemployment will result if the interest rate, determined by these demands for money and the supply of it, is too high to permit the investment necessary to generate (via the multiplier) full employment. Second, the authorities, by altering the supply of money, can influence interest rates, investment, and employment. If they buy in government bonds from the public in order to increase the stock of money held by the latter, then interest rates will fall as the increased demand for bonds pushes their prices up, inducing the public to absorb the money into larger idle balances. The fall in interest rates is likely to stimulate the demand for investment goods and possibly for durable consumer goods, and so an expansionary monetary policy will tend to increase the level of demand in the economy. If there are unemployed resources output will rise, while if the economy is fully employed the rise in demand will be reflected in rising prices.

This account of the influence on the economy of monetary factors is, of course, highly simplified, and in one important respect it may be an over-simplification. The determination of interest rates has been described in terms of a simple choice between money and bonds. But, in practice, there is a whole spectrum of assets available to the financial investor, from money at the most liquid, lowest yield and greatest security end, through short bonds, to long bonds, and then to company securities and on to highly illiquid assets which are 'real'—investment goods, for example. Some economists would go further and argue that even consumption goods (especially, but not only, consumer durables) can be regarded as 'assets' in the sense that they implicitly have a 'rate of return' in terms of the utility derived from them. A more general way of looking at the effect of an increase in the money supply can then be sketched. In equilibrium, a collection or 'portfolio' of assets will be held such that each asset is held up to the point at which its expected rate of return at the margin (allowing for the disadvantages of illiquidity, as well as for the expected capital gain and financial yield) is equal for all assets. If this were not so, one could gain over all by switching from an asset with a lower return at the margin, obtaining instead the higher return at the margin of another asset. An increase in the supply of money will then disturb this equilibrium by causing holdings of money to be too high and depressing its 'return' at the margin below those of other assets. There will be a tendency to move towards a new equilibrium as people switch their excess money holdings into other assets. The key question is how far along the spectrum of assets this adjustment will go. Keynesian economists tend to think

---

[12] The so-called 'liquidity trap'. The demand for money would become infinite in the sense that any increase in the supply of money would be held rather than moved into bonds.

that the bulk of the adjustment will take place at the 'short' end—there will be a switch into short-term bonds which will raise their price, but beyond this the adjustment will begin to weaken. Any further effects on the economy will be the consequence of any fall in longer-term interest rates—mainly on the incentive to invest, but this has in recent years been thought to be small. Those economists who have come to be known as 'monetarists', on the other hand, believe that the adjustment will proceed much further along the spectrum, ultimately increasing both investment in real assets and expenditure on consumer goods. Thus both schools agree that an increase in the money supply is expansionary, but Keynesians tend to believe that the mechanism is indirect (through interest rates), largely limited to investment, and relatively weak, while monetarists tend to think that the mechanism is direct (through adjustment of the whole spectrum of assets), wider, and powerful.

It should be stressed that the *qualitative* conclusions of Keynesians and monetarists about the effects of changes in the money supply are the same: an increase in the supply of money is expansionary, a decrease is contractionary. The differences between the two schools concern the strength of these effects and the transmission mechanism through which they occur. Empirical evidence tends generally to suggest that investment is not particularly sensitive to changes in interest rates. If this is true, even though changes in the money supply change interest rates, investment will not be much affected, and there will be little effect on demand. For monetarists, on the other hand, the effect on interest rates, though part of the adjustment mechanism, is relatively unimportant and the relative insensitivity of investment to interest rates will be irrelevant; there will, however, be a more powerful and diffused effect directly on demand for goods as people spend money in an attempt to restore their desired or equilibrium level of money balances.

It might be thought that the question could easily be settled by statistical analysis designed to discover whether there is or is not a strong correlation between changes in money and changes in demand. A number of such studies have in fact been carried out, but there are formidable complications, of which two particularly important ones stand out. First, consider the case discussed above (p. 99) of an increase in the supply of money resulting from an expansion of government expenditure not financed by increased taxation or borrowing. The increased expenditure will, through the multiplier, increase national income. At the same time, there is an expansion of the money supply. But the resulting correlation between money and income changes has nothing to do with the causal effects of money on the economy.

Second, suppose that the Keynesian analysis is correct, but that the authorities' policy is to keep interest rates stable (as it was for a good part of the post-war period in Britain). Suppose now that there is, for one reason or another, an increase in income and demand. The demand for active money balances will increase, idle balances will fall, and interest rates will rise. To prevent this rise, the authorities will have to increase the supply of money. Again, there will be a correlation between money and income which in no way reflects the causal effects of an increase in the money supply on income. In fact, in this case the correlation results from the fact that the supply of money is not, as we have previously assumed, fixed autonomously, but is made to respond to changes in demand, and thus becomes a passive factor in the economy.

Thus money and income may be strongly correlated for reasons other than those suggested by monetarists. This does not mean that the statistics disprove the monetarist view, merely that no *simple* empirical tests are possible.

One further issue tends to increase the difference between the policy recommendations of the two schools of thought. Monetarists on the whole subscribe to the Permanent Income Hypothesis of customers' behaviour. On this view it will be remembered consumption depends on some concept of *permanent* income which may be very little influenced by short-run changes in *actual* income (see above, p. 87). But the multiplier, as we have seen, depends crucially on the response of consumption to changes in *actual* income. It follows that monetarists tend to dismiss the likelihood of a powerful multiplier, and consequently to downgrade the efficacy of fiscal policy, i.e. changes in government expenditure and taxation. Thus, compared with Keynesians, monetarists not only believe that monetary policy is relatively powerful, but also that fiscal policy is relatively weak.

4. Models of the Economy

4.1. Business Cycles

Economists have drawn together the various aspects of the economy we have described in a variety of macroeconomic models. Such models are attempts to show clearly the major forces at work in generating some economic phenomenon, paring away all other factors which, although they may in reality have a part to play, are thought to be of only secondary importance. Models thus differ according to the sort of economic behaviour they are intended to illuminate, according to the theoretical framework which is believed to be correct, and according to factual judgements about which forces are of primary and which of secondary importance in a particular case. To illustrate this we take three examples, one of which is intended to throw some light on the phenomenon of the business cycle, the other two on the appropriate use of fiscal and monetary policies in controlling the economy.

The first model poses the question: 'Are there any grounds for believing that in the absence of any government policy or external influences from the overseas sector there is inherent in the economy some mechanism tending to generate fluctuations between boom and depression?' Here we are explicitly ruling out the overseas and government sectors, so the model can neglect these, and take demand to comprise simply consumption and investment. Further, since consumption itself depends (primarily) on income, it must be investment which is the prime mover. Now, suppose that over the period of the business cycle (about four to five years) the most important single influence on the rate of investment is changes in the level of demand, as explained earlier. Thus if demand is expanding entrepreneurs will wish to increase productive capacity and will order new capital equipment, whereas no new orders will be placed if demand is falling.

Suppose that demand is increasing, resulting in an increase in desired productive capacity and therefore in investment. This investment, via the multiplier, increases income, and therefore demand increases again. This results in another increase in desired capacity, in more investment, and so on. The multiplier and the accelerator interact to generate a boom. At least one factor will operate to slow the boom down, however. Constraints such as shortages of labour or capacity in the investment goods industries may, and eventually must, result in investment growing at a slower rate than previously. This means that the *level* of income as determined via investment and the multiplier will start to grow at a slower rate than before. Thus the *rises* in income will be smaller than before, resulting in less new investment being required than in previous time periods. This *reduction* in the amount of new investment will start via the multiplier to reduce the *level* of income, leading to still further falls in investment. There may indeed be virtually no expansion in investment at all, and cut-backs in even replacement and cost-reducing investment. Thus the economy has 'bounced off' the full employment 'ceiling'. Eventually investment levels out at a low level (primarily replacement). As a result income levels out via the multiplier. A constant rather than falling level of income means that the capital stock needs to be maintained rather than contracted. Replacement investment picks up, generating a new rise in income. This means some expansion investment is now required and the economy starts to move up into a new boom.

In fact, if there are significant time-lags between increases in demand and the carrying-out of investment to meet that demand then the same type of fluctuation in the economy can in certain circumstances be generated even though the full employment 'ceiling' and minimal replacement 'floor' are not reached. The inherent instability again results from the fact that investment via the multiplier determines the *level* of income, but is itself determined by *changes* in income levels. Thus a slowing in the *rate of increase* of income results in a fall in investment and so a fall in income levels, and vice versa. Hence the cyclical instability.

This model is, of course, extremely crude. Its importance lies in the fact that if it has any substantial correspondence with reality then there is a presumption that the economy, left to itself, will have tendencies to instability. There is thus a strong presumption that the government should, if it can, pursue an active stabilization policy designed to offset the investment-induced fluctuations in activity which would otherwise persist.

4.2. Stabilization Policy

Such a stabilization policy would involve the use of fiscal and monetary policies, and a second simple short-term macroeconomic model designed to illustrate the impacts of these policies may be presented, based on the analysis developed earlier. For short-run purposes, we may for the moment take expectations of future demand as given, and assume the major influence on the level of investment to be the level of interest rates, reflecting the cost of funds which are required to finance investment. The supply of, and demand for, money determine the interest rate. The model must, of course, include the government sector and, since the balance of payment is relevant to policy-making, the overseas sector. The level of output thus partly depends, through the multiplier, on government taxation and expenditure decisions as well as on investment, in the way described earlier (pp. 89–95). Consider an increase in government expenditure. This increases the level of demand both directly and through the ensuing expansion of income and demand described by the multiplier process. However, the repercussions do not end there. Assuming for the time being that the increase in government expenditure has no net effect on the money supply (i.e. that it is financed by borrowing from the public), the higher level of money income increases the demand for active money balances, reducing idle balances and pushing interest rates up. Thus there may be a tendency for investment to fall, partly offsetting the initial stimulus to demand. A variety of other repercussions may also follow such an expansionary policy. The rise in demand may raise entrepreneurs' expectations, and thus raise investment, despite the rise in interest rates (we initially assumed expectations to be constant). And—particularly important in an open economy like that of the U.K.—a rise in demand will increase the level of imports and may divert some production from foreign to domestic markets, lowering exports. There will thus be a deterioration in the balance of payments. Finally, if the increased government expenditure is not financed by borrowing from the public, the money supply will expand, with the (admittedly rather uncertain) expansionary effects outlined earlier.

It is the existence of these secondary effects—especially of expectations on investment and of changes in the money supply—which makes stabilization policy difficult. The government may be able to estimate the value of the multiplier reasonably accurately, and thus be able to calculate how great an expansion of public expenditure (or reduction in taxation) is needed to increase demand by the required amount. But uncertainty about both the magnitude and the timing of secondary effects substantially reduces the precision with which fiscal policy (or, more generally, demand management policy through both fiscal and monetary means) can be used to steer the economy.

4.3. Monetarist Stabilization Policy

Economists who believe that the supply of money has a powerful and direct influence on the economy naturally attach much greater importance to control of the money supply as a means of stabilizing the economy. As we noted earlier, fiscal policy is given a minor role and the analysis focuses on the demand for money balances. This is conceived of in real terms: a 10 per cent increase in prices leads to a 10 per cent increase in money balances demanded. The level of desired real balances is a function of income (usually conceived of as permanent income), of the yields on a wide range of other assets, both financial and physical, and of the expected rate of inflation (since the consequential fall in the value of money is itself a reason for not holding money as compared with, say, goods). A rise in the quantity of money above this level will mean people are holding real balances in excess of the desired level; the attempt to purchase other assets, including goods, will bid up prices (and perhaps stimulate output) until a desired equilibrium level of real balances is regained. To avoid such price rises the money supply should only be increased in line with the growing demand over time for higher real money balances as people's real income rises. The policy implications are complicated, however, by the long and variable lags with which the effects discussed take place. These lags mean that although control of the money supply may be a potent weapon, the authorities cannot employ it effectively on a short-term basis since they are unable to predict the timing or magnitude of the impact of a change in policy. All that can be done is to maintain a steady and moderate rate of expansion of the money supply— ideally, for price stability, at a rate equal to the rate of real economic growth.

4.4. The British Economy 1965–74

To give some idea of the magnitudes of the various kinds of expenditure and income in the U.K., Table 4.1 showing the summary income and expenditure accounts for 1973 may be referred to again (p. 86). Attention may be drawn to two aspects of the figures which are of great importance in considering the management of the national economy. These are the large size of public expenditure (excluding transfer payments), which amounted in 1973 to about 30 per cent of GDP, and the importance of foreign trade—imports and exports were both between 25 and 30 per cent of GDP.

Finally, Table 4.2 shows, for some of the most important variables in the economy, the pattern of annual changes over the last ten years. The purpose of this Table is not to present a complete picture of the British economy over the last decade, but to demonstrate the extreme difficulties which are involved not only in disentangling important from unimportant causal influences but even in distinguishing between causes and effects.

The first three columns—gross domestic product, industrial production, and unemployment—give a broad picture of the cyclical or short-run changes in economic activity. For the first three years the economy was relatively stagnant, with output growing at a lower than normal rate and unemployment gradually rising. [13] A brief upturn in output was achieved in 1968, though it did no more than halt the rise in unemployment rather than reversing it. In the next three years stagnation again set in, with unemployment rising in early 1972 to its highest post-war level. After a short but relatively sharp expansion in 1973, the decline continued.

To some extent, explanations for these changes can be found from the movements in the various components of expenditure (cols. 4–8). In the first three years fiscal policy was used to restrain consumers' expenditure in an unsuccessful attempt to cure the balance of payments problem (col. 9) by restraining imports. This attempt failed—largely through poor export performance—and the pound was devalued at the end of 1967. This was the first time that the exchange rate had been devalued since 1949. The devaluation, from £1 = $2·80 to £1 = $2·40, was intended both to stimulate

---

[13] Some increase in output can be achieved each year—perhaps 3 per cent—with an unchanged work force because of increases in productivity. Increases at a lower rate than this result in rising unemployment.

TABLE 4.2. *The Development of the British Economy 1965–74*

(annual percentage changes, unless otherwise specified)

	(1)	(2) Index of industrial production[2]	(3) Un-employment[3]	(4) Consumers' expenditure[4]	(5) Private fixed investment[4]	(6) Public expenditure[5]	(7) Exports[6]	(8) Imports[6]	(9) Balance of payments[7]	(10) Average earnings[8]	(11) Import prices[9]	(12) Retail prices	(13) Money supply M1[10]	(13) Money supply M3[11]
	GDP[1]													
1965	2·9	1·5	1·4	1·5	4·2	3·4	4·8	1·0	−27	7·1	0·1	4·8	3·7	7·5
1966	1·8	1·9	1·5	1·9	−1·1	4·1	3·9	2·5	103	6·6	1·6	3·9	0·7	3·6
1967	2·2	2·0	2·3	2·0	3·4	8·2	1·1	6·7	−300	3·5	0·2	2·5	8·3	9·6
1968	3·9	2·4	2·4	2·4	9·2	0·1	11·6	7·3	−274	7·8	12·0	4·7	3·9	7·5
1969	1·8	0·3	2·4	0·3	6·0	−3·0	9·3	2·9	460	7·9	3·1	5·4	−0·2	3·0
1970	1·7	2·4	2·6	2·4	1·7	1·8	4·8	5·0	698	12·1	4·6	6·4	9·3	8·5
1971	1·4	2·7	3·4	2·7	3·3	1·9	7·0	4·7	1052	11·2	4·7	9·4	6·0	11·3
1972	2·7	6·0	3·7	6·0	6·9	1·9	2·6	9·7	82	13·0	4·8	7·1	14·2	20·2
1973	5·3	4·7	2·6	4·7	6·6	2·8	9·4	11·3	−1117	13·3	27·3	9·2	5·1	21·6
1974	−0·1	0·1	2·6	−0·1	−5·3	1·9	5·7	0·9	−3828	17·6	55·8	16·1	10·8	12·6

Notes

[1] Gross domestic product at factor cost, at 1970 prices.　　[2] In real terms.
[3] Level, excluding adult students and school leavers, as percentage of total employees.　　[4] At 1970 prices.
[5] Current and capital expenditure, at 1970 prices.　　[6] Goods and services, at 1970 prices.
[7] Level: balance of payments on current account, £m.　　[8] Average wages and salaries, all industries and services.
[9] Unit values 1970 = 100.　　[10] Narrow definition.　　[11] Broad definition.

Source: *Economic Trends* (May 1975).

exports and to reduce the level of imports. British goods would, provided exporters did not raise prices, sell more cheaply in foreign markets (a £1,000 car would sell for $2,400 instead of $2,800), and the demand for exports should rise. If exporters raised their (sterling) prices, thereby retaining their previous foreign currency price, the consequent greater profitability of exporting could stimulate exporting efforts. Imports, conversely, would become more expensive in sterling terms, and demand should switch to domestic substitutes, in so far as these existed (which was not, of course, the case for many foodstuffs and raw materials).

The brief expansion of 1968 was mainly attributable to the devaluation-induced rise in the volume of exports and a pick-up in investment—the latter probably attributable to an increase in confidence in the expectation that the devaluation would cure Britain's 'stop–go' experience. In 1969 consumption and government expenditure were cut so as to free productive resources for export manufacture and so as to reap the full advantages of devaluation. But the response of exports was not particularly impressive and private investment, too, lost some of its momentum. Imports were restrained and the balance of payments improved, but production failed to increase very much. Continued restraint of public expenditure and a continued low rate of increase in investment carried the recession deeper through 1970 and 1971. In 1972 there was an attempt to halt the decline through a highly expansionary budget, coupled with an expansionary monetary policy. Consumers' expenditure rose rapidly through 1972, but the continued slow growth of public expenditure, the poor performance of exports, and the rapid increase in imports largely offset this stimulus so far as production was concerned, and the balance of payments deteriorated sharply.

By 1973 inflation (cols. 10–12) and the balance of payments had taken over as primary causes of concern. Import prices had risen sharply after the 1967 devaluation, and this may have led to compensatory increases in average earnings in the next year. The ensuing wage–price spiral seems to have acquired its own momentum over the next three years, despite rising unemployment, and by the time of the explosion in world commodity prices—particularly, though by no means exclusively, that of oil—in 1973–4 Britain had had over three years of double-figure inflation of average earnings and near-double-figure price inflation. By the end of 1974 Britain faced a situation in which there was failure to meet any important objective of economic policy—full employment, economic growth, balance of payments equilibrium, or stable prices.

So much is clear from the data of Table 4.2. What such a brief glance at the figures cannot provide is a clear-cut, unambiguous account of the causes of these changes. Why did investment remain so sluggish even when output grew relatively rapidly? Why did the volume of imports rise so rapidly after devaluation? Why did the wage–price spiral gain momentum despite rising unemployment? Were the rapid increases in the money supply in the latter part of the period a cause of inflation, or did they merely serve to maintain liquidity in a situation in which inflation already had its own momentum? And so on. The statistics cannot give immediate and clear answers to these questions, and it is to a more detailed examination of these problems and the difficulties they pose for economic policy that much of the remainder of the book is devoted.

Appendix 1

Let $1 + b + b^2 + b^3 \ldots + b^\infty = Z$

Therefore $b \cdot Z = b + b^2 + b^3 + \ldots + b^{\infty + 1}$

Therefore $Z - bZ = 1 + b + b^2 + b^3 \ldots + b^\infty$
$$- b - b^2 - b^3 \ldots - b^\infty - b^{\infty + 1}$$
$$= 1 - b^{\infty + 1}$$

But as a is less than 1

$b^{\infty + 1}$ is equal to zero.

Therefore $Z - bZ = 1 = Z(1 - b)$

and
$$Z = \frac{1}{1 - b}$$

Bibliography

The basic macroeconomic theory of this chapter receives much more detailed treatment in a variety of textbooks; for example:

[1] ROWAN, D. C. *Output, Inflation and Growth* (Macmillan, 1968).
[2] BROOMAN, F. S. *Macroeconomics*, 5th edn. (George Allen and Unwin, 1973).

An introduction to monetary theory and policy in a British context is:
[3] FURNESS, E. L. *An Introduction to Financial Economics* (Heinemann, 1972).

A much more empirically orientated book which, however, deals with the U.S. rather than the U.K. economy is
[4] EVANS, M. K. *Macroeconomic Activity* (Harper and Row, 1969).

An excellent book on the British economy is:
[5] PREST, A. R. and COPPOCK, D. J. (eds.) *The UK Economy—a Manual of Applied Economics*, 5th edn. (Weidenfeld and Nicolson, 1974).

Books on the management of the British economy in the post-war period include:
[6] WORSWICK, G. D. N. and ADY, P. (eds.) *The British Economy in the 1950s* (Oxford University Press, 1962).
[7] DOW, J. C. R. *The Management of the British Economy 1948-60* (Cambridge University Press, 1964).
[8] BECKERMAN, W. (ed.) *Labour's Economic Record* (Duckworth, 1972).
[9] CAVES, R. (ed.) *Britain's Economic Prospects* (Brookings Institution, 1968).

Regular surveys of the British economy are contained in:
[10] *National Institute Economic Review* (quarterly).
[11] *Bank of England Quarterly Bulletin*.
[12] *OECD Economic Survey* (annual).

5

International Economics

P. J. N. SINCLAIR

1. The Balance of Payments

1.1. Introduction

The previous chapter began to fit together the various sectors of the economy. Inevitably, its description of the foreign trade sector was purely introductory. In this chapter we expand upon this area, examining the different types of international transactions that occur, the short- and long-term determinants of each type, and the problems that can arise with a country's international economic transactions.

1.2. International Economic Transactions

In principle, international economic transactions resemble domestic transactions. Companies, governments, and households buy and sell, borrow and lend. Transactions are international when the parties to them do not all reside in the same country. Since most countries have their own currency for use in domestic transactions, international transactions will typically involve at least one party in the use of foreign currency. An example will illustrate this.

A U.K. exporter receives dollars as the proceeds of his sale of goods in the United States. He is likely to want to exchange these dollars for sterling, through a bank. The bank will probably surrender the dollars to the Bank of England, and the bank's balance with the Bank of England will rise correspondingly. The Bank of England will place the dollars in the official reserves of gold and foreign currencies held in its *Exchange Equalization Account*. To prevent any increase in bank deposits—simple or multiple—the Bank of England will then sell treasury bills equal in value to the increase in reserves, thus removing from the banks sterling deposits equal to those which the exporter originally gained.

A number of factors complicate this. First, there will be importers anxious to obtain foreign currency to carry out purchases. This process then operates in reverse, with importers demanding foreign currency from the banks as opposed to exporters supplying it. Only the excess of exports over imports will be reflected in the reserves. Second, international transactions need not be conducted in dollars. Japenese yen, German marks, or any currency—even sterling—may be used. If sterling is employed, the adjustments described will occur abroad, but not in Britain. Third, the Central Bank need not undertake offsetting open market operations in bills or bonds whenever there is a rise or fall in reserves. If it does not, it effectively permits the domestic money supply to go up (down) whenever reserves rise (fall).

Fourth, the Bank of England may choose not to buy (or sell) foreign currency. If, instead, it decides to keep its reserves constant, it will be the exchange rate—not the reserves—which bears the strain of any imbalance in the market. For example, if there is an excess supply of dollars, and an excess demand for sterling, the price of the dollar will fall in terms of sterling, to 'clear' the market; sterling will appreciate against the dollar (e.g. from £1 = $1·85 to £1 = $1·95). This will happen under a system of freely floating exchange rates. Alternatively, the Bank of England may choose some compromise between meeting any excess supply or demand for foreign exchange at existing exchange rates, and freely floating exchange rates. Some such compromises are known as 'dirty floating' or 'limited intervention'.

Fifth, international transactions are not restricted to exports and imports. They also include transactions in assets. A U.K. firm which builds a factory in Spain, for instance, will need pesetas. These pesetas must be bought, in the foreign exchange market, from exporters who have earned pesetas, or from someone lending pesetas to U.K. residents or the British Government, or from the reserves of the Bank of England. More generally, any outflow of foreign currency must be financed by an inflow of foreign currency, or out of reserves. This is true irrespective of whether the inflow is the result of export earnings, foreign investment in the U.K., or international loans to the U.K.

1.3. The Balance of Payments Accounts

A country's balance of payments accounts record all economic transactions that its residents undertake with foreigners in a given period (normally a year). These transactions are broken down in two ways. We distinguish between *credit* items and *debit* items, and between *current* transactions in commodities and services and *capital* transactions in assets; this is set out in Table 5.1.

The top left cell covers income earned from abroad. This income is earned

TABLE 5.1

	Credit Items (+)	Debit Items (−)
Current Account	Exports of Goods	Imports of Goods
	Exports of Services	Imports of Services
	Property Income received from Abroad	Property Income paid Abroad
Capital Account	Investment from Abroad	Investment Abroad
	Borrowing from Abroad	Lending Abroad
	Fall in Reserves	Rise in Reserves

from the sale overseas of a country's goods and services ('invisibles'), and 'property' income received from abroad in the form of interest payments, dividends, royalties, and repatriated profits, by any domestic resident (household or firm). The cell on the top right is the mirror image of this from the rest of the world's point of view. It includes everything the residents of other countries earn or receive as income from the home country's residents. The difference between the two cells gives the *current account balance*. This is in surplus if the value of all entries in the top left cell exceeds that of those in the top right. In contrast, a current account deficit implies that income from abroad is less than expenditure abroad.

The bottom left cell covers, first, all capital transactions which are credits in the sense that they represent an inflow of funds from abroad. These may be for the direct construction of new plant and machinery in the U.K.; the purchase of existing assets (real or financial) from U.K. residents; borrowing by individuals or firms at home; 'official' borrowing by the government (both short term and long term); and other short-term inflows, for example for speculative purposes.

Second, this cell contains any *fall* in reserves which comprise the gold and foreign currency reserves held by the country's Government or Central Bank. It may seem strange that this should appear on the credit side. This in fact is not only necessary from an accounting viewpoint: there is good reason for it. A fall in reserves will occur if total debits exceed total credits: that is, if the right-hand column exceeds the left-hand one. The difference between these two will equal the fall in reserves. Adding this to the left-hand side will, therefore, result in total credits equalling total debits. The fall in reserves is an *alternative* to an inflow of funds, and hence appears in the column identifying funds flowing in. The real significance of all entries in the cell is that they all represent decreases in the community's net wealth. This is clearly so in the case of a loss of foreign currency from the reserves, but is no less true if physical assets are bought up by foreigners or if loans are accepted from them. The bottom right cell is the opposite. It comprises all capital debits, including rises in reserves;[1] and every item in it can be thought of as a rise in the community's net wealth.

If the bottom right cell is subtracted from the bottom left, one derives the capital account surplus (a deficit if this produces a negative number).

The over-all picture could be disaggregated by country, and much can be learnt by examining the extent to which trade and capital movements *vis-à-vis* particular countries or trading blocs vary relative to those with other countries. The more fundamental disaggregation, however, is by the nature of transaction. Britain's current account balance can be split into (i) its visible part comprising net exports of foodstuffs, raw materials, machinery, textiles, fuel, transport equipment, chemicals, consumer goods (durable and non-durable), and other goods, (ii) net invisible exports comprising net earnings on tourism, insurance, banking, shipping, aviation, other services, net property income from abroad, transfers from abroad, and payments for

---

[1] In fact a rise in reserves is shown as a *minus* amount on the credit side.

government services. The main components of a capital account balance follow the distinctions already drawn: net capital inflows for government or private direct investment, net 'portfolio' investment in the form of purchases of existing real assets, bonds, equities, etc. official (government) net borrowing from overseas, net inflows of short-term capital (holdings of sterling purchased with foreign currency which may rapidly be sold again), and falls in the reserves (see above).

1.4. Measures of Imbalance

Before investigating the U.K.'s balance of payments in more detail, we must briefly examine the (in fact rather complex) question of what is meant by a 'balance of payments deficit'. If all transactions have been recorded correctly, the over-all balance of payments must balance exactly. An excess of expenditure over income implies more foreign currency going abroad than is received from abroad. The extra foreign currency must either come from borrowing or from the reserves, or both. Each of these generates a surplus on the capital account which offsets the deficit generated by the excess expenditure.

This over-all balance arises from the principles of accounting used. To see how successfully a country is performing in its foreign trade and payments, it is necessary to look at one or more sub-totals or balances between different sub-totals within the over-all accounts. For example, the movement of the reserves will be important because of the constraints imposed on a country if these are inadequate to finance temporary excesses of expenditure over income. The total value of exports will give some idea of how well a country is competing in export markets, particularly if we examine exports in real terms. In general, however, such figures provide limited information. A rise in the reserves may represent only a high level of loans; increased exports may be more than offset by increased imports. There are, therefore, a number of more useful figures each of which represents the balance between certain inflows and outflows. These are:

(i) The visible trade balance: the surplus (or deficit if it is negative) of the value of visible exports over visible imports.

(ii) The current account balance: the surplus or deficit of all visible and invisible trade items, including net property income from abroad.

(iii) The basic surplus or deficit on autonomous items: this is the excess (positive or negative) of credit (currency inflow) items over debit (currency outflow) items in the current account *and* long-term part of the capital account. The idea behind it is that it represents surplus or deficit on items which the Government cannot influence easily or quickly (hence *autonomous*— trade in commodities and services, net property income, and direct and long-term portfolio investment). The Government, presented with this, must finance it by a set of *accommodating* flows. These flows comprise short-term capital movements (which are often easy to engineer), official short-term borrowing and lending, and changes in reserves. This gives rise to the identity (with negative amounts shown in brackets):

Basic surplus (deficit) on autonomous items + balancing items for errors and omissions[2] ≡ net short-term capital outflows (inflows) + net official short-term lending (borrowing) + net gain (loss) of reserves.

(iv) Total currency flow (TCF). Formally,

TCF ≡ basic surplus on autonomous items + balancing item
     + net short-term capital inflow
   ≡ net official short-term lending + net gain in reserves

where 'net official short-term lending' is confined to transactions with overseas monetary authorities (other Central Banks and, until recently, the International Monetary Fund) and foreign currency lending by the Government. This formulation recognizes that short-term capital movements may frequently be beyond government control as well. For example, expectations of a revaluation of another currency may cause heavy short-term capital outflows.

Table 5.2 contains official preliminary estimates of the United Kingdom's balance of payments for the period 1969–74. It is illuminating to compare 1971 with 1974. In 1971 Britain enjoyed a current account surplus of £1,052 m., some 2¼ per cent of national income. A large surplus on the direct and portfolio investment and short-term capital movements elements on the capital account, with a large positive balancing item, made the TCF much bigger—a surplus of £3,228m. Britain used the TCF to repay debts to the International Monetary Fund (IMF) and other Central Banks, and to augment its reserves of gold and foreign currencies. In 1974 there was a current account deficit equal to nearly 5 per cent of national income, a figure unparalleled in peacetime. Its causes lay in the explosion (in and after 1972) in the prices of imported primary commodities, which growth in the value of exports failed to match; and in the sharp rises in the volume of imported manufactures, which invariably accompanies the end of the boom phase of the British trade-cycle. In 1974 TCF was negative, but was a far smaller figure than the current account deficit, because of the substantial overseas borrowing that took place that year.

The next part of this chapter will analyse the factors that lie behind such surpluses and deficits—the major influences at work on imports, exports, and the capital account.

1.5. The Determination of Imports

It is easiest to begin with imports. The determinants of these can be seen and distinguished by referring to the factors that generally determine the demand for any product—tastes, income, and the price of the product, relative to the price of other products. The last of these will depend partly on the relative cost of production of the goods, which in turn will depend on the cost of the

---

[2] This often quite sizeable figure covers discrepancies in the figures supplied, and is simply the figure necessary to make the two sides of the equation equal.

TABLE 5.2

	1969	1970	1971	1972	1973	1974
Current Account						
Visible Trade	−147	−11	+274	−683	−2301	−5259
Invisibles	+607	+709	+778	+765	+1184	+1431
Current Balance	+460	+698	+1052	+82	−1117	−3828
Currency Flow and Official Financing						
Current Balance	+460	+698	+1052	+82	−1117	−3828
Capital Transfers (1)	—	—	—	—	−59	−75
Investment and Other Capital Flows	−109	+481	+1871	−671	+1210	+2191
Balancing Item	+392	+108	+305	−676	+176	+1147
Total Currency Flow	+743	+1287	+3228	−1265	+210	−565
Allocation of Special Drawing Rights (+)	—	+171	+125	+124	—	—
Gold Subscription to I.M.F. (−)	—	−38	—	—	—	—
Total	+743	+1420	+3353	−1141	+210	−565
Financed as follows:						
Net Transactions with overseas Monetary Authorities (2)	−699	−1295	−1817	+449	—	—
Foreign Currency Borrowing by H.M. Government	—	—	—	—	—	+644
Official Reserves (drawings on, +/additions to, −) (2) (3)	−44	−125	−1536	+692	−210	−79

(1) Reflecting payments under sterling guarantee agreements.
(2) From July 1972 transactions with the I.M.F. affecting the United Kingdom reserve position in the Fund are included as changes in the official reserves.
(3) From 23 August 1971 valued in sterling at rates of exchange at which transactions occurred.

factors of production required and the technology which combines them. In the absence of restrictions most international trade can be explained in terms of these four aspects: cost of factors of production, technology, tastes, and incomes.

(a) *Cost of factors of production.* A country will tend to import products which require a relatively high input of those factors of production with which it is relatively poorly endowed. For example, the U.K. imports lamb and butter from New Zealand despite transport costs, because these products require much land relative to labour, and because New Zealand has an abundance of land relative to its labour force, when compared to the U.K. The abundance of land will tend to make it relatively cheap, and this would give rise to relatively low costs for such products. Similarly, a country with little capital per man compared to other countries may tend to import products which are capital-intensive in production, again because the relative abundance of capital abroad may make such products relatively cheaper.

(b) *Technology.* Another reason may be technology: Britain imports, for example, certain components for television sets from Japan, some pharmaceutical products from Switzerland, and several types of aeroplane and computers from the United States. In each case, the exporting country generally has a relative technical lead in their manufacture; indeed, because of the heavy costs of small-scale production, patents, and other obstacles to the international transmission of knowledge, these commodities may not even be produced in Britain at all. Also, the potential lead that a country might have in the production of a particular commodity might remain unfulfilled: managerial inefficiency, the inadequate exploitation of available technology, or market imperfectations could in fact be large enough for the product concerned to be imported, not exported.

Such factors will cause differences in product prices, but the crucial question is whether they generate different *relative* prices.

An opportunity for profitable commodity arbitrage exists whenever product price ratios differ between countries—or, at least, differ by enough to outweigh the costs of 'trading'. Arbitrage means buying cheap and selling dear in pursuit of a safe profit. Suppose that one ton of copper costs five times as much as one ton of coffee in London, while in New York their respective prices are $1,600 and $800. Suppose that a trader can buy and sell in limitless amounts at these prices, and that trade impediments (transport costs and government trade restrictions) are negligible. The trader can take one ton of copper from New York to London, barter it for five tons of coffee, which he can sell in New York for $4,000. This will bring him a clear profit of $2,400. If, instead, the trader took copper from London to New York and coffee in the reverse direction, he would make a substantial loss. If international trading is to be profitable, it will imply that the pattern of commodity trade between countries follows the *Principle of Comparative Advantage*: goods are taken from sources where they are (or would otherwise be) relatively cheap to destinations where they are (or would otherwise be) relatively dear. What is important is the difference in the *ratios* of the commodity prices; the result that the trader will make profits by shipping copper from New York to London and coffee back was obtained without actually stipulating the sterling prices for either good in London. The conclusion about the direction of trade would not change, either, if the New York prices doubled or halved or decupled while retaining the same ratio.

If traders cannot collude, and trading impediments are negligible, commodity arbitrage will 'unite' the two markets for coffee and copper; the new common price ratio will settle somewhere between 5 : 1 and 2 : 1. At this stage, the arbitrage profits will have disappeared, and the gains from trade will accrue as rises in real national income in either the U.S. or the U.K., or (most probably) in both. The Principle of Comparative Advantage can now be seen to have a normative implication: if planners are to decide which commodities Britain should export and import, they should ensure that the trading pattern corresponds with, and does not run counter to, the direction of trade one would predict if there were free competition in all markets. Appendix 1 presents this analysis diagrammatically.

The relative price of exports to imports is known as the *terms of trade*—the ratio of a price index of exports to a price index of imports. This therefore represents the import-purchasing power of a given volume of a country's exports. A rise in the terms of trade is known as an 'improvement', and implies that fewer exports have to be sold to obtain the foreign currency necessary to purchase a given volume of imports. Less work is required, therefore, to obtain the imports, and this represents a rise in the standard of living. Notice, however, that an improvement in the terms of trade can worsen the balance of payments if the relatively high price of exports leads to a big reduction in demand for them (see below).

Between mid-1971 and mid-1974 Britain's terms of trade fell, or deteriorated, by some 25 per cent, implying that she had to increase the volume of of her exports by $\frac{1}{3}$ if she was to 'pay for' the same volume of imports. The cause of this deterioration, with its grave implications for the standard of living in Britain, lay chiefly in the fourfold increase in the price of imported oil (1973–4) and the sharp rise in the price of food and raw materials referred to earlier.

Demand factors can also influence relative prices of products, and this leads us to the other two main influences on trade—tastes and income.

(c) *Tastes.* The third possible cause lies on the demand side. The size of British imports of tea, port, sherry, and champagne is partly explained by the lack of domestic production (for climatic reasons), but partly also because of a traditionally high level of consumption in comparison with many other European countries, reflecting different tastes. If domestic consumers were forbidden to buy these imported products, the price of them in Britain would be much higher: the price rise would be essential, to choke off the demand in excess of that which the U.K. could produce. In some cases, the product might cease to be available at any price, no matter how high.

In each example, the foreign country is a cheaper source of supply than Britain. By and large, the lower the level of foreign costs and prices, the greater the probability that a particular commodity will be imported, and —if it is already imported—the greater the volume of imports. But the effect of a change in the foreign supply price on the *value* of imports is ambiguous. In Britain's case, the demand for imported manufactures is reasonably sensitive to price: if their price goes up, all else being equal, customers may turn to domestic suppliers or buy less, the total volume of these imports falls and the total value of imports may therefore fall, despite the higher price level. This is not true, however, of imported foodstuffs, metal, and fuel. The demand for these commodities is very insensitive (inelastic) to price, at least in the short run, and it is very hard, or impossible, for domestic suppliers either to begin or to increase production quickly. So an increase in these prices leads to an almost equiproportionate rise in the total value of the imports. The period 1972–4 provides the most recent and dramatic example of this with respect to raw materials.

(d) *Income.* In addition to these price and cost influences on imports, there is the powerful effect of changes in *aggregate* demand at home. In a boom, with incomes rising, the demand for most commodities rises. In the early stages many domestic producers can increase their own sales and output roughly in pace, so imports as a whole rise little faster than demand itself. In a few sectors, however, the boom may start to eat into stocks of materials, and attempts by producers to re-stock lead to sharp rises in imports. As the boom progresses, more and more bottlenecks appear: steel, bricks, machine tools, consumer durables all run short, as the limits of current domestic production are reached. Further rises in demand then begin to spill over almost entirely into imports. After the boom breaks, and demand starts to ebb away, the ratio of imports to national income stops rising and often starts to drop back.

Can the Government affect the level of imports? The strong influence that aggregate demand can have suggests that it can do so by demand management policy (monetary and fiscal policy). Reflation will expand imports; deflation will cut them, or at least check their rate of rise. Yet these policies work slowly, taking perhaps as long as eighteen months to have maximum effect. As well as monetary and fiscal policy (which alters the *level* of expenditure), there are instruments to *redirect* expenditure away from imports towards domestically produced goods. Examples are tariffs and import quotas (which restrict the volume of imports) and devaluing the currency, which will in all probability reduce the value of imports measured in foreign currency. More formally, a devaluation will generally reduce the outflow of foreign exchange on imports if the price elasticity of demand for imports is above zero. For this implies at least *some* reduction in demand as a result of the higher sterling price of imports in the U.K. consequent upon devaluation.

1.6. The Determination of Exports

The determinants of a country's exports should now be clear—they are, by definition, the rest of the world's imports. Certain commodities are exported because endowments of resources, technology, or tastes confer a comparative cost-advantage on the home country's industries. Provided that foreign demand is sufficiently responsive to price, the total value of a particular category of exports will be enhanced if there is a fall in the export price (in particular, a fall relative to the prices and costs of overseas producers), or anything, therefore, which at existing exchange rates leads to lower U.K. prices, e.g. a fall in domestic demand, or even an expansion in the supply of domestic products. But if foreign demand responds little to price, any of these will tend to cut the total value of exports—the price will drop by a higher proportion than the resulting rise in the volume of foreign sales.

The response of foreign currency earnings on exports to a devaluation of the exchange rate depends not only on the elasticity of demand for exports but also on the extent to which exporters alter their foreign currency export prices. Suppose there is a devaluation of X per cent. At one extreme with the home currency price constant, the export price in foreign currency would drop by the full amount of devaluation, X per cent. In this case, the value of total exports in foreign exchange will rise if, and only if, there is a more than offsetting rise in the volume of exports—if and only if foreign demand is more than unit-elastic. At the other extreme, for example, if a country is a very small competitor in international markets, the foreign exchange price of its exports will be outside its control and quite unaffected by the devaluation. The home currency price will rise however, and the foreign exchange value of total exports will rise only if this induces increased supply of exports (i.e. if, and only if, the domestic elasticity of supply of exports exceeds zero). In Britain's case, there is evidence (Junz and Rhomberg [25], and two earlier articles: Worswick [36], and National Institute [32]) that foreign demand is reasonably price-elastic. This study suggests that if Britain's producers raise their export prices by 1 per cent relative to those of other manufacturing nations, the volume of their exports will drop (relative to the figure it would have reached) by perhaps 2 per cent about one or two years later (suggesting an elasticity of demand of approximately 2) and possibly even more after that. This suggests that a 1 per cent rise in export prices, all else being equal, will eventually clip about 1 per cent off the total value of sales.

It is important to note, however, that under certain conditions the initial effects of devaluation on the current account could be perverse. Suppose that British exporters always quote their prices in sterling, and importers into Britain quote in foreign currency. Balance of trade statistics measure the difference between the value of exports leaving Britain and the value of imports arriving. Since deliveries lag behind orders placed—in some cases by as much as two years or more—the volume of both exports and imports in the months after devaluation will be only minimally affected by it. In the meantime, given our assumption that international traders quote prices in the currency of the *source* country, the trade balance will actually deteriorate and may take several months to register an over-all improvement. This is the 'J curve' effect, named after the shape of the time-path the trade figures take in a diagram with time on the horizontal axis and trade balance on the vertical. The J curve depends crucially, of course, on our price-quotation assumption. If instead one is to assume that traders quote prices in the currency of the *destination* country (British exports to Holland set in prices denominated in Dutch florins, Dutch exports to Britain in sterling)—no less plausible —devaluation gives the British trade balance an artificial, temporary boost: the florin value of British imports drops while there is, temporarily, no change in the florin value of British exports. Another reason why the J curve might not appear is that devaluations are often predicted with some degree of accuracy, at least as to date. Traders expecting a sterling devaluation will advance imports into Britain and delay exports from Britain, so that exports in subsequent periods are temporarily swollen and imports temporarily cut.

Besides price, or domestic supply, the other major factor influencing a country's exports is the size of demand in other countries: just as a boom at home tends to raise imports, so a boom abroad usually stimulates exports. As well as this, mention should be made of non-price influences on exports (delivery dates, advertising, the quality of distribution and after-sales servicing, and impressions of the product's reliability) which are widely thought to have had an adverse effect on Britain's export performance in recent years.

The Government can influence exports in a variety of ways, which will be examined in greater detail later. Export subsidies increase the volume of exports, and raise the value as well, provided that foreign demand is elastic; if it is inelastic, export receipts go down. Domestic deflation of aggregate demand, through restrictive monetary or fiscal policy, should have effects similar to an export subsidy—encouraging a switch by producers from selling at home to selling overseas. In practice, however, Britain's exports tend to rise faster than average in booms and slower than average in slumps. This could be explained by the multiplier effect of exports on demand, or by some synchronization of rising demand, both home and abroad. In fact there has been a mild positive association since the war between the pressure of demand in Britain and that in other developed countries, and over all the direct effects of demand management policy on exports remains uncertain. The exchange rate can be a powerful weapon: devaluation will raise the foreign exchange value of exports if foreign demand is elastic, if domestic production of exportables can be stepped up, and if devaluation does not trigger off a burst of domestic inflation which negates the competitiveness advantage established. Incomes policy to contain domestic wage costs—provided it works—has analogous consequences.

1.7. Invisibles

Both exports and imports were seen to also contain 'invisible' elements—trade in services like tourism, insurance, shipping, and banking. In general, however, invisible exports and imports respond to the same influences as their visible counterparts. Countries will tend to have a surplus on these items if they have a comparative advantage in the generation of the services they cover, as a result of relative efficiency and abundance of the more important factors of production. The U.K. has generally been in such a position, for many years turning a visible trade deficit into a current account surplus. Rising world income will again generally improve the position.

The final item in the current account—net property income from overseas—needs further explanation. In the case of the U.K. this has been a large positive item for several decades—often over 1 per cent of national income. Traditionally, the income accruing to British owners of foreign assets (chiefly, interest on loans to foreign and Commonwealth governments and companies, dividends from overseas companies, and profit repatriation by overseas subsidiaries of U.K.-based firms) has greatly exceeded the corresponding outflows to overseas owners of assets in the U.K. Yet such has been the scale of net overseas borrowing (chiefly by the public sector) in recent years—accompanied by a sharp rise in interest rates—that net property income from overseas may fall to negative values in the late 1970s. The greater the accumulated borrowing, the higher the total cost of servicing the debt. The rise in interest rates has been important since little of the borrowing has been long term, at rates of interest fixed for long periods. On the other hand, perhaps the chief reason for the rise in 'nominal' interest rates on loans—a worldwide phenomenon since the war, but especially pronounced in Britain—has been the increasing realization and expectation of inflation.

Unless nominal interest rates rise in line with expectations of inflation, borrowers are keen to borrow, expecting to repay debts later when the real value has fallen; lenders become reluctant to lend in this form, and eventually the excess demand will force interest rates up. If inflation persists, Britain will find that the real value of her debts falls, and that the interest paid on them contains, in real terms, a concealed repayment of capital. Since Britain's overseas assets are less dominated by financial as opposed to real assets than her liabilities, there are some grounds for thinking that there might be a reversal of the downward trend of net property income from abroad in the 1980s and 1990s.

1.8. The Determinants of the Capital Account

Turning attention to the capital account of the balance of payments, we find that its determinants are much more complex. The crucial influence on international *direct* investment—the construction of industrial plant by one country's residents in another country—is the expectation of relative returns on capital at home and overseas. The higher the rate of profit expected on investment in Britain, the greater the direct capital imports; conversely, a rise in expected returns overseas will induce direct capital exports. Differences in expected returns from a similar direct investment in two countries might be explained by different unit labour costs (differences in either wage rates or productivity per man), by geography (leading to transport cost savings or natural resource cost savings in one area rather than another), or different government policies towards taxation or protection by subsidy, tariffs against imports, or preferential taxation. Other factors at work on international direct investment may include the desire to reduce risk or enhance prestige by dispersing production in several countries.

International *portfolio* investment occurs when one country's residents acquire existing assets (irrespective of location) from another's residents. Example of portfolio capital exports from Britain are purchases by Britons from Frenchmen of shares in a German company, American Government bonds, a Paris office block, or an English farm. Although it seems at first sight paradoxical that the purchase of an English farm by a U.K. resident could be a capital export, it must be remembered that, given he purchases it from a Frenchman, he will in general need francs to do it. *Ceteris paribus*, this represents a drain on the U.K.'s reserve holdings of foreign currency, and in this vital respect is exactly like the purchase of a Paris office block from a Frenchman.

The motives that underlie such investment may or may not be pecuniary. Some holders of wealth will wish to maximize the expected stream of returns from it. Others may temper concern for yield with anxiety about risk, and try to diversify their portfolio and avoid holding particularly risky assets unless there is a high average expectation of return. Yet others may hold assets abroad (holiday cottages for instance) for their 'psychic' yield. British companies may acquire foreign firms to add to profits, or facilitate expansion.

There is one important feature that direct and portfolio investment have in common: they are, by and large, non-recurrent. Suppose that expectations in Britain of profits in the Swiss chemical industry rise. British individuals will now be more likely to buy shares in these firms, and British chemical companies to consider setting up a new Swiss subsidiary. The timing of any investment that takes place is hard to predict; particularly in the latter case it may take some time, while in the former the shares may rise so much that they no longer appear worth buying. But once any Swiss assets have been acquired—financed, for example, by borrowing or the sale of assets elsewhere —further flows in that particular direction are unlikely to take place (unless, of course, expectations change once more).

Short-term capital movements (SCM) in many ways resemble portfolio investment, and the two are hard to distinguish in practice. The essential characteristic of SCM is the high degree of liquidity of the assets bought and sold. Suppose a company transfers a bank deposit from sterling into U.S. dollars, or sells British Government bonds nearing maturity and buys similar obligations of the U.S. Government. Either constitutes SCM from Britain to the United States. The bank deposits and bonds are liquid: they have a certain or near-certain value, expressed in a particular currency and can rapidly be converted back. Why should such SCM occur?

There are two major influences on SCM: relative interest rates and expected exchange rates. The first is clear. If a firm can borrow at one rate, and lend at a higher one, it can exploit the discrepancy in the market and make profits at low risk. If it can lend at one rate in one financial centre and lend at a higher one in another, we may expect it to switch any funds it has in the former to the latter, if it is adequately informed about the opportunities confronting it. Interest-rate differentials between countries may, therefore, induce SCM. Furthermore, in special conditions (if borrowers and lenders can contract at practically the same rate of interest in any one financial centre, if the costs of negotiating loans and transferring funds are negligible, and if there is general confidence that prevailing exchange rates will not change over time) SCM will tend to equalize interest rates internationally. Even a slight discrepancy in interest rates between financial centres will trigger off SCM from the centre with lower rates to the markets where they are higher. This will tend to depress the latter and raise the former, leading back to equalization of the rates of interest.

But these conditions rarely, if ever, apply. In particular, exchange rates between currencies can and do change. Even when currencies are pegged to each other—as under the Bretton Woods system for currencies which operated from after the Second World War until August 1971 (see later)—there is always a finite chance that the 'peg' may change; and the limits of permitted fluctuation of the exchange rate (perhaps 1 per cent or so either side of the 'central' rate) still expose a company moving funds to some danger of exchange loss, for example, if it borrows now for three months in sterling, and immediately lends (at a slightly higher rate) for three months in French francs, it will be faced with losses if there turns out to have been an appreciable fall in the sterling value of the franc when the three months are up. The francs he receives back are worth appreciably less in sterling than the amount he has to pay to settle his original debt.

1.9. The Forward Market

In fact, the company can insure itself against this risk, by selling francs on the three months' forward market. This involves the following: the company enters a contract (with a bank or another firm) to deliver x million French francs at a stipulated future date—in this case, three months later—in return for a promise of a guaranteed sum in sterling, which it will receive at that time. This contract eliminates the risk from exchange rate changes.

If a firm notices that it can buy 9 francs per pound *now* (the 'spot' rate) and can pre-sell them three months forward at 8·91 francs per pound, then sterling is said to be at a 1 per cent discount forward against the franc. In other words,

$$\frac{0\cdot09}{9} \text{ or 1 per cent fewer francs}$$

are required to buy back the pounds, than the pounds can currently buy, and if the interest rate that can be earned on sterling and on francs is the same, buying the francs now and pre-selling them would result in a 1 per cent profit over the three-month period. If, however, three-month interest rates in London on sterling were 3 per cent higher than those in Paris on francs, then it would be more profitable to stay in sterling rather than buy the francs and pre-sell them. There is what is known as a 'covered interest differential' of 2 per cent in favour of London, since the relevant London interest rate exceeds the relevant Paris one by more than the discount. If three-month interest rates in London fell by $2\frac{1}{2}$ per cent, the covered interest differential would favour Paris ($\frac{1}{2}$ per cent) and the company would be likely to move its funds into francs and pre-sell them—another example of arbitrage.

SCM respond, therefore, to covered interest differentials—interest differentials minus the relevant forward discount; and there is some tendency for the movements to close the gap that occasions them. In the above example sizeable SCM from London to Paris tend to raise the spot (and weaken the forward) franc relative to the pound, and to lower interest rates in Paris while raising them in London. All four effects tend to remove the covered interest differential in favour of Paris. Formally the differential is:

$$\frac{\text{spot value of pound in francs} - \text{forward value of pound in francs}}{\text{spot value of pound in francs}}$$

$$- (\text{London interest rate} - \text{Paris interest rate})$$

The spot sale of sterling and forward repurchase of them both decrease the value of the first term, while the rise in London interest rates and fall in Paris ones both raise the value of the second term. Over all, therefore, the covered interest differential diminishes. But various sorts of friction (commissions, taxes, transactions costs) usually stop the covered interest differentials from vanishing completely.

We have already examined the sort of factors which influence interest rates. Rising demand will tend to raise them, recession reduce them; Government measures to ease credit and expand the level of bank deposits may exert a sharp—but perhaps temporary—downward pressure; increased borrowing, whether by firms or Government, will tend to raise them. Expectations about future short-term rates of interest will play an important part in determining the present levels of long-term rates of interest (see Chapter 12), and any expected inflation will tend to be reflected in current nominal rates of interest.

What, however, governs forward exchange rates? A major influence here is speculation. If the relevant officials in a large number of companies and banks involved in international transactions suddenly come to expect that sterling will fall in value (spot) against the German mark over the next few months, it is fairly certain to fall in value in *forward* trading against the mark *now*. If it were not to, there would be too many willing sellers of forward sterling, and buyers of forward marks, all backing their view that the marks they are buying forward will be worth more in three months than they are at present. The three months' forward discount of the pound against the mark that emerges is an approximate measure of the market's average expectation now of what the spot rate will be in three months' time. But the measure is only approximate; there are other types of transaction, besides speculation, which impinge on the forward foreign exchange markets. Traders also have recourse to them. An importer who must pay a bill denominated in a foreign currency at a stipulated future date, and expects to receive domestic currency for the goods, may well wish to insure himself against the risk of devaluation of the home currency in the intervening period, by buying the foreign currency forward. Similarly, exporters with future receipts in a foreign currency, and costs to meet denominated in home currency, may hedge (against the possibility of revaluation, this time) by selling the foreign currency forward, thus guaranteeing the home currency value of that foreign currency against a possible fall in the value of the foreign currency. The set of forward exchange rates—generally for delivery, one, three, six, and twelve months forward—is, therefore, determined by the market forces of speculation, traders' hedging against exchange risk, and SCM 'arbitrage' on covered interest differentials. These forces may, of course, be tempered by regulation or intervention on the part of governments.

This completes the analysis of the components of a country's balance of payments, and the major influences at work on them. To summarize, factors making for a weak external position include: a domestic boom (raising imports); a recession abroad (restricting exports); a high ratio of domestic costs to foreign prices (this amounts to an overvalued exchange rate, and usually implies a weak current account, and a danger of a net outflow of direct and portfolio investment); lower interest rates at home than abroad, and/or expectations of future depreciation of the currency (stimulating adverse SCM).

2. Balance of Payments Adjustment

2.1. Automatic Equilibrium Mechanisms

To explain the parts as we have done above, is not necessarily to explain the whole. Broadly, there are two schools of thought about the balance of payments. The more optimistic one maintains that balance of payments deficits— or disequilibria—are usually transient phenomena, and that *automatic forces* are brought into play to reverse surpluses or deficits. According to this view, *Government intervention* to influence components of the external accounts is rarely justified, and often pointless or even harmful. The other more pessimistic one considers that there may be violent swings in a country's balance of payments position, with a serious danger that market forces may even be destabilizing. This school emphasizes the need for swift, intelligent Government intervention in times of trouble; it often favours controls on international capital flows, and even on commodity trade as well.

It is not hard to construct models of the economy which demonstrate that each school *can* be right, given certain assumptions. For instance, suppose that there are two countries X and Y. The exchange rate between their currencies is fixed. The capital account always balances so that the current account surplus (deficit) always accompanies some gain (loss) in reserves. Suppose that there is a positive association between each country's reserves and its money stock, and between its money stock and its price level. The current account of each deteriorates if its price level rises relative to that in the other. Suppose also that X is in surplus on its current account. X must gain reserves from Y. The money supply and, therefore, prices, in X must rise, relative to prices in Y. So X's current account surplus must fall. It will continue falling until it disappears, because the mechanism will keep operating while country X is in surplus. This is known as the price-specie flow mechanism. It was used to explain the workings of the Gold Standard (see later) and to dissuade governments from trying to increase their reserves of gold.

A similar result may follow in other circumstances. Imagine now that the two countries' currencies are free to float against each other. X is again in surplus. This means that households and firms in Y must pay more to X's residents for their imports than they are earning from exports to X, and so there is a higher demand for X's currency than the supply of it; X's currency can be expected to rise in value against Y's (which is in excess supply) pushing up the price of X's exports to Y. The effect of this will probably be to cut X's surplus. X's companies will see their profit margins on sales to country Y whittled down, or the purchases of their customers in country Y cut back in response to price rises. Again, the process may continue until X's surplus vanishes. All that is needed to guarantee this result is the assumption that the excess demand for a country's currency invariably goes down if its value rises in terms of other countries' currencies. This model constitutes the basis of the argument in favour of floating exchange rates. (It, and the price-specie flow model, are closely related to the monetarist view of macroeconomics outlined in the previous chapter.)

2.2. The Need for Intervention

By contrast, the pessimists can establish their point of view (again, given the right assumptions) in a Keynesian macroeconomic framework. Suppose that prices of goods, labour, and assets are rather inflexible, and that changes in them can be ignored. (This assumption—whether realistic or not—is far cruder than Keynes's own model of the economy). Income, or output, can change, however, via the multiplier process in response to changes in any component of aggregate demand, of which exports to other countries is one. Output in aggregate cannot exceed the limits set by productive potential, but may fall short of them. Once more, there are two countries, X and Y. There is now no reason to expect the current accounts of either to balance—now or ever—for these depend on the level of incomes (and hence imports) in the two countries. The two countries' income levels are, of course, interdependent, since a boom in one country will raise exports (and hence income) in the other, but there is no guarantee that the deficit in one country as a result of a rise in income will, via the surplus in the other country, generate an increase of income in the second country sufficient to move both countries back to balance of payments equilibrium. (Indeed in some circumstances the imbalance may get progressively bigger.) Thus a current account deficit may persist. This implies net sales of assets to foreigners, which must include the possibility of a drain on reserves. If the Government considers this dangerous for the future it may be driven to deflate home demand (using fiscal or monetary weapons), unless it can persuade the other country to reflate or accept a new exchange rate. Yet the pessimists often argue that changing the exchange rate (devaluing, if an improvement in the current account is needed) is an unreliable remedy. If domestic demand for imports and foreign demand for exports are both sufficiently inelastic (price-insensitive), the effect on the current account may well be perverse. If it is not perverse, they suggest, there still remains the possibility that the improvement in exports will give rise to such a big multiplier increase in domestic demand—and hence imports—that the final position could be little better, or even worse, than the first. Equally serious, and perhaps rather more likely, is the possibility that the higher cost of imports will raise prices generally, generating a demand for wage increases which, if granted, further worsens the country's competitive position internationally. They also fear the possibility of destabilizing capital movements (further flights from a currency if its value has recently fallen). For these reasons they often oppose the case for floating exchange rates, challenging the assumption given in the last paragraph that the world's excess demand for sterling always rises if its price comes down.

2.3. The Causes of a Deficit

It is clear that both schools' arguments are based on theoretical possibilities. There can be no general theoretical grounds for preferring one view to another. In practice, the questions of whether the Government should take action to correct balance of payments disequilibria, and if so, how, can only be answered when one knows the source of the disequilibrium, the strength of the key relationships, and the time-lags involved.

A balance of payments deficit on current account can be treated as an excess domestic demand in a particular set of markets, namely, the markets for current tradable commodities (current, because the goods are purchased now; tradables, because they comprise goods which can be imported or exported, unlike, for instance, haircuts for which international transport costs are prohibitive).

The usual explanation given for the U.K.'s tendency towards excess demand for current tradable goods is that higher or faster rising production costs in the U.K. have undermined our ability to compete either in foreign markets with our exports, or in the domestic market against imports.

This description is not wholly unreasonable, but it conflates a number of possible effects that may be at work. More formally, we can give at least four different answers to the question, Why should excess demand for current tradable goods exist? These are:

(i) Too high a real wage for labour, given its productivity level. This may well imply unemployment (excess supply of labour).

(ii) Too high a price of *non*-traded goods (restaurant meals, bricks, haircuts, and so on) in terms of traded goods. Non-traded goods will be in excess supply.

(iii) An excess supply of money in the portfolios of U.K. residents (companies and firms).

(iv) An excess supply of future goods. A borrower has an excess demand for present goods, matched by a net offer (excess supply) of future goods in exchange.[3] If reserves are constant, net borrowing by U.K. residents from foreign residents necessarily entails a current account deficit.

Similarly, a *deterioration* in the current account may be associated with a faster growth in real wages than in productivity; a faster rise in the prices of non-traded goods than in those of traded goods; a faster rise in the supply of money than in the demand for it; a faster rise in borrowing than lending.

We consider these separately. A rise in real wages relative to productivity implies a rise in the real cost to a firm of each employee relative to the real output of each employee. There will, therefore, be an incentive to reduce production and employment. Firms will, with a given level of productivity, only increase production if they can obtain higher prices relative to their wage costs or a fall in wages relative to their prices. In either case this amounts

---

[3] The hypothesis that excess demand (i.e. a shortage) in one market must be matched by an excess supply (i.e. a glut) in at least one other market, is known as Walras's Law.

to saying that they require a fall in *real* wages if they are to increase production and employment. In the meantime with the level of wages too high relative to prices, aggregate spending in money terms will exceed domestic production, and the gap in an open economy may, to some considerable extent, be plugged by imports. The optimistic view is that unemployment will reduce the real wage, thus raising domestic production and employment. Against this is Keynes's pessimistic view, amply attested by evidence, that falls in money wage rates are no longer likely in contemporary conditions; and rises in prices may well not reduce real wages if people obtain wage rises to compensate for the price rises.

Similar results occur if output per man falls or rises less rapidly than real wages. Any inefficiency, managerial or otherwise, which leads to inadequate productivity will, therefore, result in an excess demand over supply of current tradable products, and a tendency towards a current account deficit.

In the second case (non-traded goods) the explanation of the current account deficit is that the price of non-traded goods (haircuts, bricks, etc.) is too high relative to the price of goods that are imported and exported. The relatively low price of the latter means that demand for traded goods rises, but domestic production falls, giving a gap between demand and domestic supply which is filled by imports. Anything which generates a low price for tradables relative to the price of non-tradables will have this effect, but U.K. experiences suggest the major reason. More rapid increases in U.K. production costs may well increase the price of non-traded goods which face no international competition more than the price of traded goods, where international competition acts to restrain price rises. The consequent deterioration of profits in export industries gives an incentive for producers to concentrate more on non-traded goods, diminishing the domestic supply of just those products for which demand is increasing as a result of their relatively low price.

What is needed here to remove the disequilibrium is a rise in the relative price of internationally traded goods. This would tend to switch domestic production into these goods and switch domestic expenditure away from them. The optimistic view suggests that the excess supply of non-traded goods will itself tend to bring down their price, and that the excess demand for traded goods will itself tend to put up their price, thus generating the required changes in relative prices, and 'correcting' the market discrepancy. Even if this is true, however, the mechanism will almost certainly operate very slowly. It is hard to see how the price of non-traded goods can fall quickly or easily, especially if money wages are inflexible downwards. If the change in relative prices comes purely through a rise in the price of traded goods, then a general tendency to inflation may be set in motion.

If there is an excess supply of money in Britain, the portfolios (asset holdings) of a number of firms and households will be out of balance. In an economy without external transactions, this imbalance—which must induce those holding what they consider to be too much money, to attempt to run down their balances—will set in motion rises in the demand for, and prices of, alternatives to money. Houses, shares, bonds, consumer durables, and capital equipment are examples of such alternatives. Either directly (monetarist) or indirectly (Keynesian), there is likely to be upwards pressure on the price of all goods, and labour too. The inflation may continue—accompanied, perhaps, by some expansion in real output—until an increasing demand for money to finance the increasing value of transactions is brought up to meet the supply. But in an open economy (like Britain) much of the pressure from the excess money can be let off in other ways: though increased imports and capital exports. The optimistic view of this will be that it cannot go on for too long: *unless*, that is, the British Government prevents the loss in reserves from leading to a fall in the domestic money supply, or governments abroad stop their swelling reserves having any upwards effect on their own domestic money supplies. The pessimistic view is that few countries permit losses in reserves to lead to rapid or large falls in their domestic money supply, and even fewer allow rises in reserves to be reflected in rapid or large rises in it. In fact the Exchange Equalization Account of the Bank of England has operated in Britain since April 1932 to insulate domestic monetary conditions as much as possible from at least the effects of SCM on reserves. In recent years Germany and Switzerland have tried to repel inward SCM by penalizing foreign-owned deposits, and both have held their internal money supply down in periods when reserves were rising. There are also long time-lags—perhaps up to three years—which must elapse before changes in the money supply can have their full price and income effects back on the current account. The facts of the world today suggest that balance of payments deficits of monetary origin are not generally self-correcting, for at least several years, if exchange rates are fixed.

Turning to the fourth possibility, it may be that U.K. residents have decided to save less and spend more. In other words, they prefer more consumption of current goods, and less of goods in the future. This creates an extra demand for current goods, including tradables. More of these are imported, less may be exported, and the current account goes into deficit. As we saw, this must imply a net sale of assets (including reserves) to foreigners. The excess spending on imports today has thereby reduced the ability of the community to spend on imports tomorrow, and there may well be an excess supply of goods for delivery (at various dates) in the future.

The optimistic view is that when tomorrow comes the then lower demand for traded goods will result in a compensating current account surplus. On the pessimistic side, however, people may be spending more today, not because of a decision to switch from future to present consumption, but because of excessively optimistic expectations of how well off they are going to be (their long-run or 'permanent' income). In this case they may strive to keep up their expenditure later on, and regret their earlier spending, both aspects implying that it would be in the community's interest to curb the high current spending. In practice, it would be very difficult to decide whether the optimistic or pessimistic interpretation was correct.

2.4. Correcting Instruments

It therefore seems probable that the automatic market mechanism in each case works too slowly, so that Government intervention may be required. This may simply be the arrangement of official loans to offset the outflow of reserves until the relevant market mechanism removes the deficit. But if this is inadequate, and the Government has to intervene more directly, the appropriate action differs from case to case.

It is easiest to start by considering the case where the price of non-traded goods relative to that of traded goods is too high. Devaluation is the most attractive remedy here, precisely because it corrects the imbalance between higher priced profitable non-traded goods, and lower priced unprofitable traded goods. The devaluation raises the sterling price of tradables, making them less attractive to import, but more profitable to produce for export.

Meanwhile, domestic demand will switch towards non-traded goods, so the current account will improve. Devaluation is therefore a good example of an *expenditure-switching* instrument because its role is to switch expenditure from one type of good to another.

An important characteristic of devaluation is that it is likely to have negligible *permanent* effects on the current account, particularly if either of two conditions are met: (a) if the Government expands the domestic money supply to keep pace with the increased price of traded goods, or (b) if devaluation occurs when resources are already fully employed at home. In these circumstances domestic inflation will tend to remove, often quite rapidly, most, if not all, of the competitiveness advantage established.

This is a serious problem. Rising demand is frequently the *immediate* cause of a current account deficit, and historically such deficits have, until 1973, coincided with high demand, low unemployment, and general full utilization of resources. Devaluation becomes much less effective, therefore, at just the time it may be contemplated. This suggests that any underlying inability of an economy to achieve full employment and balance of payments equilibrium must be identified before resources are fully utilized, and devaluation of a pegged rate or intervention to depreciate a floating exchange rate might be carried out at a time when the balance of payments is in surplus.

If excess supply of money is the problem, the Government could take steps to cut the size or rate of growth of the money supply. Devaluation could still help, if it is not accompanied by a rise in the domestic money supply, because it will tend to raise the domestic price of all goods traded internationally. This will increase the demand for money, and thereby lower the excess supply. The monetary restriction might appear more suitable because it avoids these inflationary tendencies, and because devaluation will disturb the relative price of traded and non-traded goods—unnecessarily in this situation. Against this, monetary restriction is likely to increase unemployment for a period, whereas devaluation will tend to generate *more* employment as firms in export and import-substitute industries begin to expand production, and the multiplier repercussions of this are felt.

The next case—inadequate saving—almost certainly requires deflation of aggregate demand, for example by increasing taxes. This means that the Government ensures the abstention from consumption that is necessary to give current account balance. Any subsequent increase in personal saving can be offset in its effect on consumption by lowering taxes. The process is slow, however. The only component of aggregate demand to react quickly to fiscal cuts or tighter credit is consumers' expenditure on durables. There is a sizeable effect within three or four months, which is patricularly marked if hire-purchase regulations have been tightened or eased. The long-run effect, however, is negligible, because the main effect is only to delay such purchases. Other consumption expenditures exhibit great inertia, responding only very slowly to changes in real disposable income: it may take two or three years for the effects to be fully felt. Investment expenditures do appear—at least on some (American) evidence—to be affected by both interest rates and the level of national income; but here there is little response for up to a year, and a complicated and obscure sequence of adjustments in the five or six quarters after this.

These are both examples of *expenditure-reducing* instruments. They operate through their effect on the level of total expenditure rather than through switching expenditure from one class of goods to another.

There are several possible ways, in theory, out of the last difficulty—the excessive level of real wages relative to labour productivity.

Incomes policy might restrain money wages, and then real wages; devaluation would cut the foreign exchange value of money wages, thereby cutting import demand; longer-term policies might be designed to improve industrial productivity, lower unit costs, and improve profitability in export industries at existing world prices. But experience in recent years makes one unconvinced that any of them is likely to be very effective. Incomes policies in Britain thus far appear to have had at best a minor, temporary, and diminishing impact on money wage rises. Devaluations, particularly by small countries, seem to lead rather quickly to compensating wage demands (a matter of hours in the case of Israel in November 1974). Much of the evidence in Britain suggests that cyclical rises in output, employment, and productivity are quickly followed by higher (and possibly accelerating) rises in money wage rates: if price rises lower real wages they do so only at the cost of more rapid inflation.

One remaining possible solution to the problem is to restrict imports by quotas or tariffs. Quotas set specific upper limits to import volumes. Tariffs can discourage imports by raising the internal domestic price of importables concerned: this tends to cut home demand for them, and to stimulate domestic production to meet part of the demand at the same time. The main difference between quotas and tariffs is that the Government will receive some revenue with a tariff, while under quotas the fortunate importers gain by being able to charge the higher price (unless the Government auctions import licences). Another consequence of import restriction—given there are initially spare resources—will be to raise domestic output in the economy as a whole, unless foreign retaliation is substantial enough to damage export sales seriously. Its major disadvantage—besides its illegality under the General Agreement on Tariffs and Trade, and its dangers of inducing retaliation—is that it misallocates resources. Consumers are unable to purchase those combinations of goods that they would freely have chosen in the absence of import restrictions; production is switched (wastefully) away from industries in which the country enjoys a comparative cost advantage, towards those in which it does not. Any advantage accruing from import restriction can, in principle, always be achieved at less cost by other means. In general, no economic transaction (of which international commodity trade is an example) is entered into, unless the parties to it each expect to derive benefit from it. Any restriction on these transactions will normally be detrimental to those whom it affects—and it can be proved that, under certain conditions, everyone in the world could be made better off without them.

A final way out of the unemployment/current account deficit problem which is worth considering is an employment subsidy accompanied by a (higher) tax on household incomes. This will negate the disequilibrium directly; but besides its obvious political unpopularity it carries with it the danger of inducing compensating demands for higher pre-tax wages.

This analysis has demonstrated various possible disequilibria in other markets which can be associated with a current account deficit on the balance of payments: too much money; too many non-traded goods; a surplus of promises to deliver commodities in the future; too much unemployment. None calls for exactly the same remedy; no remedy is free from potential drawbacks; there are grounds for hoping that these disequilibria will indeed eventually disappear of their own accord, but there must be serious doubts that such automatic tendencies—if they exist—are rapid enough. In practice, the apparent causes of the deficit may be hard to identify, and be highly complicated. Some types of deficit may none the less be self-checking quite quickly: substantial stockbuilding of raw materials will lead inevitably (for countries with few natural resources, like Britain or Japan) to heavy imports of these goods. But rises in stockbuilding are always temporary: they are associated with the middle phase of an upswing in the trade-cycle. On the capital account, heavy capital exports are also, in general, a sign of stock adjustment; once assets abroad have been built up to their required level, the outflow will cease; and if the price of domestic assets falls in the face of the outflow, the capital account may swing round even more quickly. There are also grounds for expecting balance of payments deficits to disappear more quickly if exchange rates are floating, than if they are fixed—the price of the currency bears the burden of adjustment instead of reserves or SCM or official short-term borrowing; and while a fall in the value of the currency may not *invariably* improve the balance of payments, it is at least very likely to do so.

2.5. The U.K. Balance of Payments 1967–74

Apart from two years when imports were swollen for special reasons (1951 and 1955), the United Kingdom enjoyed a surplus on the current account of her balance of payments in the 1950s. Indeed, in two years (1956 and 1958) there was a surplus on visible trade, the first time this had happened in the twentieth century. There were only two worrying aspects: a persistent and rapid fall in Britain's share of world trade, and sterling's susceptibility to capital account crises. Even here, reasons could be found for optimism:

Britain's share of world trade was rendered artificially high by the low levels, in the 1940s, of production and export in Germany and Japan; some of the sterling crises were attributable to the weak payments position of other countries using sterling in international payments (the 'Sterling Area'), and not to British deficits.

In the 1960s the optimism vanished. Britain's share of world exports continued to fall severely, long after it could be attributed to Germany and Japan 'catching up'. This was mirrored in, and was probably a mere reflection of, Britain's relatively slow rate of economic growth. Domestic booms (1954–5; 1958–60; 1963–4) seemed to bring ever larger rises in the imports of materials and, above all, manufactures and semi-manufactures. Exchange rates remained unaltered until 1967, yet Britain usually experienced slightly faster inflation than most of her competitors. This implied falling competitiveness or falling profit margins in export markets, and often both. It was becoming harder to achieve a surplus on the current account; higher and higher levels of unemployment seemed to be needed to achieve it. Capital account crises became increasingly severe from 1964 onwards. Eventually, the Government was forced to devalue sterling in November 1967 by one-seventh.

The four years after devaluation witnessed a complete transformation in the current account. After a hesitant start in 1968 (when the balance actually worsened for the first few months), the deficit swung round into substantial surplus. The deflationary domestic measures taken in 1968 and 1969 contributed to this improvement, chiefly by restraining the growth of imports; and the growth of exports, meanwhile, was assisted by the multilateral 'Kennedy round' of tariff cuts by developed countries, taken at the same time. But the surplus Britain attained in 1971 was not to last.

The deterioration in the current account in the three years from 1971 to 1974 is almost unprecedented in size and speed. By 1974 the current account deficit was nearly 5 per cent of national income—about £1·50 per week per inhabitant. There were two major reasons for this—the rapid upswing in aggregate demand between 1971 and 1973 which brought in its train an inevitable surge of imports by volume, and the 25 per cent deterioration in Britain's terms of trade over this three-year period. The prices of metals and foodstuffs had raced ahead from early 1972, at a speed not seen since 1950–1. The key element here was the *simultaneity* of the boom in Japan, the United States, and Western Europe, which raised the world demand sharply for commodities whose supply was virtually fixed in the short run. Yet it was the price of oil which displayed the largest and most significant rise: a fourfold increase between mid-1973 and mid-1974. This placed an additional £2,000m. or so on Britain's import bill, if one assumes the demand-elasticity to be negligible.

This deterioration in the current account occurred despite a fall of about 20 per cent (by the end of 1974) in the value of sterling. The decision to float was taken in June 1972, in the face of a heavy capital outflow (the excess supply of sterling is thought to have been £3,000m. in the preceding week). This depreciation of sterling (which has continued, and now stands—March

1976—at 34 per cent) was larger than in the November 1967 devaluation. One might ask why the former has had so little apparent effect. The answer is, firstly, that the sinking of sterling matches quite neatly the difference in concurrent inflation rates between Britain and other countries, while the 1967 devaluation had a more pronounced effect on competitiveness; secondly, the period after 1967 was not characterized by a major boom and a very considerable deterioration in the terms of trade. In large measure, the current account deficits were not financed by falls in reserves—the cumulative deficit between 1972 and 1975 is more than twice as large as the present level of reserves—but by official borrowing. Until autumn 1974 this took the form of foreign currency borrowing by public corporations, and was then supplemented by direct foreign currency borrowing by the Government.

At the time of writing, there is evidence of some improvement on current account. The 1974 deficit was cut by half in 1975, and most recent forecasts show this trend continuing over the next year or so. The depressive effect of recession on imports, the gradual improvement in the terms of trade, and the cumulative depreciations of sterling all augur well in the near future for the balance of payments. Whether this improvement will last is a very different matter; experience suggests that the next boom—whenever it comes—will leave its familiar legacy of burgeoning imports and increased debts.

3. The International Monetary System

3.1. The Background

The analysis so far has viewed international trade and financing from the perspective of a particular country engaging in international transactions. The form these transactions take, the way in which they are financed, and the nature and consequences of policy actions undertaken by the countries' monetary authorities when the sum total of all transactions fails to produce external balance, will all depend on the characteristics of the international payments system in force at the time.

Before the First World War the international monetary system that evolved in the eighteenth and nineteenth centuries was known as the Gold Standard. Many countries employed gold as a domestic circulating medium, in the form of coins; bank notes and bank deposits were freely exchangeable into these coins at a fixed price; care was generally taken that paper money did not grow much faster than the quantity of gold on which it represented a claim. Gold would tend to leave a country with an external payments deficit—or, if it did not physically 'leave the country', it would be transferred to the accounts of foreign residents. The price-specie flow mechanism (see 2.1) gives an idealized model of how the Gold Standard was often thought to have worked. In practice, things worked differently. Sterling became the world's major reserve asset. Most other countries' currencies were pegged to sterling (for example, £1 equalled $4·86¾ approximately), by virtue of the fact that they—like sterling—had a fixed gold value. If a country experienced a drain on its reserves, held with its Central Bank, it would often raise short-term interest rates in order to attract short-term funds from overseas; on occasions it would resort to the 'gold devices' (direct buying of gold coin overseas, or interest-free loans to gold importers). While Britain disavowed import restrictions of any kind, some other countries had recourse to them for a variety of reasons, sometimes to correct a payments deficit. The system operated fairly smoothly, however.

Differing experiences of inflation and economic dislocation during the First World War rendered a return to the old pre-war parities impossible for some countries, and difficult and slow for others. A few years' experiment with floating after the war (which coincided with the famous hyperinflations in Germany and Eastern Europe) was followed by a half decade of a restored Gold Standard. This ended with the depreciation of sterling in 1931 which shielded Britain somewhat from the worst effects of the world slump. The rest of the 1930s saw a series of competitive devaluations, and the erection of very substantial tariff barriers to international commodity trade: each country reacted to a deteriorating balance of payments position and rising domestic unemployment by protectionist measures. The volume of world trade fell sharply between 1930 and 1934, and again in 1938; exchange rates altered often quite violently; and there was a conspicuous lack of international agreement on measures to combat the problems.

In contrast, the Bretton Woods conference recommended pegged exchange rates, the reduction or removal of controls on both capital movements and commodity trade, and provision for an international supervisory body (the International Monetary Fund), which, amongst other tasks, would furnish countries in temporary balance of payments difficulties with credit to act as a 'second line' of reserves.

The two main characteristics, both of which were to cause difficulties later, were the exchange rate regime and the method of providing reserves.

3.2. The Exchange Rate Regime

The currencies of all countries which agreed to abide by the arrangements were to be mutually pegged. Each had a central, or 'par', value, which was formally expressed in terms of a unit of gold. In practice, however, it was the United States dollar which was the numeraire and lynchpin of the system. The United States had emerged from the war as the world's major creditor, and as the only major developed country to escape virtually unscathed from disruption and destruction. It dominated world trade; its currency was almost unique in being freely convertible into gold; it was enjoying massive current account surpluses, and so its currency was in substantial excess demand. In practice, therefore, other currencies were quoted against the dollar. With a given dollar price of gold this implied a gold price for the other currencies, but many were inconvertible into either dollars or gold initially because of the outflow of reserves convertibility would have permitted. Other countries' currencies were allowed to float against the dollar within very narrow bands—not more than 1 per cent either side of the par rate. Exchange rates could be changed, by formal lifting or lowering of the par rate; but it was envisaged that this would occur only if the country concerned suffered from 'fundamental disequilibrium'. This was never precisely defined, but was generally taken to imply (for a country contemplating devaluation) both unemployment *and* a continuing current account deficit. Devaluation or revaluation by up to 10 per cent could occur without formal approoaval by the I.M.F.—but it had to be consulted in advance, and the country concerned could not alter its exchange rate by more than 10 per cent from the value it had when it joined the I.M.F. without approval; there would be no I.M.F. credit given to a member which acted against its wishes.

For Britain, the system did not come fully into operation until December 1958, when the pound was made fully convertible (though *de facto* convertibility was, in a sense, restored in February 1955). A brief experiment with full convertibility in 1947 (at the insistence of the United States) had proved distinctly premature.

Over all, very few exchange rate changes occurred, at least between the currencies of major countries. In 1949 sterling was devalued by over 30 per cent from $4·03 to $2·80, along with similar falls in the $ value of most West European and Commonwealth currencies. The next sterling devaluation came in November 1967, from $2·80 to $2·40; the French franc was devalued twice in the late 1950s, and once more in August 1969; the German mark was revalued in 1961 and 1969, and the Netherlands florin in 1961.

These few exchange rate changes, to a large extent, merely compensated for differences in rates of inflation in previous years. But they did nothing of themselves to remove the inequality between countries' inflation rates, expressed in their own currencies; indeed, there is some reason for thinking they increased them. The sterling devaluation in 1967 is a case in point: it is widely thought to have led to expectations of increased rates of inflation—and such expectations may become self-fulfilling when they are incorporated in wage agreements.

The general reluctance to change exchange rates was attributable to several things. There was a general fear that devaluation might preserve or even exacerbate inflation, and not merely correct its effects on the balance of payments. Memories of the interwar years were important. Surplus countries' governments were wary of the deleterious consequences of revaluation or appreciation on profits and employment in industries producing tradable goods. In Britain's case, opposition to devaluation in the 1960s was also based on considerations of political prestige, a belief that there was a moral obligation to countries holding their reserves in sterling, and worries that the role of sterling as a trading and reserve currency, and the invisible earnings thought to depend on this, would be undermined.

The consequences of this were that income adjustments were employed to correct imbalances. In this respect there was something of an asymmetry: surplus countries tended not to reflate demand—indeed, they sometimes acted virogously to prevent any increase in the domestic money supply that the surplus might otherwise have occasioned. Deficit countries, on the other hand, were often forced by shortage of reserves and the unpalatability of alternative policies into deflation: Italy's experience in 1964 is a particularly good example. Another result of the infrequency of exchange rate changes was that when at last they came, they were more substantial in size than they might have been, and were almost invariably heralded by huge speculative SCM involving Central Banks in needless losses.

3.3. Provision of Reserves

A major weakness of the Bretton Woods system turned out to be the problem of how reserves could be increased without putting severe strain on the U.S. dollar. Reserves could be held in two forms: gold, or foreign currency, in particular U.S. dollars (except for the U.S.A.). Rapid growth in world trade, and accelerating inflation (some 2 per cent per annum in the 1950s, climbing to little short of double figures by the end of the 1960s) brought rises in the demand for reserves. But the price of gold was held rigid at $35 per ounce. The production of gold became increasingly unprofitable, and the industrial and private demand for it kept growing, leaving less and less over each year available to Central Banks to increase their reserves.

But resources were not the only factor. It was seen earlier that allowing the Central Bank's reserves of foreign exchange to drop is not the only way of financing a balance of payments deficit: official borrowing and attracting inward SCM are alternatives. So we must add the degree of access to international credit markets that a particular country enjoys to the size and variability of possible payments deficits as major determinants of its demand for reserves. A firm's (or household's) demand for money is negatively associated with the 'quality' of the credit markets confronting it; similarly for a country's Central Bank. In both contexts, one observes the Natural Law of Cussedness in credit markets—those who find it easiest to get credit are in least need of it! Arrangements between Central Banks to swap or recycle reserves, and the Central Bank's ability to engineer inward SCM, have proved important substitutes for reserves themselves in the post-war world, particularly in Britain's case. But the former is easiest, and the latter cheapest, when there is general confidence that existing exchange rates will remain unaltered—in the very conditions when they are least necessary.

Against the view that credit facilities and reserves were generally inadequate, it has also been held that it was not the shortage of international liquidity that led to the collapse of the Bretton Woods system, so much as the excessive growth of the major component of it—U.S. dollars held outside the United States. (See, for example, Johnson [22 and 23].)

For much of the period, banks and individuals were prepared to hold dollars as reserves. Dollars were backed by the gold reserves of the U.S. They were thought to constitute a strong currency. They could be used readily to finance international payments. However, in the 1960s two factors emerged to change the situation. First, the American balance of payments position began to deteriorate sharply: huge long-term capital exports began to be financed by short-term American borrowing from the early 1960s, and in the late 1960s the combined effects of the Vietnam War, the space race, and the Kennedy/Johnson rises in social spending brought current account deficits as well. Second, and as a direct consequence of the above developments, the ratio of dollars held outside the U.S. to the gold reserves of the U.S. began to rise dramatically. The situation was partly alleviated when the

U.S. revoked the legal necessity to back a certain proportion of her domestic currency with gold, thus freeing another $12 billion of gold, but even this was only a temporary solution. In the view of the French, the United States was gaining claims on the rest of the world's productive assets and goods and services by flooding the world with dollars; the American reply was that, as the country whose currency formed the basis of world reserves, their balance of payments position was dictated to them by the external balance targets and policies of the rest of the world. In other words, the countries of the rest of the world were conducting their trade and exchange rate policies with the target of small surpluses. If successful, this could only mean a large deficit for the U.S. which it could not correct by exchange rate changes, because all exchange rates were quoted against the dollar as numeraire.

One solution increasingly called for was a raising of the dollar price of gold, thus increasing the effective (i.e. value of) stock of gold in the world, giving an incentive to increased gold production, and, of course, increasing the value of any new addition to the stock of monetary gold. Pressure to raise the dollar value of gold was, however, resisted as long as possible, partly because it would reward South Africa and the Soviet Union, partly because of the damage to American prestige, and partly because of potent arguments against the use of gold as a reserve medium.

The case against gold was that its use was costly. Real resources were devoted to removing gold from one hole in the ground in the Transvaal to another in Fort Knox or Threadneedle Street. The stock of gold already held also had an opportunity cost, in the form of the dental, ornamental, industrial, and private speculative demands thus frustrated. Countries had long ago ceased to use valuable commodity money as an internal circulating medium of exchange. Why should these gains from economizing on real resources not be extended to the international level too? After all, dollar deposits bore interest (at quite competitive rates), and gold could not.

The argument for gold was (i) that Central Banks' preferences for it revealed a lack of confidence in alternatives, and (ii) that the political difficulties in arranging for the creation and adequate supervision of a new international paper unit of reserves could be immense, and perhaps impossible. In particular, questions arise as to who would control its creation, its distribution, and its rate of increase, and what would be the impact of errors in such decisions.

3.4. The Breakdown of Bretton Woods

In March 1968 the pressures for a rise in the gold price became insurmountable, and the free market price was allowed to float up freely to more realistic levels. But the United States still clung to the fixed value of $35 per ounce for official (inter-Central Bank) transactions. This finally broke down in August 1971, when a massive speculative attack against the increasingly vulnerable dollar forced Nixon to suspend even this form of convertibility, and all the world's major currencies began to float against each other. In December 1971 this experiment with floating stopped, and new exchange rate parities were decided at the Smithsonian Institute. A novel feature was the wider bands on either side of the new parties, within which exchange rates were now free to fluctuate. But this system in its turn broke down, and the international monetary system now consists chiefly of two blocs, centred round the German mark and the U.S. dollar, which are floating against each other. A third group of countries (including sterling, the French franc, and the Italian lira, at the time of writing) are floating against both. The mark bloc is known at the 'snake in the tunnel': currencies in this bloc limit the extent of their mutual fluctuation to much narrower bands than the maximum range afforded by the Smithsonian agreement. The snake currencies are therefore bound together rather tightly, and tend to rise or fall in unison against other currencies. The snake is seen by some as a prelude to even closer monetary co-operation between the countries concerned (Benelux, Denmark, Norway, Sweden, and West Germany); indeed, monetary and fiscal union is seen as an eventual aim by several E.E.C. governments. One major difficulty the snake has had to face (which also constitutes a serious argument against European monetary union) is unequal rates of inflation in its member countries. The West German rate of inflation has been markedly below those in both Britain and France, for example, for most of the past twenty years, and the disparity has recently increased sharply. It has been this—and the vulnerability of sterling and the French franc to adverse SCM as a partial corrollary—that has forced both currencies out of the snake.

The floating currencies are not, however, floating freely. To a large extent the floating is managed by Central Bank intervention, to prevent exchange rates from deviating too far or too fast from the target levels that governments try to set. Such intervention takes three forms, and is periodic rather than continuous: sales or purchases of foreign exchange spot; interest rate changes to influence SCM; and intervention in the forward foreign exchange markets for the same purpose. Forward intervention can be successful, and profitable, if the authorities rightly guess that they know better than the market what the future spot value of their currency will be. But it can sometimes be disastrous: the British Exchange Equalization Account lost over £350m. in November 1967 as a result of its attempts to prop up the forward value of sterling.

Under the present system, reserves comprise gold (*de facto* if not *de jure* at free market price), foreign currencies, and special drawing rights. These last are issued by the I.M.F. and are an embryonic form of international paper reserve asset. Initially fully backed by gold (indeed they were known as 'paper gold'), their value is now based on a weighted average of the world's major currencies. One must wait to see if S.D.R.s will develop into a full international replacement for gold as the major reserve asset; there is at present some room for scepticism. It is neither possible nor desirable for an international institution to force Central Banks to hold reserves in forms, or patterns, which differ from those they want. A necessary condition for the success of S.D.R.s is that they are shown to be widely acceptable as a medium of international payments and a store of value; and this in turn requires that the doubts surrounding their supply, distribution, and rate of increase in the future be resolved. Over all, therefore, the international monetary system is facing an uncertain future and is unlikely to exhibit the stability of the 1950s and early 1960s again for some time.

Appendix 1

A figure will illustrate the Principle of Comparative Advantage. Suppose that the U.S. and the U.K. can produce only two goods, A and B. If all the productive

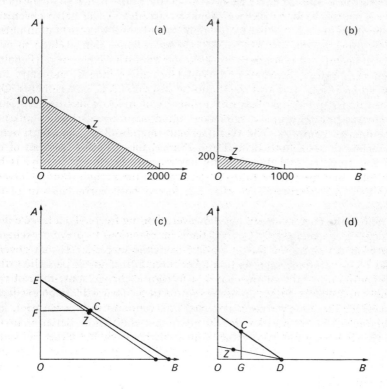

FIG. 5.1. (a) the U.S. in self-sufficiency: production and consumption at Z; (b) the U.K. in self-sufficiency: production and consumption at Z; (c) the U.S. in trade: EF = exports of A, CF = imports of B, production at E, consumption at C; (d) the U.K. in trade: GD = exports of B, CG = imports of A, production at D, consumption at C.

resources of the U.S. are harnessed to the output of A, the maximum possible annual output is 1000, with no output of B; if no A is produced, 2000 is the maximum annual production of B. Suppose that the opportunity cost of A in terms of B (the amount of B that must be foregone to secure an additional unit of A) is always 2 in the U.S., and that both A and B can be produced in any amounts subject to the limits set by productive potential. In the U.K. the relevant figures are 200 A when no B is produced, and 1000 B when no A is produced; the opportunity cost of A in terms of B is always 5. The production sets (sets of all feasible output combinations) for the two countries are shown in panels (a) and (b). The upper boundary is shown linear' since constant opportunity costs were assumed in both countries: the gradient of this boundary shows the opportunity cost of B in terms of A (A production set will have a linear boundary, in general, if industries are subject to constant retruns to scale, if no goods are produced jointly (like wool and mutton), and if there is only one priced primary factor of production or all priced primary factors are used equi-proportionately in all industries; in other circumstances, it is quite likely to curve outwards. Z is the output combination chosen by consumers in the two countries, when there is no international trade.)

Panels (c) and (d) show the effect of international trade. The U.S. has a compara-tive advantage in the production of A, since its opportunity cost in terms of B is lower than in the U.K. The U.S. will therefore specialize in A, export A and import B, while the U.K. will do the opposite. If there are no trade impediments, a common price ratio for the two goods will emerge in both countries; this is shown by the gradient of the bold line in these two panels. Production switches from Z to E in the U.S. and D in the U.K. trade takes the U.S. and the U.K. to C in each case. The gains from trade are then illustrated by the rise in consumption in both countries that international trade permits.

The Principle of Comparative Advantage can also be applied to other cases: it has implications for the most efficient allocation of people to jobs, for example, or the wisest assignment of economic policy instruments to targets.

Appendix 2

TABLE 5.3. *U.K. imports and import unit values, by commodity*

				All manufactures	Other semi-manufactures					Finished manufactures (a)			Import unit values (b)			
	Food, beverages, tobacco	Basic materials	Fuels	All manufactures	Chemicals	Total	Textiles	Iron and steel	Non-ferrous metals	Total	Machinery	Transport equipment (a)	Food, beverages, tobacco	Basic materials	Fuels	Manufactures
	Volume index numbers, 1970 = 100												*Index numbers, 1970 = 100*			
1967	101	92	82	76	64	83	87	70	89	73	72	63	87	80	94	80
1968	104	101	87	89	74	97	103	86	106	85	79	100	90	88	109	92
1969	100	98	93	94	83	98	101	86	101	92	84	116	94	94	102	95
1970	100	100	100	100	100	100	100	100	100	100	100	100	100	100	100	100
1971	100	91	109	100	103	106	125	96	91	115	106	140	107	102	122	101
1972	102	93	109	131	118	119	139	120	91	146	136	183	114	106	123	105
1973	102	104	112	159	140	136	169	139	99	186	176	219	150	141	164	127
1974	99	93	106	166	151	147	172	187	104	189	188	192	193	208	463	167
	£m., at current prices, seasonally adjusted quarterly rates															
1973 III	811	504	451	2332	239	866	133	99	175	1225	622	245	159	147	162	134
IV	839	566	570	2611	269	1031	147	124	202	1329	682	247	172	162	215	143
1974 I	858	613	1016	2819	335	1150	163	173	233	1324	731	194	183	184	393	155
II	928	659	1213	3045	392	1229	173	182	277	1406	743	235	191	207	485	167
III	988	673	1182	3035	445	1192	185	167	245	1381	723	247	193	218	482	173
IV	1005	635	1216	3029	412	1219	168	195	254	1443	772	257	202	219	494	178
1975 I	1038	592	1071	3060	349	1185	160	231	202	1526	803	281	218	217	509	183
II	991	532	959	2968	310	1114	165	184	198	1544	794	300	219	213	506	188
III	1151	510	1097	3052	329	1155	169	205	224	1569	810	300	217	213	536	194
July	1217	512	1050	2927	317	1112	168	158	238	1499	774	309	217	211	519	192
Aug.	1136	493	1149	3104	337	1198	170	259	217	1569	794	300	217	212	536	194
Sept.	1102	526	1093	3124	332	1153	170	198	218	1639	861	293	218	215	552	196
Oct.	1329	552	1242	3171	363	1179				1629	834		222	220	564	200

(a) Including U.S. military aircraft.   (b) On overseas statistics basis.

TABLE 5.4. U.K. exports, by commodity and area (a)

	Non-manu-factures	Manufactures Total	Chemicals	Textiles	Metals, metal goods	Machinery, transport equipment	Other	Total O.E.C.D. (b)	including dependencies	E.E.C.	E.F.T.A.	Australia	Total non-O.E.C.D. (c)	Non-O.E.C.D. sterling	Other non-O.E.C.D.
	Volume index numbers, 1970 = 100 (c)							*£m., quarterly rates (c)*							
1966	78	78	72	74	81	82	74	845	163	343	158	65	465	283	183
1967	85	77	76	71	83	77	75	850	160	346	160	64	454	268	185
1968	90	88	86	83	92	88	87	1061	228	433	182	80	540	290	250
1969	92	99	95	92	97	100	103	1207	226	512	221	80	618	320	287
1970	100	100	100	100	100	100	100	1343	236	589	266	86	663	366	297
1971	104	110	110	106	107	108	119	1516	274	665	290	91	770	429	332
1972	110	112	118	111	108	106	128	1677	305	734	337	79	752	394	358
1973	124	128	143	127	123	117	148	2199	380	1007	437	101	906	458	448
1974	126	135	169	125	116	125	154	2887	444	1384	567	150	1242	619	623
	£m., quarterly rates														
1973 III	452	2720	324	153	326	1248	669	2263	371	1066	445	102	971	480	491
IV	475	2785	352	155	360	1231	687	2418	388	1127	498	104	920	468	452
1974 I	553	2999	446	184	413	1309	647	2628	419	1222	552	132	1029	517	512
II	647	3415	536	203	415	1464	797	2882	448	1422	557	137	1227	603	624
III	653	3703	597	192	451	1649	813	3094	466	1485	580	161	1357	670	687
IV	576	3639	576	171	438	1671	786	2944	442	1408	581	169	1353	685	668
1975 I	714	3989	567	172	469	1910	871	3172	472	1515	640	159	1585	763	823
II	599	3975	505	162	466	2028	814	2985	419	1475	566	160	1721	788	933
III	697	4041	503	169	449	2133	787	3034	397	1515	622	155	1851	838	1013
July	700	4100	508	170	468	2125	829	3006	391	1475	630	170	1893	843	1050
Aug.	668	3893	484	164	436	2097	712	2916	389	1466	581	152	1814	825	989
Sept.	723	4129	519	173	443	2179	815	3180	410	1600	653	143	1846	845	1001

(a) The end-1973 membership of country groups is used as the basis for calculating historical figures. Monthly figures do not necessarily average to quarterly figures, nor quarterly figures average to yearly figures. (b) Includes, in addition to the areas shown, Canada, Greece, Japan, Spain, and Turkey. (c) After 1969 exports, other than by parcel post, of an individual value below £50 are omitted.

Bibliography

The theory of international trade and payments is covered admirably in the following textbooks:

[1] CAVES, R. E. and JONES, R. W. *World Trade and Payments* (Little Brown, 1973).
[2] CHACHOLIADES, M. *The Pure Theory of International Trade* (Macmillan, 1973).
[3] HELLER, R. *International Monetary Economics* (Prentice-Hall, 1974).
[4] —— *International Trade: Theory and Empirical Evidence* (Prentice-Hall, 1968).
[5] PEARCE, I. F. *International Trade* (Macmillan, 1970).
[6] SÖDERSTEN, B. *International Economics* (Macmillan, 1970).
[7] STERN, R. M. *The Balance of Payments: Theory and Economic Policy* (Macmillan, 1973).

Note: 1, 5, and 6 cover both the theory of international trade and the theory of the balance of payments; 2 and 4 are cocnerned only with the former, and 3 and 6 only with the latter. Books 2, 7, and above all 5 employ algebra widely; the other books rely on verbal and geometrical exposition.

An introduction to relevant international economic institutions:
[8] GRUBEL, H. G. *The International Monetary System* (Penguin, 1st edn. 1969, 2nd edn. 1973).
[9] VAN MEERHAEGHE, M. A. G. *International Economic Institutions* 2nd edn. (Longman, 1971).
[10] MEIER, G. M. *Problems of a World Monetary Order* (Oxford University Press, 1974).
[11] SWANN, D. *The Economics of the Common Market* (Penguin, 3rd edn. 1975).

A short list of articles and books of interest on various aspects of International Economics:
[12] BALL, J. *et al.* 'Exports and the Internal Pressure of Demand', *Economic Journal*, 1966.
[13] BHAGWATI, J. N. 'The Pure Theory of International Trade: a Survey', *Surveys of Economic Theory*, vol. ii (Macmillan, 1967).
[14] CAIRNCROSS, Sir A. *The Control of International Capital Movements* (Brookings Institution, 1973).
[15] CAVES, R. E. (ed.) *Britain's Economic Prospects* (chapters by R. N. Cooper and L. Krause) (George Allen and Unwin, 1968).
[16] CLENDENNING, E. W. *The Euro-Dollar Market* (Oxford University Press, 1970).
[17] CORDEN, W. M. 'Monetary Integration', *Princeton Essay in International Finance* (Apr. 1972).
[18] —— *Trade Policy and Economic Welfare* (Oxford University Press, 1974).
[19] CORDEN, W. M. and OPPENHEIMER, P. M. 'The Basic Implications of the Rise in Oil Prices', *Moorgate and Wall St. Journal* (Autumn 1974).
[20] HODJERA, A. 'International Short Term Capital Movements', *International Monetary Fund Staff Papers* (1973).
[21] JOHNSON, H. G. and NASH, J. E. *The U.K. and Floating Exchange Rates* (Institute of Economic Affairs, 1969).
[22] JOHNSON, H. G. 'The Bretton Woods System', *Three Banks Review* (1972).
[23] —— 'World Inflation', *Three Banks Review* (1975).
[24] *Journal of Money Credit and Banking*, 'A symposium on the Comparative Merits of Fixed and Floating Exchange Rates' (May 1971).
[25] JUNZ, H. B. and RHOMBERG, R. R. 'Price Competitiveness in Exports', *American Economic Review* (1973).

[26] KAHN, LORD. 'The International Monetary System', *American Economic Review* (1973).

[27] KAHN, LORD and POSNER, M. 'Two articles on New Cambridge', *The Times* (17, 18 Apr. 1974).

[28] KRAUSS, M. 'Customs Union Theory', *Journal of Economic Literature* (1972).

[29] KRUEGER, A. O. 'Balance of Payments' Theory', *Journal of Economic Literature* (1969).

[30] LEAMER, E. E. 'The Commodity Composition of International Trade in Manufactures', *Oxford Economic Papers* (1974).

[31] LLEWELLYN, G. E. J. 'The Determinants of U.K. Import Prices', *Economic Journal* (1974).

[32] National Institute 'Effects of the 1967 Devaluation', *Economic Journal* (1972).

[33] STERN, R. M. 'Tariffs and Other Measures of Trade Control: a Survey of Recent Developments', *Journal of Economic Literature* (1973).

[34] WILLIAMSON, J. 'International Liquidity: a Survey', *Economic Journal* (1973).

[35] —— 'The Future Exchange Rate Regime', *Banca Nazionale del Lavoro* (1975).

[36] WORSWICK, G. D. N. 'Trade and Payments', in Cairncross, Sir A. (ed.) *Britain's Economic Prospects Reconsidered* (George Allen and Unwin, 1971).

6

The Allocation of Resources

H. G. JONES

1. Introduction

The central questions of resource allocation—of how the scarce resources of any society *are, could be,* or *should be* allocated amongst the immense variety of competing activities—not only constitute some of the principal elements of the economic theory expounded in conventional textbooks, but are also at the centre of many areas of political discussion, polemical punditry, and public concern. When, for example, it appears that too few resources are being allocated to the provision of inexpensive and adequate accommodation in Britain, Parliamentary questions are asked, leading articles written, documentary television programmes prepared, and new charities formed. Government ministers and economic commentators lament the relatively low proportion of total resources that is invested in modern equipment for British industry. Newspaper headlines insist that 'too large' a proportion of the nation's reources is allocated to a particular industry, 'too little' of a certain service is available, or demand that governments, international organizations, firms, trade unions, or individuals act immediately to alleviate or eliminate a shortage or surplus of energy, paper, beef, butter, or whatever other commodity is currently a cause of sub-editorial concern. Thus, while the traditional textbook definition of economics as 'the study of the allocation of scarce resources' may be, in some important respects, too simple, it is clear that such a study, far from being just one other aspect of the so-called 'dismal science', is central to an understanding of some of the principal features and problems of any economy.

An allocation of society's resources can, at any point in time, be viewed as a complete and comprehensive description of the quantities of each and every good and service supplied or used by the government, every productive unit, every household, and every distributive unit in the economy. Although the above description is imprecise, it does convey the vast scale of the problem involved in discussing the allocation of resources.

Given the complexity of the subject-matter, it is not surprising that the economist's attempts to analyse the issues associated with resource allocation are usually couched in terms of relatively abstract theories and models—and the present chapter is, as a consequence, slightly more abstract than the rest of this book. We can, however, illuminate most of the central problems associated with resource allocation with little recourse to formal theorizing.

What, however, are these central problems? At the very least, it is necessary that we discuss:

(a) In what sense, if any, can a particular allocation be described as superior, inferior, or equivalent to some other allocation?—which leads naturally to a discussion of the possibility of a 'best' or 'optimal' allocation of society's resources.

(b) How is the actual allocation of resources in an economy determined, and can any particular method of determination be said to lead to an 'optimal' allocation?

Problem (a) is inevitably associated with the distinction between 'positive' and 'normative' economics which has become widely appreciated since the publication of a celebrated book of essays by Friedman [9] and a well-known textbook by Lipsey [13]. As was seen in Chapter 1, a 'positive' theory is concerned with what *is*—with *prediction* and *explanation* of economic phenomena—whereas a 'normative' theory is concerned with what *should be* —i.e. with *prescription*. Now, it is clear that problem (a) must lead us into the territory of the normative—with all the associated difficulties of making 'value-judgements'. Some writers would assert that if economics is to be considered a science then it has no business with the comparison of alternative allocations—with questions of '*too* much' and '*too* little' and '*better*' or '*worse*'. We return to these questions in section 2 where a relatively non-controversial method of limited comparison is discussed.

Problem (b) has been central to economics for most of the three centuries or so in which men have attempted to systematically analyse and study the economic framework of the communities in which they live. There exists, of course, a vast variety of methods whereby the actual allocation of resources in any economy can be determined. Anthropologists have discovered in primitive societies elaborate systems of custom and taboo whereby individuals are assigned to tasks, and the products of labour assigned to individuals. In the Soviet Union and other communist countries a very large part of the precise allocation of resources is determined within the context of an elaborate plan prepared by the State Planning Commission, Gosplan, and approved at various levels of the political system.[1] In the developed economies of the Western world very large corporations control a significant proportion of total economic activity, and within these corporations varying degrees of hierarchical authority can determine the allocation of resources. Nevertheless, in almost all societies at almost all periods of history at least some part of the actual allocation of resources has been determined by the more or less unfettered free trade of individuals in markets in which the relative prices of commodities, which determine the rates at which different commodities are exchanged for each other, play a central role as indicators of the relative scarcity of commodities and as incentives to individual action. That the price system can co-ordinate a myriad of individual decision-makers in the economy in an ordered manner and produce an 'optimal' allocation of resources is a proposition that has been central to economic and political

[1] For an interesting description and discussion of this system see Nove [17], Ch. 2.

thought for at least 200 years. In section 3 of this chapter we attempt to illustrate the ways in which free market competition and the associated free market prices *could* satisfy the claims to order and efficiency and, in so doing, we lay the foundations of a discussion of the strengths and weaknesses of free competition as an allocative mechanism.

2. The Efficient Allocation of Resources

2.1. Preferences and Utility

Most people have some views on the current allocation of resources in the United Kingdom—and their views often depend on their own position given the current allocation. Some maintain that too much or too little is spent on the aircraft industry, 'luxuries', education, defence, or property 'speculation'. Others argue that there are too few doctors, too many students, too many roads, or too few houses. Even when a consensus appears to exist, it often breaks down when the full implications of a choice are realized. Any allocation of resources that is considered ideal by one individual or group is likely to be anathema to another. The conflicts of interest and diversity of opinion and preference that are characteristic of most societies constitute formidable difficulties in any attempt to devise criteria whereby one particular allocation of resources can be said to be superior to another. Moreover, it is not generally thought appropriate to try and overcome such difficulties by assuming a set of 'social' preferences that are defined independently of the individuals of which society is composed—for most philosophical and political traditions have been based upon the rejection of an anthropomorphic conception of the state. Since economists traditionally assume that, in all but a very limited class of cases, the individual is the best judge of his own welfare, it should be clear that attempts to indulge in the normative comparison of different available allocations, based upon the diversity of individual preferences as to the alternatives, will at best provoke criticism and at worst be impossible.

It is useful if we state the problem formally. In general, a very large number of feasible allocations of resources will be available in any economy. An allocation can, in principle, be described by a very long list (or, as mathematicians would say, vector), $\bar{X}$, of numbers $X_1, X_2 \ldots X_n$ where the particular values of X_1, X_2, etc. are the quantities supplied or used of each input or output by the government, or each firm, household or distributor. Thus, for example, X_1 might represent the output of rolled steel and X_2 the output of candy floss in the particular allocation represented by $\bar{X}$. If we denote an alternative allocation as $\bar{X}'$ then it is necessary to discuss whether there is *any way*, based upon the preferences of individuals between $\bar{X}$ and $\bar{X}'$, in which one allocation can be said to be superior to the other.

The problem outlined above has been central to what is called 'welfare economics' for at least 150 years. Welfare economics is not, as might be expected, the economics of the social services, but that body of economic analysis which, on the basis of explicit value-judgements, attempts to assess and compare different allocations of resources. For many years welfare economics was based upon the assumption that each individual could measure the 'utility' that he or she attached to alternative allocations, that the utilities of different individuals could be compared with one another, and that, as a consequence, an allocation X could be said to be superior to an alternative allocation X' if it generated a greater sum of total utility. The conceptual problems of measurable utility combined with the profound difficulties of interpresonal comparisons of such utility led to the adoption of the so-called Pareto criterion[2] upon which much of this chapter is based.

2.2. The Pareto Criterion

The Pareto criterion is very simple and apparently reasonable.

An allocation X is said to be *Pareto-superior* to an alternative allocation X' if, and only if, (a) *some* individuals or firms are, given their own objectives, *better off* in X than in X', and (b) no individuals or firms are, given their objectives, worse off in X than in X'. Conversely, in this situation, X' is said to be *Pareto-inferior* to X.

It is important to note that if some individuals or firms are better off and others worse off in allocation X as compared with allocation X', then, given the Pareto criterion, we cannot say *anything* about the relative merits of X and X' and the two allocations are said to be *Pareto-non-comparable*. Thus it is clear that the Pareto criterion is *very limited* in its applicability, for many of the most important and interesting problems in the comparison of allocations *do* involve some individuals being better off and others worse off. If only *one* individual is worse off in allocation X compared with allocation X' then the allocations are Pareto-non-comparable *even if everybody else* is better off in X. It is, nevertheless, a useful starting-point, and has, as will be seen, been the basis of a number of far-reaching policies and decisions in the real world. It provides a relatively unobjectionable method of comparing at least some alternative allocations, and much of the remainder of the section is concerned with a discussion of the implications of the criterion. We will return to an assessment of the strengths and weaknesses of the Pareto criterion later in this chapter.

Given the Pareto criterion, it is possible to define a 'best' allocation of resources as follows:

An allocation of resources, X, is said to be Pareto-efficient or *Pareto-optimal* if, and only if, there is no feasible alternative allocation that is Pareto-superior to X—i.e. there is no possible way in which the resources can be reallocated so as to make some firms and individuals better off without making some others worse off.

This definition clearly requires some comment. First, it is necessary to notice the inherent dangers in the word 'optimal'.[3] It is easy to become bewitched by language. Casual use of the word 'optimal' can easily lead one to believe that one is referring to a 'best' allocation of resources in some absolute sense whereas Pareto optimality merely means that an allocation, X, is better than any alternative allocation *which can be compared to X using the*

---

[2] V. Pareto, an Italian economist and sociologist, devised many of the central concepts of consumer theory and welfare economics.

[3] This is the reason many writers prefer the description 'Pareto-efficient'.

very limited Pareto criterion. Thus, for example, a situation in which one man lived in incredible luxury and everybody else in the population was starving could be Pareto-optimal if improving the lot of the mass of the population involved the wealthy man becoming worse off. Such is the price of attempting to systematically eschew interpersonal comparisons of welfare. Secondly, as will become clear later in this section, there will typically exist a very large number of possible Pareto-Optima and, unless we are prepared to make further assumptions, there will not be *any way* in which we can compare one Pareto-optimal allocation with another.

The above description of a Pareto-efficient allocation of resources can be made more precise by considering its implications for (a) the allocation of the various productive inputs between the different available production activities, (b) the allocation of the outputs of production between the various consumers in the economy, and (c) the precise composition of national output—i.e. exactly which commodities are produced and in what quantities. We refer to (a) as the problem of *Technical Efficiency*, to (b) as the problem of *Exchange Efficiency*, and to (c) as the problem of *The Composition of Output*. We consider each in turn:

2.3. Technical Efficiency

If an allocation of society's resources is to be Pareto-efficient then it is clear that it must be impossible to reallocate the scarce production inputs so as to produce more of *all* outputs or *more of some* and *no less of others*. We can clarify the meaning of this condition of technical efficiency by considering just two typical production activities—say, the production of wheat and potatoes—which require the same two inputs—say, land and labour. Consider, to begin with, the production of wheat. We assume that both land and labour are required for production and they are substitutable for one another in the sense that a very large number of different *combinations* of land and labour can be used to produce the same total output of wheat. This idea is illustrated in Figure 6.1. The curve X–X in the diagram represents all the different combinations of land and labour that, given the state of the technology, can be used to produce a given output of wheat—say, 100 tons. Thus, for example, the point Y in the figure represents a combination of

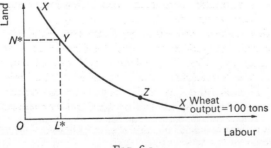

FIG. 6.1

OL* of labour and ON* of land which will produce 100 tons of wheat. Moves along the curve from left to right imply reductions in the input of land and increases in the input of labour. The curve is given a convex shape (when viewed from the point marked O) capturing the idea that it becomes increasingly difficult to substitute labour for land and keep the output of wheat constant. We define the *marginal rate of technical substitution* (MRTS) of labour for land in the production of wheat as the amount of extra labour that is required to keep the level of wheat output constant following a small, or marginal, reduction in the amount of land used.[4] It should be clear that the MRTS depends upon the initial allocation—thus it is clearly much easier to substitute labour for land and keep wheat output constant at point Y in the figure than at point Z.

Given the idea of the MRTS of land for labour, it is easy to see that any allocation of land and labour to wheat and potato production *cannot* be technically efficient if the MRTS in wheat production differs from the MRTS in potato production. Assume, for example, that the allocation of inputs is such that the MRTS in wheat production is 3 units of labour for 1 of land whereas the MRTS in potato production is 1 unit of labour for 1 unit of land. This allocation is inefficient: if 1 unit of land is transferred from potato to wheat production then 3 units of labour can be transferred in the opposite direction without any reduction in the output of wheat. But only 1 unit of labour is required to keep the output of potatoes constant following the loss of the unit of land so 2 units of labour are available to *increase the output of wheat, potatoes, or both*. The initial allocation was therefore Pareto-inefficient. Despite the very simple nature of the preceding argument it is clear that it will apply to any pair of inputs producing any pair of outputs. We have therefore deduced a very simple condition of technical efficiency which we summarize as Proposition 1:

Proposition 1 (Technical Efficiency)

If an allocation of any pair of inputs between any pair of outputs is to be Pareto-efficient then the marginal rate of technical substitution of one input for the other must be the same in the production of both goods.

2.4. Exchange Efficiency

If an over-all allocation of resources is to be Pareto-efficient then it is clear that it must be impossible to allocate the outputs actually produced between the various consumers so as to make some better off without making others worse off. Our discussion of the precise implications of this condition is very similar to the argument of the preceding section on technical efficiency. We make the same assumptions concerning the preferences of consumers as in Chapter 2. Consider the allocation of any pair of outputs—say, wheat and potatoes—between any pair of consumers—call them A and B. We have

---

[4] The reader will notice that the definition of the marginal rate of technical substitution is completely analogous to the definition of the marginal rate of substitution for a consumer discussed in Chapter 2. Following the argument of page 39 it is not difficult to see that the marginal rate of technical substitution at point Y in Figure 6.1 is measured by the slope of the curve X–X at that point.

already (see Chapter 2) defined the marginal rate of substitution of wheat for potatoes for any consumer as the quantity of wheat that would, given the personal preferences of that consumer, just compensate him or her for a small or 'marginal' reduction in the consumption of potatoes—and we have noted that this rate will depend upon the initial allocation in the sense that it is different at different points on the indifference curve. (See, for example, Fig. 2.3.)

Consider, then, a particular allocation of wheat and potatoes between A and B. It is easy to see that the allocation cannot be Pareto-efficient if A's MRS of wheat for potatoes differs from B's. Assume, for example, that the allocation is such that A's MRS is 4 units of wheat for 1 of potatoes, whereas B's MRS is 1 unit of wheat for 1 of potatoes. Then the allocation is, given their preferences, clearly inefficient. If 1 unit of potatoes is transferred from B to A then four units of wheat can be transferred in the opposite direction—and A, is given his preferences, perfectly satisfied with the deal. But B only requires 1 unit of wheat to compensate him for the loss of the 1 unit of potatoes and, consequently, *3 units of wheat are available to make B, A, or both better off.* It is, once again, clear that the preceding simple argument will apply to any pair of outputs being allocated between any pair of consumers. We summarize the basic condition for Exchange Efficiency as Proposition 2:

Proposition 2 (Exchange Efficiency)

If an allocation of goods between individuals is Pareto-efficient then their personal marginal rates of substitution between any pair of goods must be equal.

2.5. The Optimal Composition of Output

Thus far we have used simple intuitive arguments to derive two very basic conditions of Pareto efficiency—the condition of technical efficiency, implying the equality of marginal rates of technical substitution, and the condition of exchange efficiency, implying the equality of personal marginal rates of substitution. We now discuss the final condition of Pareto efficiency relating to the precise quantities of goods produced. In terms of our previous discussions, we are interested in how much wheat and how many potatoes *should* be produced. Intuitively, it is clear that this question relates both to the *preferences* of the individuals in the economy and to the *technical possibilities* of producing the different goods. It should be clear that an economy could not be Pareto-efficient if its resources were being used to produce a bundle of outputs that were considered by the populace to be inferior to another bundle of outputs that *could* have been produced using the same resources.

The necessary condition for a Pareto-efficient composition of output can be most easily appreciated if we assume that only two goods—call them, once again, wheat and potatoes—are produced. The technical possibilities of the economy can be represented in a very simple diagram. Consider Figure 6.2. The curve A–B, which is usually called the 'transformation frontier' or the 'production possibility frontier', represents all the combinations of wheat and potatoes that could be produced if the scarce resources of land and labour are allocated efficiently—i.e. if the condition of technical efficiency is satisfied. Thus, for example, if all of the economy's resources are used in producing wheat then OA of wheat can be produced. Intermediate points on the curve such as C and D represent other possible efficient combinations of wheat and potatoes—i.e. they show the absolute maximum available production of potatoes for the given levels of wheat production.

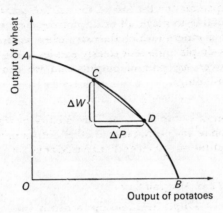

FIG. 6.2

Consider the move from the efficient combination represented by the point C to the efficient combination represented by the point D. Such a move involves the production of ΔW less wheat (the symbol Δ means, once again, a 'small change') and ΔP more potatoes. Wheat is being 'transformed' into potatoes—not by any magical method but by the simple expedient of transferring some of society's scarce resources from wheat to potato production. The ratio $\Delta W/\Delta P$ is called the 'marginal rate of transformation' between potatoes and wheat.[5] It represents the quantity of wheat that must be foregone for a small increment in potato production. The *shape* of the transformation frontier represents the idea that as more and more of society's resources are transferred from wheat to potato production the quantities of additional potatoes produced per unit reduction in wheat production become smaller and smaller.

We have already noted that if the allocation of wheat and potatoes between individuals is to be Pareto-efficient then the personal marginal rate of substitution of wheat for potatoes of any one person must equal that of all others. If, therefore, the condition of 'exchange efficiency' is satisfied, we are justified in speaking of *the* marginal rate of substitution of wheat for potatoes.

It is not difficult to see that if the precise composition of output is to be Pareto-efficient then the technically determined marginal rate of transformation between potatoes and wheat must equal the preference-determined marginal rate of substitution between potatoes and wheat. Consider, for

[5] If the amounts ΔW and ΔP are made very small then the marginal rate of transformation is measured by the slope of the transformation frontier at any point.

example, an allocation in which the marginal rate of transformation is 3 units of wheat for 1 unit of potatoes whereas 'the' maginal rate of substitution (given exchange efficiency) is 1 unit of wheat for 1 of potatoes. Then the composition of output is Pareto-inefficient. If resources are reallocated such that 1 less unit of potatoes is produced then 3 extra units of wheat will become available. Only 1 unit of wheat is, however, required given the populace's preferences, to compensate for the loss of the unit of potatoes so 2 units of wheat are now available to make all or any of the consumers better off— depending upon the manner in which the extra wheat is distributed between the consumers. This simple argument clearly applies to the marginal rate of transformation between *any* pair of outputs and we can summarize our deductions as Proposition 3:

Proposition 3

If the composition of output is to be Pareto-efficient then the marginal rate of transformation of any output into another output must equal society's marginal rate of substitution (given exchange efficiency) of one output for the other.

2.6. Marginal Product and Marginal Cost

It is useful to note a simple relationship between the marginal rate of transformation of one output for another and (i) the productivities of the inputs in producing the outputs, and (ii) the costs of production of the outputs. Let us define the *marginal product* of an input as the ratio of extra output to a small increase in the input, with all other inputs remaining constant. Thus, if ΔN extra acres of land will produce ΔP extra potatoes, then the marginal product of land is approximately[6] $\Delta P/\Delta N$. Secondly, we recall from Chapter 3 the definition of the *marginal cost* of an output as the ratio of extra costs of production incurred for a small increase in output to the increase in output, i.e. the addition to total cost per additional unit of output. Thus, if an increase ΔP in potato production generated ΔC extra cost then the marginal cost of potatoes is approximately $\Delta C/\Delta P$. We now demonstrate that the marginal rate of transformation, $\Delta W/\Delta P$, of wheat for potatoes is directly related to the marginal productivities of inputs in producing wheat and potatoes and to the marginal cost of producing wheat and potatoes.

Let us, for simplicity, assume that the only input to wheat and potato production is land, measured in acres, which is available at a rent of $£r$ per acre. Now, consider a small reduction, ΔN, in the acreage made available for wheat production. The fall, ΔW, in wheat output will clearly equal the reduction, ΔN, in available land multiplied by the marginal product of land in producing wheat—which, in this context, we denote as MPN^w. Thus we can write:

$$\Delta W = \Delta N \cdot MPN^w \ldots \tag{1}$$

where ΔW is interpreted as a fall in wheat output.

---

[6] Strictly, marginal quantities should be defined in terms of infinitesimally small changes. Nevertheless, it does no great violence to our argument if we follow the present definition.

If the acreage, ΔN, removed from wheat production is used for potato production then the increase, ΔP, in potato production will clearly equal the extra acreage multiplied by the marginal product of land in producing potatoes, MPN^p. Thus we can write:

$$\Delta P = \Delta N \cdot MPN^p \ldots \tag{2}$$

We know, however, that the marginal rate of transformation is defined as $\Delta W/\Delta P$ so, dividing equation (1) by equation (2), we obtain:

$$\frac{\Delta W}{\Delta P} = \frac{\Delta N}{\Delta N} \cdot \frac{MPN^w}{MPN^p} = \frac{MPN^w}{MPN^p} \ldots \tag{3}$$

i.e. the marginal rate of transformation of wheat into potatoes equals the ratio of the marginal product of land in producing wheat to the marginal product of land in producing potatoes. It can be shown[7] that a similar result will hold for any inputs.

Now, consider the extra costs, ΔC, of producing ΔP extra potatoes. Since we are assuming that land is the only input, total costs, C, will simply equal the amount, N, of land used multiplied by the rent, £r, (which we assume unchanged). If the amount of land used increases by ΔN, the addition, ΔC to costs will be £$r\Delta N$ and we can write:

$$\Delta C = r\Delta N \ldots \tag{4}$$

If we divide both sides of (4) by the extra potato output, ΔP, we obtain:

$$\frac{\Delta C}{\Delta P} = r \cdot \frac{\Delta N}{\Delta P} \ldots \tag{5}$$

Now, from the definitions $\Delta C/\Delta P$ is the marginal cost of potatoes, MC^p, and $\Delta N/\Delta P$ is the inverse of the marginal product of land in producing potatoes, MPN^p. Equation (5) can therefore be written as:

$$MC^p = \frac{r}{MPN^p} \ldots \tag{6}$$

Using an identical argument it is easy to show that the marginal cost of producing wheat is given by:

$$MC^w = \frac{r}{MPN^w} \ldots \tag{7}$$

Dividing equation (6) by (7) it can be seen that:

$$\frac{MC^p}{MC^w} = \frac{MPN^w}{MPN^p}$$

But we have already shown (equation (3)) that the ratio of the marginal product of land in producing wheat to the marginal product of land in producing potatoes equals the marginal rate of transformation. It can now be seen that the marginal rate of transformation between potatoes and wheat equals the ratio of the marginal cost of potatoes to the marginal cost of wheat.

[7] See, e.g., Lancaster [3], pp. 267, 268.

In the subsequent analysis we will demonstrate the importance of this simple result.

The three conditions of Pareto efficiency discussed above constitute a framework, albeit very limited, in which some questions relating to the relative merits of alternative allocations of resources can be considered. Two important points must be stressed. Firstly, as was mentioned earlier in the section, the Pareto criterion and the efficiency conditions do *not* isolate a uniquely 'best' allocation of resources. Although the conditions of Pareto efficiency *do* rule out many allocations as being unambiguously undesirable, there still remain a very large number of *different* possible Pareto-efficient allocations. Since the Pareto criterion simply makes *no* attempt to compare situations in which some are better off and others worse off, it cannot distinguish between alternative Pareto-efficient allocations that correspond to *different distributions of income and wealth*. Thus one Pareto-efficient allocation might involve substantial inequality of wealth while another might involve perfect equality. If, however, society could by some means or other decide upon and achieve what it considered to be a 'fair' distribution of income and wealth, then there would be every incentive to ensure that the precise allocation of resource corresponding to this distribution was, in fact, Pareto-efficient. Since *everybody* can be made better off in a move from a Pareto-inefficient to a Pareto-efficient allocation, there does not seem to be any obvious reason, whatever one's views on the 'fairness' of the distribution of wealth, why inefficiency should be tolerated if efficiency is available.

Secondly, although the idea of Pareto efficiency is used explicitly in the context of 'cost-benefit' analysis (see, for example, Mishan [4] and Layard [12]), it should be clear that the ideas discussed above are intended to provide an analytical rather than a practical framework for assessment. As is discussed in Chapter 9, real governments have a variety of different objectives—some of which conflict with one another. Now, Pareto efficiency is not an *explicitly* stated government objective and, indeed, it is difficult to conceive of how a real-world Pareto optimum could be identified—even if it was possible to achieve it. Nevertheless, the ideas of efficiency discussed here are not only useful for interpreting the claims to virtue of the proponents of free-market competition but do, in fact, underlie practical discussions of micro-economic policy and practical proposals. (See Chapters 16 and 18.)

3. The Price System

In the previous section we identified three basic conditions necessary for an allocation of society's scarce resources to be Pareto-efficient. In the present section we examine how the outcome of a system of unfettered and apparently unco-ordinated free competition between self-seeking individuals and firms *could* be Pareto-efficient, and we reserve for the next section a discussion of the problems associated with real-world market behaviour. We concentrate our discussion on a world of free markets and prices partly because such a system is probably[8] the most common allocative mechanism in the West and

[8] It could be argued that, even in an as ostensibly competition-oriented economy as the United States, various forms of corporate and government planning have, in many cases,

partly because many of the issues associated with communist-style command planning do, in fact, arise in the same context. We proceed in three stages. We firstly analyse an 'ideal' form of competition in the context of the market for a single commodity. Secondly, the simultaneous working of the price system for all goods and services (including labour services) is discussed. Finally, the relationship between competition and efficiency is isolated and analysed.

3.1. The Single Market

The simplest method of obtaining an insight into the workings of the competitive allocative mechanism is to examine the market for a single good. Our conception of the 'market' for the good (say beer) does not imply a single geographical location but is defined simply by the communication between potential buyers and sellers. In a world of 'free competition'[9] the quantities of beer produced and sold will depend upon the preferences of consumers, as expressed by their willingness to buy in the market, and the technical conditions of production for the potential sellers, as expressed by their willingess to sell in the market. We define a situation of *perfect competition* as one in which no trader (i.e. buyer or seller) supplies or demands more than a very small part of the total output of the good in question, any new supplier can freely enter if he wishes, all firms produce an identical infinitely divisible product, all have perfect knowledge of all aspects of any exchanges that take place, and transport costs are insignificant. In this case, the demand curve facing any one supplier will be horizontal. Any attempt to raise price above the market level would result in the loss of all demand, while any lowering of price would result in the firm obtaining all the market demand. We can now draw a cost/revenue diagram such as the one shown in Chapter 3 (p. 59), corresponding to a perfectly competitive situation. This is shown in Figure 6.3.

The average total cost and marginal cost curves are as shown in Figure 3.2. If the price were to be at P_1, the demand curve would be horizontal at this level, and is by definition the average revenue curve (see p. 59). The marginal revenue curve will be identical with it because each extra unit of output will add to total revenue an amount exactly equal to the price (equals average revenue (AR)) of the product.[10] The price P_1 will determine total market demand Q_1, and with F firms, each individual form will have Q_1/F units of demand. The profit-maximizing output will, however, be q_1^* where marginal revenue (MR) equals marginal cost (MC). Thus the situation depicted

---

replaced the market mechanism. For a famous exposition of this kind of view, see K. Galbraith, *The New Industrial State* (Penguin, 1968).

[9] It is important to note that dangers are inherent in the use of the adjective 'free'. We use it to describe a situation in which buyers and sellers are free to conclude a bargain without outside interference. Some, perhaps many, would claim, however, that 'free' competition is inextricably linked with more general concepts of freedom. Others would disagree.

[10] Any marginal amount always equals the corresponding average if the average is unchanging. An average batting score only rises if the new or marginal innings results in a score above the average. Conversely, it only falls if the marginal innings is below the average. A marginal batting score equal to the average will leave the average unchanged.

would not last. Firms would reduce price in an effort to increase output and profits.

The reduction in price increases market demand, and hence the individual firm's demand, until price P_2 is reached. The firm's demand is Q_2/F which equals the new profit-maximizing output. (The profit-maximizing output has moved from q_1^* because of the change in market price.) No firm in the industry would have any further incentive to change its price or output.

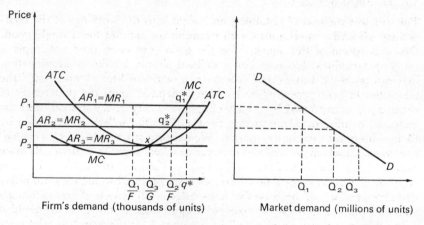

Fig. 6.3

There are three important things to notice about this situation:

(1) The price of the product equals its marginal cost. This will occur as soon as output reaches the profit-maximizing level. At this level MC = MR, but under perfect competition MR = AR which is the same as price. Hence price equals marginal cost, which is another result to be utilized in the next section.

(2) Given our assumption, the cost conditions of the producer show how much beer he will be *prepared to supply* to the market at different prices. At price P_2, profit considerations imply that he will be prepared to sell an amount q_2^*, but if the price is P_1 he will be prepared to sell the higher output q_1^*. The points X and Y represent points on the firm's *supply curve* which relates price to the amount it is willing to supply at that price. Clearly, therefore, under perfect competition the firm's supply curve is its marginal cost curve.

If *every* producer of beer is confronted by a marginal cost curve similar to the one in Figure 6.3 then it is clear that the *total* amount of beer that producers as a whole are prepared to supply will increase as the price increases. This enables us to analyse the individual market in a situation of perfect competition. Consider Figure 6.4. The curve marked DD is the market demand curve for beer showing the quantities of beer that households *plan* to buy at different prices. (See Chapter 2.)

The curve marked SS represents the quantities of beer that all the profit-maximizing producers are prepared to sell at each price—the quantities being determined by the marginal cost curves of the producers as discussed above.[11] Consider the price p*. At this price, the quantity of beer that producers are prepared to sell just equals the quantity that consumers are prepared to buy. If this price emerged in the market, consumers would find that they were actually able to buy the quantity they planned to buy—there would not be a 'shortage' of any kind. Similarly, at the price p*, producers would find that there were, in fact, just enough buyers to actually buy all that the producers planned to sell. The price p* is called the *equilibrium* price for the market—for, if it rules, no trader has any obvious incentive to try and change the situation.

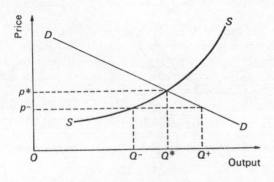

FIG. 6.4

In Chapter 2 we demonstrated how the market demand curve stemmed from households' preferences, incomes, and the prices they face. In the present chapter we have shown that market supply depends upon the marginal costs of production. Thus the equilibrium price, p*, acts as a *signal of the true relative* scarcity of beer stemming from its desirability to consumers and the resources that need to be used in its production. This is what lies behind the intuitive notion of prices equating supply and demand.

Consider the price p⁻—which is below the equilibrium price. At this price, the quantity that producers are prepared to supply is OQ⁻—which is less than the quantity that consumers plan to buy, OQ⁺. In this situation of 'excess demand' some customers will not be able to buy as much beer as they planned, and there are incentives for producers to start increasing the price.[12] Once the price has reached the equilibrium price then plans to buy will once again equal plans to sell—and there will be no more dissatisfied customers. Price acts as an *incentive to individual action* on the part of buyers and sellers and it *co-ordinates their plans* such that the quantity available exactly matches the quantity desired.

[11] It is, in fact, simply a horizontal summation of the individual marginal cost curves.
[12] There are, in fact, rather tricky logical problems associated with the argument that prices tend to the equilibrium price. If *everyone* acts as a 'price taker' who raises the price?

(3) Going back to Figure 6.3, at the price P_2, although MR = MC, average revenue is above average cost. Supernormal profits are being made and new firms will be attracted in. As F, the number of firms, rises so each firm's demand falls, and further price reductions are necessary to increase over-all market demand sufficiently to allow each individual firm to reach its profit-maximizing output. Finally P_3 is reached with G firms in the industry. Not only does MC = MR (profit maximizing) but AC = AR as well, implying no supernormal profits and no tendency for any firm outside the industry to enter (or any inside to leave). This must be at the minimum point of the average cost curve (point X at output Q_3/G). If MC = MR, MR = AR, and AR = AC, then MC = AC. But marginal cost can only equal average cost when the latter is unchanging, meaning a horizontal part of the average cost curve. Given the U-shaped curve, this only occurs at minimum average cost.

Thus, over the longer term, production at minimum average cost is ensured. Higher-cost producers will be unable to compete and will fail to continue profitable production. If there are constant returns to scale and given factor prices, the long-run price level of the product will be independent of the level of demand or output.

Perfect competition in the market for factors of production gives a rather different picture. If firms are profit maximizers they will only employ a factor of production, e.g. labour, if the gain to the firm from his production exceeds the cost of his wage. Assuming perfect competition in the product market as well, and therefore an unchanging product price, the gain from employing one more man (all other factors held constant) will be his extra output—the marginal product of labour—times the product price. The cost will be his money wage, which through perfect competition in the labour market will also be given. If the former exceeds the latter the firm will employ the man, and the next, and so on until the marginal product of labour (which is assumed to fall as more men are taken on) falls to the level of the money wage. Any further employment would depress the gain below the cost of the next man, and the firm ceases to employ more men. Its profits are now maximized. The condition is

$$P \times MPL = W$$

where P is the product price, MPL the marginal product of labour, and W the wage rate.

$$\text{This gives MPL} = \frac{W}{P}$$

indicating that under the very restrictive assumptions stated the 'price' of a factor of production (the real wage in this case) will equal the marginal product of the factor. While many things will interfere with this, it is not unreasonable to think of marginal product as one element in the determination of real wages under competitive conditions.

3.2. General Equilibrium

Equilibrium of an individual market is relatively easy to understand. What, however, is meant by the *general* equilibrium of a perfect market economy? Let us assume that the economy consists of a very large number of households, a very large number of firms, and a very large number, n, of different inputs and outputs. A general competitive equilibrium is then defined as a set of prices, one for each commodity, such that:

(a) *Every* household is in equilibrium in the sense that, given their incomes and the prices of all commodities, they are choosing a preferred bundle of commodities.

(b) *Every* firm is in equilibrium in the sense that, given its technology and the prices of inputs and outputs, it has a production plan that maximizes profits.

(c) *Every* market for each of the n different inputs and outputs is in equilibrium in the sense that planned supplies equal planned demands.

The concept of a general equilibrium is truly staggering. In such a situation, given the prices of all inputs and outputs, there would be no shortages or surpluses of any commodity, and no economic agent, i.e. firm or individual, would have any incentive to alter its pattern of production or consumption. In this situation, the *system of prices* as a whole would be acting as the co-ordinator of a myriad individual decisions by acting as an indicator of relative scarcity and as an incentive to action.

Now, it should be clear that the general equilibrium of perfect competition is an abstract concept—no real economy has been, or ever will be, in a situation of general equilibrium. But the concept of general equilibrium represents what might happen in a situation of 'ideal' competition—it shows how the competitive mechanism might co-ordinate an economy in an ordered and, as we will see, efficient manner. A clear understanding of the implications of general equilibrium enables us to understand the effects of anything less than the full equilibrium of perfect competition. We now turn to investigate the kind of allocation of resources that would be associated with general equilibrium.[13]

3.3. General Equilibrium and Pareto Efficiency

Given our definition of general competitive equilibrium and our earlier discussion of Pareto efficiency, it is a relatively easy matter to demonstrate that any general equilibrium will, in fact, be Pareto-efficient. Firstly, notice that perfect competition as we have defined it implies that only *one* price can rule for each commodity throughout the economy. All producers face exactly the same price for any input and all consumers face exactly the same price for any output. If any producer tried to charge a higher price than the ruling equilibrium price, our assumption of perfect knowledge on the part of all traders of all aspects of exchange would mean that he would immediately lose all his business. A lower price would result in normal profit not being

[13] A thorough treatment of these issues would require a discussion of (i) whether general equilibrium is logically possible, and (ii) whether forces exist that move an economy to general equilibrium.

achieved. Hence, everyone is a price-taker, unable to influence the ruling equilibrium prices. Now consider, the conditions for Pareto efficiency discussed in section 2.

(a) *Technical Efficiency*. In section 2 it was demonstrated that technical efficiency was implied if the MRTS of one input for another in the production of any good was equal to the MRTS between the same pair of inputs in producing any other good. Consider an individual producer considering what combination to buy of some pair of inputs given their general equilibrium prices. It is easy to show that he will minimize the costs of producing a given output (or, equivalently, maximize output for a given cost) if he chooses a combination such that the marginal rate of technical substitution of one input for the other is equal to their price ratio. Assume, for example, that £10 will buy 2 hours of capital services or 1 hour of labour services (i.e. the price of capital is £5 per hour and the price of labour is £10 per hour) while the MRTS is 1 hour of capital services for 1 hour of labour services. Now, if the entrepreneur purchases 1 hour less of labour services he would save £10. If he spent £5 on purchasing 1 hour of capital services then his output would remain the same (given the MRTS of 1 for 1) and he would have made a net saving of £5. Consequently, such a production plan would not have been minimizing cost nor maximizing profit. This simple argument demonstrates the MRTS between *any* pair of inputs must equal their price ratio if costs are to be minimized. Now, if all producers are in equilibrium (see the definition of general equilibrium) then they must *all* be equating the MRTSs between any pair of inputs to the ratio of the prices of the inputs. But we have already noted that in general equilibrium they will *all* face precisely the same prices for inputs. Consequently, in general equilibrium the MRTS between any pair of inputs in producing any output will equal the MRTS between the same pair of inputs in producing any other output— which is precisely our condition for technical efficiency. The price system interacts with the *desire for profit* to ensure the equality of marginal rates of technical substitution.

(b) *Exchange Efficiency*. In section 2 it was demonstrated that exchange efficiency necessitated that all personal marginal rates of substitution between any two goods must be equal. Now, in Chapter 2 we showed that a consumer freely choosing a bundle of commodities in the market will, given the prices and his income, choose a bundle such that his personal marginal rate of substitution between any pair of goods is equal to the ratio of their prices. If all consumers face uniform prices (and, therefore, uniform price ratios of different goods) then it is clear that all their personal rates of substitution between any pair of goods will be equated. Thus the general equilibrium of perfect competition, by ensuring that all consumers face the same prices, implies that the *self-interest of consumers* will ensure the satisfaction of this basic condition for Pareto efficiency.

(c) *The Optimal Composition of Output*. In section 2 of this chapter we demonstrated that the optimal composition of output necessitated that the marginal rate of transformation between any pair of commodities must equal the marginal rate of substitution. In general equilibrium, profit maximization and perfect competition generate exactly this result. This can be seen as follows.

(i) In section 2 we saw that the marginal rate of transformation between products 1 and 2 equalled the ratio of the marginal costs of production of the goods in question, i.e. $\mathrm{MRT}_1^2 = \mathrm{MC}_1/(\mathrm{MC}_2)$.

(ii) From Chapter 2 we know that household equilibrium implies that the personal marginal rates of substitution between any pair of goods will equal the ratio of their prices, i.e.

$$\frac{P_1}{P_2} = \mathrm{MRS}_1^2 = \frac{MU_1}{MU_2}$$

but we have also seen (p. 157) that Pareto optimality requires $\mathrm{MRT}_1^2 = \mathrm{MRS}_1^2$. Putting these three together we have that

$$\frac{MC_1}{MC_2} = \frac{P_1}{P_2}$$

which is the necessary condition for the optional composition of output.

(iii) In the present section we have shown that profit maximization in a situation of perfect competition implies that that the prices of all goods will equal their marginal costs of production. Therefore the ratio of their marginal costs equal the ratio of their prices which, as we have just seen, is the necessary condition for the optimal composition of output.

The conditions that
$$\frac{MC_1}{MC_2} = \frac{P_1}{P_2}$$

can be rewritten
$$\frac{P_1}{MC_1} = \frac{P_2}{MC_2}$$

saying that the ratio of price to marginal cost for each good (indeed all goods) must be the same. In fact, further considerations require that the ratio is 1. To take but one reason, some firms cover more than one stage of production. The effect of this can be shown by an example, where $P/MC = 2$.

	Stage 1 MC	Stage 2 MC	Price
(i) Production by 1 Firm			
Wages	£1	£1	
	—	—	£8
Materials	£2	—	

	Stage 1 MC	P	Stage 2 MC	Price
(ii) Production by 2 Firms				
Wages	£1		£1	
		£6		£14
Materials	£2		—	
Semi-Manufacture			£6	

In the second case marginal cost to the first firm carrying out stage 1 of the production process is £2 + £1 = £3. Its price for the semi-manufactured good is £6. So marginal cost for the second firm carrying out stage 2 is £1 + £6 = £7 and the price is £14. For the firm in case (i) with the same inputs, same production processes, and same output, its marginal cost is £4 in total and the price is therefore £8. Only if the ratio of P/MC is 1 will both cases give the same final price. Perfect competition still gives a Pareto optimum because it does generate P = MC.

We have now demonstrated that the equilibrium of an 'ideal' form of competition would, given the associated price system, imply Pareto efficiency. This result provides a precise statement of the sense in which 'free competition' is optimal, given the definition used, the limitations that have been discussed, and the limited applicability of the Pareto criterion. In the next two sections we first examine the principal factors that imply that real-world competition will not generate such attractive efficiency results, and, second, go a littler further into the problem of applying the Pareto criterion.

4. Market Failure

In the real-world, free markets often fail to perform in the idealized fashion required for allocative efficiency—hence the generic title for this section. Below we examine briefly the principal factors that prevent markets from working in the manner described above.

4.1. Monopoly and other Market Imperfections

Perhaps the principal reason for scepticism that the price system will perform effectively as a decentralized signalling system and incentive to action is the widespread existence in the real-world of monopoly and other market structures which allow individual firms considerable power in the market. Real-world markets rarely, if ever, conform to the stylized version of perfect competition described in the previous section. Traders are, as is implied by the discussion of firms' behaviour in Chapter 3, very often sufficiently dominant in the market that they can, in fact, choose the price at which they sell their product. As was demonstrated in Chapter 3, profit maximization in the general situation implies that firms will choose output such that marginal cost equals marginal revenue. Since marginal revenue for this kind of dominant firm is *less* than price, prices must be greater than marginal cost. We have already seen in the previous section that the composition of output will be optimal only if *all* prices equal marginal costs of production. No general statement about the desirability of setting price equal to marginal cost can be made if some other prices do not equal the marginal cost of their product. We are in what is known as a 'second-best' world where a more *ad hoc* approach has to be adopted. Thus any element of market power or monopoly will militate severely against the claims to efficiency of free competition. This simple, but powerful, resource allocation argument against monopolistic market structures is not, of course, the whole story. These matters are discussed in Chapter 16.

4.2. External Effects

Many real-world production activities involve side effects or 'externalities' which are a pervasive problem if competition and the price system are to live up to the claims to efficiency summarized in the previous section. Externalities arise when the activities of one economic agent directly affect the outcome of the activities of another economic agent in a way not covered by the price mechanism. Thus, for example, a factory may pollute a river which is the source of water to another factory, or the air that the local community breathes, etc. In the absence of a system of licensing or a system of compensation, the price system *alone* will not provide incentives to minimize this pollution, and legal prohibition may be essential.

The effects of externalities may be unfavourable—as in the case of the polluting factory—or favourable—as in the case of the bee-keeper who benefits from living next door to an orchard. At the heart of the problem of externalities is the fact that, in the case of many activities, it is difficult to *exclude* others from the costs and benefits of the activity. If exclusion is impossible (or very difficult) markets may not exist for the commodity in question—in which case the price system will not provide incentives to reduce harmful externalities and increase beneficial externalities.[14]

The factory has no incentive to reduce its pollution because it does not bear the cost of the pollution, nor would it reap any gain from reducing it (indeed it would incur the cost of prevention). The orchard-owner receives no payment from the bee-keeper despite the benefit of the orchard to the bee-keeper, and hence has no incentive from this source to maintain it, unlike a hive-maker for example.

Such considerations lead us to distinguish between *private* cost or benefit—the actual cost or benefit incurred by a private transactor such that he will pay for the benefit or need payment to incur the cost—and *social* cost or benefit, which is the cost or benefits which accrue to *anyone* in society irrespective of whether they were involved in the transaction or mode or received any payment. There has in recent years been increasing effort in some parts of the public sector to identify such social costs and benefits before taking major resource allocating decisions.

A problem closely related to that of externalities involves the problem of *public* goods, such as street lighting, the provision of 'defence', or a clean-air programme, where the 'consumption' of these goods by one individual in no way excludes someone else also 'consuming' or enjoying their benefits. Such goods form a significant proportion of the collective purchases made by government on behalf of the community (see Chapter 11).

4.3. Intertemporal Efficiency

The ideas of Pareto-efficient general equilibrium developed in the previous section referred to the allocation of resources at a single point in time. A central characteristic of the real-world economy is that resources have to be allocated *now* for the provision of outputs in the future. Thus, for example, a decision to allocate resources for the construction of a new factory must depend upon the demand for the factory's products when it is eventually

[14] This is a very terse statement of a profound problem. For an excellent discussion see Bator [7].

completed. Now, in principle, all the arguments concerning efficiency in the previous section could be duplicated *if* there existed 'future markets' for all commodities—i.e. markets that quote prices *today* for delivery of goods at future dates. In the real-world, however, futures markets are rather rare. Thus the real-world price system does *not* provide signals of scarcity in the future and cannot properly co-ordinate current activities whose outcome lies in the future. Today's beer price reflects today's costs and today's preferences—it will not, in general, provide any information of future costs and future preferences. The price of a raw material might remain very low because of an abundance of it today, irrespective of the fact that it will soon run out altogether. A long-term futures market would allow the future scarcity to be reflected in a high futures price, giving suppliers the incentive to reduce supplies now in favour of supply in the future. This would drive up the current price and lead to an economizing in the use of the ultimately very scarce resource. Many of the ideas of indicative planning stem from this weakness of real-world price systems.

4.4. Risk and Uncertainty

All our discussions thus far have involved an implicit assumption of certainty. In the real-world, however, the outcomes of activities are frequently uncertain. Now, if insurance companies provided markets for *all* risks it is conceivable that the price system could generate an efficient allocation of resources between activities involving different degrees of risk. But insurance markets are far from perfect and it may be that the price system produces a bias against risky activities, which is inefficient from the point of view of society.

4.5. Information and Disequilibrium

The central strand in our argument that the equilibrium of perfect competition would be Pareto-efficient was the idea that all buyers of inputs and outputs would face exactly the same prices—and this proposition stemmed from our assumption of perfect knowledge. In the real-world, however, information is far from perfect and is *costly* to obtain. Thus it is not difficult to find two adjacent supermarkets charging different prices for identical products. Consumer organizations frequently reveal astonishing variations in prices for identical commodities. Whatever else may be said about competition in the real-world it certainly does not involve uniformity of prices at any point of time—although there are, of course, tendencies to equalization. The costs of acquiring information are a strong reason for believing that equilibrium may never come about—the microeconomy might be in persistent disequilibrium. All the results of section 3 are jeopardized by this fact.

5. Limitations of Pareto Efficiency

Finally, we return to consider the Pareto criterion itself. Many limitations on its use have been demonstrated; we mention three of these.

5.1. Compensation

How do we deal with situations (which are the typical sort) in which some gain by a move from situaton A to B, but some lose? Are we unable to say anything at all about the desirability of the change?

It has been suggested that the move could be judged beneficial as long as the gainers gain more than the losers lose, implying that the gainers could compensate the losers for the change. This is only acceptable, however, if the gainers *actually* do compensate the losers. If they compensate the losers sufficiently for them to voluntarily agree to the change then we may presume that they are not worse off at the end. The gainers are still net gainers, however, and thus the Pareto criterion again becomes operative and allows us to judge the move *plus* compensation as Pareto-efficient.[15] The compensation that can be paid, however, and the amount required are both generally dependent on *the distribution* of income, and this may make the compensation procedure unacceptable.

5.2. Income Distribution

We have already referred to the problem of income distribution, views on which are explicitly value-based judgements. If decisions determining the distribution of income were independent of those determining resource allocation then, in principle, society could decide through its political system on the distribution of income it desired, independent of its allocation of resources, which could then be made Pareto-efficient separately. In fact, of course, this is largely not possible. A non-Pareto-efficient allocation may be preferred to a Pareto-efficient one because the income distribution associated with the former is preferred, but is not in practice obtainable in conjunction with a Pareto-efficient allocation of resources. At best it is only possible to indicate the loss of potential satisfaction that one or more people are suffering in order that a measurable improvement in income distribution is achieved so that society can take an informed value-judgement between the two situations. This in turn will clearly depend on people's views of the importance of equity, incentives, property rights, etc.

5.3. Preferences and the Means of Payment

Perhaps the biggest problem of all is the fact that within the Pareto system preferences are only recognized if they are backed up by the necessary money for payment. The strength of a preference for chocolate is assumed to be indicated by willingness to pay for it. For many products this may be acceptable but for a whole range of other products it is not. Inability to pay for a life-saving operation clearly does not indicate the lack of any desire for it, and there is probably general agreement that it is desirable to make such things available irrespective of payment, and hence outside the market system. More controversial, however, are products such as housing, education, minimum standard of consumption, etc. It is generally thought desirable that everyone should have adequate amounts of these irrespective of prices or costs. Clearly, the Pareto-efficient criterion is inadequate to reflect this type of view.

[15] Many difficulties arise in practice, and even some theoretical inconsistencies may arise, but in principle this compensation principle can sometimes offer a way forward.

In conclusion, therefore, one can only go a little way with the Pareto criterion. Later on, various situations will be examined in which it has been applied, albeit in conjunction with other criteria. There appear to be relatively few examples in the modern market economy where there is both a general agreement that a Pareto-based criterion is paramount and also a sufficient degree of competition to *guarantee* the achievement of the Pareto optimum. The existence of other value-judgements, of externalities, public goods, monopolistic elements, and excessive risk all contribute towards a system in which resource allocation decisions may be extremely complex, political, and subjective.

Bibliography

Section A consists of various expositions of the economic theory of resource allocation. Section B is a selective list of books on welfare economics. Several of the books and articles cited (e.g. Mishan [4]) contain detailed bibliographies.

SECTION A

[1] BATOR, F. M. 'The Simple Analytics of Welfare Maximization', *American Economic Review* (Mar. 1957).
A very well-known geometrical exposition of most of the central ideas of welfare economics.
[2] DORFMAN, R. *The Price System* (Prentice-Hall, 1964).
A good relatively short account of the theoretical working of the price system.
[3] LANCASTER, K. *Introduction to Modern Microeconomics* (Rand McNally and Co., 1969).
Chs. 9 and 10 constitute a good textbook exposition of most of the issues discussed in this chapter.
[4] MISHAN, E. J. 'A Survey of Welfare Economics 1939–1959', *Economic Journal* (1960).
A well-known survey of welfare economics.
[5] SCITOVSKY, T. *Welfare and Competition* (George Allen and Unwin, 1971).
Contains a very clear account of the resource allocation implications of free competition.
[6] WINCH, D. M. *Analytical Welfare Economics* (Penguin, 1971).
A succinct textbook treatment of welfare economics.

SECTION B

[7] BATOR, F. M. 'The Anatomy of Market Failure', *Quarterly Journal of Economics* (Aug. 1958).
[8] DOBB, M. *Welfare Economics and the Economics of Socialism* (Cambridge University Press, 1969).
[9] FRIEDMAN, M. *Essays in Positive Economics* (University of Chicago, 1953).
[10] GRAAF, J. DE V. *Theoretical Welfare Economics* (Cambridge University Press, 1967).
[11] KOOPMANS, T. *Three Essays on the State of Economic Science* (McGraw-Hill, 1957), Essay 1.
[12] LAYARD, R. (ed.) *Cost-Benefit Analysis* (Penguin, 1972).
[13] LIPSEY, R. G. *An Introduction to Positive Economics*, 4th edn. (Weidenfeld and Nicolson, 1975).

[14] LITTLE, I. M. D. *A Critique of Welfare Economics*, 2nd edn. (Oxford University Press, 1957).

[15] MISHAN, E. J. *Elements of Cost-Benefit Analysis* (George Allen and Unwin, 1972).

[16] NATH, S. K. *A Reappraisal of Welfare Economics* (Routledge and Kegan Paul, 1969).

[17] NOVE, A. *The Soviet Economy*, 3rd edn. (George Allen and Unwin, 1968).

[18] PIGOU, A. C. *The Economies of Welfare*, 4th edn. (Macmillan and Co., 1932.)

[19] ROWLEY, C. K. and PEACOCK, A. T. *Welfare Economics: A Liberal Restatement* (Martin Robertson, 1975).

[20] SEN, A. K. *On Economic Inequality* (Oxford University Press, 1973).

PART III

7

Inflation

A. W. M. GRAHAM

1. Introduction

Inflation is the process of the aggregate price level rising. We want to know why a pound today only buys about half as much as ten years ago, and why aggregate money incomes have doubled in an even shorter period. We are not mainly concerned with why prices of meals in restaurants are rising relative to the price of colour television sets. But no explanation can be regarded as very adequate if it does not explain why particular prices or particular wages do rise—the whole has to be the sum of the parts. Inflation is the aggregate result of thousands of separate decisions by firms, employees, and consumers about prices, wages, and expenditure. We shall therefore need to see how the tools of analysis developed in Chapters 2–5 above interact. Moreover, since inflation is a problem for policy rather than a definable area of economics, this chapter will not only draw on the earlier analysis, but also to some extent overlap with material in later chapters, particularly in the fields of fiscal and monetary policy, in incomes policy, and (in considering the international aspects of inflation) balance of payments policy. Another problem with inflation is that explanations of it, and 'cures' for it, are both highly controversial. In this situation any account will be partly subjective.

2. Demand Inflation

'Too much money chasing too few goods' is the most widely quoted and most misunderstood saying about inflation. It should be clear from the model of Part I that money in the bank (a stock) is *not* money chasing goods. For it to chase goods it must change hands in exchange for goods, i.e. it must *flow*. So what we are interested in is not too much money sitting idle, but too much *expenditure* chasing too little *production*.

2.1. Demand as a Sufficient Condition

One way of being sure of starting inflation—a demand inflation—is to consistently raise the pressure of demand; i.e. by increasing expenditure plans faster than the trend growth in supply. For example, if planned expenditure increases by 5 per cent in one year in an economy with a stable population of working age, while output per man hour only grows at 3 per cent, then the 2 per cent difference has to be met by some mixture of reduction in stocks, longer hours, increases in employment, and greater use of the existing capital equipment. But if this continues, the economy will approach the limit of its resources and all the classic symptoms of a demand pull inflation will occur. These are:

(i) In the *goods market* consumers find shortages (queues and delivery delays). The price of such goods as are available rise. Stocks tend to be low and profit margins high.

(ii) In the *labour market* firms compete against each other to attract new labour and to hold on to the labour they already have—there is no question of them reluctantly giving in to wage demands. Wage rates and earnings therefore increase rapidly—actual earnings usually faster than nationally negotiated rates as the result of many small bargains struck at the level of the plant. Unemployment and short-time working will be low, overtime and vacancies will be high.

(iii) In the *foreign exchange market* a country with a fixed exchange rate will tend to lose reserves. Because of the shortages and the high cost of home-produced goods, some demand is diverted to imports and the country's balance of trade deteriorates.

If the pressure of demand remains high these features then interact with each other. The rise in prices leads employees to demand higher money wages so as to avoid a fall in their real wages. This increases costs, which manufacturers rapidly pass on in further price rises.

In this aggregate picture it makes no difference *why* demand increased in the first place. It could have been the result of government policy, or autonomous increases in investment and/or consumption in the private sector, or increases in foreign demand. It matters even less whether the government policy was fiscal (cuts in taxation or increases in government expenditure) or monetary (easier credit conditions and a larger money supply). The only relevant factor is that demand increases and continues to increase *relatively faster* than the economy can expand production. The identical process can therefore also occur through a reduction in supply combined with attempts to maintain roughly pre-existing levels of demand. In fact some of the classic hyperinflations have had elements of both of these.[1]

2.2. *Demand as a Necessary Condition*

In the explanation just given, excess demand is a *sufficient* condition for inflation to occur—and no one disputes this. But many economists have made the much stronger claim that excess demand is also a *necessary* condition for continually rising price levels. It is this second view which is so controversial,

---

[1] The fastest inflation this century was in Hungary in 1946 when reparations payments were imposed at a time when every bridge across the Danube had been destroyed. Germany was in a similar situation in 1919 to 1923, particularly after the occupation of the Ruhr (the main industrial area) by the French in 1923; and supply shortages because of strikes were certainly contributing to inflation in Chile in 1973 just before the military *coup*.

and we must look at the reasons why it is held. At the theoretical level two influences have been important:

(i) At the *micro* level we know that *if* markets are perfectly competitive, and *if* firms try to maximize profits, and *if* the conditions of production show constant returns to scale then prices will only rise when there are supply constraints. (The three conditions give (i) P = MR (ii) = MC (iii) =constant AC if input prices are constant.) Hence is has been thought that a *general* and *continuing* rise in prices—as opposed to increases in some and falls in others as resources shift from one industry to another—could *only* occur when supply constraints were general—i.e. at full employment.

(ii) At the *macro* level the Keynesian model (which we have seen in Part II) predicts that if there are under-employed men and machines in the economy then any extra demand will tend to be met by changes in output and employment—money wages and prices remaining relatively constant. Rising prices therefore again seem to be a symptom of demand being greater than the economy can supply.

2.3. The Phillips Curve

The theoretical presumption that excess demand was a necessary condition for inflation was powerfully reinforced by empirical work on the labour market by Phillips [64].[2] He examined data for changes in money wage rates and the level of unemployment from 1861 to 1913 and found that low unemployment was associated with large increases in money wages, and vice versa. Moreover, data for the periods 1913–48 and 1948–57 still 'fitted' the original curve quite well (see Figure 7.1). Now, if—as many have supposed—this association were causal, the rate of change in wages could be traded off against the level of unemployment. Moreover, other work has shown that for the U.K. in the 1950s and early 1960, prices were determined by a fairly stable mark-up over trend unit costs (of which wages form the largest part). The implications for policy are obvious. If Phillips had been right, the U.K. could have achieved price stability at an unemployment level of about 2–2½ per cent. (At this level, wage rates would have increased by about 3 per cent p.a., roughly equivalent to the growth in output per man in the U.K., and unit wage costs would have remained constant.) As a result of this analysis it became increasingly part of the conventional wisdom of economic policy in the U.K. that her inflation resulted from running the economy at an unemployment level of 1½–2 per cent, i.e. at too high a pressure of demand.

3. Cost Inflation

The explanation above has been challenged by those who argue that inflation —cost inflation—can take place without excess demand. Their most fundamental criticisms are of the theoretical assumptions of the demand inflation school. We must therefore look at these and at the alternative assumptions

---

[2] Phillips himself took care to stress that cost push factors (particularly large increases in import prices) could provide exceptions to this.

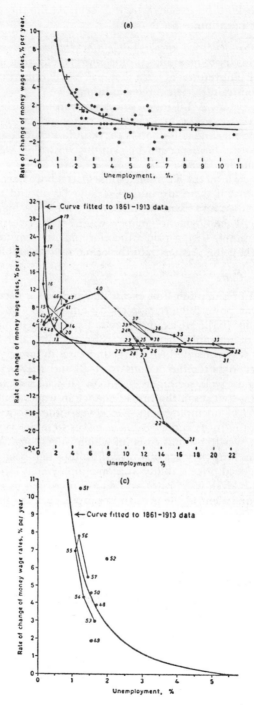

FIG. 7.1. The Phillips Curve   (a) 1861–1913   (b) 1913–1948   (c) 1948–1957

which they make in some detail. (They also give a different interpretation of Phillips's evidence—see below, section 8.) They argue:

(i) That in the labour market there are a large number of bargaining agents, but these are *not* directly in competition with each other. In many sectors of the U.K. economy the situation is more that of one union facing one employer (or federation of employers).

(ii) That in the goods market there is often an oligopolistic situation. The number of firms ranged against one another is therefore small enough for each to be thinking about the reactions of the others.

(iii) That under oligopoly firms try to keep prices fairly stable. They set prices to cover average costs plus a relatively unchanging conventional mark-up to provide a margin of profit, and then take the sales they can get at that price. Small variations in cost or output do not lead to revision of price lists. However, when significant cost increases occur, prices are raised to cover them, because the expectation is that such a move will be matched by the other firms (see Chapter 3, p. 61). Moreover, this expectation is virtually certain if the other firms face (or are about to face) similar cost increases—as will be the case when a series of wage bargains are being struct in an industry.

(iv) That this structure of industry (oligopoly) and the consequent pricing policy (covering costs plus a mark-up) make a crucial difference to the settling of wages. Whereas in a competitive industry, with firms as price-takers, for *one* firm to give in to a wage increase may mean bankruptcy, under oligopoly the expected impact on profits is small—indeed, often much less than could be expected from a strike. This is because other firms and industries are also raising their prices, or are expected to do so—a process which the firm thinks it can reinforce. Thus, with other prices being increased, the demand curve for both the firm and the industry is shifting outwards. The firm therefore thinks it can grant the wage increase and raise its prices without major loss of profits, if any loss at all.

(v) Finally, and most importantly, these micro expectations can be self-fulfilling at the macro level. For the economy as a whole, higher money wages (i.e. higher nominal incomes) flow back as higher levels of expenditure and so the outward shifts in the demand curve, which had been anticipated, are able to occur.

Explanations of cost inflation stress two other features of micro markets. Firstly, in the public sector, when dustment, nurses, or civil servants bargain for more pay it makes little sense to talk of a demand curve for their services which will be any less because *aggregate* demand falls. The reverse may even be true if the Government is happy to run a deficit in a recession. Secondly, the way in which micro level price and wage movements work through the economy is emphasized. Four links can be distinguished: (i) Prices/prices: prices rising in one sector may raise costs in other sectors or make it easier for the price of substitutes to rise. (ii) Wages/wages: there are a multiplicity of links, both formal and informal, between wages in one sector and wages in another sector. In the U.K. system of collective bargaining, wage claims (granted for whatever reason) tend to spread to other firms, industries, and occupations, as bargaining groups either press similar claims on grounds of comparability or press to re-establish their differentials. (iii) Prices/wages: as prices rise real wages fall and employees try to raise their money wages to offset this. (iv) Wages/prices: if prices are based on average cost plus a mark-up then increases in wages will automatically be reflected in higher prices.

Of course, many of these effects also occur in a demand pull situation and where there are competitive labour and product markets. But the essence of *cost* inflation is that these effects can take place without the presence of general excess demand and that money wage demands are pressed and met with little or no fear of an increase in unemployment. The more general, and the more rapid, the transmission process—prices, wages, prices—the more this is true. And the more this is true, the better the transmission.

To recap: demand pull explanations of inflation lay emphasis on the *macro* conditions in the economy (the level of aggregate *real* demand and its relation to supply) and see prices and wages at the level of the firm as a response to these. In contrast, cost push explanations emphasize the structure of firms and unions at the *micro* level and see inflation as the aggregate result —the fallacy of the demand pull argument is seen as its (hidden) supposition that the macro level of expenditure, in *nominal* terms (i.e. in current prices), is unaffected by the micro decisions.

4. Monetary Inflation[3]

In some sense all inflation is monetary since without money there is no generally perceived price level and without a price level there can be no inflation. With this thought as background we now examine the views of those economists who are known collectively as 'monetarists', and who maintain that in the long run prices rise if, and only if, the money supply increases faster than the economy can grow in real terms.

To understand the monetarist explanation it is helpful to imagine a simple economy in a pre-monetary state. Consider a self-sufficient farmer: his wage is his production, and unemployment and leisure are indistinguishable. There is no *money* wage, no price *level*, and no *in*voluntary unemployment. More-over, since the same person takes both savings decisions and investment decisions, there cannot be a lack of effective demand. Now, suppose the farmer engages in barter (so many pints of milk for a bale of hay), there will be *relative* prices but still no price level. A price level generally only occurs if one good is used as a medium of exchange (i.e. held in its own right and used as money). When this happens all other goods will have their prices expressed relative to the price of the one good now used as money. All these prices aggregated into an index then constitute the price level.[4, 5]

[3] Readers may find this section more difficult. It may be helpful to read it in conjunction with Chapters 4 and 12.

[4] Indices are usually either base weighted (in which case the value of a typical basket of goods bought at an earlier period, $\Sigma P_0 V_0$, is compared with the value of the *same* basket of goods at today's prices, $\Sigma P_1 V_0$) or current weighted (which compares the value of a typical basket of goods bought today, $\Sigma P_1 V_1$, with the same basket at the prices of an earlier period, $\Sigma P_0 V_1$).

If a price level only exists when we have money, one can see why money might be thought to play a special role. It seems similarly reasonable that if the quantity of money doubles its worth will be halved (i.e. prices double) but nothing real changes. This view—that money only effects money things (i.e. that the real and monetary economies are separate)—is known as the Classical Dichotomy. With some refinements, it is the view held by monetarists.

On closer inspection the monetarist position is seen to depend on two separate propositions:

A. that increases in the money supply cause changes in nominal expenditure (i.e. expenditure measured at current prices), and
B. that such changes in nominal expenditure result in different levels for all prices and all wages, but have consequences neither for the level of real activity and employment nor for the distribution of activity between different sectors.

The first of these (A) requires that the demand for money is stable (implying that if the demand for money depends only upon the level of nominal income then the income velocity of circulation, $(P \times Y)/M$, is constant), and that the relationship between nominal expenditures and the money supply occurs in the way that monetarists claim (i.e. that changes in the money supply cause changes in nominal expenditure rather than the other way round). These points have been briefly examined in Chapter 4 and are further discussed in the context of monetary policy in Chapter 12. The important extra point to note here is that inflation is itself likely to influence the demand for money in two conflicting ways. On the one hand, the faster the expected rate of inflation the *less* money the community is likely to want to hold (as money is falling in value). On the other hand, the more inflation there has been the higher will be the price level and the *greater* the demand for money for current transactions. These conflicting influences mean it is particularly difficult for the monetary authorities to judge what the appropriate money supply should be when the rate of inflation is fluctuating.

The second proposition (B) needs greater examination since it is the central contribution of monetarists to inflation theory and since it appears to deny the existence of a Phillips Curve. In fact such denial is not absolute since, in modern monetarist analysis, propositions A and B above are both claims about what happens to the economy in equilibrium (i.e. in the long run) and monetarists think that the long run could be a period of many years or even decades. Monetarists therefore believe that the Phillips Curve may apply in the short run, but not in the long run.

To see why the short-run and long-run situations might be different we must return to the Phillips Curve and introduce the factor of *expectations*. The Phillips Curve plots money wages. Employees and employers in bargaining base their decisions on their own views about future prices. If expectations about these change the Phillips Curve may shift. To illustrate this imagine

---

[5] Technically, money acts as the numeraire. In principle, any good could be used as the numeraire and a price level could therefore be defined without the presence of money. However, in practice, the price level is only of interest in monetary economies.

that we can construct supply and demand curves for labour for the economy
as a whole as in Figure 7.2 (a). Here DD represents the derived demand for
labour given an expected demand for goods and an expected price level,

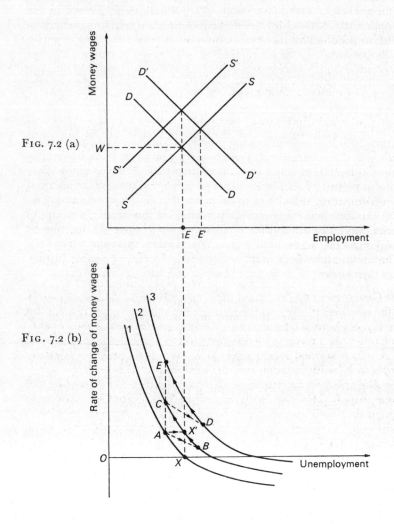

FIG. 7.2 (a)

FIG. 7.2 (b)

and SS represents the supply curve of labour—again given an expected price
level. Suppose that initially, prices are stable (i.e. the money wage equals the
real wage) and have been so for some time. The economy is then in equilibrium at E. However, if employers believe that prices will rise (e.g. because
the Government is expanding the money supply) the demand curve will
shift to D'D' and they will be prepared to pay higher money wages. But,

if employees suffer temporarily from money illusion (i.e. they look only at their money incomes and fail to allow for changes in prices) the supply curve will remain at SS, and so employment will expand from E to E'. 'Unemployment' will thus be lower. However, if, as seems likely, employees are actually interested in *real* wages, the supply curve will gradually shift to S'S' (i.e. the labour supplied depends on the level of real wages, so that as a result of inflation, less is supplied at any given money wage). Employment therefore returns to E. On these assumptions employment can only stay above E either if employees suffer from *permanent* money illusion *or* if expectations of inflation are continually revised upwards but employees' expectations constantly lag behind those of employers.

This had led the monetarists to call E (in Figure 7.2 (a) the 'natural rate of unemployment' and to argue that attempts to maintain a lower level of unemployment will lead to accelerating inflation—since only in an accelerating inflation will the expectations of employees about the rate of inflation be consistently too low. This can be seen in terms of the Phillips Curve if we imagine that in Figure 7.2 (b) the economy is initially at X (the 'natural' rate) but the Government regards this as too high a level of unemployment, and so reflates (by expanding the money supply) with the intention of moving to A. At A prices would be rising, and as employees adjusted to this they would demand higher money wages at any given level of unemployment. Thus the Phillips Curve would shift from 1 to 2. According to monetarists, three possibilities then occur:

(i) The Government can maintain the rate of growth of the money supply at the new higher level. In this case the expectations of employers and employees about the future price changes gradually become equal to each other. As a result the temporary shift to profits and the expansion to A which seemed worth while both disappear and the economy moves to X' with inflation now proceeding at a steady rate.

(ii) The Government can react to the rise in prices by restricting the money supply. However, with the shift in the Phillips Curve, we go to a point such as B instead of returning to X. If this level of unemployment is then regarded as unacceptable, repetition of the same cycle takes us to CDE, etc.

(iii) The Government can try to maintain the economy at the lower unemployment level corresponding to A. This can only be done if the price expectations of employers have again risen so that they are willing to pay the higher money wages now demanded at A. In other words, a further acceleration in the money supply is required. But in this case employees again eventually adjust to the rise in prices and we move to C. But this point in its turn is unsustainable. In fact, the monetarists maintain that any continued attempt to stay to the left of X in Figure 7.2 (b) (or to the right of E in Figure 7.2 (a) must lead to permanently accelerating inflation, and ultimately be unsuccessful. We have no long-run trade-off, only the vertical line through X.

The monetarist analysis leads, therefore, to the conclusion that in the long run it is the price level which adjusts to the money supply, with real output and employment tending to their 'natural' levels.

This is a persuasive line of argument which brings out very well the important role played by expectations. However, there are three areas of difficulty: (1) the underlying micro assumptions about the structure of markets, (2) the relatively little that is known about the formation of expectations, and (3) the question of whether the economy is stable at the macro level.

At the micro level the monetarist explanation assumes that all markets are competitive. However, it will be recalled that cost push theorists argue that, in the U.K., such markets are now the exception. Further, it can be argued that the very process of exchange which money makes possible also allows specialization; and specialization and economies of scale are part of the explanation for our current form of industrial society in which large firms and unions predominate and markets tend to be oligopolistic. If this is accepted then Figure 7.2 (a) is certainly a misleading representation of the micro situation. If wages are determined in a bargaining situation there is not necessarily a single equilibrium wage (W in Figure 7.2 (a)). Moreover, if firms and unions are price-setters then reductions in demand will lead to reductions in output and employment rather than to reductions in prices and wages.

In the case of expectations the monetarist view requires that these adapt smoothly and slowly and above all that over the long run divergences between the expectations of employers and employees (and between borrowers and lenders) will gradually disappear.[6] Moreover, emphasis is usually placed on the past experience of price movements and the rate of growth of the money supply in determining price expectations. However, expectations may change, perhaps quite sharply, for all sorts of reasons. In the modern world economic and political events (devaluations, strikes, wars, etc.) are given rapid and wide publicity—and even when predictions about inflation are fulfilled it will often be rational to hold a different view for the next time period. In addition, there is no reason why the expectations of different groups should necessarily change by the same amount. Expectations may therefore be frequently disturbed. And, at least in the short and medium term, they may even move further apart.

At the macro level monetarist analysis suggests that, in the long run, point E in Figure 7.2 (a) is a unique equilibrium position. It also implies that the economy is dynamically stable, i.e. it would find point E if left to itself. Furthermore, if this is so, there can be no 'unemployment' because the only people unemployed are those to the right of the line SS, and so are unemployed because they *choose* not to work at the wages being offered. However, this ignores the effect of uncertainty. The rational response to an increase in this is a greater unwillingness to commit oneself to the future. One way of avoiding commitment is by reducing current expenditure in order to hold more money (or other liquid assets) for use at a later date. Since less expenditure now means less employment Keynesians argue that involuntary or

---

[6] As Friedman says, 'you can't fool all the people all the time'.

Keynesian unemployment may result. This can be seen from Figure 7.3 (which is identical to Figure 7.2 (a) except that the vertical axis plots real wages instead of money wages). Here, if DD represents the derived demand for labour given full employment expenditure in the goods market, then E represents full employment in the labour market. However, if lower real expenditure is expected in the goods market, the derived demand for labour will be less at all levels of real wages, i.e. DD shifts to D'D'. As a result, and if the real wage rate is rigid downwards, we *could* reach a point such as A.

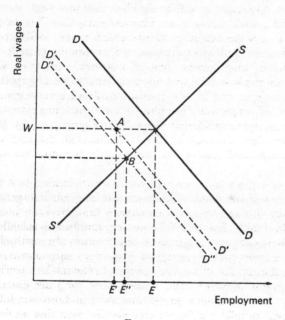

FIG. 7.3

Here, even though W still represents the full employment equilibrium real wage, there is involuntary unemployment of E' to E. Moreover, at the macro level, wages are a major part of aggregate income which in turn influences DD. Thus SS and DD cannot be independent of each other. In other words, Keynesian analysis stresses that it is only possible to say anything about DD (and about the eventual equilibrium position, if any) by examining the *time path* of the economy in successive phases of disequilibrium. Keynesians also link these points to the previous discussion of expectations (which will both influence, and be influenced by, the time path) and argue that the decentralized savings, investment, price and wage decisions, which money makes possible, may well lead, in the absence of government intervention, to an unstable economy or to one which settles at a point of chronic unemployment for long periods.

Finally, this unemployment issue cannot be resolved merely by asking unemployed individuals whether they remain so out of choice or through an absence of jobs at the going wage rate. Suppose, as above, that DD shifts to D'D' but real wages are, in fact, flexible downwards. In this case, after the lower real wages react back on expenditure (via the multiplier), we might reach some new equilibrium at, say, B. This is on the supply curve and so represents a voluntary choice. But because of insufficient effective demand in the goods market there will still be Keynesian unemployment of E'' to E.[7]

The importance of this debate between Keynesians and monetarists for policy towards inflation is obvious. Monetarists think that control of the money supply is a necessary and a sufficient condition for the control of inflation. Keynesians, however, think that control of aggregate demand (by both fiscal and monetary policy) is necessary to achieve full employment, but concede that, once full employment is guaranteed, prices and money wages may be unstable upwards—and so advocate an incomes policy.

The relationship of this debate with policy-making also helps to explain the heat and confusion which it has generated. The former occurs because a monetarist policy appears to be compatible with leaving wages and prices to be determined in a decentralized market economy, whereas an incomes policy appears more collectivist—a highly political and controversial issue. The confusion arises because we do not have equivalent evidence of the consequences of pursuing the two alternative policies. Keynesianism has been tried. Monetarism (at least in its most severe form) has not. As a result, even though monetarists point to an impressive array of empirical evidence which they claim demonstrates the stability of the demand for money and the stability of expectations, Keynesians are able to argue that this stability could have occurred largely because since the war the main industrialized countries have achieved relatively full employment levels and significantly reduced the trade-cycle—and that some of this reflects the benefit of Keynesian policies.

This section has been concerned with difficult ideas which require much further research. Disagreements in the subject are many and have been emphasized in order that the reader may, to some extent, form his own judgements. However, it is worth summarizing the following points on which many economists would agree:

(i) Monetarists have been right to remind economists of the very important role played by expectations (about which Keynes himself wrote a great deal) and to emphasize that if inflationary expectations are increasing then inflation is itself likely to increase irrespective of the state of demand.

(ii) The possibility of changes in expectations means we have no simple way of distinguishing cost push and demand pull inflation. If we observe points lying above and to the right of the Phillips Curve (i.e. combining unemployment and rising wages) it is an open question whether these result from different expectations (i.e. a shift in the Phillips Curve) or whether trade unions are successfully pressing for

[7] No significance should be attached to the fact that in this figure, E'' lies to the right of E'.

wage increases for some other reason (thus invalidating the Phillips Curve).

(iii) Increases in the quantity of money can affect demand and monetarism is a special case of demand pull inflation in which the excess demand occurs because of an excess money supply.

(iv) A change in the quantity of money is likely to have its first impact on the demand for financial assets and then on those real assets whose demand is particularly responsive to changes in the rate of interest. Where the assets in question exchange in markets with many buyers and many sellers (e.g. housing and to a lesser extent property) changes in demand result in changes in price—particularly where supply is inelastic. Since increases in property and house prices tend to add to inflationary expectations governments must therefore be cautious of rapid increases in the money supply.

(v) In an inflationary situation a constant money supply normally acts (after a lag) as a constraint on nominal expenditure. The only two exceptions to this are: (a) if money substitutes are rapidly created, and/or (b) under conditions of hyperinflation, when a 'flight from money' might cause nominal expenditure to *increase*. However, in the normal case, nominal expenditure will eventually fail to grow. If, then, prices and wages continue to rise they can only do so at increasing cost in terms of falling real output and rising unemployment. The crucial question which remains is whether this stops inflation. Is there a trade-off? This is examined in section 8 below.

5. International Factors

No account of inflation would be complete without an examination of its international aspects—particularly when it is realized that currently there is inflation in every industrialized country in the world and in most of the non-industrial countries as well. As Figure 7.4 illustrates, inflation declined after the end of the Korean War at the beginning of the 1950s but since the beginning of the 1960s it appears to have been accelerating. The rate of change has slowed down occasionally, e.g. in 1968 and 1972, but each successive trough and peak has been higher. And Table 7.1 shows that although experience has varied in different countries, in all of them inflation has been at a higher rate in recent years. These facts have focused attention on mechanisms which may transmit inflation from one country to another, and on whether features of the international economic and monetary system may contribute to inflation. There is no space here for a full examination of the spate of theories which have been put forward. However, a brief look at the arguments they embody will help in our understanding of possible inflationary causes as well as illustrate different ways in which inflation in one country may affect inflation in others.

5.1. Fixed and Floating Exchange Rates

Both fixed and floating exchange rates have been blamed for inflation. It is argued that with a flexible exchange rate a country is more likely to pursue inflationary policies because its balance of payments no longer acts as a constraint. In contrast, if exchange rates were to be immutably fixed (as in a monetary union) the only way to correct a deficit would be by deflation.

Against this it is argued that if the rest of the world is inflating faster than the domestic economy then a fixed exchange rate will force the domestic

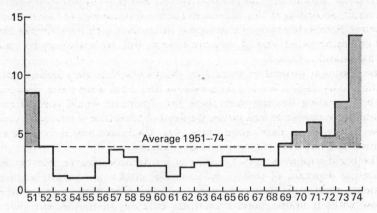

FIG. 7.4. Inflation in the Industrialized Economies. Percentage increase in Consumer Prices in O.E.C.D. countries.

Source: *O.E.C.D. National Accounts. O.E.C.D. Main Economic Indicators.*

economy to 'import' inflation through the rising prices of the goods it buys from abroad. If, on the other hand, the exchange rate is allowed to float upwards, the price of the imported goods stays unchanged in terms of the domestic currency. The floating exchange rate thus 'insulates' the domestic economy from world inflation.

A fixed exchange rate regime has also been criticized in the reverse situation of the domestic economy having more inflation than the rest of the

TABLE 7.1. *Average Annual Percentage Rates of Change in Consumer Prices in the Main O.E.C.D. countries*

	1959–64	1964–9	1969–74	1973–4
U.S.A.	+1·3	+3·4	+6·1	+10·9
Canada	+1·4	+3·7	+5·8	+12·2
Japan	+5·4	+5·2	+8·7	+13·1
France	+4·0	+3·8	+7·4	+13·7
Germany	+2·4	+2·6	+5·6	+7·0
Italy	+4·5	+2·8	+9·0	+19·4
U.K.	+2·8	+4·3	+9·1	+16·0
O.E.C.D. Total	+2·2	+3·7	+7·2	+13·4

Source: *O.E.C.D. Main Economic Indicators.*

world. This is on the grounds that a fixed exchange rate will cause some of the inflation to be 'exported'. The price of its exports will rise and increase the costs of other countries. In addition, if there is excess demand some of this will be satisfied by imports. Because of this leakage, the demand on domestic resources is lower than would otherwise have been the case and so the domestic economy avoids the full internal consequences of such excess demand. As a result, according to this approach, there is less urgency to take corrective measures. Also, other countries may find themselves with more demand than they had anticipated, and, if they are close to full capacity, may be pushed into a demand inflation.

The common ground of these two theories is that they both attribute inflation to too high a level of demand and they both want more 'discipline'. Those advocating floating rates think this discipline would come if excess demand were unable to leak out in the form of a balance of payments deficit. Those in favour of fixed rates think that discipline would be stricter if countries did not have the option of devaluation.

Whether discipline is in fact greater or less when exchange rates are fixed or floating depends, of course, on countries' attitudes to their balance of payments position. If they can finance a deficit from large reserves, or can borrow without undue international surveillance, then it is true that the deficit need not lead to corrective action. But this is not the normal situation. And as far as the U.K. is concerned most economists would argue the reverse, i.e. that the fixed exchange rate in the 1950s and 1960s led to demand being lower rather than higher.

5.2. International Liquidity

The one country which for a long time was able to ignore its balance of payments deficit was the U.S.A. The dollar is both her domestic currency and the major international currency. The U.S.A. (particularly in the 1960s) was therefore able to finance her deficits by printing dollars (to pay for the excess of imports) which other countries were prepared, or forced, to hold.[8]

This special position of the U.S.A. led to a theory which attributes inflation to too much international liquidity. This alleges that the vast increase in the dollar deposits of banks in Europe (the Euro-dollar market) which occurred in the 1960s and early 1970s created large inflationary monetary inflows into countries like Germany, Japan, and Switzerland. In other words, it was the world money supply which was too large and which was causing worldwide inflation. However, it is essential here to remember that much of this was 'hot' money which was moved in anticipation of currency changes. Such flows are not in themselves inflationary to the recipient country. The people concerned who buy D-marks want the D-marks—not Volkswagens. It is a good example of the speculative demand for money.

Of course, when monetary inflows occur, an accompanying feature is a large increase in the deposits and reserves of the commercial banks in the

---

[8] They did not have many options since there was little else they *could* hold. Their domestic currency was of no use in world trade, they fought shy of sterling which was likely to depreciate, and gold earned no interest and, *de facto*, after March 1968 was unobtainable.

recipient country in question. Their response to this may be to increase their holdings of interest-earning assets (e.g. bonds or overdrafts). This pushes down interest rates, and may encourage an increase in expenditure. However, there are several weak links in this chain. Firstly, the domestic government can decide to neturalize the inflow by simply increasing the supply of bonds for sale to the banks—in which case that is the end of the affair. Secondly, even if the Government does not do this, one would expect banks to be cautious about increasing holdings of highly illiquid assets (e.g. overdrafts and long-term bonds) when they must know that the inflow is mainly 'hot' money which is likely to leave the country within a matter of months, weeks, or even days. In this case all that one would expect is a fall in very short-term interest rates (which is what in fact occurred in Germany). Thirdly, there is little conclusive evidence that, on average, demand has been any higher in those countries receiving dollar inflows, during the period of the inflow, than in the same countries in earlier periods. And Germany, one of the major recipients, has had *lower* inflation than most other industrialized economies. Finally, suppose the 'hot' money flows were a contributory factor in the revaluations of the relevant currencies. Can we say that these revaluations caused inflation? Certainly not by the normal mechanism, since a revaluation (a) tends to reduce demand (remembering that *too much* demand is supposed to be the problem), and (b) reduces the cost of imports (in domestic currency) and so lowers domestic prices. In both cases inflation is reduced, not increased.

5.3. *The Bretton Woods System*

A further important explanation emphasizes the possible asymmetry of the world monetary system. The essence is that:

(a) the system operates in such a way that more countries devalue (or float downwards) than revalue; and

(b) as an observed fact, money wages adjust upwards following devaluations but not downwards following revaluations. As a result, inflation is increased.

In more detail, this theory claims that the international monetary system operating since 1945 tended to force countries with persistent balance of payments deficits to devalue, but did not put equivalent pressure on countries with persistent surpluses to revalue. The asymmetry arises as follows. If the U.K., for example, is trying to avoid devaluation it supports sterling with its dollar reserves, of which it has only a limited supply. A surplus country, such as Germany, however, can avoid a revaluation by selling D-marks which, for the Germans, are in virtually unlimited supply. In addition, by virtue of their role as official lenders to the deficit countries, the surplus countries are in a powerful position. Since reserves have meant power, the surplus countries have tended to play safe with their balance of payments. As a result, those who have been in surplus cannot be *forced* to revalue, and equally have been unwilling to dissipate the surplus by reflation. This has created tension. The deficit countries have had no choice but to correct their deficits and in any case have wanted to do so in order to reduce their international borrowing and the surveillance involved. Whereas the surplus countries, despite their pro- testations of reluctance to continue lending, really preferred to stay in surplus. Resolution of this tension occurs when deficit countries devalue—provided the surplus countries do not follow them down.

However, this resolution may be only temporary because in the devaluing country wages and prices gradually adjust upwards. The relative price change, which is the aim of devaluation, tends to disappear and a further devaluation may become necessary. This reinforces any already existing inflationary tendencies, and the result is a series of devaluations, e.g. in countries such as the U.K. and Italy. If this theory applies then (a) it is a powerful argument against floating exchange rates—the downward float might well become self-reinforcing, and (b) balance of payments disequilibria should be met by *revaluations* in the surplus countries.

Unfortunately, this last point ignores another argument which casts doubt on whether such revaluations would in fact help very much. This suggests that international inflation is caused by countries 'exporting' inflation, but this time through a form of *oligopoly pricing* rather than through excess demand spilling over externally. This may work in two ways (not mutually exclusive). Firstly, an international but oligopolistic industry may be able to pass on cost increases in higher prices more easily than a more competitive one. Secondly, if a particular country acts as a price-setter then when its prices rise the prices of competitors' goods will follow. This latter point is interesting since the price-setters in world trade in the recent past may well have been Germany and Japan—both have rapidly increased their share of the world market (Germany in the 1950s and Japan in the 1960s). It seems likely, therefore, that other countries struggling to maintain their own shares of world markets have tried to set prices to meet competition from these two sources. Looked at in this way, the large revaluations of the D-mark and the yen in the early 1970s removed one of the major constraints on prices in the, competing industrialized countries. Firms in the U.K., the U.S.A., and Italy, for example, were then able to concede wage claims and raise prices with less fear of losing sales.

One implication of this analysis is that inflation may greatly reduce the effectiveness of exchange rate changes as a means of correcting the balance of payments. Indeed, if the countries which tend to run surpluses (and thus float upwards under a flexible exchange rate system) are those which are already the least inflation prone, and vice versa, then in the long run floating exchange rates may just result in a wider dispersion of inflation rates and little or no reduction in the balance of payments disequilibria.

5.4. Demonstration Effects

The acceleration of inflation in most industrialized countries in recent years could also be explained by *demonstration or expectation effects*. This could be the case if wage claims in one country influence unions in other countries about what the 'going rate' for the job should be (in much the same way that unions in Liverpool or Scotland now expect to receive a similar wage as those in, say, Dagenham or Luton). Equally there may be greater pressure for money wage increases if expectations of rising real income levels are rein-forced by a growing awareness of conditions in other countries. As a statement about real wage levels, this can neither be proved nor disproved since it merely describes a motive for pushing for money wage rises (average real wages will primarily depend on levels of productivity). However, it is inter-esting that until the early 1970s, when exchange rates were allowed to float, there was a greater dispersion between European countries in the rates of productivity increase, than in the rates of growth of money wages—which is at least consistent with this view. Moreover, one is bound to notice that the French strikes in 1968, the Italian 'hot' summer of 1969, and the increased militancy in the U.K. in 1970 coincided with an acceleration in world inflation.

5.5. Primary Product Prices

The final factor to be examined in the acceleration of world inflation is the impact of increases in the prices of *primary products* (food, commodities, oil, etc.) feeding through into the prices of other goods. Two things are worth noting about this:

(i) With the exception of the oil price rise, inflation is poorly correlated with changes in primary product prices. This suggests that movements in primary product prices are at most an additional factor, rather than part of the underlying cause of inflation.

(ii) If one accepts a demand pull explanation there is no reason why shortages of *some* goods should lead to a *general* price rise. If money wages are flexible the prices of goods in short supply would rise but others would fall. Even in the case where money wages are rigid downwards, demand pull alone would merely predict a once and for all increase in the price level. The only case where prices would rise *and go on rising* is where the increase in primary product prices repre-sents a long-run shift in the balance of supply and demand *and* where the consequent reduction in real living standards is resisted by con-sumers in the industrialized countries. In this case the *relative* price change needed to call forth extra supplies of primary products would be eroded by the inflation in the industrialized economies. As this happened shortages would reappear and primary product prices would again rise—so triggering off another round of wage and price increases in the consuming countries. (A similar series of events could occur with oil prices, even though this particular price rise did not result from supply shortages.)

Looking back at these various theories of international inflation, it is clear that the first three (fixed exchange rates, flexible rates, and international liquidity) are all appealing to demand pull explanations of inflation. The only real differences between them are that the first two concern themselves with how governments can be 'disciplined' to run their economies at lower levels of demand and the third claims that too much liquidity is the reason for demand being too high. The fourth theory claims there is asymmetry in the international monetary system and requires a cost-based explanation— wages in the domestic economy react upwards as import prices rise. The fifth theory is also cost-based but this time stresses the role of price leadership under oligopoly. The sixth theory, appealing to demonstration and expectation effects, is a sociological explanation of *why* wage earners press for wage increases. The last explanation (primary products) can be either demand pull or cost push; but in the case of demand pull it would at best provide an explanation of a temporary acceleration in inflation, not of any continuing change. Finally, it is helpful to note that this last theory is a special case of the need for a change in *relative* prices. If the structure of demand or supply changes for whatever reason and *money* wages are rigid downwards, then (ignoring differences in productivity) a net upward movement in the *general* price level is inevitable if relative prices are to readjust.

This consideration of the international aspects of inflation makes one thing very clear. Unless one holds to a strong view of monetarism in which inflation everywhere is caused by an excessive money supply, then one is no longer looking for a unique cause of inflation. Experience is likely to vary from country to country depending on its particular historical context, economic circumstances, and position in the world economy. Some countries may have attitudes which are particularly resistant to inflation (e.g. Germany, as a result of hyperinflation in the past). In other cases a conjunction of socio-economic forces may suddenly lead to increased wage pressure, as occurred in France in 1968. Commodity price increases may have a ratchet effect on the price level and hit some countries worse than others—e.g. Japan in 1974. In other countries periods of excess demand may be added to a propensity to cost inflation—as was probably the case in the U.S.A. from 1966 to 1968 and in some sectors of the U.K. from 1964 to 1966, and in the latter part of 1973. And relatively small open economies such as the U.K. will always be more heavily affected by inflation in other countries than will an economy such as the U.S.A.

6. A Marxist View

To complete our review of the various causes of inflation we turn now to the Marxists. The main Marxist explanation of inflation focuses on the inevitability of conflict between labour and capital. Marxists emphasize the share of national income going on the one hand to employees (labour) in wages and salaries, and on the other hand to the gross trading profits of companies (i.e. capital), and inflation is seen as the outcome of the struggle between these two classes—a struggle in which the shares of national income demanded by each side are incompatible. Inflation, and the money illusion associated with it, provide a solution—albeit temporary. Modern Marxists tend to argue that in the long run capitalism is bound to collapse because of the continuing and growing tension between inflation on the one hand and the unemployment consequences of attempting to control it by deflation on the other. Moreover, they believe that when this crisis occurs the inevitable outcome will be the disappearance of the classes of capital and labour, together with the antagonism between them.

In the case of the U.K., the analysis above is built round data showing a decline in the share of profits in national income (Table 7.2). It is claimed that associated with this is a decline in the profit rate, i.e. the profitability of investment. It is very difficult to judge whether this latter claim is true,[9] but

TABLE 7.2. *Gross Trading Profits as a Percentage of Gross National Income (1954–1974)*

	Including stock appreciation	Excluding stock appreciation
1954	16·1	15·7
1955	16·9	15·8
1956	15·9	14·8
1957	15·4	14·7
1958	14·6	14·6
1959	15·4	15·0
1960	16·3	15·8
1961	14·8	14·2
1962	14·0	13·4
1963	15·0	14·4
1964	15·3	14·4
1965	15·0	14·0
1966	13·8	12·9
1967	13·2	12·7
1968	14·0	12·5
1969	12·9	11·1
1970	12·4	9·8
1971	12·4	10·1
1972	12·5	10·1
1973	13·5	8·6
1974	13·1	5·1

the important point for the analysis of inflation is that this squeeze on profits is attributed to the conjunction of upward pressure on wages from trade unions and downward pressure on prices from international competition. This links directly to our earlier discussion of international factors, because this downward pressure on prices is released if the country in question devalues or if other countries revalue. However, if a devaluation is to work it must, as we have seen, cut real wages (or reduce their growth). The essential point of the Marxist argument is that workers resist this by pressing for wage increases—in other words, *real* wages, and not just money wages, are

[9] If P = profits, Y = National Income, and K = the stock of capital goods, then P/Y is the *share* of profits and P/K is the amount of profit per unit of capital, i.e. the profit *rate*. But $P/Y = P/K \times K/Y$ so that a declining profit share only implies a declining profit rate if K/Y (the capital/output ratio) is constant or rising, and it is very difficult to know whether over time we need more or less machines to produce a given quantity of output. We know that technical change is occurring but is it labour-saving or capital-saving?

rigid downwards. If this happens, then the effect of the devaluation gradually wears off and the pressure on profitability reasserts itself.

Of course, Marxists are not the only ones to make this particular point. Upward pressure on wages following a rise in prices (whether or not caused by a devaluation) is a standard part of any cost push explanation, and the interaction between a falling exchange rate and rising wages is the basis of the cost push argument against floating exchange rates. But in the eyes of Marxists, the result of these pressures is an accelerating inflation, and the demise of capitalism. However, the inevitability of this only follows from positing two classes necessarily in conflict. In modern industrial societies this picture needs considerable modification. Much of company profits goes to finance new investment on which employment and rising real wages partly depend, and even that portion of profits which is distributed to shareholders accrues partly to the pension funds of employees. The result is that, although the distribution of wealth is still unequal, the collapse of profits and of the stock market is now of concern to trade unionists as well as to more traditional capitalists.

In addition, although it is conventional to describe the wage bargain in terms of 'them' and 'us', the distinction between salaried management and other employees is much more blurred today than in the days of the nineteenth-century bosses. Moreover, the constant leap-frogging in pay claims suggests that the struggle for shares in national income now takes place just as much between groups of workers as between workers and owners.

7. Demand Pull and Cost Push Reconsidered

In the extreme cost push explanation of inflation, of which Marxism is one version, demand seems to play no part at all. Money wages are entirely exogenous. But a closer analysis suggests that demand ought to influence wage settlements in two ways:

(i) At the micro level the cost push explanation is based on the bargaining situation in the labour market, and the level of demand is likely to affect this. When demand is high and rising and profit margins can be increased, employers are more likely to give in to wage claims. Similarly, when there is little fear of redundancy, trade unions are likely to be more insistent in their wage claims—their leaders know as well as anyone the right moment to press a wage claim.

(ii) At the macro level, ever since the Second World War governments have been committed to full employment, and have been held responsible for ensuring it. This has almost certainly had a critical effect on the general context in which wage bargains have been struct. Even in periods of depressed sales and employment, the prospect of general and continuing unemployment has not seemed too large. Employees have therefore felt able to press for wage increases at least to the level of the 'going rate' with little fear for their own jobs. Similarly, employers faced with wage demands have clearly thought it better in most cases to settle, even if this involves a temporary loss of sales, rather than to face a strike. In the limiting case companies have preferred to go bankrupt slowly rather than quickly—but they have not really expected to go bankrupt at all, since they think the Government will reflate (or even bale them out).

Thus from this viewpoint the level of demand may affect the timing of claims and settlements, as well as having some effect on their level. But provided the commitment to full employment is maintained, there is no upper limit to the rate of wage and price change and the likelihood is that inflation will accelerate. On the other hand, no firm or union wants its own price (or wage) to get too far out of line. These is thus a constraint on the rate of acceleration of inflation.

There is no space here for a full analysis of why pressure for wage increases should build up at particular times. However, one possibility is that in a growing economy employees become adjusted to relatively regular increases in their real consumption, and the money wage increase in any particular year is an attempt to achieve this. But if the money wage increase turns out to represent only a small increase in real take-home pay (or even a decline) then this in turn may result in further pressure for money wages.

At the level of the economy as a whole, the scope for an increase in real living standards depends upon (a) the real growth in the economy, and (b) how much of this growth is available for private consumption by employees. In the case of the U.K. in the 1950s and early 1960s, private consumption rose slowly but moderately steadily. However, this increase in private consumption was achieved by (a) an improvement in the terms of trade, (b) a declining share of resources devoted to defence, and (c) an increasing balance of payments deficit on current account. This situation was reversed at the end of the 1960s and was combined with an expansion of the resources going to public consumption and with a slower growth in the economy. The inevitable consequence was that less resources were available for private consumption (see Table 7.3), that taxation was increased, and that workers found their real take-home pay almost stagnant. This may have been a contributory factor to the acceleration in money wages after 1968.

It is important to realize how much this explanation differs from that of demand pull. In demand pull inflation too much expenditure chases too

TABLE 7.3. *Percentage Increases in Consumers' Expenditure and Gross Domestic Product at 1963 prices*

	1953–7	1957–61	1961–5	1965–9
Consumers' Expenditure	+11·7	+13·8	+11·6	+6·7
Gross Domestic Product at factor cost	+11·3	+12·0	+13·4	+8·8

Source: *National Income and Expenditure.*

little production and pulls up prices, whereas in the explanation above people *want* to consume more but are not making the goods to do so. As a result, money wage claims are made and granted, but cannot be met out of increased production, and so are passed on in higher prices. The net result looks much the same—prices and wages rise. But the policy implications are quite different. In the demand pull case a reduction in demand would cause inflation to diminish. In the wage pressure case a reduction in demand, brought about, for example, by increased taxation, would reduce real output and real take-home pay and so exacerbate money wage claims and inflation.

The implications of the pressure for real wage increases may be clarified if one imagines an economy in which *all* claims are fully indexed. In this case every wage, salary, pension, etc. would be linked to the price index, and the money value of the wages, etc. would automatically adjust upwards or downwards so that they retained a constant real value. Now, what is true of one part of the economy viewed in isolation need not be true of the whole. A single wage earner can make a wage contract which represents a real claim on the year's output. However, one inescapable feature of a monetary economy in which exchange takes place is that it is not possible for everyone to contract for a real wage at the moment of settling a money wage and have their claims fulfilled except if, and only if, the total amount of real output happens to equal the sum of their individual claims.

In general, there is no reason why this should occur, and this particular cost push version argues that because it is *not* occurring we have inflation. The demand for real wages, as expressed in wage claims, totals to more real output than the system makes available. Inflation is the result and reconciles temporarily the inconsistency of the total claims. In these circumstances any attempt to index *all* claims would indicate their inconsistency and inevitably lead to an explosive inflation. On the other hand, if output grew rapidly enough to absorb these real claims then full indexation would lead to an equally rapid deceleration of prices. From this viewpoint the period 1973-4, with output virtually stagnant and the terms of trade moving against the U.K. (so that real incomes grew less than real output) was a particularly unfortunate time to introduce threshold payments.

This explanation with its emphasis on the inconsistency of claims obviously shares common ground with the Marxist view that inflation is the outcome of a struggle for shares in national income. However, one must not confuse the fact that the inconsistency is more likely to occur when demands for real wages rise or when growth is particularly low, with the claim that this is always the case. People's perceptions of their interests can change and during the £6 pay policy workers were clearly prepared to accept cuts in real wages.

8. Is there a Trade-Off Between Unemployment and Inflation?

Finally, we must tackle the central question which has arisen in this chapter— is there a trade-off between unemployment and inflation? The honest answer to this question—certainly as far as the U.K. is concerned—is that no one knows. However, a re-examination of earlier views will prove suggestive:

(i) The original demand pull explanation based on the Phillips Curve emphasizes the trade-off as a potential tool for economic policy, but fails to account adequately for cost inflation, or for changes in expectations.

(ii) The extreme demand pull version (particularly associated with the monetarists) argues that in the long run no trade-off exists, but requires one to assume relatively competitive markets and no involuntary or Keynesian unemployment.

(iii) The extreme cost push view (of which Marxism is one version) treats money wages as exogenous and implies that there is no relationship of any kind, but then can give no very coherent account of the wage bargaining process.

The difficulties associated with each make it more fruitful to pursue an eclectic view based on the cost push version considered in Section 7. This is a cost push theory but demand is still one of the important influences affecting the context within which wage bargains are struck. Fully competitive markets are not assumed, but changes in expectations are seen as an important further influence.

In this situation rising unemployment could mitigate inflation, firstly because the greater availability of labour would tend to reduce competitive wage bidding by employers, and secondly because some wage bargains might be delayed as a matter of tactics. On the other hand, perverse responses are also possible. Faced with loss of overtime, unions may press for increases in wage rates or reductions in normal hours to recoup their position, and firms (particularly in capital intensive industries) faced with higher overheads may react to lower demand by raising their prices. In addition, expectations of continuing inflation could exacerbate wage demands and so reduce still further the already rather weak pressure, exerted by rising unemployment, on wage settlements.

In this situation the only way that a reduction in aggregate demand could stop inflation would be if firms became convinced that they could not pass on wage rises into prices. At the same time, either union members would need to realize this and so expect that further wage claims would lead to redundancy, and/or union cohesion would need to materially weaken in the face of competition for jobs from the unemployed. Three things follow from this:

(i) It is highly unlikely that any of these would occur except with unemployment on a much larger scale and/or for a much longer period than anything experienced in the post-war period. Effectively, employers and employees would have to believe that the post-war commitment to full employment no longer applied.

(ii) It is impossible to say exactly what this level of unemployment would be. It would depend on how people's expectations changed, on how militant, organized, and cohesive the trade unions were, and on the actions and attitudes of the Government.

(iii) If people think that full employment has been abandoned, it is very probable that the increase in unemployment *whether or not* created intentionally by the Government will be larger (possibly much larger) than the initial deflationary impact plus multiplier effects. Consumers would be likely to increase their savings as a precaution against unemployment, and firms to reduce investment in anticipation of a long period of depressed demand. The slump would be particularly large if firms' views about expected prices were revised downwards before there was any impact on wages. Expected profits would then be very low, or even negative, and output plans curtailed. Moreover, if the reduction in demand were the result of a contraction in the money supply, the effect of rapidly falling asset values on balance sheets would probably render some companies and financial institutions bankrupt when they were still trading profitably.

Most of the argument in this chapter can now be summarized in three propositions. Firstly, if one finds the arguments above persuasive, governments can probably stop inflation by large-scale unemployment. Secondly, by means of controlling demand, governments can start a demand pull inflation (and can also avoid adding to inflation generated from some other cause). Thirdly, the conjunction of these two propositions does *not* mean there is a trade-off in the normally accepted sense between inflation and unemployment—there is certainly no Phillips Curve. Attempts to stop inflation by reducing demand are likely initially to have only small or perhaps perverse effects, while continuation of the attempt will probably set in motion forces leading to much larger unemployment than the policy-makers intend.

Moreover, these propositions are reinforced if we reconsider the time periods which were linked together in Phillips's analysis. The data covers the following groups of years:

(i) *1861–1913*—a period when unemployment ranged from 1 per cent to 11 per cent, when there was virtually no public sector and no government, and when product and labour markets were less oligopolistic than at present.

(ii) *1914–19 and 1941–5*—periods of almost certain excess demand but in the latter case suppressed by wartime controls.

(iii) *1921–39*—unemployment continually above 10 per cent and with money wages and prices lower at the end of the period than at the beginning.

(iv) *1945–57*—unemployment nearly always between 1 per cent and 2 per cent and changes in wage rates ranging from approximately 1 per cent to 11 per cent.

When the data are looked at in this way we find one clear period of un-suppressed demand pull inflation (the First World War). Unemployment was below 1 per cent for the last three years of the war and the rate of change of wage rates accelerated rapidly (see Figure 7.1(b)). In contrast, the inter-war period is a clear example of deficient demand and chronic unemployment—conditions under which no one would expect even cost inflation.

However, these are two discrete observations and provide no evidence in favour of a smooth trade-off. The data which provide the best apparent evidence of a trade-off between inflation and unemployment is that for the years 1861–1913 when unemployment varied between 1 per cent and 11 per cent—and it is on this evidence that Phillips first postulated that a trade-off existed. However, at that time conditions were fundamentally different from the present. Markets were more competitive, labour was less well organized, unified, and cohesive in wage bargaining, and above all neither firms nor employees expected governments to pursue full employment policies. As a result, bankruptcies and loss of jobs were seen as real possibilities. In other

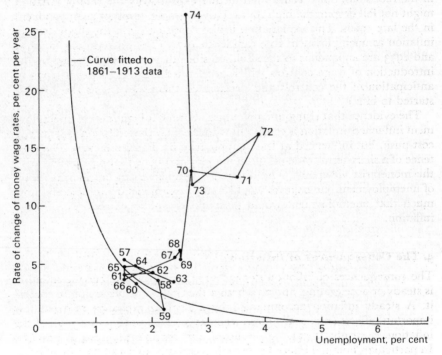

FIG. 7.5. The Phillips Curve 1957–74.

words, a paradoxical situation arises. Although the trade-off appears to us today to have existed, this is only because governments, trade unions, and firms at the time did not base their actions on the assumption that the Government believed in such a trade-off. If they had done so, the evidence would be different.

For an empirical validation of the trade-off we must therefore look at the post-war period. Between 1948 and 1966 a possible trade-off is apparent in the unemployment range 1 per cent to 2½ per cent. (This can be seen in Phillips's data reproduced in Figure 7.1(c) above and in Figure 7.5, which extends Phillips's data from 1957 to 1974.) The difficulty is that any trade-off which may have existed breaks down after 1966. From 1967 to 1969 money wage rates continued to increase despite relatively high unemployment, and then accelerated sharply in 1970. Indeed, from the viewpoint of the Phillips Curve, 1970 is particularly puzzling since this deviation cannot be explained away by reference to a rapid rise in import prices (as partially explains 1968 and at least some of the further acceleration in 1974).

This evidence may therefore be better explained by the hypothesis that inflation slows down, not when unemployment is high, but when it is *rising*. In this case the apparent trade-off up to 1966 would merely be a reflection of demand pull inflation in the booms and tactical delaying of wage claims in the recessions. This would then further explain why the rate of inflation might not fall despite the high, but relatively stable, levels of unemployment in the late 1960s. This explanation is also consistent with the slight drop in inflation as unemployment rose rapidly in 1971. (The observations for 1972 and 1973 are anomalous to the situation since they are both distorted by the introduction of wage controls which accelerated wage pressures in 1972 in anticipation of the controls and decelerated them in 1973 as the controls started to bite.)

The evidence that rising unemployment but not a high level of unemployment influences inflation is consistent with the view that inflation is primarily cost-push, but influenced at least temporarily by demand factors. The existence of a short-term trade-off but not a long-term one is also consistent with the monetarist viewpoint. The difference between them lies in what level of unemployment one believes would result from monetary control and how much that unemployment would permanently influence the rate of wage inflation.

9. The Consequences of Inflation

The consequences of inflation depend very much on whether the inflation is steady or accelerating, and on whether the Government is trying to control it. A steady inflation accompanied by a floating exchange rate has few important effects (except for those who are on fixed money incomes). If the inflation is steady it can be predicted and sensible planning is possible. In particular, nominal interest rates will eventually adjust to the rate of inflation and neither borrowers nor lenders gain. However, a steady, fully anticipated inflation is a very special case. Indeed, our interest in inflation occurs primarily because, in the real world, inflation is always either a symptom and/or a cause of disequilibrium.

As far as this is concerned there is very little of a general nature which can be said about an economy in disequilibrium since what may be under-anticipated in one time period may be over-anticipated in the next time period. However, despite this qualification it is usually the case that in an accelerating demand inflation profits rise as a share of national income, and real interest rates on financial assets such as bank deposits and fixed interest shares tend to fall below those on physical assets. As a result, investment and growth may be encouraged. Also, wages which are being pulled up by demand tend to rise most rapidly in the competitive sectors and hence the distribution of wage income shifts in their favour and against the unionized sectors. In the case of an accelerating cost inflation the opposite effects seem to occur. Profits tend to be low (since prices lag behind current costs), and the distribution of income shifts to those who have the most power to push. Real interest rates, however, are again usually low or negative and once more borrowers gain and lenders lose (though with profits low there is less of an incentive to investment). In both cases the Government, being a major borrower, benefits.

Beyond these simple points the effects depend critically on whether the Government is trying to control the inflation, and if so on the means that it uses and on the expectations which its attempts create. Generally speaking, governments do attempt to control inflations, because:

(a) Rising prices are unpopular even when wages are rising equally, or more, rapidly. (This may be because of redistribution within the family.)

(b) Those on fixed incomes lose.

(c) In most cases inflations are neither steady nor predictable. Changes in the distribution of income and wealth are therefore arbitrary. The uncertainty associated with this is probably unpopular with both gainers and losers. Tension between social classes also seems to increase.

(d) Attempts by governments to live with inflation often result in the inflation accelerating. This is because when they compensate those who would otherwise have lost (e.g. pensioners) they must raise taxation. As a result they remove from the wage earner his relative gain and renewed pressure for money wage increases reappears.

(e) The Government's own macroeconomic control becomes more difficult. With unpredictable rates of inflation, company and consumer behaviour is more than usually difficult to forecast and the Government's own taxation and expenditure planning is disrupted.

(f) In an open economy such as the U.K., inflation makes it more difficult to finance balance of payments deficits, because foreign lenders are uncertain about the future exchange rate (and in the extreme case are uncertain whether debts will ever be repaid).

Conflicting pressures are set up as a result of attempts by governments to control inflation. Firstly, as far as *consumers* are concerned, if it looks as if the inflation will accelerate, then those who can will anticipate the rise in prices by bringing their consumption forward in time. This will have its biggest impact on consumer durables like cars and housing which do not have to be purchased regularly (see Chapter 2). An upward shift in the prices expected in the future will, other things being equal, lead to more consumption now. On the other hand, consumption is also a function of expected income. If, therefore, consumers think that the Government is about to give greater priority to the control of inflation than to maintaining full employment, then their expectations of future real income will be lowered and they may react by increasing savings.

Similar uncertainty exists for *firms*. The most important impact is on investment planning. As we saw in Chapter 3, investment plans depend on an assessment both of future cash flow and of the interest rate. In the presence of inflation both of these will be more than usually difficult to predict. If the firm could be certain that inflation would be allowed to continue or accelerate, it would expect its future cash flow to rise in line with inflation and a high nominal rate of interest would seem low in real terms. But the firm is uncertain whether or not inflation will continue. It also does not know whether it should borrow long term (in the expectation that interest rates will rise) or short term (expecting them to fall). Faced with this uncertainty the most likely effect is that firms will increase their liquidity—both in the sense of building up liquid assets rather than investing, and in the sense of preferring short-term to long-term investments.

Other pressures on firms will depend on the form of control used. For example, if the Government attempts to maintain a fixed exchange rate, export sales will tend to decline. But if domestic price controls are used and the exchange rate allowed to depreciate then the relative profitability of exporting is increased. In general, following the analysis of Chapter 3, any Government measure which reduces sales revenue (whether price controls or deflation) leaves the firm with the options of attempting to reduce its cost conditions (e.g. by resisting wage claims), of reducing dividends, of cutting back investment in stocks or in fixed equipment, of increasing short-term borrowing—or some mixture of these.

The effects on income distribution also vary with the form of control. At the aggregate level, price and wage controls can be used to shift the profits/wage share and this can have important side-effects on demand management. Firms have a higher propensity to save out of profits than do consumers out of wages, so that shifting the distribution of income towards profits probably reduces aggregate demand now. It may also increase investment later. But, since this depends so much on the expectations created, this latter effect is considerably less certain. In addition, it is worth noting that similar effects can occur even without controls if firms base their prices on past costs and inflation first accelerates and then decelerates (as occurred in the U.K. from 1973 to 1976). In this case, as inflation accelerates prices lag behind current costs and profits are squeezed and real wages are increased. The opposite follows as inflation decelerates. These effects cause problems for demand management, since during the deceleration phase consumption is reduced and this may coincide with lower investment lagging behind the earlier squeeze on profits. (Given this it is not surprising that unemployment rose so much in the U.K. from 1975 to 1976.)

At the micro level the main consequence of inflation in the U.K. for the distribution of income has been that it has favoured those who have borrowed for house purchase, which has probably most benefited the middle class. At the same time there has been a shift away from unearned income towards earned income. The conjunction of rising nominal interest rates (which depress gilt-edged prices), price control squeezing profits, and capital gains taxation on nominal values, has almost certainly reduced unearned income and also acted as a partial tax on wealth. In the short run it is, of course, also true that certain groups have lost (or gained) through the operation of particular incomes policies (e.g. the £6 pay policy squeezed differentials), but there is as yet little evidence that these effects persist in the longer run.

It is because the consequences of inflation are so unpredictable that its most important effect is the uncertainty it creates. As it accelerates a paradoxical situation arises. Firstly, people become gradually adjusted to inflation and increasingly expect it to continue. Secondly, as expectations of inflation become widespread, people anticipate that governments will act to restrain it. Rightly or wrongly, the experience of the last twenty-five years has suggested to many people that incomes policies do not work and that the only solution to an accelerating rise in prices is unemployment on a scale comparable to the interwar years. Thus we have a situation in which each increase in inflation fulfils people's expectations while at the same time making them think that the Government is bound to take policies to bring it to an end—perhaps rather suddenly.

This links back directly to consideration of the trade-off between unemployment and inflation. It is very improbable that governments can maintain good control of the economy when consumers, firms, etc. are so schizophrenic about the future. Moreover, this would be a strong reason why one should not use a tight money policy to stop inflation. The effects of monetary policy are only predictable if expectations remain stable or change gradually. But if they are as volatile as suggested above, the danger is that monetary policy will either have little or no effect, or that the effect will be much larger than intended.

10. Conclusions

Demand management policies can start demand inflations. However, in the industrialized countries the maintenance of full employment tends to be associated with accelerating cost inflation generated within the economy, even without general excess demand. The rate at which this occurs varies from country to country as a result of different social attitudes and institutional arrangements and with the extent to which wage pressures can be absorbed by economic growth. There may also be important effects between economies, and commodity price increases can exacerbate domestic inflationary trends. Moreover, in the longer run exchange rate changes (unless accompanied by incomes policies) may reinforce the difference between inflation rates rather than correcting balance of payments disequilibria.

Demand management, whether fiscal or monetary, can probably stop cost inflation but only by creating unemployment on a scale unprecedented in the post-war period—the exact scale of this cannot be known but is likely to be greater the longer inflation has been sustained and the more rapid it has become. The political consequences of this make it unlikely in the short term as an intentional act of policy in the U.K. This means that the only function of demand management with respect to inflation is to avoid adding to cost inflation. However, if unemployment is the only way of stopping even a cost inflation then Keynesian economics seems hoist with its own pétard—Keynesianism solved unemployment, but this has created inflation which requires unemployment as its cure.

This dilemma might be avoided by some form of incomes policy, but this still presents very significant problems. Keynes, as he was understood by his disciples, appeared to repeat the trick of the Classical Dichotomy. In this classical explanation relative prices and wages were determined by real factors, while money determined the prive level. Neither one affected the other and full employment was taken for granted. The only role for Government was to control the money supply and, via this, the price level. In the Keynesian system it looked as if one could substitute control of the aggregate output level for control of the price level. The Government was thus responsible for fixing the level of employment and the level of national income, but was still *not* involved in the micro determination of relative wages or prices. It determined the size of the cake, *not* who got what. But once Keynesianism requires an incomes policy, whether statutory or voluntary, then micro price and wage decisions are inevitably involved and *either* there is extensive Government intervention *or* wage bargainers (at *all* levels) have to show much more self-restraint than has so far been the case. The latter is difficult to expect when the distribution of income and wealth correlates only weakly with the power of groups within society.

Governments are still grappling with these dilemmas. Given the political consequences of unemployment and the very obvious loss of welfare involved, large-scale unemployment remains only a policy weapon of last resort. Nevertheless, the difficulties of stabilizing the economy in the presence of inflation using only fiscal and monetary policy could mean that it will occur unintentionally. Moreover, the political consequences of an accelerating inflation and the difficulties and social tensions of establishing a long-run incomes policy could leave a government with no option but heavy long-term unemployment.

In contrast, the hope for incomes policy lies in contemplating the unpleasantness of the alternatives. Accelerating inflation and large-scale unemployment are both very costly. One followed by the other would be an even greater failure and would place severe strains on society. There is also little evidence that societies organized on Marxist lines offer a solution. In such societies a suppressed conflict over income shares still remains, and full-scale central planning contains its own problems—to say nothing of the possible loss of personal liberties. A *continuing* voluntary incomes policy, combining some self-restraint with some institutionalized discipline, is no easy solution to inflation but it may nevertheless eventually come to be seen as the least of all evils.

Bibliography

SECTION A

The danger of a demand pull inflation was originally set out very clearly in [43] J. M. Keynes, *How to Pay for the War* (1940), reprinted in *Essays in Persuasion*

(Macmillan, 1972). This concept is further examined in [64] A. W. Phillips, 'The Relationship between Unemployment and the Rate of Change of Money Wage Rates in the U.K. 1861–1957', *Economica* (1958), and Professor Paish in, for example, [58] F. W. Paish and J. Hennessy, *Policy for Incomes* (4th edn.), Hobart Paper 29, Institute of Economic Affairs (1968) emphasizes the relation of demand to productive potential. On the other side of the debate the most persistent believer in cost push inflation (advocating an incomes policy as early as 1943) is Thomas (now Lord) Balogh, and the fullest exposition of his views as well as the origin of the 'social contract' is given in [4] Balogh, *Labour and Inflation* (Fabian Society, 1970). Balogh also deals with the importance of asymmetry in the international monetary system arguing that it manages both to deflate output and inflate prices, see [5] Balogh *Fact and Fancy in International Economic Relations* (Pergamon, 1973).

Two other attacks on the post-war international monetary system are [73] Triffin, *Gold and the Dollar Crisis* (Yale University Press, 1960) and [66] Rueff, 'Gold Exchange Standard a Danger to the West', reprinted in H. G. Grubel, *World Monetary Reform* (Stanford, 1963). Although surprisingly similar in their diagnoses, these two authors offer very different prescriptions. Triffin would like to see the I.M.F. develop into a World Central Bank. Rueff, epitomizing the opposition to thirty years of supposed Government mismanagement of money and especially to its inflationary consequences, advocates a return to the 'gold standard'. Similar opposition to Government intervention is expressed by the monetarists. The clearest exposition of their position is in [28] M. Friedman. 'The Role of Monetary Policy', *American Economic Review* (Mar. 1968) and, most recently, in [30] M. Friedman. *Unemployment versus Inflation?* Institute of Economic Affairs, Occasional Paper 44 (1975). In contrast, the case for thinking that the money supply may be endogenous rather than exogenous is given in [40] Professor (now Lord) Kaldor, 'The New Monetarism', *Lloyds Bank Review* (July 1970). The main British Marxist contribution to the debate on inflation is [31] A. Glyn and B. Sutcliffe, *British Capitalism, Workers and the Profits Squeeze* (Penguin, 1972). A relatively brief analysis of the international transmission of inflation is available in O.E.C.D., *Economic Outlook* (July 1973). A stimulating piece, which emphasizes the importance of take-home pay, and which gives interesting data covering inflation in a wide variety of countries is [36] D. Jackson, H. A. Turner, and F. Wilkinson, *Do Trade Unions Cause Inflation?* Department of Applied Economics, Occasional Paper 36 (Cambridge, 1972). A useful collection of readings which contains some, but unfortunately not all, the articles referred to above is [6] R. J. Ball and P. Doyle (eds.), *Inflation* (Penguin, 1969). There is a highly competent, though slightly dated, survey of the literative in [13] M. Bronfenbrenner and F. D. Holzman, 'A Survey of Inflation Theory', reprinted in *Surveys of Economic Theory*, vol. i, Royal Economic Society, 1965 and a more recent survey article which gives a thorough coverage of the economometric evidence is [46] D. E. W. Laidler and J. M. Parkin, 'Inflation: A Survey', *Economic Journal* (Dec. 1975). Those interested in history might enjoy two contrasting accounts of the German hyperinflation in the early 1920s, [12] C. Bresciani-Turroni, *The Economics of Inflation* (New York, 1968) (originally published in 1931, this takes a classical monetarist position) and [48] K. Laursen and J. Pedersen, *The German Inflation 1918–1923* (North Holland Publishing Co., 1964). The latter adopts a mainly Keynesian analysis, together with some emphasis on the potential power—both for good and evil—of trade unions.

Finally, some of the best insights into the process of inflation are contained in the very readable essays on 'Inflation and Deflation' recently reprinted in [41] J. M. Keynes. *Essays in Persuasion* (Macmillan, 1972). A more complete bibliography is given below.

SECTION B

[1] ACKLEY, G. 'Administered prices and the inflationary process', *American Economic Review*, (1959).

[2] ARTIS, M. J. and NOBAY, A. R. 'Two aspects of the monetary debate', *National Institute Economic Review* (Aug. 1969).

[3] BALOGH, T. 'Productivity and Inflation', *Oxford Economic Papers*, ix (1958), 220–45.

[4] —— *Labour and Inflation* (The Fabian Society, London, 1970).

[5] —— *Fact and Fancy in International Economic Relations* (Pergamon, 1973).

[6] Ball, R. J. and Doyle, P. (eds.) *Inflation* (Penguin Education, Harmondsworth, 1969).

[7] Bank of England 'The Importance of Money', *Bank of England Quarterly Bulletin*, x (2) (1970), 159–98.

[8] BARRO, R. J. and GROSSMAN, H. I. 'A General Disequilibrium Model of Income and Employment', *American Economic Review*, 61 (1) (1971), pp. 82–93.

[9] BEHREND, H. 'Price and Incomes Images and Inflation', *Scottish Journal of Political Economy*, xi (2) (1964), pp. 85–103.

[10] BOWERS, J. K., CHESHIRE, P. C., and WEBB, A. E. 'The Change in the Relationship Between Unemployment and Earnings Increases', *National Institute Economic Review*, No. 54 (1970), pp. 44–63.

[11] BOWERS, J. K., CHESHIRE, P. C., WEBB, A. E. and WEEDON, R. 'Some Aspects of Unemployment and the Labour Market 1966–71', *National Institute Economic Review* (Nov. 1972).

[12] BRESCIANI-TURRONI, C. *The Economics of Inflation: A Study of Currency Depreciation in Postwar Germany* (Kelly, New York, 1968) (earlier editions 1931, 1937).

[13] BRONFENBRENNER, M. and HOLZMAN, F. D. 'A Survey of Inflation Theory', *American Economic Review*, 53 (4) (1965), pp. 593–661. (Reprinted in *Surveys of Economic Theory*, American Economic Association and Royal Economic Society, 1965.)

[14] BURTON, J. *Wage Inflation* (Macmillan, London, 1972).

[15] CAGAN, P. 'The Monetary Dynamics of Hyperinflation', in Friedman, M. (ed.) *Studies in the Quantity Theory of Money* (University of Chicago Press, 1956).

[16] CLOWER, R. W. 'The Keynesian Counter-Revolution: A Theoretical Appraisal', in Hahn, F. H. and Brechling, F. P. R. (eds.) *The Theory of Interest Rates* (Macmillan, London, 1965).

[17] —— (ed.) *Monetary Theory* (Penguin Education, Harmondsworth, 1969).

[18] CORRY, B. A. and LAIDLER, D. E. W. 'The Phillips Relation: A Theoretical Explanation', *Economica* (N.S.), 34 (134) (1967), pp. 189–97.

[19] CRAMP, A. B. 'Does money matter?', *Lloyds Bank Review*, 98 (Oct. 1970), pp. 23–37.

[20] DAVIDSON, P. *Money and the Real World* (Macmillan, London, 1972).

[21] DICKS-MIREAUX, L. A. 'The Inter-Relationship Between Cost and Price Changes, 1945–1959: A Study of Inflation in Postwar Britain', *Oxford Economic Papers* (N.S.), 13 (3) (1961), pp. 267–92.

[22] DICKS-MIREAUX, L. A. and Dow, J. C. R. 'The Determinants of Wage Inflation in the United Kingdom, 1946–1956', *Journal of the Royal Statistical Society*, Series A (General), 122 (2) (1959), pp. 145–84.

[23] Dow, J. C. R. 'Analysis of the Generation of Price Inflation', *Oxford Economic Papers* (N.S.), 8 (3) (1956), pp. 252–301.

[24] Dow, J. C. R. and DICKS-MIREAUX, L. A. 'The Excess Demand for Labour', *Oxford Economic Papers* (N.S.), 10 (1) (1958), pp. 1–33.

[25] ECKSTEIN, O. and FROMM, G. 'The Price Equation', *American Economic Review*, 58 (5) (1968), Pt. 1, pp. 1159–84.

[26] ECKSTEIN, O. and WILSON, T. A. 'The Determination of Money Wages in American Industry', *Quarterly Journal of Economics*, 76 (1962).

[27] FRIEDMAN, M. (ed.) *Studies in the Quantity Theory of Money* (University of Chicago Press, 1956).

[28] — — 'The Role of Monetary Policy', *American Economic Review*, 58 (1) (1968), pp. 1–17.

[29] — — *The Counter-Revolution in Monetary Theory*, International Economic Association (for Wincott Foundation), Occasional Paper 33 (London, 1970).

[30] — — *Unemployment versus Inflation?* Institute of Economic Affairs, Occasional Paper 44 (London, 1975).

[31] GLYN, A. and SUTCLIFFE, B. *British Capitalism, Workers and the Profits Squeeze* (Penguin, Harmondsworth, 1972).

[32] GODLEY, W. A. H. and NORDHAUS, W. D. 'Pricing in the Trade Cycle', *Economic Journal*, 82 (327) (1972), pp. 853–82.

[33] GRIFFIN, K. B. 'A Note on Wages Prices and Unemployment', *Bulletin of the Oxford University Institute of Economics and Statistics*, 24 (3) (1962), pp. 379–85.

[34] HICKS, J. R. 'Economic Foundations of Wage Policy', *Economic Journal*, lxv (1955).

[35] HINES, A. G. 'Trade Unions and Wage Inflation in the United Kingdom, 1893–1961', *Review of Economic Studies*, 31 (3), no. 88 (1964), pp. 221–52.

[36] JACKSON, D., TURNER, H. A. and WILKINSON, F. *Do Trade Unions Cause Inflation?* University of Cambridge Department of Applied Economics, Occasional Paper 36 (Cambridge University Press, 1972).

[37] JOHNSON, H. G. and NOBAY, A. R. (eds.) *The Current Inflation* (Macmillan, London, 1971).

[38] JONES, A. *The New Inflation: The Politics of Prices and Incomes* (Penguin and André Deutsch, London, 1972).

[39] KALDOR, N. 'Economic Growth and the Problem of Inflation', *Economica* (Nov. 1959).

[40] — — 'The New Monetarism', *Lloyds Bank Review*, No. 97 (July 1970), pp. 1–18.

[41] KEYNES, J. M. *Essays in Persuasion* (Macmillan, London, 1972).

[42] — — *The General Theory of Employment, Interest and Money* (Macmillan, London, 1936).

[43] — — *How to Pay for the War* (Macmillan, London, 1940).

[44] KNIGHT, K. G. 'Strikes and Wage Inflation in British Manufacturing Industry 1950–1968', *Bulletin of the Oxford University Institute of Economics and Statistics*, 35 (3) (1972), pp. 281–94.

[45] KNOWLES, K. G. J. C. and WINSTEN, C. B. 'Can the Level of Unemployment Explain Changes in Wages?', *Bulletin of the Oxford University Institute of Economics and Statistics*, 21 (2) (1959), pp. 113–20.

[46] LAIDLER, D. E. W. and PARKIN, J. M. 'Inflation: A Survey', *Economic Journal*, 85 (1975), pp. 741–809.

[47] LAIDLER, D. E. W. and PURDY, D. (eds.) *Labour Markets and Inflation* (Manchester U.P. and Toronto U.P., 1974).

[48] LAURSEN, K. and PEDERSEN, J. *The German Inflation 1918–1923* (North Holland Publishing Co., Amsterdam, 1964).

[49] LEIJONHUFVUD, A. *On Keynesian Economics and the Economics of Keynes* (Oxford University Press, 1968).

[50] LIPSEY, R. G. 'The Relationship Between Unemployment and the Rate of Change of Money Wage Rates in the U.K. 1862–1957: A Further Analysis', *Economica* (N.S.), 27 (105) (1960), pp. 1–31.

[51] LIPSEY, R. G. and PARKIN, J. M. 'Incomes Policy: A Reappraisal', *Economica*

(N.S.), 37 (146) (1970), pp. 115–38 (reprinted in Parkin, J. M. and Sumner, M. T. (eds.), 1972).

[52] MUTH, J. F. 'Rational Expectations and the Theory of Price Movements', *Econometrica*, 29 (3) (1961), pp. 315–35.

[53] NEILD, R. R. *Pricing and Employment in the Trade Cycle* (Cambridge University Press (for National Institute of Economic and Social Research), London, 1963).

[54] NORDHAUS, W. D. 'The World-Wide Wage Explosion', *Brookings Papers*, No. 2 (1972), pp. 431–63.

[55] Organisation for Economic Co-operation and Development *Inflation: The Present Problem* (O.E.C.D., Paris, 1970).

[56] PAGE, S. A. B. and TROLLOPE, S. 'An International Survey of Indexing and its Effects', *National Institute Economic Review*, 70 (1974), pp. 45–59.

[57] PAISH, F. W. *Studies in an Inflationary Economy—The United Kingdom, 1948–1961.* 2nd edn. (Macmillan, London, 1966).

[58] —— 'The Limits of Incomes Policies', in Paish, F. W. and Hennessy, J. *Policy for Incomes*, 4th edn., Hobart Paper 29, Institute of Economic Affairs (1968).

[59] PARKIN, J. M. and SUMNER, M. T. (eds.) *Incomes Policy and Inflation* (Manchester U.P. and Toronto U.P., 1972).

[60] PARKIN, J. M. and ZIS, G. (eds.) *Inflation in the World Economy* (Manchester, 1975).

[61] PHELPS, E. S. 'Phillips Curves, Expectations of Inflation and Optimal Unemployment Over Time', *Economica* (N.S.), 34 (135) (1967), pp. 254–81.

[62] PHELPS, E. S. *et al.* *The Microeconomic Foundations of Employment and Inflation Theory* (W. W. Norton & Co., New York, 1970).

[63] PHELPS-BROWN, E. H. 'The Analysis of Wage Movements Under Full Employment', *Scottish Journal of Political Economy*, 18 (3) (1971), pp. 233–43.

[64] PHILLIPS, A. W. 'The Relationship Between Unemployment and the Rate of Change of Money Wage Rates in the U.K. 1861–1957', *Economica* (N.S.), 25 (100) (1958), pp. 283–99.

[65] POLAK, J. J. 'Monetary Analysis of Income Formation and Payments Problems', *I.M.F. Staff Papers*, vi (1957–8), pp. 1–50.

[66] RUEFF, J. 'Gold Exchange Standard a Danger to the West' (1961), reprinted in Grubel, H. G. *World Monetary Reform: Plans and Issues* (Stanford University Press, 1963).

[67] RUNCIMAN, W. G. *Relative Deprivation and Social Justice* (Routledge and Kegan Paul, London, 1966).

[68] SHACKLE, G. L. S. *Uncertainty in Economics and Other Reflections* (Cambridge University Press, London, 1955).

[69] SOLOW, R. M. *Price Expectations and the Behaviour of the Price Level* (Manchester University Press, 1969).

[70] STREETEN, P. 'Wages, prices and productivity', *Kyklos*, 15 (1962), pp. 723–31.

[71] TOBIN, J. 'Inflation and Unemployment', *American Economic Review*, 62 (1) (1972), pp. 1–18.

[72] TREVITHICK, J. A. and MULVEY, C. *The Economics of Inflation* (Martin Robertson, London, 1975).

[73] TRIFFIN, R. *Gold and the Dollar Crisis* (Yale University Press, 1961).

[74] WEINTRAUB, S. 'The Keynesian theory of inflation: the two faces of Janus?', *International Economic Review*, i (1960), pp. 143–55.

[75] WILES, P. 'Cost Inflation and the State of Economic Theory', *Economic Journal*, 83 (330) (1973), pp. 377–98.

8

Economic Growth

C. J. ALLSOPP

1. Introduction

Economic growth is now firmly established as one of the policy objectives of modern governments. But on both theoretical and practical levels understanding of the processes involved remains very limited. Growth models abound, which even their authors do not think of as having practical application; and on the empirical side the field is beset with complications, some theoretical and some mundanely practical, like the absence of the relevant data to test various hypotheses. This chapter surveys some of the approaches that have been suggested, focusing on the problem of explaining why different developed countries have grown at such different rates. The policy problems of intervention at the industrial level to foster growth is taken up in Chapter 19.

In the United Kingdom there is a widespread feeling that growth performance has been inadequate, and it is true that, compared with most other developed countries, the British growth rate has been low. Nor is it possible to explain the poor performance in terms of other countries catching up. It is now well known that the major countries of Western Europe have substantially surpassed the United Kingdom in levels of National Income per capita. Table 8.1 shows Britain's comparative position in the 'growth league table' for the period 1951–70. Although there is a margin of error in computed growth rates due to differences in national accounting procedures, such large differences as are displayed are obviously significant. The general picture is not particularly sensitive to small changes in the time period considered. For the data shown, the actual years used for each country have been chosen to eliminate, as far as possible, the influence of the business-cycle.

A consideration of importance when looking at the table is that it is the *fast* growth of some countries which is the new phenomenon. Britain's performance is more or less in line with historical experience, and in fact Britain has been growing faster, in the post-war period, than in any historical period of comparable length. When looking at explanations of differences in growth this should be kept in mind. It may be that the interesting question is why some other countries were able to grow so much faster, rather than why Britain grew so slowly. The shift of emphasis to the positive factors that favoured fast growth in some countries may be important.

Before considering some of the approaches to the problem of growth, it is as well to look at some of the explanations, which, in their naïve form at least, just will not do. One problem is that many 'explanations' are not explanations of growth at all, but of the level of output. Most commonly, this includes efficiency arguments, where the efficiency of someone, management or labour, is to blame for slow growth (and conversely gets the credit for fast growth). The point is simply that it is perfectly possible for an 'inefficient' economy to grow fast, or an efficient one to grow slowly. In the

TABLE 8.1. *Growth Rates of Gross Domestic Product (GDP) and GDP per Employee for 12 Developed Countries, for the Period 1951–70.**

Per cent per annum

	GDP	Employment	GDP/Employee
Japan	9·5	1·6	7·9
West Germany	6·0	1·2	4·8
Italy	5·3	0·6	4·6
Netherlands	5·2	1·2	4·0
Austria	4·9	−0·3	4·6
France	4·7	0·3	4·4
Canada	4·5	2·3	2·2
Denmark	4·4	1·1	3·3
Norway	4·1	0·4	3·7
Belgium	3·7	0·5	3·2
U.S.A.	3·6	1·7	1·9
United Kingdom	2·6	0·6	2·0

Sources: *O.E.C.D. National Account Statistics; Manpower Statistics.*

* The period 1951–70 was used except in the following cases:

Japan	1953–69	Denmark	1954–69
France	1951–69	U.S.A.	1951–69
Canada	1951–69	U.K.	1951–69

first instance the effect of inefficiency should be on the *level* of output rather than on growth. To be sure, whilst inefficiencies are being removed, growth accelerates—in exactly the same way as when an economy moves from slump to boom—and it may be that inefficiencies can go on being removed for a long time with marked effects in the medium term. But to establish an effect on long-run growth it is necessary to establish that the degree of efficiency is changing over time. Of course, this does not imply that 'efficiency' of various kinds can never affect growth in the long run. There may be reasons why the *level* of efficiency might influence, for example, the rate of innovation and hence growth. The important point is that a connection must be established between the level and some such factor—in many arguments no attempt is made to do this.

Another set of 'explanations' which are suspect are those that associate certain factors with growth and then assume that these factors cause growth.

The problem is always that they might be a result of growth, or perhaps have nothing to do with it. It would be wrong to say, for example, that because Japan has a high growth rate and invests a lot, that investment causes growth. On the other hand, it clearly is interesting that Japan has both high investment and high growth, and we might want to make use of the hypothesis that there is a causal connection. The point here is simply that the association, by itself, does not imply any causality whatsoever; it may, however, suggest that certain causal hypotheses are reasonable.

2. Productive Potential

The development of Keynesian policies of demand management has meant that there is now no particular difficulty in altering the rate of growth of the economy, from year to year, by altering demand. As demand rises, however, constraints appear as the economy nears its supply potential—or productive potential. This concept of productive potential is important for short-term policy—targets for demand must always be set in relation to some concept of productive potential—and it is with the *growth of productive potential* that we are usually concerned when economic growth is discussed. Actual growth rates of the economy obviously differ from the growth of productive potential —being higher when, for example, the economy moves from slump conditions to boom conditions, and lower, in a situation when unemployment and excess capacity are building up. It is not too misleading to think of the growth of productive potential as that rate of growth which would maintain a constant level of unemployment.

There are many techniques in use for assessing productive potential. One of the simplest is to extrapolate growth between peaks of the business cycle. Though this may be adequate for many short-term applications it hardly contributes to an explanation of the growth of the economy. Much the same can be said of the techniques which rely on modifying observed levels of national output to take account of variations in unemployment, or capacity utilization indices to give estimates of full employment or full capacity output. However, many measurements are based implicitly or explicitly on a theory of the growth process.

The traditional approach to the problem of determining the productive potential of an economy (and by extension its growth) is to look at it in terms of the co-operating factors of production. In the last century these factors were often thought of as labour and land, a classification which reflected the importance of agriculture in the economy. Nowadays, the usual breakdown is in terms of labour and capital, and considerable weight is given to technical progress as an additional source of growth.

A simple approach is to assume that output depends on the inputs of the factors of production, according to some stable relationship which retains the same form over time. Such a relationship is often called a *production function*. Usually, the function is allowed to shift over time, so as to allow more output for a given input—the shifts representing the influence of increasing technical knowledge and of other factors which are not specifically included in the analysis. Normally, the relationship is assumed to be fairly flexible in that it allows capital and labour to be combined in different proportions to produce a given output.

The earliest results using this approach were obtained in the 1920s by Cobb and Douglas; and a particularly simple version of the production function, which is often used in empirical work, still bears their names. The Cobb-Douglas production function assumes that the elasticity of output with respect to either of the two inputs is constant. This means that if the labour input is increased by 1 per cent, output is assumed to increase by a fixed percentage, say a per cent, whilst if capital increased by 1 per cent, output increases by b per cent; these constants, a and b, being independent of actual output, or of the proportions in which capital and labour are combined.[1] This function has convenient properties, not least the implication that the growth of output can be thought of as composed of a part dependent on labour and a part dependent on capital. Thus in symbols we can write

$$\dot{q} = a\dot{l} + b\dot{k}$$

where $\dot{q}$ stands for the rate of growth of output, and $\dot{l}$ and $\dot{k}$ for the rates of growth of labour and capital.[2]

In order to make the analysis more applicable to the real world, it is usual to introduce a residual term, which allows output to rise over time at a constant trend rate even if labour and capital do not rise. In that case, the above equation becomes

$$\dot{q} = r + a\dot{l} + b\dot{k}$$

and the rate of growth of output (or, strictly, productive potential) is now seen to be broken down into three components, one due to increase in labour, another due to increase in capital, and a third (r in the above equation) being simply a time trend, which, apart from genuine advances in technology, may represent anything else left out of the analysis.

The above approach, using the Cobb-Douglas production function (or more complex formulations), can be used in order to try to establish an empirical relationship between the inputs into an economy and its output. Given the data, this is a statistical problem, and statistical measures of how well the hypothesis of a production function fits the data can be derived, as well as measures of the significance of individual coefficients. Such production functions can be fitted to data for one country, for a number of years

---

[1] The mathematical formulation of the function is

$$Q = \text{Constant } L^a K^b$$
$$\text{or } \log Q = \log C + a \log L + b \log K$$

where Q = output
      L = labour input
      K = capital input

[2] The assumption made in many empirical studies that there are *constant returns to scale* can be seen to amount to the assumption that a and b add up to unity—for, then, a 1 per cent increase in capital and labour together would mean a 1 per cent increase in output. This assumption is not necessary, however, and the function can be used with either diminishing or increasing returns to scale. In the latter case a particular increase in the inputs would result in a more than proportionate rise in output.

(the time series approach), or to data drawn from a number of different countries (the cross-section approach). Ideally, perhaps, both cross-section and time series information should be used.

Although it is an attractive idea to fit production functions, there are a number of very acute difficulties. When production functions were first fitted to time series data, they seemed to give good results (a close fit) and the co-efficients came out sensibly at about ⅓ for the capital coefficient (b) and ⅔ for labour (a). However, difficulties soon appeared. It was found, for example, that the time trend 'explained' most of the growth. Since the time trend is really no explanation at all, this is a serious defect. Moreover, capital and labour usually grow together and their effects tend to get mixed up in time series analysis.

Quite apart from these problems, there are a number of difficulties which make the interpretation of the results in terms of an aggregate production function very suspect. In the first place, is it right to expect a stable relationship between aggregate output change and the change in capital and labour inputs? Surely we might expect different results depending on which industries or firms were expanding? Secondly, there are grave theoretical and practical difficulties in using the concept of capital. The capital goods in use are a heterogenous collection of physical objects. If they can be valued, they can be added up; but what values should be used? What about obsolescence and technical progress? When they were installed they represented a sum of money, but their cost even after allowance for depreciation may be a poor indicator of their value in production now. Finally, it may be wrong to interpret a fitted relationship between capital labour and output as being due to a production function. There are many other relationships which are likely to be important in the analysis of growth which could also lead to observed relationships between output, labour, and capital.

Though some of these problems can be dealt with, it is true that there is widespread dissatisfaction amongst economists with the aggregate production function. All sorts of sophisticated modifications have been tried, but, on the whole, the interpretation of the results remains problematical. If enough assumptions about the world are made, the results can be interpreted in terms of these assumptions. But there is something unscientific about such a procedure.

Since so many of the difficulties, both practical and theoretical, arise because of the concept of capital, it is tempting, at least for short-term applications, to leave it out, and pick up its effect in the extrapolation of labour productivity (which will tend to rise the more capital labour has to work with). In the United Kingdom productive potential is usually assessed simply in terms of the labour force—and changes in productivity. The rate of growth of output can be written as the sum of the rates of growth of employment, and the rate of growth of productivity (output per man). The rate of growth of labour supply can be projected on the basis of demographic data and assumptions about participation rates[3] and so on. It is common practice to

[3] The participation rate is defined as the proportion of a given group that is economically active—i.e. that is at work or actively seeking work. The labour supply is usually projected

add to this a trend rate of growth of productivity in order to project productive potential. This usually results in an assessed growth of productive potential, for the British economy, of the order of 3 per cent per annum.

Though such crude estimates are usually good enough for short-term policy purposes, they are subject to serious limitations for medium-term work. A number of comments can be made. In the first place, there is an assumption that productivity growth is independent of output. If productivity is influenced by output growth, because of economies of scale, for example, then procedures should reflect this. Secondly, productivity is often projected simply as a trend. It would seem better to allow explicitly for the influence of capital accumulation on productivity growth, but it has, in fact, proved extremely difficult to establish empirically significant effects of capital accumulation on productivity for the British economy. Thirdly, it is questionable whether productivity projections for the aggregate of the economy are very useful. Better results might be achieved by disaggregating, at least down to broad sectors of the economy (Agriculture, Industry, Services, etc.). Indeed, many would argue that a fairly fine industrial breakdown is necessary for productivity projections to be useful. For these reasons, amongst others, estimates of productive potential growth should be treated with care. In particular they do not imply that there is an immutable supply-determined growth rate which it is difficult to exceed.

3. The Neo-Classical Approach

An approach which is of considerable importance in the literature on comparative growth rates makes use of a production function as described in the previous section, but with additional assumptions about the world which justify (if they are true) a particularly easy estimating procedure. The major additional assumption necessary is that capital and labour markets are *perfectly competitive*. Under perfect competition factor prices are determined by the *marginal products* of the factors. This type of system has been described above, in Chapter 6.

The importance of the competitive assumption is that it allows estimation of the elasticities of output with respect to labour and to capital (the coefficients of the Cobb-Douglas production function, as in the previous section) simply by looking at the shares of National Income which accrue to labour and to capital respectively—data which are nearly always available. There are obvious defects in the procedure, but let us see how it is justified under competition.

Marginal products are defined as follows. Given a production function, we can ask how much extra output an additional unit of labour would produce if all other inputs into the system were to remain fixed. The value of this extra output is the marginal product of labour, and under the competitive assumptions it is equal to the wage that labour receives. In a similar way the marginal product of capital is defined and set equal to the rental on capital.

Going back to the Cobb-Douglas production function of the previous

by assuming that participation rates for particular age/sex groups of the population remain unchanged, or at least, are predictable.

section, the constant a, the labour coefficient, is defined as the *elasticity* of output with respect to the labour input

$$a = \frac{\text{proportionate change in output}}{\text{proportionate change in labour input}}$$

given that capital is not varying. But this elasticity can be rewritten as

$$a = \frac{\text{change in output}}{\text{change in labour input}} \times \frac{\text{level of labour}}{\text{level of output}}$$

where all we have used is the definition of a proportionate change.

The first term in the last expression is, however, the marginal product of labour as defined above. If the competitive assumptions apply, then it is equal to the wage rate, and the whole expression is equal to the value of the total labour input divided by the value of output; that is, a is equal to *labour's share of National Product*. By a precisely similar argument we can show that b, the capital elasticity, is equal to capital's share of National Product—it is equal to total profits as a proportion of the National Income.

The assumptions of perfect competition under which the above 'factor shares' method is justified may seem so unrealistic that it may come as a surprise to find that the method is widely used in practice. In fact, a weaker justification is possible. It is rather natural to look for a measure of the growth of total input—a measure which includes both capital and labour. One such measure which has the virtue of simplicity is to define the growth of Total Factor Input as the weighted sum of the growth rates of labour and capital input, the weights used being the shares accuring to labour and capital in the National Income accounts. Such a measure can be regarded as a useful starting-point for the analysis of growth, even if it is not felt that the perfect competition assumptions apply. Total Factor Input is a concept widely used by economic historians.

As in the case of 'fitted' production functions, one of the main difficulties with the factor shares approach turned out to be that Total Factor Input appeared to contribute very little to the explanation of growth. Most of growth appeared to be due to the 'residual factor', the unexplained rises in productivity. Moreover, differences in growth between countries appeared to be associated with differences in the residual, rather than differences in factor inputs. This led to attempts to refine the measurement of the inputs, and to cut down on the apparent importance of the residual.

Denison [3], in one of the best-known books on comparative growth rates uses an extension of the factor shares approach. In a cross-country analysis he estimates Total Factor Input for each of nine countries. The inputs are 'corrected' to reflect increasing levels of education, changes in composition and utilization, and so on. Beyond this, differences in the residual between countries are in part explained by estimating the importance of structural shifts in the disposition of the labour force, and the influence of economies of scale. By appealing to a wide range of factors, Denison does succeed in cutting down the apparent importance of the residual very considerably.

It is not possible to do justice to such a major study in a short survey. We are concerned with the approach.[4] The difficulties are obvious. The assumptions may not apply. Even if they do the estimates may be rather inaccurate. Moreover, the approach does not really explain growth—rather it imputes growth to various contributory factors. If it does this correctly it is a very useful starting-point, but at some stage it is necessary to consider the causal problem of how actually to affect growth in practice. It is implicitly assumed in the factor shares method that the way to affect growth is to have more of the factors such as capital and labour; and that the causality runs from input to output. It is difficult to test this against the alternative hypothesis that, say, investment (and hence capital accumulation) is induced by output growth (probably through some mechanism involving expectations of future growth).

Finally, Denison's procedures do not involve fitting a production function to the data, so there is no *test* of the idea of a production function involved. It is assumed that the economy works in a particular way. If it does then the importance of various factors can be estimated in a mechanical way (apart from data difficulties). The only problem is how much of observed growth is left over at the end to be explained by 'residual factors'—i.e. is left unexplained.

Professor Denison is well aware of the difficulties. His view appears to be that this is a worthwhile exercise since one must start somewhere, and quantification of the effects is an exceedingly important, if hazardous, task. Certainly, his estimates are interesting even to those who may not agree with the underlying methodology.

Table 8.2 shows Denison's estimates for the contributions of Total Factor Input and the 'residual' output per unit of input (productivity) to the growth of National Income for the nine countries he studied. The period covered is 1950–62.

It can be seen that though the imputed contribution of the factor inputs is substantial, there is still much to be explained. More importantly, differences in growth between countries appear to be largely due to differences in the contribution of output per unit of input. Denison's estimates thus serve to emphasize the difficulty in explaining differences in growth rates by appeal to differing rates of growth of capital or labour inputs. As noted, however, Denison does not stop at this point, but proceeds to 'explain' the growth of output per unit of input by appeal to other influences such as economies of scale and structural shifts in the disposition of the labour force. The latter factor, in particular, is estimated to be an important reason for differences between countries. The method used is discussed below.

4. Demand and Supply

The approaches to the growth problem described so far all concentrated on the development of supply potential—and explain the development of the economy in terms of the growth of labour and capital resources, and changes

[4] Innumerable estimates are involved, many of which depend on special procedures and assumptions and cannot be understood simply in terms of the 'factor shares' method.

in the state of technology. Though there is clearly a need for some concept of the short-term supply potential of the economy (i.e. productive potential) it is not so self-evident that the explanation of growth in the longer term should run in terms of the supply of resources.

In the first place, a supply-oriented approach itself needs some supplementation. It may be reasonable enough to assume that the growth of the labour supply is an independent factor determined 'outside' the model by demographic factors; but the growth of the capital stock is itself influenced by the

TABLE 8.2. *Contributions to the Growth of National Income 1950–62*

Per cent per annum

	Growth of National Income	Labour	Contribution of		
			Capital	Total Factor Input	Output per unit of Input
Germany	7·26	1·37	1·41	2·78	4·48
Italy	5·96	0·96	0·70	1·66	4·30
France	4·92	0·45	0·79	1·24	3·68
Netherlands	4·73	0·87	1·04	1·91	2·82
Denmark	3·51	0·59	0·96	1·55	1·96
Norway	3·45	0·15	0·89	1·04	2·41
United States	3·32	1·12	0·83	1·95	1·37
Belgium	3·20	0·76	0·41	1·17	2·03
United Kingdom	2·29	0·60	0·51	1·11	1·18

Source: Denison [3], Table 15.3.

level of investment. In the pure supply-oriented approach it is not capital that is constraining, but the supply of investible resources—i.e. savings. In the short to medium run an increase in savings (a reduction in consumption) allows more to be invested, and speeds up capital accumulation.[5] Thus this view of the growth process often carries with it the policy prescription that the way to faster growth is to increase savings as a proportion of National Income. Clearly, there may be problems of a Keynesian kind in ensuring that increased savings, which reduces consumer expenditure lead to, or are at least balanced by, increased investment expenditures.

In sharp contrast to those approaches which concentrate on the supply side, many explanations of growth emphasize the development over time of the various categories of expenditure (consumption, investment, etc.)—that is, the development of aggregate demand. It is natural to label such approaches 'demand-oriented'—or 'demand-side'. Clearly, the idea of a demand-side growth path develops out of the Keynesian model of income determination—by extension, the growth of the economy is seen as deter-

[5] In the long run, on this theory, the capital/output ratio would rise—so that the growth of the capital stock would slow down again to its previous rate. Thus the growth rate would ultimately be independent of the proportion of savings. The *level* of output and output per head would, however, still be raised by the increased savings ratio.

mined by the growth of aggregate demand. The growth of aggregate demand is, in turn, seen as dependent upon the behaviour of businessmen and households, as well as government policy, and of course export demand. Variants of this general approach include some of the best-known hypotheses—such as that of export-led growth.

The terminology may suggest that demand-side growth paths are very easy to change—for example, by Keynesian policies. This would, however, be an incorrect inference. Any rate of growth, if established for some time, may be difficult to alter, and indeed may appear supply-constrained. There are a number of reasons for this. In the first place, there may be a built-in tendency for things to continue unchanged if expectations are rigid. More importantly, it is natural to suppose that businessmen would, if a growth path were maintained for a reasonable length of time, adjust their capital stock to that growth path, so that the development of capital capacity would tend to be consistent with the growth that was achieved. Expansionary policies would tend to lead to supply problems and bottlenecks. The concept of productive potential would still appear to be applicable—defined, perhaps, in terms of capital capacity—but would, in fact, be of little use in explaining longer-term growth tendencies.

The obvious problem with the concept of a demand-side path is that there is no particular reason to suppose that such a path would be consistent with *full employment*, in that the rate of growth of demand for labour might not be equal to the rate of growth of supply of labour. It is this possible inconsistency which has attracted most attention from economists. It appears that the consequences of such a problem—either an increasing proportion of the labour force unemployed, or an increasing demand for labour in relation to its supply—are just not observed. Most developed countries appear, since the war, to have had growth at reasonably full employment, with no longer-run tendency for the amount of unemployment to either increase or decrease. Surely, therefore, there must be some interaction to ensure that demand for labour grows at the appropriate rate?

There are several possible answers to this. In the first place, it may be that the supply of labour is, in real economies, very variable, due to a potential for shifts between occupations, regions, and so on. The massive shifts in the disposition of the labour force in some fast-growing countries since the war would support this view. If such shifts occurred in response to growth, then growth itself can be explained as largely due to the development of demand. Even in the absence of such potential movements it may be that technology is such that shortages of labour are very easily overcome—so that labour supply is unimportant. Conversely, the labour force policies of firms (hoarding, etc.) may be such as to disguise unemployment even if it exists—at least for a time.

The problem of how the demand side and the supply side interact is exceptionally important for practical policy but there are many difficulties in the way of getting any answer. It is probable that different countries at different times are in different situations—in some, it may be that it is the supply of resources that is the crucial constraining factor. In others it may be a demand-side problem, requiring a different policy approach. In general, it is likely that the two sides of the picture interact in a complex way.

5. Keynesian Problems in Growth Theory

Though the idea of a 'demand-side' or 'expenditure-side' growth path is easy enough, there may be difficulties in achieving it. One problem has already been discussed. A demand-side growth path may not automatically give rise to full employment of the labour force. Another problem is that demand-side paths, if they exist, may have a tendency to be unstable—a divergence, once it starts, may tend to develop into a cumulative movement away from equilibrium.

The formal analysis usually starts from the simple Keynesian 'multiplier' model, with only two categories of expenditure—consumption and investment. Such models are usually considered statically—a simplification that is only valid in the short run (see Chapter 4). In particular, when considering growth, investment cannot be taken as 'autonomous'—given from outside the model. It is necessary to consider why businessmen invest, and also the results of a given level of investment.

Over time, the investment expenditures that are going on are, clearly, adding to capital capacity. Aggregate demand, however, only expands to utilize the extra capital capacity that is produced if investment *rises*; it is a *rise* in investment which, through the multiplier, leads to a *rise* in aggregate demand. The problem is that there is no particular reason to suppose that the extra capacity produced in a given period will be fully utilized—no more and no less. There may be an inconsistency between the growth of capacity and the growth of demand—which if prolonged would, of course, tend to lead to a revision of investment expenditure—downwards if excess capacity is developing, upwards if a shortage of capacity appears.

Although, in general, there may be inconsistency between the development of capacity and the development of demand, the question arises as to whether it is possible to find a special case in which there is no inconsistency—in which capacity develops in line with demand. It turns out that there is; there is a particular rate of growth of the economy (often called the 'warranted' growth rate g_w) which allows capacity and demand to grow in line with each other. For any other rate of growth the problem of inconsistency would arise (see [4]).

There are many different ways in which the problem of inconsistency can be analysed. The approach adopted here is intended to focus as closely as possible on the likely behaviour reactions of businessmen and householders—so as to bring out practical problems. The point is that if inconsistency develops then either households or businessmen are likely to be in 'disequilibrium' in the sense that they would not be satisfied with the way things were turning out and would, therefore, tend to change their expenditure plans.

Consider first the question of why businessmen invest. What determines aggregate investment expenditures? A simple hypothesis is that businessmen invest in order to expand capacity in line with expected changes in output or demand.[6] Formally, we may write:

[6] Neglecting, for simplicity, other reasons for investment such as capital deepening, or replacement.

$$I = v_r \Delta Ye$$

where $I =$ Investment

$\Delta Ye =$ Expected change in output ($Ye =$ expected output)

$v_r = (I/\Delta Ye)$ is a coefficient—the desired incremental capital/output ratio.

Since we are concerned with growth it is more convenient to consider proportions and proportionate changes, so it is useful to divide the above equation through by output Y, to get

$$\frac{I}{Y} = v_r \frac{\Delta Ye}{Y} \quad \text{or} \quad \frac{I}{Y} = v_r g_e$$

—and the hypothesis is that the investment/output ratio (I/Y) is directly related to the expected rate of growth of demand ($\Delta Ye/Y = g_e$) by some coefficient v_r which represents some desired, normal, or required incremental capital to output ratio.

In aggregate, this amounts to the hypothesis that the investment/output ratio for the economy depends upon the rate of growth expected by the business community. It is a simple idea. Suppose, for example, that the normal capital/output ratio were about 2. Then according to the formula, if expected growth were 3 per cent per annum than a (net) investment/output ratio of 6 per cent would be required. If, however, expected growth were 6 per cent per annum, then the investment/output ratio would have to be twice as large, at 12 per cent.

This is all very well and appears reasonably realistic. But under what circumstances will the investment that satisfies businessmen also lead to people being satisfied with the amount they are saving? Assume that investors invest as above. Then it follows that the *actual* savings rate is determined (for actual savings always equals actual investment—so much is a matter of accounting). So the condition that savers as well as investors should be satisfied with the situation is simply that *the growth expected by businessmen should lead them to want to invest the same amount as people want to save*. Formally, this means that

$$\frac{I}{Y} = v_r g_e = s_r$$

The expected growth rate (g_e) must therefore be s_r/v_r if savers and investors are to be satisfied simultaneously.

So it is possible to solve the problem and satisfy the requirements (or desires) of both investors and savers—but only if the expected growth rate is appropriate. The particular growth rate that is appropriate, s_r/v_r, is what we have termed the warranted rate of growth (g_w) because it has the property that no inconsistencies arise. Investors are adding to capacity at the appropriate rate—and savers are saving what they want to save.[7] Since the

---

[7] This latter condition is simply the condition that the 'multiplier' relationship holds. In fact the warranted rate can also be written as

$$g_w = \frac{1}{mv_r}$$

warranted rate of growth depends upon two independently determined behavioural characteristics of the private sector—the desire to save, and the desired (incremental) capital/output ratio—it can be appreciated that the determination of a 'demand-side' growth path by expectations may not be quite so simple as at first appears. In fact, only if expected growth is equal to the 'warranted rate' (g_w) will the actual growth that comes about tend to correspond with expectation. If any other growth rate were expected, the result would tend to be inconsistent with the maintenance of that expectation over time, in that inconsistency and disequilibrium would result.

This problem was first analysed by Harrod [19], who pioneered growth theory and first used the formula for the warranted rate in 1939. Using a rather more general approach, Harrod defines the 'warranted' rate of growth (g_w) as that rate of growth 'which is consistent with people saving what they want to save, and having the capital goods they require for their purposes' ([4], p. 19). The warranted path can be thought of as that growth path that would keep the private sector happy, and continuing to do what it was doing in the past—i.e. continuing to grow at a steady rate. The warranted path thus depends on the concept of the desired savings ratio, and on the concept of the required capital/output ratio—that relationship between increments in output and increments in capacity which, if it obtained, would leave businessmen feeling 'in the upshot that they have done the right thing'. Put thus generally, it can be seen that the idea of the 'warranted' path has nothing to do with the constancy or otherwise of savings behaviour, or of the required capital/output ratio. It depends on the idea of there being two independent conditions for equilibrium (one for savers, one for investors) with no automatic mechanism for making sure that they will be simultaneously satisfied.[8]

The interpretation of the 'warranted' rate of growth is problematical. There are reasons for supposing that warranted paths, if they exist, would tend to be unstable—a chance divergence might set up forces taking the economy even further away from the warranted path. The point is quite straightforward. If by chance, say, the economy were to grow at a different rate, the inconsistency problem would arise, and either savers or investors would be dissatisfied with the results—they would be out of equilibrium. But the likely reactions to the disequilibrium are such that they would tend to lead to further divergence from the warranted rate.

The easiest way to analyse this problem is to note that any *actual* growth rate can be written in a way which allows it to be compared with the war-

---

where m is the multiplier. This follows since in the simple model the multiplier is the reciprocal of the *desired* saving ratio

$$\left(m = \frac{1}{s_r} \right)$$

[8] Most growth models solve the problem posed by Harrod in rather unsatisfactory ways. The neo-classical school ignores the problem by dropping the idea of an independent investment function. The neo-Keynesian school usually allows savings to adjust to investment by changes in income distribution between wages and profits. Though this is a way out of the consistency problem, there remain problems as to the actual mechanism of adjustment in a dynamic setting. See, for example, [7], [8], [44].

ranted rate. Actual growth (g_a) can always be expressed as s/v, where s is the actual or observed savings ratio, and v is the actual, observed, incremental capital/output ratio. This is derived as follows:

$$g_a \equiv \frac{\Delta \Upsilon}{\Upsilon} \equiv \frac{\Delta \Upsilon}{I} \times \frac{I}{\Upsilon} \equiv \frac{\Delta \Upsilon}{I} \times \frac{S}{\Upsilon} \equiv \frac{s}{v}$$

This is *always* true since all that has been used is the definition of v $(=I/\Delta \Upsilon)$, the definition of s $(= S/\Upsilon)$, and the accounting identity that, ex post, savings is always equal to investment $(S = I)$.

Let us suppose that actual growth is above the warranted growth—perhaps by chance, or due to a wrong expectation. Then we have

$$g_a > g_w$$

But from the definitions, this means that

$$\frac{s}{v} > \frac{s_r}{v_r}$$

Such a divergence thus implies *either* that the actual savings rate (s) has turned out to be bigger than the desired savings rate (s_r) or that the actual incremental capital/output ratio (v) has turned out to be less than required (v_r). Thus *either* savers have saved more than they desired, *or* businessmen have invested less than they required. In either case there would be a tendency for expenditure plans to be revised upwards, further raising the growth of the economy and tending to lead to a cumulative upswing in the economy. In the case where actual growth turned out to be less than warranted, cumulative recessionary forces would tend to develop.

The tendency towards cumulative movements away from the warranted growth rate is suggestive of the phenomena of the business-cycle. A fuller analysis would aim to develop a model of growth and cycles. The nature of the movements away from equilibrium is, however, very sensitive indeed to the precise assumptions made about the formation of expectations and the reactions of businessmen and households. But it is easy to see why there may be a problem. In the long run there are no 'autonomous' variables—everything is induced by everything else—and it is not surprising that 'instability' should be a problem.

In practice, instability may not be as severe as might be suggested by the above analysis. For an individual country, foreign trade may be powerfully stabilizing (so long as countries do not all move together).[9] Moreover, the problem of short-term instability over the trade-cycle may be regarded as a problem for short-term demand management policy. But what about the problem of a divergence between the warranted rate of growth and that rate of growth that would seem best for the economy in question? If the government has a target—for example, that the economy should grow at a rate which would lead to full employment over time—should policy action be

---

[9] Cf. Chapter 14 where it is suggested that the increased coincidence of policy problems and movements in demand and output have increased problems of instability on an international scale.

designed to bring the warranted rate of growth into line with the target? This is not a problem that has been faced in practice.

The argument that the warranted rate should be brought into line with a target rate of growth for the economy (such as the growth of 'productive potential') can be presented as follows. Suppose the authorities do succeed in managing the economy so that it grows in line with productive potential. Then it would seem natural to suppose that businessmen would come to expect such a growth rate. It would clearly be desirable that their expectations should lead to the right rate of growth—this would minimize the need for policy action. But the condition that expectations should, by and large, be fulfilled is that growth should be at the warranted rate. If the warranted rate of growth were different from the growth of productive potential, then disequilibrating reactions would tend to occur and the task of maintaining growth in line with potential would be much more difficult.

This is a powerful argument. But there is a catch. If investment is in any case appropriate to the 'target' rate of growth, the policy amounts to controlling consumption to be appropriate to the investment that is going on. This is a highly likely response, and lends plausibility to the idea that favourable expectations can generate high investment and hence high growth —a feature of many explanations of rapid growth since the war. But what happens if investment is not high enough for the target growth? In the United Kingdom, for example, policy targets usually involve the objective of raising growth. It turns out that the normal short-term response may be perverse from a medium-term point of view.

If it is desired to raise actual growth, then if 'warranted' growth is also to be raised, consumption needs to be lowered (desired savings needs to be raised). What this amounts to is the policy prescription of lowering consumption to 'make room' for the extra investment required for higher target growth. The difficulty is very well known—there is no reason for investment to rise, and the policy might just swell unemployment. However, if the alternative of lowering taxes and stimulating consumption were pursued, the target growth might be achieved for a time—but only at the cost of instability. For such a policy *raises* actual growth but *reduces* the warranted growth—thus increasing disequilibrium. In practice, when investment does respond, there is then too much demand. This tendency for consumption-led booms to be unstable is beginning to be given the attention it deserves. Thus policy to raise growth needs simultaneously to lower consumption and to raise investment. The first is easy. No one has yet solved the problem of controlling investment.

6. Demand-Side Emphasis

Some analyses and some policy suggestions concentrate on the 'demand side' of the growth issue. A practical example of such an approach—in fact, an extreme one—is the 'expectations' approach. According to this view, businessmen's expectations are thought to be the most important factor affecting growth rates. If the business community believes that a certain growth rate s normal, then, so goes the argument, that is the growth rate that will tend to be achieved. There is clearly a great deal in this; it is known that expectations affect investment and that investment will affect the growth of the economy. Moreover, the expectations held by businessmen may easily frustrate governmental targets if inconsistent with them.

This view of growth can easily be abused. As it stands, it does not really explain anything. It can be much improved, however, if something is said about what affects expectations. In its naïve form, what is more, it says nothing about supply-side influences at all—it just assumes their absence. It is necessary at least to specify what is happening on the supply side. It could be that there is unemployment; in which case the assumption that there are no supply limitations is reasonable. Often, however, the implicit assumption is not that there is unemployment, but that the combination of capital accumulation and technical progress is so powerful that almost any supply bottleneck can be overcome. If the labour is available, it will be used —if not, then technology will come to the rescue. This is an assertion about the nature and speed of technological advance which is in principle testable.

A related approach has been spelled out by Beckerman [1], writing in 1965—when, of course, exchange rates were still 'fixed'. There are many strands to his analysis, but a crude sketch would be as follows. Growth depends on expectations, but these in turn depend upon the balance of payments position of the country in question. The idea behind this link is that the business sector is well aware of the constraints that operate on a modern government, and if the balance of payments is in surplus, they will expect expansionary policies; whereas if it is in deficit, they will expect deflationary policies. Thus the climate of expectations is modified by the payments position.

To this expectations hypothesis are added certain other interactions. The first is between the rate of growth of the economy and the rate of growth of productivity in the economy. That such a relationship exists is well attested empirically, but of course it can be explained in many different ways. The effect of this relationship is that the balance of payments position affects not only the growth rate (because of expectations) but also the rate of growth of productivity in the economy. But a fast rate of growth of productivity will lead to a tendency for costs per unit of output to decline, and under a regime of fixed international exchange rates this will improve the country's competitive position in international markets.

Thus we get a feedback effect. A good balance of payments position stimulates fast growth which stimulates productivity, which lowers unit costs, which improves the competitive position, which improves the balance of payments position, and so on. Corresponding to this virtuous circle, there is a vicious one, where slow growth leads to a worsening payments position, and so to slower growth.

This analysis is obviously closely related to the idea of an export boom, or export-led growth, which is often put forward as an explanation of growth in France, Italy, and Germany in the post-war period. It is also related to the idea of 'indicative planning' as a technique for stimulating growth. If the expectations of the business sector are inappropriate for fast growth, increased aggregate demand by itself would not be much of a help. It is necessary that expectations be revised upwards so that investment plans become consistent with a target rate of growth. No individual in the private sector can affect growth by himself—but in concert, if the business sector as a whole revised its expectations upwards, then the whole economy would grow faster. The idea behind indicative planning is that the publishing of a target rate of growth with a set of consistent plans for each sector of the economy can help to modify expectations and investment plans so that they are in fact consistent with the targeted growth. Clearly, if the business sector believes that the targets will be achieved, then they are more likely to behave accordingly, and the plan may have the desired results.

In practice, of course, indicative plans, whilst relying on expectational phenomena, do not concentrate exclusively on the demand side. It is an essential purpose of such plans to identify potential supply constraints, bottlenecks, etc.—and to break them. The government's role on the supply side may be very important. Much depends, of course, on the over-all credibility of an indicative plan. They are vulnerable once they start to go wrong, and much depends upon there being policies to implement them. The greater the government role, and the more it is seen to be committed to the plan targets, the more likely is the private sector to react in the desired way.

It is often claimed that indicative planning played a major role in stimulating French growth rates. In this country the closest approach to indicative planning was the National Plan of 1965. The plan and its failure are discussed in Chapter 17 below. In the event it was balance of payments problems that led to the abandonment of the plan. There is a question, however, of whether it would have been feasible in the absence of payments problems. The plan suggested some shortage of labour if the targets were achieved. Would it have been possible to surmount this supply-side constraint? Would productivity have responded? We shall never know, but there is much international evidence which suggests that the labour supply position may be very important.

7. The Importance of Labour Supply

The previous section outlined certain approaches that concentrated on the development of the expenditure side (or demand side) of the economic growth problem. Such approaches are much more plausible if it can be shown that the labour supply is unlikely to be constraining. In recent work a number of studies have stressed the importance of shifts in the labour force from one sector of the economy to another in the post-war decades. The potentiality for such shifts makes approaches which concentrate on demand factors look much more reasonable.

There is no doubt that in the fast-growing countries of Western Europe and in Japan such shifts in the disposition of the labour force did in fact take place. Indeed, these shifts are the reason that, in a cross-country comparison, differences in growth appear to be almost entirely due to differences in the growth of productivity (output per man). With widely differing degrees of structural change, it is hardly surprising that there is no simple correlation between observed rates of growth of output and observed rates of growth of total employment. There are a number of different ways, however, in which the importance of these shifts might be assessed.

As noted above, Denison [3] finds changes in the disposition of the labour force to be important. He estimates the contribution of shifts in the labour force, both from agriculture to other sectors of the economy, and from self-employment into other activities. His method is to estimate the productivity of the labour force in the two sectors. Conceptually, imagine the transfer of a worker from agriculture to, say, industry and assess (i) how much extra output is produced by that worker in industry, and (ii) how much output is lost due to the worker leaving agriculture. If the productivity in the two sectors is different, there is certainly a gain due to the transfer—which would not already have been picked up in terms of total factor input (since no change in measured labour supply is involved). For the economy as a whole, the total effect can be found by multiplying the net effect per worker by the number of workers who transferred in a given time period.[10]

The problem with this method is to decide on the gains and losses in the two sectors, and any such estimates are rather arbitrary. Denison assumes that the proportionate gain in output in the non-farm sector is four-fifths of the proportionate gain in the non-farm labour force for the north-west European countries, and three-quarters for the United States and Italy. The figures for the loss in agriculture due to the transfer vary from country to country—from zero in Italy to one-third of average agricultural productivity in the U.K. and the U.S.A.

On the results of this method of calculation Denison ([3], p. 215) observes 'The reduction in the over-allocation of resources to agriculture emerges as a principal source of growth in several countries and an important source in all but the United Kingdom. Differences in the gains from this source are responsible for much of the difference among countries in growth rates of national income per person employed.' The actual order of magnitude of the combined effect of movements from both agriculture and from the self-employed can be gauged from the largest figure, for Italy, where on Denison's method the shifts accounted for 1·26 percentage points of their annual growth rate for the period 1950–62. The corresponding figure for the United Kingdom was 0·1 percentage points.

It is important to realize that Denison's estimates are concerned only with the effect of the shifts on productivity and growth as part of his general approach of imputing the growth that was achieved to various sources. It may well be that the true importance of the labour force transfer may have been much greater if such a transfer was a necessary condition for the achievement of other 'sources' of growth. For example, without the expansion of the labour force in the non-agricultural sectors, it might have been impossible to have so much capital accumulation. If so, the true importance of the labour transfer would be much understated by this method.

[10] If the total employment changes between the two years used, the number who 'transferred' cannot be measured simply by the decline in agricultural employment.

An approach which gives a much more central role to intersectoral shifts in the labour force is that of Kindleberger [6]. He conceptualizes the problem of the fast rates of growth achieved by some European countries in the post-war period (he uses the term 'supergrowth') in terms of a model of the growth process which was designed to be of use when considering underdeveloped countries. The Lewis Model [30] is a model of a *dual* economy which has an advanced modern sector co-existing with a backward non-monetized sector, which is usually thought of as agriculture. The backward sector is usually considered to be underemployed, so that labour can be taken out of it without adversely affecting the output of the sector. The importance of the backward sector in the Lewis Model is that it provides the more modern sectors of the economy with a supply of labour over time—the labour force in agriculture can be run down without lowering the output of agriculture; and secondly, since there is an abundance of labour available for the industrial sector, real wages in industry are kept low. The mechanism of growth is that the profits that arise in industry are reinvested and increase the growth of industry. Labour is always available, and since the real wage is depressed due to the existence of the low productivity sectors, profits in industry rise over time.[11] The rising profits generate an accelerating growth process. The rapid and accelerating growth process ends when so much labour has been taken out of the low productivity sectors that they are no longer underemployed. At this point wages start to rise, cutting into profits and slowing the growth process.

Kindleberger suggests that some such mechanism as the Lewis process is behind the 'supergrowth' experience of some Western European countries. As evidence of this he examines the labour supply situation in a number of countries in some detail. The thesis of the book is best put in Kindleberger's own words:

The major factor shaping the remarkable economic growth which most of Europe has experienced since 1950 has been the availability of a large supply of labour. The labour has come from a high rate of natural increase (the Netherlands), from transfers from agriculture to services and industry (Germany, France, Italy), from the immigration of unemployed and underemployed workers from the Mediterranean countries (France, Germany and Switzerland). Those countries with no substantial increase in the labour supply—Britain, Belgium and the Scandinavian nations—on the whole have grown more slowly than the others ([6], p. 3).

Though it would not be right to think of the labour supply as merely a permissive factor for Kindleberger, his analysis of the supply side is not really an explanation of the fast rates of growth achieved in parts of Western Europe. Kindleberger, as others, tends to appeal to demand-side factors such as the growth of exports, and policy action by governments as additional factors making for fast growth.

Professor Kaldor, in a lecture given in 1966 [5], also stressed the importance of shifts in the disposition of the labour force in explaining the fast rates of growth achieved by some countries. He suggested, moreover, that the slow rate of growth achieved by the United Kingdom could be explained by the

[11] In the formal model the stricter assumption of a constant real wage is made.

impossibility of such shifts, which meant that the United Kingdom should be regarded as labour-constrained.

The starting-point for this analysis is the by now familiar finding that the rates of growth of output of developed countries seem almost totally unrelated to the rates of growth of employment.[12] Kaldor, however, used a more disaggregated approach and turned his attention to the growth of the manufacturing sector. For this sector, in sharp contrast to the results for the economy as a whole, it is found that there is a very close relationship between the growth of output and the growth of labour input. The explanation of the contrast is, of course, simple enough. In those countries that were growing fast (such as Japan and Italy) intersectoral shifts in the labour force were important, and for these countries the rates of growth of employment in manufacturing substantially exceeded the rates of growth of the total labour force.

The finding that, for a subsector of the economy (Manufacturing) there is a close relationship between labour input and output, is hardly surprising. It is in fact just what would be expected. It serves to illustrate, however, the dangers of aggregative analysis. Many had drawn the conclusion from the cross-country results for the total economy that labour supply was unimportant. Kaldor's results served to re-establish the possibility of a labour-constrained growth process.

Kaldor examined data from twelve developed countries. For the period he used (1953/4–1963/4) the relationship he found between rates of growth of output and rates of growth of employment in manufacturing, was, approximately,[13]

$$\dot{e} = -1 \cdot 0 + 0 \cdot 5 \, \dot{x}$$

where

$\dot{e}$ = rate of growth of employment

$\dot{x}$ = rate of growth of output

This relationship suggests that employment in manufacturing would tend to decline at about 1 per cent per annum if there were no increases in output, and that a 1 percentage point increase in the growth rate would have about half that effect on the growth of employment. The relationship thus indicates that faster growth is associated with faster growth rates of output per man. Apart from suggesting that labour matters, its form indicates that there may be economies of growth in manufacturing. Kaldor himself, in explaining the relationship between growth and productivity, stressed economies of scale, both of the static kind and also 'irreversible' economies of scale due to the extension of the division of labour and markets, organizational economies, effects of 'learning by doing', and so on. Some of the effects could also be imputed to capital accumulation, and technical advance 'embodied' in new

---

[12] In the discussion of Denison's work above, we have seen that even if productivity is defined as output per unit of *total* factor input, differences between countries still appear (in large part) as differences in productivity growth or as differences in the 'residual'.

[13] For simplicity of exposition, the coefficients have been rounded. The actual equation estimated by Kaldor was: $\dot{e} = 1 \cdot 03 + 0 \cdot 52 \dot{x}$. The correlation coefficient (squared) $R^2 = 0 \cdot 84$.

equipment. It should be noted that a relationship between growth and productivity is also a part of many other analyses of economic growth.

If the hypothesis of a relationship between labour input and output is accepted for the manufacturing sector, then a high rate of growth of labour input may be a necessary condition for a fast rate of manufacturing output. Kaldor expressed the view that it was the lack of an expanding labour supply to manufacturing that was the major explanation of Britain's relatively poor performance, and that, by contrast, in the fast-growing countries, intersectoral shifts in the disposition of the labour force occurred in response to the demand for labour from manufacturing. He discussed the ease with which shifts could occur in terms of the 'maturity' of a country's economic structure.

There are two elements in the concept of maturity. The first is simply the relative size of the various sectors of the economy—in particular, the size of the agricultural sector. Traditionally, industry (and also services) has attracted labour from the land, and the size of the agricultural sector has a major influence on the possible magnitude of flows of labour to manufacturing. The larger the primary sector relative to industry, the more 'immature' is the economy. The second element is the relative levels of wages and productivity in the various sectors of the economy. The greater the differential in favour of manufacturing, the more 'immature' is the country. The importance of this second element is that, if there exist large sectors of the economy where wages and productivity are lower than in industry, labour is likely to leave these sectors for industry automatically in response to demand. Such differentials would tend to suggest a situation of underemployment.

Britain appears to be relatively mature by either of these criteria. In 1968 3 per cent of the labour force was left in agriculture compared with 4·8 per cent in the United States, 10 per cent in Germany, 15½ per cent in France, 20 per cent in Japan, and 22 per cent in Italy ([38], Table 8). The comparison is more dramatic if the beginning of the post-war period is examined. In 1950, whereas the U.K. had 5 per cent of employment in agriculture, the U.S. had 12 per cent, Germany 25 per cent, France 30 per cent, and Italy 43 per cent ([3], Table 16.4).

The ratio of real National Income per worker in agriculture to that in non-agricultural activities was just over one in the U.K. in the year 1962. In the United States, Germany, France, and Italy it was just over one half. Belgium and the Netherlands are similar in this respect to the United Kingdom ([3], Table 16.1). It does not, of course, follow that wage differentials are very closely related to productivity differentials, nevertheless the productivity figures are striking enough to suggest that wage differentials also vary greatly between countries.

If the disposition of the labour force between sectors can respond to demand, then this is an explanation of why differences in growth rates appear to be largely differences in the growth of 'productivity'. There remains a question, however, as to the effect of labour transfers on the output of the sectors that lose labour (or increase their labour forces less than would otherwise be the case). Kaldor took the view that the labour transfers in the fast-growing countries could take place without any adverse effect on the output of these sectors. For agriculture this is a familiar enough assumption, similar to that made by Denison. Kaldor's cross-section results suggest, however, that there is no relationship between labour input and output for the service sectors either.[14] For those parts of the services sector where output is independently measurable, rates of growth of output vary closely with over-all growth rates; whereas the growth of employment input does not. Growth experience in these sectors is more diverse than is generally realized.[15]

Though 'immaturity' and labour transfers may explain why labour was not constraining in the fast-growing countries, it does not explain the positive factors that led to fast growth. Here Kaldor's analysis bears similarities with other approaches which we have labelled 'demand-side emphasis'. He appeals to the growth of the exogenous elements of demand for industrial products as his explanation. He cites two factors especially. The first is the stage of development of a country. When a country is developing its own capital goods sector, one would expect a great reinforcement of demand for industrial products which would be largely self-generating. Increased demand for goods would lead to increased demand for capital goods which would reinforce incomes, and so on. He regards this stage as a characteristic of an intermediate stage of development such as that achieved by Japan in the 1950s. Secondly, the export sector is exceedingly important as an initiating factor in the expansion of demand (cf. [1] and [6]).

What about a country that is not immature? In this case, Kaldor would regard the labour supply as constraining. This can happen for two reasons. First and rather obviously, certain sectors which are traditionally suppliers of labour run out and become very small in relation to total employment —agriculture and low productivity self-employment sectors especially. Secondly, wage and productivity differentials may be eliminated so that there is no longer any economic meachanism by which industry can attract the labour it needs for expansion. It is important to recognize that this stage can be reached even though it is *technologically* possible to remove labour from a sector without adversely affecting output. The lack of wage differentials would still make it impossible for industry to attract labour, unless special policy measures were adopted.

In his lecture, Kaldor suggested that the U.K. was 'mature' and that, in consequence, conditions had been much less favourable for fast growth than in many other countries. The implication he drew was that greater attention should be devoted to the efficient utilization of labour in all sectors of the economy, with a view to improving dynamic performance. It was his view that a fast rate of growth of manufacturing production is necessary for fast self-sustaining growth, and that in order to achieve this it might be necessary to encourage labour to move into industrial activities.

[14] The real output of many service activities—particularly in the public sector—is often measured by factor input. In such cases the idea of an employment/output relationship is meaningless.

[15] Time series data for the U.K. also suggest that there is no clear relationship between variations in output and variations in labour input in service sectors, such as Distribution.

8. Other Explanations

The previous sections have outlined some of the major strands of analysis that have been applied to the problem of why growth rates differ. But some analysts stress quite different aspects, focusing not so much on aggregative questions about the supply of resources or the development of exports or government policy, but on more microeconomic elements such as the degree of initiative or of innovation. It is particularly true that in discussions of the United Kingdom's poor performance, it is common to come across diagnoses which run in terms of poor innovative record, the inefficiency of British management, or the power of the British trade unions. It is even sometimes suggested that it is all to do with the British National Character—whatever that is.

It is as well to start by reiterating a caveat made at the beginning of this chapter. It is perfectly possible for inefficient economies to grow fast, and for efficient economies to grow slowly. In considering growth it is necessary to look for changes in efficiency over time or for those inefficiencies which might specifically affect growth performance. There is another problem. Objective factors such as the labour supply position did obviously differ greatly between countries. So, for example, did export competitiveness and exchange rate policy. It would, in fact, seem unreasonable to try and explain the larger differences between the United Kingdom and her competitors in terms of general sluggishness and inefficiency. There would still be a problem of explaining what led to the inefficiency—and it might be slow growth. But there may be something in these views, and certainly from a policy point of view, it is desirable that inefficiencies, if they exist, should be identified and eliminated.

One suggestion is that the low growth of productivity in the United Kingdom is due to inadequate expenditure on research and development. On the surface, however, there is fairly strong negative evidence. The United Kingdom spends a lot relative to European competitors, and, in fact, it is the two slowly growing countries, the United Kingdom and the United States, which seem to have concentrated most heavily in expenditure on research and development. However, it is possible to point to aspects of the British programme which appear unfavourable—such as the relative proportion spent on basic research compared with developmental work, and so on (for a useful survey of this aspect see [40]).

The most difficult assertions to test are those which suggest that the United Kingdom's growth rate is slow relative to competitors' due to the inefficiency of British management or the structure of labour relations. How should one measure the efficiency of a manager? Even more problematic is the question of how one should measure the supposedly adverse effect of Britain's complex industrial relations structure. One measurable aspect, the strike record, suggests that Britain was not particularly strike-prone compared with other countries (see, for example, [45]). Of course, the fact that influences are difficult to quantify does not mean that they are unimportant—only that we do not know how important they are. It does mean, however, that assertions about relative efficiency and its effects on growth should be treated with some scepticism.

9. Concluding Remarks

It should be clear that the problems involved in explaining why different economies have had such different growth rates do not arise because of a shortage of plausible explanations. Quite the contrary. But it is possible that some degree of consensus can be detected. It does appear that nearly every study that has examined structural shifts in the disposition of the labour force has found that they were important—though the weight given to such shifts varies greatly with the methodology adopted. In the fast-growing countries it would appear that the shifts that were observed may have been necessary or permissive factors on the supply side. If the potential for such shifts had not been there, perhaps fast growth would have been frustrated. It is possible, however, to interpret the shifts as originating on the side of supply, or of demand. On the supply-side view the shifts provided a large effective supply of labour which, by some mechanism, was then utilized. On the demand-side view the shifts themselves would be explained largely as a response to growth, rather than as a cause. Most studies also stress demand-side factors as a reason for fast growth. Explanations vary, of course—differing weights are given to expectations, to exports, to government policy, in the various studies —but there would appear to be reasonable agreement that fast growth needs favourable conditions on both demand and supply sides.

There is much less agreement on the reasons for slow growth. This is especially true of the reasons given for the slow rate of growth of the United Kingdom. Kaldor and Kindleberger both stress the labour supply situation. Others stress different supply-side factors such as a low level of investment, sluggish innovation, restrictive practices, and so on. But another group of explanations suggests that the problem does not arise on the supply side at all. Many argue that the low growth rate in the U.K. is due to unfavourable factors on the demand side. Of these explanations, the most common are those that stress the balance of payments position, or the exchange rate and the development of exports. (As noted above, if growth has been low for a long period it may easily appear supply-constrained even if it is not.)

Recent experience in the U.K. (and also in some other countries) may tend to favour the view that low growth in Britain is not due to any fundamental supply-side factor, such as a restricted labour supply. In the manufacturing sector, where there did appear to be a good relationship between employment and output, and hence the possibility of the operation of a labour constraint, productivity growth has recently accelerated as a result of 'shake-outs' of labour. The normal relationship between output change and employment change has broken down since the mid-1960s. The international cross-section evidence also suggests that there was little relationship between the growth of output and the growth of employment in the late 1960s and early 1970s. In a number of countries the absorption of labour in manufacturing has been substantially less, recently, than might have been expected on the basis of past experience. If the manufacturing sector can, in fact, grow fast without a fast rate of growth of labour input, then this means that the idea of a labour-constrained economy is much less plausible.

In fact, Kaldor, who, as noted, in 1966 propounded the view that a slow rate of growth of labour supply to manufacturing was the cause of Britain's problems, has, on the basis of evidence since then, modified his position. He still stresses the role of manufacturing production as the engine of growth, but diagnoses Britain's poor performance in terms of the wrong exchange rate policy (an over-valued pound) together with mistakes in demand management policy. (See, for example, [27] and [28].) In particular, he recommends 'export-led' expansion as a way to faster growth. It will be recalled that in the discussion of Keynesian problems above, it was suggested that a policy for growth would need to lead the way with investment. In practice, going for export-led growth via a managed exchange rate may be the only practicable way for an individual country to achieve an investment-led expansion. Meanwhile, in other countries, the world recession of 1974–5 has led to worries about the buoyancy of their investment expenditure.

No solution can be offered to the problem of the fundamental cause of Britain's problems. From a policy point of view it may not even matter very much, as improvement of export performance, and improvement of productivity at the industry level, are both well established as governmental policy objectives. Whatever the diagnosis, policy is likely to have to operate on both supply and demand sides of the problem if it is to be effective.

Bibliography

SECTION A

[1] BECKERMAN, W. and Associates. *The British Economy in 1975* (Cambridge University Press, 1965).
Part I presents information on Britain's comparative performance and develops the thesis of export-led growth.
[2] BOLTHO, A. *Japan: An Economic Survey 1953–73* (Oxford University Press, 1975).
An up-to-date and readable analysis of two decades of rapid growth in Japan.
[3] DENISON, E. F., assisted by POULIER, J.-P. *Why Growth Rates Differ* (Brookings Institution, 1967).
Probably the most influential book on comparative growth experience—described in the text. See also a summary of the United Kingdom position in [15] below.
[4] HARROD, R. F. *Economic Dynamics* (Macmillan, 1973).
A recent exposition of the Harrod growth model, and much else.
[5] KALDOR, N., *Causes of the Slow Rate of Growth of the United Kingdom* (Cambridge University Press, 1966).
Kaldor's controversial inaugural lecture. Should be read in conjunction with [26] and [28] below.
[6] KINDLEBERGER, C. P. *Europe's Post-War Growth: The Role of Labour Supply* (Harvard University Press and Oxford University Press, 1967).
An analysis of growth in Europe stressing the role of the labour supply—especially as a permissive factor allowing 'supergrowth' in some countries.
[7] KREGEL, J. A. *The Theory of Economic Growth*, Macmillan Studies in Economics (Macmillan, 1972).
A good non-technical introduction to modern growth theories.

[8] Sen, A. K. (ed.) *Growth Economics* (Penguin, 1970).
A collection of many of the most important articles on growth theory, with a very useful introduction by the editor.

SECTION B

[9] Aldcroft, D. H. and Fearon, P. (eds.) *Economic Growth in 20th-Century Britain* (Macmillan, 1969).

[10] Beckerman, W. 'Projecting Europe's Growth', *Economic Journal*, lxxii (Dec. 1962).

[11] —— (ed.) *The Labour Government's Economic Record 1964–1970* (Duckworth, 1972).

[12] Balassa, B. 'Some Observations on Mr. Beckerman's Export-Propelled Growth Model', *Economic Journal*, lxxiii (Dec. 1963).

[13] Caves, R. E. and Associates. *Britain's Economic Prospects* (Brookings Institution, 1968).

[14] Cripps, T. F. and Tarling, R. J. *Growth in Advanced Capitalist Economies 1950–1970* (Cambridge University Press, 1973).

[15] Denison, E. F. 'Economic Growth . . ., Chapter VI of [13] above.

[16] —— 'Some Major Issues in Productivity Analysis: An Examination of Estimates by Jorgenson and Griliches', *Survey of Current Business* (1969).

[17] Gomulka, S. *Inventive Activity, Diffusion and Stages of Economic Growth* (Aahus, 1971).

[18] Hahn, F. and Matthews, R. C. O. 'The Theory of Economic Growth: A Survey', *Economic Journal*, lxxiv, (Dec. 1964).

[19] Harrod, H. F. 'An Essay in Dynamic Theory', *Economic Journal*, xlix (Mar. 1939).

[20] Heathfield, D. F. *Production Functions*, Macmillan Studies in Economics (Macmillan, 1972).

[21] Henderson, P. D. (ed.) *Economic Growth in Britain* (Weidenfeld & Nicolson, 1966).

[22] Jones, H. *An Introduction to Modern Theories of Economic Growth* (Nelson, 1975).

[23] Jorgenson, D. W. and Griliches, Z. 'The Explanation of Productivity Change', *Review of Economic Studies* (July 1967).

[24] —— 'Issues in Growth Accounting. A Reply to Edward Denison', *Survey of Current Business* (1972).

[25] Kaldor, N. *Strategic Factors in Economic Development* (New York, 1967).

[26] —— 'Productivity and Growth in Manufacturing Industry: A Reply', *Economica*, xxxv (Nov. 1968).

[27] —— 'Conflicts in National Economic Objectives', *Economic Journal*, lxxxi (Mar. 1971).

[28] —— 'Economic Growth and the Verdoorn Law', *Economic Journal*, lxxxv (Dec. 1975).

[29] Kregel, J. A. *The Reconstruction of Political Economy. An Introduction to Post-Keynesian Economics* (Macmillan, 1973).

[30] Lewis, W. A. 'Economic Growth with Unlimited Supplies of Labour', *Manchester School* (Jan. 1958).

[31] Maddison, A. *Economic Growth in the West* (New York, Twentieth Century Fund, 1964).

[32] —— 'Explaining Economic Growth', *Banca Nazionale del Lavoro* (Sept. 1972).

[33] Matthews, R. C. O. 'Why has Britain had Full Employment Since the War?' *Economic Journal*, lxxviii (Sept. 1968).

[34] —— 'Why Growth Rates Differ', *Economic Journal*, lxxix (1969).

[35] —— 'Foreign Trade and British Economic Growth', *Scottish Journal of Political Economy* (Nov. 1973).

[36] Command 2764, The National Plan (H.M.S.O., Sept. 1965).

[37] OPIE, R. G. 'Economic Planning and Growth', in [11] above.

[38] Organization for Economic Co-operation and Development (O.E.C.D.). *The Growth of Output 1960–1980* (Paris, 1970).

[39] —— *The Outlook for Economic Growth* (Paris, 1970).

[40] PEAKER, A. *Economic Growth in Modern Britain*, Macmillan Studies in Economics (Macmillan, 1974).

[41] PRATTEN, C. F. 'Reasons for the Slow Progress of the British Economy', *Oxford Economic Papers* (July 1972).

[42] ROWTHORN, R. E. 'What Remains of Kaldor's Law?' *Economic Journal*, lxxxv (Mar. 1975).

[43] —— 'Reply to Lord Kaldor's Comment', *Economic Journal*, lxxxv (Dec. 1975).

[44] SOLOW, R. M. *Growth Theory: An Exposition* (Clarendon Press, 1970).

[45] TURNER, W. A. *Is Britain Really Strike Prone?* (Cambridge University Press, 1969).

[46] WOLFE, J. N. 'Productivity and Growth in Manufacturing', *Economica*, xxxv (May 1968).

[47] VICIAGO, G. 'Increasing Returns and Growth in Advanced Countries', *Oxford Economic Papers* (July 1975).

PART IV

9
Objectives and Instruments

A. W. M. GRAHAM

1. Introduction

People often lose sight of the fact that there is no point in decision-making unless one has some goal, or goals, in mind. The important thing is to assess realistically *what* one wants to achieve and *how* to achieve it. This chapter therefore looks at the economic objectives which industrialized societies have tried to pursue and the means which they have had available. Some of these are fairly obvious. Judged either by what governments said or by their success in elections most people would agree that providing reasonably full employment, raising the material standards of living, and keeping prices stable have all been important objectives for society throughout the post-war period (not that they have all been achieved). But there has been less agreement about how benefits from these policies should be shared within society. For example, in general the Labour party has wanted the distribution of income and wealth to be made more equal, whereas the Conservatives have placed more emphasis on the preservation of traditional values. The political parties have also disputed the degree of intervention by the State which is either desirable or necessary to achieve such goals as economic growth and greater equality. So although we may talk about economic policy, economic objectives, and economic instruments, all these are also deeply political. This chapter therefore considers whether it is possible to draw boundaries between the economic and the political and of whether or not the ends and means of policy are separable.

In discussing these questions it will be necessary to deal with the detail and confusion of the real world, though we must of course simplify and select in order to understand. But the real world is neither simple nor unchanging, and indeed its complexity may significantly alter our initial theoretical outline. The challenge for the good decision-taker is to find the correct mix between the generality of theory and the detail of real life. However, to examine both of these at once has obvious difficulties, so we begin with some theoretical simplifications.

2. The Theory of Economic Policy

In many textbooks economic policy (if it is discussed at all) is presented as merely a technical choice. In the simplest case society is said to have only one aim—to achieve the greatest economic welfare—and this is equated with maximizing consumption over time subject only to the physical constraints of the land and labour available, and the technological constraints of the existing stock of knowledge. In a more complex case society is assumed to have a number of objectives. The formulation of these and the individual weights to be given to them is seen as the subject-matter of politics, while the means of achieving them is regarded as economics. *What* people *want* is expressed at the ballot box and through the interpretations placed on the results by politicians. *How* the 'wants' are then put into practice is a technical matter for the economist.

This view of macroeconomic policy choice can be put into the same framework as that of individual choice outlined in Chapter 6. Where objectives conflict and trade-offs are involved the job of politicians is to interpret society's utility (or welfare) function. For example, faced with a choice between price stability and unemployment the politicians (acting on behalf of society) say how much of one they would be prepared to give up to gain more of the other. The economist then advises on how much of one it is necessary to give up in order to have more of the other. Politicians are concerned with the values, economists with the facts.

An alternative approach is the idea that specific policy instruments can be assigned to specific policy objectives (though the formulation of these objectives is still the job of politicians). In fact, the models of the economic system outlined in Part II already suggest the way this might be done. Thus changing taxes or government expenditure (fiscal policy) would be expected to alter the level of demand, output, and employment, but changing the exchange rate would be expected to alter the balance of payments. This thought has been developed into a rule (first formulated by Tinbergen) that one needs as many independent *instruments* of policy as one has independent *objectives*. For example, there is no reason why the level of demand which gives (1) full employment, should also give (2) equilibrium in the balance of payments, (3) price stability, or (4) adequate economic growth; and, by extension, there is no reason why an exchange rate policy to achieve (2) should also give (3) and (4). One could only be sure of being able to move towards four separate objectives if one has four independent instruments, e.g. demand management for full employment, the exchange rate for the balance of payments, an incomes policy for price stability, and tax incentives to investment for economic growth.

One other rather obvious, but important, point ought to be made at this stage. Discussion of economic policy is often unnecessarily confused by a failure to distinguish genuine policy instruments from other variables, which may be no more than part of the causal link between the instrument and the objective. For example, higher investment in the private sector may be a means of achieving economic growth, and greater retention of profits may encourage investment, but neither investment in the private sector nor retained profits is a policy instrument, because they are not directly within the Government's control. What we need is a way of *starting* the chain of causation. In this case a possible *instrument* of policy would be the introduction of different tax rates on retained and distributed profits.

The importance of this last point can be appreciated if one asks whether it is correct to regard an incomes policy as an instrument. If a government has the support of its back-benchers (which cannot always be taken for granted) it can legislate for controls on prices, wages, dividends, etc. These controls, if combined with the co-operation of employers and employees, would constitute an incomes policy. However, if unions and firms only acquiesce to controls, and with increasing reluctance, there will come a point when the Government no longer has a workable policy instrument.

In addition, although policy instruments like raising taxes or cutting public expenditure are within the Government's control, it is only possible to give effect to them by raising particular taxes or cutting particular forms of expenditure. Do we change direct or indirect taxes, and if direct, income tax or corporation tax, and if income tax, which rates? Such decisions may be of subsidiary importance in terms of controlling aggregate demand, but nevertheless have important implications for the distribution of income between individuals and groups and for the pattern of output between industries and regions.

The situation would therefore appear as follows: with any given model of the economic system, certain causal relationships will be implied between the exogenous (or independent) elements and the endogenous (or dependent) elements. Some of the endogenous elements are objectives and some of the exogenous elements are policy variables. The role of economic policy (once politicians have determined the desired levels for the objectives) is therefore (a) to predict those exogenous elements which are not instruments of policy (e.g. the level of world trade); (b) to set the policy instruments at those levels which, combined with the other exogenous elements, give the desired outcome; (c) if this leaves any of the objectives either at an unsatisfactory level, or undetermined, to introduce an extra instrument which impinges particularly on that objective. According to this account once he has the relevant set—of objectives, causal links, and predictions—the economist's job is complete.

3. Complexities and the Real World

In the real world life is more complex. In what follows three concepts should be remembered:

(i) Objectives—these are what we want to achieve (e.g. more output).
(ii) Instruments—we use these to affect the economy in order to achieve the objectives. They must be within the Government's power to implement (e.g. higher taxes).
(iii) Constraints—these are conditions that cannot be broken while we try to achieve the objectives (e.g. not running out of foreign exchange).

However, we must also remember the difficulties. We may have many objectives and they may conflict with each other. There is disagreement about what the objectives ought to be and on their relative importance.

There are many instruments and some instruments may also be seen as objectives—and vice versa. There may also be ignorance of, and disagreements about, the causal relationships which link instruments to objectives. And even where the direction of causality is agreed there is frequently uncertainty about the magnitudes and the time-lags involved. Finally, constraints can be of many kinds—political and social as well as economic.

3.1. Multiple Objectives

The objectives which governments have been held responsible for in the post-war period would be agreed generally to include:

   (a) full employment
   (b) maintenance of a *high* standard of living (i.e. consumption now)
   (c) achievement of a *rising* standard of living (i.e. economic growth to give more consumption over time)
   (d) price stability
   (e) equilibrium in the balance of payments.

Some economists argue that (e) should be thought of as a constraint rather than an objective, on the grounds that equilibrium in the balance of payments is not desired for its own sake (in fact, consumption can be higher when there is a deficit), but that it is impossible in the long run to be constantly borrowing. Taking this view to extremes one could say that only maximizing consumption over time is an ultimate objective and that all the others are merely constraints on, or means to, this end. For example, the desire for present consumption acts as a limit on investment, and full employment is one requirement for maximizing output. But no matter how logical this view, it is none the less a false description of how governments and their electorates have behaved. Many people regard both full employment and price stability as objectives in their own right, and governments have clearly acted as if choosing between conflicting objectives. Indeed, for much of the post-war period additional objectives which governments have pursued include:

   (f) liberalization of trade
   (g) liberalization of capital movements
   (h) maintenance of a stable exchange rate
   (i) a more equitable balance of output between the different regions of the economy
   (j) greater equality in the distribution of (i) income, and (ii) wealth.

And, of course, the more objectives there are the greater are the number of potential conflicts and the less likely it is that they can be achieved simultaneously.

3.2. Conflicts between Objectives

Many of the conflicts are obvious both at a theoretical and empirical level. At full employment, consumption *now* conflicts with investment now. Liberalization of trade and capital movements may conflict with equilibrium in the balance of payments. Greater equality of income may be incompatible with the desire for more output (if high marginal tax rates act as a disincentive). Regional balance may conflict with economic growth. Full employment has increasingly conflicted with price stability. And full employment plus a stable exchange rate has created balance of payments problems.

Further difficulties can appear when the objectives are analysed more closely. For example, if full employment is taken to include job security this will result in a degree of inflexibility which may well reduce the possible *growth* of output. Thus, in principle, there could be at least four target levels of employment, (i) to give price stability, (ii) to give equilibrium in the balance of payments, (iii) to maximize growth, and (iv) to maximize present output. The problem for the policy-maker is, firstly, that there is no reason why these should necessarily coincide; secondly, that rather little is known in practice about the levels required (these will depend on the particular historical circumstances and on the other policies being pursued); and thirdly, none may be the socially desirable level.

3.3. The Formulation of Objectives

In the account given earlier in section 2 above, objectives were formulated exogenously by the politicians, acting on behalf of the electorate. But, in practice, objectives are determined within society. Politicians and the electorate will both be influenced by their own experiences, by various interpretations of the past, and by both theoretical and wishful thinking about what is possible for the future. For example, Beveridge, remembering the high unemployment of the interwar years, stated in 1944 that full employment was represented by a national unemployment rate of 3 per cent. In contrast by the early 1960s there had been twenty years of unemployment close to 2 per cent and the Keynesian revolution in economics had become part of the conventional wisdom. As a result, a level of 3 per cent was regarded as a disaster. Still more recently priority has shifted to price stability and the level of unemployment has been allowed to rise. Moreover, faced with this apparent conflict between full employment and price stability the trade unions have been willing to co-operate in incomes policies and to abandon (temporarily at least) free collective bargaining. However, a Marxist interpretation of history would argue that this unemployment/price stability experience is a symptom of a deeper conflict of interest between the proletariat and the capitalists that is irreconcilable within the existing social and economic structure—in which case the objective is nothing less than the transformation of society.

Objectives cannot therefore be thought of as wholly separate from the analysis of the situation. Fact and value are interdependent, not independent. Indeed, a potential source of frustration in society is created when aims become unrelated to a realistic analysis and the gap between the desired and the possible becomes too great. This may have been the case in the U.K. in the post-war period when it increased the number of its objectives (full employment, growth, and regional balance were all added to the inherited objectives of a fixed exchange rate and freedom of external payments) at a time when the war had made the U.K. financially and economically much weaker.

3.4. Multiple Instruments

To achieve their objectives governments have a range of instruments. These derive from the following four sources:

(i) *Fiscal powers*. This is the power of the purse. It allows a government to levy taxes and to undertake expenditure (see particularly Chapter 11 on fiscal policy). Its forms are many and varied. It includes not only direct and indirect taxation, but also all government expenditure whether in the form of direct purchases of goods and services or in the form of transfers to individuals (e.g. pensions), to firms (e.g. investment grants), or to regions (e.g. regional employment premiums).

(ii) *Monetary powers*. The Government via the Central Bank is the monopoly supplier of legal currency. This allows it to influence the quantity and price of credit (see Chapter 12). In addition, the Central Bank is the manager of the country's foreign exchange reserves. It therefore regulates foreign exchange transactions and influences the exchange rate (see Chapter 5).

(iii) *Public ownership*. The Government owns the nationalized industries and has a controlling interest in some companies. In these sectors it can therefore directly influence pricing, investment, and employment policies (see Chapter 18).

(iv) *Legal powers*. Broadly speaking there are two forms:

    (a) The creation of a *legal framework* within which the private sector operates (e.g. Monopolies and Mergers legislation, and the Restrictive Trades Practices Court). (See Chapter 16.)

    (b) The regulation of specific activities via *direct controls*. These range from traffic regulations through wage and price legislation to the extensive controls of a wartime economy.

These instruments and their relationship to objectives are considered in greater detail in later chapters. However, there is a more general point. In virtually all areas of policy there is a choice between using direct controls and/or using instruments simply to change relative prices. Should consumption be lowered by imposing rationing or by raising taxes? Should firms be encouraged to move from congested regions by requiring Industrial Development Certificates to be applied for or by investment incentives? (See Chapter 19.) Should a balance of payments deficit be corrected by introducing import quotas or by changing the exchange rate?

Unfortunately there is no 'right' answer to these questions. The main case for using relative prices is that this best takes account of the preferences of consumers and firms. Taxes (or subsidies) affect decisions at the margin so that in response to a price rise it is the marginal units which are foregone. A strong preference for a product can, therefore, still be expressed. This, however, does not take account of *ability* (as opposed to willingness) to pay. Direct controls, by constraining the rich, may therefore be more equitable in some cases (e.g. food rationing). On the other hand, direct controls affect everyone concerned, irrespective of their particular needs or circumstances and do not allow the individual to decide. The other argument for direct controls is that sometimes they may be more efficacious. Potentially, therefore, we have three considerations. Firstly, does the State or the individual know best? Secondly, what importance do we attach to achieving certainty of effect? And thirdly, is equity or efficiency more important? Given these considerations we can make the following generalizations. First, direct controls are most effective where society as a whole has a clear objective (as in wartime), but are least appropriate where goals are diverse and information is decentralized. Second, direct controls are normally only worth serious consideration where the quantity of some activity needs to be reduced—they cannot usually initiate new activities. Third, arguments based on equity will be relatively more important when income is thought to have been inadequately redistributed by fiscal means. However, the very nature of these generalizations makes it obvious that selecting instruments is not just a technical matter for economists.

3.5. Instruments can be Objectives and vice versa

Some instruments are themselves objectives. This was the case with the exchange rate in the 1960s, but there are many other examples. In the 1970s public ownership has played a similar role. This can certainly be an instrument of economic policy towards, say, greater investment, but for some is also an end in itself. In addition, some people want equality of incomes for its own sake, others see greater equality as a means of reducing the conflicts in society.

3.6. The Boundaries of Politics and Economics

If ends and means overlap then any dividing line between politics and economics is already very blurred. This ought not to be surprising. One of the main concerns of economics is the allocation of resources. But in all societies resources are allocated in varying degrees by two very different processes: by the State and by the market place. Quite different principles underlie these. In the ballot box one man's vote is as good as another's, but the correlation between the wishes lying behind the ballot box and decisions by the State may be weak or non-existent. In the market place one man's pound is as good as another's, but some people have greater income or wealth than others. The dividing-line between politics and economics, and indeed whether there is any such line, is therefore the concern of both politicians and economists and is always, in principle, disputable. The relevance of this for economic policy is twofold. First, the *range* of policy instruments and the particular policy instruments which we use, are, at least partly, a matter for political judgement and debate. Second, the frequency of disagreement about economic policy may be as much the result of (hidden) disputes about the importance to be attached to different objectives as to differing views about the causal relationships. Political issues are often involved even when the subject-matter appears to be purely technical economics.

3.7. Instruments, Objectives, and Models

To be clear about instruments and about objectives we need a series of causal relationships (i.e. a model) which links one to the other. However, most policy instruments affect many objectives. For example, changing the exchange rate will alter not only the balance of payments, but also the level of demand and the level of prices; it will shift output between industries, and change the distribution of income between profits and wages. This means that it may be arbitrary to assign one instrument to one objective (as the strongest form of Tinbergen's approach requires). It may also be difficult to identify these relationships. There are three reasons for this. First, as we shall see in later chapters (particularly Chapter 12 on monetary policy), different models of the economy imply different primary relationships. Second, causation can never be proved. Third, there is no necessary reason to assume that because an economy behaved in a particular way in the past it will repeat that behaviour in the future. Under different historical circumstances (see section 3.9 of this chapter below) the patterns of causation may alter.

3.8. Constraints and Time Scales

In the real world, constraints are the most difficult problem of all for economic policy. What are we to take as 'given'? What is it possible to change? Closely related to this is the time horizon. Many constraints can be relaxed by a policy decision (the law can be changed, new institutions can be established, etc.). But some policies take a long time to implement, others a long time to have their effects. For example, in the U.K. it is helpful to distinguish the following:

(a) short-term forecasts and budgetary policies aimed at controlling the level of unemployment and the balance of payments over the next 2 to 3 years;

(b) medium-term planning and public expenditure decisions looking 4 to 5 years ahead. On this time scale the achievement of the target level of unemployment and the need to balance the external accounts are both taken as given, and decisions focus on the allocation of resources between consumption and investment and between public and private use;

(c) longer-term industrial and social planning for 5 to 10 years ahead and aimed at the supply side of the economy and the social and institutional structure.

In other words, the further ahead one is looking the greater is the room for manœuvre. On the other hand, looking into the future is a hazardous business, and saying how the future might be *changed* is even more speculative.

Beyond this there is rather little of a general nature that can be said. Most constraints are particular to particular situations. What we can do, however, is indicate the types of constraints and the ways in which these might influence policy.

(i) *Economic*. Economic constraints are the physical quantities of the existing land, labour, capital, and the state of technical knowledge. They also include the need to balance the external accounts. How binding this is as a constraint depends on the level of the country's reserves and its potential borrowing facilities. (The latter is difficult to judge as under I.M.F. rules and now also under E.E.C. rules, it is possible to borrow successive 'tranches' only at the cost of increasing surveillance of the conduct of economic policy by the respective international bodies.) In addition, in the real world economic constraints include the cost of changing policy.

(ii) *Political.* At a technical level the major political constraint is the need for a majority in the Cabinet, and, if legislation is required, in the House of Commons. More generally, political parties are elected, in part, as a result of advocating particular objectives and particular policies. These commitments cannot simply be discarded the day after an election. Democracy requires *some* correlation between promises and action. And a government's room for manœuvre is almost always constrained by the need for popular support, particularly when approaching an election which in the U.K. cannot be delayed more than five years. One almost inevitable result of this is that more attention is given to the short-term than to medium- and longer-term policies.

(iii) *Social.* Social constraints are many and varied, ranging from traditions surrounding the family, social group, or job, to general concepts of fairness. Policies to increase the labour force may be constrained by attitudes towards the employment of women or immigrant labour. Regional policy may be constrained by the conservatism of employers (unwilling to establish new sites) and by employees with close family or community ties unwilling to move job location. Attempts to change long-established traditions can have distressingly small or even perverse consequences. The U.S.S.R. discovered this to its cost—when it introduced collectivization in the 1920s the peasantry responded by slaughtering the livestock. And the Conservatives who hoped to reduce strikes and the power of militants by insisting on ballots among union members found that the ballots invariably displayed strong loyalty by trade unionists towards their leaders.

(iv) *Institutional.* Institutional forms are central to much of economic policy —as the insistence of trade unions on the maintenance of free collective bargaining makes clear. More generally, the power of the T.U.C. *vis-à-vis* the unions, the relationship of the Nationalized Industries and the Local Authorities to departments in Whitehall and to Ministers, bodies such as the Monopolies and Mergers Commission and the National Enterprise Board, the contacts between the banking system and the Bank of England, all affect what economic policy is implemented, how it is implemented, and what effects it has. These cannot be abolished overnight, and new laws are by no means sufficient to change an institution as the case of the Industrial Relations Act illustrated.

(v) *Legal.* All governments are constrained by the legislation of their predecessors and by international law (see (vi) below). Many of the bodies referred to above have powers legally vested in them. For example, about half of government expenditure on goods and services is controlled by the local authorities and central government influence on this is, at best, indirect. New domestic legislation can be introduced but this takes parliamentary time, and everything cannot be changed at the same time.

(vi) *International*. Finally, the U.K. is a member of a series of overlapping international institutions, e.g. the International Monetary Fund, the United Nations, the European Economic Community, and the Organization for Economic Co-operation and Development. And it is a signatory of still more international conventions (e.g. the General Agreement on Tariffs and Trade). Each of these has its own charter or treaty (e.g. the Treaty of Rome) and each of them constrains the U.K. either *de facto* or *de jure*. At the same time these institutions constrain other countries. Whether or not these systems of mutual restraint and co-operation are in the U.K.'s interest in particular circumstances is often difficult to judge, but what is certain is that economic policy must take them increasingly into account.

3.9. The Historical Context

To formulate economic policy we need to generalize and to predict. However, the historical context is always unique and our generalizations and predictions may therefore mislead more than they illuminate. To guard against this we must constantly question our assumptions and allow for changing behaviour. To take just one example: Chapter 7 on inflation has illustrated that there are good reasons for thinking that the commitment to full employment has radically altered the operation of the labour market. In addition, even where the direction of causation remains the same, time-lags can be very different if expectations change. In other words, we have come full circle. We emphasized earlier the need to know the impact of a policy instrument upon an objective and said that this depended upon our model of the economy. But behavioural relationships change over time, and once useful models become inappropriate. Moreover, sometimes this occurs simply because of feedback from the initial government intervention.

3.10. Uncertainty

The Government is never fully in control of the situation and cannot be. An open economy is part of a world most of which is outside its control. In addition, even within the economy there are many unpredictable factors. The magnitude, the timing, and sometimes even the direction of policy effects may therefore be uncertain. Moreover, even when economic relationships behave as predicted, there may still be a major strike, a war, or a discovery of new natural resources, which could not possibly have been foreseen, and which throws the economy off course.

3.11. The Need for a Strategy

All these features mean that economic policy is *not* a neat mechanistic choice about the correct levels of policy instruments. Rather it is the attempt to pick one's way forward from a present which is highly constrained to a future which is highly uncertain. Policy must be seen as a package—as a strategy. Moreover, given uncertainty we must ask how sensitive any given strategy is to particular assumptions—and what happens if these assumptions go wrong. What contingency plans do we have and what do these assume? Policy formulation is incomplete without an analysis of the risks.

4. Simplicity and Complexity: An Example

Many of the points made above will be clarified if we take a specific problem and look especially at:

(a) The *theoretical framework* applicable to such a problem in order to see the simplification, and thus the insight provided by theory.

(b) The same problem in *particular historical circumstances* to see how the real world modifies and complicates the analysis.

4.1. Simplicity: The Theory

Consider a government with two objectives—full employment and equilibrium in its balance of payments. The models of Part II tell us that fiscal policy can be used to control aggregate real domestic demand, and that by controlling demand we can raise or lower unemployment. In addition, changing aggregate demand affects the demand for imports and hence the balance of payments. Thus reflation makes unemployment lower but imports higher and the balance of payments worse.

The models of Part II also tell us that the exchange rate can be used to *switch* expenditure away from or towards domestic production by altering relative prices. Thus following a devaluation, domestic production becomes relatively cheaper, domestic consumers buy fewer imports, and foreign consumers switch towards our exports. As a result, aggregate demand increases and unemployment falls, and the balance of payments probably improves. (This improvement requires (a) that the price elasticities of exports and imports are large enough to induce changes in volume which more than offset the price changes, and (b) that net domestic savings rise—with more resources going to foreigners less is available domestically.)

These two arguments may be summarized as follows (horizontal arrows indicate causation, vertical arrows changes):

(a) reflation → *domestic* demand ↑ →
$$\begin{cases} \text{unemployment} \downarrow \\ \text{import volume (income effects)} \uparrow \end{cases}$$

(b) devaluation → $\begin{cases} \text{export prices in \$} \downarrow \to \text{export volume} \uparrow \\ \text{import prices in £} \uparrow \to \text{import volume} \downarrow \end{cases} \to$

aggregate demand ↑ → $\begin{cases} \text{unemployment} \downarrow \\ \text{import volume} \uparrow \end{cases}$

Thus, while reflation lowers unemployment and worsens the balance of payments, devaluation lowers unemployment and improves the balance of payments. These two sets of relationships can be depicted diagrammatically as in Figure 9.1. In this the vertical axis represents the relative price of foreign to home production. Devaluation moves us upwards and revaluation downwards. The horizontal axis represents real domestic demand (C+ I + G). Reflation moves us to the right, deflation to the left.

Now suppose that the centre point (o) represents both internal equilibrium (full employment) and external equilibrium (a satisfactory balance of payments). The model described above predicts that deflation lowers output and improves the balance of payments. In the figure, starting at o (i.e. equilibrium) deflation will move us leftwards, e.g. to point X. X must therefore represent unemployment and a balance of payments surplus. All other points in the figure can be deduced by similar reasoning. Z, for example, indicates very high domestic prices relative to foreign prices, lack of international competitiveness, and so unemployment and a balance of payments deficit.

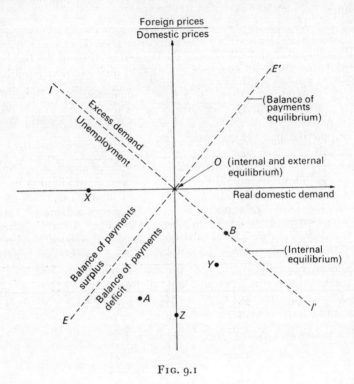

FIG. 9.1

We can therefore trace out a curve II' to show the *mix* of policies which would leave aggregate demand unchanged[1] and a curve EE' which would leave the balance of payments unchanged (reflation and devaluation have opposite effects on the balance of payments, and there is therefore a combination of them, shown by a north-easterly line, which maintains external equilibrium). Thus points above II' represent excess demand and below it unemployment; points above EE' a balance of payments surplus and below it a deficit.

This model immediately makes Tinbergen's point clear. At any point Y (with unemployment and a deficit) one can only obtain the twin objectives of internal and external equilibrium (represented by point o) by using the

[1] Only *aggregate* demand remains unchanged. At each point on the curve a given level of aggregate demand consists of differing proportions of domestic demand (C + I + G) and net foreign demand (X − M).

two instruments of devaluation and deflation. It is only in the special, and unlikely, case of points such as X and Z that one policy would be sufficient. However, we should note that although a point such as A (which has the same basic characteristics as point Y of unemployment and a deficit) still requires *two* policies, the policies are *different*. This time devaluation and *reflation* are required. One other important lesson emerges. If we observe a deficit *and* full employment (e.g. point B) this can only be corrected provided that expenditure switching is combined with the reduction of domestic expenditure.

We can now use this theoretical framework to provide an insight into the U.K.'s economic problems of the 1950s and early 1960s. The data in Table 9.1 shows unemployment and the level of the current account of the balance of payments. Using these as measures of internal and external equilibrium respectively, a pattern emerges of the U.K. oscillating from full employment in the years 1954, 1955, 1960, and 1964 to equilibrium in the balance of payments in 1957, 1962, 1963, and 1966. But there is increasing conflict

TABLE 9.1. *Alternative Measures of Internal and External Equilibrium 1954–74*

	(1)		(2)	(3)	(4)	(5)	(6)
	Unemployment in G.B.		Vacancies in G.B.	Visible Balance	Current Balance	Balance of Current and Long-Term Capital	Total Currency Flow
	(000's)	%	(000's)	£m.	£m.	£m.	£m.
1954	272	1·3	247	−204	+117	−74	+126
1955	209	1·0	305	−313	−155	−277	−229
1956	226	1·0	263	+53	+208	+21	−159
1957	289	1·3	185	−29	+233	+127	+13
1958	402	1·9	136	+29	+344	+148	+290
1959	433	2·0	157	−117	+152	−103	+18
1960	337	1·5	212	−406	−255	−447	+325
1961	305	1·3	213	−152	+6	+74	−339
1962	419	1·8	149	−102	+122	+24	+192
1963	502	2·2	144	−80	+124	−31	−58
1964	362	1·6	221	−498	−353	−710	−695
1965	308	1·3	265	−223	−27	−254	−353
1966	323	1·4	255	−64	+103	+18	−547
1967	510	2·2	174	−554	−300	−401	−671
1968	538	2·3	188	−666	−274	−402	−1410
1969	531	2·3	200	−147	+460	+355	+743
1970	568	2·5	186	−11	+698	+444	+1287
1971	737	3·3	129	+274	+1052	+1135	+3228
1972	816	3·6	145	−683	+82	−679	−1265
1973	581	2·6	304	−2301	−1113	−1030	+210
1974	572	2·5	298	−5259	−3771	−2595	−565

Sources: *Economic Trends*; *U.K. Balance of Payments*; *Department of Employment Gazette*.

between these objectives. The deficits get successively larger and unemployment successively higher.

Although any precise representation on our original figure is arbitrary, the situation might look roughly as in Figure 9.2. The reason for the conflict is then very obvious. First, the U.K. had a fixed exchange rate and (with the exception of the import surcharge in 1965 and 1966) was only using the single policy instrument of reflation/deflation (this was the period known as 'stop–go'). Second, the U.K. was tending to inflate faster than other countries so that with a fixed exchange rate her competitiveness was decreasing.

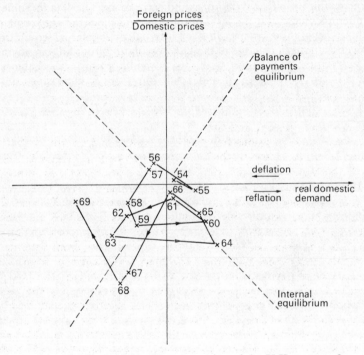

FIG. 9.2. An Approximate Representation of the U.K. 1954–1969.

Thus the U.K. moved gradually down the vertical axis of Figure 9.2 and away from equilibrium. Eventually, devaluation to offset this became inevitable.

4.2. Complexity: The U.K. 1954–74

The theoretical framework above has provided some lessons and some insights into the real world—as good theory should. But we must beware of applying any theory too rapidly to particular situations. We need to look more closely at the particular context and at the problems of applying the theory to the real world.

Deciding on objectives and how to measure them is the first problem.

Some alternative measurements of external and internal equilibrium are offered in Table 9.1. (Before proceeding the reader should consult this and consider for himself which measures he would use, why he would use them, and what implications for policy follow from different choices.) For example, is internal equilibrium to be measured by the level of unemployment, or by the number of job vacancies, or defined by equality of the two?[2] Are these indicators of the labour market the relevant ones for measuring internal equilibrium? Or should one examine product market indicators, e.g. order books, and/or indices of capacity utilization? (Remember: there is no guarantee that different indicators will point in the same direction.) Similar difficulties occur with external equilibrium. Should we use the visible trade account, or the current account, or current and long-term capital combined, or the total currency flow? Even when the measure of the objectives is settled there is still a decision about the appropriate level. If unemployment is the measure of internal equilibrium, should it be 1 per cent, 2 per cent, 3 per cent, or 4 per cent? If the state of the current account is the measure of external equilibrium should it be in balance, or in surplus (to pay off previous debts), or in deficit (because others are certain to run large surpluses, e.g. the oil producers in 1974 and 1975)?

To answer these questions fully would require a major study of the U.K. in particular years. However, the following points may be helpful in illustrating how the historical context may alter our initial theoretical framework.

(i) *Sterling as a Reserve Currency*. No account is taken in the model of sterling's role (alongside the dollar) as a major reserve currency. Because of this banking role there can be large capital movements in the U.K.'s balance of payments, which are entirely unrelated to the U.K.'s domestic situation or its trading account position. Such movements may arise from interest rate differentials, from expectations about exchange rate changes, or from changes in the balance of payments on current account of countries who hold their reserves in London (in the 1950s and 1960s these were mainly the 'sterling area' countries which pegged their currencies to sterling and held their reserves at the Bank of England). From this viewpoint the rational approach would be to ignore capital movements in defining external equilibrium for the U.K. (since they are not necessarily a direct function either of U.K. fiscal policy or of the *level* of the U.K. exchange rate). However, it is possible to do this if, and only if, at least one of the following three conditions is satisfied: (a) that the U.K. has sufficient liquid assets (i.e. realizable in the short term) to finance the withdrawal of liquid liabilities, (b) that the withdrawal of such funds is automatically offset by changes in other parts of the balance of payments, or (c) that the withdrawal of funds can be offset by raising U.K. interest rates.

For most of the period under discussion condition (a) was *not* satisfied.[3]

---

[2] Many students choose the last. However, we know that many vacancies are not reported, and many of the unemployed are not registered—and even if the figures were quite accurate it is not clear that the equality of one with the other has any particular significance.

[3] The one minor qualification is that under the Basle Agreement of 1968 a group of Central Banks agreed (on certain conditions) to finance withdrawals of sterling.

The U.K.'s gold and convertible currency reserves were consistently less than her short-term liabilities, and the position was worsening because in most years there was a deficit on the long-term capital account which the U.K. financed by more short-term borrowing. This was profitable, but made the U.K. increasingly vulnerable. In contrast, during the 1950s and the first few years of the 1960s, condition (b) was partially satisfied because of the balance of payments pattern of the sterling area, i.e. when the U.K. was in deficit on current account with the non-sterling area (and so losing dollar reserves), the other sterling area countries tended to be in surplus (and so gaining dollar reserves)—and vice-versa. The actual loss of foreign currency reserves from London was therefore minimized. For most of the 1950s condition (c) was also satisfied. The U.K. was not expected to devalue (except during a brief period in 1957) and raising U.K. interest rates was therefore an effective way of attracting funds. However, by the middle of the 1960s the situation had changed. As the sterling area countries industrialized, their balance of payments movements began to coincide with the U.K.'s—thus exacerbating the reserve losses. In addition, the U.K.'s recurrent balance of payments deficit on current account increased the expectation of a devaluation. As a result neither condition (a), nor (b), nor (c) was fulfilled and U.K. policy-makers were forced to shift away from their 1964 policy of gradually correct-in the current account deficit to their policy of 1967-9 of rapidly eliminating the reserve losses. The policy objective changed and the time scale shortened.

The reserve currency role of sterling coupled with the low level of U.K. reserves acted as a further constraint on policy. Since the capital account is partly a function of the *future* level of the exchange rate, policy-makers worried that lowering the exchange rate (after many years of a fixed rate) might cause holders of sterling to become more pessimistic. If this occurred, they feared that speculative outflows (which could not be offset from the reserves) might cause the exchange rate to fall much further than was justified by the U.K.'s trading position, so creating a new disequilibrium.

(ii) *Price Stability, Incomes Policy, and Growth.* The model also needs modification to take account of price and wage behaviour. U.K. prices appear on the vertical axis in Figure 9.2. Implicitly, therefore, the model assumes either that the level of unemployment which we desire for internal equilibrium also happens to give us price stability, or that U.K. wages and prices are formulated independently of both the level of demand and of the exchange rate. Neither of these seems accurate. British governments and their electorates have been unwilling to tolerate the levels of unemployment necessary to produce price stability and British trade unions appear to react to rising import prices by pressing higher wage claims. At the very least we therefore need to qualify the conclusion reached above that we should devalue to offset the U.K.'s tendency to inflate faster than other countries. This may work in the short run, but in the long run the devaluation may itself add to the inflation. Partly for this reason the Labour party from 1964 (and the Conservatives from 1972) tried to establish an Incomes Policy. If successful, this reduces the need to use unemployment to achieve price stability, and if it brings the rate of growth of domestic prices down below that of foreign prices, it also acts like a slow devaluation—which, in the political circumstances of 1964, was what the Labour Government wanted.

Another omission from our model is any mention of the U.K.'s longer-term industrial decline relative to her main competitors. This is obviously of importance if competitiveness depends not just on price but also on technical progress. In practice, both parties tried (though by different means) to deal with this through industrial policies aimed at raising investment, innovation, and productivity. Indeed, incomes policy and industrial policy were supposed to be complementary means of improving the U.K.'s competitiveness, the first by slowing down the growth in wage costs, the second by raising output per man (both in quantity and quality). In addition, a high level of demand was regarded as desirable in order to encourage investment and to increase the acceptability of incomes policy. But industrial policies take a long time to bring benefits, incomes policies are difficult to achieve, and maintaining a high level of demand by allowing domestic demand to expand increases the likelihood that the balance of payments will remain in deficit, which in turn makes it more difficult to maintain the exchange rate.

(iii) *Constraints.* In addition to the problems imposed on the U.K. by the reserve currency role of sterling there were at least two other constraints which no economic model can capture:

(a) From 1964 to 1966 the Labour party had a majority of only 3 and an early election was inevitable. Moreover, it had been elected on an 'anti-stop–go' platform. Although devaluation plus deflation would have made it possible to maintain full employment, the small majority meant that it would have been political suicide to impose the resultant rapid cut in real wages. Moreover, most people would have confused this with 'stop–go'. Financing the balance of payments deficit in order to correct it only slowly therefore seemed the only political option.

(b) The alternative to devaluation was incomes policy. But all attempts to establish voluntary incomes policies were handicapped by a relatively weak T.U.C. and Trades Union movement—in the sense that the T.U.C. was unwilling or unable to ask for restraints on money wages or on normal forms of collective bargaining.

(iv) *Analysis and Forecasting.* Finally, the experience of the U.K. in this period reminds us of three further hazards of policy-making in the real world. To make sensible policy decisions one needs:

(a) An accurate *diagnosis.* We may observe unemployment and a deficit in the balance of payments but our model does not tell us whether this is the result of too high an exchange rate or of a slump in world trade. To even begin to decide this we need accurate and up-to-date information (both of which are often sadly lacking).

(b) A *forecast* of what would happen in the absence of policy, e.g. will world trade recover? Will import prices rise? If companies are being squeezed financially will they react by reducing stocks, cutting investment plans, laying off manpower, or by raising prices? In the U.K., forecasts have often been seriously misleading—and events such as the Middle East War in 1967 or the oil price rise of 1973 can make even the best of forecasts almost useless.

(c) An *assessment* of the impact of a policy—its magnitude, direction, and timing. In practice, we have no such precision. The higher levels of unemployment after 1968 were accompanied by higher levels of inflation (contrary to what many economists expected), and the Conservatives' attempt at legal reform of the trade unions was wholly negated by the hostility it created.

This analysis of the U.K. has necessarily been brief, but even the small complexity considered here has changed our simple model almost out of recognition. Crudely, one might say that the failure of the Labour party from 1964 to 1970, and of the Conservatives after 1970, was not that they left devaluation too late (as our simple model seemed to imply) but that they failed to precede this with a workable incomes policy. But the failure to establish an incomes policy is itself only a reflection of deeper questions about the relations between governments, firms, and trade unions operating in a democracy. It may be nearer the truth to say that both governments came to power overestimating the extent to which they could introduce new policies. They were constrained by the economic situation, by the demands of society, and by the 'conventional wisdom' of the Civil Service. In addition, they had too many prior policy commitments, placed too much faith on policies which were largely unproven, and made too little allowance for the risks and uncertainties in their strategies.

5. Conclusions

At this level of generality it is impossible to lay down precise rules or to teach one *how* to reach decisions—and economics can never tell one *what* to decide. It can, however, suggest ways of thinking about problems: conceptual frameworks within which information can be organized and facts and objectives assessed. The very action of doing this may itself suggest what is to be done. Much of this chapter may not have seemed like economics at all, but at times more like politics, or management, or common sense. This should not be surprising. Management of the economy ought to involve all three. Moreover, it is inevitable that there can be no real dividing-line between politics and economics. As society's goals change, or become more obviously in conflict—as has occurred recently between full employment and price stability— so the balance may shift between decisions taken by the individual and decisions taken collectively by the State. And the peaceful reconciliation of these interests is itself an objective of economic policy.

To summarize: deciding on economic policy ought to be an iterative process. Objectives are formulated in the light of past experience and then assessed against the means available for achieving them. If the initial set of objectives is unobtainable, either the objectives must be revised, or new instruments to achieve them be introduced, or constraints (originally taken as given) relaxed, and the situation reconsidered. To assess the objectives and their relation to particular policies requires a view of the causal links involved—a model—with estimates of the quantitative relationships and the time scales. But this is not sufficient to decide on a strategy. Our control of the situation is incomplete, our interpretation of the past is debatable, our knowledge of the future is uncertain, and many of our estimates are judgemental. Thus we must try to examine the plausibility of alternative views of the world and assess how well they correspond to reality—a task which is both theoretically and empirically demanding. Finally, in choosing a strategy we should ask (1) what risks do alternative strategies involve (allowing for a normal degree of poor information and human fallibility)? (2) How sensitive is this or that strategy to particular assumptions? (3) How much do they depend on *particular* policies? (4) In what ways could the chances of success of each strategy be increased? And lastly, (5) what contingency plans should be prepared in case the strategy decided upon goes wrong. Ultimately, therefore, economic policy is *not* a technical choice of particular policies, but the assessment of the applicability ,the reality, the desirability, and the coherence of a *package of policies*.

Bibliography

The original discussion of the required relation between policy objectives and policy instruments is [1] J. Tinbergen; *The Theory of Economic Policy* (North Holland Publishing Company, Amsterdam, 1952)—and it is notable that this contains many warnings overlooked by later writers. The trade-off approach to economic policy has been most explicitly formulated by [2] H. Theil in 'On the Theory of Economic Policy', *American Economic Review* (1956) and in *Economic Forecasts and Policy* (North Holland Publishing Company, Amsterdam, 1961). The problem of formulating a social welfare function is discussed from a theoretical viewpoint in a relatively difficult book by [3] K. Arrow, *Social Choice and Individual Values* (Wiley, New York, 1951). In stark contrast, almost any of the writings of Thomas (now Lord)Balogh emphasize the complexity of economic policy in practice, the need for realism, and the inappropriateness of simple rules. The best introduction to his thought is [4] *The Economics of Poverty* (Macmillan, New York, 1966) and [5] *Unequal Partners*, vol. i (Basil Blackwell, 1963). Also in a realistic vein are [6] S. Brittan, *Steering the Economy* (Penguin, 1971) and [7] Sir Alec Cairncross, *Essays in Economic Management* (Allen and Unwin, 1971)—though both of these are mainly concerned with the short-run regulation of the economy rather than with economic policy as a whole. The case for thinking that economists have an influence on the formulation of objectives is made in [8] P. Streeten (ed.), *Value in Social Theory* (Routledge and Kegan Paul, 1958), and the reason why economics and politics cannot be separated is considered in [9] A. Graham, *Impartiality and Bias in Economics* in A. Montefiore (ed.), *Neutrality and Impartiality* (C.U.P., 1975). An interesting attempt to analyse the relationship between different objectives is [10] M. Lipton, *Assessing Economic Performance* (Staples, 1968). The conflicting considerations about both objectives and instruments which face governments in particular instances are well brought out in [11] W. Beckerman (ed.), *The Labour Government's Economic Record 1964–1970* (Duckworth, 1972). The question whether one should maximize output or maximize employment is illuminatingly examined by [12] F. Stewart and P. Streeten, 'Conflicts between Output and Employment Objectives in Developing Countries', *Oxford Economic Papers* (1971). Other conflicts are studied in [13] N. Kaldor (ed.), *Conflicts in Policy Objectives* (Blackwell, 1971). Contrasting views about the particular objective of economic growth are [14] E. Mishan,

The Costs of Economic Growth (Staples, 1967) and [15] W. Beckerman, *In Defence of Economic Growth* (Cape, 1974). A short, but subtle, analysis of why some decisions need to be decentralized and others taken centrally is [16] G. Richardson, 'Competition versus Planning', *Soviet Studies* (1971). Finally, a brief and stimulating pamphlet which discusses some of the questions raised in this chapter is [17] A. Lindbeck, *The Political Economy of the New Left. An Outsider's View* (Harper and Row, 1971).

10

Government Pay Policy

D. ROBINSON

1. Wage Bargaining

1.1. The Textbook Model

It is not unusual in many basic economic textbooks for wages to be regarded as determined by supply and demand in that individual workers, or potential workers, consider the wages, fringe benefits, and other aspects of reward offered by employers for different occupations and jobs, and after comparing these with the skills, nature, and extent of work required, decide which job to take on the basis of the resulting net advantages. On the demand side the employer considers the wage necessary to obtain the amount and type of labour he requires and either pays it or alters his requirement by increasing or decreasing his demand for labour, and possibly other factors of production which can be substituted for labour. The resulting interplay of forces is held to lead to a situation where labour is paid the value of its marginal product (see p. 163), i.e. the rate of pay for a class of labour is determined by the value of output received from the employment of the marginal unit of that labour, or, if the wage level is determined by market forces, i.e. it is regarded as given to any individual employer, the marginal productivity of a class of labour will determine how much of it any particular employer will seek to recruit. Essentially wages and/or employment levels are determined by the exercise of maximizing choices by individuals and employers. The individual worker maximizes his net advantages by choosing which occupation and which job to take, and the employer maximizes profits by choosing how much of what sort of labour to employ. Trade unions are thus seen as 'distortions' in that they hinder or prevent the workings of these mechanisms of choice or adjustment. They may do this by insisting that a certain type of labour be paid a particular wage level, determined either in absolute terms or in relation to the pay of some other type of labour, or by insisting that a certain amount or combination of types of labour be employed. They may also restrict the entry of prospective recruits to a particular occupation or job.

1.2. Real-World Bargaining Systems

The real world is frequently much different from this highly simplified model.

If employers were to say to workers, through their trade unions, that if they did not like the wages offered they should maximize their net advantages by moving elsewhere, the reaction would more likely be industrial action, loss of production, and perhaps plant closure. Neither firms nor governments are generally willing to take this risk, although some individual politicians may be prepared to do so.

As far as real life is concerned, wages, and salaries, are determined not only by economic forces but also by social and political forces, and in particular by people's views about fairness. Of all economic questions and issues there is none in which the importance of people's beliefs about what is or is not fair is as great, as pervasive, or as influential as the question of wages and relative wages.

There are still a number of people whose terms and conditions of employment—their rate of pay, hours of work, job content, fringe benefits, and so on—are determined by individual bargaining and agreement between themselves and an employer. However, some of these apparently 'free market' wage and salary levels are in practice, very much influenced by views as to what is the trade union or 'going' rate. For the majority of blue-collar employees, however, terms and conditions of employment are determined by collective bargaining between trade unions and employers or employers' representatives such as an Association or Federation. At the same time there is a substantial number of manual workers whose basic or minimum terms and conditions of employment are fixed by Wages Councils whose Orders have statutory effect in that it is an offence for employers to employ workers in the industries concerned below the terms set out in the relevant Orders.

There are some four million workers subject to Wages Council or similar provisions.[1] They are mainly in low-paid industries, and the origins of Wages Councils is in the Boards set up to provide special protection for the old 'sweated' trades. Currently trade unions are undecided whether Wages Councils are the most effective way of helping the lower-paid and are undecided whether Councils do help stimulate collective bargaining which is one of their objectives.

Even where wages or salaries are determined by collective bargaining there can be considerable differences between industries and groups in the methods of bargaining and the ways in which pay is actually determined. In many industries there is bargaining at various levels while in others a single industry-wide agreement may determine the actual rate of pay.

At one end of the spectrum an industry-wide agreement, probably made by a Joint Industrial Council (J.I.C.) or some other joint body composed of representatives of trade unions and employers, will establish a negotiated rate of pay which is in effect standard throughout the firms covered by the agreement. In some other cases the industry agreement (which is often referred to as the national agreement) lays down only a minimum rate of pay which individual firms can improve upon if they so wish. In many parts of the public sector, particularly where white-collar workers are concerned, an

[1] House of Commons Hansard, 15 Nov. 1974, cols. 262/3 gives figures of those covered by Wages Councils as 3,409,000. There are others covered by the Agricultural Wages Board.

effective rate of pay or incremental salary scale will be determined by collective bargaining, arbitration, or some other form of wage determination. While these public sector agreements are also frequently referred to as national agreements they differ in one important respect from the J.I.C. or similar agreements in the private sector, namely that there is basically only one employer on the employer's side of the bargaining table and it is administratively easier to ensure that the standard rates of pay will be adhered to.

One of the historical objectives of trade unions in the public sector has frequently been the establishment of a national rate for the job in the industry concerned. While companies in the private sector have also sought, often under pressure from trade unions or in response to national trade unions which are believed to have greater power than an individual company, to create national or industry-wide bargaining machinery, they have, particularly in times of full employment or shortages of labour in their trades, also sought to retain some elements of individual discretion in deciding the pay they will offer. For one of the built-in difficulties of an employers' association is that while the various companies may have common interests in joining together to negotiate across the board with the unions in their various establishments they also have some competing interests when faced by labour shortages or to meet what they see as the special needs of their own establishments.

However, many blue-collar workers receive some part of their pay from piecework or other types of payments by results systems. There is an extremely wide range of incentives and bonuses in addition to a bewildering assortment of methods of relating pay to output or performance. But all payments-by-results schemes and particularly piecework schemes where the pay (or more usually part of the pay of the individual or group) is directly related to changes in output or in the price paid for each unit of output, have one thing in common. The amount of pay that a worker will receive in a week is not laid down in the national agreement, although the agreement may contain a clause such as 'a pieceworker of average ability should receive one-third more than a timeworker'. This is because it is generally expected that a pieceworker or incentive-scheme worker will work harder than a worker on time rates. This view is in some process of change with the development of Measured Day Work pay systems whereby workers are guaranteed high time rates of pay in return for agreeing to a 'norm' or standard effort input which is higher than that regarded as normal under ordinary time rates.

2. Factors in Pay Determination

2.1. The Level of Bargaining

Trade unions in a Western society are fundamentally and necessarily bargaining organizations. It is their purpose to bargain to defend and improve the conditions of their members and if, at certain levels or at certain times, they cannot bargain about pay, they will bargain about something else. This is particularly important when changes are made in the bargaining system. For example, if plant, industry, or company-level bargaining is introduced to replace fragmented shop-floor bargaining, the shop stewards will have lost an important role and it is unlikely that they will be content to give up bargaining altogether.

The level at which bargaining takes place can influence the type of bargaining and the way in which it is carried out. Even in theory it is difficult to produce an explanation that would satisfactorily lead to the same level of pay emerging from a single industry negotiation as would from a series of fragmented or plant-level bargains. A single national bargain which settles the effective rate of pay will channel all the *pay* pressure into the one negotiation (although of course there may be bargaining at lower levels about such things as grading and regrading which can be equivalent to a pay rise, manning ratios, the effort bargain, and so on). This is one reason why pay negotiations in the public sector may more frequently lead to national or industry-wide strikes or work-to-rule activities.

With a piecework payment system there is frequently almost constant bargaining. Changes in methods of working, materials, product design, etc. all provide opportunities for a revision of the piecework prices. It is never clear from the outside, nor sometimes from the inside, whether pieceworkers' earnings have increased because they are producing more output at constant piecework rates, because the rates have been increased, or because of some combination of these, complicated by new work for which new rates have had to be set. The actual weekly gross pay may also vary considerably from week to week as a result of changes in the amount of overtime worked (or paid whether it is actually worked or not) and the incidence of shift working, which usually attracts an additional premium.

The combined effects of these factors is that an employee's pay packet may be composed of a number of different items which have been determined at different levels of bargaining or determination, by different groups of people and representatives, in response to different pressures or arguments and which may, or may not, be integrated through a coherent relation of pay to effort, labour shortages, or concepts of equity and fairness. There is considerable scope for adjustment and manipulation of many pay packets from week to week and the plethora of allowances and bonuses plus the opportunities for regrading into a higher pay category all provide different employers with some variety of opportunity to adjust pay. These factors should be borne in mind when considering incomes policies.

They are also relevant to questions of measuring and comparing pay levels and movements in pay. There is an Index of Basic Rates of Wages and Minimum Entitlements (weekly and hourly) for manual workers, an annual figure of average weekly and hourly earnings of manual workers which includes overtime and all bonuses and premiums, a monthly Index of Wages and Salaries (actual amounts not shown), and the New Earnings Survey published annually which provides considerable detail about wages and salaries. The important point is that the various measurements differ in coverage and content and that any interpretation of them and conclusions drawn from them must be confined to the questions for which they can reasonably be expected to be relevant. It is crucial in this respect that the

Department of Employment notes about each series be read carefully and the limitations on their use accepted.

2.2. Pay Claims: Defensive

Pay determination through bargaining with trade unions can be separated into two parts. There is the pay claim and the pay settlement. Unfortunately, there does not appear to be any explanation, simple or complicated, that will satisfactorily account for the level of claims that are forthcoming or factors which it is believed influence these claims. On some occasions the economic arguments may dominate a trade union's behaviour, on others more political considerations, perhaps the perceived obligation on trade union leaders not to fall behind other unions, or the tactics of a group within the union which is seeking to obtain control (the nearest analogy might be the behaviour of directors in relation to dividends when a take-over threat is made and resisted), or the fact that some officials are seeking re-election, or a new leadership is seeking to establish its own mark on the union, or a membership drive, and so on. Similar possibilities arise if it is a workgroup rather than a union which is submitting the pay claim. On some occasions the processes by which a claim is formulated may influence its size. If a union conference determines the specific size of the claim it may represent aspiration more than a realistic assessment of what is obtainable (assuming this can be made), or it may be an attempt to embarrass those who will actually have to negotiate. It does appear that claims formulated by those who will subsequently have to negotiate for them are generally lower than those formulated by people who do not have the responsibility for attaining them. It is useful to separate claims into defensive claims which seek to maintain some previously established position or relationship, and offensive claims which seek to improve on past positions or relationships.

There are two aspects to a defensive claim:

(i) Normally a change in price levels, sometimes an anticipated change, provides a minimum floor to a wage claim on the grounds that living standards should be at least maintained. As unions become more sophisticated in their bargaining, increases in direct taxes may provide grounds for a defensive claim. Although the Retail Price Index is generally taken as an indication of price movements there may be some particular items that are more sensitive than others so that an increase in, say, rents may have a greater effect on stimulating claims than an equivalent increase in the overall R.P.I. which was spread more evenly over other items.

(ii) The maintenance or restoration of past pay relationships which may have changed as a result of a pay settlement by some other group generates strong defensive claims even if the cause of an increase in pay of the comparison group is supply and demand. Frequently, past relationships and history are regarded as powerful arguments in support of fairness. While there may not always be certainty as to which other groups a particular union will use for these comparisons there are a number of broadly recognized orbits of comparison. Here a distinction should be made between internal comparisons and relativities, which are made with other groups in the same industry, company, or plant but which have their pay determined in a separate bargaining unit, and external relativities which are made with groups outside.[2] Differentials are used to refer to pay relationships within the same bargaining unit.

2.3. Pay Claims: Offensive

Offensive wage claims arise from a group's attempts to *improve* its relative position or living standard. These can be based on such things as changes in productivity, altered job content, changed skill requirements, or profitability. Just as defensive claims are based on a perception of fairness so too can fairness influence or determine an offensive claim. For example, it may be regarded as fair, at least by the union or workgroup, that some past relationship between pay and productivity should be maintained so that if productivity increases there should be an increase in pay. If job content is changed it is seen as fair that the workers affected should receive more pay, and this perception of fairness is independent of the prevailing state of supply and demand for that type of labour. The particular criterion adopted to justify an offensive claim may change with circumstances.

A successful offensive claim by one group often leads to defensive claims based on past pay relationships by others. This can make it extremely difficult to change pay relationships in an accepted or agreed way as different interpretations of fairness are introduced by different groups. It is because pay claims are often based on pay movements elsewhere, which may themselves have been strongly influenced by economic factors, that the interaction between offensive and defensive claims, or between claims based on fairness and those caused by economic factors, that a system of 'free' collective bargaining often leads to repercussive actions which can add force to a wage–wage spiral. It is crucial to bear in mind that claims will be generated as a result of the views and perceptions of those who believe they are affected by changes elsewhere. It is less important whether 'outsiders' consider the pay relationships fair than that the 'insiders', those concerned, do so.

2.4. Pay Settlements

If pay claims are determined by a range of complicated factors, which make them difficult to analyse, pay *settlements* are either determined by a simple set of factors or by even more complicated ones. The simple explanation would use market forces, supply and demand, as the sole determinants of pay levels and pay increases. The discussion of the Phillips Curve in Chapter 7 suggests that at the aggregate or macro level such an explanation is not satisfactory, and if earnings rather than wage rates are used no real improvement occurs. At the micro (industry and firm) level the evidence, although patchy and incomplete in coverage, is even less convincing.[3] Various institutional factors, bargaining practices, payment systems, militancy, union and workgroup attitudes, as well as a range of factors on the employers' side need

---

[2] See Pay Board Advisory Report 2, *Relativities*, Cmnd. 5535, Jan. 1974, and Advisory Report 1, *Anomalies*, Cmnd. 5439, Sept. 1973 for a more detailed discussion of this approach.

[3] See K. G. J. C. Knowles and D. Robinson, 'Wage Movements in Coventry', *B.O.U.I.E.S.*, 31, No. 1 (Feb. 1969).

to be brought in if some even roughly realistic explanation is to be forth-coming.

In practice, there need be little systematic relationship between claim and settlement. Many people believe that settlements are about half-way between the claims and the employer's offer, but even in arbitration cases where this is supposed to hold most firmly there is little evidence to justify the interpretation. Clearly, it is an unsatisfactory explanation in itself. In present conditions, and since the end of the Second World War, employers have not generally sought to obtain pay cuts. The lowest offer in arbitration might therefore be seen as zero. If arbitrators merely split the difference, unions seeking to maximize increases in rates of pay ought to ask for as large an amount as they like, knowing they will get half of it. But unions do not in fact do this. One reason is that their own views of what is fair and reasonable impose constraints. Also they have views as to the number of people, primarily their members, who should be employed to receive that rate of pay. This is influenced by their view of the employer's ability to pay certain levels, and so in some way depends on profitability. In the public sector this might be influenced by views of government policy on nationalized industries' deficits or pricing policy. This probably leads to an area of acceptable settlements rather than a precise figure, but if a defensive claim is pursued based on a specific relationship then the union and its members may be committed to a precise amount.

The more that a pay packet is composed of a number of items each of which is decided by different people in response to different factors or for different purposes, the more difficult it may be to say that anyone actually determined the level of pay, although of course the various decision-taking levels or elements may have paid some regard to what happened elsewhere. In other cases, while there may have been the performance or ritual of bargaining the increase in pay has been employer-led in response to his views of the need to recruit or retain labour in a tight market.

It does not follow, of course, that a union's views of fairness necessarily leads to the appropriate settlement, nor that those making defensive claims will receive exactly what the comparison group received. Much depends on how similar the settlements are expected to be, and while there is some consistency in some pay relationships this is not necessarily the same as rigidity, and there is often more variation than either an extreme 'labour market' or 'coercive comparisons' view would suggest. The observed results will vary according to the particular measurement of pay that is used.

There is, then, no agreement about the factors that actually do cause pay movements. Nor is there agreement about what *should* cause pay movements. Both collective bargaining and arbitration in this country are marked by an absence of agreement about the criteria that should determine pay. (The main exception is the adoption of pay research in the Civil Service as a method of determining principles and the Pay Research Unit which discovers the facts. For an account of this system see Pay Board Advisory Report 1, op cit., and Advisory Report 3, *Civil Service Science Group*, Cmnd. 5602, Apr. 1974.) While this leads to an agnostic view of pay determination, it is clear that many groups and unions believe that fairness and comparability in some sense *should* influence pay. Conflicts between normative views and actuality lead to pressures to change the existing situation, and because normative views themselves change one ought not to expect any permanent solution.

The strength and the weakness of job evaluation schemes is that they deliberately make explicit and focus upon the criteria thought important in wage bargaining and attempt to weight these different criteria in a generally acceptable way. This tries to get to the heart of the matter but perhaps at the cost of discovering that there is no generally accepted weighting of the criteria mentioned.

3. The Government's Role in Pay Settlements

3.1. The Basis of Government Involvement

In theory it might be possible for a government to take the view that what happens to pay is the result of either market forces or institutional and bar-gaining processes and that it is no part of its duty or obligation to become involved. In practice this choice is not open to it for two main reasons. Firstly, it is itself a large employer, and is widely regarded as responsible, directly or indirectly, for the pay of a large number of public sector employees. Secondly, as discussed in Chapter 9, Government is expected to accept responsibility for the general management of the economy, inflation, income distribution, full employment, and so on. Government cannot therefore choose to opt out of concern for pay developments. However, it can choose how it will accept its responsibilities, and the types of policies it will introduce to seek to attain some form of combination of different objectives.

Government's choice has been from three main types of policies, although, of course, it has not confined itself to only one of them at any given time. There has been a tendency to switch the main emphasis from one to another, sometimes, perhaps, with insufficient regard for the necessity to ensure that all policy approaches are, so far as is possible, co-ordinated and consistent. Often we are impressed by the difficulties and failures of the type of approach most recently adopted with perhaps an underestimation of the difficulties that will be faced by the alternative policies.

3.2. Demand Management Policies

These are discussed in the following chapter. From a pay determination viewpoint there are two important features. Firstly, it is hoped that pay levels will change as a result of changes in the general level of economic activity. The intention is that pay (and price) decisions will be influenced by the changed economic environment as decision-takers respond to the pre-vailing economic forces. In addition to these 'pure' economic forces, *expecta-tions* will be changed as a result of easing or tightening economic pressures, and these expectations will feed through on the workers' and trade union side to influence their wage demands, and on the employers' side by affecting their demand for labour and thus their willingness to increase pay in order to recruit or retain a satisfactory labour force. If there was a single or single set of determinants of expectations that was related in a constant way to the economic circumstances or to some economic variables, then we could bypass expectations and relate pay developments directly to the variables. It is because there is not, or we have not been able to discover any firm, consistent, and constant relationships, that we introduce the concept of expectations. This does not mean, however, that we know how these expectations are determined or how they will react to changing economic circumstances.

Those who place rather less weight on economic factors than, say, a simple Phillips Curve approach would imply (see Chapter 7) would also wish to introduce other factors of an institutional political and social nature. The view, therefore, of whether demand management works, or can work, in an effective way on pay development, depends on two judgements. First, that the pressure of economic forces is the sole important criterion. The evidence would seem to be against this position. Moreover, even if economic forces are the sole or major determinant it is still unclear as to what exactly will happen; for example, there could be fewer jobs at higher wages or more jobs at lower wages. Second, it has to be decided, if the pure economic view is rejected, whether the other factors are constant over time or whether they can and do vary. What we can say with some certainty is that the old economic relationships do not seem to hold in the same form and that this is probably due to changes in attitudes on the part of workers and trade unions.

Unions do not seem to act in the same way when unemployment is high as they did in the past. It is as though they have questioned the belief that they are necessarily weaker, or all of them are weaker, when unemployment rises. We have experienced rising unemployment at times when prices are rising quickly and defensive pay claims are being pushed. Also a contracted or depressed economy affects firms too and it may be that some of them conclude that they cannot afford to have a strike, and so they opt to pay what they do not appear to be able to afford in the long run because they cannot afford not to do so in the short run.

Secondly, there is the question of the effect of demand management policies on the public sector. On occasions governments have tried to use the public sector to set the pace for the rest of the economy. On other occasions the needs of the public sector to give relatively large pay rises has generated comparability pay claims.

At this point in time, therefore, it is difficult to resist the conclusion that demand management policies as exercised do not seem able satisfactorily to contain the inflationary pressures within our economy, whether the initiating pressures are domestic or international in origin. As we have suggested above, this is in part because the reactions and responses of people who are able to influence the rate of inflation and pay developments are uncertain and changing. It is also due to the fact that governments have believed that there are certain limits beyond which they cannot use demand management policies. For the containment of inflation is only one of Government's objectives. Amongst other things it also seeks to maintain a high level of employment, encourage economic growth, affect the distribution of income, pursue a regional policy, and maintain free collective bargaining. Whether demand management 'works' partly depends on the effect on unemployment, income distribution, etc. of successful control of inflation.

If workers hold the view that increased prices, whatever the cause (e.g. higher unit costs, higher import prices, or higher indirect taxation), provide sufficient grounds for increase in money wages, then demand management measures which lead to increased prices might well themselves generate additional pay demands. Contractionist measures require that there be reductions in living standards somewhere in the economy and the crucial question is whether people will accept this. While workers and unions react more quickly and directly to measures which increase the cost of living they are increasingly adopting a more sophisticated approach, so that the effect of direct taxation, national insurance contributions, and social security provisions are taken into account in the formulation of their pay claims. This tendency is strengthened when unions and Government seek to obtain general agreement on economic and social policy in order to develop a pay policy. While it might be a little extreme to say that all contractionist measures have inflationary consequences, there is sufficient validity in the statement to give concern about the ability of demand management measures alone to moderate inflation and even perhaps to question the contribution they make when used in association with other policies.

3.3. Structural Changes

The second main type of measures open to Government can be regarded as structural. This approach rests on a belief that there are distortions, blockages, or impediments in the way in which the economy operates such that if they can be reduced or removed it might be possible to reduce some of the undesirable features of the economy. For example, a particular skill or occupation may be in short supply. We might expect employers to bid up wages for that sort of labour which in turn might have the effect of reducing the total demand and of increasing its supply as more people are attracted to it by the relatively higher wages. However, if in the process other occupations press for higher wages to maintain some past pay relationship then general inflation occurs, relative wages do not change quickly, and the time period of adjustment, if left to the market, is lengthy. Government-introduced or -sponsored training schemes might therefore be established in order to speed up the adjustment process and perhaps moderate the inflationary effects.

A more comprehensive approach is an active manpower policy. The original Swedish advocacy of an active manpower policy was related to the Swedes' solidaristic wage policy. The manpower side was seen as an essential link in a comprehensive approach which included trade union wage strategy, concern for the lower-paid, economic development, macroeconomic policy, and other narrower questions of labour supply.

Similarly, anti-monopoly legislation or provisions against restrictive trade practices can be seen as structural measures designed to reduce the rate of increase of prices. Other measures to help regional development, encourage investment, provide redundancy pay to help workers adjust to job change are part of the same approach.

In recent years the structural approach has also tried to tackle the *processes* of industrial relations and collective bargaining by proposals for industrial relations reform. There has been running through the various proposals the view that changes in the way in which industrial relations are carried out, and some shifts in the balance of power either between unions and management, or union leaders and their members, would make some contribution to easing inflationary pressures. This was spelled out very clearly by Mr. Roy Jenkins, then Chancellor of the Exchequer in the 1969 Budget statement. He said that the then existing climate of industrial relations was a serious obstacle to the attainment of economic objectives and that there was a need to facilitate the smooth working of the process of collective bargaining to prevent the occurrence of unnecessary and damaging disputes which were totally incompatible with the nation's economic objectives. It was for this reason the Government had decided to implement without delay some of the more important provisions incorporated in the White Paper 'In Place of Strife'. In the event the Government was unable to get its legislation through the Commons. What is important, however, is that both the then Labour Government and the succeeding Conservative administration believed that reform of industrial relations was either necessary or desirable not only to reduce the incidence of industrial disputes but also to ease the inflationary pressures from wage settlements.

Both the Labour Government's White Paper and the subsequent Conservative legislation appeared to support the view that some disputes and wage pressures were the result of trade union leadership pressing for larger pay rises than the rank and file would themselves press for. There seemed to be a belief that trade union leadership was more militant than the membership and that members might be led or coerced into action to support excessive demands. Legislation which changed the structure of decision-taking and the processes by which decisions were taken and strike action initiated therefore appeared attractive. The issue of whether the balance of power in collective bargaining should be shifted, assuming that legislation is able to do this, focuses on two issues: first, whether the workers' side is considered to have too much power vis-à-vis the employers, and second, whether trade union officials accurately reflect the views of their members.

The answer to the first question will be based primarily on judgements about what one thinks *ought* to happen. These judgements will necessarily involve various views about the distribution of income, the causes and effects of trade unions, industrial democracy, and the general distribution of power and decision-making authority in industry and society generally. On the second question there is frequently a tendency for people to allow their view of the content of the decision to influence their judgement of why or how the decision was made. This is perhaps nowhere more prevalent than in the question of whether trade union officials lead and manipulate the views of their members or whether they reflect them, sometimes in a moderating way. If, as seems to be currently the case, there is a general movement towards the rejection of authority by individuals, and this is reflected in a work situation by the rejection by workers and workgroups of the traditional authority of both management and formal trade union structures, then the view that trade union officials, particularly national officials, lead workers into acts of more militancy than they would themselves initiate requires re-examination. It may also mean that the view that a trade union, as a collective or corporate body, is responsible for the actions of its members, or of various lay representatives such as shop stewards and conveners, while possibly a tenable value-judgement, nevertheless implies a state of control over members that is unrealistic or unenforceable.

3.4. Prices and Incomes Policies

The third main group of measures is prices and incomes policies. The essence of all these policies is that those responsible for taking wage and price decisions are expected to take decisions which are different from those which they would take in the same economic circumstances but without the existence of the prices and incomes policy. Thus instead of seeking to reduce the pressure of demand to obtain lower wage increases, or shift the balance of power by restricting the use of the strike weapon or some other form of sanction, a prices and incomes policy seeks to reduce the rate of increase of money wages (or prices) by inducing people to take decisions that they know are different from what they *could* and *would* have taken. In practice, of course, it may not be possible to know precisely what they would have done.

Thus an incomes policy can be seen as saying to wage bargainers 'you could get a settlement of ten per cent but we want you to settle for eight'. Or it might say, 'If you settle for the ten per cent you would have got anyway, we want you to do so on certain additional conditions which will increase efficiency and so reduce costs and prices'. While there may well be a whole series of other features of a prices and incomes policy, this one is essential, and if it is thought that it is not possible to obtain decisions that are different from those imposed by economic or market forces, there is no point in pursuing an incomes policy. It is therefore a necessary condition for the successful operation of a prices and incomes that there is enough flexibility in price and wage determination to allow changes in the decisions actually taken. There is a wide range of possible methods of inducing changed behaviour in pay determination, ranging from exhortation and moral pressures on the one extreme to strict legal control on the other. At various times since 1945 British governments have tried the whole range of options.

The Labour Government operated an incomes policy between 1948 and 1951 which consisted essentially of no pay increases and the non-operation of such sliding scale agreements as existed until prices had risen by the then relatively large amount of 5 per cent. The standstill on pay was not legally enforceable but was announced by Government and received the support, increasingly grudgingly, of the T.U.C. Subsequent governments introduced pay standstills with legal backing (the Labour Government in July 1966 and the Conservative Government in November 1972). Both of these were followed by periods of statutory control of pay increases of differing complexity and severity with organizations created to apply the rules. In the case of the Labour Government's policy there was already an organization, the National Board for Prices and Incomes in existence, but its powers were considerably increased after the standstill. The Conservative Government created the Pay Board and Prices Commission to apply its rules from April 1973. Attempts to obtain an incomes policy as a result of voluntary agreement took place in December 1964 with the Declaration of Intent, agreed by Government, unions, and employers, and in 1974 with the Social Contract agreed by Government and the T.U.C. It is not intended to provide any detailed history of these various approaches, but only to draw some general conclusions about the use of various forms of incomes policy.

Exhortation alone may not be sufficient to obtain moderation in pay settlements. A crucial factor is whether those whose actions are subject to the exhortation believe that it is in their interest to change their behaviour. This requires that there be some view as to which set of people is responsible for making pay settlements. As we have seen, sometimes this may be trade union officials, sometimes shop stewards, sometimes arbitrators and third parties, and sometimes employers. It is reasonable to believe that they are much more likely to change their behaviour if they believe that their own interests will be furthered by their so doing, although, of course, it is possible that they might do so in order that some other interest, that of another group or society as a whole, might be furthered.

For it to have much chance of success exhortation needs to be in somewhat specific terms. Even if we assume that 'men of goodwill' will respond, they need to know what they are supposed to do. Some indication of the extent of restraint or modification to their behaviour is necessary. In the early post-war years Government's approach was based on macroeconomic considerations; the aggregate rate of increase in money incomes should be kept in line with the aggregate or average rate of increase of productivity. This can be done in two ways. The first is to tie all pay increases to the increase in national productivity. This means that some industries face rising costs as pay rises faster than productivity, giving price rises, and some face falling costs, giving offsetting price reductions. But this divorce of pay increases from the productivity of the industry or firm concerned creates great pressures on the policy, particularly from the sectors with fast-rising productivity.

In some cases it may be that with existing payment systems pay in a firm will automatically rise perhaps on a par with productivity, for example, if there is a piecework system which links them together. If employees believe they are 'entitled' to a pay settlement based on the national increase in productivity, they may well conclude that there is no need for them to participate in measures to increase productivity in their employment, so that the actual increase in productivity could be less than expected.

If, as an alternative, the approach is to link pay and productivity in each plant, firm, or industry, so that a group of workers receive an increase related to the change in their productivity, there will be different reactive pressures emanating from defensive pay claims based on comparability. Tight links between pay and productivity on this basis would require significant changes in attitudes towards fairness and comparability. There are also many workers for whom it is extremely difficult to measure productivity, because of the problems in quantifying the output of the workers, e.g. policemen or teachers. In many situations, even though it may be possible to indicate that there has been a rise in productivity it is unclear why this has happened, whether it was the result of a direct contribution by the workforce or because of increased or improved capital equipment or technological progress.

An important conclusion, which is relevant whether the approach is based on exhortation or legislative intervention, is that while the macroeconomic relationship between pay movements and productivity increases may be the central theme in the package of Government economic objectives, the implementation of pay policies or approaches to attain this objective must recognize the microeconomic realities of the processes of pay determination and the existence of extremely powerful, albeit variable and varying, concepts of fairness.

A modification of exhortation is the creation of some degree of concensus between Government and those responsible or mainly responsible for pay determination. Government may seek to obtain tripartite agreement to a set of rules which should govern pay movements, or bipartite agreement with either the trade unions or, less frequently perhaps, the employers. The success of this approach will depend on the extent to which those responsible for making the agreement, in good faith, are actually able to ensure that their good intentions are translated into modified behaviour. For obvious institutional and representational reasons the concensus or agreements are likely to be made with the national leadership of unions and/or employers. In practice, this leadership may not be able to exert dominant influence over the actual pay decisions. This may depend on the structure of bargaining as well as the extent of the opportunity for national leadership to influence the behaviour of members. Thus if the Donovan Commission's [13] interpretation that trade unions, particularly in their relationships with shop stewards, workgroups, and members, are too weak rather than too strong, and its view that this is the fundamental explanation of the creation of the two systems of industrial relations as well as a result of it, are correct, then consistency of approach would suggest that Government should not expect the trade unions to be able suddenly to obtain greater strength in the sense of being able to commit their members to pay restraint. They may not have the *de facto* power to do so. Clearly, it is contradictory to recognize the relative weakness of the official trade union organization on many issues and then expect it to act in a way which rests on its having considerable strength. Similar arguments apply in the relationships between representatives of employers and their member companies.

The use of voluntary agreements, or preference for them over statutory methods, rests on a belief that voluntary commitment to moral obligations, perhaps in a bargained situation where Government has altered its economic and social policies to allow the unions and/or employers to obtain some of their objectives through government policies, is a more effective way of influencing behaviour than the use of coercion through legislation. It also appears that there is a strong commitment to the view that the moral obligations are more likely to be accepted if the enforcement of the agreed rules, or the responsibility for ensuring that they are followed, is left to the bargaining parties rather than to some external agency.

The 1975 Social Contract reflects this approach. The T.U.C. and Labour Government arrived at a concensus on the broad social and economic policies to be implemented by Government and in return the T.U.C. agreed to support a pay policy which limited increases to £6 with no increases being received by those earning £8,500 or more per annum. This involved the T.U.C. in accepting some responsibility for ensuring that member unions accepted the obligations imposed upon them. It also meant that the unions within the T.U.C. had to agree on the content of the policy, a flat rate increase rather than, say, a percentage increase, with the consequential effects on differentials. Both of these points subjected the T.U.C. to considerable internal pressures and stresses. The great virtue of this approach is that the unions themselves will seek to ensure the observance of the policy. A weakness is that if they believe that the Government has not delivered the economic policies or circumstances that they expected, they will withdraw their support, and, of course, there are circumstances in which Government believes that it is unable to guarantee the creation of specific economic situations, e.g. a particular level of employment, because of factors outside its own control. Similarly, there may well be situations in which the T.U.C. will find itself unable to ensure the observance of its members because they cannot actually control the behaviour of all negotiating groups in all affiliated unions. If the labour market tightens so that employers begin to compete for labour through pay increases then the strains will become much more severe and it may be that a bipartite policy between governments and unions will prove insufficient in a tight labour market as it does not require observance by employers (unless there be additional legislative restraints on them).

A consequence of tripartite or bipartite approaches to incomes policy is that there will be much more 'bargaining' about the Government's economic policies and this will focus attention much more on the effects of these policies on such things as real disposable income, income distribution, employment levels, etc.

If the Government believes that voluntary enforcement or compliance is unlikely to prove sufficient, it may introduce legislation limiting the increases which are permitted. Legislative intervention has not hitherto taken the form of insisting that certain increases by given.[4] The rules have been permissive maximums. Settlements could be allowed up to the declared maximums if certain rules were followed and if the parties chose to go to the permitted limits. The adoption of legislative controls requires two main decisions to be taken. First, who is to apply the rules? Second, what should be the content of the rules? The questions have been put in this order because it is generally the case that the method of administration imposes constraints on the type of rules that can be introduced.

The 1965 Labour incomes policy was implemented by the appropriate Government departments with the National Board for Prices and Incomes asked to provide advisory reports when departments wished them to do so. The 1974 Pay Board created by the Conservative Government was different

---

[4] The normal position of the Wages Councils is an exception to this general rule.

in that it had statutory authority to implement the rules which Parliament had laid down in a Pay Code. (The advisory reports of the Pay Board had no legally binding effects but were much more like the previous N.B.P.I. reports.) A very rough analogy is that the N.B.P.I. was in a similar position to the Monopolies Commission while the Pay Board was more like the Restrictive Trade Practices Court, except that it had no power to judge on wider 'interests', e.g. of consumers, purchasers, etc. (which would have given an element of discretion) (see Chapter 16, p. 399).

The choice of the rules reflects both the social and economic objectives sought. If the decisions of the agency are, in the absence of specific intervention by a minister or Parliament, to be legally enforceable, it follows, given our system of parliamentary democracy and accountability, that the agency will not be empowered to make decisions which are discretionary, based on its own value-judgements. Thus terms such as 'in the national interest' or 'desirable re-structuring of a payment system' are unlikely to be introduced as grounds on which the agency can permit exceptionally large pay increases. The provisions of the Pay Code for the Pay Board were therefore much more prescribed (in the sense that they were expressed in objective or quasi-objective and measurable terms) than were the terms and exception clauses of the document which provided guidance for the N.B.P.I. What this means is that Government can provide for differentiated but not discretionary treatment in the code. If an exception clause cannot be stated in objective terms it is extremely difficult for it to be included in a statutory policy that is implemented by an independent agency whose decisions are legally enforceable. If discretionary clauses are introduced it is unlikely that an independent agency can implement them, as opposed to the offering of advice to a minister, and therefore the implementation and enforcement will ultimately have to lie with ministers. In so far as this requires decisions on individual settlements, the implementation of the policy is much more likely to become a political process rather than an administrative one.

The simplest policy consisting only of a permitted maximum increase expressed in either flat-rate or percentage terms is the easiest to implement and to check whether observance is taking place. Even here there can be some sticky problems connected with the calculation of the base to which a percentage is to be applied or with the date of the previous settlement if there is a specified time gap between increases [40]. If other exception clauses are introduced which permit additional pay increases on other, specified, grounds the complications and difficulties become much more serious. This is one reason why a purely voluntary policy ought to be a very simple one. The 1965 Labour policy had for much of its life four 'exception' clauses and it was widely believed that one of them—the productivity clause—was frequently abused by management and unions entering into collusive agreements to sign phoney productivity agreements [2 and 35]. The 1973 Conservative policy had various exception clauses in Stage III but because they were stated in terms which required quantification before they could be invoked there was not the same alleged abuse.

Perhaps the most striking difference in the approach of the Pay Board and the N.B.P.I. was that the former in its advisory reports[5] placed great emphasis on the importance of relative pay and concepts of fairness and the effect these had on influencing the acceptability of a policy, while the N.B.P.I. discounted these factors and emphasized productivity. The use of the concept in the Conservative policy of a pay kitty for a negotiating group to allocate as it wished also reflected the view that relative pay is crucial and parties ought to be given some element of freedom within a statutory policy to alter these if they so wish. Stage III also contained a threshold provision whereby if pay rose by 7 per cent above the base-date level additional payments of 40p a week could be made for each 1 per cent increase in the Retail Price Index. In part this was to offer guarantees against inflation and might also have influenced the size of the pay limit which it was thought would be acceptable. The vital question is whether a threshold provision or some other form of indexation makes inflation worse by ensuring an increase in labour costs when prices rise, or helps by reducing the size of the general norm. There are models, but currently no satisfactorily empirical explanations. A major problem arises if Government believes that it has to obtain a reduction in living standards, perhaps because of a significant change in the terms of trade. Any policy here can face difficulties, but indexation may make these far worse.

Policies have not simply been measures to hold down money wages and prices. They have contained varying provisions designed to make some changes in the distribution of income or to change relative pay. In all cases they sought to inject some element of value-judgement into pay relationships. This is crucial. If trade unions and workers are to be induced to settle for less than they could have obtained in money terms they will need to be persuaded that they will receive other benefits which are considered worthwhile by them. Income redistribution is often one such benefit which is offered, or, perhaps more accurately, the possibility of achieving some degree of redistribution is offered if those responsible for decision-taking wish or are able to take advantage of it.

When Government seeks to influence the development of wages at the macro level it has to do so by influencing developments at the micro level, i.e. it must seek to influence the actual changes in pay at whatever level these are determined and this varies considerably from industry to industry, and job to job. Moreover, it is reasonable to expect that changes will be made in the levels at which decisions are taken as a response to the creation of the incomes policy itself. In a modern economy such as the United Kingdom where trade unions represent an important part of the work force, it is essential that Government should try to obtain the agreement and consent of the unions to its measures, and if this is not possible, then at least their acquiescence and the avoidance of overt and direct rejection. Government will therefore seek

[5] See especially [39] Advisory Report 2 on Relativities, which proposed setting up a special Relativities Board to consider claims for special treatment within a statutory incomes policy. This reflected the belief that no matter how well the permitted exception clauses were written there would be occasions when special treatment might be necessary, but determined on grounds which could not satisfactorily be set out in the quantifiable and objective terms; some element of judgement would be necessary.

discussions with the Trades Union Congress as the representative body of the trade union movement, and, in seeking to induce unions to alter their behaviour in collective bargaining, will itself have to bargain with unions about the quid pro quo.

Once it is accepted that Government may have to become involved in a form of bargaining with the unions, and possibly employers, in order to obtain their support or acquiescence in an incomes policy it is clear that Government's freedom to choose from the full range of policy options which are in principle open to it has been reduced. Thus, without reopening the question of whether demand policies are actually effective, if Government believes that they are or might be, or that certain measures might have to be introduced either because there appears to be no viable alternative or because perhaps foreign opinion believes that they should be introduced and it is desired to maintain foreign confidence in sterling, then it could well be the case that incompatibility arises between the measures necessary to obtain trade union support and the measures which Government would like to introduce. Unless it is thought that an incomes policy can be imposed on unions, employers, and workgroups irrespective of the prevailing economic and social policies of Government, it has to recognize that there might well be a trade-off between incomes policy and demand management measures. Government might well not be able to choose the combination of items it wishes from the full range of possible measures which are, *prima facie*, open to it. If, at the same time, it is accepted that various themes of policy should be mutually supportive then the possibility may easily arise that an acceptable and effective combination of measures is not politically available. The selection of certain items for the policy package may by itself rule out the choice of other items of policy measures. Even if 'fairness' and Government macro-economic objectives are compatible it is by no means certain that labour market requirements will also be met.

Even if we ignore the labour allocation point, we do not know whether it is possible to arrive at sufficient concensus so as to reduce the areas of dispute about pay relationships in a society in which well-organized trade unions perform an economic function of influencing pay determination. It does appear, however, that leaving pay relationships to a series of *ad hoc*, even though somehow interrelated, decisions is not likely to produce an acceptable solution. To some extent the growth of white-collar unions is a response to the perceived success of blue-collar unions in pushing up their wages and the extension of white-collar unionism will probably make the resolution of pay relationships more difficult.

There is a tendency to condemn incomes policies on the ground that they have always failed, or always lead to a subsequent explosion which results in the over-all position being no better or even worse. Several points should be borne in mind when considering these criticisms. The policy is frequently judged against one or both of two criteria, (a) the statement of policy objectives made by its advocates when it was introduced, and (b) the extrapolation of some past trends to provide a yardstick against which the actual economic out-turn can be measured.

One of the difficulties of using the declared objectives of those introducing incomes policy as the criteria for evaluation is that an important part of the declaration of objectives is to influence behaviour. Sometimes this may lead to the policy being couched in terms that overstate the extent of change that is really expected. The difficulty is that if the actual results are too far removed from the expectations generated by the public advocacy, credibility is lost for the next phase of the policy.

If the extrapolation of past trends is used as a yardstick the appropriate test is to compare what happened with what *would* have happened in the absence of incomes policy. This of course requires some forecast of what would have happened in the absence of the policy, and this is notoriously difficult to make. While there are econometric techniques for producing these forecasts they depend heavily upon assuming fairly constant relationships between various economic variables, e.g. wages, unemployment, and productivity, and if, as has been suggested earlier, these relationships have been changing, the usefulness of the forecasts is accordingly reduced. Moreover, the forecasts or the econometric equations from which they are derived tend to regard economic policies as consisting of only two types, 'incomes policy on', or 'incomes policy off'. If the 'off' periods consist of various and changing combinations of *other* policy measures it cannot be assumed that there is a contant relationship between pay awards and unemployment in the absence of incomes policies.

The most comprehensive series of econometric tests of the impact of a policy was carried out by the Department of Employment for the period 1951–69 [37]. This showed that the 1965 Labour policy had some effect in its first two years which was followed by two years in which pay rose by about the same amount *more* than it would otherwise have done so that over all there may have been no effect on pay development other than one of timing. However, devaluation took place at the end of 1967 and this might well have had an effect in leading to pay increases which the econometric models could not satisfactorily include. Other tests have suggested that incomes policy have not had particularly pronounced, if any, effects, other than the periods of freeze. However, some of these measure wages only by the Wage Rate Index and so are of much less relevance to the objectives of the policy [30] [31] [33]. The Pay board concluded that on the whole the 1973–4 policy was well observed [41] [40].

There are finally two other points relevant to evaluation of incomes policies. People paradoxically seem to adopt much more stringent tests for incomes policies than they do for other policy measures. Thus demand management measures which notoriously have not been successful in containing inflation while maintaining full employment are not condemned merely on that ground, yet incomes policy may be. All evaluation of policies, in the real world of government decision-taking, should be between the policy adopted and the other policies which were considered as realistic reasonable alternatives. It is of little value to make comparisons with perfect systems; perfect systems of running an economy are not given to man.

The other point is that a distinction needs to be drawn between the content of the policy and its application. If it is concluded that an incomes policy failed it must be decided whether this was because the policy provisions were inappropriate and perhaps excessively generous in an anti-inflation sense, or whether it was because people did not observe the policy provisions. If it is for the former reason then incomes policies as such should be condemned only if it is also concluded that any policy that is to have a chance of being implemented must be sufficiently generous to fail to reduce inflationary pressures, or alternatively that a 'tight' incomes policy will prove to be incapable of implementation. But these are different arguments and not established by examination of the outcome of a specific policy and its application.

4. Conclusions

Government cannot ignore pay developments nor can it choose to opt out and leave pay developments to be determined by market forces or whatever else determines them. To do so would mean that the rest of economic policy was in effect dependent on what happened to pay, and this would involve too great an abdication over too many crucial areas of policy. The real choice facing Government is in the selection of methods or combination of methods to influence pay developments. But choose it must. Because pay levels and pay changes are influenced by social and institutional factors, particularly people's conceptions of fairness, any measures which affect one group will have repercussions on others. The implementation of policies determined by consideration of macroeconomic factors must pay regard to the actualities of pay determination at micro level. If people's perception of fairness and equity coincided with economic realities and with such changes as may be necessary on economic grounds, for example to obtain a necessary allocation or reallocation of labour, it might be much easier to influence pay development. But they do not, or at least do not seem to do so sufficiently well to permit significant changes to be introduced quickly and easily.

Incomes policies create some additional problems. By making certain issues surrounding relative pay levels explicit they focus attention upon these very sensitive areas. If they are successful they emphasize that many people are receiving smaller increases in *money* wages than they might otherwise have done, although the increases may be larger in real terms in the longer run. This inevitably creates problems inside trade unions as the leadership is pressed to obtain the larger money increases in the shorter run. At a time when the national leadership of trade unions is less able to commit its membership to any policy as a result of the decentralization of decision-taking and the effective devolution of power inside unions, the stresses thus generated makes the implementation of a policy more difficult. A paradox is that at the same as it is more difficult for national leadership to commit their membership in this way to the effective observance of restraint, the development of tripartite or bipartite discussions or agreements on general economic policy measures requires that the national leadership should take part in realistic discussions with Government about quid pro quos.

None the less, it is difficult to foresee any government abandoning for long the option of incomes policy. Even governments which are politically or philosophically opposed to the concept will no doubt be compelled by the force of economic events to use this range of policy measures. At the end of the day the lack of effective alternatives will lead governments to turn to incomes policies; these policies may have disadvantages but when the disadvantages of alternative policies are experienced the possible advantages of incomes policies will seem relatively more attractive. Each policy will also be a response to the perceived lessons of the last one(s).

At the same time the problems of Government as an employer with responsibilty for the whole public sector will compel it to take a more positive role than merely reacting to general economic circumstances which can be handled by demand management policies alone. Indeed, this area of Government responsibility might well prove to be one of its most difficult.

Because incomes policies have been regarded as short-term measures imposed by the overwhelming necessities of current adverse economic circumstances there has been relatively little attempt to work out longer-run policies. If expectations and attitudes really do lie at the heart of the problem then measures which are seen as only short-run ones will not be sufficient to secure the necessary changes. Incomes policy would have a much better chance of success if it were to seek to obtain these longer-term changes even at the expense of some of its more immediate effects, but it is doubtful whether this is politically feasible at the present time.

Bibliography

SECTION A

[1] CLEGG, H. A. *The System of Industrial Relations in Great Britain*, revised edn. (Basil Blackwell, Oxford, 1972).
A standard text on industrial relations with good chapters on the development of incomes policies. The various types of bargaining institutions and methods of payments are described in their historical setting.
[2] — — *How to run an Incomes Policy and why we made such a mess of the last one* (Heinemann, London, 1971).
A short very readable account of the Labour Government's policy 1965–70 by a former member of the N.B.P.I. It brings out very well the difficulties of implementing a policy and demonstrates the importance of taking account of industrial relations factors in an economic policy.
[3] CORINA, J. *The Development of Incomes Policy* (Institute of Personnel Management, London, 1966).
Although written ten years ago this pamphlet raises a number of issues which are central to incomes policy.
[4] FELS, A. *The British Prices and Incomes Board* (Cambridge University Press, 1972).
The most comprehensive survey of the role, operation, and methods of inquiry of the N.B.P.I. yet published.
[5] JACKSON, D., TURNER, H. A., and WILKINSON, F. *Do Trade Unions Cause Inflation?* (Cambridge University Press, 1972).
Discusses British experience of inflation in comparison with other countries' experiences. The second part argues that Government tax policy influences pay claims by affecting take-home pay.

[6] JONES, A. *The New Inflation: The Politics of Prices and Incomes* (Andre Deutsch and Penguin, London, 1973).
The former Chairman of the N.B.P.I. discusses the need for an incomes policy. He emphasizes the importance of productivity and the way in which pressures for wage increases spread. The role of incomes policy in the over-all framework of economic policy is well discussed.

[7] LAIDLER, D. and PURDY, D. E. (eds.) *Inflation and Labour Markets* (Manchester University Press, 1974).
A collection of papers dealing with issues in a more theoretical way which presents some challenges to incomes policies. Rather advanced reading.

[8] McKERSIE, R. B., and HUNTER, L. C. *Pay, Productivity and Collective Bargaining* (Macmillan, London, 1973).
A good account of the development of productivity bargaining with emphasis on the Labour Government's experience with incomes policy. Plenty of factual material.

[9] National Board for Prices and Incomes, various Reports but especially Nos. 23, 36, and 123 on Productivity Bargaining, 65 on Payment by Results, and 83 on Job Evaluation.

[10] PAISH, F. W. *Rise and Fall of Incomes Policy*, Hobart Paper 47 (Institute of Economic Affairs, London, 1971). Critical survey of incomes policy which argues that it might well do more harm than good and emphasizes the limitations which inevitably face an incomes policy.

[11] ROBINSON, D. *Wage Drift, Fringe Benefits and Manpower Distribution* (O.E.C.D., Paris, 1968).
An introductory discussion of various methods of payment bringing out the wide range of possible components of pay.

[12] — — *Incomes Policy*, Ditchley Paper No. 38 (Ditchley Park, 1971).
Short discussion of benefits and disadvantages of incomes policy. Compares other methods of influencing inflation open to governments based on an Anglo-American conference.

[13] Royal Commission on Trade Unions and Employers' Association 1965–1968 Report, Cmnd. 3623 (H.M.S.O., 1968): The Donovan Report. Good survey of industrial relations practices at the time but very little indeed on incomes policy. Essential reading for industrial relations questions.

[14] ULMAN, L. and FLANAGAN, R. J. *Wage Restraint: A Study of Incomes Policy in Western Europe* (University of California Press, Berkeley, 1971).
A comparison of incomes policies in a number of countries which combines statistical analysis with an understanding of collective bargaining processes.

SECTION B: OTHER WORKS

[15] BAYLISS, F. J. *British Wages Councils* (Basil Blackwell, Oxford, 1962).
[16] BOWER, A. and LUPTON, T. *Job and Pay Comparisons* (Gower Press, London, 1973).
[17] BROWN, WILFRED. *The Earnings Conflict* (Penguin, London, 1973).
[18] BROWN, WILLIAM. *Piecework Bargaining* (Heinemann Educational, London, 1973).
[19] CLIFF, A. *The Employers' Offensive: Productivity deals and how to fight them* (Pluto Press, London, 1970).
[20] DANIEL, W. W. 'Beyond the Wage-work Bargain', P.E.P. Broadsheet 519 (1970).
[21] DANIEL, W. W. and McINTOSH, N. *The Right to Manage* (MacDonald, P.E.P., London, 1972).
[22] FAY, S. *Measure for Measure: Reforming the Trade Unions* (Chatto and Windus, Charles Knight, London, 1970).
[23] FISHER, A. and DIX, B. *Low Pay and How to End It* (Pitman Publishing, London, 1974).

[24] FLANDERS, A. *The Fawley Productivity Agreements* (Faber and Faber, London, 1964).

[25] GOODMAN, J. F. B. and WHITTINGHAM, T. G. *Shop Stewards* (Pan Management Series, London, 1973).

[26] HYMAN, R. and BROUGH, I. *Social Values and Industrial Relations* (Blackwell, Oxford, 1975).

[27] INGHAM, G. *Size of Industrial Organisation and Worker Behaviour* (Cambridge University Press, 1970).

[28] McCARTHY, W. E. J. and WILLIS, N. D. *Management by Agreement* (Hutchinson, 1973).

[29] MACKAY, D. I., BODDY, D., BLACK, J. and JONES, N. *Labour Markets Under Different Employment Conditions* (George Allen and Unwin, London, 1971).

[30] PARKIN, J. M. 'Incomes Policy: Some Further Results in the Determination of the Rate of Change of Money Wages', *Economica* (Nov. 1970).

[31] — — 'United Kingdom Inflation: the Policy Alternatives', *National Westminster Bank Review* (May 1974).

[32] ROBINSON, D. (ed.) *Local Labour Markets and Wage Structures* (Gower Press, London, 1970).

[33] — — 'Labour market policies' in Beckerman, W. (ed.), *The Labour Government's Economic Record 1964–1970* (Duckworth, 1972).

[34] — — *Solidaristic Wage Policy in Sweden* (O.E.C.D., Paris, 1974).

[35] SEGLOW, P. (ed.) *The Future of Productivity Bargaining* (Brunel University, 1973).

[36] WEEKES, B., MELLISH, M., DICKENS, L. and LLOYD, J. *Industrial Relations and the Limits of the Law* (Blackwell, Oxford, 1975).

[37] Department of Employment. *Prices and Earnings in 1951–69: an Econometric Assessment* (H.M.S.O., May 1971).

[38] Office of Manpower Economics. *Wage Drift: Review of Literature and Research* (H.M.S.O., 1973).

[39] Pay Board. Advisory Report 2, *Relativities*, Cmnd. 5535 (Jan. 1974).

[40] — — Experiences of Operating a Statutory Incomes Policy (Mimeo, July 1974).

[41] — — Quarterly Reports.

[42] Trade Union Congress. Annual Reports with verbatim reports of debates on incomes policy, industrial relations, and Government's economic policies.

I I

Public Finance

P. J. N. SINCLAIR

1. Introduction

This chapter investigates why, and how much, governments spend, and also how their disbursements are paid for. The analysis concentrates mainly on Britain, but some historical and international comparisons will be made. The methods governments employ to raise revenue will also be examined: their merits and drawbacks, their evolution in the recent past, and their likely development in the future.

The chief revenue-raiser is, of course, taxation. No society on which records exist—past or present—has managed without them. The reasons for having taxes fall under four headings. First, *public goods* have to be paid for. This technical term will be defined and illustrated below. Second, for reasons good or bad, society frequently needs to defray *losses or subsidies* on a number of other undertakings. The third function of taxes is to *redistribute*, in cash or kind, to those whom the Government thinks deserve more than inheritance, luck, and the market place give them. The fourth reason for taxes is to meet the costs of the community's financial obligations to pay *interest on the National Debt*.

Table 11.1 gives a comprehensive breakdown of Public Expenditure (expressed in real terms, in 1975 prices) for the fiscal years 1970–1 to 1974–5, with forecasts for the following five years, in the United Kingdom. Expenditure under rows 1, 9, and (in part) 8 and 11 can be classified as public goods; that under rows 3, 4, 5, 6, and the remainder of 8 comes under the heading of subsidies considered in section 3; most of the expenditure in rows 10 and 11 is on merit goods (section 4); rows 7 and 12 can best be treated as redistributive (section 5.3); debt interest is examined in section 6; the remaining rows are *sui generis* and do not fit neatly into our classification. Row 2 could be interpreted as redistributive, while 13, 14, and 15 might be categorized as public goods expenditure.

2. Public Goods

Public goods are goods which can be consumed collectively. One person's enjoyment of a public good in no way prevents someone else's. What is more, no one can be prevented from enjoying public goods if he wishes to: exclusion is impossible. They are contrasted with a private good (apples, for instance) from which generally only one person can derive satisfaction; and from other goods or amenities from which exclusion is possible, although they may share other characteristics of public goods. Because exclusion is impossible, direct charges for consumption are impossible.

One example of public goods is collective defence. Any benefits X feels it confers on him are in no sense at the expense of someone else's deriving them either. This is not to suggest that everyone must benefit from expenditure on defence. X may be a pacifist: he may consider that some types of defence spending are more likely to jeopardize his security than increase it; he may feel that it threatens something dear to him. The point simply is that, good or bad, defence can only be 'consumed' collectively.

Other types of public good are not hard to find. The task, assumed by public authorities, of containing, and eliminating, contagious diseases. TV and radio waves: the fact that X's set receives them does not stop Y's doing so as well. Good architecture, at least on the outside of buildings, displaying a public face. The judiciary and the police are also public goods. One of the most important of all public goods, with profound economic effects, is knowledge—knowledge, at least, which is unappropriable. The saving in the costs of gathering information afforded by the Yellow Pages of Telephone Directories is a simple example.

A decentralized market system will probably not, by itself, provide public goods in the required amount. This is because the extent to which X contributes towards the provision of public goods will only to an insignificant extent affect how much X can himself consume. What matters for X's consumption is what is provided by everyone together; and that in turn depends on what the millions of others provide. In these circumstances it will pay people to understate their demand for public goods and this may make it hard for public authorities to decide how much to provide. If a city council sends a questionnaire to all inhabitants, asking them to put a monetary value on the benefit they would get from a doubling of the local police force, but pointing out that each household will be called on to pay some proportion of the value it states, plenty of households will reply, 'Nothing'—not because the extra policemen are valueless to them but because the increase in their numbers, and the benefit each household derives, will be seen to depend primarily on the answers of others. All you really get from being honest is a bigger tax demand.

The only realistic solution to this problem involves communal action, organizing our collective affairs together. Application of the Pareto criterion (discussed in Chapter 6) requires that the ratio of the *sum* of individuals' marginal benefits (or utilities) from a public good to the price (as a measure of marginal benefit) of a private good be equal to the ratio of their respective marginal social costs, if the allocation of economic resources between public and private goods is to be correct under ideal conditions. Public goods are, of course, costly to provide in aggregate, and, clearly, some limit must be placed on them. In practice, the decision on how much should be provided lies with governments; and their guesses of 'the sum of individuals' marginal

TABLE 11.1. *Public Expenditure by Programme in Volume Terms: 1970–1 to 1979–80*

£ million at 1975 Survey prices

	1970–1	1971–2	1972–3	1973–4	1974–5	1975–6	1976–7	1977–8	1978–9	1979–80
1. Defence	4,531	4,593	4,494	4,426	4,426	4,538	4,586	4,573	4,541	4,541
2. Overseas aid and other overseas services	598	646	788	825	798	734	882	953	1,027	1,085
3. Agriculture, fisheries and forestry	632	718	635	751	1,468	1,438	987	840	641	612
4. Trade, industry and employment:										
Investment grants	808	635	384	233	102	63	23	5	2	1
Other	1,080	1,234	1,755	2,538	2,763	2,618	2,249	2,085	2,121	2,113
5. Nationalized industries' capital expenditure	2,669	2,554	2,519	2,281	2,822	2,358	3,050	2,647	2,789	2,907
6. Roads and transport	1,790	1,727	1,848	1,964	2,181	2,316	2,193	2,032	1,860	1,852
7. Housing	2,827	2,492	2,555	3,330	4,429	4,018	4,097	4,064	4,014	4,090
8. Other environmental services	1,855	1,888	2,014	2,156	2,088	2,217	2,045	2,062	1,991	1,981

9. Law, order and protective services	1,093	1,175	1,189	1,260	1,339	1,444	1,470	1,462	1,439	1,438
10. Education and libraries, science and arts	5,073	5,434	5,799	6,081	6,104	6,164	6,234	6,141	6,024	5,995
11. Health and personal social services	4,235	4,405	4,701	4,934	5,056	5,285	5,317	5,384	5,465	5,548
12. Social security	7,200	7,646	8,078	8,080	8,582	9,463	10,002	10,014	9,964	9,963
13. Other public services	520	560	757	587	628	682	686	686	675	679
14. Common services	545	582	599	606	606	713	678	697	716	739
15. Northern Ireland	767	802	896	1,015	1,200	1,321	1,336	1,306	1,263	1,258
Civil Service staff costs								—50	—140	—130
Total programmes	36,223	37,091	39,011	41,067	44,497	46,372	45,835	44,901	44,392	44,672
Debt interest	4,142	4,031	4,048	4,764	4,757	5,000	6,200	7,000	7,500	7,500
Contingency reserve							700	900	1,200	1,400
Shortfall						—200	—250	—250	—250	—250
Total	40,365	41,122	43,059	45,831	49,254	51,172	52,485	52,551	52,842	53,322

Source: *Public Expenditure to 1979–80*, Cmnd. 6393 (Feb. 1976), Table 1.4, p. 14.

benefits', however intuitive or inaccurate, are often influenced by pressure groups and periodic elections. What must be noticed, however, is that public goods have to be paid for by some system of levies or taxes on the citizens themselves.

3. Subsidies

3.1. The Economic Efficiency argument and its Applications

The second category of public expenditure we identified was the losses or subsidies on various undertakings, which governments assume.

A common justification for an economic undertaking to run at a loss is as follows. Everyone should be free to buy another unit of any private good at the same price; and this 'same price' should equal the extra costs, to society as a whole, involved in making another unit of the good available. The first of these two precepts presumes relatively little for proof; the second is necessarily true only in an ideal world, and very probably needs modification in the presence of distortions elsewhere in the economy. The implication is that everyone should be free to buy at a price equal to marginal cost: the detailed argument for setting price equal to marginal cost can be seen in Chapter 6.

Marginal cost need not equal average cost. Marginal cost means the addition to total cost involved in providing the last or the next unit, when the size of the unit is very small. The average cost is the total cost divided by the number of units provided. Only when average cost does not alter with output will the two be equal. This could occur in some cases—labour intensive operations, for instance, like services or baking bread, where the technical advantages or disadvantages to be had from altering the scale of provision are minimal. But in other cases there can be a wide gap between marginal cost and average cost. Two obvious instances are bridges and museums, two goods usually provided publicly. One extra journey across a bridge or visit to a museum costs those providing the service hardly anything at all. Until the facilities become congested, it costs other users nothing either; but when the point of congestion is reached the *external* marginal cost—in the form of extra delay imposed on *other* users—becomes appreciable; even though the 'internal' marginal cost stays negligible. The average cost, however, is a considerable one. The correct price to charge people who cross the bridge or visit the museum is (in ideal conditions) the *marginal cost to society*. Unless the facility is congested, this is nothing. So the bridge toll and museum entry charge should be set at zero except when they are congested. Any positive charge will produce economic loss—society is, as a whole, the poorer (in terms of time and fuel wasted) for having the toll. But there is one obvious and awkward implication of not having tolls or charges. The fixed costs of providing the facilities are not met. Taxation is an obvious possible source.

Several nationalized idustries are in a similar position to the bridge- or museum-owners. Transport and telecommunication are the obvious cases. The marginal cost of allowing another passenger on a train or a bus is very low, so long as the facilities are uncongested. Similarly with a telephone call. But these organizations have heavy costs to bear in total—a large wage bill to pay and a large debt on which to pay interest. These can be met, in part, by charging the higher social marginal cost which occurs when the facilities are congested—peak-time railway travellers and telephone callers impose external costs (delays, inconvenience and so on) on other would-be users. (This point will be developed in Chapter 18.) Another method of raising revenue to meet losses otherwise resulting from optimal pricing rules is to levy fixed contributions to meet the fixed costs, although this often merges at national level into taxation. Just as a club levies subscriptions on members to defray fixed costs, and charges marginal costs only for the use of facilities whenever they are used, telephone subscribers are charged quarterly rentals, and owners of vehicles and television sets charged for annual licences, which are independent of the use of the service made. All such charges are fixed, and so do not affect the *marginal* price which everyone who pays them faces. But there may well still be an over-all loss; general taxation is then needed to meet it.

3.2. Subsidies to Agriculture

Subsidies are given sometimes to specific industries. The best British example is perhaps agriculture. This has been subsidized since 1928 through exemption from rates, since 1930 through cheap loans, and since 1932, starting with wheat, through price regulation and price support. A major purpose of these subsidies has been to conserve a domestic agricultural industry in the face of competition from frequently low-priced imports; it has been felt to confer strategic and aesthetic social benefits; hence the marginal *social* cost of domestic output is less than the marginal commercial cost faced by farmers. So the price farmers receive for many of their products has been stabilized at levels often much higher than import prices. The device employed is 'deficiency payments', a system now being dismantled in conformity with E.E.C. regulations. The deficiency payment scheme keeps prices to consumers at the world level (plus the obvious mark-ups for distribution), and shields farmers from the losses this would involve by paying them, when necessary, a deficiency payment above this. By contrast, the E.E.C.s Common Agricultural Policy keeps the domestic price to farmers and buyers within prescribed limits, and taxes or subsidizes imports of food to keep their price in line with the domestic price. Until the world explosion in food prices in 1973–4 this always meant taxing food imports with tariffs, a policy seen earlier to be suspect.

3.3. Subsidies to Aviation

Another British instance of an industry subsidized heavily is aviation. The subsidy is often indirect, as the Government is a major purchaser of military aeroplanes, and the price paid is calculated to cover all costs and give a 'fair' rate of profit. The Government also defrays all the costs of abortive projects; and it has been known to require the State airlines to buy British, if necessary even subsidizing them as the price for this. The justification of the subsidy must be that the strategic importance of a domestic aircraft industry, and 'spill-over' benefits to other industries from research and development, keep marginal social costs below the marginal commercial costs confronting the manufacturer. The need to keep unemployment down or the exchange rate up have also been offered as reasons, but they are uncompelling, since economically more efficient means are at hand to reach these objectives.

3.4. Other Subsidies to Private Industry

Other subsidies paid to private industries have usually had a more specific purpose, and a more complicated method of operation. For something over a year after September 1966 manufacturing industry was paid a small subsidy for each employee. This was part of the Selective Employment Tax. The idea was to shift resources out of services into manufacturing, upon which the economy's over-all growth rate was felt to depend (see Chapter 8). Since the 1930s, and more especially the 1960s, increasingly lavish subsidies on investment (and, from 1967, employment) have been available for manufacturing firms operating in various regions of Britain where unemployment was seen to be below the national average. The Department of Scientific and Industrial Research was set up in 1916 to encourage and subsidize research in industry; and in recent years quite generous tax treatment has been given for research and development expenditure. Investment in manufacturing, irrespective of location, has been encouraged at various times by tax allowances (from 1959 to 1966 and from 1970), cash grants (between January 1966 to 1970), and increasingly generous depreciation allowances against tax. The purpose of the research and investment incentives has been to guide industry towards a 'socially correct' set of choices between consumption now and investment for consumption later. This can be done by offering the incentive of greater expected profit, or by increasing the cash flow for such projects if capital markets are imperfect, and do not therefore provide the funds.

The common thread between all these subsidies or losses has been that attempts to justify them depend on *economic efficiency*. Pricing at average cost for bridges, museums, telephones, and railways was seen to lead to waste; in ideal conditions, they, and all other goods, should be priced at marginal cost. In these four cases—to which one might add many others—pricing at or near marginal cost is likely to lead to losses. The agriculture and aviation cases were slightly different. Here the crucial factor was the *external* benefits (greater security and so on) alleged to accrue from domestic production. Subsidies were one method—perhaps the most efficient method—of ensuring that these benefits were reaped to the correct extent. Then we saw specific subsidies or allowances (for regional development or investment, for instance) being given. In this case, the justification must be that the market place *malfunctions*. Unemployment in a particular region ought to lower wages there, relative to other areas, and so induce a double switch: workers to the work in the other areas, and work to the workers in the area concerned, but this does not happen sufficiently. If society invests too little and consumes too much, the shortage of capital should be signalled in the form of a high enough reward to investors and savers to correct the misallocation. But, for various reasons, this does not happen either, or happens too slowly. Hence the subsidy. Research may combine the external benefits and market malfunctioning arguments—not all the gains from successful research go to the researcher, and some may accrue free, at once or after the patent expires, to others; also there may be an 'intertemporal' fault in the market which places too low a value on any form of investment, of which research is one.Unfortunately, some subsidies given cannot easily be justified under any of these criteria; and the calculation of 'correct' prices, 'external' benefits, and 'marginal' costs is so beset with mathematical, political, or philosophical problems that all we can attempt are the crudest and most tentative of guesses. But before moving on to the third object of taxation—redistribution —we should look at the last type of justifiable subsidy.

4. Merit Goods

Merit goods are goods which buyers may for some reason undervalue. Education is an often-quoted example. The point is that if there were no State subsidy or State provision of education, then parents would decide on the level of education their children received. In many cases the parents could be feckless and·disregard their children's interests. The children themselves might indeed be no better judges of their interests at the time either. So education is subsidized, and also attendance made compulsory. In many societies, it is avi+lable free. The argument does not necessarily imply that the State should itself control all the schools, merely that education should be cheap, in relation to costs, *or* compulsory. The fact that it is generally *both* is partly explained by the income-distribution argument we consider next. Health is similar to education; both the merit good and income-distribution arguments are relevant. We may bitterly regret not having visited our doctor for an early diagnosis; cheap, or free, or, alternatively, compulsory access to him may guide us to make 'better' decisions. And again, parents may pay inadequate attention to their children's health. But the provision of a free medical service may also be a way of making the distribution of income less unequal, and of compensating those unlucky enough to be prone to illness. Also, in contagious disease we have a case of a pure public 'bad'; so anything to halt or cure it is a public good. These two merit goods—education and health—are dominant items of public expenditure, frequently consuming, together, one-seventh or more of society's total economic resources.

5. Income Redistribution

5.1. Factors Influencing the Distribution of Income

How the market place parcels out income to the citizens in a society is a complex matter. It is described in some detail in the chapter on pay policy. National income may be decomposed into earned income (wages and salaries) and unearned income (rent, profits, and interest). Virtually everyone receives unearned income, in cash or kind. Consumer durables, houses, inherited stocks and shares, accumulated savings, and pension rights all confer a yield of services or income. These assets constitute wealth (a stock), and unearned income, both psychic and pecuniary, is the yield (a flow) of wealth. About two-fifths of the population are also workers: usually some

90 per cent of the male population aged between 20 and 65, and about 35 per cent of the female population in this age range, receive earned income in return for work. Nearly the entire population—all but the youngest and oldest—are workers in a wider sense: at the least they perform jobs, as it happens unpriced in the market place, for themselves or their household, in the house or the garden. The fruits of labour, and, more particularly, the income from wealth, are unevenly spread over the population; but there can hardly be any family with no income at all from both sources, even before the substantial adjustments by the Government are carried out. The inequality in wealth and income arises from differences in ability, inheritance, accumulated savings, market power, and luck.

5.2. The Welfare Arguments

No area in economics elicits greater controversy than the question of what constitutes an optimum distribution of income. Any answer is necessarily normative, not positive; and this difficulty is further compounded by the fact that individuals will differ in their answers, and even disagree about whether or how they can formulate general principles for debating the topic.

Marx and Proudhon challenged the moral basis of property rights, and the unearned income that accrues from them in capitalist or pre-capitalist societies. Marx also believed that labour income (earned income) should be spread evenly. Complete equality was a moral precept, for which no independent justification was offered or thought to be necessary. The utilitarian approach to the question suggests that the distribution of income is best when redistribution has equalized the marginal utility of money for everyone. This implies complete equality of incomes if, and only if, everyone has the same relationship between money and utility—the same utility function.[1] It produces strange results when, for example, poor health prevents someone enjoying money as much as others. It is also open to other objections: can one individual's marginal utility of money be measured, or compared with that of someone else? A recent attempt to answer the problem has relied on the concept of a hypothetical social contract which would be drawn up between everyone if they were unaware of what their actual position in the hierarchy of incomes would actually be. They would be so alarmed, the argument runs, of falling into the poorest set that they would assent to a distribution of incomes which maximized the absolute income of the poorest set. This would result in complete equality provided that the volume of work done, and goods produced, did not fall as the marginal rate of tax on incomes was raised to 100 per cent—or if individuals were deprived of any freedom to choose their hours and intensity of work. But if these liberties are protected, and the disincentive effects of high marginal rates of income tax are perceptible, the hypothetical contract to maximize the absolute income of the poorest set will impose less than total equality of incomes [26, 11, 25].

It has sometimes been held that the income a person receives is a true reflection of the value placed by society on the (marginal product of) his

---

[1] With the further assumption that the marginal utility of money diminishes the more money one has.

wealth and work; and that this constitutes a case against any redistribution of incomes. The first proposition is falsified in practice by the imperfections in factor and other markets; the second is no less a value-judgement than any of the pleas for complete or limited equality discussed earlier.

5.3. Methods and Scale of Redistribution

Redistribution has its origins in the 1563 Poor Law, and has been transformed and extended beyond recognition in this century. Since the war the scale of assistance has steadily risen in real terms, although there is much evidence that the take-up rate of this assistance is still quite low.

The beneficiaries of redistribution may receive income in cash or kind. The redistribution in kind takes the form primarily of merit goods freely available to all in equal amounts. Although these goods can be enjoyed (if they will) by the better off, (at least, in the case of 'blanket' provision) the provision of merit goods is still redistributive since the costs are not spread equally over the population, but bear much more heavily on the higher-income groups. Education and health are the obvious examples. But there are other types of redistribution in kind as well: cheap butter (1973-4) and beef (1974) for old age pensioners.

Cash benefits include unemployment and sickness benefit; old age pensions; supplementary benefit; since 1971 family income supplement (for those on low earned income); child allowance; maternity benefits and assistance for widowhood or disablement; rent rebates for local authority and private tenants on low income (introduced by the Housing Finance Act, 1972); abatements in prescription charges for medicines bought by families in need or old age pensioners (an exception to their general reintroduction in 1968). Attempts to suppress politically sensitive symptoms of inflation led to 'blanket' subsidies on mortgage interest rates (1973, 1974) and some items of food (milk, 1973- ; bread, cheese, and butter, 1974-).

Redistribution has gainers; it also, obviously, has losers. So it must generally involve taxes. How redistributive taxation in fact is depends on its degree of 'progessivity'. A tax is progressive if the *proportion* of income paid in tax is higher for higher-income groups, regressive if it is lower for them. Assessing the effect of the tax system on the distribution of income is difficult, since incomes are spread over a continuous scale, and it is possible for a tax to cut the ratio of the highest 25 per cent to the lowest 25 per cent, let us say, but raise it between the highest and lowest 10 per cent. In general, income taxes are strongly progressive, since an increasingly large chunk of income is lopped off in tax for every increase in the scale above about £6,000 p.a. Taxes on consumption may be regressive or progressive, depending on whether expenditure on the goods concerned is a higher or a lower proportion of low-income budgets than high-income budgets. The net effect of taxation in Britain in much of the nineteenth century has been thought to be slightly regressive. The picture is different now, although some commodities with a low income-elasticity of demand do bear a heavy rate of tax (see section 7.2 of this chapter). Tables 11.2 and 11.3 give some impression of the effect of income tax on the distribution of income.

TABLE 11.2. *Distribution of household incomes before and after tax 1972–3*

Range of incomes		Number of tax units	Income before tax	Taxes on income	Income after tax
Income before tax		Thousands	£ million	£ million	
Not under £	Under £				
	595	4,868	2,104	—	2,104
595	750	2,265	1,573	2	1,571
750	1,000	3,409	3,020	120	2,900
1,000	1,250	2,648	2,981	235	2,746
1,250	1,500	2,491	3,423	368	3,055
1,500	1,750	2,406	3,903	480	3,423
1,750	2,000	2,238	4,179	516	3,663
2,000	2,500	3,500	7,803	1,091	6,712
2,500	3,000	2,133	5,812	908	4,904
3,000	4,000	1,472	5,009	911	4,098
4,000	5,000	455	2,022	459	1,563
5,000	6,000	157	860	226	634
6,000	8,000	146	999	297	702
8,000	10,000	68	605	216	389
10,000	12,000	39	426	172	254
12,000	15,000	26	345	155	190
15,000	20,000	17	289	147	142
20,000 and over		13	411	269	142
Total		28,351	45,764	6,572	39,192
Income not included in the classification by ranges			8,754		
Total income of households (including pensions and other benefits from life assurance and superannuation funds)			54,518		

Not under £	Under £				
	595	4,871	2,105	—	2,105
595	750	2,594	1,822	25	1,797
750	1,000	4,164	3,910	222	3,688
1,000	1,250	3,227	4,085	438	3,647
1,250	1,500	2,945	4,638	581	4,057
1,500	1,750	2,686	5,005	639	4,366
1,750	2,000	2,280	4,929	665	4,264
2,000	2,500	3,154	8,241	1,223	7,018
2,500	3,000	1,273	4,197	731	3,466
3,000	4,000	769	3,347	736	2,611
4,000	5,000	183	1,138	325	813
5,000	6,000	95	780	263	517
6,000	8,000	81	913	360	553
8,000	10,000	20	355	177	178
10,000	12,000	5	124	71	53
12,000	15,000	3	91	55	36
15,000	20,000	0·5	24	16	8
20,000 and over		0·5	60	45	15
Total		28,351	45,764	6,572	39,192
Income not included in the classification by ranges			8,754		

Total income of households (including pensions and other benefits from life assurance and superannuation funds) 54,518

Source: *National Income and Expenditure 1964–74* (H.M.S.O., 1975), Table 28, p. 31.

6. The National Debt

Lastly, we come to our fourth need for taxes: to pay interest on the National Debt. The National Debt is the sum total of the *Government's* interest-bearing obligations. In large measure, these debts are explained by the excess of Government spending over the tax receipts in the two World Wars. The First War more than decupled the Central Government's interest-bearing debt £650m. to over £7,000m., and the Second War nearly trebled it by adding another £14,000m. or so. The thirty years after 1945 saw it rise by another £25,000m. Table 11.4 gives the most recent estimate available, and shows how the debt is broken down by the type of obligation, and nature of its holder. Fortunately for the tax-payer most of these debts are in the form of

TABLE 11.3. *Official estimates of distribution of income, before and after tax, United Kingdom 1949–67*

	Percentage share of total income					
	Before tax			After tax		
	Top 10	Next 60	Bottom 30	Top 10	Next 60	Bottom 30
	%	%	%	%	%	%
1949	33·2	54·1	12·7	27·1	58·3	14·6
1954	29·8	59·3	10·9	24·8	63·1	12·1
1959	29·4	60·9	9·7	25·2	63·5	11·2
1964	29·0	61·4	9·6	25·1	64·1	10·8
1967	28·0	61·6	10·4	24·3	63·7	12·0

Source: Atkinson, *The Economics of Inequality* (Oxford University Press, 1975), Table 4.1, p. 51. These were based upon Nicholson, R. J., 'The Distribution of Personal Income', *Lloyds Bank Review* (Jan. 1967).

long-term fixed-interest bonds; he has been shielded from much of the unparalleled rise in nominal interest rates that has occurred since the last war. To the luckless holder, of course, this has meant a sharp fall in the nominal value of his bonds, and a remorselessly negative real return apart from brief periods. Inflation (the growing expectations of which were the main cause of the rising interest rates) has helped to whittle away the real value of interest payments, too. But for fresh debt, newly issued to cover the current budget deficit, or to redeem old bonds falling due, the expectation of inflation has an odd effect: if the new debt is not indexed,[2] the interest payments will reflect fears of inflation and effectively force the Government into a fast rate of amortization of the debt in real terms. At the time of writing, for example, the Government must offer £14 per year interest to borrow £100 for a long period (say, thirty years)—and if inflation occurs as expected, some two-thirds of the real value of the loan will have been already paid off after seven years. If the annual rate of inflation comes down to single figures, however,

[2] A bond is fully indexed against inflation if both the interest payments (coupon) and redemption value are guaranteed in real terms.

the burden of debt-serving on future tax-payers becomes very onerous indeed. These points constitute some of the justification for indexing Government borrowing. The case for continuing to pay interest on Government borrowing from the public is both moral and prudential: it will have to pay prohibitive interest on future borrowings if it has reneged in the past. It is interesting to note that substantial increases in the real burden of National Debt servicing charges are forecast for the remainder of the 1970s—a rise from about $10\frac{1}{2}$ per cent of total public expenditure in 1974–5 to nearly 17 per cent only five years later. This estimate is based on a pessimistic view of continued Government borrowing, and an optimistic view of the rate of inflation—but not (one trusts) on the view that bond-holders will begin to anticipate any possibility of default!

The National Debt has grown simply because of budget deficits. These are likely in wartime, as military expenditure soars. Inflation may produce deficits too—'fiscal boost' as it is known because tax payments on average lag behind Government spending. There is also, as was seen in Chapter 4, an argument for being prepared to deliberately 'unbalance' the budget when the pressure of aggregate demand is too low or too high and if the alternative weapon, monetary policy, works too slowly. This argument is originally due to Keynes but is also supported by Milton Friedman. The idea is that 'fiscal stabilizers' should be 'built-in'; when demand is high, tax receipts should exceed Government spending; when low, fall short. We must, however, distinguish the effects of a change in the budget deficit from the budget deficit level itself. Keynes's theory is that a *rise in the deficit* or *fall in the surplus* will be expansionary, raising output if there are spare resources, and raising prices in any case, but especially if there are none. This is because Government spending must rise, or consumption spending must rise somewhat if tax rates fall; and the multiplier chimes in, steadily if slowly, to amplify the effect. For Friedman, two things are important: the *level* of the deficit, and whether the gap is covered in part or whole by raising the *money supply*. Demand, and perhaps prices, will go up if the existence of a deficit leads the Government to raise the money supply. We shall return to this macroeconomic aspect of public finance after analysing the British system of taxation.

7. Sources of Government Revenue

The sources of Government revenue can be broken down in several ways. Some is precepted by local authorities, through rates; most accrues to Central Government; some comes from the gross trading surpluses of public corporations. A second distinction is between current receipts and capital receipts; a third between direct taxation (levied on income and capital) and indirect taxation (from taxes on expenditure).

7.1. Taxes on Income and Capital

For many years the biggest single revenue-raiser has been income tax. It is expected to yield some £14,000m. in the financial year 1975–6. All income—wages, salaries, commissions, bonuses, dividends, interest, and rent—is subject to tax. There is a personal allowance for a single persion, which is un-taxed: this is £675 per year in 1975–6. Married couples receive a combined

TABLE 11.4. Estimated distribution of the national debt: 31 March 1975

£ million
Nominal values: [a] *percentage of total debts in italics*

	(i) Total	(ii)	(iii) Treasury bills	(iv) Total (v)+(vi)+(vii)	(v) Up to 5 years to maturity	(vi) Over 5 and up to 15 years	(vii) Over 15 years and undated	(viii) Non-marketable debt
Official holdings	12,785	*28·8*	4,859	6,871	2,491	1,841	2,539	1,055
Market holdings								
Public bodies:								
Public corporations	32	*—*	—	32	26	4	2	|
Local authorities [b]	20	*—*	··	20	6	4	10	··
Total public bodies	52	*0·2*	··	52	32	8	12	··
Banking sector: [c]								
Deposit banks	1,878		323	1,555	1,402	153 (vi+vii)		—
National Giro	23		—	23	17	6 (vi+vii)		—
Accepting houses, overseas banks and other banks	479		94	385	213	172 (vi+vii)		—
Discount houses	457		424	33	30	3 (vi+vii)		—
Total banking sector	2,837	*6·4*	841	1,996	1,662	334 (vi+vii)		—
Other financial institutions:								
Insurance companies	5,341		26	5,315	643	1,085	3,587	··
Building societies	1,651		—	1,651	1,224	400	27	|
National Savings Bank, investment account	378		3	375	44	95	236	|
Trustee savings banks, special investment departments	647		—	647	97	287	263	|
Local authority superannuation funds	487		··	487	98	57	332	|
Other public sector superannuation funds	408		1	407	129	94	184	|
Private sector superannuation funds	1,278		2	1,276	338	214	724	|
Investment trusts	137		—	137	77	48	12	|
Unit trusts	44		—	44	16	27	1	|
Other	107		12	95	70	6	19	|
Total other financial institutions	10,478	*23·6*	44	10,434	2,736	2,313	5,385	··

	Total	%						
Overseas holders:								
International organizations	1,277		4	140	48	92	—	1,133
Central monetary institutions	2,996		1,716	1,280	462	374	444	
Other	1,700		7	1,679	226	234	1,219	14
Total overseas holders	5,973	12·9	1,727	3,099	736	700	1,663	1,147
Other holders:								
Public Trustee and various non-corporate bodies	251		26	223	34	60	129	2
Private funds and trusts	9,297		..	5,514	1,789	1,298	2,427	3,783
Industrial and commercial companies	109		25	77[d]	{ 2,019	{ 517[e]		{ 7
Other (residual)	2,713		..	2,459				{ 254
Total other holders	12,370	28·1	51	8,273	3,842	{ 4,431[f]		4,046
Total market holdings	31,710	71·2	2,663	23,854	9,008	4,635	10,211	5,193
Total debt	44,495	100·0	7,522	30,725	11,499	6,476	12,750[g]	6,248
of which, nationalized industries' stocks guaranteed by the Government	908			908	654	30	224	

.. not available.
— nil or less than £½ million.

[a] With some exceptions: see notes on sources and definitions.
[b] At end-March 1974 this classification included municipal banks' holdings of £68 million, which now form part of other financial institutions.
[c] Stocks shown at book value or cost except for those of the discount market where nominal values are used.
[d] Represents a sample only of companies' holdings: see notes on sources and definitions.
[e] On the assumption that the banking sector holds approximately £230 million of medium-dated and £100 million of long-dated stock, this figure represents mainly long-dated stock.
[f] On the above assumption, this figure comprises approximately £1,380 million medium-dated and £3,050 million long-dated.
[g] Of which undated £3,385 million.

Source: *Bank of England Quarterly Bulletin*, xv, No. 4 (Dec. 1975), p. 362.

allowance of £955, although since 1971 they have been able to opt, up to a certain limit, for separate tax assessment. There are further allowances for children (£240 for the first child, £188 for the second and subsequent), for aged dependent relatives, certain necessary working and other expenses, life insurance premiums, covenants, and—a very substantial item—all interest paid on loans or mortgages secured on the family house. When these allowances have been subtracted, all income is taxed at a standard rate (35 per cent in 1975–6). Any excess over £4,500 is taxed more heavily: the rate goes up by 5 per cent steps, until a level of 75 per cent is reached on any income (less allowances) between £15,000 and £20,000 per year. Above that, there is a top rate of 83 per cent. Investment income derived from the ownership of assets (receipts of dividends, interest, and rent) is subject to an additional levy of 15 per cent if it exceeds £1,000 per year. So the highest rate of tax (on investment income above this limit, received by a person with an annual income over £20,000) is 98 per cent. Similar, if not even higher, rates of tax are levied on high incomes in New Zealand and some Scandinavian countries; but British tax rates in this range are considerably heavier than in North America or the rest of Western Europe.

At present levels, income tax receipts amount to some 12 per cent of GNP. This compares with 7 per cent in 1929 and 10½ per cent in 1960. In recent years the burden of income tax has increased most on sections of income between £1,000 and £2,000 per year, and above £5,500 (in 1975 values). Since 1961 the steepest increases in the average rate of tax have occurred in the £1,000 to £3,000 range. This is explained chiefly by the fact that the thresholds at which the higher rates start to operate have been changed very little in money terms despite inflation, and have consequently come down sharply in real terms. The reason why the share of income tax in GNP has risen so little, in spite of sharp rises in the average rate of tax on upper incomes, is the increasing equalization of pre-tax incomes.

Nearly all sources of Government revenue have the drawback that they distort choices. Income tax is no exception. It distorts the individual's choices between leisure and commodities. It is (in general) a necessary condition for economic efficiency that the rate at which an individual is prepared to exchange his leisure for commodities at the margin should equal the marginal rate at which firms can transform his leisure into commodities. If these marginal rates were unequal, the individual and the owners of a firm could both become better off—to no one else's detriment—by bargaining some other exchange of labour for goods. Suppose, for example, a man will only give up one hour of leisure for £2, but that a firm can produce a commodity value at £3 by employing him for that hour. It would be to everyone's benefit if the firm employed him for any sum between £2 and £3. The firm would make a profit and the man would gain more than the £2 necessary to compensate him for the loss of his leisure. A 50 per cent income tax would prevent this occurring because £1.50 is not sufficient to induce the man to work. A good illustration of the distortion this brings is the way it persuades individuals to forsake comparative advantage, to some extent, by 'doing it yourself'. Furthermore, as the marginal rate of income tax is increased, the leisure of the individual concerned comes to acquire more and more the character of a public bad (the opposite of a public good). This is so because all other citizens have to forgo the advantages they would derive from his work, through his tax payments. Against this, increases in tax rates can often lead people to work longer hours, especially if they treat the leisure they retain as complementary with the commodities they buy.

In fact, the case for taxes on income is based on two points: they are often a relatively costless way of obtaining some of the vast financial resources the State needs to support its transfers and expenditure; and they are a very convenient way of achieving whatever redistribution it is aiming for. Yet it might be noted that some research on the latter has come up with recommendations for far lower marginal rates of tax—especially on top incomes—than present British levels [18]. A final point on marginal tax rates: the effect of the recent trend to selective welfare benefits (e.g. income-related rent and rate rebates, Social Security payments, and Family Income Supplement) has been to increase substantially the effective marginal rate of tax on those who take them up. In some cases this can reach 100 per cent. So the effective marginal rate is often at its maximum on both very low and very high incomes.

The other major direct tax is Corporation Tax: tax on the profits of companies. In recent years it has come to yield about £2,500m. per year. The figure fluctuates: profits themselves are a volatile element in the national income, rising in booms and falling in slumps; companies can now set off against Corporation Tax the depreciation of their investments virtually when they like; and the timing and rates of charge do change. Since 1973 Corporation Tax has been based on an 'imputations' system. Profits, net of permissible depreciation and other allowances (e.g. interest on borrowing), are taxed (since 1974, at 52 per cent). The company can then split the residue as it chooses between dividends for its shareholders and retained earnings. Dividends are then deemed to have paid income tax at the standard rate; the shareholder pays more tax only if his income from all sources exceeds about £5,500, or his investment income exceeds £1,000. If his income is very low, he gets a refund.

The system previously in operation (from 1965 to 1973) had favoured profit retention in the company (see Chapter 3); this was achieved by double taxation on dividends, which were liable to income tax and paid out of profits net of Corporation Tax (then at lower rates, which oscillated between 40 and 45 per cent). There is controversy about the wisdom of the 1973 changes [16, 30].

On levels of tax, comparisons are hard, since systems differ; but British rates of Corporation Tax—at least until the 1975 reform which deferred tax due on profits attributable to stock appreciation—were on average somewhat above equivalent rates abroad. On the question of incidence—who finally pays Corporation Tax—there is little firm evidence to suggest that it is passed on fully or quickly to the customer in the form of higher prices, and some impressive American evidence [14] to suggest that it is not. In certain circumstances, it may be passed backwards on to employees in the form of lower wages than otherwise. But probably the major burden is borne by the owners of companies.

The direct taxes on capital yielded £899m. in 1974–5: £381m. from Capital Gains Tax (introduced in 1961, extended in 1965, and much modified since); £339m. from estate duties (introduced in their modern form in 1894 and greatly extended later); and £179m. from Stamp Duty (an ancient tax on the transfer of assets, doubled to 2 per cent in 1974). In the years to come a new Capital Transfer Tax will replace estate duties: under the rates now envisaged, the two will have similar yields, if differing incidence. It is also planned to bring in a Wealth Tax, which is now operating in several European countries, although often at lower rates than those suggested by the British Government.

7.2. Taxes on Expenditure

Central Government's taxes on expenditure are estimated to have yielded £8,095m. in 1974–5. Of this, nearly one-third came from Value Added Tax (V.A.T.). Brought in in 1973 to replace other types of indirect tax (purchase tax on 'luxuries' and S.E.T. on the employment of labour in service industries), V.A.T. is charged at various rates on businesses' valued-added—the excess of gross sales over their payments to other businesses. This amounts to paying the V.A.T. rate on sales value and recovering the tax paid by suppliers on their sales value. Some activities are zero-rated, paying no tax on their sales, but recovering the tax paid on purchases from other firms; food and housing are important examples. Others are exempt: the tax paid on purchases is not recovered, but tax is not charged on their sales. About one-third of the value of total output of goods and services is liable to V.A.T., at a rate (since July 1974) of 8 per cent. There is a higher rate of 25 per cent, applied first to petrol (November 1974) and then extended to a wide group of consumer durables (May 1975). France and Germany introduced V.A.T. in January 1968; the telling case for bringing it in here was perhaps the need to conform with Common Market practice. Collection costs—borne in large part by the businesses themselves—appear to be higher for V.A.T. than for the taxes it replaced. One important feature is that it is rebated on exports and applied to imports. The effects of the switchover to V.A.T. on the distribution of income are thought to have been negligible—the rates of tax on the chief items of expenditure in low-income budgets remained the same (often zero)—and there was little over-all impact on the cost of living. One can assume that V.A.T., like all expenditure taxes, is generally passed on fully to the customer. Two further arguments were made for V.A.T.: the previous tax base for expenditure was held to be too narrow (and hence inefficient for demand management policy) and too uneven (in an ideal world, the relative price of two goods facing consumers should deviate as little as possible from their relative marginal costs of production). Both these defects could, however, have been remedied by evening up the old taxes. It is too early to give a final judgement on V.A.T. [30].

Central Government's other receipts from taxes on expenditure come chiefly from motoring (in 1974–5 £1,549m. from petrol and oil, £532m. from

Motor Vehicle Duty—Road Fund—and £122m. from a special tax on top of V.A.T. on the sale of new cars); from smoking (£1,337m.) and alcoholic drink (£1,133m.); and from gambling (£268m.). Virtually all countries have substantial taxes on these activities. The goods concerned are usually treated as 'demerit' goods, or at least, relatively inessential; and they all have low price-elasticity of demand—implying that they are lucrative sources of tax revenue to the Exchequer, and that heavy taxation on them has less serious consequences for consumers' welfare than it would on more price-elastic goods. As most of these duties are specific (a tax on a unit of *quantity*) they tend to drop in real terms during inflation: the fact that they were held roughly constant in money terms between December 1968 and March 1974, for instance, meant that they fell by over 35 per cent in real terms in that period. Since inflation may raise the State's spending faster than its tax receipts, this can produce 'fiscal boost', mentioned earlier. There is therefore a strong case for keeping indirect taxation in line with the general price index. One property that these taxes have is widely felt to be opprobrious. They tend to be regressive: consumption of petrol, drink, and tobacco usually accounts for a higher share of low-income budgets than high-income ones. Expenditure on, for example, tobacco, appears to be virtually indpendent of income levels.

7.3. Other Sources of Central and Local Government Revenue

Other Central Government receipts include the proceeds of tariffs on imports ('Protective Duties' brought in some £500m. in 1974–5, with a further £24m. estimated to have come from agricultural levies imposed in conformity with the Common Market's Common Agricultural Policy). As was seen in Chapter 5, duties on imports must be inefficient, at least at the world level— for they contravene the rule that the price ratios for goods that one buyer faces should be as close as possible to the price ratios facing others. But import duties have usually proved cheap to collect; and it has to be remembered that virtually all other taxes create some distortion. Besides tariffs, £164m. was estimated to have come from television licences, £9m. from other small duties, £171m. from interest and dividends received by the Government on assets it owns, £1,103m. from various other sources, and £5,435m. from contributions from employers and employees to National Insurance.

The National Insurance Fund is designed to be self-balancing. Contributions are levied upon employer and employee in roughly equal measure, to defray the costs of providing pensions, and sickness, disability, unemployment, and other benefits. In 1974 there was a pronounced increase in the graduated, or income-related, element in the employee's contribution. The purpose of this was redistributive: the non-graduated part of the contribution is regressive.

Turning attention to the Local Authorities, one finds that the majority of their income takes the form of grants from Central Government, and that much of their spending is financed by borrowing. In 1974–5 less than one-quarter of their spending was raised locally through rates on residential, commercial, and industrial property. In that year rates generated some £3,127m. The other major local source of revenue is rents on municipally owned property, which, together with interest and dividends, brought in nearly £1,900m. that year. Rates are levied on the imputed rentable value of property; for a number of reasons, they are unpopular. Inflation and recent increases in the real volume of local authority spending have increased them sharply in money terms; they are more conspicuous than taxes on income or expenditure; it is often felt unfair that they are not related to income, or any measure of ability to pay, and are not paid by tenants. Yet there is something to commend rates. The structure of national taxation creates a large bias in the relative desirability of saving through house-buying and saving through other means (for instance, by buying shares). Dividends from shares, and interest from loans, are liable to Corporation and/or income tax, and a 15 per cent surcharge when income from this source exceeds £1,000 per year. But the imputed rent on an owner-occupant's dwelling is untaxed in Britain (although it is liable to tax in the Netherlands, for example). Interest on mortgages or loans to buy houses can be set off against the borrower's income for tax purposes, at least for the first house, whereas interest on borrowing to buy shares is not tax-deductible. There is no tax on any capital gains made on the sale of a house, if effected more than two years after purchase, but capital gains on shares are taxed. Rates go some way to redress these biases. Furthermore, if rates were replaced by additions to income or expenditure taxes, there could be a serious added disincentive to work, since the effective marginal rate of tax would have to go up sharply.

7.4. Microeconomic Criteria for Taxes

There are two *microeconomic* criteria on which to assess a tax: economic efficiency, and equity. Taxes inevitably affect the allocation of resources, usually, but not necessarily, for the worse. They influence consumers' choices between goods, and between goods and leisure; they alter wealth-holders' allocation of assets in their portfolios; they bear on production and factor-hiring decisions by firms. There are also the costs of collection, never wholly borne by the State, which represent a deadweight loss. Taxes can improve economic efficiency, if they are applied on the output of industries experiencing increasing costs of production (where marginal cost exceeds average cost) or firms imposing external costs on other firms or citizens (pollution, for example). The damage they bring will be low, if they are levied on the consumption of goods for which demand is inelastic, or on factors of production of which the supply is inelastic. The second criterion—equity—is hard to apply for many reasons. Individuals' views about the 'ideal' distribution of incomes are bound to vary. The actual effects of a tax on the distribution of income are difficult to assess. The correct balance between efficiency and equity—in so far as they conflict—can only be a matter of subjective judgement.

8. Note on Demand Management

Besides those already mentioned, there is a further use to which Government spending and taxation can be put. Both can be altered for *macroeconomic* purposes: they can and do alter the level of aggregate demand. To a great extent this purpose can be achieved simply by changing tax rates on income and on certain items of expenditure. None the less, this demand management aspect has to be integrated into the determination of taxation for all the reasons we have already seen, and vice versa. The effect on the economy in general and the level of demand in particular of budgetary changes is complex. The fiscal changes generally have monetary effects; the time-lags involved are often considerable and differ according to the tax rate changed, the type of expenditure directly affected, and the other influences at work in the economy at the particular time. Consideration of these matters is therefore left to a later chapter, so that monetary aspects of the economy already briefly referred to in Chapter 4 can be amplified and the impact of monetary policy examined.

Bibliography

The following books give an excellent coverage of the theory of public finance:
[1] ALLAN, C. M. *The Theory of Taxation* (Penguin, 1971) (introductory).
[2] BLINDER, A. S., SOLOW, R. M., *et al. The Economics of Public Finance* (Brookings Institution, 1974).
[3] MILLWARD, R. *Public Expenditure Economics* (McGraw-Hill, 1971).
[4] MUSGRAVE, R. A. *The Theory of Public Finance* (McGraw-Hill, 1959).
Note: [2] is particularly recommended as a comprehensive, modern, and readable work. [1] is a good introduction.

On Britain, the Central Office of Information has published a very useful summary of recent changes and the system (with some modifications) now in force:
[5] Central Office of Information. *The New British System of Taxation*, Reference Pamphlet 112 (1973).

The most recent document on the recent level and projected changes in public expenditure is:
[6] *Public Expenditure to 1979–80*, Cmnd. 6393 (H.M.S.O., Feb. 1976).

On income distribution and redistribution the following are strongly recommended:
[7] ATKINSON, A. B. *The Economics of Inequality* (Oxford University Press, 1975).
[8] SEN, A. K. *On Economic Inequality* (Oxford University Press, 1973).

On the macroeconomic significance of changes in the share of national income represented by various sorts of public expenditure, the reader is urged to consult:
[9] BACON, R. and ELTIS, W. A. *Britain's Economic Problem: Too Few Producers* (Macmillan, 1976).

Other works of general interest on aspects of public finance include:
[10] ATKINSON, A. B. (ed.) *Wealth, Income and Inequality* (Penguin, 1973).
[11] BARRY, B. M. *The Liberal Theory of Justice* (Oxford University Press, 1973).
[12] CAVES, R. E. (ed.) *Britain's Economic Prospects* (chapter by R. A. and P. Musgrave) (George Allen and Unwin, 1968).

[13] DIAMOND, P. A. and MIRRLEES, J. A. 'Optimum Taxation and Public Production', *American Economic Review* (Mar., June 1971).

[14] GORDON, R. 'The Shifting of Corporation Tax', *American Economic Review* (1967).

[15] HICKS, Lady U.K. *Public Finance*, 3rd edn. (Oxford University Press, 1968).

[16] KAY, J. A. 'The Taxation of Corporate Income and Capital Gains', *Oxford Economic Papers* (1974).

[17] LITTLE, I. M. D. and FLEMMING, J. S. *Why we Need a Wealth Tax* (Methuen, 1974).

[18] MIRRLEES, J. A. 'An exploration in the Theory of Optimum Income Taxation', *Review of Economic Studies* (1971).

[19] MOODY, T. and SMITH, K. G. D. 'An Evaluation of Subsidies to British Manufacturing Industry', *Oxford Economic Papers* (1975).

[20] NICHOLSON, R. J. 'The Distribution of Personal Income', *Lloyds Bank Review* (1967).

[21] NORDHAUS, W. D. 'The Political Business Cycle', *Review of Economic Studies* (1975).

[22] PEACOCK, A. T. and WISEMAN, J. *The Growth of Public Expenditure in the U.K.*, 2nd edn. (Unwin, 1967).

[23] PHELPS, E. S. (ed.) *Economic Justice* (especially chapters 16 (Atkinson), 18 (Phelps), and 19 (Arrow)) (Penguin, 1973.)

[24] PIGOU, A. C. *A Study in Public Finance* 3rd edn. (Macmillan, 1947).

[25] *Quarterly Journal of Economics* 'Symposium on Rawls' (Nov. 1974).

[26] RAWLS, J. *A Theory of Justice* (Oxford University Press, 1972).

[27] SAMUELSON, P. A. 'Diagrammatic Exposition of a Theory of Public Expenditure', *Review of Economics and Statistics* (1955).

[28] WARD, T. and NIELD, R. 'Public Spending and Taxation', *Economic Policy Review* (1975).

[29] WEBB, M. G. *The Economics of Nationalized Industries* (Nelson, 1973).

[30] WHALLEY, J. 'A General Equilibrium Assessment of the 1973 U.K. Tax Reform', *Economica* (1975).

12

Monetary Policy

R. G. SMETHURST

1. Monetary Theory and Monetary Policy

1.1. Portfolio Adjustments

The relationship between monetary policy and monetary theory is a complex one. At the most general level there is the question of whether, and if so how, a monetary economy differs from an economy which uses barter. Clearly, as an economy grows in complexity it will be more convenient to conduct exchanges between goods and services by means of some socially accepted medium of exchange—but does the interposition of money in this way affect the essential nature of the transaction? It is the fundamental proposition of Keynes's *General Theory of Employment, Interest and Money* that a monetary economy is essentially different, in particular that the demand for money as an asset, dependent on the interest rate on bonds (see Chapter 4, section 3.3), could prevent an economy in which prices were fully flexible from reaching equilibrium at full employment. But there is an alternative view that money can only affect 'money' things—the aggregate price level—and not real things—relative prices (the exchange ratios between goods), the real interest rate, and employment. The second view, expressed, as we saw in Chapter 4, in the crude quantity theory which involved a mechanically stable velocity of circulation, seemed to have been refuted by the *General Theory*, but has been revived in a more sophisticated form by Professor Milton Friedman and the monetarist school.

Keynes's simple model included a transactions and precautionary demand for money, dependent on money national income, and an asset demand for money, which involved the choice between money and bonds. Subsequent theoretical work has integrated the demand for active money balances (the 'transactions' and 'precautionary' demands) with this 'speculative' demand for idle money balances, and has extended the kinds of asset which can be held as alternatives to money to include a range of bonds of different maturities and equities. Thus instead of a situation where the asset-holder, worried about a possible fall in bond prices, puts all his wealth into the bank, we now allow the wealth-holder a variety of choices across a spectrum of short- and long-term financial assets. Indeed, as we also saw in Chapter 4, the wealth-holder's choice is thought by monetarists not to be confined to a portfolio of financial assets alone, but to include capital assets themselves and consumption goods, especially, but not only consumer durables.

Along with these theoretical developments have gone attempts to reveal empirical demand curves for money: economists have tried to find out whether the money held by people is empirically related in a systematic way to other economic variables, in particular, of course, the level of money national income and the level of interest rates (short and long term, real and nominal). Early attempts were concerned with discovering whether there was any empirical evidence for the Keynesian liquidity trap—an interest rate at which the demand for money became infinite so that no increase in the supply could induce people to buy bonds, lower interest rates and therefore stimulate investment expenditure. Later attempts were concerned more generally to measure the interest elasticity of the demand for money. This is the proportional change in the demand for money divided by the proportional change in the level of interest rates, a high value suggesting that the demand for money is very sensitive to a change in interest rates. In addition, there was increasing focus upon the stability of the demand for money as a function of money national income. These empirical questions, devolving from theoretical work, have profound importance for policy. If the demand for money is a stable function of a few determinate variables and therefore predictable, then monetary policy may offer a better method of controlling the economy than fiscal policy. If the demand for money is not at all interest-elastic, implying little significant 'speculative' demand for idle money balances, then the quantity theory of money holds and the monetary Authorities can directly control money national income (either real income or prices) by controlling the money supply.

On the other hand, the complex set of assets, financial and real, between which wealth-holders can choose makes agreement on empirical testing very difficult. The concept of money as a means of payment suggests that money is comprised of notes, coins, and current account deposits, but once this simple concept of money gives way to the notion of money as part of a spectrum of assets whose yields at the margin are equalized in wealth-holders' portfolios, it becomes difficult to differentiate money from non-monetary liquid assets. If then it becomes difficult to differentiate these theoretically, it also becomes difficult to define money for empirical purposes. Do we mean by money just cash and bank deposits against which a cheque can be drawn, assets which can be transferred between transactors without affecting the market for loans, or do we mean a reasonably liquid asset, such as money in interest-bearing deposits, whether in banks, hire-purchase finance houses, Building Societies, etc.?

A further example of the complex interaction between theory and policy is to be seen in the case of the money supply. This is often assumed to be reasonably under the control of the monetary Authorities (usually so called because they consist of both the Finance Ministry and the Central Bank—in the U.K. the Treasury and the Bank of England). So that, given a demand for money schedule, either the money supply could be chosen by the Authorities, or it could be set to match the demand for money at a chosen price (the interest rate). But the large part of the money supply in modern developed economies consists of deposits with financial intermediaries. Such intermediaries grant loans according to their own needs to earn income with reasonable security. The same portfolio theory which we have just been describing in relation to the demand for money is therefore applicable to the supply of it: banks grant loans as part of their portfolio management (see p. 318 on the asset structure of commercial banks) just as borrowers come to borrow as part of *their* portfolio changes (for instance, a firm may want to have more new plant and machinery, more new capital assets). So the Authorities' control of the money supply becomes a complex problem, and is only possible within limits: even if the Authorities want to expand the money supply the banks may not wish to grant more loans, and even if the loans are available, people may not wish to borrow. If the Authorities wish to contract bank deposits, the banks may try to circumvent this because advances earn relatively high interest.

Monetary policy can therefore be described in the most general terms as policy designed to produce reactions in the portfolios of banks, financial intermediaries, companies, and persons which involve changes in the demand for real assets. There is general agreement that monetary policy works by altering a given set of interest rates on a spectrum of assets, but there is considerable disagreement on which interest rates are affected, which real assets are affected, by how much, and over what time period. Yet these empirical questions are the critical ones for the policy-maker.

Of the areas where the disagreements between monetary economists have important policy implications, we may distinguish four: the definition of money; the nature of the demand for money; the nature of the mechanism which links changes in the money stock to changes in real expenditures on goods and services; and the inferences to be drawn from monetary history.

1.2. The Definition of Money

In Chapter 4, section 3.1 we saw that money had two main purposes—to act as a means of payment and as a store of value. If the portfolio approach sees a wide selection of financial and real assets as being involved in any monetary change, how are we to distinguish precisely which assets are to be counted as money and which as near-money substitutes? One approach would be to decide beforehand, on theoretical grounds, what *effects* money had on the economy, and then select that group of assets as 'money' which could be shown statistically to be closest to fulfilling that theoretical role. For example, we might try to identify that group of assets, changes in the supply of which best correlated with changes in money national income, and then define that group as the money supply.

An alternative approach is to ask what is the *essential nature* of money. This relates to the cost and uncertainty involved in barter as soon as society becomes at all complex. Firstly, there is the search cost involved in looking for an exchange partner who wishes to swap what one wants for what one has to offer—but this could be overcome, and frequently is in the development of monetary economies, by the use of some intermediate good which is in more general demand. (For example, suppose I bring a cow to market to obtain cooking pots. I am unlikely to find a potter willing to look after cows, at least if the economy is at all specialized. But I may find another farmer willing to swap eggs for my cow, and I now have a commodity readily acceptable to potters.) Secondly, however, even the use of intermediate goods for convenience in the barter process does not remove the uncertainties of valuation as the barter exchange ratios are determined—is the cow healthy, are the eggs fresh, will the pots last? So 'fiat money' (normally notes and coins) evolves as a *unit of account* and *means of payment*—and to the powerful individual or group issuing such money there accrues the 'seignorage'—the difference between the cost of the commodities and services which go into minting the coins or printing the notes, and the value of the resources which can be obtained in exchange.

But this kind of gain, the difference between the cost of producing fiat money and what can be bought with it, also offers a reward to *any* institution which can issue something which others can hold as an asset and which can be turned easily and with certainty as to its value, into fiat money (legal tender). For institutions issuing such liabilities in return for fiat money then have the use of funds to lend to others at a fee. In essence, all financial intermediaries act in this way, acknowledging their liability to provide fiat money (e.g. by issuing cheque books to customers against current accounts, which are the liability of the bank and the asset of the customer) and making their profit on the difference between their costs, which may include the payment of interest and the opportunity cost of keeping some legal tender in case of withdrawals, and the charges made for lending.

Thus not only legal tender (fiat money) but also bank deposits come to serve as the acceptable medium of exchange. But in a developed economy there are many kinds of financial intermediary, offering deposit facilities differing slightly from each other in respect of ease of withdrawal and interest rate paid (or providing other ancilliary facilities—like the clearing mechanism whereby banks settle transfers between their customers as instructed by the cheques drawn). If we count bank deposits against which cheques can be drawn as money, what about bank 'time deposits', which cannot technically be transferred by the writing of a cheque and therefore earn interest from the bank in return for the greater certainty that the deposits will stay put? For in practice it is very unlikely that a bank would dishonour a cheque overdrawn on a current account if a sufficiently large deposit account existed to meet it. Further, it is possible to draw cheques against agreed overdraft facilities, where *no* deposit exists to the credit of the person writing the cheque. And even in the absence of an agreed overdraft, I could draw a cheque in excess of my demand (current account) deposit, relying on the two or three days' credit afforded to me, in effect by the shopkeeper, whilst my cheque is going through the clearing mechanism to replenish my account, perhaps by drawing down my Building Society deposit, or by selling a government bond or industrial share. On the other hand, even if I have a large demand deposit (current account) balance a shopkeeper may refuse to accept my cheque.

Thus it is difficult to make a clear distinction between financial intermediary deposits which are money and those which are not. There is no obvious break in the spectrum of highly liquid assets, and transactions may occur on the basis of non-transferable assets which can very readily be converted into transferable ones. Attempts have been made to draw an analytic distinction by arguing that for an asset to be truly money the transfer of it in payment of a debt should complete the transaction. On this basis overdraft facilities are not money, since the use of an overdraft to pay a debt to a shop merely lands the transactor with a debt to his bank instead. We shall see in the next two sections that this issue is not just a matter of elegant theorizing but has a considerable bearing on the nature of monetary policy.

1.3. The Nature of the Demand for Money

If we write the pre-Keynesian Quantity Theory of Money as

$$MV = PY$$

where M is the money stock

PY is national income at current prices

then V, the income velocity of circulation, is determined statistically by dividing national income at current prices by the money stock. In fact, pre-Keynesian monetary theory tended to argue that velocity was determined rather mechanically: as money was thought to be used very largely as a medium of exchange, the amount of it required depended upon the length of time that elapsed between one pay-day and the next, and the nature of the banking mechanism. So the demand for money was considered stable and predictable. The amount of money required as a proportion of income is the reciprocal of velocity $(1/v)$: if a given money stock circulates four times during a year, the demand for money is one-quarter of national income in that year, or, more formally:

$$M = kPY$$

where

$$k \text{ is } \frac{1}{v}$$

Keynes retained a flavour of this mechanistic approach in his transactions demand for money, but post-Keynesian work has integrated this component of demand with the speculative demand, giving a single demand for money function which is, as we saw in Chapter 4, section 3.3, affected by expectations of future changes in bond prices. Not only is the Keynesian demand for money affected by changes in expectations about yields on alternative assets, it is also sensitive to a 'change in the news', which causes revisions of expectations.

We can observe this graphically, as in Figure 12.1 which plots interest rates up the vertical axis and the supply and demand for money along the horizontal axis. The distance OM_{t+p} indicates the transactions and precautionary demand for money, dependent on the existing level of money national income. To this is added the speculative demand which is higher the lower the rate of interest, giving the curve LP^1. The money supply is presumed to be determined by the monetary Authorities at MS_1. This produces the interest rate

r^1. (A higher rate of interest would give an excess of supply of money over the demand for it and the ready availability of money would bring down the interest rate. Similarly, a lower interest rate would lead to a rise.)

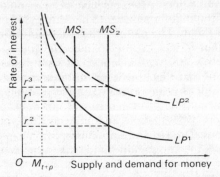

FIG. 12.1

The fall in interest rates from r^1 to r^2 is caused by an increase in the money supply from MS_1 to MS_2: the monetary Authorities are buying bonds on the open market, thus raising their price and lowering their yield. If, however, there is a change in the state of the news which causes a complete shift in the demand for money schedule from LP^1 to LP^2, then interest rates will rise to r^3. In this case the change in the state of the news has shifted the whole market's views of the normal rate of interest (though as before different investors have different notions of that normal rate) and caused a revision in portfolios, which are diversified between bonds and cash. The 'news' causes investors to try to sell bonds both for fear of impending capital loss and to hold their portfolios in a more liquid form: bond prices fall and yields rise.

So the Keynesian demand for money was not only interest-elastic but unstable, a 'will-o'-the-wisp, shifting erratically and unpredictably with every rumour and expectation', as Professor Friedman described it.

Friedman's own rehabilitation of the Quantity Theory was a restatement of it as a theory of the demand for money. To the productive enterprise, he argued, money was a capital good, a source of productive services which combined with other productive services to yield the products which the enterprise sold. To the ultimate wealth-owning units in the economy money was one kind of asset, one way of holding wealth, and the demand for it could be made formally identical with the demand for any other asset (or the service from an asset). The demand is a demand for *real balances*, that is, for nominal money balances corrected for expected price changes. Transactors do not suffer from *money illusion*—they require money balances to allow them to purchase given quantities of physical goods and services. Other things being equal, a uniform rise in all prices should lead to an exactly proportional increase in desired money balances.[1] This demand for money is

---

[1] The emphasis on real balances, and the consequent dependence of the demand for money on expected price changes, means, of course, that money can no longer be regarded as a 'safe' asset.

thought by Monetarists to be stable—i.e. it depends only on a number of specified variables in a relationship which, if it changes at all, does so only slowly. In general terms these variables include the composition, returns at the margin, and total value of assets owned by firms and individuals. More specifically they include the following:

(i) Permanent Income. The major 'asset' that people have is their ability to generate in various ways a stream of income for themselves both now and in the future. Indeed, just as a machine is an asset whose value depends on the income it can produce for its owner, so one can imagine an individual owning a collection of physical, financial, and intangible assets whose value depends on the income they can generate. Current income, being subject to all sorts of temporary fluctuations and influences, would not necessarily be related to this imputed value, but permanent income, which measures the longer-term 'normal' income stream that can be expected, would be a good indicator or 'proxy' for this asset value.

(ii) The ratio of human to non-human wealth. Part of the total wealth one has, as measured by the permanent income it could generate, is in non-human readily realizable form, and part is in human capital—education, job skills, etc.—which is not so readily realizable. This is seen clearly when it is recognized that one can generally borrow much more easily against non-human assets than against human ones, i.e. one's prospects of future earnings (even a mortgage agreement requires the house itself as security). So if human assets are a high proportion of total assets more money may be held because of the difficulty of obtaining it quickly if required.

(iii) The yield on different non-human assets—on bonds, equities, and real assets. As we have seen, this will have an effect on the demand for money.

Of these three, monetarists regard the first as by far the most important. The second will tend to change very slowly, if at all, over time. The third will exert relatively little long-term influence. The unique characteristics offered by money mean that the responsiveness of the demand for money to a change in the yield of other assets will be low.

The money which is thus demanded is defined by monetarists as that set of assets which are a 'temporary abode of purchasing power', a set which possesses capital certainty in nominal terms and can readily be used as a means of payment. These assets are usually regarded as currency, demand deposits, and time deposits.

So to simplify by emphasizing the differences rather than the similarity of the basic approach, Keynesians hypothesize the demand for money as being very sensitive to changes in the yield on alternative assets. They emphasize that in a modern developed economy there are many financial assets which are interest-bearing, liquid, and capital-certain, and are therefore very difficult to distinguish from time deposits in banks. They also emphasize the potential instability and unpredictability of the demand for money. Monetarists see certain financial assets as possessing unique characteristics which distinguish them from other financial assets and make them money. They therefore expect the demand for money to be relatively insensitive to changes in the yields on alternative financial assets, to be a stable function of (permanent) income, and to be a demand for *real* balances. These differences have great importance for monetary policy. If the demand for money is not stable, there is little point in using the supply of it as an instrument with which to control the economy. If the demand for money is highly interest-elastic, changes in the money supply may simply change interest rates without having any significant influence on the level of income (especially if investment is not very sensitive to interest rates); whereas if it is highly interest-inelastic, monetary policy must be very effective, since this in effect means that if a transactor is short of money balances he is more likely to attempt to restore the position by forgoing expenditure than by selling some financial asset.

Empirical tests on whether the demand for money is a stable function of income have tended to show much more stability than at least the immediate post-war Keynesians implied. But it is difficult to determine whether this stability is the result of a long period of stability in the basic monetary environment, and hence to decide whether policy-makers could rely on this stability persisting in a different environment. For example, British evidence on the demand for money following the major change in the rules by which banks were controlled in 1971 (see below, section 2.7) shows that demand relationships estimated from data for earlier periods were not good predictors after the new approach was adopted.

Tests of the interest-elasticity of the demand for money come up against the difficulty we saw earlier (section 1.2) of defining money. Keynesians, who emphasize the substitutability of financial assets, especially the number of substitutes for bank time deposits, tend to favour a narrow definition of 'money proper' and to suggest that the greatest switches occur where transfer costs are low—e.g. between money (defined as cash and demand deposits) and bank time deposits, local authority short-term deposits, etc. Monetarists favour a broad definition. This might be expected to show a lower interest-elasticity, since switches between demand and time deposits go unmeasured and only switches into less liquid assets get picked up in the measurement. A second problem concerns whether short-term or long-term interest rates would be used in the calculation. All interest rates tend to move together; but rates on short-term assets move more widely than those on longer-dated ones, so the statistics tend to show a larger interest-elasticity of demand for money with respect to changes in long rates than short rates.

There has been a very great deal of empirical work on this question, but the results are rather inconclusive. Broadly, studies using a Keynesian approach (narrow definition of money, long-term interest rates) show a high interest-elasticity of demand for money, those using a monetarist approach (broad definition of money, short-term interest rates) show a low interest-elasticity. Thus the results of the tests on stability and interest-elasticity seem to show that the demand for money is more stable than Keynesians may have supposed, but also that it is certainly not completely interest-inelastic.[2]

---

[2] Notice that a low interest-elasticity means that a given change in the money supply has a *large* effect on interest rates—if money and bonds are not good substitutes for each other the price of bonds will have to rise a long way to induce people to sell them and hold money instead.

1.4. The Transmission Mechanism

The basic portfolio-adjustment approach is thus compatible with either a Keynesian or a monetarist approach to the crucial policy question of how changes in the money stock affect what and when. As Friedman himself puts it:

the crucial issue that corresponds to the distinction between the 'credit' (Keynesian) and 'monetary' effects of monetary policy is not whether changes in the stock of money operate through interest rates but rather the range of interest rates considered. On the 'credit' view, monetary policy impinges on a narrow and well-defined range of capital assets and a correspondingly narrow range of associated expenditure. . . . On the 'monetary' view monetary policy impinges on a much broader range of capital assets and correspondingly broader range of associated expenditures.

A Keynesian analysis of the portfolio adjustment sees an increase in the money stock as bidding up the prices (lowering the yields) of short-term financial assets, which are likely to be particularly close substitutes for money. This initial disturbance is then transmitted through the whole market as investors seek to equalize yields at the margin: as they shift out of the now lower-yielding shorts into medium and long bonds they drive the prices of these assets up, lowering their yields. As these substitution relationships are not confined to assets which have been issued by the public sector, the prices of equities rise and company borrowing becomes cheaper. This may induce new capital investment, but Keynesian analysis now tends to play down the role of the cost of capital in investment decisions.

More important are what are known as 'wealth' and 'availability' effects. The monetary disturbance will cause changes in the price of bonds and hence changes in the wealth of those holding bonds (or other financial assets whose price changes). This may affect expenditures on which wealth is a significant influence. There may, for example, be quite large effects on consumption if bond or equity prices rise. Equally, 'availability effects' may be important: if some institutions fail to respond quickly enough to changes in yields on deposits elsewhere they may experience large inflows or outflows from their own deposits—e.g. if a restriction of the money supply drives up the rates of interest available on bank time deposits and Building Societies do not decide to raise their rates to depositors for some time, the Building Societies may lose deposits to banks, and may have to ration their advances to those wishing to buy houses. Finally, as a kind of mixture of the wealth and availability effects, financial institutions may be unwilling to reallocate their portfolios if there has been a serious fall in the prices of the assets they are presently holding. If they feel themselves to be thus 'locked in', particular institutions may be very cautious in lending. The loss of wealth therefore results in lack of available funds to potential borrowers.

These effects may tend to be rather unpredictable, especially if the overall spectrum of assets is at all segmented. If particular institutions have preferences for portfolios covering specific ranges of the asset spectrum then there will be barriers to smooth substitution between assets. This will diminish

(a) Short-term interest rates in London

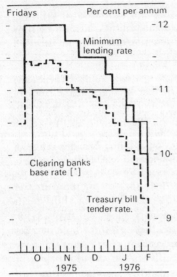

Fridays   Per cent per annum

Minimum lending rate

Clearing banks base rate [˙]

Treasury bill tender rate.

O   N   D   J   F
1975   1976

[˙] Changes are recorded when at least three of the major London clearing banks have changed their rate.

(a)

(b) U.K. and U.S. three-month interest rates

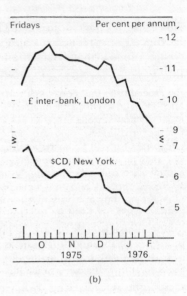

Fridays   Per cent per annum

£ inter-bank, London

$CD, New York.

O   N   D   J   F
1975   1976

(b)

(c) Time/yield curves of British government stocks

Per cent per annum

31 January 1975

31 October 1975

30 January 1976

x = 3½% War Loan

5   10   15   30   50
Years to maturity

[˙] The lines measure the nominal rate of interest which a stock at each maturity should bear if issued at par. The curve runs from the shortest-dated stock with a life of more than one year to the longest-dated stock. The construction of the curves is discussed in the September 1973 *Bulletin*, page 315.

(c)

(d) Security yields

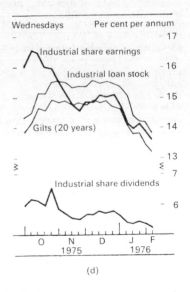

Wednesdays   Per cent per annum

Industrial share earnings

Industrial loan stock

Gilts (20 years)

Industrial share dividends

O   N   D   J   F
1975   1976

(d)

FIG. 12.2. Interest Rate Indicators.

Source: *Bank of England Quarterly Bulletin* (Mar. 1976).

NOTES

Figure 12.2 (a) shows in detail movements at the short end of the spectrum of financial assets. On 3 October the rate bid by the money market for Treasury Bills rose to 11½ per cent, and the Bank of England minimum lending rate (MLR), which automatically follows the market rate, remaining ½ per cent above as a penalty against excessive borrowing from the Bank of England by the money market (see p. 322), rose from 11 per cent to 12 per cent. MLR had been established at 11 per cent on 25 July, when Treasury Bill rate had risen to 10½ per cent, but Treasury Bill rates had begun to fall towards the end of August. In early September the Bank signalled its displeasure at the way rates were edging downwards by forcing the market to borrow at the penal MLR rate for seven days, and the market rate began to rise again. After the rise in MLR, the Clearing Banks raised their base rate (the rate from which they calculate deposit and advances rates) the following week. During November and December large sales of government bonds, heavy tax payments, and the usual Christmas increase in the note issue meant a shortage of funds coming into the money market, but because the Bank of England did not wish to see any further rise in short-term rates, it relieved these shortages by buying Treasury and local authority bills. Further pressures from the payment of taxes prompted the Bank to release 1 per cent of Special Deposits on 19 January to be paid back when pressures had eased, on 10 February. Despite large issues of Treasury Bills towards the end of January competition for bills was keen, so that rates declined rapidly, bringing with them falls in MLR and in the Clearing Banks' base rate. The latter was not lowered as much as it might have been because the Building Societies made it clear that they were unwilling to lower their deposit rates, at any rate until after the Budget in April: this meant that the banks began to lose deposits to the Building Societies.

Figure 12.2 (b) shows one of the reasons for the keen competition for Treasury Bills, namely the expectation that the fall in U.S. rates would lead to a further fall in U.K. rates. The comparison plotted is between the rates prevailing on short-term loans between banks in London and the rate on a dollar-denominated certificate of deposit (a CD is a negotiable certificate issued by a bank acknowledging a deposit for a fixed period, frequently of about one year. The issuing bank knows that it has the deposit for the life of the CD; the lender knows that he can easily realize his asset by selling the certificate).

Figure 12.2 (c) shows the yields of British Government securities (plotted on the vertical axis) of varying dates to maturity (plotted on the horizontal axis). There is extensive literature about the relationship between short and long rates, but the basic explanation for higher yields at the longer end is the increased uncertainty, which affects the prices investors are prepared to pay for bonds if we assume that they wish to avoid risk (as opposed to being indifferent to, or even preferring, it). Any empirically drawn curve must reflect a theory of the determination of the term structure: the Bank of England's assumes that investors do not have the information to make useful forecasts of the future movements of rates beyond some horizon. The best fit of the model was obtained on the assumption that the bond market was segmented into two parts, a long market consisting of bonds with over five years to maturity (where the investors' horizon was three to four years) and a short market of bonds up to five years (horizon one year). These two segments overlap and interact in the range four to eight years. The curves drawn in Figure 12.2 (c) show the counterpart over the whole range of the movements in the money market shown in 12.2 (a). They also show how the shape of the yield curve can change: over the range of bonds over ten years to maturity the yield curves for 31 January 1975 and 31 October 1975 are virtually the same, but shorter rates were lower in January, reflecting in part the different inflow of oil funds in the two periods.

Figure 12.2 (d) shows the change for one particular maturity of government bond—twenty years—plotted against two indices of the yields on equities—earnings and dividends—and industrial loan stock. The time/yield curve (12.2 (c)) is drawn for assets of the same risk class, so that the relationship between yield and time is brought out. But portfolios obviously contain private sector liabilities (company loan stock and equities) as well as Treasury Bills and gilt-edged securities (bonds), which are the liabilities of the Government. This figure, then, gives an indication of the substitution relationships between public sector debt

the disturbance to interest rates caused by the initial change in the money supply and make the effect on particular sections of the money market more uncertain. Figure 12.2 shows recent movements in various interest rates, and has an extended note attached describing the effects operating at the time.

The monetarist transmission mechanism includes all these Keynesian readjustments. But it emphasizes the *direct* consequences upon expenditure of changes in the money supply. Since money is a unique asset, no closer a substitute for financial assets than for real assets, differences between actual and desired real money balances cause *direct* changes in final expenditures, as well as in the financial markets where reactions can only *indirectly* change expenditure on goods and services.

1.5. Monetary History

For Monetarists, changes in the money supply brought about by the monetary Authorities act upon a stable and predictable demand for money and cause direct impacts on national income. When this view is compared with historical experience, for instance in Friedman and Schwartz, *A Monetary History of the United States 1867–1960*, Monetarists claim to find that sizeable changes in the rate of change in the money stock are a necessary and sufficient condition for sizeable changes in the rate of change in money income. Further tests in the laboratory of history involve estimating the direct relationship between income and autonomous expenditure (the Keynesian multiplier) and income and money (the monetary multiplier). Monetarists claim that such tests have shown consumers' expenditure to be more closely linked with changes in the money stock than with autonomous expenditure, but it has been shown that money stock and autonomous expenditure together explain only a relatively small amount of consumption expenditure, and that different definitions of autonomous expenditure reverse the result, as do the introduction of time-lags into the equations and the utilization of data from different periods or different countries.

Similar problems arise in connection with direct tests of fiscal and monetary actions, where United States experience seemed to suggest that monetary policy had larger, quicker, and surer effects than fiscal policy: these findings, too, are less conclusive if different specifications of fiscal policy are used, or if different time periods are considered. (British evidence, furthermore, seems to suggest that fiscal policy is more powerful than monetary.)

A number of issues are involved when we appeal to historical experience in this way. One problem is to establish *causality*. For example, an increase in the budget deficit to expand the economy will probably result in at least some increase in the money supply (for a more detailed investigation of such interrelationships see Chapter 13). Similarly, if the monetary Authorities

---

and private sector liabilities. Industrial loan stock yields follow the pattern of gilts closely, whilst equities move in the same direction but are affected by other considerations (for instance, by the degree of 'inflation-proofing' offered by the fact that the revenue accruing to firms—from which dividends are paid—comes from selling goods and services *at current prices*, and should therefore roughly keep pace with inflation).

decide to stabilize nominal interest rates, any increase in economic activity which would otherwise have raised interest rates will call forth an increase in the money supply from the authorities—but in neither case have the money supply changes *caused* the changes in economic activity.[3] As Professor Kaldor has remarked, the rise in the money supply just before Christmas does not *cause* Christmas—whilst to the objection that *restriction* of the money supply would curb the spending spree Kaldor argues that new money substitutes would emerge (shop and trade credit, for example), so that statistically the velocity of circulation would rise, i.e. PY rises even though M as defined remains the same, so that V which equals PY/M rises. This, of course, is part of the problem of whether the observed stability of the demand for money is actually the result of stable conditions, so that it would change if those 'ground-rules' changed. Finally, quite apart from the question of whether the Authorities have simply allowed the money supply to expand to 'meet the needs of trade', there is the question of whether the money supply is in fact under the Authorities' control. This was referred to in Chapter 4 but we now go into it in more detail.

1.6. The Portfolio Approach to the Money Supply

We have analysed the demand for money and the impact of monetary changes in terms of reallocation of funds amongst assets. It is clear that many of the most important portfolio changes are made by financial institutions, those who *intermediate* by borrowing—issuing liabilities of a type preferred by lenders (and thus at lowish yields)—and lending—investing these funds in higher-yielding assets of the form issued by borrowers.

Since banks are one type of financial intermediary, the peculiar characteristics of whose *liabilities* (i.e. bank *deposits*) we have been exploring, we ought to be able to describe changes in, and the control of, the money supply (bank deposits) in terms of portfolio adjustments amongst the *assets* held by the banks. A simplified account of this process was given in Chapter 4, section 3.2. There we saw that if ordinary commercial prudence on the part of banks suggested that they hold 10 per cent of their assets in the form of cash, then the total deposits in the system (deposits are liabilities of the bank, and must be equal to the banks' assets) would be ten times the amount of cash. So if the Authorities could devise some method to deprive the banks of some of that cash (the American term 'high-powered' money seems very appropriate), deposits will have to fall by £10 for every £1 of cash the Authorites have removed. The method the banks should adopt, in this simple textbook approach, is to call in their overdraft loans to customers.

In practice, British banks not only hold a variety of assets which offer a

---

[3] The effect on interest rates of a discrepancy between the supply and demand for money will, as we have seen, be greater the lower the interest-elasticity of demand for money. Therefore a past concern on the part of the Authorities to stabilize interest rates (whether sensible or otherwise) plus a low interest-elasticity of demand for money will ensure not only that the supply is generally matched to the demand, giving a correlation between money stock and money national income, but also that no autonomous change in the money supply will be attempted.

mixture of combinations of certainty and yield (see p. 322), they have also been *obliged* to hold these assets *in a particular form*. Before the Second World War they held 8 per cent in cash ('till money' at branches and their own interest-bearing balances at the Bank of England, i.e. Bankers Deposits). In 1951 the banks were required to hold a 30 per cent 'liquidity ratio', defined as 8 per cent cash and a further 20–2 per cent in 'liquid' form (money at call and short notice, bills). In 1971 the system was again changed: the liquidity ratio, renamed the 'reserve asset ratio', was lowered to 12½ per cent; till money was excluded and bonds with one year or less to maturity were included. We explore the rationale for these changes in section 2.7 below.

But from the point of view of portfolio allocation, some further remarks need to be made here. First, if a given asset or group of assets, originally held because of the ease whereby they could be converted into legal tender, become assets which the Authorities *require* banks to hold, then they also become *illiquid* in the original sense. For they are *not* available to meet sudden withdrawals. Thus whatever the designated set of assets which the banks are told to hold, the genuinely liquid assets (in the original sense of available to meet sudden withdrawals) are the most liquid set *outside* the designated set .It is to the selling of these that the intermediary will look if it is in difficulties; it is these assets whose prices will therefore fluctuate (yields change) at such times. Secondly, the Authorities will be imposing losses on banks the more they require them to hold their assets in a form different from that which the banks would themselves choose. If the banks are made to lose income in this way they will, subject to their need for 'genuine liquidity', minimize their holdings of low-yielding assets and maximize their holdings of high-yield assets. So banks will, other things being equal, hold less government debt and more advances. Thirdly, the supply of the reserve assets should be under the Authorities' control. Considerations two and three point to control via a small *cash* ratio; but consideration one shows that if this were adopted the brunt of genuine adjustment would be borne by Treasury Bills, whose yields the Authorities may well wish to stabilize, for instance, because of the attractiveness of such assets to foreign holders, or because such short-term interest rates have close substitutes in politically sensitive areas (Building Society deposit rates, for instance). A wider reserve asset ratio, on the other hand, implies that longer-term bonds will feel the effect more.

Thus the distribution of banks' assets is a portfolio decision determined at base by the considerations of equalizing yields at the margin (where liquidity has a 'yield' in terms of security). But the choice is impinged upon by the need on the part of the Authorities to control the level of advances, and the level and structure of interest rates, party through reserve asset requirements and partly through other instruments to be examined below.

Finally, in so far as a bank chooses to make advances, these are profitable and create deposits in the system as a whole; but they are the liability of another transactor—the borrower. His decision on whether to incur a liability on certain terms (interest rate, repayment period) will be determined by his estimate of his ability to meet his obligations, given his own or his company's earning capacity. If he feels he will not be able to meet these terms, he will not ask for a loan. What is not demanded by the private sector will go as a residual into public sector debt. Thus the Authorities do not have complete control over the money supply, since advances are demand-determined: nor can they fully control the distribution of banks' assets between lending to the private sector (both companies and persons) and lending to the public sector. Purely mechanical models, where the money supply is completely exogenously determined by the Authorities, are therefore incorrect.

1.7. Objectives and Instruments, Targets and Indicators

Any discussion of policy should seek to delineate ultimate objectives and proximate targets. It should assign instruments to their appropriate targets, and choose indicators by which the instruments' progress can be monitored. The ultimate objectives of monetary policy are the familiar ones of growth, full employment, external balance, and price stability. But in practice monetary policy is intimately linked with fiscal and exchange rate policy—indeed, this is to be seen in its history: clipping the coinage was a familiar way in which the monarchy attempted to pre-empt resources it could not secure by taxation, and preserving the exchange rate was the major role of sound monetary policy. These complex issues are explored further in Chapter 13. Here it is sufficient to observe that, faced with important theoretical and empirical disagreements about how money affects what and when, it is difficult to select targets for monetary policy.

For Monetarists the objectives of monetary policy are clear. Monetary policy cannot peg interest rates for more than very limited periods. An increase in the money supply may exert an initial downward movement on interest rates, but will also tend to increase money national income partly or completely through price rises. These effects increase the demand for money balances which starts to push interest rates up again, and the inflationary pressures also require higher nominal rates for a given real rate. Monetary policy cannot peg unemployment for more than very limited periods—because of the behaviour of price expectations and their effect on the Phillips Curve (see Chapter 7, section 4). Further, both these arguments lead to the conclusion that nominal interest rates are a misleading indicator of monetary ease or tightness. The relevant rates of interest are *real* rates and these may be moving in a different direction.

Suppose, for example, that expectations of future rises in the price level make fixed interest securities less attractive, resulting in falling bond prices and a rise in interest rates in line with the rise in the expected rate of inflation. If the Authorities step into the market, buying bonds in order to reduce the fall in bond prices, nominal interest rates will rise by less than the rise in the expected inflation rate. Even though nominal rates are still rising the Authorities will in fact have brought about a fall in real rates of interest which is basically expansionary. Observation of nominal rates of interest can therefore be a bad indicator of whether the Authorities are following a tight or easy monetary policy.

What monetary policy can do, argue the Monetarists, is prevent money itself being a major source of economic disturbance, provide a stable background for the economy, and contribute to offsetting major disturbances arising from other sources. Monetarists therefore emphasize the importance of the money stock, their belief in a stable demand for money, and the relative change in the money supply and money national income as the measure of monetary policy, rather than movements in interest rates. The monetary Authorities should adopt a target of a steady rate of expansion of the money supply in line with the projected demand for real balances and avoid wide swings in the money supply.

By contrast, the Keynesians focus on the complexity of the financial structure and the role of specialized financial intermediaries in issuing liabilities which are good substitutes for each other. Monetary policy is thus focused upon the structure of interest rates, for two reasons. First, it is changes in interest rates which are the transmission mechanism between monetary changes and changes in aggregate demand, though these changes are brought about by wealth and availability effects, as we saw, rather than by substitution relationships involving real assets in portfolios (the Keynesian pessimism about the low interest-elasticity of investment coupled with the belief in the high interest-elasticity of the demand for money). Secondly, if the Authorities focused upon some narrow monetary aggregate, evolution in the financial structure would mean that deposits in other institutions, not at present regarded as part of the money supply, would grow rapidly, circumventing proper control. Monetary policy is seen as important in affecting particular credit flows—expanding finance for export, reducing credit for personal consumption, so much of which at the margin is imports of manufactured goods. As such, monetary policy is a useful adjunct to fiscal policy, but it is the latter whose stance is central and crucial.

2. Monetary Policy in Action

2.1. The National Debt and its Management

British monetary policy has followed an exclusively Keynesian pattern, except for some monetarist influences which can be traced in the period 1968–71. Whilst this undoubtedly reflects the influence of Keynesian theory it also meshes well with the size of the U.K. National Debt, and the importance attached to its management. Of the total national debt of nearly £45,000m. 70 per cent—about £32,000m.—is held by the banking sector; by other financial institutions (Building Societies, Insurance Companies, superannuation funds, both public and private sector, etc.); by overseas holders like the I.M.F., other Central Banks, and overseas banks, institutions, and individuals; and by private funds and trusts. The average life of dated stocks is about twelve years: about 45 per cent of total market holdings are Treasury Bills and bonds with up to five years to maturity, 20 per cent between five and fifteen years, and 35 per cent with maturities over fifteen years or are undated (see Table 11.4). Thus the Authorities face the task of getting the market to accept an orderly roll-over of £2,000m. of National Debt each year to refinance maturing bonds, without considering the effect of the borrowing requirements for the current fiscal year, which arises as a result of the difference between Government expenditure and revenue.

The traditional approach of the Authorities to this nagging problem has been cautious. Pointing out how much greater the British national debt is in relation to GNP compared with other countries, the Authorities have laid stress on the aim of maximizing sales of debt, and have argued that such a policy is best pursued in a situation of 'orderly markets' where holders can rely within reasonable limits on the capital value of their portfolios. The argument is that in the short run at least, expectations about movements in the bond market are *extrapolative*, a fall in price leading to expectations of a further fall. Thus in situations where interest rates are rising (gilt-edged prices falling) investors are unwilling to buy bonds. This behaviour circumscribes the Authorities' willingness to see rapid or substantial changes in interest rates, and gives them a marked predilection for a monetary policy focused on *gradual* adjustments in the structure of interest rates. We now go on to examine how they tried to carry out this policy, and the problems inherent in it.

2.2. Interest Rate Instruments

For a hundred years or so until Bank Rate formally gave way to Minimum Lending Rate in 1972, the prime technique of British monetary policy was (a) to raise Bank Rate—the rate at which operators in the short-term money markets could borrow from the Bank of England to balance their books—and (b) 'make it effective' by sales of debt in the open market. If the Bank of England sells financial assets in the open market it has to offer them at an attractive (lower) price to induce the portfolio change which will accompany someone's decision to buy. This slight fall in asset prices edges yields up; but it will also mean the transfer of bank deposits from the investor who has bought the bonds to the Bank of England. The banking system is thus losing bankers' balances, which are part of their required reserve assets. So further portfolio adjustments will ensue as the financial intermediaries try to get back to their preferred portfolio distribution. In particular, the banks would call in their loans to the Discount Houses (money at call and short notice) in order to replenish their cash base. The Discount Houses would then attempt to replace these loans (at least temporarily) from elsewhere, but if the sales of debt by the Authorities were sufficiently vigorous, there would be an over-all shortage of cash in the money markets. In principle, this could lead to a multiple contraction of advances as banks attempted to re-establish their minimum cash ratios (though this could be circumvented by sales of Treasury Bills) but the main impact was to force the Discount Houses 'into the Bank'. The shortage of cash would mean that at the end of the chain there would be some borrowing from the Bank of England, which always stood ready as 'lender of last resort' to relieve the shortage. But for the privilege of borrowing to balance their books in this way, the Discount Houses would have to pay Bank Rate, which, because it stood above the market established rate, involved them in losses. This generally induced them to raise their lending rates, triggering off a more general rise in interest rates.

From the 1930s, and particularly from 1951 to 1971, Bank Rate came to stand as the pivot of an elaborate set of conventional borrowing and lending rates. Instead of waiting for the Bank to make its Bank Rate change effective by open market sales designed to drive the Discount Houses to borrow, changes in lending and borrowing rates were 'administered', so that if Bank Rate rose by ½ per cent, all administered rates (rates paid on time deposits with banks, charged on overdrafts, etc.) rose by the same amount. In 1972 Bank Rate was formally abolished, and the new Minimum Lending Rate (MLR) substituted. This rate follows the market-established rates for short-term assets, but is always above them. Despite the abolition of the cartel on rates between the Clearing Banks, the banks do not in practice compete for small deposits: the result is that there is still a conventionally determined set of rates, whilst the Authorities use market operations and informal contacts with institutions to edge rates up, and MLR then follows.

2.3. Conflicts between Policy Objectives

The very large size of the U.K. National Debt as described above presents the Authorities with an important conflict between their responsibilities as debt managers (in which role they wish to ensure that existing debt continues to be held and market conditions preserved which will enable the Government to finance its continuing borrowing requirements, consistent with minimizing interest payments) and their responsibility for monetary control, with its implications for interest rates. This conflict of roles has been behind much of the evolution of monetary policy since the 1950s and we go on to consider this against the background of that policy conflict.

2.4. The New Orthodoxy and the 1950s

The first development was the abandonment in 1951 of the cash ratio as the fulcrum of the Authorities' control of the commercial banks. In the post-war world the changes in short-term interest rates caused by open-market sales designed to affect the commercial banks' cash reserves were unacceptable. War finance and the post-war nationalization programme had greatly increased the national debt, and the greater part of the much larger Treasury Bill supply was bound to be held by the banks. Since banks could always very easily obtain cash by selling some of these Treasury Bills the changes in short-term interest rates required to engineer a shortage of cash for the banks' reserve ratios were much larger, and fell more directly on the Government as borrower, than in earlier periods when commercial bills were much more important. So the banks were requested to observe a 'liquidity ratio' as well as a ratio of cash to deposits. This ratio included not only the former cash ratio (till money and Bankers Deposits) (8 per cent) but also other short-term assets—Treasury Bills, Commercial Bills, and money lent short term by the banks to the London Discount Market—to a total of 30 per cent. Thus in principle the Authorities now faced a simpler task in their open-market operations. Instead of depriving the banks of cash by selling Treasury Bills (and facing the interest-rate consequences), they now had only to deprive the banks of some officially defined 'liquid assets' by selling bonds (bonds were *outside* the definition of 'liquid assets'). Since bonds were widely held outside the banking system, the penalty of monetary control for the Authorities was less—high substitutability in portfolios meant that quite small changes in bond prices (yields) persuaded people to buy bonds, thus draining the banks of cash. The banks could then freely sell their bill holdings to the Bank of England to restore their cash ratio, but a mere swap of bills for cash left the banks short of required 'liquid assets'.

2.5. Special Deposits

Yet by the end of the 1950s this 'new orthodox' method of control by the 'liquidity ratio', as it was called to distinguish it from the 'old orthodox' method of control by the cash ratio, was not satisfactory. Empirical evidence suggested that the Authorities' control of the total supply of liquid assets was not succeeding in controlling the money supply, if that was what it was designed to do. In particular, the banks had proved willing, when their holdings of liquid assets were threatening to fall too low to sustain their profitable advances, to sell their holdings of bonds rather than reduce advances. Furthermore, it was generally the Authorities themselves who duly bought these bonds. As a regular part of their aim to maintain orderly markets, the Authorities would buy back over a period bonds nearing maturity. This arrangement was convenient to them since it smoothed out the disturbance which would otherwise be caused in the markets when a large issue came to maturity; for market-holders it meant that short bonds were highly liquid, being readily and reliably exchangeable into cash. But of course this liquidity, which the Authorities saw as stabilizing the market and encouraging bond-holding, did offer an escape from having to reduce more profitable advances if the banks' liquidity ratios were being squeezed by open-market operations.

The answer to this problem was the technique of Special Deposits, the introduction of which in 1960, two years after their invention, is the second major instance of the conflict in roles of the Authorities. Special Deposits were a new attempt to achieve what open-market operations were designed to achieve, but more effectively and with less cost in terms of higher interest rates. Now instead of depriving the banks of 'liquid assets' by open-market operations in bonds, which would require increases in bond yields if the banks were not to evade the measures by selling bonds back to the Authorities, the Authorities *required* the banks to place Special Deposits with them. Interest is paid on these but they do not count as part of the required liquid assets base. Thus the banks had to meet the call for special deposits by adjusting elsewhere in their portfolios, preferably by cutting back on their loans to the private sector. Yet this attempt to again minimize the interest rate effect of monetary policy was frustrated almost from the start: although the Authorities did not have to operate in the market, altering interest rates thereby, in order to squeeze the banks' liquidity ratios, the banks met the call for special deposits by again running off their holdings of maturing bonds. [4]

---

[4] This should not be interpreted entirely as a move to frustrate the intentions of the new scheme. In a sense Special Deposits act like an increase in the required reserve ratio—by

2.6. Direct Controls

Such behaviour was countered by the Bank of England by the use of direct controls—or rather, the more discreet version known as 'moral suasion'. The 1946 Bank of England Act seems to give the Bank of England power to issue directives, but in practice it is so powerful, and has such a informal network, that 'requests' by it are normally respected. Such 'requests' to bankers had become common since the mid-1950s, but had previously covered advice as to the amount and direction (e.g. 'give advances for exports but not for home consumption') of bank overdrafts. By the early 1960s advice had been extended to the hire-purchase companies, supplementing the control of initial downpayment and repayment periods which remained in the hands of the Board of Trade. With the recurrent balance of payments crises of the 1960s such requests became the major mechanism of monetary control, qualitative guidance being accompanied by explicit quantitative instructions on the growth of bank advances from the Budget of 1965 to the Budget of 1971, when the abandonment of such guidance anticipated a new policy.

Under the category of direct controls too come the Capital Issues Committee controls (suspended in 1959) and exchange controls. Hire-purchase controls are not technically under the Bank of England but under the Department of Trade and Industry, reflecting their origins as controls for consumer protection. H.P. controls have an excellent profile for stabilization policy—a strong immediate effect through the changes in minimum downpayments and the maximum repayment period, which then dies away. But they are heavily directional, particularly affecting the sales of cars and other consumer durables, with potentially damaging effects on the planning, investment, and profitability of the firms making these products.

Quantitative and qualitative guidance certainly provided tight monetary control, and helped to reduce the impact of monetary control on debt management. For if the growth of bank advances to the private sector was limited, the only outlet for the profitable deployment of bank deposits lay in lending to the Government and other public sector bodies. But in such circumstances the banks were under no pressure to compete in efficiency, preferring rather to engage in what was to some extent conspicuous consumption by proliferating branch networks. There was no incentive for the banks to compete with each other, and control of advances meant that they tended to lose business to other financial intermediaries, like Finance Houses (hire-purchase companies), Building Societies, and merchant banks. The report by the National Board for Prices and Incomes on Bank Charges (1967)

---

forcing the banks to hold more lower yielding assets than they would wish, Special Deposits may encourage them to reallocate the rest of their portfolios to bring higher yield in compensation, that is to substitute out of middle-yielding bonds into the required Special Deposits and to expand further high-yielding advances. Since Special Deposits pay a rate of interest ($\frac{1}{16}$ per cent nearest to the average Treasury Bill rate of the previous week), the loss of income from the larger required reserve assets is not as great as if, say, the banks were required to hold bigger bankers' deposits at the Bank of England: on the other hand, Special Deposits may be thought more genuinely liquid, since they could readily be released by the Authorities.

and the Monopolies Commission's comments on the proposed merger between Barclays, Lloyds, and Martins the following year highlighted the consequences of this lack of genuine competition. Yet an important part of the lack of competition was the banks' own collective agreement on interest rates paid to depositors and charged to borrowers, institutional arrangements between the banks and the Discount Houses, and the agreement of the Discount Houses to take up all of the Treasury Bills issued each week and not purchased by higher bidders. These complex agreements were supported, so the Monopolies Commission stated, by the Treasury 'because they believed that they enabled the major part of the credit requirements of the country's industry and commerce to be satisfied at lower [interest] rates than would otherwise be the case'.

2.7. Competition and Credit Control

In 1968-9 the Authorities began to change their tactics in the gilt-edged market. Their readiness to support bond prices by buying bonds near to maturity was reduced, constraining the banks' ability to unload these easily, but generating larger fluctuations in interest rates. This implied an increasing concern with the level of advances rather than with the level of interest rates. Although these very important changes can in the first instance be traced to pressure from the I.M.F., whose inclination is much more towards controlling the money supply than the structure of interest rates, econometric evidence also played its part by suggesting that the demand for bonds was more stable than market opinion had supposed. It seemed that the Authorities had less need to beguile the market into holding bonds by offering high liquidity, and that though expectations might over the short term be extrapolative, in the longer run they were regressive—that is, although for some time falling bond prices might induce less bond-holding as operators feared further capital losses, after a time falling prices induced purchases as expectations grew that bond prices could now only move upwards.

The withdrawal of support from the gilt-edged market became complete on the publication in May 1971 of the proposals for a new system of control known as *Competition and Credit Control*. This immediate removal of gilt-edged support, together with the other arrangements proposed but not put into effect until September 1971, was designed to restore control through market mechanisms, and to stimulate efficiency in the whole financial sector. The proposals combined Special Deposits with a further widening and refinement of the 'liquidity ratio', now lowered to 12½ per cent. This new 'reserve assets ratio' did not include till money but was widened to include bonds with one year or less to maturity. These bonds could, as we saw, be sold by the banks to the Government broker, who was willing to buy them at prevailing market prices to ease the problem posed by a large amount of debt maturing at the same time. By including such bonds *within* the required reserve ratio, the Authorities preserved their ability to ensure orderly market conditions whilst plugging the hole in monetary control whereby the bond broker, to preserve orderly markets, supplied the cash which enabled the banks to evade a monetary squeeze. Two other 'leaks' which had threatened the efficacy of control via the liquid assets ratio in the 1950s were also stopped up by the new definition of required reserve assets. Both leaks were due to the inclusion in the old liquidity ratio of assets whose supply was not determined by the Authorities: commercial bills are a liability of the private sector, and 'money at call' a liability of the Discount Houses, whereas cash, Treasury Bills, and bonds are all liabilities of the Authorities themselves. Thus until the redefinitions of *Competition and Credit Control* banks could expand their holdings of commercial bills when short of 'liquid assets', perhaps by inducing some companies to borrow via commerical bills instead of via overdraft. Similarly, the banks could increase money at call if short of 'liquid assets' by lending to the Discount Houses money which the Houses agreed to use to buy bonds from the banks; such a book transaction representing a shuffling around of assets preserved the old liquidity ratio but without any change in deposit liabilities. Under the new system a *maximum* ratio of commercial bills to deposits was specified, whilst the ability of the Discount Market to increase its money at call liabilities was also circumscribed. Thus both leaks were blocked.

The major changes, however, were the changes in the gilt-edged market already discussed, and the imposition of a *uniform* reserve ratio ($12\frac{1}{2}$ per cent) upon *all* banks (previously reserve ratios had applied only to clearing banks, thus handicapping them by a kind of tax in competition for deposits with other non-bank financial intermediaries). Special Deposits were now to be called uniformly from all these reserve ratio banks: a very similar arrangement was applied to Finance Houses. Such changes were intended to promote competition and efficiency in the banking structure, by allowing competition for deposits and rationing of credit by price: the banks agreed to abandon their collective agreements on interest rates and the Discount Houses to abandon their collective bid for Treasury Bills.

The new control measure showed the conflict between the Authorities as managers of the national debt and as controllers of monetary policy very clearly. The changes in the gilt-edged market, where, as we saw, the Authorities no longer guaranteed to intervene, except on occasions and terms of their own choosing, were undoubtedly a move towards the primacy of the second, monetary policy, role over the policy of debt management. Yet the retention of Special Deposits and the widening of the assets eligible as reserves seemed to re-establish concern over the level of interest rates as most important. Explanations by official spokesmen reinforced this impression: the new control measures were intended, they said, to work through their effects on the interest rate structure. Nor did the Authorities pledge themselves not to seek to influence particular credit flows by 'guidance'. Indeed many commentators believed from the start that the monetary Authorities might intervene from time to time to preserve orderly markets, or to influence the terms and direction of credit. Within a year moral suasion had been employed to moderate lending for property development, and the clearing banks had been rescued from difficulties caused by their policies at the time the pound was floated; and within two years the Building Societies had been subsidized to hold down mortgage interest rates and then protected from bank competition by the imposition of a ceiling interest rate on bank deposits up to £10,000.

But the clearest example of the ambivalence of the Authorities towards letting the interest rate structure go free is to be found in the 'merry-go-round' in 1973. 'Blue-chip' borrowers (large companies, local authorities) could borrow up to their overdraft limits at rates below those they could obtain by lending such overdrafts back to the banking system via the 'wholesale' credit markets. The higher rates in these markets reflected the willingness of 'fringe banks' (outside the *Competition and Credit Control* scheme) to offer high rates to depositors to sustain their portfolio of rapidly inflating property, and the ability of the banks proper to bid high rates for *marginal* funds because of the relatively low rates they paid to the ordinary depositors who supplied the bulk of their funds. One solution to the problem lay in letting market forces have free play (with some nudging to provoke the collusive oligopoly arrangements, which succeeded the clearing banks' cartel, into raising rates for depositors). The other solution involved full intervention, forcing the clearing banks to control their overdraft lines by collective action to prevent 'blue-chip' customers playing off bank against bank by threatening to move their funds between the accounts they each keep at the different banks. In fact, direct intervention was the method belatedly chosen: in December 1973 the Bank of England reacted to a developing crisis in the fringe banks by limiting competition for interest-bearing deposits by imposing target rates of increase, the exceeding of which attracted harsher and harsher penalties as the excess interest-bearing deposits increased. This was despite the fact that adherence to the market-orientated philosophy which had supplied the initial impulse for the rapid growth of 'fringe' banks would have suggested allowing them to fail.

The imposition of these penal Supplementary Special Deposits (for funds up to 3 per cent in excess of the target rate, a special deposit of 5 per cent on which interest would not be paid, for an excess of 3–5 per cent a special deposit of 25 per cent, for an excess of over 5 per cent a special deposit of 50 per cent) had similarities to the French system of monetary control, and perhaps reflected a growing concern to harmonize British control methods with those proposed in draft E.E.C. banking regulations. At all events, even though operation of the Supplementary Special Deposits scheme was suspended in early 1975, it marked a significant change from established British practice. Instead of concentrating controls on the assets side of the banks' balance sheet (liquidity and reserve asset ratios), control was related directly to the growth of bank deposits on the liabilities side of banks' balance sheets.

2.8. *Unification of Markets*

One final comment on *Competition and Credit Control* is that it to some extent recognized a process of unification of different money markets that had been occurring gradually since the war. In 1959 the Radcliffe Committee saw British financial structure as comprising basically a single market for credit, though still divided by imperfections which it took effort to overcome. In the 1960s the unification of previously rather separate markets continued apace. Clearing banks bought Finance Houses or set up their own hire-purchase subsidiaries. Foreign banks flocked to London, attracted by the development of international capital markets (Euro-dollar market) and other 'wholesale' money markets. Non-bank financial intermediaries, such as Finance Houses and Building Societies, competed for deposits whilst the clearing banks were constrained—or imagined that they were—by limits on their lending. New, sophisticated markets for assets appeared—the certificate of deposit market, the market in inter-company debts.

As London's financial markets became more unified not only within themselves but also with respect to foreign markets, so the hotchpotch of different regulations and controls was becoming all the more inappropriate. This unification of financial structure was reflected in *Competition and Credit Control*'s uniform reserve ratio of $12\frac{1}{2}$ per cent (10 per cent for deposit-taking Finance Houses) but it undoubtedly adds another source of complexity to monetary policy. Even if the background of monetary theory and empirical investigation is ignored, and monetary policy is regarded as being primarily concerned with credit flows rather than with the money supply, there are important conflicts of aim. The appropriate interest-rate structure may require a particular level or shape of the time/yield curve (see Figure 12.2)—for instance, high short-term rates to attract or retain short-term capital from abroad, lower long-term rates to encourage investment. If financial markets are separate, such policies may be feasible, but the unification of markets may reduced such freedom to manœuvre. In addition, social or political interests may desire a monetary policy which favours low interest rates in general, or low interest rates in particular markets—e.g. in housing, or rates which can discriminate in favour of certain types of borrowing within the same market— say, discrimination within bank advances in favour of industrial investment and export promotion and against consumption or property development. Here again the unification of financial markets makes such monetary policies more and more difficult, even if they were desirable.

3. Conclusion

Monetary policy reflects clearly the numerous policy objectives of modern governments and the constraints within which such objectives have to be pursued, both domestic and foreign. At a more fundamental level monetary policy suffers from confusion both in theory and investigation about its relative importance, its effects, and how these effects are brought about. There is no empirical evidence which settles conclusively the disputes about the stability of the demand for money, or the degree to which other financial assets are substitutable for a group identified as 'money'. There is disagreement about the extent to which it can be shown that changes in the money supply *cause* changes in prices or output. There is dispute about the nature of the mechanism which links changes in the money stock with changes in real expenditures, and about the timing and power of such effects. There is room for much more work on how the effects of monetary policy are divided between changes in prices and changes in real output. And there is controversy about the effects of monetary policy upon the labour market, particularly upon expectations and the bargaining process.

In the face of such uncertainty, can we reach any general conclusions about monetary policy? Perhaps two. First, that policy-makers should think very carefully about the consistency of their policy as a whole, about the place of monetary policy within that policy mix (particularly its relationship to the fiscal stance and the balance of payments), and about the internal consistency of the various strands of policy. These issues are explored further in Chapter 13. Second, that however monetary policy works, its effects, save only for changes in H.P. terms, are likely to be somewhat unpredictable in extent and long delayed in timing. Keynesians and Monetarists can unite on the desirability of more consistent and stable monetary policies. Unfortunately, since monetary policy can be changed by executive action, very quickly, and without the need for lengthy Finance Acts and debates in Parliament, it is often politically handy to use monetary policy rather than fiscal. But the fact that a weapon can be used easily does not make it the most suitable: monetary policy is important but it is not a particularly suitable instrument for 'fine tuning'.

Bibliography

SECTION A

On the whole area covered by this chapter:

(a) Introductory

[1] DAY, A. C. L. The Economics of Money (Oxford University Press, OPUS 31, 1968).
[2] FURNESS, E. L. An Introduction to Financial Economics (Heinemann, 1972).
[3] CROCKETT, A. Money: theory, policy, and institutions (Nelson, 1973).

(b) Intermediate

[4] BAIN, A. D. The Control of the Money Supply (Penguin, 1970).
[5] CRAMP, A. B. Monetary Management (Allen and Unwin, 1971).
[6] REVELL, J. The British Financial System (Macmillan, 1973).
[7] SAYERS, R. S. Modern Banking, 7th edn. (Oxford University Press, 1967).

Day, Bain, Cramp and Sayers do not include the changes in control methods introduced in 1971, but are nevertheless excellent introductions to the problems which led to the adoption of Competition and Credit Control. The details of Competition and Credit Control can be found in:
[8], [9], [10] Bank of England Quarterly Bulletin (June, Sept. and Dec. 1971), with subsequent modifications in [11] June 1972 and [12] March 1974.

The subsequent developments, especially in the secondary banks and the property market, can be followed in the quarterly issues of the Bank's [13] Bulletin.

SECTION B

A more institutional approach can be found in:
[14] FERRIS, P. The City (Penguin, 1974).
[15] CAIRNCROSS, F. and McCRAE, H. Capital City (Eyre, Methuen, 1973).

Both of these are more journalistic than the books cited in Section A, but are great fun to read and contain some important background to recent problems.

The best short description of financial institutions is to be found in:
[16] *British Banking and other Financial Institutions*, Central Office of Information Reference Pamphlet 123 (H.M.S.O., 1974).

SECTION C

More advanced books on monetary theory and policy:
[17] PIERCE, D. G. and SHAW, D. M. *Monetary Economics* (Butterworth, 1974).
[18] GOODHART, C. A. E. *Money, Information and Uncertainty* (Macmillan, 1975).

Both excellent modern textbooks: Goodhart is the more advanced.

[19] JOHNSON, H. G. (ed.) *Readings in British Monetary Economics* (Oxford University Press, 1972).
[20] GIBSON, W. E. and KAUFMAN, G. G. (eds.) *Monetary Economics: Readings on Current Issues* (McGraw-Hill, 1971).

These contain a wide selection of classic articles on both theory and policy, the latter exclusively about the United States, whilst
[21] CLOWER, R. W. (ed.) *Monetary Theory* (Penguin, 1969) concentrates on theory.
[22] HODGMAN, D. R. *National Monetary Policies and International Monetary Co-operation* (Little Brown, 1974) looks at the interrelationship between financial structures and the tools and targets of monetary policy in Benelux, France, Germany, Italy, Holland, and Britain.

13

Demand Management

P. J. N. SINCLAIR and R. G. SMETHURST

1. The Budget Deficit in a Closed Economy

In the chapter on monetary policy we saw how the management of the national debt had impinged upon monetary control since the war. This chapter explores further the relationships between monetary and fiscal policy, and between the monetary/fiscal mix and the balance of payments. It then provides a basis for evaluating different approaches to the problem of simultaneously achieving two or more government economic objectives, requiring management of the level and structure of demand.

The central feature of the analysis is the budget deficit, the difference between what the Government takes in taxation and spends on goods and services, both capital and current.

1.1. The Budget Deficit and the National Income Multiplier

As we saw in the basic model (Chapter 4, p. 94), an increase in public expenditure (G) will increase national income via the multiplier. Assuming a closed economy in which there are unemployed resources, and assuming further that investment is unchanged and that there are no interest rate effects:

$$\Delta Y = \frac{\Delta G}{1 - b(1 - t)} \text{ or } \Delta Y = \frac{\Delta G}{s + t}$$

Two other points from the basic model are worth recalling at this stage. First, if the Government balances its budget when it increases expenditure by also increasing direct taxation, the level of GNP will normally still rise. The simple explanation is that the repercussions of both changes, both ΔG (injection) and ΔT (leakage), are the same (i.e. the same multiplier process is at work in both directions), but the initial Government purchase of goods and services was also itself a direct component of aggregate demand (GNP), whereas the initial round of tax payment was simply a transfer of purchasing power away from households, which does not count against GNP. If, then, the same marginal propensity to consume applies to the taxpayers as to the recipients of the income accruing in the first instance from government expenditure, the rest of the multiplier processes will be equal and opposite, and the over-all difference between the two processes will therefore be the initial Government expenditure.

More formally:

$$\Delta G \text{ produces } \Delta Y_1 = \Delta G + \frac{b}{1-b}\Delta G$$

$$\Delta T \text{ produces } \Delta Y_2 = b\Delta T + \frac{b}{1-b}b\Delta T$$

since for a balanced budget $\Delta G = \Delta T$, the *net* change $\Delta Y_1 - \Delta Y_2$ is

$$\Delta Y = \left(\Delta G + \frac{b}{1-b}\Delta G\right) - \left(b\Delta G + \frac{b}{1-b}b\Delta G\right) = \Delta G.$$

Secondly, for national income to be in equilibrium, injections and leakages must be equal. Thus in our closed economy

$$I + G = S + T$$

and therefore

$$G - T = S - I.$$

That is, in other words, an excess of government expenditure over taxation requires an excess of private sector saving over investment. This forms the first link between the multiplier effects of a change in the government's deficit and the monetary implications of financing it. For what this equation tells us, in simple language, is that if the Government is to run a budget deficit, it does so by issuing debt $(G - T)$ which must be held as a surplus by the private sector $(S - I)$.[1] That this is the private sector's surplus can most easily be seen by adding and subtracting private consumption expenditure. The expression becomes $(C + S) - (I + C)$ which equals private sector income minus private sector expenditure in a given period—the surplus of the private sector.

1.2. Debt-Holding and the Public's Portfolios

Now, clearly, if a budget deficit must be *financed* by issuing debt, which must be *held* by the non-government sector, there are two aspects of an excess of government expenditure over tax receipts which go beyond the national income multiplier effects. First, there is the question of the way in which the deficit is financed—does the Government print cash, or issue I.O.U.s of various types (Treasury Bills; gilt-edged securities of various maturity dates)? Secondly, how does it induce the public to accept its debts, and what further changes result?

To see the basic principles, we might first consider a medieval monarch who wishes to engage in some military campaign, but who knows he will meet fierce opposition if he tries to raise taxation. The monarch is already gaining 'seignorage' from the coinage he issues and the most obvious way of

---

[1] The deficit to be financed by increased government expenditure of ΔG is in the first instance the full amount ΔG. Eventually it will be less because the rise in income consequent upon the increase in government expenditure will itself generate increased tax receipts at current tax rates. The eventual deficit is:

$$\Delta G - \frac{t\Delta G}{s + t}$$

financing the campaign is for the king to debase the coinage. Providing the populance does not lose confidence in the currency (which subtle debasement should avoid) the seignorage gain will increase: the monarch will be able to get hold of more resources.

The modern counterpart of this would be if the Government financed its excess expenditure over taxation by simply printing more money for the purpose. (This reminds us that notes and coin are part of the National Debt.) It does not cost £1 to print a pound note, so there is a seignorage gain involved. Provided confidence in the currency was undiminished, the Government could be confident that its increased debt would be held by the public.

There will, however, be changes in the public's financial portfolios as a result of the increased note issue in circulation. For as we saw earlier (p. 104) we can regard transactors' portfolios as distributed across the spectrum of cash and all other financial assets, equalizing yields at the margin. Even though cash may have no obvious yield it does provide liquidity—convenience and certainty. So for the public to hold more cash, which will at the margin, other things being equal, yield less convenience, the yields on other financial assets must fall. If money is ultimately no more closely substitutable for financial assets than for real assets (see p. 105) then the yield on real assets must also fall.

If the Government wishes to avoid this increase in the supply of money, it must borrow the sum it requires by issuing bonds. Just as the holding of more cash involves reallocation of portfolios, so the consequences of the Government's financing its deficit by issuing other types of debt will also be to cause changes in relative yields to induce the debt to be held. Put simply, extra units of a good, which we assume are worth less at the margin, will only be purchased if the price falls, since for equilibrium the marginal utilities of goods per unit price must be equal. Similarly for equilibrium in financial portfolios: if the Government is to induce wealth-holders to take up more debt it must normally lower the price (increase the yield).

An additional complication in financial markets arises from the fact that the amount of the budget deficit to be financed over any given year is much smaller than the existing stock of debt. Thus in issuing its new debt at a price attractive enough to induce wealth-holders to accept it, the Government has to pay attention to the repercussions of this decision on existing debt, and thus on the term structure of interest rates as a whole.

1.3. Financing the Deficit

This need to ensure that the new debt corresponding to the current budget deficit is held in portfolios obviously feeds back to the other aspect of the deficit—in what *form* the debt should be issued. It is important to issue debt which will readily be taken up by the public, at prices which minimize the interest cost of servicing the National Debt. This implies issuing those bonds, the demand for which is most buoyant. But there are two related aspects of the financing decision which need to be considered further.

The first is whether to finance by long-term or short-term debt issues; the second, whether the Authorities are prepared to accept the implications of either for interest rates. If long-term bonds and short-term bonds, or bills, are perfect substitutes for each other, the choice of length of the borrowing by the Government is immaterial. That they will be at least limited substitutes is incontestable: a long-term loan by the Government is, in a sense, equivalent to a sequence of short-term loans covering the same period. But there are important differences between long-term bonds and short-term bonds or bills. The long-term lender knows on buying the bonds what interest he will receive throughout the whole period to maturity, and knows what he will be repaid (in cash) at the end, if he chooses to hold the bond that long. What he does not know is the value that the bond will command in the meantime. The short-term lender has much greater confidence in the value of his assets (his loan to the Government). For the value at maturity of any bond is certain, and the maturity date is nearer for the short-term lender. But he cannot know if he will be able to lend again at the same rate. Hence he cannot predict the income from a sequence of short-term loans. Therefore the short-term lender will face a different sort of risk from the long-term lender. Because of the greater certainty of their capital value short-term bonds tend to have a lower yield than long-term bonds. If there are many institutions which prefer to hold bonds with particular periods to maturity (so that they can match the maturity date of these bonds with the period to maturity of their own debts) then the market for government debt may not be completely unified. There may be segments of particular maturity dates where it is easier or harder for the Government to get its debt taken up.

Evidence in Britain, in fact, tends to suggest that the market for different maturities of government debt is segmented. The implication is that if the Government finances its deficit by long-term borrowing, long-term interest rates will rise absolutely, *and* relatively to short rates; borrowing short, meanwhile, would raise short rates quite sharply, and long rates only rather slowly.

The *over-all* level of interest rates will probably also rise. This is because there has been a net addition to the supply of bonds, unmatched by any change in the demand. If the budget deficit were to be maintained for only one year there would be no further change in the supply or demand for bonds, and interest rates *ceteris paribus* would stick at their new, somewhat higher, level. If, however, the Government continues to run a budget deficit in subsequent years there will be subsequent increases in the supply of bonds, further depressing the price of bonds. Thus a constant level budget deficit will imply continuously rising interest rates. Of course, if there is an increase in the demand for bonds, e.g. because of growth in the economy, this rise in interest rates will be mitigated.

The next point is whether the Government is prepared to accept these increases in interest rates. It will not view them with favour. They imply growing costs of servicing the National Debt.[2] This means cuts in government

---

[2] The higher interest rate is represented by the higher coupon on the debt newly issued to cover the deficit. Since *existing* debt with a *lower* coupon would now be unattractive the price of old bond must fall, raising their yield to a level comparable with that on the new debt.

spending, or rises in taxes, if the budget deficit is to be prevented from rising. Higher interest rates are resented by the politically important group of those buying houses on mortgages. They are also likely to damage industrial investment, by making it more expensive for firms to borrow; and they have harmful effects on the balance sheets of financial institutions which lend long term because the value of long-term assets goes down. So the Authorities may try to peg interest rates.

There are two ways of doing this: the Authorities could support the bond market by buying bonds on the open market at the previously existing price. Alternatively, they may try to make room for increased lending to the public sector by telling the banking system to reduce the loans to the private sector. The former method of holding interest rates down must imply an over-all increase in the money supply. The latter method, as we saw in Chapter 12, cannot successfully be operated for long without either structural inefficiency or evasion.

To summarize: a budget deficit implies that the Government is disbursing a higher value of funds than it receives. The excess will always increase the money supply, unless offset in some way. Issuing bonds to cover the deficit will be an offset. But if bonds are issued, on balance, to cover only *some* of the deficit, because of open-market purchases to cut the rise in interest rates, there will still be a net expansion of the money supply. Thus financing the deficit generally implies either continuous rises in the money supply or continuous rises in interest rates, or both. It follows from this that there will be considerable ongoing effects from any fiscal stance, that is from an excess of expenditure over tax revenue or vice versa. Any budgetary change must therefore be assessed against these ongoing effects.

Had the public Authorities inherited a fiscal surplus, but decided in their first budget to raise G by less than enough to remove it, there would still be a falling trend over time in the Government's obligations, because the *over-all* budget is still in surplus. Of course, after the new budget's *deficit* stance the rate of decline would be lower than otherwise. The demand effect on expenditure, however, would still be expansionary.

1.4. Expenditure Effects on Interest Rates and Prices

These are all consequences in the financial markets. The rise in National Income brought about by the rise in government expenditure will itself also exert an influence on interest rates. This is because the demand for money will rise to finance the growing amount of transactions. Unless the supply of money increases to match the rise in demand, interest rates will go up. This may have an adverse effect on investment, and also on the buying of consumer durables. On the other hand, both may be stimulated by the boom itself. So the over-all effect on investment is unclear. We shall return to this later.

There will be a number of effects on the level of prices. If the increase in

---

Thus the general level of interest rates will rise, but this will *not* involve an increased cost to the Government of financing its *past* debts except in so far as these debts mature and need refinancing.

government expenditure is represented by, for example, a new hospital, one may predict that *particular* prices may begin to drift upwards as a result: the wages of building workers, the prices of concrete and other materials, etc. Secondly, there will tend to be a *general* effect on the price level. As prices of particular products rise, and as wage levels rise, so both demand and costs rise throughout the economy, and both influences tend to stimulate price rises. This effect may be small if there is initially substantial excess capacity in the economy, but it cannot be ignored even then, and is a central feature if there is little or no excess capacity. In particular, as the economy approaches full employment of labour, there will be upwards pressure on wage rates: the rate of rise may even accelerate if the inflation it produces comes to be expected, and allowed for in subsequent wage rises. These wage rises will be followed—perhaps slowly, perhaps less than fully, but followed none the less—by increases in prices (unless it so happens that productivity is increasing even faster). If the rise in government expenditure occurs in the context of a fully employed economy, inflation will be àn inevitable result.

1.5. Monetary Effects on the Budget Deficit

While fiscal policy has monetary implications, changes in the money supply have budgetary effects too. A boom initiated by monetary expansion will lead to swelling income tax receipts, tending to cut (raise) the budget deficit (surplus). A rise in the money supply may well lower interest rates initially, which, by cutting National Debt servicing charges somewhat, can have the same effect. But persistent monetary expansion may be associated with persistent inflation, which may come to be expected, and thus discounted in higher (nominal) interest rates. Inflation can also produce reverse effects on the budget if indirect taxes levied on goods the demand for which is price-inelastic are kept constant in money terms and/or if government expenditure plans are maintained irrespective of their increasing cost.

2. The Budget Deficit in an Open Economy

2.1. Financing and Expenditure Effects

The situation changes when the closed-economy assumption is dropped. The main effect on the financing of the deficit is that *foreigners* may take up some or all of the State's increases in debt. If they do, there are two consequences to notice. First, the rising trend in interest rates that is needed to keep selling the extra debt may be gentler than if the State had only domestic firms and households to borrow from. The second consequence is on the money supply. We saw that a budget deficit implied an increase in the money supply unless domestic residents kept lending to the Government to finance its budget. If the latter happened the monetary expansion was neutralized by the sale of bonds. But this neutralization does *not* occur if foreigners take up the debt. For in this case the money paid over for the bonds is not part of the domestic money supply. So the initial increase in the domestic money supply is not counterbalanced. To do this would require a *further* issue of bonds to domestic purchasers.

As for the real effects of the increased government expenditure, in an *open* economy, multiplier-induced additions to aggregate demand will spill overseas into extra imports, thus somewhat alleviating the pressure on domestic resources (see p. 94 for the open-economy multipliers).

On the other hand, the deterioration in the balance of payments puts strain on the existing exchange rate, which will tend to fall (relative to what would have happened otherwise) if it is freely floating. Depreciation of the exchange rate implies higher prices for imported commodities in terms of domestic currency, the ability to raise export prices in terms of home currency, and inflationary repercussions on all related wage and price levels.

2.2. Summary of Impacts

Before proceeding, it is worth just summarizing all the impacts that are likely to occur as a result of a change in the Government's deficit (surplus) for demand management reasons. We do this by describing the main repercussions of a *fall* in government expenditure unaccompanied by any change in tax rates. Assume, for example, that the Government cancels a planned capital project—a new motorway—which was to have begun in six months and cost £X per month for two years. Instead of government expenditure continuing at a given level, therefore, it will temporarily dip over this period, as shown in Figure 13.1.

The immediate effect will be to lower demand for the products of the civil engineering industry, or, at least, ensure that the demand will be lower than it would have been otherwise. But this—with its implications for the demand for building labourers, concrete, bulldozers, and so on—will only start to occur in six months' time, and continue for the two-year period over which the motorway would have been built. The fall in aggregate demand over this interval will be amplified by falls in consumption (again relative to what it otherwise would have been). Consumption of durables (or, strictly, the acquisition of consumer durables) will begin to tail off quite quickly, since expenditure on them is sensitive to current income. Non-durable consumption displays considerable inertia; habits acquired in the past, and memories of old income levels, will ensure that there is only a gradual build-up in the fall of this component of aggregate demand. This effect will be protracted, while the drop in durable buying will be temporary. Companies' investment expenditure may also be curtailed—especially in the industries immediately affected—although (as with durables) the dip in spending here is not likely to last long; unlike the durables case, however, the dip may well not be noticeable for up to a year after government expenditure has fallen. The possible course of investment, total consumption expenditure on durables and non-durables, government spending and national income is shown in Figure 13.1.

There are also other effects. The drop in national income—which will not, of course, be permanent—will cause a drop in tax receipts. It will also lower imports (relative to trend). The slump in business at home may raise exports as companies switch their sales abroad; but this effect may be small. If the money supply is not changed, interest rates may well weaken during the recession as the demand for money and credit falls off; and a fall in interest rates will tend to stimulate durable buying and (though with a lag) investment as well. There is also a second implication of all this for interest rates. Government spending has fallen, for a twenty-four-month period, and tax receipts have fallen too (but by a good deal less). This suggests an increased probability of budgetary surplus, or a reduced probability of deficit. A continuing deficit implies a continuing rise in interest rates: bond prices have to

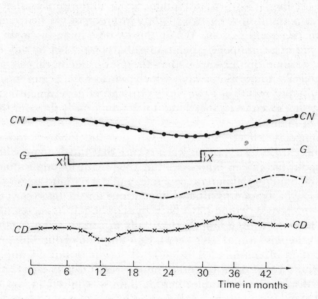

FIG. 13.1. The Course of National Income and its Components During and After a Temporary Fall in G. Y = National Income; CN = Consumption, Non-Durables; CD = Consumption, Durables; I = Investment; G = Government Spending.

keep falling to ensure that the growing debts of the State are willingly taken up. (This need not happen if the Authorities take action to keep interest rates steady, by buying bonds back to keep their price up—in which case the money supply will rise. It is also possible, especially if the trend in national income is upward, that the demand for bonds may keep up with their supply.) Conversely, an increased probability of budgetary surplus amounts to an increased probability that there will be a falling trend in interest rates; whether interest rates do in fact keep falling depends on the initial budgetary position, and any action the Authorities take to influence interest rates. Falls in interest rates have an initially unfavourable effect on the balance of payments. And interest rates are not the only prices upon which there is likely to be downward pressure. The fall in government spending will probably lead to a small fall (relative to what would have happened otherwise) in the prices directly affected—building wages, and relevant materials. The decline in consumption this induces will have similar effects on the prices of a wider range of goods. The unemployment this gives rise to may reduce the rate of rise—and conceivably even the level—of general wage rates; and any fall in wages (relative to trend) is likely to be followed by a broadly parallel movement in prices, since labour costs are such a dominant element in manufacturing prices.

In total, the repercussions even of one simple expenditure change are diffused, complex, somewhat unpredictable, and heavily spread out in time.

2.3. The 'New Cambridge' Approach

Some economists take the view that in an open economy the most pronounced effect of the new budget deficit will in fact be on the balance of payments: their view has been christened 'New Cambridge'. New Cambridge starts with the national income identities.

(1) Y factor cost $\equiv Y$ market prices $- T$ indirect (net of subsidies)

that is (2) $\qquad Y \equiv C + I + G + X - M - T_I$

but by definition (3) $\qquad Y \equiv C + S + T_D$

i.e. income after (direct) tax is either consumed or saved. Subtraction of (3) from (2) reveals that

$$0 = I + G + X - M - T_I - S - T_D$$

and therefore

$$(4) \quad X - M \equiv S - I + (T_D + T_I - G)$$

$(S - I)$ is the domestic private sector's surplus retained from income after payment for tax, consumption, and investment, and therefore (5) the current account surplus of the balance of payments $(X - M) \equiv$ Non-Government domestic sector surplus $(S - I)$ + Government's budget surplus $(T - G)$ where

$$T = T_D + T_I$$

The non-Government domestic sector can be split into (i) the household sector, and (ii) the company sector. Therefore, the current account surplus of the balance of payments (F_b) must equal the surplus of the household sector (F_h) plus the surplus of the company sector (F_c) plus the surplus of the Government sector (F_g), or:

$$(6) \quad F_g \equiv F_b - F_c - F_h$$

Note (i) that the final term could be split up into central government (cg), local authorities (la), and nationalized industries (ni), giving

$$F_g = F_{cg} + F_{la} + F_{ni}$$

and (ii) that any sector or subsector surplus is the difference between its saving and its investment.

These equations are pure tautologies so far. The novel feature of New Cambridge is their suggestion that F_h and F_c are small enough to be ignored, so that

$$(7) \quad F_b \simeq F_g$$

The current account balance is approximately equal to the public authorities' combined financial surpluses.

The view that F_h and F_c are negligible, both in level and rate of change in response to changes in National Income, is supported first by two hypotheses: that the household sector's savings are often approximately balanced by private investment in house-building (one explanation being that much of their savings are channelled into Building Society deposits, which finance house purchase and so, indirectly, new house construction); and that private industry's savings (i.e. business retained earnings) finance the great majority of company investment. Second, by empirical evidence showing that in the ten years up to 1974 there was little change in either of these sectors' financial positions, and that F_b and F_g were roughly of the same magnitude.

This theory has three related implications:

(i) That a financial deficit run by the State will be associated with a balance of payments deficit on current account. It follows that any increase in the State's debt will be matched by an increase in indebtedness to foreigners, and in effect the State debt will have been 'bought' by foreigners.

The consequences of State borrowing from foreigners are only too clear: the debts will have to be serviced, and, in all probability, redeemed if and when the creditors wish to repatriate their assets. While foreign borrowing expands the society's ability to spend now, it must restrict it in future years. These debts will have their adverse effect on the balance of payments in the future, in the form of higher interest payments abroad on the current account. It is always possible, furthermore, that the Central Bank will be faced with a serious liquidity crisis, if its foreign creditors wish to recall their funds quickly. These points suggest that there is more to be said for foreign borrowing if the deficit it finances represents genuine investment with a sufficiently high pay-off, than if it is merely spent on consumption.

(ii) It was seen in Chapter 4 (p. 95) that if investment expenditure is regarded as dependent on income, then the multiplier can be written in simple form as $1/(s + t + m - i)$. If private investment and saving tend to stay in line in the manner suggested then the marginal propensity to save (s) will roughly equal the marginal propensity to invest (i) and the multiplier will become $1/(t + m)$. If t, the marginal 'propensity' to pay tax, is small, this reduces to $1/m$. In this case devaluation may have little long-term effect on the balance of payments. A rise in exports of ΔX will increase national income via the multiplier by $\Delta X/m$. Imports will increase by this rise in national income multiplied by the marginal propensity to import (m) which equals m. $\Delta X/m$ which equals ΔX. Thus the additional imports which follow a devaluation-led boom more or less cancel the initial export improvement.

(iii) If a government surplus/deficit has its impact primarily on the balance of payments, and devaluation to improve exports has little effect on the balance of payments, then there appears to be a case for using fiscal policy to obtain external balance, and devaluation to increase the level of employment via exports and the very high multiplier of $1/m$. This is the reverse of the traditional view of assignment of policy instruments.

Against this it may be argued, firstly, that the t term is so big in Britain—about 50 per cent when poverty-trap considerations, indirect taxes, and graduated national insurance contributions are added to the standard rate of income tax—that the multiplier is probably much lower than $1/m$. Secondly, while F_b and F_g have been numerically quite close for the ten years up to 1974, the estimates for 1975–6 show very substantial divergence.

The New Cambridge approach should probably, therefore, be thought of as a special case of the general open-economy model, for which there is qualified empirical support; it remains controversial, and its dependence on the equality of s and i prevent it from being a good guide to policy.

3. Government Objectives and the Policy-Mix

3.1. Review of Objectives and Instruments

Let us now try to relate policies to the objectives of the Government. The objectives can be summed up as the optimum use of resources. We have seen that there are several ways in which this optimum may not be attained. One is the existence of unused capacity, which signifies a waste of resources. The same is true of involuntary unemployment, but this in addition is a direct cause of welfare loss. Another cause is misemployed resources—too much output of some products, too little of others. The composition of final output could be wrong if there are externalities, monopolies, or firms who do not maximize profits; and also if there is an incorrect intertemporal division of aggregate output between present consumption and investment for future consumption. Balance of payments disequilibria may violate the optimum, since current account deficits imply a sacrifice of future consumption for extra present consumption. Inflation can also violate the optimum: it introduces further uncertainties and social friction, arbitrary redistribution of income and wealth, the extra costs of changing prices, and the nuisance of money circulating more quickly as everyone tries to spend, depreciating cash. A final violation of the optimum will arise if the allocation of incomes and goods between households and individuals is not that for which the Government aims (always assuming Government accurately reflects social choices).

Fiscal policy was shown to affect all these targets: it can alter the level of employment, the pattern of output, the balance of payments, the level of prices, and—in many cases—the distribution of incomes. So too with monetary policy: a rise in the money supply will usually tend to raise output and employment, stimulate expenditure on houses, durables and capital equipment, and, to a lesser extent, non-durable consumption; increase imports, raise prices, and, in certain conditions, redistribute incomes. A change in the exchange rate is also likely to have effects on each target too; similarly with commercial policy, and quite possibly incomes policy as well. There are

obviously many sets of instruments; the effects of the use of each may be
temporary or lasting.

3.2. Assignment of Instruments

Where two or more instruments affect the same targets simultaneously, it
has been proposed (see Chapter 9 for a discussion of this approach) that
particular instruments should be assigned to *particular* targets. Consider, for
instance, two broad targets (internal and external balance) and two instruments (monetary and fiscal policy) which the Government could employ to
guide the economy to the simultaneous attainment of both targets. Suppose
that although fiscal policy affects the balance of payments, monetary policy
acts more effectively (because the fiscal effects operate through aggregate
demand, whereas monetary policy, by raising interest rates on short-term
debt, induces capital inflows as well). Suppose also that fiscal policy has a
more powerful affect on aggregate demand than monetary policy because
interest rates have only a weak affect on expenditure. It would then appear
sensible to use monetary policy for external balance and fiscal policy for
internal balance, because each is then applied in the area where it has an
absolute advantage. (In fact, it can be shown that the crucial factor in assignment of instruments is *comparative advantage*: if instrument a has a stronger
effect on target x than target y, but β has an even more powerful influence on
x relative to y, then β should be tied to the target for x, and a to that for y.)

The weakness in assigning monetary policy to external balance, and fiscal
policy to internal balance, is that it ignores the distinction between short-
and long-term effects. On the external side a rise in the level of domestic
interest rates will not keep on attracting funds from overseas, and so the gain
will tend to be a once-and-for-all gain. Yet one *permanent* effect it has on the
balance of payments is adverse. Both because obligations to foreigners have
risen, and because those obligations are now more costly to service, there is
a deterioration in the interest payment and dividends section of the current
account of the balance of payments. Similarly, although fiscal policy may be
more effective in achieving internal balance in the short run, expansionary
fiscal policy in the long run may involve budget deficits whose adverse effect
on interest rates has already been described (see p. 334). It is now accepted,
because of these conflicting short-run and long-run effects, that no general
rules can be given for the assignment of monetary and fiscal policy.

A second suggestion is that *exchange rate* policy should be contrasted with
monetary and/or fiscal policy for their relative external and internal effects.
The New Cambridge view, as we have seen, is that fiscal policy (in particular,
the public authorities' financial balance) should be assigned to the external
balance and the exchange rate to internal balance.

The more traditional approach opposes this, suggesting that exchange rate
policy should be assigned to the external balance and fiscal (and/or monetary)
policy to the internal one. In order to see which is correct and under what
circumstances, we utilize the Swan diagram again (see Chapter 9).

To state our conclusion first, the New Cambridge assignment (fiscal policy
to external balance EB, exchange rate to the internal balance IB) is correct

if the EB curve is steeper than the IB curve; if not, the standard assignment is correct. This can be seen as follows. The traditional approach can be represented as in Figure 13.2.

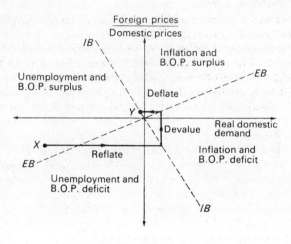

FIG. 13.2

Starting from a position of unemployment and balance of payments surplus X, suppose reflation to achieve full employment (IB), and then devaluation to correct the resulting balance of payments deficit (EB). This requires some deflation to avoid excess demand as a result of increased export demand (and import substitution). The economy homes in on internal and external balance (perhaps stopping at Y—internal balance and a small balance of payments surplus).

Consider what happens if the slope of IB is flatter, and that of EB much steeper. This is shown in Figure 13.3.

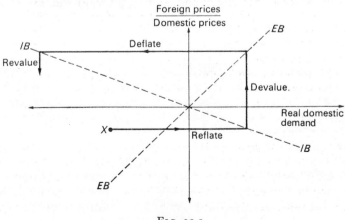

FIG. 13.3

In this case, although the starting-point and the equilibrium point are the same, the policy assignment is destabilizing, with progressively bigger and bigger adjustments required for each type of balance to be achieved. In this situation it would be necessary to devalue to obtain internal balance, and reflate for external balance, etc. This is the New Cambridge theory, and is shown in Figure 13.4.

What then determines the relative slopes of the IB and EB lines? It is shown in Appendix 1 that the traditional approach will work if $s + t + x$ is greater than $i + m$ where these are the marginal propensities to save, pay tax, export, invest, and import, respectively. Most of the time in Britain one would expect this to be the case. t is the largest of these terms (about $\frac{1}{2}$);

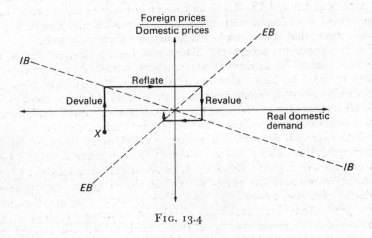

Fig. 13.4

s is certainly no smaller than i, and in the short run likely to be considerably above it (non-durable consumption displays great inertia, and although durables spending is very sensitive to current income, investment is strongly lagged); and while x is probably very small, m will only exceed about $\frac{1}{3}$ at times of very high demand. The chances that $s + t + x$ exceed $i + m$ are greater if the money supply is kept reasonably tight (so as to produce an interest-rate drag effect on spending in a boom) than if the money supply is adjusted passively in line with the demand for it.

Two other factors must be added to the above analysis:

(i) Deflation/reflation and devaluation/revaluation will generally take different periods of time to have their effect. It has usually been thought that the former acts more quickly.

(ii) The cost of being out of internal and external equilibrium may be different. Unemployment may be regarded as more serious than a balance of payments deficit, even though the latter must eventually be removed. On the other hand, a balance of payments deficit may *have* to be corrected very rapidly if international loans or adequate reserves are not available.

3.3. Rules versus Discretion

There are those who disagree with discretionary intervention to attain either external balance or internal balance. They argue that the money supply should be kept growing at a constant rate, G and T should be set so that there is approximate fiscal balance at full employment, and the exchange rate should be allowed to float to its natural level. They believe that the economic system, if left to itself under these rules, will tend to simultaneous external and internal balance, without discretionary intervention. The case *for* discretionary intervention, as opposed to set rules governing policy instruments, rests on three premises: one, that there is no reliable inherent mechanism—or at least no mechanism that works fast enough—to push the economy into the state (e.g. EB and IB) the Government wishes it to attain; two, that the Government is endowed with adequate information and forecasting techniques; three, that it can employ instruments which work well.

The first premiss is acceptable. There have been prolonged slumps, many of which cannot be attributed to conscious attempts by governments to restrict demand by fiscal or monetary deflation. Slumps have been caused by a sudden burst of pessimism about the economic future: consumers cut back on consumption, producers feel saturated with capital equipment and reduce investment expenditure. The multiplier and accelerator can interact to reduce aggregate demand still further. A check to the recession can come, in principle, from falling prices—prices of factors (wage rates and interest rates) and prices of goods. But wage rates are sticky downwards in advanced capitalist economies; the prices of manufactured goods are, in practice, similarly inflexible downwards; and there is some evidence that interest rates—particularly long-term rates of interest, of more relevance to investment decisions—cannot always be relied upon to fall fast enough either. There is also clear evidence that external imbalance can persist for quite long periods; and that the composition of total output or distribution of incomes brought about by market forces may be felt by society to be undesirable or unfair. Information is expensive to acquire and often faulty. Imperfect competition, externalities, problems over public goods, and markets which are missing altogether (especially for goods in the future) can and do generate microeconomic waste, and can and do conflict with the objectives of the public authorities.

It is not so clear that the Government is endowed with adequate information and forecasting techniques. Intervention is required in the economic system, partly because of the informational deficiencies and false expectations that can arise in markets. But the Government does not have costless access to information; that information is not perfect, and in particular it cannot know the future. Even short-term macroeconomic forecasting is hazardous. In Britain most studies have concluded that post-war fluctuations in aggregate demand have, on balance, been amplified by intervention. 'Too much, too late' has been a general verdict. The trouble has been caused by excessive reaction to indicators of the pressure of demand—unemployment in the slump, sterling crises in the boom—which lag behind the cycle in production by up to a year; and by the use of slow-acting policy instruments, the long-run effects of which are underestimated and the short-run effects of which are overestimated.

The third requirement is the availability of instruments which work well. What does 'well' mean? Primarily, it means four things: (i) the instruments must work *quickly*, or within the desired time horizon ('desired' being a political datum); (ii) they must work *predictably*; (iii) with *sizeable* effect on the target concerned; and (iv) without *harmful side-effects*—or, at least, with side-effects which are both predictable, and offsettable by the use of alternative instruments. It is interesting in the light of these to evaluate the Keynesian-based monetary and fiscal policy of the post-war period. It is widely, if not universally, accepted that both work slowly—the effects on aggregate demand building up to maximum impact at least four or five quarters later. (The only clear exception to this is hire-purchase or credit policies to influence consumer durable buying, which work much faster, while leaving few, if any, permanent effects.) Both sets of instruments also score rather poorly on the criterion of predictability—the major problem here being over the speed of the effect, and to some extent, too, on its final size. Both instruments also have side-effects—monetary expansion may raise house and land prices, and stimulate durable buying relative to non-durable consumption; fiscal expansion will tend to have effects on relative prices; both will induce some inflation, and a deterioration in the balance of payments. Whether these side-effects are harmful depends partly on the existing position, and partly on the Government's preferences, but they are probably hard to offset in the short term.

What can we conclude about the dilemma of rules or discretion? On fiscal policy, it is definitely unwise to have a general rule about the actual fiscal balance: tax receipts swell in booms and ebb in recessions. If the Authorities try to keep the budget balanced irrespective of the level of demand, they will destabilize demand by, for example, cutting taxes at the top of booms and raising them in recessions. A much better rule is a balanced budget at the target level of unemployment, which implies the built-in fiscal stabilizer of deficits at the bottom of the cycle and surpluses at the top. But given the possibility of sharp, non-cyclical shifts in aggregate demand, fiscal policy should be used—when there is clear evidence of such phenomena—with more discretion particularly if the evidence favours fiscal weapons on the four criteria of efficiency discussed above.

Turning to money, the case for discretion here may be based on the Keynesian suggestion that the demand for money function may become highly volatile, and that the Authorities should adjust supply towards demand to stop the swings in interest rates which would occur if the two got out of line. Empirical evidence so far has not supported this: the demand for money function has rarely displayed much volatility (see Chapter 12).

If prices are neither rising nor falling, the best monetary rule might be: keep the supply rising at the speed of population growth, plus the long-run rate of increase in real incomes per head multiplied by the observed long-run income-elasticity of the demand for money. This ensures that the supply of money would rise to meet increased demand resulting from a rise in real income, but no more. If prices are rising at an unacceptably high rate, the rule might be changed to: keep the money supply rising at the previously stated rate, plus something rather less than the present inflation rate (how much less will depend on how much and how quickly the Authorities wish to sacrifice jobs—at least temporarily—to bring inflation down). These monetary rules carry with them the responsibility for supervising the balance sheets of banks, and also for intervening to prevent bank failures (which would otherwise lead to a sharp drop in the money supply). The use of monetary policy in this way as a counter-inflation weapon implies that alternatives (in particular incomes policy) do not work, work inadequately, or work only at too high a cost in terms of arbitrary distortions to wages, restrictions on wage differentials as incentives to labour mobility, and removal of links between wage rates and productivity.

There are many other examples of the issue of whether to use rules or discretion, e.g. competition policy, regional policy, or even incomes policy. Chapters 5 and 7 provided arguments concerning the type of exchange rate system to be employed, and both a free floating and a fixed rate (either against a group of other currencies or against gold) represent simple rules for obtaining equilibrium which may or may not work. A genuinely adjustable peg or 'managed' floating system are examples of discretionary approaches. As in the case of monetary policy so here the argument for the rule depends on the belief in the efficiency of an automatic equilibrating mechanism. The case for intervention implies that these mechanisms will not work, or not quickly enough. In this area too there can be no simple answers to the rules versus discretion dilemma.

4. Conclusion

This chapter has examined the relationship between monetary and fiscal policy. There are two main kinds of relationship. First, the fiscal stance—the budget surplus or deficit—has inevitable monetary consequences. A budget deficit must have financial repercussions, involving changes in interest rates and/or in the money supply, as well. Secondly monetary and fiscal policies may be deployed to attain certain targets of economic policy. The way in which these two policies are combined or used in combination with other instruments of economic policy, such as exchange rate policy or incomes policy, depends upon their relative strengths and the time it takes for them to be effective. It also depends more fundamentally on the degree to which policy-makers feel justified in intervening at their discretion or wish to bind themselves by rules of action. Although these complex problems would be easier to solve if empirical evidence was clearer, the issue is not solely a technical one. For instance, the question of whether one can frame fiscal and monetary policies on the assumption that a reliable incomes policy will be operating will be largely outside the competence of the economist. Similarly, international demand management may require that the Authorities suit their policy-mix to that of the rest of the world. This issue is explored in the next chapter.

Appendix 1: Instrument Assignment in New and Old Cambridge Approaches

Definitions:

$B \equiv$ balance of trade (excess of exports over imports)

$A \equiv$ absorption (consumption + investment + government spending)

$R \equiv$ price of foreign currency in domestic currency (so that a rise in R is a depreciation or devaluation of the home country's currency)

$F \equiv$ a financial policy parameter: a rise in F is expansionary. (F may be thought of as government expenditure, but might equally well stand for a set of tax rates, or even a monetary variable)

$Y \equiv$ domestic income

Lower case letters denote changes in the relevant variables

Assumptions: All variables are measured in real terms; all relative prices of goods are fixed.

The rest of the world is assumed to be very large: no explicit account is taken of the effects of any repercussions on the rest of the world. B varies positively with R and negatively with Y so that

$$(1)\ B = B(R,Y) \text{ with } B_1 \equiv \frac{\partial B}{\partial R} > 0,\ B_2 \equiv \frac{\partial B}{\partial Y} < 0.$$

A varies with R, and positively with Y and F so that

$$(2)\ A = A(R,Y,F) \text{ with } A_1 \equiv \frac{\partial A}{\partial R} \gtrless 0,\ A_2 \equiv \frac{\partial A}{\partial Y} > 0,\ A_3 \equiv \frac{\partial A}{\partial F} > 0.$$

Y is the sum of A and B:

$$(3)\ Y = A + B$$

Differentiating, and eliminating $a\ (= \partial A)$, we have

$$b = B_1 r + B_2 y$$
$$y = A_1 r + A_2 y + A_3 f + B_1 r + B_2 y$$

which, after substitution and rearrangement, yields

$$b = k[((1 - A_2)B_1 + B_2 A_1)r + B_2 A_3 f]$$
$$\text{where } k = (1 - A_2 - B_2)^{-1}$$
$$y = k[(A_1 + B_1)r + A_3 f]$$

For *external balance* (EB), $B = b = 0$: consequently

$$(4)\ \lambda \equiv \frac{f}{r}\bigg|_{b\,=\,0} = -\frac{1 - A_2}{A_3}\frac{B_1}{B_2} - \frac{A_1}{A_3}.$$

For *internal balance* (IB), Y is at some target level and $y = 0$: consequently

$$(5)\ \mu \equiv \frac{f}{r}\bigg|_{y\,=\,0} = -\frac{A_1 + B_1}{A_3}.$$

Now λ is positive if and only if $A_2 < 1 + A_1 B_2 / (B_1)$ and μ is negative if and only if $B_1 > -A_1$. These conditions are generally met.

The figures show various combinations of f and r which bring EB and IB. In panel (a) (Fig. 13.5), the gradient of the EB line is steeper than that of the IB line; in this case, the New Cambridge assignment (f to EB, r to IB) is stable. In case (b) it is the IB line which is steeper—and the New Cambridge assignment is destabilizing; the orthodox assignment (r to EB, f to IB) is stable. In case (a), $\lambda + \mu < 0$; in case (b), $\lambda + \mu > 0$. On what does the sign of $\lambda + \mu$ depend? For $\lambda + \mu > 0$,

$$- \frac{B_1}{B_2} (B_2 + 1 - A_2) > 2A_1.$$

This in turn implies that $1 - A_2 > -B_2 + \dfrac{2A_1B_2}{B_1}.$

Now $1 - A_2 = s + t - i$ (the rise in savings and taxes, less the rise (if any) in investment, induced by a rise in Y); and $-B_2 = m - x$ (the deterioration in the trade balance brought about by a rise in Y). If A_1 (the direct effect of an exchange rate change on absorption) is thought to be negligible, we can conclude that the New Cambridge assignment is stable (unstable) when and only when $m + i$ exceed (fall short of) $s + t + x$.

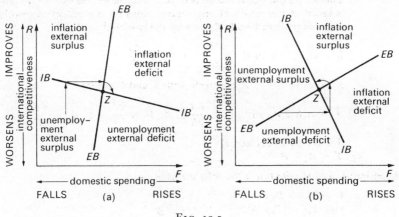

FIG. 13.5

(a) EB steeper than IB: New Cambridge Assignment stable.
   Clockwise adjustment converges on Z, counter-clockwise adjustment explodes.
(b) IB steeper than EB: Orthodox (Old Cambridge) Assignment stable.
   Counter-clockwise adjustment converges on Z, clockwise adjustment explodes.

Some further comments are in order. A_1 is unlikely to be large; but it is more likely than not to be negative. This strengthens the orthodox position: case (b) becomes likelier. The sign of i (the effect of a rise in Y on investment) is ambiguous: it will be positive, in general, if the domestic monetary Authorities keep the rate of interest rigid and raise the supply of money when the rise in Y raises the transactions demand for it. But if they keep the money supply fixed, we are likely to experience rises in the interest rate when Y increases, which may well be appreciable if the interest-elasticity of the demand for money is low. If investment responds negatively to the rate of interest—as most empirical evidence suggests it will, to some extent, after a lag—the sign of i could easily be negative. Once again, this strengthens the orthodox case. The value of m will probably alter over the business-cycle—it is likely to rise sharply in the late phases of a boom, as domestic producers are less and less able to meet rises in demand; in these circumstances it is the New Cambridge view which is strengthened. The sign of x is unknown: a rise in Y may pull back into the domestic market goods otherwise destined for sale abroad; but if we relax the assumption that the rest of the world is large enough for us to ignore foreign repercussions of domestic policy decisions, it could become positive—if a rise in Y raises imports, foreign incomes are likely to go up, since home imports are by definition foreign exports; and this will, if anything, tend to raise domestic exports. Lastly, it should be remembered that this model is exceedingly simple—it ignores all types of price change in particular markets for example—and that universal applicability should not be claimed for its results. None the less, given that the value of t in contemporary Britain exceeds $\frac{1}{2}$ (when indirect taxes, graduated insurance contributions, and means-tested benefits are allowed for), there is reason to prefer the Old Cambridge assignment (f to IB, r to EB) to the New.

14
The International Demand Management Problem

C. J. ALLSOPP

1. Introduction

Economic policies are, by and large, formulated at the national level. It is important, however, to consider the ways in which national economic policies interact to bring about favourable or unfavourable results for the world economic system as a whole. Moreover, some problems are international in character, and cannot be adequately analysed from the viewpoint of any particularly economy. Recent developments such as the oil crisis and the world recession have raised the spectre of a marked increase in international instability. How real are the difficulties? Does economic analysis point to a rational solution, or have traditional modes of analysis ceased to be adequate in the new situation? Focusing on the commodity price rise of 1972-3, the oil crisis, and the subsequent move to recession, this chapter analyses some of the problems involved as a kind of case study of the considerations that are relevant, and of the additional difficulties that arise when economic policy is considered in the international context.

The emphasis of this chapter is on interactions amongst developed industrialized countries in the short term. Longer-term considerations, such as the development of the international monetary system, the position of developing countries, resource availabilities, and so on, form the background to short-term policy, but are not themselves under discussion. In keeping with the objective of illustrating the problems involved, no policy recommendations are made; and, since the situation is, at the time of writing, still evolving, judgement on the most recent events cannot even be tempered by hindsight.

2. The Framework of Short-Term Policy Formation

Though there is no supranational authority with powers in any way comparable to those of national authorities, economic policy formation can at times be greatly influenced by the international environment. Consultation and information exchange are continuous; countries have international obligations of both formal and informal kinds, and, on occasion, international pressure may have a decisive influence on economic policies.

Many contacts are formalized under one or other of the International Institutions, such as the International Monetary Fund (I.M.F.), or the

Organization for Economic Co-operation and Development (O.E.C.D.), but others may be more *ad hoc*, concerned with particular issues. Committees are set up at many different levels, ranging from purely technical working parties to ministerial meetings. Often the same set of problems will be discussed simultaneously in many different contexts; gradually a consensus may emerge, or there may be a formal agreement. The whole process is rather amorphous, often shrouded in diplomatic language, but is none the less an important element in policy formation.

Expected developments in the world economy are vital inputs into any national forecasting exercise. National forecasts and, for that matter, policy targets may, however, be inconsistent with each other. It is one of the roles of international consultation to try to remove as far as possible these inconsistencies so as to arrive at a better over-all consensus as to likely developments in the international economy. To this end, institutions such as the O.E.C.D. produce their own forecasts for individual countries and for world trade and payments. Of necessity, these forecasts have consistency thrust upon them. As an example, balance of payments positions must be compatible with each other, whereas it is not uncommon for the aggregate of individual country forecasts to violate the condition that one country's surplus is another country's deficit. An organization specifically looking at the total picture may be more likely to get certain aspects of it right—such as the growth of world trade. Even where such forecasts are not accepted, they may, nevertheless, have a substantial influence.

Discussions cannot stop at the technical level of forecasting. In part this is a result of a methodological problem. Forecasts, such as those of the O.E.C.D. or of the E.E.C., are intended as a basis for policy discussion, and as such are usually conditional on a continuation of present policies. On the other hand, the forecasts most appropriate for a national authority would assume a continuation of present policies in that country—so that the need for policy action could be identified—but would normally assume 'most likely policies' for other countries. There is a need, therefore, for an understanding of policy positions elsewhere. Beyond this, international discussions are designed to influence policies; to promote a co-operative approach to common problems. The views of the I.M.F., or the O.E.C.D., or of individual trading partners may, on occasion, be ignored, but they are heard in national capitals. Sometimes international pressure is more than diplomatic, as when, for example, conditions (usually to deflate) are attached to the granting of an I.M.F. loan.

The difficulties in achieving international consensus and a co-operative approach are too well known to require restating. One aspect should, however, be stressed in an economics book. Meaningful co-operation requires consensus on the diagnosis and economic analysis of common problems. The problems raised by disagreement are nowhere more obvious than in the field of short-term demand management policy. Is there a trade-off between inflation and unemployment? Should use be made of fiscal or monetary policy? Should demand management policy be used to correct international payments disequilibria? Fundamental disagreement on how to run a rational world is an important stumbling-block, even if there are no other difficulties, such as national self-interest, in the way of achieving co-operation.

3. The Trade Cycle since the War

The outstanding characteristic of the post-war period has been the generally high rate of expansion of the industrialized countries. Between 1954 and 1973 the rate of expansion of the non-socialist industrial world was of the order of 5 per cent per annum—a rate unprecedented in any historical period of comparable length. This was a general expansion, with all industrial countries participating. Fluctuations have been shorter and smaller, and in most countries have often taken the form of fluctuations in growth rather than absolute declines in output as in the traditional definition of depression.

Many explanations for the moderation of the business cycle have been advanced, and the subject is still controversial. Clearly, Keynesian policies of demand management have played a role; but the weight that should be given to this factor is uncertain. Many countries were slow to adopt Keynesian policies and some have not accepted them yet. The extent of intervention by Governments can also be questioned—was counter-cyclical policy, where practised, powerful enough to stabilize the economy? Others would point to automatic stabilizers such as improved unemployment benefits which help maintain expenditure during a recession, and the progressivity of the tax system, which increases taxation as incomes rise. The increasing role of Government—of public expenditure generally—may be an important stabilizing factor even if not used as a counter-cyclical tool, since a larger proportion of the national economy may be independent of cyclical conditions. A related point is that the time-scale of investment in major capital projects is now so long that decisions cannot be influenced as much as before by short-term considerations.

It would seem likely that all these explanations have some validity. Econometric model simulations of industrialized countries tend to display stability in the sense that, left to themselves, the models do not generate even the relatively minor fluctuations observed since the war. They are perhaps best thought of as tracking the cycle—the fluctuations being induced by movement in exogenous variables. For example, changes in exports, or changes in policy, may set off cumulative tendencies of a cyclical kind—but if the 'shocks' are not repeated the fluctuations would, in time, tend to die away.

There are, however, two qualifications that need to be made to the view that industrial economies have become inherently more stable. The first is that any analysis or model for a particular economy treats exports as an exogenous component of demand. But for the world as a whole, there is no exogenous component of demand in exports. We do not trade with Mars. Technically this means that the world economy may be less stable than analysis of individual economies would suggest.

This point can be seen as follows. The 'multiplier' in most economies is rather small—probably less than two. Apart from personal savings, 'leakages' occur due to taxation (its net effect on disposable incomes after tax) and due to imports. For the world economy as a whole, however, there can be no 'leakage' due to imports—so the multiplier appropriate for the analysis of the world economy is higher.[1] This leads to the familiar point that if an impact on the world economy affects all countries at the same time and in the same direction, then it is likely to be much more destabilizing in its effects than if it affected only a single country or if it affected different countries at different times.

World trade has grown rather steadily since the war. Countries have generally not been in phase—when one group of countries has been expanding fast others have been moving towards recession. Exports have remained buoyant in the face of domestic recessionary forces, or policies. Equivalently, the import leakage has operated for individual economies in that imports have fluctuated *relative* to the rest of the world. Until recently the most nearly coincident movement of industrialized countries was in the 1958 recession. Importantly, however, some major countries took reflationary action before or during 1958, and Japan, Germany, and Italy maintained relatively strong rates of expansion. The recession was short-lived.

The lack of close coincidence between major economies, and the resulting buoyancy of world trade must be counted as a major contributory cause for the relative stability of economies since the war. It is in marked contrast to the experience of the 1930s. As a diagnosis, however, it must be worrying. It explains stability in terms of the primacy of domestic economic aims, or as a happy accident, and does not rule out the possibility of major cyclical problems occurring should the major countries start to move in phase.

The second qualification relates to the difficult area of expectations and confidence. As noted, there is doubt as to the extent to which Keynesian demand management policies can explain such stability as we have had— even in Britain where they have been most consistently applied. Nevertheless, the commitment to full employment and growth may have been vitally important. After the war, in Britain, the Government took formal responsibility for the maintenance of employment, and, with Keynesian policies, had the means to achieve it. The success was phenomenal compared even with the expectations of the architects of such policies. Once it is accepted that the Government can and will maintain employment, there is an important effect on the expectations of both investors and consumers. In recessionary periods their best guess is that the economy will be back to full employment within a few years. Consumption is maintained, investment plans are geared to the growth of productive potential. In other countries also, commitments were made to maintain employment and to foster growth. Governments nowadays are expected to run the economy—and until recently they were expected to succeed.

If there has been a favourable feedback from government action to expec-

---

[1] Consider an illustrative example. Suppose the multiplier is $k = 1/(s + m + t)$, where s, the marginal propensity to save and, t, the marginal 'propensity' to pay tax, pick up *domestic* leakages, and m, the marginal propensity to import, picks up 'foreign leakages'. Dropping the import leakage would raise the multiplier to $k' = 1/(s + t)$. If domestic and foreign leakages were equally important, the multiplier appropriate to the 'world' would be double that appropriate to domestic economies on average $[(s + m + t)/(s + t) = 2]$.

tations (partial, of course), then all the relationships in forecasting and policy models, together with the rules of thumb used by policy economists, will reflect this phenomenon. There is no statistical way of identifying the separate contributions of governmental policy and changes in expectations; the latter is largely unobservable. If long-run expectations change, or if the way in which expectations follow or lead the cycle changes, then all our current models and quantitative guesses may be a bad guide to short-run policy in the future. To take a specific example: if a forecasting model suggests a relatively stable economy this may reflect fundamental economic relationships, or it may reflect a more fragile set of expectational factors—such as a tendency for longer-term investment plans to be maintained in spite of short-run difficulties. In the latter case, the system could cease to be so stable if longer-term expectations became adverse, and if investment plans were subject to greater downward revisions than would normally be expected. Policy action to reflate the economy would then have to be of quantitatively greater significance than usual.[2]

One of the most worrying aspects of the situation that developed in the 1973 boom and subsequent recession is, of course, that the normal stabilizing elements seemed to be absent, or to be operating with much diminished force. Whereas in 1958 world trade stagnated for a short period, in 1975 it collapsed. For the O.E.C.D. area as a whole imports declined in 1975 compared with 1974 by nearly 10 per cent. Total exports declined by about 6 per cent [8, Table 2.2]. Moreover, the climate of expectations became highly adverse, affected by the oil crisis, the world recession, and rapid inflation.

4. Recent Developments

The most notable features of the period since 1967 are the breakdown of the fixed exchange rate system set up after the war, and the emergence of inflation as an international policy issue. Moreover, in the 1970s the degree of coincidence between major economies—though difficult to measure—appears to have strengthened. Policy problems and policy responses have tended to coincide in major economies and, especially in the boom period of 1972–3, so have movements in demand and output.

We start by briefly reviewing the collapse of the Bretton Woods system. When sterling was devalued in 1967, the existing set of exchange rates was called into question, and the dollar was in the front line of speculative attack. Persistent United States balance of payments deficits—due largely to an outflow on capital account—had vastly swelled the quantity of externally held dollar balances. The first casualty was the price of gold, which had been stabilized at $35 to the ounce by the mechanism of the London Gold Pool. Fears about the position of the dollar led to massive buying of gold in March 1968. The system was, however, patched up. Gold continued to enter transactions between Central Banks at the official price, but was allowed to find its own level on the free market.

---

[2] In the normal case this would not suggest that policy would not work; but that reactions to it would tend to be delayed. In a reflationary situation this would seriously increase the risk of overshoot as expectations were revised upwards again.

Uncertainty and speculation continued, however, and by the middle of 1971 convertability of the dollar into gold was suspended, and all the world's major currencies were *de facto* floating. This period of floating ended with the formal devaluation of the dollar and revaluations of other currencies with the Smithsonian Agreement of December 1971. At the time the realignment appeared to mark the end of a period of extreme uncertainty—but the newly established parities were themselves destined to be short lived. A little over a year later the dollar was again devalued, and floating currencies again the rule.

These monetary uncertainties and exchange rate changes cannot, however, be seen in isolation from other developments. The year 1967 was one of low world growth due to policy action taken to lower demand pressure in the three major economies. In the United States severe restrictive action was taken by the Federal Reserve to slow the growth of the economy, which had been enjoying a long period of uninterrupted growth and which appeared to be overheating in 1966. The result was a sharp credit crunch, and a collapse of the house-building sector. Industrial production flattened out in 1967. In Germany deflationary measures were a response to overheating in 1965, and led to a recession which continued through into 1967. The low growth in the United Kingdom was a result of the deflationary July 1966 package of the Labour Government. This recessionary period did not develop, however. Japan and Italy continued to expand strongly through 1967: the German economy recovered quickly, and, most importantly, the Federal Reserve changed course to relieve the credit squeeze, and United States growth was resumed.

Overheating continued to be a worry. In the United States a tax increase—the other side of the coin to the 1964 tax decrease which had maintained expansion—was proposed as 10 per cent surcharge on income and corporation taxes. This was resisted for a reason that illustrates well the difficulties of pursuing Keynesian policies in the United States. It was felt by many that a tax increase would only be justified if the Federal Government also did its part and reduced expenditure. Thus the greater the expenditure reduction, the greater the tax increase that was likely to be let through. After delays, the tax increase was enacted in the summer of 1968—together with a proposed government expenditure reduction of 6 per cent, significantly increasing the demand-reducing effects of the package. The effects of these policies were somewhat delayed, and were subsequently reinforced with tight monetary conditions. Internationally the deflationary action in the United States was taken as an indication of seriousness of purpose in correcting the dollar outflow—one of the reasons why the dollar was relatively immune to the monetary crisis of November 1968, which centred on the French franc and the German mark.

Other countries also moved towards a restrictive posture, with the result that most major economies were in a recessionary phase in the period 1970–1. The reasons for the policy moves differed, but external considerations were part of the explanation. In the United Kingdom restrictive policies were related to the slow response of the balance of payments to devaluation, and in many countries the general climate of monetary uncertainty must have been influential. But, as in the United States, a most important factor was that price and wage rises were accelerating in many countries. The problem of inflation had become generalized. In the countries concerned, however, it was the domestic wage-price spiral that was the policy issue, and this phase of demand management policy can be seen as an attempt in a number of countries to make use of the traditional assumed trade-off between inflation and the pressure of demand to slow the rise in prices.

The period of low pressure of demand in 1970 and 1971 set the stage for the worldwide coincident boom of 1972 and 1973. In part this was the result of normal cyclical developments from a starting-point in which many countries had a larger degree of slack than usual. But economic policies changed sharply to induce and to reinforce the expansion.

There were several elements in the reversal of policy positions. In the first place, deflation, in a number of countries, appeared to be going too far. The United States recession was larger and more prolonged than many had expected. The policy position was reversed; there were rapid increases in the money supply and the Federal Budget position became more expansionary. It was not until the end of 1970 that the economy really started to grow again, and the turn-around in industrial production was even further delayed. In the United Kingdom, 1971 was marked by a severe rise in unemployment. The second element is that the slow-down appeared to have disappointingly small effects on the course of price and wage inflation. In Europe consumer prices continued to accelerate through to the middle of 1971. In the United States consumer price rises were somewhat lowered in 1971 and 1972. But even here there is a question as to whether the improvement reflected the lagged effect of lower demand pressures, or, alternatively, the beneficial effects of productivity gains at the beginning of the upswing, combined with the move to policies of prices and incomes control. It began to look as if the demand management weapon for controlling price and wage rises was a very blunt instrument: if it worked at all, the costs in terms of unemployment and output forgone appeared to be great—so great in some countries as to be beyond the limit of political feasibility.

By 1971 nearly all major countries were in a strongly reflationary policy position. This coincided with strong pressure on the dollar. When convertibility of the dollar was suspended in the summer of 1971 an extra twist was given to expansionary policies. In the subsequent period of floating there was a tendency for Authorities to want to maintain their competitive position, and to resist upward movements of their exchange rates. Monetary expansion, general reflation, and Central Bank intervention accompanied the float, leading to a sharp increase in the world money supply and a marked stimulus to demand. In addition, it is arguable that the fixed exchange rate system, up to this time, had tended to lead to a deflationary bias in economic policy, as the onus of adjustment fell on weak currency countries who resisted devaluation by restrictive monetary and fiscal policies. When countries floated, the tendencies were reversed; it was strong currency countries which were resisting revaluation by expansionary policies. Confidence factors, however, due to the turmoil on exchange markets, probably acted as a brake on expansion, until world monetary uncertainties were sharply reduced as a result of the Smithsonian realignment of December 1971.

The boom that followed was very sharp. It was led by North America; Japan and Italy joined in the general upswing rather later, but were soon expanding very fast indeed. By the first half of 1973 it appeared that the industrial countries as a group were expanding at a rate of about 8 per cent per annum; a rate which was clearly unsustainable. The boom was marked by some unusual features. Inflation accelerated sharply, stimulated in the main by rapidly rising commodity prices. Supply constraints appeared early on, particularly in primary processing sectors, so that capacity limitations became a brake on expansion earlier than might have been expected. Many governments acted to restrain demand quite early in the boom. In the second half of 1973 the oil crisis erupted, with marked effects on industrialized economies which were already slowing down.

5. The Commodity Price Rise in 1972–3

The world boom of 1972–3 started from a position of slack in many countries, but soon ran into trouble. There was a marked increase in the rate of inflation—an extremely worrying phenomenon given that the recessionary policies of the previous few years had had only a small effect, so that prices were already rising fast. At this time, however, the increased inflationary pressure arose, not from an intensification of the domestic wage–price spiral, but from a worldwide rise in the prices of food and raw materials. The terms of trade started to move sharply in favour of primary producers. To an individual country this raised a difficult policy problem in that the phenomenon was largely outside the scope of domestic control. Even for the United States, a large exporter of primary commodities, the inflationary stimulus had a quasi-exogenous character, arising as it did from increased export demand. For the world as a whole, however—or for the industrialized countries as a group, which are about 80 per cent self-sufficient in primary products—this inflationary stimulus could not be regarded as 'exogenous'. It arose in part owing to sharply increased demands, reflecting the speed and generality of the upswing in activity, and in part from supply-side difficulties.

In the post-war period primary commodity prices have fluctuated in response to world activity and changes on the supply side, but on the whole the terms of trade to primary producers have been reasonably stable, or declining. In most agricultural markets—food and raw materials—there have been periodic problems of over-supply, and continued discussion and implementation of policies to support prices. Domestic agricultural production has typically been supported or protected to maintain farm incomes and continuity of production. Non-agricultural raw materials have fared better— with especially fast trend rises in the prices of non-ferrous metals. It is characteristic of most primary commodity markets that prices, if left to themselves, are particularly vulnerable to the vagaries of supply and demand shifts. Typically, supply changes take a considerable time, and demand is relatively inelastic so that any imbalance has to be met by large price changes. It is this vulnerability that accounts for the many arrangements that have been set up to interfere with these markets. But for most commodities, free markets, of varying importance, exist, and prices on the free market are the most readily available, and the easiest to collect. The spot prices, on these free markets, are much more volatile than the average prices at which actual transactions take place. These are often based on longer-term contracts between producers and consumers. Transaction prices may lag behind movements of the spot price by as much as six or nine months.

In 1972 and 1973 primary commodity prices in general—both food and raw materials—took off, and rose very sharply. The Economist index of world commodity spot prices[3] fell during 1971 to 90 (taking 1970 as 100), rose to 109 in 1972, to 164 in 1973 as an average; was 193 in December 1973, and rose to over 200 in the first part of 1974. The food component rose earlier (to 120 for the average of 1972) and to an even greater extent. In October 1974 the index stood at no less than 262. Spot food prices had risen $2\frac{3}{4}$ times compared with the situation in 1971. Wheat and soya beans went up about fourfold.

These dramatic figures considerably overstate the effects of the commodity price boom. As noted, transactions prices lag developments on the free markets, and, moreover, much food is domestically produced, and the prices tend to be much more stable. Nevertheless, food prices in the United States rose by $14\frac{1}{2}$ per cent in 1973 compared with 1972, and alone contributed about half the rise in the consumer price index of that year (6·2 per cent). In the United Kingdom the food price rise was smaller ($11\frac{1}{2}$ per cent), but the weight of food in the consumer price index is greater. For the United Kingdom also, the food price rise contributed about half the total rise in the C.P.I. of 9·2 per cent. It is probable that the rise in price of *imported* primary products (excluding oil) was about 30 per cent in 1973 on a *transaction* basis. It was about the same in 1974. If industrial materials are included as well, it is clear that the contribution to inflation of the rise in commodity prices was very great.

The reasons for the rise vary between commodities. In the case of food, prices rose rapidly from the middle of 1972, reflecting global supply deficiencies and sharp increases in demand. Crop failures in the Soviet Union, Australia, and China, and many parts of South-East Asia, led to a 3 per cent fall in world grain production, exacerbated by a low stock position. The temporary collapse of the Peruvian anchovy catch worsened the situation with respect to animal feed—especially the price of soya. The initiating cause of the rise in industrial raw materials was the sharp increase in world industrial production—but here too the situation was exacerbated by supply-side difficulties. In many products the low prices of the 1960s combined with increasing costs, and interest charges had deterred investment in increased capacity. Problems were not confined to the primary industries themselves, but also appeared at the primary processing stage, where widespread capacity bottlenecks developed. In relation to the expansion of industrial production

---

[3] The weighting of this index is based on imports into industrial countries rather than on world production. Fuel and oil prices are excluded.

the spot price of industrial materials rose to a far greater extent than usual.

An end to the boom was widely expected in the summer of 1973. But in October the Middle East War occurred, followed by the oil crisis. The general effect on expectations and speculation was such as to keep the commodity price boom going into the first half of 1974, when industrial materials did start coming down with characteristic sharpness. Food prices remained high, however, throughout 1974, as it became apparent that the crop year was not going to be as good as had been expected.

The policy problems posed by the commodity price rises were very great. The additional stimulus to inflation came on top of inflation rates which were already regarded as highly unsatisfactory. In retreat from demand manage-ment policies as a cure for inflation, many countries were relying on prices and income controls to stem inflationary pressures during the upswing. The most notable example was the introduction of the various phases of price and incomes policy in the United States, starting with the price and wage freeze introduced during the second half of 1971. In the first half of 1972 there were grounds for optimism that the rate of rise of consumer prices was moderating in North America, Europe, and Japan. But there was soon a dramatic acceleration, reflecting the effects of the commodity price boom. There was then a retreat from reliance on prices and incomes controls, which simply could not operate successfully in such unfavourable conditions. The price rises for food and raw materials were in such sensitive and important areas that incomes policies and the like could be of little help.

It is necessary to distinguish between different phenomena, all of which are often loosely described as inflation. A rise in the price of primary commodities has a direct effect on final goods prices—especially consumer prices. But the most important aspect is that the real incomes of those who pay the increased prices are reduced. There is a change in the distribution of income away from consumers in favour of those who gain from primary commodity production. If the deterioration in living standards were accepted by the consumers there would simply be a once and for all increase in consumer prices. Inflation, as measured by consumer prices, would rise as commodity price rises worked their way through; but then stop. The process can be thought of as analagous to an increase in indirect taxation—which raises prices and lowers consumer real incomes. The really serious inflationary consequences of rising com-modity prices are the effects that occur at the next stage. If the erosion of real income positions is resisted, there is an attendant increase in wage-price pressure, and the likelihood of spiralling inflation of a continuous kind. This is especially likely when increases occur in areas such as food prices which are important in the wage bargaining process. Higher money incomes may, in turn, further bid up commodity prices.

Seen in this way, there were two possible approaches to the policy prob-lem. In the first place, it could be argued that the price rises were exceptional, brought about by excess world demand for commodities. Policy should be concentrated on lowering demand and increasing supply. The difficulty was that the problem arose in a global way, and any particular country could have only limited impact. The other possibility was that the change in terms of trade of primary producers was more permanent. In this case policy would have to concentrate on the problem of making sure that the changes in the distribution of real income were accepted without too great an acceleration in the wage-price spiral. Here again, however, there was room for disagreement. It could be argued that this case also called for deflationary policies. But it has to be remembered that deflation itself has an unfavourable effect on real income positions, and it is possible that this could further exacerbate cost-price pressures. In fact, the situation did lead to a move towards deflationary policies. In part this was seen as acting on commodity prices themselves. In part it was felt that domestic wage-price pressures would be minimized in this way—the trade-off again; but, most importantly, it became apparent that domestic demand pressures were building up in a number of important economies; and there is of course no disagreement that generalized excess demand is a cause of inflation, and should be avoided.

The analysis of the commodity price rise in terms of implied distribution of income changes brings out clearly the effects on aggregate demand. When income is transferred from one group to another, the impact depends on the relative spending propensities of the groups concerned. Thus if primary producers, who gained, spent on current goods and services exactly the same proportion as those who lost, there would be no aggregate demand effect. In fact, many primary producers—the less-developed countries—are high spenders, so that on balance the effect may have been stimulating to demand. Though consumer real incomes were reduced, demand returned in the form of increased demand for exports. Lags are involved, of course, and as it turned out less-developed country demand for industrial-country exports grew very fast in 1973, and was maintained in 1974, when industrial countries were slowing down. Within a large primary producing country such as the United States it is more difficult to be sure what the effect was. In fact, wage earners' real incomes were considerably eroded, and the farming sector, which gained, is, traditionally, a high saver. It is probable that the income distribution changes were an important reason for the recessionary trends that developed in the United States.

It should be noted that the commodity price rise did *not* lead to any overall worsening of the balance of payments situation for the industrialized countries. This is in contrast to the oil price increase considered in the next section. The reason is quite straightforward. The impact was balanced by increased export demand from primary producers. There was no reason to suppose that less-developed countries, in particular, would maintain balance of payments surpluses—there was no consequent tendency for world savings to increase. But relative balance of payments positions were affected. There was an improvement in the United States balance; and a reduction of the Japanese surplus, thus contributing to an adjustment that the exchange rate changes of previous years had failed to achieve. For some countries, such as the United Kingdom, the adverse effects were in part responsible for further downward movement of the exchange rate; exacerbating inflationary problems. Germany and some other countries received some relief from the inflationary situation as their currencies rose in relation to the dollar.

6. The Oil Crisis

In October 1973 the Middle East War erupted. This was followed by the oil embargo, with a restriction on supplies and a rise in price. Up until the end of 1973 the major concern of policy-makers was the threat of severe shortages of energy, which would have an immediate effect on industrial supply potential and bring about widespread disruption. On 23 December the supply restrictions were relaxed, but a massive price rise was announced, which brought the (landed) crude oil price to about $10½ or about four times its October 1973 level. The oil crisis brought about massive political and economic problems, which, at the time of writing, are still far from resolved. The following sections are intended to illustrate the analytical problems involved: the situation may, of course, change again markedly.

6.1. The Embargo Period

In the event the embargo was not very effective; crude oil shipments did not decrease very much. Industrial production was not cut for lack of energy. [4] No Government could know this at the time, however, and policy had to respond to the threat of shortage. Most countries introduced measures to cut energy demand—of varying severity; the effects of these were in some cases quite substantial. The main effects, however, were indirect. Confidence and expectational factors became highly adverse, affecting particularly the demand for automobiles; and governmental policies became more cautious, and more restrictive. In general, demand management policies moved considerably further towards restriction than might have been expected on the basis of the previous situation. In some countries, notably Japan, curbs on certain types of expenditure, especially investment, were designed both to reduce aggregate demand and to economize on energy.

Awareness of supply-side problems in general was considerably heightened, especially with respect to primary commodities and the primary materials producing industries. Together with the heightened uncertainty this produced a further rise in commodity prices, the rise appearing to have a strongly speculative element. The hoped-for decline in spot commodity prices failed to materialize and was replaced with further substantial rises. [5] With the further oil price rise of December 1973 it was clear that it was the problem of commodity prices that would dominate economic policy discussions in the short term; it was certain that the price rises would lead to a very substantial acceleration of inflation, to rates in the 10–20 per cent per annum range; rates which a few years previously would have been unthinkable.

6.2. The Oil Price Rise

In terms of its effects on domestic price levels, a rise in the price of oil has

---

[4] In the United Kingdom the 'oil shortage' was exacerbated by the miners' strike, which led to the introduction of the three-day working week in the early months of 1974.

[5] The threshold payment arrangements introduced in the United Kingdom in the autumn of 1973 became a source of great problems owing to the rises in oil and other commodity prices. The adverse effects of the U.K. terms of trade were bound to trigger the thresholds—contrary to the expectation of officials when they were introduced.

similar effects to other price rises affecting essential commodities. From this point of view, the massive oil price increase added to, rather than changed, the problems faced by consuming countries. The unfamiliar aspect of the price rise was that there was no possibility that the increased oil revenues could be spent in the short term. Thus producers—or some of them—were bound to run very large balance of payments surpluses, and consumer countries, as a group, would have to run a correspondingly large deficit. For the same reason, the oil price rise was deflationary, tending to lower aggregate spending in real terms.

There are many ways in which the deflationary impact of the oil price rise can be conceptualized. In the first place, since there was a transfer of income to countries which could not spend all their increased revenue, there was a tendency for world savings to rise, with deflationary effects according to standard Keynesian analysis. An analogy which goes further is with an indirect tax increase (such as a rise in Value Added Tax—or an increase in the excise duty on oil). An indirect tax lowers, other things being equal, the real spending power of households and companies that pay the tax. The total effect, however, depends on what is done with the proceeds of the tax. If it is spent by the Government, there is an 'injection' to balance the 'withdrawal' and the deflationary impact is neutralized, or even reversed.[6] In the analysis of the commodity price boom we have already come across this situation— the increased revenue to producers was largely spent so that the deflationary impact was offset. In the case of the oil impact, the increase in revenue (to oil producers) could not be fully spent in the short run, so the impact was deflationary. The increase in tax was external to the consuming countries, so that the balance of payments on current account was affected adversely.

The quantitative importance of the oil price rise can be gauged in terms of the approximate magnitude of some of the financial flows relative to the aggregate Gross National Product of industrialized countries. The total increased expenditure on imported oil by O.E.C.D. countries was of the order of $65 billion in 1974—or about $1\frac{1}{2}$ per cent of their aggregate GNP. Thus, on average, the oil price impact was analogous to a rise in indirect taxation of about $1\frac{1}{2}$ per cent of GNP. However, the average includes the United States and Canada. For other countries the impact was much larger— about $2\frac{1}{3}$ per cent of GNP for Europe as a whole, and about 3 per cent for the United Kingdom. These figures also indicate the direct mechanical effect on domestic price levels. There were additional effects on other coun-tries—the non-oil-producing less-developed countries being adversely affec-ted by about $10 billion.

But even in 1974 there was additional expenditure on imports by oil-

---

[6] If an 'income stream' is transferred from one group to another, the demand effect is neutral if the spending propensities of the two groups are the same. For then the depressive effect on the losers is exactly offset by increased expenditure by those who gain. In the case of a tax which is spent, the effect is usually stimulatory in that the Government spends all the tax, whereas the private sector would have saved a proportion of the income forgone. See p. 331.

producing countries so that the net effect on current balance of payments positions of O.E.C.D. countries was smaller than $65 billion—perhaps $50–5 billion. This impact is a measure of the effect of the increased world savings on industrialized countries—as far as they are concerned it represents that part of the impact which is not 'recycled' in the form of increased export demand.

In the event, however, the balance of payments position of industrialized countries only worsened by about $35 billion between 1973 and 1974—the reason being that there was a large increase in the surplus of O.E.C.D. countries with other non-oil producing countries.[7] The surplus of O.P.E.C. countries increased by about $63 billion; the deficit of the non-oil-producing less-developed countries rose by about $15 billion [8, Table 2.9].

The special feature of the oil impact was that, in effect, it was not possible for consumers to pay fully for the increased oil bill at the time. Though the commodity price rise and the oil price rise have similar effects on inflation, the commodity price impact implies an immediate transfer of real resources to the beneficiaries—in the form of increased exports—whereas the oil impact implies a future or potential demand for exports rather than a current one. This is because, initially, to the extent that oil producers increase their savings, there must be a transfer of 'claims'—money, or other assets—from the consumers to the producers rather than export of real goods. To the extent that 'claims' are transferred, rather than real goods and services, there is no necessity for the consumer countries to lower their real expenditure flows—of consumption and investment—in order to make 'room' for increased exports.

In fact, by 1975 the surplus of oil producers was much reduced, and the absorptive capacity of oil producers is likely to go on rising. As this occurs, the problem changes from one of debt management to the problem of an increased transfer of *real* resources with an attendant effect on potential real living standards in consumer countries. These problems are exactly those of the increase in the price of non-oil commodities. The assets accumulated by the oil producers represent a deferred demand for real commodities, which eventually has to be met.

One aspect of the situation which may appear confusing needs to be brought out. In 1975 the current account deficit of O.E.C.D. countries was almost eliminated.[8] The major reason for this was the world recession. The lower activity had a substantial effect in lowering the demand for imported oil, thus lowering the deficit directly. Even more importantly, low activity led to a cut-back in imports other than oil from developing countries, so that much of the 'oil deficit' was passed to them. It is estimated that in 1975 the deficit of the non-oil-producing less-developed countries worsened further to $27 billion. In fact the surplus of oil producers was still substantial at about

---

[7] The increased surplus of industrialized countries with less-developed countries was not, of course, due, directly or exclusively, to the oil impact. The two major reasons were a favourable build up of reserves by less-developed countries in 1973 reflecting the commodity price rise, and the slump in activity in industrial countries.

[8] A figure of $6 billion is given as an estimate in O.E.C.D. *Economic Outlook* 18.

$40–5 billion [8]. Clearly, a revival of activity would lead automatically to a re-emergence of the industrialized countries' deficit position.

6.3. International Payments Problems

If the increased balance of payments surplus of the oil-producing countries is acceptable as inevitable, it follows that other countries must suffer a deterioration in their aggregate current account position of similar magnitude. The danger, in such circumstances, is that countries may be unwilling to accept the inevitable, and individually attempt to improve their position. This could involve competitive devaluations, competitive deflations, and trade restrictions which would be very damaging to the world economy. Such beggar-my-neighbour policies would, moreover, be self-defeating in that the over-all balance of payments position would not be improved.

In order to avoid competitive reactions, it is necessary for countries to accept a modification of traditional balance of payments targets, and aim, in effect, to run deficits to the required extent. International debtors are needed to balance the saving of the oil-producing countries. In an ideal world some concept of a fair distribution of the burden would be worked out, and it would be clearly recognized that surplus positions were as damaging internationally as excessive deficit positions.

In 1974 and 1975, the first two years since the oil crisis, there has been no serious scramble for balance of payments positions. Nevertheless, the problem is one that cumulates in that indebtedness to foreigners rises for as long as there is a payments deficit. The increasing indebtedness has to be accepted, is in fact inevitable, for so long as the surpluses of the oil producers continue. It is very difficult indeed for some governments to countenance.

Though 'willingness' to run balance of payments deficits is extremely important if competitive reactions are to be avoided, it is not by itself sufficient. There is a supply side to the problem in that finance must be available to the 'willing' debtors. Indeed, attitudes to balance of payments deficits cannot be regarded as independent of the supply of finance, and the terms on which it is available.

In aggregate there can be no problem of financing the deficits. The oil producers have to accumulate assets and these must be the assets of the deficit countries. For the world as a whole there can be no problem of 'recycling'. In this context the term itself is misleading. The financial counterpart to the surplus of the producers and the deficit of the consumers is a transfer of ownership—of financial claims or real assets—from oil consumers to oil producers. Nevertheless, there may be considerable difficulties for individual countries.

To simplify somewhat, the 'recycling' problem arises in that the surplus countries may not want to build up assets from different countries in proportion to the deficits they run. For example, if they want to accumulate assets entirely as dollars (claims on the United States), there may be a financing problem for a deficit country such as Italy. Though the balance of payments account, like other accounts, always balances—*ex post*, deficits are always financed—a deficit may not be financeable at existing rates of exchange, or with existing economic policies. If a deficit country wishes to maintain its exchange rate (and other aspects of its economic policy) it has to make sure that there is a capital inflow to balance the current deficit, or make use of its reserves. The deficit country, in effect, must be able to borrow—or be in a position to run down a stock of internationally acceptable assets. There is no need for direct borrowing from oil producers. There may be a long chain of intermediaries; and in the process the composition of all sorts of asset portfolios may alter. The new claims on the deficit country or the assets released by it must be accepted somewhere in the system—but not necessarily by the oil producers. Thus it is the acceptability of claims on particular countries to the international financial community *in toto*, rather than to the oil producers, that is important.

The recycling problem is therefore simply the problem of making sure that those with balance of payments deficits can finance them with reasonable stability of the exchange rate, and on reasonable terms.

In 1974 and 1975 the major mechanism for ensuring that the demands for funds and the supplies of funds matched was the international capital market, i.e. the market in internationally mobile currencies and loans. The free market performed its function reasonably well, but there may be limits to its capacity over the medium term. One problem can be mentioned as illustrative. The oil producers showed a preference for holding their assets in rather liquid form, as short-term deposits. Borrowers, however, typically wanted loans of longer maturity. The market therefore had to act as intermediary, borrowing short from the oil producers and lending longer term to the deficit countries. The extent of intermediation of this type imposed considerable strains. In principle, this problem should be much mitigated by market forces with the return on short-term deposits tending to fall and on longer-term loans tending to rise.

The difficulty inherent in relying on private capital markets to perform the intermediation between surplus and deficit countries is that there is no guarantee that particular deficit countries can always obtain finance, so that they might be forced into actions which would be judged to be internationally damaging. Furthermore, it is just those countries which most need finance which may have most difficulty in obtaining funds on the free market. For this reason, more formal, official schemes to aid in the recycling process have been proposed and introduced. The basic principles of operation of various schemes are simple enough. The 'oil facility' of the International Monetary Fund, introduced in 1974, and considerably extended for 1975, is perhaps the simplest. Its basic mechanism is for the I.M.F. to borrow directly from oil producers and other countries in a strong economic position, and to lend on the funds to deficit countries with financing needs. The 'safety net' scheme, run through the O.E.C.D. (with the Bank for International Settlements as agent) is more complex, with two basic elements. In the first place, countries may subscribe convertible currency to the Fund directly, according to a set of quotas. As an alternative, however, countries may act as guarantors (up to an agreed amount) for international borrowing by the Support Fund.

The problems with official intervention in the recycling process are political as well as technical. There are two particular areas of political disagreement which are important in the discussion of any official scheme. The first is the question of the appropriate policy response of a deficit country. On one side, there are those who feel that deflationary policies are the appropriate remedy for any deficit, so that any facility that allows countries to be 'irresponsible' is therefore regarded as unacceptable. On the other side, many would stress that policy reactions to deficits and surpluses already tend to be asymmetrical—favouring over-all deflation—and that beyond this, the oil deficits would tend to produce a strong deflationary bias. For this group, the object of a recycling scheme is not just to avoid particular financing difficulties, but to actively encourage more reflationary policies than would otherwise be the case. The other area of political divergence is the question as to how favourable any scheme should be to oil producers. One view is that they should have no special treatment, and be, therefore, as subject as others to declining financial asset values as a result of inflation. Against this, it is sometimes argued that if oil supplies are to be maintained, some favourable 'home' for the oil monies must be provided—otherwise supply cut-backs would look increasingly attractive to producers.

Concern over the 'recycling' problem was much reduced in 1975. The most important reason for the increased optimism was that industrialized countries, as a group, improved their balance of payments position substantially. As we have seen, however, only part of the improvement reflected increased demand for imports by oil producers. To quite a large extent, the problem was being disguised—or displaced—by the recession. The huge deficits being run by the non-oil-producing less-developed countries obviously raised questions as to whether they could go on being financed—and also point to the possibility of downward adjustments of imports by the affected countries, which could become an additional deflationary factor in the world situation.[9] Another aspect is that, amongst the group of industrialized countries, there remain some very difficult balance of payments positions—especially amongst the smaller countries.

6.4. Domestic Implications

Though the international problems raised by the oil price rise were reasonably clear and well understood, there was much less agreement on the implications for domestic demand management policies.

It is useful as a first step to consider an artificial case, where the oil impact is completely neutralized. For this purpose it is convenient to simplify and to assume that all increases in revenues to oil producers are saved; there is no increased export demand. The inflationary and deflationary domestic effects could be offset completely if oil were de-taxed to the extent of the price rise. In practice, this could be approximated by lowering existing taxes and duties. As far as the domestic economy is concerned there would then be, in effect, no oil price rise, and no effects on aggregate demand *or inflation*. The

[9] By maintaining imports in spite of declining exports the less-developed countries (as a group) operated as a powerful stabilizing force on the world economy in 1974.

implication, however, would be an increase in the public sector deficit to the extent of the oil impact, for government revenues would fall to the extent of the de-taxation, whilst government expenditure was maintained. We would have: oil impact equals change in current balance of payments deficit, equals change in public sector deficit.

The increase in the public sector deficit has to be financed. For simplicity, suppose it is financed by an increase in the money supply, or by an increase in the bond issue, or some mixture of the two. If oil producers, or more generally foreigners, are prepared to hold, as assets, some mixture of money and government bonds or bills at existing exchange rates and interest rates then there need be no monetary impact either. The *domestically* held money supply and the domestically held bond supply could be unaltered.[10] The only thing that would have happened is that there would be an increase in externally held currency and/or debt instruments—and hence, of course, some increase in debt servicing costs. In effect, we would have the oil, whereas they would have some pieces of paper representing a future claim on national resources and there would be no other effects.

This neutral case can be made less unrealistic. In the first place, it is not necessary to de-tax oil itself. If economy in the use of oil were desired, it would be better, for example, to lower other indirect taxes to the extent of the oil impact. The difference between the two cases is a standard exercise in budgetary analysis.

Secondly, it is unlikely that foreigners would so conveniently desire to hold public sector assets. If they wanted private sector assets instead, this would present a problem of intermediation, but no serious difficulties from a monetary point of view. In effect, the private sector would get the increased public sector debt and release the other assets for foreigners to hold. There would, however, normally be some changes in relative asset prices.

The most serious difficulty is one we have already come across. If the oil producers or, more accurately, international creditors in general, do not want to hold *any* of the debt instruments of the country concerned, there is a 'recycling' problem; the balance of payments deficit could only be financed if exchange rates or interest rates changed. It is notable that this is not an unfamiliar problem; it is simply an example of the general difficulty that international considerations limit domestic monetary freedom—though admittedly the problem appears in rather an extreme form.

If the impact is *not* offset by the public Authorities, broadly along the lines of the simplified analysis above, then the private sector must run a deficit—i.e. its net asset position must deteriorate in line with the balance of payments deficit.[11] It is this deterioration that leads to the deflationary effects,

---

[10] This is a simplification. In practice, externally held assets of certain types can affect domestic credit creation, and hence the domestic money supply. The impacts depend, however, on the precise institutional and legal provisions surrounding banking ratios, and hence vary between countries.

[11] Cf. the discussion of the identity underlying the 'New Cambridge Approach', p. 339. The Balance of Payments surplus equals the Private (Household + Company) sector surplus + the Government sector surplus. If there is an imposed swing to balance of payments deficit then necessarily one or other of the sectors must also move towards deficit.

and which may also increase inflationary pressure. It is convenient to analyse the impacts separately for households and for companies. In an actual case, of course, both sectors would be affected, simultaneously, so that the over-all result would depend on some mixture of the two 'pure' cases considered.

Consider first the case where the household sector takes *all* the oil impact— by which it is meant that the deterioration in the financial position of the country (the adverse effect on the current balance) is entirely reflected in the household sector's financial position. This will be the case if there is no change in the government deficit, and no change in the net acquisition of financial assets by companies. In this situation the relation between the household sector's receipts and its expenditures must worsen to the extent of the oil impact. Consumers must be going more into debt or saving less than before. So much is a matter of accounting.

Though the worsening of the relation between household receipts and expenditures must happen—*ex post* it is a truism—the new situation may induce disequilibrating reactions. Of course, consumers might simply be willing to countenance the deterioration in their financial position, without altering real expenditures.[12] In this case there would be no effects on real aggregate demand. A more likely reaction, however, is that they will reduce expenditures in an attempt to restore their financial position—thus reducing real demand. For so long as the balance of payments deficit continues, however, they cannot be successful in lowering their expenditures in relation to their receipts. Their reduced expenditure simply works through, *in aggregate*, to produce a reduction in their income to the same extent. A cumulative process is likely to be set in train, which continues until households are willing to accept the deterioration in their financial position without further attempts to cut expenditure. This is nothing more than the familiar Keynesian multiplier effect. Equilibrium occurs when desired savings have fallen to the required extent, which, according to standard consumption function theory, only occurs at lower levels of demand and output.[13]

Another reaction is possible: faced with a deteriorating financial position, individuals may struggle harder to raise their income. The attempt to restore their real income position (again doomed to failure in aggregate) could lead to a sharp increase in inflationary pressure.

Now consider what happens if *companies initially take all* the oil impact. (Suppose, for example, that consumers are protected, or somehow manage

---

[12] No change in real expenditures, since they are paying more for oil, would imply increased expenditure in money terms—hence with unchanged money incomes their savings must fall, or they must be going more into debt.

[13] The example is artificial in that most of the normal stabilizers are absent. (1) If the balance of payments deficit is unaltered, there is no 'import leakage'. (2) If the public sector deficit is unaltered, there is no automatic stabilizing effect due to unemployment benefit or tax decrease. (3) If the company sector deficit is unaltered, in effect company investment must decline *pari passu* with company income. The multiplier in this artificial example really would be the reciprocal of the marginal propensity to save out of personal disposable income —or about ten. If consumer investment—largely expenditure on housing—were also adversely affected, the full effects could be even larger. In the short run, of course, lags could be highly stabilizing. In practice, household savings tended to rise in 1974 and 1975—adding to instability.

to avoid any deterioration in their financial position—so that households' net financial surplus or deficit position remains unchanged.) If the assumptions of no change in the foreign balance[14] and of no change in the public sector deficit are retained, then the 'pure' effect of the oil impact on the company sector can be analysed. In standard Keynesian forecasting models little attention is paid to the effect of financial variables on company expenditure. Here, however, it is suggested that financial changes may be very important.

The deterioration in the current balance now implies, as an accounting identity, that the company sector must be spending more in relation to its receipts—it must be increasing its indebtedness—or lowering its surplus earnings. The extent of the deterioration is great; under the artificial assumptions adopted, it is equal to the oil impact itself. For the U.K. this would give a swing in 1974 relative to 1973 of nearly $6 billion or slightly less than £3 billion. If the oil impact is accepted as inevitable, and the other sectors of the economy do not 'allow' their financial positions to deteriorate, then this deterioration is inevitable, no matter what evasive action is taken.

The problem in this case is that though the corporate sector's position *must* deteriorate to this extent, company policy may be affected. In exactly the same way as for households, expenditures may be lowered—leading to lower investment and increasing unemployment. There may also be pressure from company accountants to raise prices—stimulating inflationary pressure. Equilibrium would occur, as before, when no further cuts in expenditure are induced, that is, when the deterioration in financial positions is accepted as inevitable.

The problem is cumulative, and the effects may be delayed. Adverse cash-flow positions can be tolerated for a time; if prolonged, however, difficulties get worse, and reactions follow.

The domestic problem, for companies, is entirely analogous to the international balance of payments problem. There is a demand side—are companies willing to change their traditional operating criteria and take on increased debt, or lower surpluses? If not, deflationary reactions will be set in train. Secondly, there is a *domestic* recycling problem. Those companies which are prepared to keep up expenditure, in spite of lower income, may look bad credit risks; they may not be able to raise the finance even though they desire to. Bankruptcy may follow, if they are not bailed out. The situation can be made easier if credit conditions ease; but the problem remains. They have to be willing to take on more debt (including, of course, floating new equity issues)—which they will only do if they feel that it is profitable on a long-term basis.

Surprisingly, perhaps, the possible effects on company liquidity were relatively neglected in early analyses of the oil crisis. It was felt by many that, if consumers—through wage pressures—succeeded in protecting themselves, the deflationary impact would be lost. Experience through 1974 has shown how wrong—at least in some cases—that view was. But there *can* be offsets, in certain circumstances, if the impact is taken by companies. Certain types

14 Other than the initial impact.

of investment may be stimulated (energy exploration and saving). It is possible also that in some countries there is a typically *excess* demand for finance in the sense that firms are always willing to borrow more at existing interest rates if they can get credit—the system being kept in check by monetary availability factors. In circumstances of extreme willingness to accept higher liabilities—presumably due to profit expectations—there is no need for a deflationary response, unless monetary policy tightens further to contract the supply of credit.

But, in general, a relaxation of monetary policy may not easily counteract the flow impact on corporate financial positions. A relaxation may increase willingness to take on additional debt liabilities—either for cost or availability reasons—but need not. The liquidity difficulties do not arise from a tight monetary policy, but from a changed relationship between current receipts and current expenditures. The problems posed by such a situation can be considerably exacerbated by high interest rates and the difficulty of obtaining loans, but there may still be reactions of an expenditure-reducing kind even if monetary conditions are relatively easy.

We have considered three 'pure' cases corresponding to the oil impact being taken by Government (public sector), by households, or by companies. Clearly, any actual case is a mixture of the pure cases. Some of the impact falls on households, some on firms, and the Government takes some. In fact, however, it is likely that most of the impact will end up being taken by the Government, *whether that is the intention or not*. The reason is that not much stabilization can be expected from either households or companies. The actions of the Authorities make a great difference to the level of activity that results at the end of the disequilibrium process. At one extreme, if the Authorities act to offset the impact there may be no downswing in activity. At the other extreme, if no action is taken, the offsetting increase in the public sector deficit position occurs automatically as a result of recession—due to increased transfer payments (especially unemployment benefits) and a decline in tax receipts.

An imposed swing in the current balance of payments position is like a change in the public sector deficit. When it happens, the economy is in disequilibrium. The impact may, in fact, be passed around from sector to sector before equilibrium is re-established. Suppose, for example, that the initial impact falls on consumers. Through a combination of reduced expenditure and successful wage demands the impact could be passed to companies. As we have seen, the response of companies could be to reduce expenditure (thus creating unemployment) and also, perhaps, to pass the impact back to consumers via price rises. The process of disequilibrium continues until the deterioration in financial positions is 'willingly' accepted by some sector or sectors. In practice, however, no great reduction in savings can be expected from consumers—in the 1974–5 recession savings actually rose. In the short term, dramatic increases in the deficit of the company sector are possible; but in the longer run these may not be sustainable. So the main stabilizing force is an induced rise in the public sector deficit as a result of the recession, which offsets the impact on the private sector. It is perhaps interesting that

Keynes, writing at the start of the Depression in 1931, saw demand stabilizing due to government deficits—he did not appear to expect much stabilization from household savings [4, 5].

An interesting example of the sort of interactions that can occur is provided by price control in the United Kingdom in 1974. Consumers' real income positions were protected by threshold payments under Stage III. Companies were unable to pass on fully the effects of increased expenditure on inputs—back to consumers—because of price control, and also because of increased competition. Pressure developed, however, for a removal of price controls—and ultimately price control was relaxed. Paradoxically, however, the reduction in price control might not have been able to improve company financial positions. Obviously, if higher prices led to higher wages (because of threshholds) they would be self-defeating. But even if the price rises had 'stuck', it is arguable that they would not have improved the situation. By passing the impact back to consumers they would have set in train further reductions in consumer demand, adversely affecting company income, and so on. Only if the price rise led to a reduction in consumer savings would the financial balance of the company sector be improved.[15] But the reduction in price controls was not the only aid to companies in the second half of 1974. Part of the help to companies fell directly on the government deficit, and, in any case, it was found that the public sector deficit (combined capital and current account) had been rising very rapidly: so rapidly, indeed, that 'liquidity' difficulties looked like being temporary anyway.

7. Conclusion

Industrialized countries, as a group, decelerated extremely sharply from the peak of 1973 into the worst recession since the Second World War. By the middle of 1975 recorded unemployment in O.E.C.D. countries had risen to about 15 million or about 5½ per cent of the civilian labour force. Industrial output fell dramatically during the recession—by over 20 per cent in Japan, and by about 15 per cent in Germany and the United States. In the United Kingdom the fall was somewhat less—but still substantial. In the United States GNP fell by about 7½ per cent from its peak in 1973 to a low point in the first half of 1975. For other industrialized countries taken as a group, GNP roughly stagnated over the same period. The volume of world trade which had been buoyant since the war was rapidly contracting in late 1974 and in the first half of 1975. The move to recession was accompanied by unprecedented rates of inflation and some very difficult balance of payments situations.

By the end of 1975 it was apparent that the three major countries which had led the way into recession—the United States, Japan, and Germany—had bottomed out during 1975. The United States recovery appeared well established. The extent of recovery in Japan and especially in Germany was more debatable. Many European countries, however, were still experiencing the full effects of the world recession.

---

[15] Of course, the reduction in price control was very important for some particular companies.

It is natural to ascribe the development of world recession to the commodity price boom and the oil crisis. But the direct effects of these events was probably less important than the indirect effects that came about owing to the policy response of governments. As noted, the demand depressive effects could have been offset. In most cases they were not offset, and indeed demand management policies (especially monetary policy) moved further towards restriction. Particularly in the three largest countries, the United States, Japan, and Germany, restrictive policies were pursued as a conventional response to rapid rates of inflation.

There is no doubt that aggregate demand on a global basis was excessive in 1973. Some restriction was necessary, both to remove the supply constraints which were appearing and in order to stem the rise in commodity prices. Policy disagreements appeared, however, as to the extent of deflation and of unemployment that was desirable.

It was, of course, accepted as more or less inevitable that consumer prices would accelerate dramatically in 1974 as the increased oil and commodity prices were passed through. But the major fear was that after that stimulus tailed off, inflation would continue at high or even accelerating rates due to a domestic wage-price spiral. Some argued that the best way to minimize the ensuing wage-price spiral, and to make sure that inflation rates come down, was to deflate substantially and to rely on the traditional trade-off between inflation and unemployment. Others took the view that deflation beyond the point necessary to remove excess demand would have little effect on inflation, and might indeed intensify the struggle over income shares. Proponents of the latter view naturally tended also to favour the use of incomes policies or other 'non-conventional' anti-inflation policies. It is not surprising that the conventional policies of deflation and monetary control found least favour in those countries where past experience (and especially experience in 1970–1971) suggested that the trade-off between inflation and unemployment was particularly unfavourable.

The large falls in domestic demand in the United States, Japan, and Germany largely account for the very uneven pattern of balance of payments surpluses and deficits that developed. The relative conjunctural positions meant that the over-all deficit of the O.E.C.D. area was concentrated on the smaller O.E.C.D. countries. Though the United Kingdom found external finance easy to obtain, Italy and some of the smaller countries were more or less forced to take deflationary action as a result of financing problems. Nevertheless, the more extravagant fears of an immediate scramble for balance of payments positions turned out to be unfounded. In fact, by the first half of 1975 the deficit position of the O.E.C.D. area had been almost eliminated. The most important reason for the turn-round was the world recession, which had the twin effects of sharply lowering oil imports and of lowering imports from the non-oil producing less-developed countries so that the 'deficit' was passed to them. As noted above, a recovery by industrialized countries would tend to lead to a re-emergence of the problems of a current balance of payments deficit for the O.E.C.D. countries as a group.

The oil price rise did mean that deflationary impulses were more likely to be transmitted from one country to another. Those countries which did not deflate immediately (or deflated only moderately) were subject to a double impact. The recession in the large countries was bound to affect the development of their exports and worsen their balance of payments position; the oil crisis added to the problem in that the swing in the balance of payments was that much larger. This swing in turn tended to lead to a direct response through deflationary policy; and even in the absence of an explicit policy response tended to produce recessionary forces anyway, for the reasons explained above. Particularly where the impact fell on companies, the response tended to be delayed and it was easy to underestimate its magnitude.

Perhaps the most puzzling aspect of the world recession is that it was not more widely predicted—at least by official forecasters. Though in many countries the rise in unemployment was an intended response to the inflation problem, the recession took on a cumulative character which was not generally anticipated. Some speculative remarks about the reasons for the underestimation of the deflationary forces can perhaps serve to draw together some of the points raised in previous sections.

A distinguishing feature of the 1973 boom and subsequent recession was that practically all countries were simultaneously affected. By the beginning of 1975 recessionary forces appeared to be operative in almost all countries. As noted in section 3 of this chapter, when countries move together, rather larger multiplier effects are to be expected. Moreover, the impact of the oil crisis and inflation on expectations and confidence was very substantial indeed. It is probable that many of the usual stabilizing elements were absent during the development of the recession, so that any adverse impacts would tend to have larger effects than usual.

Another element that should be given weight is the situation in 1973. It seems probable that many countries had already passed the turning-point and that a slow-down was already occurring. The deflationary moves and the effects of the oil crisis therefore came on top of a situation which was already recessionary. This illustrates that one of the most difficult elements in any forecasting exercise is the diagnosis of the current situation.

Forecasting procedures should capture the cumulative effects due to simultaneous movements. But forecasting is difficult when the situation passes outside the range of recent past experience. There was no precedent, for example, for the sharp contraction in world trade that occurred. But another element is that the lags appear to have been rather lengthy. For example, world trade was stabilized in 1974 to a remarkable extent by a maintenance of imports by less-developed countries. It was only at the end of 1974 that world trade started to drop sharply. As noted, some of the financial effects in the deficit countries were delayed; such effects cumulate and appear to build up to some kind of a threshhold. The result of the long lags was that it was easy to underestimate the effects still to come. Since in most countries inflation fears and balance of payments worries combined to produce deflationary or at least cautious policies, the recessionary forces developed considerable momentum.

In the course of the recession two further deflationary elements appeared.

Households, which in more normal times would have been expected to stabilize the situation by lowering their savings, in fact sharply increased their savings with strongly deflationary results. The reasons for the rise in savings which occurred in many countries are debatable. Some of the rise may have been due to wealth effects following the extremely severe fall in stock-market values all over the world. But much of the rise was probably precautionary—a response to rising unemployment and the general climate of uncertainty. In support of this it is notable that a large part of the increase can be accounted for by a reduction in consumer indebtedness. The other element is that there was a very sharp adjustment of inventory levels by companies. Contrary to the experience of most post-war business cycles, voluntary inventory accumulation appears to have continued well after the turn-round in final demand. In early 1975, however, there appears to have been an absolute reduction in the level of inventories for the O.E.C.D. area as a whole.

In general, due to the long lags and the additional deflationary elements that appeared, it seems that disequilibrium in the world economy continued for much longer than usual, and so the recession developed much further. One major stabilizing element was that as the recession developed public sector deficits rose, in many countries, to unprecedented levels—far exceeding the oil impact. Much of the rise reflected the automatic stabilizer effects referred to above, but there were fiscal relaxations as well. The rise had to go far beyond the oil impact or the balance of payments impact to offset the increased desire to save of consumers—and, in some countries, to allow for a build-up of financial assets to more normal levels by the company sector as well.

The situation at the beginning of 1976 illustrates well a major difficulty in forecasting economic development. A number of the elements that contributed to the development of recession are self-reversing in character. Most obviously, inventory run-down comes to an end—as it did in the United States in mid-1975. High savings allow a reduction of consumer indebtedness and contribute to a revival of consumer spending. If companies are saving more than they are investing, they are building up their asset position, and as this happens this contributes to a revival of investment expenditure. These two elements mean that public sector deficits (the counterpart to increased saving by companies and households) may have cumulative effects on the level of activity. Most importantly, as activity recovers so do expectations— thus reinforcing the upswing in activity. These elements mean not only that it is hard to forecast turning-points, but also that it is very difficult to judge the strength of any upswing that develops. Much of course depends upon policy action. But there is a worry that if reflationary action is large enough then it may, almost inevitably, be too large, and tend to bring about a kind of political cycle as governments oscillate between the objectives of full employment and price stability.

As the recession developed, it became widely agreed that the three largest countries, Japan, Germany, and the United States, which had the strongest balance of payments positions, and which apparently had had greatest success in bringing down the rate of inflation, should make the earliest moves to get out of recession. Indeed, it has now become an objective of international co-operation to move away from the coincidence of policy problems that can cause such destabilizing effects.

Bibliography

Many of the works suggested at the end of other chapters are also relevant to the issues discussed in this chapter. The list that follows is highly selective—intended only to give an indication of where some of the issues can be followed up.

[1] Bank for International Settlements (B.I.S.). Annual Reports (June each year). Various issues. These reports contain topical description and analysis of major economic developments. Chapter 1 of the 1972 Annual Report is a useful summary of the history of the dollar and the lead-up to the Smithsonian Agreement, December 1971.
[2] Cambridge Department of Applied Economics *Economic Policy Review* (1975). Analyses the situation in the United Kingdom and discusses important world developments. Contains a chapter on North Sea oil.
[3] HIRSCH, F. *Money International* (Penguin, 1967; revised edn. Pelican, 1969). Useful description and analysis of many aspects of the international monetary system.
[4] KEYNES, J. M. 'An Economic Analysis of Unemployment'. Three lectures contributed to the Harris Foundation series in Chicago, June 1931. Reprinted in *The Collected Writings of John Maynard Keynes*, xiii (Macmillan, 1973), pp. 343–67.
[5] —— *The General Theory of Employment, Interest and Money* (Macmillan, 1936).
[6] National Institute for Economic and Social Research (N.I.E.S.R.) *Economic Review* (quarterly), various issues.
Presents forecasts for the United Kingdom. Many issues of national and international importance are discussed and evaluated as part of the regular assessments or in special articles.
[7] ODELL, P. R. *Oil and World Power* (Penguin, 1970; 4th edn. 1975). Background to the oil crisis.
[8] Organisation for Economic Co-operation and Development (O.E.C.D.) *Economic Outlook* (June and December annually), various issues, but especially No. 18. Forecasts for the world economy are presented biennially together with extensive discussion and analysis of major issues of current interest.
[9] RYBCZYNSKI, T. M. (ed.) *The Economics of the Oil Crisis* (Macmillan, 1976). A useful collection of articles on various aspects of the energy crisis.

15

Assessing the Economy

M. J. C. SURREY

1. Developing the Theoretical Model

1.1. The Basic Flow Model

In Chapter 4 we developed a basic model of the economy which served as a framework for much of the analysis of subsequent chapters. This basic model was highly schematic: it was intended to focus attention on the main lines of determination of the level of economic activity, the level of employment, the state of the balance of payments, and so on, rather than to provide a realistic model of the way in which an economy such as that of the U.K. actually functions. The purpose of this chapter is to extend the basic model of Chapter 4 in the light of the analysis of the intervening chapters so as to arrive at a model which is sufficiently close to reality to serve as a tool with which to assess the economy. 'Assessment' here means both understanding the primary causes of the past behaviour of the economy and providing reasonably trustworthy forecasts of its future behaviour.

The most basic model comprised the expenditure identity for the economy,

$$Y = C + I + G + X - M - T_I$$

together with the assumptions of a consumption function,

$$C = f(Yd)$$

an investment function,

$$I = f(r)$$

an import function,

$$M = f(Y)$$

and the assumptions that government expenditure and exports of goods and services are exogenously determined, that direct taxes (the difference between Y and Yd) are given, or are a simple function of the level of national income, and that the interest rate is either exogenously determined or is given by the equation of the supply of and demand for money. Figure 15.1 represents the simplest possible flow diagram.

This schematic model fails to correspond at all closely with reality in three distinct ways. First, it is incomplete, in the sense of omitting important macro-economic variables and relationships—the most glaring omission is the price level and its determination. Second, it is excessively aggregated: for example, no distinction is drawn between different kinds of private investment, and there is no breakdown of income into wages and salaries, profits, and so on. Third, the relationships, the consumption function, the investment function, and the export and import functions (which take no account of changes in relative prices and exchange rates) are oversimplified.

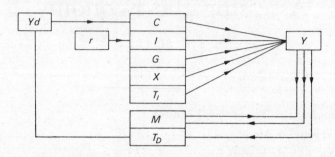

FIG. 15.1

What is the minimum degree of complication which is necessary to arrive at a 'realistic' macroeconomic model? The best way of answering this is to take each of the expenditure aggregates in turn.

1.2. Consumption

The first problem here is that the national accounts' aggregate 'consumers' expenditure' lumps together both personal consumption proper (i.e. current expenditure by the personal sector on goods and services) and expenditure on durable goods. While consumption may depend only on disposable income, expenditure on durable goods is likely to be significantly affected by changes in the cost and availability of finance to persons, notably through hire-purchase and bank overdraft facilities. There is thus a strong case for treating the two components of consumers' expenditure separately.

The relevant concept of income is real personal disposable income (RPDI) which bears an extremely complex relationship to national income. There are several factors to be taken into account in passing from national income to RPDI:

(i) the distribution of national income between sectors,
(ii) transfers between sectors,
(iii) direct taxation,
(iv) changes in the price level.

(i) *The distribution of national income between sectors.* Income accruing directly to the personal sector comprises income from employment (wages and salaries together with income from self-employment), rent, and net receipts of interest. The wage and salary bill is the product of average earnings and the level of employment. Average earnings depend on both negotiated standard rates of pay and on a variety of other factors reflected as 'wage-drift'—that is, the tendency for the gap between standard rates and actual earnings to vary independently of changes in standard rates (because of changes in the scarcity of labour, changes in the extent of piece-working, and so on). Changes in standard rates of pay may be affected by the general pressure of demand for labour, but will tend to be strongly affected by incomes policy, whether statutory or voluntary, and by the rate of price inflation and the extent to which central negotiations attempt to compensate for past inflation or anticipate future inflation.

The volume of employment is generally dependent on the levels of real output and of labour productivity. There is a tendency for labour productivity to increase over time, but an increase in output in excess of the increase in labour productivity will raise employment, and a lower rate of increase of output will reduce employment. However, this relationship is likely to be characterized by a significant lag: the initial response to a rise in the volume of employment desired by employers may be to increase overtime working until new workers can be hired.

The remainder of income accruing directly to the personal sector is influenced by a variety of factors. Incomes from self-employment seem to move broadly in line with employment incomes, while incomes from rent and interest—though growing fairly steadily over time—are influenced by a host of factors, including monetary policy and legislation. However, little is known about the precise determinants of changes in incomes from these sources, and in forecasting, for example, projected movements are very much a matter of guesswork.

(ii) *Transfers between sectors.* The next step is to add in transfers of income from the company and public sectors to the personal sector. Transfers from the company sector—notably dividends—tend to depend, after a lag, on company profits (though companies' dividend policies generally mean that fluctuations in dividends are smaller than fluctuations in profits). Transfers from the public sector—pensions, social security benefits, and so on—are primarily determined by government decisions on rates of benefit, though a number of such payments (unemployment benefit and earnings-related benefits) will clearly reflect the pressure of demand and its effect on the levels of unemployment and earnings.[1]

(iii) *Direct taxation.* The main component of direct taxation of personal incomes is income tax. The amount of tax paid will depend primarily on the rates of tax and on the level of personal income, but because of the distinction between 'earned' and 'unearned' income the distribution of personal income between income from employment and other income will also be relevant.

(iv) *Changes in the price level.* Consumer prices (the index of prices which is relevant in arriving at the real value of personal disposable income) are generally considered to be calculated (before indirect taxes) on a cost-plus basis (see Ch. 3). A given profit margin is added to the average unit costs of production, which comprise labour costs and the unit costs of imported

---

[1] Employers' contributions to National Insurance and private pension funds are treated in the national accounts as imputed personal sector income which is automatically saved.

materials. Unit labour costs vary directly with earnings and inversely with labour productivity. The existence of lags in price-setting means that the assumption of an unchanging target profit margin does not entail an unchanging profit share: if costs of production are increasing at an accelerating rate, actual profit margins will fall (if the lag in adjusting prices stays constant) even though the target profit margin remains unchanged. The contribution of indirect taxes to the consumer price index depends primarily on the rates of the taxes, though it will also be affected by any shifts in the composition of consumers' expenditure between high- and low-taxed items.

The final stage is to relate consumers' expenditure to real personal disposable income. Even in its simplest form, this relationship must also take account, as we have already noted, of the effect of financial conditions on the availability of credit to finance expenditure on consumer durables. Another important aspect of the relationship is that it will almost certainly be characterized by a significant lag between changes in disposable income and changes in expenditure.

Figure 15.2 summarizes in diagrammatic form these relationships as they appear in the National Institute of Economic and Social Research forecasting model.

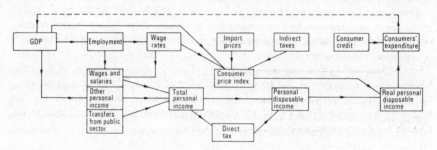

FIG. 15.2. Flow Chart of the Personal Sector.

1.3. Investment

The first need, in reaching a realistic model of the behaviour of private investment, is to recognize the importance of distinguishing several different kinds of investment. The most obvious distinction is between fixed investment and investment in stocks (or inventory investment). Within fixed investment, it is obviously necessary to treat investment in dwellings separately. The remainder of fixed investment can be classified by industry (notably manufacturing and non-manufacturing), or by type of asset (plant and machinery, new buildings and works, vehicles), or both.

The main reason for distinguishing manufacturing investment from investment in other industries is that fluctuations in both output and investment in manufacturing industries tend to be more violent than in other industries. A distinction is usually drawn between investment in different types of

assets because of the differing lifetimes of different capital assets. Thus investments in plant and machinery which have relatively short lives will tend to be
influenced predominantly by expectations of future output levels, and much
less by small changes in the cost of finance. Investments in new buildings and
works, on the other hand, have a much longer life and a more certain rate of
return (given long-run trends in production), so that the cost of finance can
be expected to have a powerful influence while short-run fluctuations in
output will have relatively little effect.

Private investment in dwellings is powerfully influenced by financial
factors. This reflects the factors governing both the demand for and the supply
of new houses in the U.K. Demand is highly sensitive to the liquidity position
of the building societies, which in turn depends on the structure of interest
rates among the various financial institutions competing for funds, and on
the relationship between interest rates and levels of personal income (since
the building societies normally operate according to rules setting maximum
allowable repayments—largely interest—in relation to income). On the
supply side, most private house-building is speculative—that is, houses are
not built to order—and thus builders are heavily dependent on the availability of credit during the period of building and before the sale of the
completed house.

Investment in stocks is generally related in a simple—though lagged—way
to changes in output. The presumption is that, other things being equal,
stock-holders will wish to maintain some fairly constant ratio of stocks—
whether of raw materials, work in progress, or finished goods—to output.
The desired level of stocks will thus vary directly with the level of output.
Short-period changes in the level of stocks, or stockbuilding, will, however,
be erratic both because of lags in the adjustment of actual stocks to the
demand level and because of involuntary changes in the level of stocks
caused by sharp changes in output or demand.

1.4. Other Items

Public expenditure—both current and capital—is generally treated as wholly
exogenous. Decisions, whether by Central Government, local authorities, or
public corporations, are not normally regarded as having passively or
systematically to follow short-term fluctuations in the economy.

Exports of goods and services are, at the most aggregate level, determined by
world demand and the relative prices of U.K. and foreign goods. Because of
differing movements in demand and relative prices in different parts of the
world and for different commodities, a case is often made, however, for
disaggregation of exports by destination or commodity or both. Information
about demand in different countries can often be obtained from forecasts
made by international organizations such as the O.E.C.D. With the exception
of the effects of changes in the levels of U.K. prices (effects which are hard
to ascertain except when there are very marked changes such as those attributable to a devaluation), these determinants of the demand for exports are
largely exogenous to the U.K. economy. It has, however, sometimes been
argued that the profitability of production for export relatively to production

for the home market and the pressure of domestic demand will both influence the supply (as opposed to the demand) for exports.

Similarly, *imports of goods and services* will depend on both the volume of demand at home and on relative prices. Again, a distinction may be drawn between different commodities—for example, between basic raw materials, where demand is likely to be insensitive to cost but highly sensitive to changes in output, and finished consumer goods where price relative to domestically produced substitutes will play a much larger role.

The net sum of all these aggregates gives *gross domestic product at market prices*—that is, prices which include indirect taxes. Since we are primarily interested in gross domestic product at factor cost in real terms (since the payment of the indirect tax element does not represent a demand for real resources), net indirect taxes must finally be deducted.[2] The effects of changes in indirect tax rates are reflected, as we saw above, in changes in (mainly) the consumer price index, which alter the real purchasing power of given money incomes.

The above outline shows that a realistic 'Keynesian' model of the economy, while remaining broadly within the familiar framework of the national income expenditure identity, needs to account on the way for a wide variety of economic variables which the simple model ignores—the price level, average earnings, the distribution of income, the level and structure of interest rates the availability of credit, and so on. The resulting larger model may be summarized by means of a further flow chart, again representing the National Institute's forecasting model (Figure 15.3).

2. Models of the Economy in Practice

2.1. Simulation

There are in existence several models of the U.K. economy constructed broadly along the lines set out above. The best known are those used in the preparation of forecasts by H.M. Treasury, the NIESR and the London Business School (see Bibliography).

In principle, the analysis of such models should settle a number of fundamental questions. For example, is the economy subject to a persistent business cycle? Are monetary factors important? Is the wage–price spiral stable or unstable? How powerful is the multiplier? And many more. These questions should be answerable using the techniques of *simulation*. The procedure is as follows: the model is 'solved'—i.e. the paths of the endogenous variables like GNY found—for chosen paths of all the exogenous variables. One exogenous variable is then changed and the model solved again. The differences between the two solutions then reflect the consequences of the change in the exogenous variable. Thus, for example, if the two exercises differ in having a

---

[2] This raises a technical point. Working at constant prices (in the case of the current U.K. national accounts, 1970 prices), this means that net indirect taxes must be valued at 1970 'prices'—that is, 1970 tax rates. This adjustment is known as the *factor cost adjustment*. Changes in this adjustment thus reflect only changes in the pattern of real expenditure between high- and low-taxed items.

uniformly different path of public expenditure, the resulting differences in the paths of GDP will show the resulting multiplier effect. Because of the lags in the system, the GDP differences will not be constant over time, even though the difference in public expenditure is. The multiplier value in the first period is known as the *impact multiplier*. The subsequent response of GDP will reflect any cyclical characteristics of the model—damped or explosive oscillations may be produced, or there may be a steady move towards or away from an equilibrium. If the model does tend towards an equilibrium,

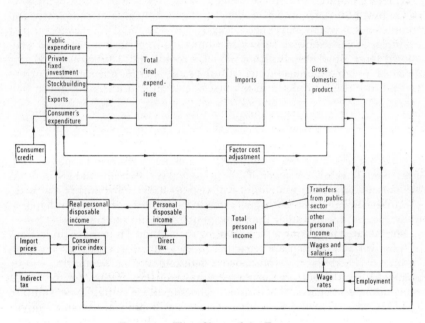

FIG. 15.3. Flow Chart of the Economy.

the multiplier in the new equilibrium is known as the *dynamic multiplier*. Similar exercises can be conducted to show the effects of changes in taxation, or in monetary variables, or wage rates, and so on.

Unfortunately, little has so far been published on the results of such experiments with models of the U.K. This is partly because the approach is a relatively new one, but also because the models, being designed primarily for the production of forecasts, are often not well suited to this kind of analysis. For example, it may be found much more satisfactory to forecast private investment by means of investment intentions surveys than by means of a formal investment function. But a model which does not contain an investment function will throw little light on the behaviour of the economy under differing assumptions, for there will be no means of estimating effects on investment—one of the most crucial determinants of the dynamic behaviour of the economy. In addition, the models may be incomplete simply because of the absence of knowledge about the precise functioning of some parts of the economy—notably the financial sector and its influence on real variables.

Such evidence as is available suggests, very tentatively, that the U.K. economy is characterized by very highly damped oscillations, and that both impact and dynamic multipliers are rather low—perhaps of the order of $1\frac{1}{2}$–2 respectively. Even more tentatively, there is little evidence of powerful monetary influences.

These conclusions are on the whole consistent with the results of analyses of the much greater number of models (of generally greater complexity and completeness) which have been constructed for the U.S. economy. For example, in an extensive survey of simulation experiments with the well-known large Brookings Institute model, Fromm and Taubman found evidence of a highly damped cycle, with the multiplier for government current expenditure rising from 1·4 in the first quarter to 2·9 after two and a half years.

2.2. Economic Forecasting

Most of the models of the kind described in general terms above have been constructed primarily for the purpose of making short-term economic forecasts. Such forecasts are generally for up to two years ahead, and are in terms of quarter-to-quarter (sometimes half-year to half-year) paths of the main variables, though these paths are intended to reflect the general 'shape' of future developments rather than precise quarterly movements.

The first step in making a forecast using such a model is to make projections of those variables which are regarded as 'exogenous'—that is, those which, because of the absence of simultaneous determination or 'feedbacks', will be unaffected by the outcome of the remainder of the forecast. Of the broad expenditure aggregates, this is usually thought to cover public expenditure and (largely) exports, while other elements will probably include import prices, tax rates (unless future changes have already been announced), public sector transfer payments to persons,[3] and, perhaps, 'liquidity', wage rates (under an effective incomes policy), and so on. The assumption that existing public expenditure programmes will be realized and that tax rates will remain unchanged reflects the assumption of 'unchanged policies' on which such forecasts are usually made. It depends on the acceptability of the outcome of such a forecast whether clear recommendations for *changes* in policy can then be made.

The remainder of the model consists, broadly speaking, of a set of equations. These represent the economic relationships described in earlier chapters (which are presumed to operate together). Thus a rise in consumption will raise GDP, but this in turn will raise employment and average earnings, and thus further increase consumption. If all the equations were linear the whole set could be solved algebraically, but this is extremely unlikely to be the case.

[3] Note that changes in inflation and unemployment rates can change these semi-automatically (see p. 379).

Iterative methods are therefore used: a provisional likely path for GDP is selected; through the various relationships of the model, this allows consequential paths for consumption, investment, and so on to be calculated. When these are added up, the resulting path for GDP will not normally agree with the initial assumption. A new revised path for GDP is therefore specified in the light of the consumption, investment 'forecasts' etc. and the solution of the model repeated. This process is repeated until consistency is achieved between the path of GDP and the total of the expenditure components given autonomously plus those dependent on GDP itself. Normally, of course, this is done with the aid of a computer.

Described thus baldly, the forecasting process seems comparatively mechanical. In practice, however, this is far from being the case. A wide variety of ambiguities and uncertainties must be taken account of. Some of these are mentioned very briefly below: interested readers are referred to the Bibliography at the end of this chapter for more detail.

Firstly, since economic data appear only some time, often considerable, after the event, the 'forecast' actually starts in the past. Partial information—on retail sales, industrial production, international trade, and so on—will be available for the recent past, but the picture of the economy over the last six months remains relatively incomplete.

Secondly, even the full national accounts data are subject to revisions, often substantial, so that even the more distant past is not known with complete certainty.

Thirdly, the formal, econometric relationships which comprise the model can only be treated as rough guidelines to the behaviour of the economy in future. In particular, such relationships will normally have 'fitted' the recent past with some inaccuracy and the problem arises of what degree of 'inaccuracy', one should assume in the future.

Fourthly, the forecast will be influenced by all kinds of unquantifiable factors for which a formal model cannot allow—the effect of the general level of 'confidence', to take only the most pervasive example.

Finally, although forecasts are generally made on the basis of the assumption of unchanged policies on the part of the Government, it is frequently difficult to lend precision to the notion of what 'unchanged' means. No real problem arises with, for example, tax rates, but an 'unchanged' monetary policy cannot normally be uniquely defined,[4] still less the notion of, for example, 'continued severe restraint' on pay or prices.

Against these uncertainties, the forecaster can derive some help from various 'extraneous' or 'leading' indicators. Examples of the former are investment intentions surveys and surveys of business confidence. The latter, e.g. statistics of new orders, are variables that have been found generally to move up and down prior to a corresponding movement in GDP, and are thus of some help in predicting the latter.

It follows that a forecast made using any particular model will reflect not

---

[4] Does it, for example, mean that the money supply will continue to grow at the same rate as in the recent past, or that interest rates will be stabilized at their current levels?

merely the character of the basic formal model, but, often more importantly, the judgement and intuition of the forecaster in employing the model.

2.3. The Use of Economic Forecasts

The main purpose of most macroeconomic forecasts is as an aid to the rational discussion of economic policy-making. As we have observed, the forecasts are generally based on the assumption of the continuation of existing policies; if the resulting forecast shows an unacceptable pattern of development of the economy, then some of the existing policies must be altered. Until the mid-1960s, this meant almost exclusively the use of fiscal policy and some aspects of monetary policy—notably the use of hire-purchase regulations—to control the level of aggregate demand: in particular, to attempt to maintain a constant pressure of demand in relation to capacity. This concentration on 'demand management' or 'fine tuning' reflected the beliefs, explicit or implicit, firstly, that forecasting techniques and policy manipulations were adequate for the task of maintaining balance over a period of eighteen to twenty-four months ahead, and, secondly, that the preservation of a stable pressure of demand at the right level would simultaneously prevent fluctuations in output and employment, prevent anything more than creeping inflation, preserve a stable balance of payments, and even raise the rate of economic growth. The techniques of demand management were in principle simple: confronted with a situation in which, on existing policies, unemployment was projected to rise to an unacceptable level, a reflationary demand policy was called for. The forecasting process would be repeated with different, lower, sets of tax rates prevailing from the next Budget, and that policy package chosen which produced a stable level of unemployment. The changes would duly be made; a new forecast would be produced some months later which might again suggest some adjustment to the level of demand . . . and so the process continued. 'Brakes', 'accelerators', and 'tillers' became common terms in chancellors' Budget statements.

It gradually became clear, however, that short-term demand management of this kind was failing to produce the desired results. In the first place, it became increasingly apparent that simply controlling the level of demand was not sufficient to produce a tolerable rate of inflation, a satisfactory balance of payments, or an adequate rate of growth of production. The recognition of cost rather than demand factors in governing the rate of inflation reduced the relevance of demand management as a counter-inflationary policy. There was a realization that after allowing for cyclical fluctuations there was a persistent and growing fundamental disequilibrium in the balance of payments. And there was increasing dissatisfaction with the underlying rate of growth. The retreat from near-exclusive preoccupation with demand management was reflected in the adoption of prices and incomes policies, devaluation (and later floating) of the exchange rate, and indicative economic planning. There was even mounting scepticism about the Government's basic ability to manipulate demand so as to even out the vestiges of the business-cycle in real output and employment. This inability seemed to stem from inadequate recognition of the lags involved both in implementing decisions and in the effects of their implementation on the economy at large. Changes in income tax rates, for example, cannot normally be put into effect for some months—to allow for P.A.Y.E. codes to be changed; the consequential reduction in personal disposable income affects consumers' expenditure only with a lag; and the effect of the subsequent rise in output on the level of private investment may extend well beyond the forecast period. Furthermore, caution on the part of government decision-takers may have led them to delay acting in accordance with the forecasts until the projections were confirmed by the actual behaviour of the economy as reflected in, for example, the unemployment figures. But the delays already noted in connection with the collection of statistics (and the fact that unemployment, in particular, lags well behind changes in output) meant that such information was not available until far too long after action should have been taken. The total of all these lags, stretching from a change in the economy to the final impact of policy designed to redress the change, could be two or even more years. In the meantime, self-correcting forces might well have been in operation. In short, there is probably a broad consensus—with hindsight—that demand management measures were generally 'too much and too late'.

This change of emphasis in the use of economic forecasts is sharply pointed up by a comparison of the policy recommendations made by the National Institute of Economic and Social Research in its Reviews for February 1964 and February 1974. In 1964:

To sum up: in the absence of government intervention total demand in real terms seems likely to rise . . . at a rate of some 5½ per cent a year. . . . At some time fairly soon, the rate at which demand is rising will almost certainly have to be slowed down: 5½ per cent is not a rate which the British economy is likely to be able to sustain in present conditions, once it is fully employed. . . . It is important that the measures should not shake the confidence of those who are beginning to plan ahead on the basis of a faster long-term growth rate. . . . We suggest a cut of about 1 per cent in the rate at which real expenditure, public and private, is rising. This would require an increase in personal taxation of around £200 million, or a reduction in government expenditure of rather less than this. If this is done soon, there will be time later to make further adjustments if needed. (pp. 10–11)

And in February 1974:

The policy problems presented by this outlook are formidable. It is not often that a government finds itself confronted with the possibility of a simultaneous failure to achieve all four main policy objections—of adequate economic growth, full employment, a satisfactory balance of payments and reasonably stable prices. . . . The initial problem with the balance of payments will be to cover the deficit of the first half-year, and to prevent it forcing the exchange-rate substantially down for any length of time. . . . On prices, the policy problem will be to decide whether to let Stage 3 [of the prices and incomes policy] run its course, or to attempt to tighten it up in some way. The assumptions underlying Stage 3 have, of course, gone by the board. . . . On balance, a neutral Budget might be best now, so long as there is the clear intention of taking reflationary action later in the year if unemployment continues to rise (as we think it probably will). It would be wrong, in our view, to allow unemployment to rise simply in order to improve the balance of payments. There should be some international agreement about a sensible pattern of deficits among the industrial countries; if other countries are unwilling to allow us a 'full employment' balance of payments deficit in the interim between now and the arrival of North Sea oil, then we would be justified in imposing import restrictions. (pp. 4–7)

These developments do not, of course, mean that economic forecasts are now less valuable than formerly as a basis for the rational discussion of economic policy—rather the contrary. It is abundantly clear that forecasting is more hazardous now than a decade ago—but this makes forecasting and the careful assessment of forecasts even more vital. What has changed is the scope of policy choice. The policy implications of a forecast can no longer be discussed simply in terms of the amount and timing of reflation or deflation required; rather, attention is now focused on a number of (often conflicting) policy targets and on the wide variety of policy instruments which are available, of which demand management is only one.

There have, however, been two more radical attacks on fine tuning—from the Monetarists and from a group of Cambridge economists. In both cases, it is asserted that policy-makers have tried to do too much, rather than too little.

The monetarist position, as we have seen, has two basic planks. The first is that there is a 'natural' rate of unemployment consistent with constant *real* wage rates, and which can be reduced only at the cost—in the long run—of inflation. Secondly, it is held that only a steady moderate expansion of the supply of money is consistent with the steady expansion of economic activity without price inflation.[5] (See Chapters 7 and 12 on this.)

It is debatable to what extent the neo-monetarist view *per se* precludes attempts at fine tuning: fiscal policy is not explicitly mentioned. But it seems reasonable to infer that, under conditions of steady monetary expansion of the sort proposed, fiscal policy measures are supposed only to affect the level of employment in the short run; in the longer run the 'natural' level of employment must be regained. Thus short-run stabilization measures are in the long run irrelevant as far as real output and employment are concerned. Yet if Friedman's Permanent Income Theory of Consumption holds, fiscal changes will have little effect on short-term consumer demand either. Both fiscal and monetary fine tuning should thus on these views, be eschewed.

If this interpretation is correct, this attack on fine tuning is clearly not specifically a monetarist attack: the relative efficacy of fiscal and monetary policies is a separate question. What is asserted is that *any* measures which attempt to hold the economy away from the 'natural' level of employment are ultimately futile. This is a straightforward neo-classical contention of the kind rejected by Keynesian analysis, with the exception that the old presump-

[5] Professor Friedman has summarized the implications of this view: 'Other forces would still affect the economy, require change and adjustment, and disturb the even tenor of our ways. But steady monetary growth would provide a monetary climate favourable to the effective operation of those basic forces of enterprise, ingenuity invention, hard work and thrift that are the true springs of economic growth. That is the most that we can ask from monetary policy at our present state of knowledge. But that much—and it is a great deal— is clearly within our reach'. (Concluding lines of 'The Role of Monetary Policy', *American Economic Review*, 58 (1), 1968).

tion that the economy would inevitably tend towards full employment equilibrium is replaced by the new presumption that it will tend towards equilibrium at the 'natural' employment level.

2.4. Sector Flows of Funds

The second attack on fine tuning has come from disillusioned forecasters (now at Cambridge) who came to feel that the existing framework was inadequate for the analysis, forecasting, and regulation of, in particular, the balance of payments. As we saw in Chapter 13, they have derived a simple relationship between the balance of payments and fiscal policy, the latter broadly conceived as the public sector's surplus or deficit (that is, its excess or deficiency of revenue over expenditure). As a matter of accounting, such a relationship was easily derived (see p. 339).

For any *given* level of the private sector's financial balance, the balance of payments deficit will vary directly with the public sector deficit. In practice, the private sector's financial balance does vary, but it is claimed that these variations are relatively small and are in any case predictable, so that a simple policy implication follows: the balance of payments deficit will be higher the higher is the public sector deficit. If fiscal policy is to be directed towards the balance of payments, the Government can thus follow an extraordinarily simple prescription: all that need be done is to fix, and achieve, the appropriate public sector financial deficit surplus.

Appealing though this approach is, it is open to objections, quite apart from the problems about whether empirically it has continued to be valid, noted in Chapter 13. Firstly, nothing is said about the levels of real output and employment. As the examination of the oil crisis in the last chapter showed, a balance of payments deficit may well end up as a public sector deficit but have caused a very severe contraction in the level of activity in the meantime as the household and company sectors attempt to shift the impact of the balance of payments deficit. Removal of the public sector deficit, if it removed the balance of payments deficit, would almost certainly cause more contraction, with the private sector attempting to avoid the impact again falling on itself. It could be argued, therefore, that the identity merely expresses the truism that a given balance of payments target can always be achieved with sufficient deflation (decrease in the public sector deficit) if the level of employment is ignored. Secondly, the crucial contention that the private sector's financial balance is stable and/or predictable is a remarkable one. The suggestion is that for firms and households taken together, the sum of firms' investment and households' consumption bears a systematic relationship to the total of their disposable income. No behavioural hypothesis is advanced for this remarkable assertion—indeed, it is difficult to see what kind of hypothesis could be offered to replace the familiar relationships between households' incomes and consumption and between firms' incomes and investment which figure so prominently in orthodox macroeconomic analysis.

The 'New Cambridge' approach must therefore—unless and until a satisfactory theoretical underpinning is provided, together with the 'missing' determination of the levels of output and employment—be rejected as an *alternative* to the conventional analysis. There is, however, one way (though it is not novel) in which the identity of the new approach can be used. This is as a cross-check on the plausibility of conventional forecasts.

The equation stating that the balance of payments deficit must equal the sum of the private and public sector deficits follows from the national expenditure identity and it is evident that it must be satisfied by any set of data which satisfy the latter—in particular, by any consistent short-term forecast (expressed in current prices). It is possible—particularly if the private sector is split into households and firms—that the *pattern* of financial balances (surpluses and deficits), or *flows of funds* (which will be reflected in the acquisition or sale of financial assets) implied by the forecasts of expenditure patterns will be implausible or unlikely. In particular, if firms or households must, for consistency with the forecast, acquire or divest themselves of unprecedented amounts of financial assets this *may* (though not necessarily *must*) suggest that there is an implausibility in the basic forecast. For example, an unprecedented company sector deficit may suggest that the forecast of investment is too high, or that of prices too low. In this way the examination of the financial balances of the different sectors implied by a forecast can serve to identify possible errors.

3. Summary and Conclusions

The difficulties in assessing the past and current behaviour of the economy and predicting its future evolution have increased dramatically in the last ten or so years. Up until the early or middle 1960s it appeared that the economy was subject to relatively mild cycles in economic activity. The task of the authorities seemed to be the (in principle) relatively simple one of using the tools of demand management to counteract these fluctuations. If this were done successfully, the resulting high and stable level of employment could, it appeared, co-exist with balance of payments equilibrium (without recourse to alterations in the exchange rate), relatively stable prices (without an incomes policy), and high rates of growth of investment and output (without planning).

In the last decade it has become clear that these objectives of economic policy can no longer be achieved simultaneously merely by the manipulation of (particularly) fiscal policy to manage aggregate demand. We have moved much closer to a position in which the authorities probably need to employ as many policy instruments as there are targets to be achieved. This change of attitude has produced a variety of reactions. First, the absence of experience of the use of new policy instruments has made it difficult to assess or employ them with much confidence. The experience of the 1967 devaluation and the current floating of the exchange rate has shown how little we know of the extent to which depreciation improves the balance of payments—or, indeed, given a price–wage–price spiral to which it is likely to contribute, whether its longer-run effects may not actually be perverse. We have little experience of import controls. We still have not solved the problem of devising an effective and equitable long-run prices and incomes policy. And the experience of the hastily abandoned National Plan of 1965 taught us little about the effects of planning.

By the same token, economic forecasters have necessarily become much more tentative in their assessment of past policies and their views and recommendations about the future. Assessing the accuracy of past forecasts is a difficult task: the 'unchanged policies' assumption is naturally rarely realized, and there are formidable problems in allocating inaccuracies between (i) errors in the forecasts of exogenous variables, with consequential errors in the forecasts of endogenous variables, and (ii) independent errors in the endogenous forecasts. Such evidence as there is suggests that while short-term economic forecasts made with the help of a model of the economy are better than simple rules of thumb (such as assuming steady growth in all variables), the improvement is not startling. Nor is there any real evidence that the forecasts have got better over time—though, as we have suggested, this may well be because the economy has become more difficult to predict.

Two groups of commentators have reacted to the increased difficulty in managing the economy by proposing a much reduced degree of policy interference. The New Cambridge School argues that the poor performance of demand management policies suggests that short-term changes in fiscal policy should be eschewed. Both employment and the balance of payments might have been more stable if tax rates were fixed for several years at a time. This (given a reasonably steady growth in public expenditure) would tend to stabilize the public sector deficit. In an analogous way, Monetarists have argued that a steady and moderate expansion of the money supply represents the greatest degree of monetary stabilization which the authorities should seek. Conventional forecasters, by contrast, while conceding that 'fine tuning' has not had a notably successful record, tend to believe that the task of the authorities is to employ a wide variety of policy instruments so as to attempt to attain the varied targets of economic policy-makers.

Bibliography

Regular assessments of the British economy appear in:
[1] *National Institute Economic Review* (quarterly).
[2] *Bank of England Quarterly Bulletin.*
[3] *O.E.C.D. Economic Survey* (annual).
[4] Department of Applied Economics, Cambridge, *Economic Policy Review* (annual)

The forecasting models used by the London Business School, the Treasury, and the National Institute are described in Part 1 of:
[5] RENTON, A. (ed.) *Modelling the Economy* (Heinemann/S.S.R.C., 1975).

A fuller account of the National Institute model, together with a description of its use in forecasting, is given in:
[6] SURREY, M. J. C. *The Analysis and Forecasting of the British Economy* (Cambridge/N.I.E.S.R., 1971).

An attempt to evaluate the accuracy of short-term economic forecasts is:
[7] ASH, J. C. K. and SMYTH, D. J. *Forecasting the UK Economy* (Saxon House, 1973).

In addition to the books on the post-war management of the British Economy given at the end of Chapter 4, reference may also be made to:

[8] BRITTAN, S. *Steering the Economy* (Penguin, 1971).

[9] COHEN, C. D. *British Economic Policy 1960–69* (Butterworth, 1971).

[10] WORSWICK, G. D. N. and BLACKABY, F. (eds.) *The Medium Term* (Heinemann, 1974).

16

Anti-Trust Policy[1]

C. J. M. HARDIE

1. The Need for Anti-Trust Policy

1.1. Monopoly and Competition

The economic case for a free enterprise industrial system rests on the proposition that such a system will develop and produce the goods and services the community requires, and do so at the lowest attainable cost to society. This proposition itself depends on three basic conditions:

(i) There must be an identity between the 'private' costs which producers take into account in their commercial decisions and the 'social' costs to society as a whole which those decisions entail. In other words, any cost —pecuniary or otherwise—incurred by anyone as a result of the decision must be reflected in the actual cost the producer pays.

(ii) Similarly, there must be an identity between the private benefits (i.e. revenues) accruing to producers and the social benefits of their decisions. With the first condition, this will mean that the pursuit of private profit—the difference between private costs and revenues—will entail the pursuit of maximum social 'profit', i.e. the maximum net benefit to society of the individual decisions concerned.

(iii) In addition, this result requires that producers have as their objective the pursuit of maximum profit. If other objectives intrude then maximum social net benefit might not occur even though private and social costs and benefits were equal.

Given these conditions, the case for a perfectly competitive free enterprise system can be seen by contrasting the case of a monopolist (depicted on p. 59 and reproduced here) with that of a firm in a perfectly competitive market (depicted on p. 161 and reproduced here—see Figure 16.1). The average and marginal cost curves are the same in each case. The horizontal demand curve of perfect competition ensures that the profit-maximizing firm produces at the minimum point on the average cost curve, with the minimum prices consistent with continued production in the long run and no supernormal profits. Comparison of the two cases immediately indicates the potential advantages of perfect competition. These are:

[1] Any opinions expressed in this chapter are personal to the author, and do not represent the views of the Monopolies and Mergers Commission, of which he is now a member.

(a) It leads to a situation in which price equals marginal cost. Profit maximization requires that marginal revenue equal marginal cost. Only under perfect competition does price equal marginal revenue and so equal marginal cost. This, as we saw in Chapter 6, is a necessary condition for optimal resource allocation as defined there. Under monopoly, price is above marginal cost, and therefore too little of the product will be bought by comparison with the optimal production of goods, because its price is in excess of the optimum.

(b) The monopoly permits excess or super-normal profits to be made, but they do not act effectively as a signal for new firms to come into the industry to increase production, because of the barriers, natural or man-made, which enable the monopolist to preserve his position. This also effects the over-all distribution of income in the economy.

(c) The combination of a horizontal demand (giving price equals marginal revenue), profit maximization (giving marginal revenue equals marginal cost), and free entry (giving only normal profits, with price equals average cost) ensures that perfectly competitive firms will end up producing at average minimum cost, where marginal cost equals average cost. No such automatic tendency exists under monopoly conditions.

These three advantages can all be seen directly from the diagrams in Figure 16.1. But there are additional advantages which are not so obvious.

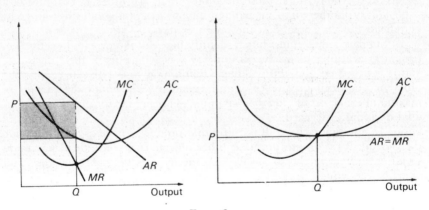

FIG. 16.1

(d) The monopolist has less incentive to improve his product or in other ways increase his efficiency because unlike the perfectly competitive firm he can survive perfectly well on less than the maximum profits obtainable. He can therefore choose if he wishes to reduce such efforts and still make a more than adequate profit. In terms of the figure, the monopolist may have average costs above those indicated by the average cost curve, for the latter shows only the *minimum* average cost for each possible output level.

(e) The obvious advantages of such market dominance may easily mean that maintaining it becomes a major company objective. Not only may this violate basic condition (iii) above, but means that monopoly no longer just happens to occur sometimes but is actively promoted and pursued, tending to make it more widespread and more difficult to remove or control.

(f) Finally, we have so far made only a crude comparison of two extremes. The above points become much stronger if it can be establishep that a tendency to dominate even just a large proportion of a market will generate a corresponding tendency for the monopolistic factors described to appear. The most likely reasons for this to occur are that a large firm may well be able to enforce its own price leadership by threatening a price war if other small firms do not follow its price lead. The threat of takeover, saturation advertising, and so on, may also be used to enforce its dominance.

Profit is an important element in the functioning of the perfectly competitive system. It creates the incentive on the sales side to develop and produce successfully the goods and services which customers want, and on the cost side to minimize the use of inputs for the level of output chosen so as to minimize cost for that level. It acts as the incentive and signal for firms to expand production of goods in high demand and for new firms to add to production, or for firms to leave the industry if profits are inadequate.

It is clear from all of this that the perfectly competitive model is an important part of the background to anti-trust policy, the belief in a free enterprise system, and the profit motive. It is none the less open to objections on both theoretical and practical grounds. For example, many dominant firms will, because of large size, be able to obtain economies of scale—that is, lower long-run unit costs of production. In this case Figure 16.1 is inaccurate because it presumes equal cost structures in the two cases it depicts. The existence of economies of scale may mean that prices will be lower under monopoly than perfect competition despite extra profits being made in the former but not the latter.

Although economies of scale are the most obvious potential gain from the larger size which will accompany market dominance, they are by no means the only one. The reduction in uncertainty about competitors' behaviour may stimulate more investment. More finance may be forthcoming to such firms, and they will tend to be more effective in export competition with large foreign firms. Some of the earlier drawbacks listed may be reversed. For example, *more* innovation may occur than under a more competitive situation because there are economies of scale in providing finance for it, and a greater incentive because the profits from it can be more readily protected from competition.

This list of the gains that may accrue from dominance ignores many aspects of actual company behaviour, the effect of which is in general uncertain. Firms use a range of pricing procedures and other competitive weapons like advertising, have different degrees of management skill and efficiency, and attempt to integrate different stages of production. Each of these may be a source of gain or loss to the company and to the community.

So the case for the free market is not conclusive. It indicates some potential gains which may result from free enterprise and the promotion of competition.

In practice there will be other important considerations. Competition may not operate in the way assumed by the theory, profit may not be an effective incentive, and so on. The arguments outlined here make an *a priori* case for government concern with industrial structure and business behaviour. But they do not prove that the free market system is the best, nor show what measures would be necessary to make it work competitively.

If in a particular case investigation reveals a clear discrepancy between private profit and the public interest, this does not in itself justify government interference. Such interference might lead to even worse results than the operation of the unfettered and admittedly imperfect market. But if intervention is justified, it is still necessary to decide upon the appropriate form of intervention. Some very obvious types of discrepancy are dealt with by direct legislation, backed up by inspection and fines, e.g. provision of unhealthy or unsafe working conditions; allowing pollutants, chemicals, and waste products which are a danger to health to be discharged into the public drainage system; or inadequate safety devices in products. Another case (already referred to) is when companies are discouraged from investing by fear of the risk and uncertainty involved, ignorance, or short-sightedness. The aggregate of such micro decisions may well represent a level of aggregate investment well below what the community thinks desirable at the macro level (where, among other things, the individual risks matter less because they are pooled). Hence the taxation system is used to bring private and public benefits closer together—either by subsidizing investment in general in the interests of growth, or by subsidizing investment in particular geographical areas. Still others are dealt with by a full-scale examination of all the social costs and benefits involved. Decisions on the M1 motorway, the Victoria Line, and a third London airport are all examples of this approach.

Anti-trust policy arises from the existence of market power. It is concerned with those discrepancies between maximum private and social net benefit that occur because of the malfunctioning of the competitive mechanism; where single firms (monopolies) or groups of companies (cartels) escape the discipline of competition by virtue of their control of a high proportion of a market and the absence of any potential rivals. It is therefore concerned with the consequences of the free market failing to operate properly— excessive prices and profits, sub-optimal output, lack of incentive to increased efficiency, and failure to improve products.

1.2. Remedies

The most obvious remedy for such situations is to reinstate or promote competition in some way or another, so that the market power is destroyed, and with it the anti-social behaviour. In some cases this is quite easy. Where the companies involved have drawn up a formal agreement to fix prices, without which they would find it difficult to co-operate, then essentially all that has to be done is to forbid them to make or operate such agreements. This is the effect of the 1956 Restrictive Trade Practices Act (see below). There are many British industries in which the number of competing companies is large enough, or their suspicion of each other great enough, that they cannot work together to raise prices without quite elaborate, often legally enforceable, provisions. In those cases, the elimination of the agreement goes much of the way to restoring competition.

This will not of course result in Berfect competition, the concept of which is a hypothetical extreme only. put it may be competition of a sufficiently vigorous type so that the problems of market imperfection, if they exist, will be relatively minor.

In other industries, however, escape from competitive pressure may not require any agreement between companies. There may be price-leadership, implicit or half-conscious understanding not to rock the boat by price cuts which will harm everyone, or a long history of mutual accommodation and respect, which amount to an industry solidarity very like a cartel, but without any formal co-operation. In that case, the remedy is not so clear because there is no agreement to be prohibited. It is impossible to order the companies to 'behave competitively' since that would be irrational and inefficient by the standards of their profit objectives, and very difficult to enforce or even observe. For example, uniformity of prices may be the result either of intense competition or of a collusive agreement. Heavy advertising may be part of an aggressive competitive strategy, or just the result of an implicit understanding that price competition would be mutually disadvantageous.

The existence of a single dominant firm is an extreme example of a case where no agreements are necessary to avoid competition and no easy solution exists for creating competition. It may be possible in theory (though frequently not in practice) to break up such a firm or encourage entry into the industry, particularly if tariff barriers exist which can be removed to stimulate import competition. But where such remedies are impossible or inadequate, the only answer will be regulation of prices, profits, and commercial behaviour—a strategy of which nationalization is the ultimate form.

In most anti-trust policies—certainly in the United Kingdom—there are therefore two strands. First, there is an attempt to promote competition, so that the industry can be left to set prices, plan production, and trade freely in a free market. In this case, competition automatically tends to regulate behaviour in the desired way and therefore prevents any major abuse. Second, there is a more or less explicit regulatory function. The behaviour or performance of the monopolist is examined with a view to modifying that behaviour, rather than seeking a remedy via the promotion of competition. For example, if the problem is excess profits, it may well be that renewed competition would have eliminated them. But if that is impossible, the alternative is simply to force the company, by administrative decree, to lower prices. Or if market power is associated with wasteful or misleading advertising, the obvious remedy is to tell the company to stop the practice.

There are therefore in principle two ways of dealing with anti-trust problems. First, to change the environment in which the company operates; second, directly to change its behaviour. There are great difficulties with both these approaches; and they will be discussed later. But first it is necessary to outline the present legal and institutional situation in the U.K. and the E.E.C. on anti-trust policy, both of which reflect this dual approach.

2. The Legal Background in Europe

2.1. Anti-Trust Regulations in the U.K.

Until after the Second World War there was no anti-trust policy in this country. Indeed, the Depression of the 1930s had the opposite effect. It induced governments to persuade industries to concentrate and rationalize, thereby ensuring their survival in times of low demand and inadequate profits. Since 1948, however, with the general improvement in the level of aggregate demand, there have been a series of Acts designed to deal with dominant firms (or monopolies), mergers, restrictive practices (of which price-fixing is the most obvious but by no means the only example) and resale price maintenance agreements, whereby e.g. a retailer must sell a product at the price laid down by the manufacturer.

Since the Restrictive Trade Practices Act of 1956,[2] the Restrictive Trade Practices Court deals with agreements between companies which relate to the supply or production of goods or services in the United Kingdom, and with the enforcement of Resale Price Maintenance (R.P.M.) by individual companies. All agreements must be notified to the Director General of Fair Trading, who has to take them to Court, unless they are previously abandoned. The Court has to decide whether the Agreement can be justified in terms of Section 21(1)—which allows eight 'gateways', or grounds for justification, of which the most general is (b) 'that the removal of the restriction would deny to the public . . . specific and substantial benefits. . . .'[3]

Passing a 'gateway' is not sufficient, however. If this occurs (and *only* if it does) the Court then has to decide whether the advantage outweighs any detriment that can be shown to arise from the agreement. This provision is known as the 'tailpiece', and can result in a court decision against an agreement, despite its passage through a 'gateway'. Similar procedures and provisions apply to R.P.M.

The *Monopolies and Mergers Commission* was established in 1948, and its powers extended to mergers in 1965. It deals primarily with situations where one company supplies 25 per cent or more of a particular good or service. It deals also with the case where two interconnected companies (e.g. a parent and a subsidiary) control a quarter of the market; and where two quite distinct companies operate in such a way as to restrict competition without any formal agreement—e.g. the case of price-leadership or tacit collusion. In relation to mergers, the criterion is that a merger must involve assets over £5m., or a market share of 25 per cent or more, if it is to be examined.

The Monopolies Commission machinery differs in important respects from that of the Restrictive Trade Practices Court. First, companies do not have to notify a dominant position or the intention to merge—it is for the authori-

---

[2] Here and in what follows the account of the legislation is necessarily summary. Much legal detail which may be of great importance in specific cases must therefore be ignored and anyone who wishes to know the provisions of the legislation in detail must refer to the relevant Act—see Bibliography.

[3] See Appendix 1 for the 'gateways' and the 'tailpiece' in full.

ties to identify the situation for themselves. Second, the authorities have no obligation to refer a monopoly position or a merger. The vast majority of situations which fall within the 25 per cent or £5m. criteria have not been, and are unlikely to be, referred to the Commission. This means that though all cartel and R.P.M. agreements have to be examined, few monopoly/ merger situations are. Third, the criteria to be used by the Commission are much more general than the 'gateways' prescribed under the 1956 Restrictive Trade Practices Act appear to be. There are certain specific matters which the Monopolies Commission must take into account, which are given in Section 84 of the 1973 Fair Trading Act as follows:

In determining for the purposes of this Act whether any particular matter operates, or may be expected to operate, against the public interest, the Commission shall take into account all matters which appear to them in the particular circumstances to be relevant, and among other things, shall have regard to the desirability—

(a) of maintaining and promoting effective competition between persons supplying goods and services in the United Kingdom;

(b) of promoting the interests of consumers, purchasers and other users of goods and services in the United Kingdom in respect of the prices charged for them and in respect of their quality and the variety of goods and services supplied;

(c) of promoting, through competition, the reduction of costs and the development and use of new techniques and new products, and of facilitating the entry of new competitors into existing markets;

(d) of maintaining and promoting the balanced distribution of industry and employment in the United Kingdom; and

(e) of maintaining and promoting competitive activity in markets outside the United Kingdom on the part of producers of goods, and of supplies of goods and services, in the United Kingdom.

But the Commission must take into account all relevant matters, and there is nothing to say that the factors in Section 84 are to be given any special weight. So the scope of 'the public interest' remains wide, and undefined by statute.

2.2. E.E.C. Regulations

The E.E.C. legislation—of which the most important provisions are Articles 85 and 86 of the Treaty of Rome—differs most obviously from the United Kingdom legislation in having no straightforward provision (outside the Coal and Steel Community) for dealing with mergers. Otherwise, there is an obvious parallel between Article 85 and the Restrictive Trade Practices legislation; and between Article 86 and the Monopolies legislation. The E.E.C. provisions deal only with situations where interstate trade is affected. But the coverage is in other ways similar to that in the U.K. Under Article 85, agreements have to be notified, and their chances of being allowed to continue are quite small, as in the case of the U.K. legislation. The major exception is that a whole range of exclusive dealer and agency relationships are caught under Article 85, but not under the U.K. legislation. However, block exemptions are available for many such arrangements.

Article 86 deals with abuses by dominant firms (including, as an abuse, attempts to consolidate market power by merger). There is no arithmetic definition analogous to our 25 per cent to say what constitutes a prima facie case for investigation. However, it is difficult to say what Article 86 amounts to, because there have been no important cases to provide a basis for any general conclusions. The impression is, however, that the European Commission staff—who are predominantly responsible for the operation of the policy—are in favour of the promotion of competition rather than the regulation (or cost-benefit) approach to anti-trust matters. See Appendix 2 for Articles 85 and 86.

2.3. Impact of the Legislation

The impact of the anti-trust legislation is very hard to determine. At the macroeconomic level, the number of factors influencing prices, profits, and investment is so large that it would be very difficult to identify the impact of anti-trust legislation alone. At the microeconomic level, agreements likely to be banned may be replaced by more informal understandings that are difficult to detect, and firms are for obvious reasons unlikely to provide information on such activities. Nevertheless, some useful work has been done on investigating the consequences of the judgements of the Restrictive Trade Practices Court (see [14]). This suggests a significant impact. Over 10 per cent of a sample of agreements existing in 1956 were formally abandoned, others were modified in the light of the legislation, and of the cases where an agreement was struck down by the Court, over 50 per cent showed an increase in competitive behaviour, predominantly with respect to prices and discounts.

On the other hand, perhaps half of the agreements condemned appeared to have been replaced by some alternative means of restraining competitive pressures, in particular by information agreements. These involve only the publication of prices, but can easily form the basis for implicit understandings. Price-leadership to a lesser extent also took over the role of banned agreements. There is also some evidence that industry continues to operate restrictive agreements which are not registered, and are therefore unaffected by the legislation.

A further likely effect of the restrictive practices legislation is that mergers will have been encouraged. If prices cannot be maintained by agreement with competitors, an obvious alternative is to merge, and thereby increase the effectiveness of price-leadership.

The merger legislation has on the face of it had much less impact than has the Restrictive Trade Practices Act. Few mergers have been referred to the Commission, and still fewer prevented. There is no doubt that some potential mergers are abandoned because the parties fear, or are advised by the authorities, that a reference would ensue; and that is enough, given the delays involved, to kill the proposal. In particular cases, therefore, the legislation will be of decisive importance. But they are few enough to make it unlikely that there has been any significant effect on industrial structure.

Similarly, in the case of monopoly references, there are a number of companies—Courtaulds and Hoffman La Roche to name but two—whose businesses have been substantially affected by Monopolies Commission recommendations. And any company with a large market share will, if it is prudent, watch its behaviour carefully in order to avoid the danger of a reference. But as a proportion of total economic activity in the United Kingdom such cases are small. Again, therefore, the over-all impact, even if useful, will not be of great significance.

3. The Alternative Approaches Considered

3.1. The Problem of Natural Monopoly

At the beginning of this chapter a distinction was drawn between those aspects of anti-trust policy which aimed at the promotion of competition, and those essentially regulatory in purpose. This section deals with these alternatives, and the general question of cost-benefit or 'trade-off' approaches to anti-trust, in greater detail.

The central purpose of the 'competition promotion' alternative is to identify and eliminate those factors which obstruct new entry, rivalry, and other challenges to market power. Such obstacles may be 'natural', that is, not deliberately created by the dominant company (or, for that matter, by anyone else). The clearest example is where geography, transport costs, economies of scale, and the size of the market combine to create a local monopoly (which may be as large as a state, or a region, or a country). In that market there can only be one major supplier; and he is necessarily protected from competition because there is no room for any producer of similar size in the same place, nor cheap access to the market from the outside. Another problem arises when there are obvious economies in providing a single network of services. Duplicate gas pipes up the same street are evidently wasteful; so too are duplicate railway systems. Where this is so, the least cost solution is to have one company to establish and operate the network. But that immediately creates a monopoly situation.

The main difficulty with situations of natural monopoly is not to identify them, but to find a remedy. It is possible, of course, to accept the costs of breaking up the dominant position by subsidizing transport into the local market, or setting up a State competitor, or allowing duplication. But this amounts to the promotion of competition for its own sake, that is, even though it is a less cost-efficient solution. Price control is an obvious alternative —either via regulation or nationalization. But this is only a partial answer. It deals with prices and price/cost ratios, but can do nothing to substitute for competition as a stimulus to efficiency in product development and production. The regulated prices will necessarily be on some kind of cost-plus basis, with all the dangers that involves to incentives and effort.

Some man-made obstacles are in principle easier to deal with. If a company controls all or a high proportion of distribution outlets or supplies, then potential rivals are foreclosed from competing, and the dominant firm can relax. In this case, the company can be made to give up control. Other cases are more difficult, for example that of patents. It is plain that the possession of a key patent can—if not as often as is popularly supposed—be a crucial protection from challenge. Is this barrier to be condemned? Surely not, since the patent system itself results from government action to protect an inventor, and to allow him to reap the fruits of his successful ingenuity. The most general difficulty is that the major obstacle to new competition is the existing skill and experience of the historically successful large company. Is that a natural or a man-made barrier? Is it desirable or undesirable? In principle the rules of free enterprise allow companies to compete against each other rather like runners in a race—save for the advantages of effort, energy, and natural ability, all start equal. It may then be argued that the winner deserves the credit for having developed and displayed the virtues which the system is designed to reward. If he gains experience by persistent competition and success, and thereby becomes even more difficult to defeat, it is further to his credit. Rivals are not entitled to complain that his skill constitutes an undesirable obstacle to their success.

3.2. Regulation, Trade-Off, and Cost-Benefit

The competition-promotion approach is comparatively simple. It is based on the proposition that if only competition can be enforced, then efficiency will be achieved—at least so far as it is within the power of anti-trust policy. The approach is admittedly limited—both because competition cannot achieve everything, and because in some circumstances (natural monopoly) competition cannot practicably be achieved.

The alternative approach (which is more like that adopted in the United Kingdom by the Monopolies Commission) can be explained as follows. Competition is not desirable *per se*, but only as a means to socially desirable ends such as efficient production, technical progress, low prices, high exports, and so on. Competition certainly has an important contribution to make to the achievement of these ends—and perhaps for most industries most of the time it is the most appropriate mechanism. But in many cases—not only those of natural monopolies—it will be not simply unattainable, but undesirable. Large scale may be necessary to achieve optimum efficiency in plant, organization, management, distribution, and research. Co-ordination, either via cartel or via single ownership, is essential when plant has a long and unpredictable gestation period, is large scale, and has to rely for its operation on complementary inputs from other companies. The petrochemical industry, for example, cannot operate on an arm's-length basis. The advantages of planning are not simply an ideological matter: they arise from unavoidable technical features of the world, which cannot be reconciled with competition. Efficient economies are full of desirable market imperfections (of which the patent system is one); and it is dangerously simple to pretend that anti-trust policy should aim at the reimposition of competition regardless of its disadvantages.

Considerations of natural justice may also be against a whole-hearted competition-promotion policy. The free enterprise system will from time to time throw up victors. These victors will be dominant. But all they have done is to take the prizes which the system offers. It is not right to change the rules after the game has started—particularly not when it has been won. Unless, therefore, the victory has been achieved by foul means, the verdict should stand, even if it involves accepting the temporary dominance of a single company. There is, of course, a practical reason for this attitude, as well as a feeling for natural justice. The incentive system which makes companies strive to be efficient will not operate successfully for long if rewards once achieved are promptly removed.

The theory of competition in its simplest form assumes crudely that it is only by fear of failure or desire for financial success that managers can be successfully motivated. This is plainly a narrow view of human behaviour. Many people, not only inventors, work hard and ingeniously simply from a desire for craftsmanship and doing a good job for its own sake. Moreover, internal competition between individuals or decisions in a company can be a very good substitute for outside pressure. Management systems such as 'management-by-objectives' or more mundanely efficient budget setting and monitoring can have a substantial effect on efficiency. Of course, the vigour with which the management at the top of the company strives to introduce and operate systems of this kind will depend on what forces are operating to motivate them. But it is evident that the vast majority of people working in industry are motivated not by the direct impact of competition or even of financial gain/loss; and that therefore the effectiveness of these other sources of discipline and efficiency must be assessed before it can be assumed that the absence of competition is associated with lack of efficiency.

The main problem with a broad approach to anti-trust is that it provides no calculus for making a trade-off. That is, suppose a company to be dominant, and that consequently prices are somewhat higher than they would be in the absence of dominance. But the same dominance has the effect that the company is a good deal more successful in exports than it would otherwise have been. What are we to conclude? Does the export disadvantage outweigh the price disadvantage or not? How can we decide these things? There is at present no good answer to this question. However, it is plainly no answer to concentrate solely on the fact of dominance; condemn it as anti-competitive; and therefore seek its elimination. As well as this general difficulty, there are a number of major problems which recur in the practical operation of anti-trust policy when particular industrial situations are examined. A common feature of these problems is that there is a discrepancy between what the investigated company thinks is or was reasonable behaviour and what an investigating body thinks is advisable or permissible. This is the discrepancy between private and public good emerging in a new form. For example, a commercially minded company will make profit a major objective. Of course, the law constrains the unbridled pursuit of profit, by regulating such matters as conditions of employment, working conditions, and trade descriptions. And decent behaviour sets a limit where the law does not. Nevertheless, many things which a businessman would consider a cause for self-congratulation and applause will be suspect to a public body—not because profits *per se* are frowned on, but because such behaviour damages the public interest in some way. An increase in market share is admirable for the company and its shareholders; but if it is a step toward dominance, the rest of the community may condemn it.

4. The Evaluation of Business Practices and Industrial Structure

4.1. Profitability

For most businessmen profit is a major objective; and hence an important yardstick of success. From the point of view of the public interest, however, high profits can be a prima facie indication of the exercise of market power. The company may have deliberately set out, by market segmentation, advertising, the development of a brand name, or otherwise, to establish for itself a secure niche in the market, and hence premium profits. Such behaviour is admirable in terms of profitability and serving the shareholders' interests. It represents, however, a deliberate attempt to create quasi-monopoly and to enjoy the extra profits which such dominance allows. There will therefore be a conflict between the valuation of such behaviour and profits by business and the attitude of the community. What is more, governments have recently been at pains to encourage companies to set clear objectives, pursue the interests of the shareholders rather than of the management, and in general run their businesses in a purposeful and rational way instead of by allegedly sleepy and old-fashioned routines inherited from the inefficient past. It is odd and even offensive therefore for managers who have tried to adjust to these new standards, and have laboured through courses at government-subsidized management schools, to be told that their hard-won profits are a sign of vice rather than virtue.

Of course, profits may be, and often are, associated with wholly admirable qualities. Where a company operates in a competitive market, high profits must mean that the company has reduced costs and developed new products to satisfy that market. But there is no way of discovering from the figures alone whether a rate of return on capital employed of, say, 30 per cent is the reward of virtuous efficiency and risk-taking, or of monopolistic exploitation, or both. What matters is not what profits have been earned, but how they have been earned: and that is a matter for detailed investigation.

It follows that notions of 'reasonable', 'fair', or 'normal' profits are not very helpful. To compare a dominant firm's profit with the average for British industry as a whole, or of that particular industry, or of foreign competitors, only reveals the trivial arithmetic fact that they are higher or lower. If they are higher, no conclusions can be drawn as to whether they are deservedly so. If they are lower, this may reflect greater competition or greater inefficiency. If by normal is meant not average or typical, but rather the economist's technical notion of the level of profit required to retain capital in or attract it to that industry, then the question is at least being considered from a useful point of view—that is, what is the minimum profit which has to be offered to this company to induce it to do what the community wants? But very little help can be gained in answering this question from simple arithmetic comparisons. The answer depends on the amount of risk involved, the opportunity cost of the particular resources to the company and to the community, and a number of other factors which required detailed individual examination.

Finally, the accountancy problems associated with the use of rates of return on capital employed are formidable, and of more than merely technical importance. It is well known (see p. 71) that true profitability must be calculated by taking into account the duration and time profile of the profits or cash flows associated with a product, which is why the use of discounted cash flow techniques is encouraged. Rates of return as conventionally calculated are, however, defined simply as the ratio of net profits to net assets employed. Both the computation of profit and the valuation of net assets are notoriously difficult. The most striking example of this is the problem of taking into account inflation in the computation of profits. This is discussed in Appendix 3 to this chapter. Moreover, accountants and managers can differ quite legitimately as to the treatment of R & D, or depreciation, or stocks, and so on. These variations in treatment will produce quite different calculations for return on capital employed even where the actual experience and profitability of companies is identical. More important, the rate of return on capital employed is a snap-shot concept. Where, for example, a product has a pronounced life-cycle, to be told that in a particular year it has been highly profitable says nothing about its profitability over its whole life.

4.2. Advertising

For the businessman advertising is an important and often inseparable part of the marketing mix—particularly for consumer goods, but also in a less flamboyant way for producers' goods. To achieve sales by successful advertising is a common and generally admired characteristic of well-run businesses. The peculiar contribution of advertising is not simply that it communicates the existence and characteristics of the product to potential customers. More important, it can be used to distinguish the advertiser's product from the competition, establish its identity and brand name as separate and distinct, and thereby turn it into a branded product where higher profits can be earned than on an anonymous commodity. To establish a clientele which is loyal and captive gives a company to that extent an opportunity to raise prices and profits. This, or something like it, is plainly the purpose and effect of much advertising; which is not, of course, to say that any advertising is wholly effective in capturing and tying up any customer, nor that advertising can sell inherently unsatisfactory goods.

All this can look a great deal less admirable from the public policy point of view. In the first place, there is the problem of whether advertising is misleading. To some extent this is an easy matter to deal with—and nothing particularly to do with large or dominant firms. If an advertisement makes factual claims about the slimming properties of bread, or the performance of a stereo set, and those claims are false, plainly harm has been done, and the advertiser is culpable.

But very little advertising is straightforwardly of this kind. The real difficulty is that advertising may be used to persuade people to attach non-existent, ill-defined, but psychologically important characteristics to different versions of a product which are essentially the same, or at any rate differ much less than the advertising leads people to believe. Detergents are the classic case. The objection to this sort of situation is that although it may be quite harmless if a customer is induced to buy Brand A rather than Brand B (they are, after all, essentially the same), resources, in particular management time, will have been wasted in inducing the switch, to no purpose save that one company's sales increase at the cost of the other.

Other objections to advertising arise simply from its effectiveness, whether that involves misleading the customer or not. When advertising achieves its commercial purpose, it succeeds in appropriating a part of the market and attaching it more or less permanently to the advertised product. This means that higher profits can be earned, even after charging the costs of the advertising. This extra profit arises directly from the exercise of market power in the sub-market so created; and cannot in any way be attributed to any socially useful behaviour by the advertiser—whose only skill has been to devise a successful advertising campaign. What is more, advertising is often expensive. When it works, it creates barriers to competition. Its effect, therefore, is to limit threats to the position of the advertised product to rivals who have the time and money to break down the barriers.

Of course, the harm done by advertising will vary a great deal from case to case. Where there are a good number of competing firms, who incur small advertising expenditure, all at about the same level, very little harm will be done; although, of course, to the extent that advertising by competing firms does *not* over all affect their competitive position and the market shares then resources have been wasted in self-cancelling rivalrous effort.

Advertising can often be justified on more positive grounds. It is in the interests of both the company and the community that new products should be diffused rapidly through the community. It is difficult to know what the optimum rate should be; but it will be faster than that achieved by word of mouth. Advertising not only informs people that the product exists, but induces them to try it out. It is socially desirable that information on the range and quality of available products should be good; indeed, the simplest models of competition require that it be perfect. Moreover, the company will get its return more quickly if diffusion is fast. This is desirable for the company. From the social point of view, the faster the return if the product is successful, the more willing will companies be to risk money and effort in research and product development. R & D is risky enough anyway; it would be doubly so if advertising were not available to market any saleable products which are created.

4.3. Pricing

The question whether prices are reasonable is to a considerable extent the same as whether profits are acceptable. A price which results in an acceptable level of profits will itself be acceptable; and vice versa. All the same difficulties then arise in the evaluation of prices as were outlined in the section on profits.

But an additional set of problems arises when price/cost relationships are considered. In any business there will be substantial differences in the gross and net margins[4] earned from product to product at any moment of time. These differences result in part from the fact that products are at different stages in their life-cycle. Quite apart from this, it would be a miracle if every product were equally successful in every market. Hence it is an inevitable feature of business life that margins (or price/cost ratios) vary. Even where the company makes only a single product, or only the prices of a particular product are under scrutiny, that product will be sold in a variety of markets (for example, at home and for export); and the margins will differ.

This fact of life is for various reasons suspect. Elementary welfare theory suggests that price should be equal to marginal cost in all parts of the economy if welfare is to be maximized and resources correctly allocated (see Chapter 6). Leaving aside the problem that in particular inquiries the investigation deals not with all prices but with a particular price (which should not necessarily be equal to marginal cost unless all others are), and that average cost may well be different from marginal cost, this welfare proposition can be translated into the rough-and-ready criterion that prices should all bear the same relation to average cost; which is to say that price/cost ratios, or margins, should be uniform.

This criticism is concerned with resource allocation. The second main line of concern is to do with fairness, or distribution of income. If two products bear different margins, then the purchasers of one are paying more than the other for the same amount of resources. A very common situation is where the margins earned on export business are a good deal lower than those on home business. In this case, it is said, the home buyer is unfairly treated; the export buyer is being subsidized by the home buyer.

Again, criticism of this kind appears odd to the businessman not only because it is based on unfamiliar proportions of welfare economics, but also because it purports to criticize business practices which are both universal and unavoidable. The consequence of advocating uniform price/cost ratios seems to be that products should all be priced on a cost-plus basis. But this is an odd recommendation when at other times businessmen are asked to pursue rational pricing policies, and abandon ritualistic and mechanical procedures such as cost-plus.

It is plain, however, that the naive application of uniform price/cost ratios is wrong for more reasons than that it is impracticable or fails to fit with business reality. If it is accepted that there is no such thing as a standard 'reasonable profit' to be applied to all situations (because the reward to risk and enterprise must differ from case to case) then different margins on different products become quite acceptable. As for different margins on the same product in different markets, what needs to be considered is not whether price/cost ratios differ (which they do), but whether the profit earned over all in the product is reasonable or not. In many cases price-discrimination (which is a term synonymous with variations in price/cost ratios) is necessary if adequate profits are to be earned at all. How could

---

[4] 'Gross margin' means the price less direct costs (that is, the gross profit per unit) expressed as a percentage of the price. Net margin means the price less both direct and indirect costs (the net profit per unit) expressed as a percentage of the price.

airlines cover their costs unless they charged first-class passengers more than
the difference in the cost of providing first-class seats can justify? An imposition of standard margins may mean that the producer standardizes on the
high-margin market and abandons the low-margin market completely—
because that is the most profitable way of adjusting. But in that case resource
allocation is made worse, because the low-margin market where price was
close to cost is abandoned; and the output of the product is even further
away from the optimum than previously.

4.4. Efficiency

It would be nice to be able to solve the problem of whether high profits were
justified or not by assessing whether the company that earned them was
efficient or not. High profits cannot themselves be taken as an index of
efficiency, because their source may just as well be market power.

But estimates of efficiency are extremely difficult to make, and very difficult
to know what to do with when you have got them. One measure of efficiency
is units of output per unit of input—or productivity. Static labour productivity is quite easy to calculate when you can count the output in physical
units (apples) and the input in terms of physical units (men). But there are
severe difficulties when there are a number of different kinds of products
(apples and pears) and of labour input (skilled and unskilled labour). You
cannot use market prices to weigh the different products/inputs, because
those market prices themselves reflect market power; and all you end up
with is profitability per unit of input. The situation is worse when the value
of the capital input has to be calculated; machines are even more difficult to
count than men. And all these problems are multiplied when comparisons
are made over time to estimate improvements in efficiency, because the
nature of the product and the inputs will change, and the valuation measure
be further distorted by differential inflation.

Suppose heroically that these problems have been solved, and that productivity is estimated to be currently at such and such a level, and to have
improved at such and such a rate over the last ten years. It is very difficult to
know whether this performance is creditable or not. If the company were
just one among many, it might be possible to compare the company with
the average, or the best, of the industry. But the characteristic of dominant
firms is that they are often the only, or only significant, member of the
industry and that there is, therefore, nobody else to compare them with.
In that case, it may be possible to make comparisons with other similar
companies in other countries. But international comparisons are very
difficult to make in a way which is fair to the company concerned. Exchange
rate problems add a new set of difficulties to the valuation of inputs and outputs. Different countries have more or less skilled work-forces—and hence
differences in production efficiency cannot fairly be imputed to the company
alone. And so on.

These problems arise not only with those aspects of efficiency which are
in principle quantifiable, but also with the whole range of more general
company characteristics which consideration of efficiency should cover. A

company has a record of high and increasing exports; or has steadily improved its production process by research and innovation. But should it not have done even better? How can we tell what it would have achieved in a more competitive environment?

Even if we were able to attribute high profits to superior efficiency, problems remain. Should not the company have passed on more of its cost savings in lower prices? Thereby the consumer would have been benefited directly. Demand for the product would have been increased, and resources diverted to the efficient manufacture of the product. Alternatively, it may be that a high price/profit will attract resources to that activity more effectively, because capital is drawn to the most profitable opportunities.

4.5. Equity

An attractive anti-trust policy, following the arguments of the first part of this chapter, is to make sure that companies cannot earn profits illegitimately —for example, by vertical foreclosure, predatory price cutting, or purchase of patents; and then let them set whatever prices the market will bear, and enjoy the resulting profits.

It must be admitted, however, that this policy may result in unacceptably high profits. Just as in the case of personal incomes it is almost universally recognized that the taxation system should limit the take-home salary of the most successful to below what they would earn in a free-market situation, so too certain levels of profit are simply unacceptable, even if properly and openly earned within the rules. For example, the producers of a life-saving drug should not be allowed to charge what the market will bear when that means charging a user his whole earnings to save his life. Even where morality restrains companies from such extremes, very high rates of return by comparison with those earned elsewhere may be unacceptable, both because they represent too high a reward to the producer, and because they result from too high a price to the customer.

It must be recognized, therefore, that a regulatory body must from time to time criticize and reduce profits simply on the grounds that they are inequitably high.

5. Conclusion

The scope and effectiveness of anti-trust policy is necessarily limited. Even if it is possible to identify successfully what is wrong with an industry, there may be very little one can do about it. It is often very difficult and damaging to promote competition by breaking up large firms—economies of scale are lost, management morale shattered, and the new smaller firms may still collude and fix prices as effectively as did their parent. Regulating prices and profits is possible but it is very difficult to increase exports, or investment, or R & D if those are the areas in which you believe that the monopolist has been inefficient.

If anti-trust cannot do the job, then other instruments of economic policy will have to be used. Some of these may be general—price codes; export subsidies; investment grants and tax allowances—and designed to change the behaviour of all companies, large or small, dominant or not. A catch-all remedy for situations where private enterprise does not serve the public interest is nationalization. Whether the problem is to do with employment, or investment, or industrial relations, the Government can put it right—or at least believe that it can—by taking direct control of the industry, and removing certain of its decisions from the influence of market forces.

Anti-trust policy must therefore be seen as part and part only of industrial policy. It is one option from a range which extends from whole-hearted *laissez-faire* to centralized State planning. Different diseases will require different remedies.

Appendix 1: The Restrictive Trade Practices Court 'Gateways' and 'Tailpiece'

(a) That the restriction is reasonably necessary having regard to the character of the goods to which it applies, to protect the public against injury (whether to persons or to premises) in connection with the consumption, installation or use of those goods;
(b) That the removal of the restriction would deny to the public as purchasers, consumers or users of any goods other specific and substantial benefits or advantages enjoyed or likely to be enjoyed by them as such, whether by virtue of the restriction itself or of any arrangements or operations resulting therefrom;
(c) That the restriction is reasonably necessary to counteract measures taken by any one person not party to the agreement with a view to preventing or restricting competition in or in relation to the trade or business in which the persons party thereto are engaged;
(d) That the restriction is reasonably necessary to enable the persons party to the agreement to negotiate fair terms for the supply of goods to, or the acquisition of goods from, any one person not party thereto who controls a preponderant part of the trade or business of acquiring or supplying such goods, or for the supply of goods to any person not party to the agreement and not carrying on such a trade or business who, either alone or in combination with any other such person, controls a preponderant part of the market for such goods;
(e) That, having regard to the conditions actually obtaining or reasonably foreseen at the time of the application, the removal of the restriction would be likely to have a serious and persistent adverse effect on the general level of unemployment in an area, or in areas taken together, in which a substantial proportion of the trade or industry to which the agreement relates is situated;
(f) That having regard. to the conditions actually obtaining or reasonably foreseen at the time of the application, the removal of the restriction would be likely to cause a reduction in the volume or earnings of the export business of the United Kingdom or in relation to the whole export business of the United Kingdom or in relation to the whole business (including export business) of the said trade or industry; or
(g) That the restriction is reasonably required for purposes connected with the maintenance of any other restriction accepted by the parties, whether under the same agreement or under any other agreement between them, being a restriction which is found by the Court not to be contrary to the public interest upon grounds other than those specified in this paragraph, or has been so found in previous proceedings before the Court.

(h) That the restriction does not directly or indirectly restrict or discourage competition to any material degree in any relevant trade or industry and is not likely to do so.

The 'tailpiece' states that the Court must be 'further satisfied that the restriction is not unreasonable having regard to the balance between these circumstances and any detriment to the public or to persons not party to the agreement . . . resulting or likely to result from the operation of the restrictors'.

Appendix 2: European Economic Community: Articles 85 and 86

Articles 85 & 86, Treaty Establishing the European Economic Community

ARTICLE 85

1. The following shall be deemed to be incompatible with the Common Market and shall hereby be prohibited: any agreement between enterprises, any decisions by associations of enterprises and any concerted practices which are likely to affect trade between the Member States and which have as their object or result the prevention, restriction or distortion of competition within the Common Market, in particular those consisting in:

(a) The direct or indirect fixing of purchase or selling prices or of any other trading conditions;

(b) the limitation or control of production, markets, technical development or investment;

(c) market-sharing or the sharing of sources of supply;

(d) the application to parties to transactions of unequal terms in respect of equivalent supplies, thereby placing them at a competitive disadvantage; or

(e) the subjecting of the conclusion of a contract to the acceptance by a party of additional supplies which, either by their nature or according to commercial usage, have no connection with the subject of such contract.

2. Any agreements or decisions prohibited pursuant to this Article shall be null and void.

3. Nevertheless, the provisions of paragraph 1 may be declared inapplicable in the case of:

—any agreements or classes of agreements between enterprises,

—any decisions or classes of decisions by associations of enterprises, and

—any concerted practices or classes of concerted practices

which contribute to the improvement of the production or distribution of goods or to the promotion of technical or economic progress while reserving to users an equitable share in the profit resulting therefrom, and which:

(a) neither impose on the enterprises concerned any restrictions not indispensable to the attainment of the above objectives;

(b) nor enable such enterprises to eliminate competition in respect of a substantial proportion of the goods concerned.

ARTICLE 86

To the extent to which trade between any Member States may be affected thereby, action by one or more enterprises to take improper advantage of a dominant position within the Common Market or within a substantial part of it shall be deemed to be incompatible with the Common Market and shall hereby be prohibited.

Such improper practices may, in particular, consist in:

(a) the direct or indirect imposition of any inequitable purchase or selling prices or of any other inequitable trading conditions;

(b) the limitation of production, markets or technical development to the prejudice of consumers;

(c) the application to parties to transactions of unequal terms in respect of equivalent supplies, thereby placing them at a competitive disadvantage; or

(d) the subjecting of the conclusion of a contract to the acceptance, by a party, of additional supplies which, either by their nature or according to commercial usage, have no connection with the subject of such contract.

Approved March 25, 1957
Effective January 1, 1958

Appendix 3: Inflation and Profits

Traditional accountancy uses historic costs as the basis for the computation of profits —in particular, for the calculation of depreciation and the treatment of stocks. A machine costing £10,000 with a life of ten years will therefore be written off to profits at a rate of £1,000 p.a. Similarly, the profit and loss account for a particular year will be charged with the stocks brought forward from the previous year at the cost of acquiring them, and credited with stocks carried forward on the same basis.

So long as there is no, or little, inflation, this works reasonably well. But suppose that prices/costs in general are rising at 20 per cent a year. This means that the machine which cost £10,000 this year will cost £62,000 to replace in ten years. Since the depreciation charge is designed to recover sufficient from gross profits to pay for replacement, it is plain that £1,000 p.a. over ten years will be grossly inadequate for this purpose. And any profits computed after this inadequate depreciation charge will be grossly overstated.

The problem with stocks can be illustrated as follows. Suppose a company start the year with £10,000 worth of new materials. At the end of the year it holds precisely the same quantity, but the price level has risen by 20 per cent. The charge for the year for raw material usage will be as follows:

stock brought forward	£10,000
add purchases during year	£50,000
	£60,000
less stock carried forward	£12,000
	£48,000

Since the company ended up with the same stocks as it started with the correct charge is at least £50,000—that is, the materials purchased during the year. But the charge as computed here is reduced by the fictitious profits of £2,000 arising from the revaluation of stocks at the new higher price level. No real profit has been earned; indeed, the main effect is unfavourable since the company has £2,000 more tied up in working capital.

Although these examples show clearly that there is something wrong with using historic cost figures, it is not nearly so clear what should be done instead. There are both theoretical and practical difficulties in deciding between inflation accounting based on replacement cost or on a general index of inflation such as the retail price index. And the distortions relate not only to depreciation and stocks, but to such matters as net monetary liabilities and the valuation of assets, the treatment of which can materially affect the computation of profit and of capital employed.

Bibliography

SECTION A. THE LAW

The relevant *United Kingdom* legislation is as follows:

[1] Fair Trading Act, 1973.
[2] Resale Price Maintenance Act, 1964.
[3] Restrictive Trade Practices Acts, 1956 and 1968.
Details of decisions of the Restrictive Trade Practices Court can be found in [4] the Law Reports of Restrictive Trade Practices Cases.
[5] The Reports of the Monopolies and Mergers Commission give a full account of the arguments and conclusions of Monopolies Commission cases.
[6] The Annual Reports of the Registrar of Restrictive Trade Practices, now succeeded by the Director General of Fair Trading, give a good general account of anti-trust policy for the preceding year.
The position in the *United States* can be seen most easily from [7] Neale, A. D. *The Anti-Trust Law of the United States* (Cambridge University Press, 1960). For the E.E.C., see [8] Ballamy and Child *Common Market Law of Competition* (Sweet & Maxwell, 1973).

SECTION B. GENERAL

The best general introductions are:
[9] HUNTER, A. *Competition and the Law* (George Allen and Unwin, 1966).
[10] ROWLEY, C. *Anti-Trust and Economic Efficiency* (Macmillan, 1973).
For a book of readings from the theoretical and applied literature see:
[11] HUNTER, A. *Monopoly and Competition* (Penguin, 1969).

More detailed books include:
[12] ROWLEY, C. *The British Monopolies Commission* (George Allen and Unwin, 1966).
[13] SUTHERLAND, A. *The Monopolies Commission in Action* (Cambridge University Press, 1969).
[14] SWANN D. *et al. Competition in British Industry* (George Allen and Unwin, 1974).
[15] KORAH, V. *Competition Law of Britain and the EEC* (Penguin, 1974).
[16] HEATH, J. (ed.) *International Conference on Monopolies, Mergers and Restrictive Practices* (Dept. of Trade and Industry, H.M.S.O., 1971).
[17] GEORGE, K. and JOLL, C. (eds.) *Competition Policy in the U.K. and the E.E.C.* (Cambridge University Press, 1975).

For analysis of the causes of mergers and take-overs see:
[18] NEWBOULD, G. *Management and Merger Activity* (Guthstead, 1970).

More advanced are:

[19] SINGH, A. *Take-Overs* (University of Cambridge, Dept. of Applied Economics, Monograph 19, Cambridge University Press, 1971).
[20] KUEHN, D. *Take-Overs in the Theory of the Firm* (Macmillan, 1975).

Finally, the further reading for Chapter 3 contains many books on other specific topics referred to above, in particular cost structure, advertising, pricing, and company objectives.

17

Medium-Term Policies

D. K. STOUT

1. The Medium-Term Perspective

1.1. Introduction

In this chapter we shall be looking at the policies of Government towards private industry to try to achieve a less dismal rate of economic growth. The central difficulties are to reduce the pain and dislocation attaching to the needed faster movement of productive resources between industries and between firms, and to help to organize and encourage these movements.

The conditions of 'equilibrium' growth in a long-term steady sense can be described without reference to changes in industrial structure. As was described in Chapter 8, the 'growth of productive potential' can be derived on the supply side from the rate of growth of the labour force and the stock of capital, together with an assumed independent factor, the rate of technical progress. On the demand side, the policy task might then be seen as the maintenance of a balanced growth of consumption and investment so that neither growing unemployment nor excessive pressure on resources results in the long term.

However, the growth of output per head that this implies may be unsatisfactorily low compared with the 'abnormal' rate that can be achieved for many decades on end in an industrial (or rapidly industrializing) economy in which the allocation of resources between industries is rapidly altering, and in which there are continuous increases in plant and company concentration, in product specialization, and in average closeness of approach in each industry to current best practices of production. Models of such economies (when they work with equations covering the whole economy) often include a residual trend term which describes, without explaining, this vital element of growth that depends on changes in industrial structure.

Rapid growth requiring structural change has important consequences for other facets of economic policy. For example, such structural change may add to some of the inflationary pressures described in Chapter 7. Or the Government may find itself locked in, in the longer term, to a stable framework of policies (on regional incentives and aid to investment, for example) which reduces the freedom of manœuvre to match instruments to short-term policy targets.

In fact, growth policies over the past fifteen years have been unsuccessful and discontinuous, both because industrial intervention is a political issue, and because of the disappointment which has so far attended each endeavour. There has also been an undercurrent of tension between the competition policy described in Chapter 16 (which is largely indifferent or antipathetic to industrial planning) and medium-term growth policy.

1.2. The Medium-Term Problem

The main problems are the same today as they were in 1960, when attention in Britain first began to fasten upon the slow rate of economic growth. High regional employment still inhibits the redeployment of both capital and labour; re-equipment and the efficient application of new techniques proceeds slowly; products are too heterogeneous; industrial relations are damaged by suspicion, conflict, and the abuse of power; and the confidence and expected profitability required for new industrial capacity remain depressed. Uncertainty about the long-term growth of demand, about the balance between competition and concentration, about the sources of industrial finance, and about the extent of public supervision and control over the private sector are all greater than ever before.

We know for certain hardly any more today than we did fifteen years ago about the effect of general economic conditions upon the rate of growth of industrial productivity. Does a higher ratio of wages to profits help or hinder? There are arguments on both sides. On the one hand, labour saving is encouraged; on the other, the supply of finance for investment and the expected return are reduced. Is it better that the pressure of demand on capacity should be high (so that investment is encouraged) or low (so that underemployed factors of production are shaken out)? Is higher growth associated with more stability or less? (Industrial opinion insists more, but international evidence suggests less.) Is there more to be gained from information-sharing than from competition? Is the chance that an indicative plan will fail, create disillusionment, and inhibit future growth, greater than the chance that it will succeed and raise future self-justifying expectations? Is all that is needed for this second result the power to vary the exchange rate which we denied ourselves in 1965? Does the trick of faster economic growth depend upon a multitude of microeconomic measures to reproduce in unregenerate plants and firms the practices of the most progressive? Or is it mainly a question for social and industrial psychologists—a matter of our attitudes to each other at work and towards individual effort; and of our responses to the threat of change?

The U.K. industrial economy has for decades been growing at about the same rate as the U.S., but, of course, at a very much lower *level* of productivity. Partly because of the smaller size of our market, because of the limits to specialization imposed by a large population of establishments and by product heterogeneity, and also because of lower relative wage costs and technical information lags, we advance at a greater (if unchanging) distance than the U.S. below the moving horizon of highest obtainable productivity within individual industries.

Other relatively fast-growing economies, like the German, the Japanese, and the French, have been growing for some time at 'abnormal' rates: that is to say, they are in transition from low-level productivity to the moving frontier of minimum feasible distance behind best practice. (This minimum feasible distance is itself lower, the higher the rate of growth, because more rapid investment permits a higher proportion of the capital stock to be very new.) In Figure 17.1 the problem for the U.K. can be described as to discover and apply industrial policies that make it possible to shift over, say, a generation from the low-level line LL to the high level line HL, transitionally enjoying the 'abnormal' growth rate AB which Germany, for example (whose *broad* industrial composition is quite similar to ours), is experiencing now.

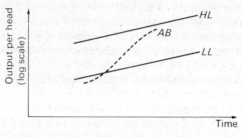

FIG. 17.1

There is nothing very new about this approach to the industrial productivity problem, and in this very limited description it is based too simply upon a 'vintage' theory of growth which relates average industrial productivity to the share of output produced using new techniques, embodied in recent capital stock. There have been special circumstances in other economies which do not obtain in Britain, like the scope for large movements of labour from low-productivity agriculture into secondary industry, and the past success of *dirigiste* planning in France. It remains to be discovered how relevant this structural view is; how far it explains the across-the-board differences between industrial productivity growth here and in Germany, for example; what obstacles prevent the more rapid movement of resources into relatively high productivity industries, firms, plants, and products; and what policies can best overcome the obstacles (see [30]).

1.3. The Spectrum of Policy Options

The Government can influence industry in a wide variety of ways ranging from general exhortation to selective discretionary *quid pro quo* action; from seeking to make market mechanisms more competitive (so that individual choices determine the allocation of resources), though Planning Agreements and participation by the National Enterprise Board all the way to nationalization (Chapter 18).

In a mixed economy there are fields of decision in which social welfare is likely to be increased if free consumer choice is permitted to determine what goods are produced and in what ways, subject to qualifications about the distribution of income; while there are other allocative decisions where social benefits and costs diverge widely from private benefits and costs so that either goods and services need to be produced and distributed by the State, or rewards, penalties, and prohibitions devised which will change resource allocation.

The Government is the ultimate custodian of the public interest, and can and does bring its influence to bear in a number of ways. The main ones, with examples, some of which we have already seen, are these:

(a) as a customer of the private sector, e.g. buying pharmaceuticals for the National Health Service;

(b) as an employer, e.g. paying incomes to workers in the electricity industry, in competition with private employers;

(c) as the framer of tax and subsidy laws, setting the framework within which individual decisions are taken, e.g. determining the relative burden of indirect tax upon value added in food, electrical appliances, and construction; or the relative cost of employing workers inside and outside the Development Areas;

(d) as the authority prohibiting by law, for example, the pollution of rivers by industrial waste;

(e) as the agent ultimately responsible for the level of demand and employment, through its control over such instruments as the rate of exchange, the budget balance, and the quantity of money;

(f) as the collector and disseminator of statistical indicators and forecasts likely to influence industrial decisions—everything from the Public Expenditure White Paper to figures of monthly car registrations.

The extend of the Government's influence in all these respects tends to increase over time. But there are also other powers, sometimes active, sometimes latent, which can be in the industrial policy armoury. The Government may:

(g) make commitments (in return for reciprocal commitments) to instil the confidence required if faster economic growth is not to be frustrated by failures to invest or retrain; or in pursuit of a voluntary pay or prices policy;

(h) channel savings to industry, through the tax system or by borrowing, to restore liquidity or to augment the investment funds available from the private capital market;

(i) influence the quantity and quality of investment decisions through *discretionary* controls over industrial pricing; or

(j) intervene directly to change the structure of an industry (its concentration, product diversity, capital intensity, management span of control, rate of diffusion of new techniques, and economies of scale at plant level) either be encouraging mergers, providing conditional capital or aid, entering into planning agreements, or taking over a particular firm in whole or in part.[1]

---

[1] The strategic importance of this type of government influence in 1974–6 is developed in [19] and [8]. A much earlier and at the time isolated example was the assistance provided to redundant workers and compensation for the scrapping of obsolescent equipment in the cotton textile industry in the late 1950s, following a decision of the Restrictive Practices Court which ended a pricing agreement in yarn spinning.

In some of these roles the Government acts directly and selectively on economic decisions; in others it sets broader conditions within which resources are allocated by the market. They do not simply provide two alternative routes to the same set of industrial policy objectives. The decision how far to try to co-ordinate actions under these several headings into a policy for industry is largely a political one.

1.4. The Recent History of Medium-Term Industrial Policy

By 1960 it was becoming clear that the faster growth of most other industrial economies was not a temporary result of post-war reconstruction. In Britain both price stability and the balance of payments were progressively undermined by its slow growth of industrial productivity relative to other countries.[2] This inability to match their growth and productivity entailed a progressive undermining of Britain's ability to compete profitably in international markets, and a consequent long-term decline in the U.K.'s balance of payments position. Each cyclical recovery was therefore likely to be cut short by earlier deeper policy-induced unemployment to restore the balance of payments at the fixed rate of exchange.

Investment and the movement of resources into the areas of strongest demand were sluggish in the upswings. Perhaps what was needed was the confident expectation that faster growth was going to take place if the constraints on the supply side were removed.

In its Fourth (and final) Report, the Council on Prices, Productivity and Incomes urged in 1961 that a planning institution should be set up along French lines to collate the plans of the main sectors, enabling a consensus to be formed about a higher rather than a lower growth rate, with the exchange of information leading to simultaneous and mutually justifying commitments to investment. There might be, it said, a 'projection of the extent to which productivity in the national aggregate may be expected to advance' whose compilation would be based upon open discussion. There would be the further task of 'persuading those in responsible positions to accept the projection as a guide, not only in the interests of those whom they represent but also of the community as a whole. This calls for a high degree of leadership, both on the part of the Government and of both sides of industry' ([16], paras. 48, 67, and 68).

This report heralded the institution of the National Economic Development Council later in that year. The Council's first main business was to consider a feasibility study of faster growth prepared by its Office [27]. This was closely followed by the 'Orange Book'—a set of recommendations to the three parties to the N.E.D.C. (unions, management, and Government) on overcoming the obstacles to faster growth [6].

---

[2] Although industrial productivity growth has tended to rise between 1950 and 1973, it has done so by much less than for our E.E.C. neighbours. From 1955 to 1972 the U.K. growth of industrial output was less than half the rate achieved by the Six. And between 1960 and 1971 real GDP per head rose by 79 per cent in the U.K., but by 140 per cent in the E.E.C.

Looking back at the Orange Book, *Conditions Favourable to Faster Growth*, its eight sets of prescriptions, arranged by chapter, fell into three categories which have changed very little; though the weight attached by successive governments to the different topics has varied, and some new topics of a more structural kind would now be added. One category comprised the setting-up of a framework within which private decisions are freely taken. Here belonged the tax recommendations: a neutral V.A.T. in place of profits tax and purchase tax; a wealth tax; a Swedish-style Tax Reserve Scheme to encourage the rephasing of investment over the cycle; and social security contributions based upon payroll. Here too were demand management recommendations (a steady increase to a much higher level of employment over a four-year period). The second category contained measures designed to overcome a key constraint on faster sustained growth; measures designed to improve the balance of payments; and the recommendation that there should be some sort of (unspecified) agreed policy to moderate the increase of incomes. The third category consisted of the long-term changes in policies directly and specifically calculated (whatever their other advantages) to increase economic growth. These were increased education and training; measures to increase the mobility of workers and capital through retraining, and regional policies; and the identification of Government, trade unions, and management with 'an agreed growth objective', the achievement of which could be seen to depend upon their joint efforts.

In 1964 the economic work on indicative planning was taken out of the N.E.D.C. and carried on in a new Ministry, the Department of Economic Affairs, which consulted with the Economic Development Committees for particular industries (the little Neddies) about the consequences of a predetermined growth target for individual industries' output, investment, manpower, productivity growth, exports, and imports. What seemed to have been added by this change of place and status was a more credible commitment by Government to macroeconomic policies which would sustain the planned growth rate. This credibility was fragile and the National Plan to increase output by 25 per cent between 1964 and 1970 was shattered within ten moths of its publication by the measures taken to deal with the sterling crisis in July 1966.

There followed a period of growing preoccupation with the immediate problems of inflation and the the balance of payments. After the long-delayed devaluation of October 1967 the overriding concern of policy was to manage the economy in such a way that devaluation would work. Without much heart for it, the D.E.A. (and, after its demise, the Treasury) in consultation with the National Economic Development Office prepared and revised another economic assessment, *The Task Ahead*, describing the possible use of resources from 1967 to 1972 [4], [39]. This was confessedly not a plan, but the basis for consultation between the Government and both sides of industry about 'major issues of economic policy'. It looked at the prospects for output, investment, employment, and the balance of payments within a 'wedge' of two alternative growth rates. Industrial detail was sketchy.

At the same time, the Government was becoming more deeply involved than it had been since 1950 in highly selective industrial intervention and assistance, through the Industrial Reorganization Corporation, and through sponsoring Departments like MinTech., to help bring about increases in concentration under efficient management, and to encourage innovation.

The need for 'more concentration and rationalization to promote the greater efficiency and international competitiveness of British industry' was stressed in the White Paper which introduced the I.R.C. [18]. To act as a catalyst for industrial restructuring the I.R.C. was given wide powers, a great deal of freedom from government departments, and what at the time seemed large financial resources (£150m.) to be used as a revolving credit, not as a fund for permanent equity holdings. The main *raison d'être* of the I.R.C. was the sound one that, left to themselves, market forces had not led to anything like a rapid enough elimination of inefficient and out-of-date industrial organizations. But it acted also as the Government's intermediary in supporting prestigious individual companies (like Rolls-Royce and Cammell Laird) and in representing a British interest in cases of expansion by multinationals (like S.K.F. and Phillips) in the U.K. Its principal functions were none the less to give financial support to well-managed companies, to tie assistance to managerial reforms (Davy Ashmore), and to steer structural changes by *ad hoc* encouragement of specific mergers, like the favouring of G.E.C. over Plessey in the bidding for Elliott Automation.

I.R.C. lent to newly merged companies (like B.L.M.C.) and to individual companies for modernization (as in the Textile Re-equipment Scheme). It guaranteed future funds following mergers, and bought shares on the market to influence bid situations. It was perhaps most successful in reducing the population of small firms (in the textile industry, for example) and less so where units were already large but increasingly uncompetitive (as in ship-building, motors, and aircraft). What was lacking was a clear view of conditions for increased efficiency other than the obvious one of economies of scale. After an attempt at disengagement in 1970 and 1971 the Government of the day has been drawn increasingly into the affairs of some key firms, usually because of the imminence of their financial failure. The industrial policy of the 1974 Labour Government was to participate, along with the work force, much more directly in decision-taking at the level of the individual large firm.

Meanwhile, the idea of consultative medium-term reviews of growth prospects, which began with the N.E.D.C. Growth Study 1961–6 [27] has not quite evaporated. The last review was a N.E.D.O. responsibility [29]: again with two alternative sets of assumptions about over-all growth provided by the Treasury (3½ and 5 per cent), covering 1971–7 and published in 1973. This was avowedly an Industrial Review, covering only those eleven industries still represented by E.D.C.s. It showed the feasibility, on the supply side, of what seemed (until the energy crisis) a moderate rate of growth, starting from a year of quite high under-use of resources. And it presented the obstacles, industry by industry, that would have to be overcome in the illustrative case of very high (5 per cent) growth. Eleven companion volumes set out for each industry demand and output projections, resource requirements, and balance of payment effects for the two illustrative economy growth rates; described the (usually very small) expected effect of entry into the E.E.C.; and made policy recommendations to the firms in the industry and to Government on how to improve industrial performance.

Successive reviews have moved away from trying to make optimistic assumptions about over-all economic growth come true by means of the favourable influence of these assumptions upon decisions to invest and recruit manpower. The trend has been towards investigating the changing shares of different sectors in resource use, and towards a more detailed consideration of the reasons for the low underlying growth of industrial productivity. This development is unlikely to be reversed, since the long-term redistribution of income away from corporate profits and the increase in the share of government expenditure and transfer payments have reinforced the dependence of individual companies upon the Government of the day.

At the same time, in the field of prices and incomes, there has been the notable development, since the summer of 1972, of high-level bargaining, involving simultaneous policy commitments of greater or lesser strength by Government and T.U.C., with and without the C.B.I. as a third party.[3]

A natural extension of this from 1975 onwards is the attempt at the comprehensive and co-ordinated planning of balanced recovery to try to secure the moderation of inflation, the recovery of employment, and the flow of resources into investment and the balance of payments over the next five years. So far as industrial productivity growth is concerned, the approach that is gradually being developed is a much more piecemeal, industry-by-industry one, seeking out the requirements for higher average performance within each important industry and with lessons learnt from one industrial situation applied to others with similar characteristics [8].

2. The Nature and Performance of Industry Policy in the U.K.

2.1. The Meaning of Medium-Term Policy

Medium-term economic policy is an unfortunate phrase. It suggests a distinction which is false between policies with only temporary consequences and policies with only delayed ones (see Budd in [9]). Almost all policies have longer-run or lagged effects which must be allowed for. Tax relief for capital spending, for example, has a small effect in the year it is imposed, but a large effect in year two. Suppose that in the first year excess capacity in the capital goods industry is expected. Suppose, further, that an attempt is made to set the investment incentive at a level which will, from the first year, maintain investment demand at the full capacity level. The relief that was just sufficient in the first year would tend to stimulate too much investment in the second year and have to be reduced, only to be increased again the

---

[3] Mr. Heath's Downing Street and Chequers talks on Pay and Prices and the unsuccessful attempt to reach a *quid pro quo* agreement incorporating voluntary restraint are described from the T.U.C.'s viewpoint in [38]. In 1974 the contents of Mr. Healey's two budgets may be compared with the T.U.C.'s published Budget recommendations. The Social Contract proposals were published by the T.U.C. in September 1974, and the £6 limit to pay increases, endorsed by the T.U.C., in a Government White Paper in summer 1975.

following year with, possibly, ever-increasing fluctuations in policy until the measure broke down. It is the essence of medium-term economic policy to take account of the later effects from the outset, and to try to settle incentives for considerably more than one year ahead.

Most industrial policies tend to have their main effects many years ahead. Furthermore, they may have almost no influence if it is expected that the policies will change. Large payments of the Regional Employment Premium can have had little effect upon employment in the Development Areas from the moment that the Conservative Government announced its intention of phasing out R.E.P. in September 1974, until its reprieve announced in February 1974.[4]

Medium-term industrial policy consists of a framework of conditions which will not be varied unpredictably, and hence is of special relevance to investment decisions which have long-term consequences, to location decisions, to research and development activity, and to training and choice of occupation. Because of policy conflicts (for example, between job security in depressed regions and the enhancement of economic growth by the movement of resources into expanding industries), medium-term policies ought to set out the priorities between the different objectives (or the weights implicity attached to them in the attempt to maximize social welfare). The probable changes in policies which might follow if economic conditions should deteriorate in important but unpredicted ways, should be described, provided that the effect of doing so will not be to make that deterioration more likely. For instance, if a Government was to announce that should inflation persist at a certain rate beyond a certain date a freeze would be imposed upon all wages, the announcement would itself make the unpleasant contingency it sought to cover more likely. If, on the other hand, the Government announced that a freeze would be imposed only upon those wages which had risen by more than the past rate of inflation, while increases might be permitted to those who had settled for less than this, then—whatever the demerits of such a policy—a *lower* rate of increase of wages would be likely than would occur in ignorance of the Government's intention. In general, selective rather than general policies are required to achieve this, as the above example illustrates.

2.2. The Set-back to Indicative Planning in Britain

If the slow growth of GDP in Britain was because of the continuous disappointment of demand expectations through the combined effects of caution (of investors, principally) in the face of uncertainty, then the preparation and contemplation of a detailed plan showing the feasibility of a higher growth rate than before could lead to a set of simultaneous decisions which make this growth possible. But it is not enough to ask everybody what they would do if they believed in, say, 4 per cent growth; and to show that, under favourable assumptions about the balance of payments consequences and the

---

[4] An incentive designed to affect the *timing* of a decision—to rephase investment within the cycle, for example—is more likely to be effective if its duration is specifically announced as being limited.

movement of manpower, these hypothetical actions could lead to 4 per cent growth.

The main advantage of this kind of indicative plan is the steadier and higher rate of industrial investment that may result from more confident expectations. But investment may languish in spite of the plan. If this is not to happen, the government needs to do two things. First, it should state the measures it is prepared to take to ensure that expansion is not halted by a worsening balance of payments. In fact it has to convince investors that the *only* thing that stands in the way of faster growth is their own timidity—not a very plausible proposition. Second, it has to be able to persuade or oblige firms to act upon those changed expectations. There were no *directives* for actions by firms in the 1965 National Plan. And there is a logical difficulty about expecting firms to act voluntarily in accordance with such a plan.

A simplifying selection out of the possible future states of the environment has to be made to reduce the number of paths and the corresponding sets of hypothetical questions to a manageable level [26]. In the case of the National Plan this reduction was down to a single path. Since one does not know what confidence is attached by industrialists to the chosen outcome, one cannot know for sure how they will behave. All that is known for certain is that producers are likely to make more flexible decisions than would be optimal if they believed that the plan was self-fulfilling. This almost certainly implies less investment, postponed investment, less product specialization, and less training and manpower planning.

It is a pity that the idea of consultative industrial planning across the board should have received such a severe set-back because of the mistakes that were made by rushing the National Plan in 1965 and expecting too much from the 'virtuous circle' theory of growth. With hindsight, the main mistakes are apparent. First, the target growth rate was too high. Since Neddy had chosen 4 per cent in its 1961–6 study, the D.E.A. did not want to aim at less.[5] Second, only one growth rate was considered. But a lower one alongside might have defeated one of the objects of the exercise, which was to raise growth by raising expectations of growth. Third, the increase in the volume of exports required to maintain the balance of payments was $5\frac{1}{4}$ per cent p.a. The rate of growth in the five years before 1964 had been about 3 per cent, and an optimistic view of trends in world trade might have raised this figure to 4 per cent for the Plan period. But $5\frac{1}{4}$ per cent was the needed increase, and the document observed baldly that 'this figure has been taken for the purposes of the Plan' [3, Ch. 7, para. 65]. In justification, the planners offered two straws of comfort: 'many of our competitors have expanded exports considerably faster' (which was irrelevant) and 'the Industrial Inquiry has

[5] Neddy settled on 4 per cent in order to bring out the problems of faster growth. Since the rate achieved from 1950 to 1960 was 2·6 per cent, this might have been done by the choice of, say, $3\frac{1}{2}$ per cent. However, the figure was to some extent a compromise between the T.U.C.'s desire to countenance as high a growth rate as people could bring themselves to swallow and the Federation of British Industry's equally understandable interest in a rate not too far from what was being used by the corporate planners in their own forecasting. Neither of these reasons ought to have been allowed to influence the D.E.A.'s choice of a target growth rate.

shown that industries themselves believe an increase of this order to be attainable' (which meant little more than that if the export demand was there it could be supplied).[6] The paragraph concluded 'the task will not be easy and will require a major effort by all concerned'. It did not show why such an effort should be made by individual firms, given the relative un-profitability of exports at the old rate of exchange. As a matter of fact, the required growth of exports would have been even higher, since the ratio of the growth of imports to the growth of consumption over the Plan period (despite devaluation in 1967) turned out to be not the 1·2 assumed in the Plan, but 2·7. The balance of payments measures in the Plan's check-list of action included 'the impact of a successful prices and incomes policy', a con-dition which would have been all the more necessary had devaluation come in 1965 in time to make the Plan's export target more credible.

Fourth, even if the 1966 sterling crisis had been avoided, the Plan would almost certainly have run up against supply constraints. The forecast man-power requirements exceeded the work force by almost half a million, a gap which it was optimistic to suppose could be filled by movement between regions or by changes in the organization of work. There were few industrial policies built into the Plan to raise the rate of growth of productivity by the amount the Plan required: rationalization by means of the I.R.C. was foreshadowed; the investment of nationalized industries was to be based upon the Plan assumptions; the switch to investment grants and the dis-crimination in favour of profit retentions under the newly introduced Corporation Tax were expected to boost industrial investment; and lump sum payments to redundant workers and transferable pension rights to increase worker mobility. Apart from this, beneath the surface of the 1965 National Plan lay the assumption that the growth of productivity was *demand-determined* and could be raised simply by the expansion of capacity which was presumed to follow increased demand.

It is instructive to contrast this Plan with indicative planning in France in the 1950s and 1960s. In France the Budget was based on the Plan; general economic policy was co-ordinated around it; the Plan allocated the growth increment, concerning itself with distribution as well as growth; prices and incomes policy were fully tied in; and the industrial detail in the Plan encouraged optimism; but the prime condition of the Plan was a healthy balance of payments surplus. Contracts with individual firms were entered into in the spirit of the Plan, and (to a decreasing extent after the Fourth Plan) financial rewards and penalties attached to their performance [33, Ch. 3].

[6] The export growth forecast was heavily weighted by absurdly optimistic figures for three of the four largest exporting industries: mechanical engineering (7·8 per cent per annum), electri-cal engineering (7·7 per cent), and vehicles (5·2 per cent). The report qualified these estimates in terms that exposed them: 'the forecasts represent the rates of growth which industries think are feasible in the context of a rate of growth of 25% in the economy as a whole by 1970'. Some industries made it clear that their ability to secure the rise in export sales they were 'forecasting' was subject to 'certain more specific conditions' which remained unspeci-fied, but were probably connected with the regulation and taxation of domestic sales [3, para. 64].

Table 17.1 compares, for the three U.K. growth studies of the 1960s, planned or projected increases over the period in GDP (and its principal components) with what happened. The ratio of the actual to the projected increases (o/p) is also shown.

TABLE 17.1

(all figures are expressed as percentages)	Growth 1961–6			National Plan 1954–70			Task Ahead 1967–72 (basic plan)		
	plan	out-come	o/p	plan	out-come	o/p	plan	out-come	o/p
GDP	22	16	71	25‡	14‡	56	17	13	74
consumption	19	14	72	21	11	52	12	14	119
investment	30	27	89	38	24	64	21	12	55
public current	19	12	65	27	12	44	9	7	82
exports (vis.)	28	20†	73	36	37	102*	32	35	110
imports (vis.)	22	19†	86	26	29	112*	22	36	163
import growth/ GDP growth (%)	100	119		104	209		129	284	
invest. growth/ consump. growth (%)	158	160		181	224		175	81	
consump. growth/ GDP growth (%)	86	94		84	78		71	113	

* affected by devaluation
† goods and services; goods alone in other columns
‡ GNP

Sources: N.E.D.C. *Growth of the UK Economy to 1966*; D.E.A. *The National Plan*; D.E.A. *The Task Ahead*; C.S.O. *Nat. Inc. & Expend. 1974*, Blue Book.

It is plain that all three projections or requirements were optimistic. In the third exercise, when higher and lower cases were considered, as well as a basic case, the growth of GDP and investment were well below even the lower case. The expected relation between consumption growth and income growth in the first two exercises was not much different from the actual; but in the third, the share of consumption increased markedly. The income elasticity of demand for imports was 2 over the period of the National Plan, about double the target elasticity, in spite of devaluation.[7] In 1967–72 the growth of imports was almost three times as fast as the growth of GDP, and the income elasticity more than twice what was projected. In all three stages, manufacturing investment grew less than had been projected or required; and in *The Task Ahead*, investment as a whole rose more slowly than consumption, instead of very much faster.

The verdict on all three of these episodes must be that throughout the 1960s Britain failed to develop industrial policies to permit the sustained

[7] Income elasticity of import demand is approximately the percentage growth of imports, divided by the percentage growth of income.

faster growth of GDP: consumption and imports grew much too rapidly, and industrial investment (whose quantity is a necessary, but by no means sufficient, condition of faster growth) much too slowly. Above all, employment policy and competition policy and our inadequate understanding of industrial economics prevented us from encouraging the rapid changes in industrial structure upon which mobility of resources and industrial growth depend.

2.3. Industrial Restructuring

There are in Britain some recent institutions and arrangements (like Finance for Industry, the Manpower Services Commission, the National Enterprise Board, the Planning Agreements system, and 39 Sector Working Parties in N.E.D.O., making recommendations to develop the Industrial Strategy outlined in [8]) which are at least potentially capable of constructively promoting industrial movements along the abnormal growth lines described in section 1.2—even though it is far from clear yet that they will succeed. Furthermore, reorganization within the Treasury created, late in 1975, a key division with responsibility for co-ordinating industry policy.

Since the failure of the National Plan, industrial policy has been increasingly directed at bringing about the sort of changes in the organization of output within industries which will cause resources to be concentrated in more efficient units. This policy trend was reinforced by both theoretical and practical doubts about the growth benefits of general inducements to increase industrial investment. It is certain that the relative stagnation of investment in manufacturing in recent years has severely damaged the prospects for future growth. Real fixed capital formation typically grows faster than real output. This relationship was broken by manufacturing industry between 1969 and 1973, with investment actually declining over the four-year period (recovering quite strongly in 1974 but falling back heavily again in 1975).

This under-investment in manufacturing has followed partly from the long-term downward trend in company profitability (accentuated until 1974 by the effects of inflation on the cost of stock-holding) and partly from increased uncertainty—about the future application of price controls and their effect

TABLE 17.2. *Annual Growth Rates at Constant Prices*

	1965–9 %	1969–73 %
Manufacturing		
output	+3·2	+2·6
investment	+4·0	−1·3
Other industrial (incl. agric. and services):		
output	+2·3	+3·7
investment	+2·8	+4·1

Source: *Nat. Inc. & Expend. 1974*, Blue Book.

upon profit margins; about the future of the capital market and the prospects for replacing short-term debt with longer-term loans and reducing the very high ratios of debt to equity finance without cutting back fiercely on new investment; and about the nature and degree of government participation, the sharing of control implied, and the amount of discretion companies will have in this matter.

There is, therefore, a very strong case for continuing to remove, as far as possible, some of the main discouragements to investment. However, this is not the same as prescribing an investment boom as a cure for slow growth. International comparisons over time show that there is a correlation between the ratio of industrial investment to output and the rate of growth of GDP; but it appears that the rate of growth 'predicted' for the U.K. from this relationship is higher than the rate we have achieved, and there are many problems about inferring causal relationships from statistical ones (see Ch. 1).[8]

So while adequate investment is a necessary condition of growth, an indiscriminate increase in industrial capacity cannot be guaranteed to raise medium-term growth prospects. Except in times of high unemployment, such a general increase could not occur unless resources were released as the result of a simultaneous increase in international competitiveness,[9] or unless there was such a cut in consumption as would disappoint the expectations on which the expansion had been based.

General increases in investment allowances, or cash grants, are not what is required. To encourage investment in a selective way, one has to pick out three areas: for expansion, those sectors where future international comparative advantage is likely to be found; for modernization and re-organization, those sectors which have fallen furthest behind best practice (where there is most to be gained from imitation) provided the reasons they have lost ground are well understood and the cures can be swiftly applied; and for restructuring, where there is a wide dispersion of productivity within a sector, with capital and labour slow to move out of the efficient plants and firms.

An active industrial policy, selective in these sorts of ways, is bound to rely to some extent upon intervention *within* industries.[10] Across-the-board industrial policies which lead to more flexible attitudes to resource use are

---

[8] The investment ratio-growth rate relationship is examined by T. P. Hill in 'Growth and Investment According to International Comparisons', *E.J.* (June 1964); and in O.E.C.D. *The Growth of Output 1960–1980* (Dec. 1970), Appendix VI.

[9] i.e. if product quality, reliability, after-sales service, etc. could be improved so that imports could be matched by fewer exports at higher prices, then less resources would be needed for export production and would be made available for increases in investment.

[10] There were plenty of recommendations of this selective and structural kind from the earliest days of N.E.D.C. See, for example, [27] paras. 162–3: 'the iron and steel industry, where output per worker in many new plants is several times as high as in old plants and significantly higher than the average for industry. . . . a greater concentration of output in more efficient plants and firms with a large scale of operation will increase productivity in a number of industries'. And later (paras. 170–1), 'a key factor will be the degree to which new investment embodies the results of up-to-date technical advance—largely through the development and application of research results already achieved'. These are recommendations about reducing productivity spread by levelling up; about the faster diffusion of new techniques; and about increased industrial information.

also indicated: like policies designed to reduce conflict and increase the involvement of workers in company planning.

The most important agency of such intervention, up to the National Enterprise Board proposals, had been the Industrial Re-organization Corporation, set up at the end of 1966, and abolished, along with the National Board for Prices and Incomes, by the Conservatives in their short-lived mood of disengagement in 1970 (see section 1.4 of this chapter, and [10], Chs. 4–10).

At a meeting of the N.E.D.C. held at Chequers in November 1975 the Government tabled its proposals for the evolution of an industrial strategy. It described a process of setting-out annually the main components of the Government's medium-term projection, identifying thirty-nine key sectors for individual attention, and involving tripartite working parties for each sector, as well as the N.E.D. Office, which is working in a complementary way on performance and its dependence on structure at the particular industry level. (See [8], paras. 7, 19–21 and 24–7, and [30].)

2.4. General Measures and Selective Measures

It is a mistake to regard discretionary selective measures and conventional non-discretionary market measures as strict alternatives from the viewpoint of their economic effects, so that *all* that matters is the philosophical or political principal at stake. This proposition is nowhere more evident than in the field of growth policy. The corporate control of capital, the oligopolistic organization of workers, and the vested interest of managers in the survival and growth of the activities in which they are engaged all impede industrial mobility (since power is exercised by those involved in relatively declining activities, blocking the development of those whose expansion would increase the rate of growth) unless the Government acts to reduce the costs of movement, to direct new capital to growth points, or to speed up the release of scarce factors of production by persuasion, compensation, or penalties.

If our individual resistance to change were less, our organizations less entrenched, or our demands for higher living standards less avid, the conflict between growth and freedom from government intervention would not arise as actively as it does. More information-sharing and more concentrated and collective decision-taking in industries producing internationally traded goods need not be in conflict with competitive incentives to reduce costs and improve products, provided that the increasingly transnational organization of production or a resurgent protectionism do not weaken the impact of competition from abroad.

2.5. Industrial Policy and Collective Decisions

Behind early statements of the advantages of collective decision-taking in the industrial field (like the one quoted earlier from [16], two separate threads of argument were entangled. On the one hand, the exchange of information about intentions which depend upon the simultaneous actions of other decision-takers can lead to a mutually compatible set of decisions taken in a context of much reduced *market* uncertainty. If these decisions lead to a higher rate of investment and to less waste of resources (avoiding over-expansion in one sector and under-expansion in another) then the aggregate of economic growth may be increased to the potential benefit of each decision-taking group.

On the other hand, it would be wrong to suppose that responsible leaders can be persuaded (and can persuade others) that there is necessarily an identity between personal and community interest. Industrial interest groups are understandably motivated by the desire to change the *distribution* of output and wealth. Such attempts to redistribute eventually cancel each other out to some extent. The most pervasive example is provided by the wage–price spiral. If the deterioration of the balance of payments which this spiral exacerbates is the effective constraint on sustained growth, then faster economic growth will require not just the honest exchange of information about intentions. It will require disengagement from the battle for shares, for the sake of a common interest in higher living standards all round. Since there have been particular winners and losers in this battle over the past decade, disengagement will be very difficult to bring about. Voluntary restraint is not just a matter of the high degree of leadership which the Cohen Council (C.P.P.I.) appealed to in 1961. The Government may have to make enforceable rules if it can, so that the gains from aggressive wage bids are reduced.

In the company sector, commercial interest, independently advanced, and higher over-all growth, can conflict in all sorts of ways. There is no point in expensive in-house training schemes if the effect is that your rivals can afford to offer higher wages and bid your trainees away. It may be good policy not to be the first firm to introduce an untried production technique, if others will benefit from your mistakes and avoid some of the teething troubles. There may be a strong case, in a cyclical industry, for operating a small vertically integrated plant to provide one's own raw material, building it on a scale where it will just supply all one's requirements at the lowest point in the cycle—residual supplies being bought outside from the specialist suppliers, over the rest of the cycle. To the firm integrating in this way the gain from getting most of its requirements from a plant used at full capacity throughout the cycle more than offsets the loss of scale economies and the somewhat higher price that must then be paid for its bought-out supplies from specialists whose average plant utilization over the cycle is now somewhat lower. But productivity in the industry as a whole is reduced since there is an over-all loss of economies of scale.

Much of our social organization consists of institutional arrangements to bring individual and public interests closer together. Some of these are market-oriented (like the subsidization of Research and Development expenditure); some are government regulations (like industrial training levies); some are direct and selective interventions by government agencies (like the enforcement of mergers by the I.R.C. in the late 1960s or the *contrats fiscaux* between the French Government and particular firms in successive National Plans); and some follow judicial recommendations (like those on proposed mergers by the Monopolies Commission). Typically, the Government has a role wherever externalities are important: that is, where social returns are different from private returns. (See Schelling and Olsen in [25]).

The role of the Government is likely to be more interventionist (and more often resented) when the social benefits from collective actions are *unevenly* distributed. It is difficult to have a voluntary agreement not to pollute a river, or an agreement to exchange market information, because there is always somebody further up-stream, or someone with the most valuable information, who gains little from the commitment.

The role of the Government is most propitious when what is required by individual planners is knowledge of the contingent plans of other industries and of the Government itself. 'Indicative planning' can be an efficient means (though not the only one theoretically available [26]) of achieving equilibrium growth, and reducing the uncertainty that otherwise affects individual plans. The functions of the Government are then usually those of convenor; of participator (as one whose own plans, if not revealed, are an important source of environmental uncertainty); and—if the exchange of information has gone as far as a social contract—those of policeman, ensuring that no one fails to carry out his part of the plan.[11]

3. Government, Industry, and Unions

3.1. A Model of a Contract

Because price stability, income distribution, and economic growth are jointly dependent upon decisions taken by industry, trade unions, and Government, economic policy in these respects depends upon interlocking decisions by all three parties. We can try to represent schematically the very large number of separate decision-takers involved by these three representative entities. It is apparent that the common objectives of all three can only be achieved by co-operative decisions arrived at contractually after a process of bargaining.

What follows is a highly stylized and oversimplified illustration of this interdependence. It can be thought of as the bare bones of a more realistic

---

[11] Selwyn Lloyd's statement of the remit of the N.E.D.C., which he made at its inaugural meeting in March 1962, enshrines the first two of these functions: 'I would define our task as follows:

To examine the economic performance of the nation with particular concern for the future in both the private and the public sectors of industry.

To consider what are the obstacles to quicker growth, what can be done to improve efficiency, and whether the best use is being made of our resources.

To seek agreement upon ways of improving economic performance, competitive power and efficiency, in other words to increase the rate of sound growth.'

On another occasion, the Chancellor observed that he was anxious to secure that both sides of industry, on whose co-operation the fulfilment of our objectives must significantly depend, should participate fully with the Government in all stages of the process. It could be argued that on this occasion, as many times later, Ministers allowed themselves to be beguiled by a collective noun into supposing that agreement about the desirability of a set of actions by representatives of 'both sides of industry' would actually result in any voluntary collective action. One notable unilateral counter-example was the C.B.I.'s voluntary price restraint in 1971–2.

and intricate model. It shows some of the working parts of a highly institutional economy. It differs from most traditional models of the working of the economy by admitting three separate economic agents, each of which individually controls only one of three levers of the economy—the growth of demand, the growth of money income per man, and the growth of prices. The participants have three principal objectives which they hold in common and which can be achieved only by the concerted action of all of them.

The relationship between the decisions of the three principals in the economy are shown in the circuit-diagram represented in Figure 17.2. There are three controlled inputs, one from each of the three principals. These inputs are circled. There are three outputs—the three common objectives, These are boxed. The wages/profits distribution is assumed to be a common goal, which might be negotiated after exploration of the model and agreement about the dependence of real wage growth upon investment and hence upon profits. (At worst, consideration by all three parties of the model's relationships would make disagreement on the distribution goal explicit. At best, it might make it possible to resolve the disagreement by negotiation against a background of other particular policy objectives.) There are a number of intermediate steps described below, which connect the inputs and the objectives by way of changes in other key economic quantities like employment, productivity, unit costs, prices, consumption, exports, and imports. The order of cause and effect is shown by arrows. Continuous lines show the links between principal production and expenditure quantities. The dashed lines show the relationship between different components and shares of income.

Starting at the top of the figure, the three levers which the three principals control are these:

(1) (by the Government) additional real government expenditure, G, which can be set so that, after the consequent increases in the other sorts of domestic expenditure—consumption and investment—are calculated, and the growth of exports is added, the required growth in real domestic product, Q, is attained. G stands for the much more complicated measures, including changes in taxation and monetary policy which the Government takes in practice.

(2) (by the T.U.C.) the annual rate of growth of earnings per man employed (w in the figure).

(3) (by the C.B.I.) the mark-up (m) which, when applied to the change in unit costs (c), determines the change in price (p).

These three instruments (circled) are the only three 'independent' variables; and together, by way of the principal loops and feedbacks shown in the figure, they determine the behaviour of the economy. In particular, the values they take will determine the degree to which the three collective goals (boxed in the figure) are achieved.

The instruments and the targets (full employment growth, currency stability, and fair distribution) are connected by a number of pathways through dependent real and money changes.

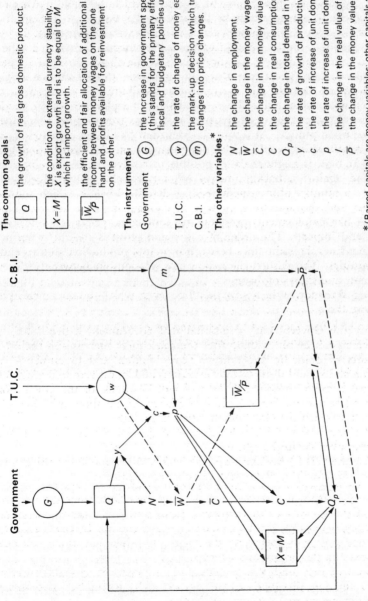

The common goals:

Q the growth of real gross domestic product.

$X = M$ the condition of external currency stability. X is export growth and is to be equal to M which is import growth.

$\overline{W}/\overline{P}$ the efficient and fair allocation of additional income between money wages on the one hand and profits available for reinvestment on the other.

The instruments:

Government G the increase in government spending in real terms (this stands for the primary effects of government fiscal and budgetary policies upon spending).

T.U.C. w the rate of change of money earnings per employee.

C.B.I. m the mark-up decision which translates cost changes into price changes.

The other variables:[*]

N the change in employment.

$\overline{W}$ the change in the money wage bill.

$\overline{C}$ the change in the money value of consumption.

C the change in real consumption.

Q_p the change in total demand in the private sector.

y the rate of growth of productivity.

c the rate of increase of unit domestic costs.

p the rate of increase of unit domestic prices.

I the change in the real value of investment.

$\overline{P}$ the change in the money value of profits.

[*] (Barred capitals are money variables; other capitals are real variables; small letters are rates or ratios)

FIG. 17.2

This may be summarized as follows (see figure) : the current rate of growth of real gross domestic product will be reflected partly in changes in employment, and partly in productivity changes (for much of the 1950s and 1960s these relationships were stable and reasonably predictable, but have become rather less so since then for reasons which are still not clear). Productivity growth, coupled with the rate of change of money wages per employee, determines the rate of increase in domestic unit costs. This, together with the chosen average mark-up, determines the rate of domestic price increase. In addition, the rate of increase in money wages per employee and the change in the level of employment determine the change in total money wages. This in turn determines the change in consumption expenditure in money terms. Coupling this with the rate of price increases sets the rise in real consumption while the rate of price increases also determines international competitiveness, hence balance of payments performance over time, and the stability or otherwise of the external value of the currency. (This would also, of course, depend on the rise in real incomes which will result from the growth of money wages and prices.)

Thus changes in consumption, exports, and imports will be determined, and these are three of the four components of the change in total demand facing the private sector. The fourth component—investment—depends partly on over-all private sector demand itself (i.e. the accelerator relationship) and partly on the profitability of meeting that demand. This will depend on the mark-ups industry wants, or can get, in the light of the prevailing demand conditions. The proportion of profits retained will also be important because of its effect on the supply of funds for investment. Finally, adding this total private sector demand increase to that which occurs as a result of government expenditure gives the real rate of growth of domestic product which can therefore be controlled by the Government's policy on expenditure and taxation. (In this sketch of the structure time-lags have been omitted, and so no notice has been taken of the fact that investment may not respond *swiftly* to increases in private product if there is excess capacity in manufacturing industry.)

Even this very simple crude sketch illustrates clearly the interdependence of objectives and the dependence of each on all three participating agents. The rate of inflation depends on mark-ups, wage increases, and demand management policy, and in turn directly or indirectly determines the external value of the currency and the growth of real output. The distribution of additional income between wages and profits also depends on the mark-up, money wage, and demand-generating decisions of the three agents respectively.

Some flesh can be put on the bare bones of this model. Specific values of the targets Q and $\overline{W/P}$, and a manageable rate of growth of prices, may be set which will permit the objective of external stability also to be met. Using the model, mutually consistent values can then also be established for w and m and for the rates of growth of productivity y and of employment N.

Some important details of the structure have not been included in this sketch—for example, the derivation of the growth of *real* earnings per head of those employed. This would call for the subtraction of p from w and an allowance for the changing burden of taxation to derive disposable real earnings per employee. Furthermore, p is strictly the change in the price of *domestic* production and ought to be modified by the effect of changes in the cost of imports upon this price level. But these are elaborations that do not affect the framework of triple responsibility, triple decision, and triple consequence. No one objective can be attained in isolation, and the value chosen for one target will influence the possible values of the other targets. Finally, of course, if there is *irreconcilable* disagreement among the three parties about the objectives, the model will not have an equilibrium solution.

3.2. Government Medium-Term Models

The macroeconomic input into investigations of the possibilities of industrial growth is provided by models of the relationship between the main components of demand and output in the medium term. As part of the Public Expenditure Survey system the Treasury now estimates public expenditure five years ahead. Assuming that policy targets are achieved (a target level of employment and a target balance of payments, in particular), the model projects total output (based upon alternative assumptions about the rate of growth of productive potential). Total output, in turn, is the main influence on the volume of imports. The balance of payments target and the volume of imports together determine export requirements, and these requirements are achieved by changing the assumed exchange rate. Thus it is possible to estimate the part of total output that has to be devoted to exports. The faster domestic output grows, the larger this proportion has to be, for the only way of financing a faster growth of imports is to reduce the exchange rate and so the unit value of exports. Private investment is also related to the growth of domestic output, for investment is induced by growing markets. Private consumption then emerges as a residual balance, making up the difference between total domestic output and the output pre-empted by public spending, the balance of trade and investment.[12]

The main shortcoming of this approach is the amount of uncertainty attaching to the key domestic variable, the growth of productivity. To explore the effects of alternative policy packages and growth rates of demand upon industrial productivity, it is essential to have a disaggregated model showing inter-industry inputs and outputs, showing the effects of shifts of resources between low and high productivity sectors as the composition of demand changes, and basing industry resource requirements upon production functions (see Barker in [9]. pp. 25–44).

Industrial consultation, if it is comprehensive enough, can usefully be combined with illustrative growth cases drawn from a model like this, provided some forecast is also provided of the changing pattern of final consumption demand. The consultation, industry-by-industry, can provide a

---

[12] For further information on the Treasury's medium-term model and its use in Public Public Expenditure surveys, see Budd, A. P. 'Economic Policy and the Medium Term' and McLean, A. A. 'The Treasury Model', in [9]; *Public Expenditure: a New Presentation*, Cmnd. 4017 (H.M.S.O., 1969); *Public Expenditure White Paper* (H.M.S.O., Dec. 1972 and Feb. 1976).

set of domestic outputs and import, investment, and manpower requirements. These can then be faced with the same sets of hypothetical requirements produced for each industry by an input–output model which articulates the technical interdependence between them. Further consultation may then make it possible to remove inconsistencies between the view of the various industries about their output and resource requirements. Perhaps the main precondition that must be met if macroeconomic models are to help industry planning at industry or company levels is that the assumptions on which they are operating should be revealed.

4. Prospects

In the circumstances of early 1975 (the extreme weakness of the London capital market and the intense pressure upon company profitability and liquidity) the opportunity for government intervention, either for better or worse, became very much greater than it was in 1966. The National Enterprise Board is now empowered to acquire permanent (and in some cases controlling) equity holdings in companies it assists; and many companies, in severe financial difficulties, may voluntarily seek government help and participation, as indeed they have done under the wide powers created by the Conservative 1972 Industry Act.[13] In addition, in the White Paper *The Regeneration of British Industry*, published in August 1974, more detailed and continuous collaboration between Government, management, and workers was foreshadowed by way of planning agreements. The powers to make such agreements have since been enacted. The purpose of such agreements is to harmonize with national objectives the plans of large firms three years ahead, and they may have much in common with the *contrats fiscaux* with which the French Government has sought to ensure the success of its National Plans. Both the N.E.B. and Planning Agreements are discussed further in Chapter 19.

There is now much less risk than there was in early 1975 that powers under the Industry Acts will be used less to support 'alert and vigorous' companies than to maintain employment in declining industries, hit especially hard by recession. Picking past winners is not a difficult job, but industrial recovery cannot be based on it: there are altogether too few such industries or firms. The problem is to identify from among the temporary losers those firms which deserve to succeed, and to establish and create the conditions for their success. The over-all level of productivity has most to gain from the transformation of a firm that has drifted farthest behind the horizon, but most to lose if it is supported without being transformed. This doctrine is easy to state but hard to apply—in engineering and in the motor industry just as it has been in shipbuilding.

---

[13] It was the failure of Rolls-Royce and Upper Clyde Shipbuilders in 1971 that interrupted the Conservative policy of industrial disengagement. There was, in fact, already some ambivalence in the policy statements of John Davies, the Secretary of State of the Department of Trade and Industry, 1970: 'Simply to abandon great sectors of our productive community at this moment of maximum weakness would be folly indeed . . . but . . . I will not bolster up or bail out companies when I can see no end to the process of propping them up.'

It is too early to say whether this is going to provide the sort of machinery that might lead the British economy back to a more disaggregated and more credible attempt at industrial planning than in 1965. A somewhat higher priority than heretofore is now given to industrial regeneration and to sector-by-sector analysis of the means to improve industrial performance and increase world trade shares—with co-ordinated policies at national, industry, and company levels. The November 1975 N.E.D.C. meeting and the Government's Industrial Strategy White Paper [8] gave grounds for hope that Britain may now be closer to realistic microeconomic industrial reform than in earlier planning or assessment experiments. The danger is that targets may be set for output and employment before the requisite policies have been chosen and their effects measured.

For the next two or three years, the most that the strategy can achieve is probably rather modest. It may make it possible for large firms to increase their share of resources in exchange for more detailed public accountability; it may lead to greater investment confidence and better directed investment; and by involving workers and improving industrial relations, it may speed up a little the diffusion of new processes and the development of new markets. It may slowly widen understanding of the dependence of full employment in the *long term* upon the sorts of changes in industrial structure which are usually resisted because of their short-term impact on jobs or on the survival of independent businesses.

Bibliography

SECTION A

[1] BECKERMAN, W. *Labour Government's Economic Record 1964–73* (Duckworth, 1972). (Chapters by A. Graham, W. Beckerman, and R. Opie.)
First-hand account of heady early days of D.E.A. planning and what went wrong (Opie); and excellent descriptions of later beginnings of a more selective policy (Graham).
[2] BRITTAN, S. *Government and the Market Economy*, I.E.A. Hobart Paper (1971).
A highly critical view of intervention when it is not based upon research into the effects of structural change on performance in individual industries.
[3] D.E.A. *The National Plan*, Cmnd. 2764 (H.M.S.O., Sept. 1965).
Enshrines (or embalms) the U.K.'s only attempt at comprehensive indicative planning.
[4] D.E.A. *The Task Ahead: Economic Assessment to 1972* (H.M.S.O., Feb. 1969).
The 'Planning document' that succeeded the failure of the 'National Plan'.
[5] DELL, E. *Political Responsibility and Industry* (Allen and Unwin, 1973).
View of industrialist turned Minister on purpose and conduct of policy up to 1972; need to maintain competition; inevitability of responsible intervention.
[6] N.E.D.C. *Conditions Favourable to Faster Growth* (H.M.S.O., Apr. 1972).
The 'Orange Book' whose chapter-headings cover what are still most of the background conditions of faster industrial growth, though not the required changes in industrial structure.
[7] O.E.C.D. *The Aims and Instruments of Industrial Policy, A Comparative Study* (Feb. 1975).
The only comparison—although rather too vague and polite—of the aims and method of longer-term industry policy in various O.E.C.D. countries.

[8] Treasury and Dept. of Industry. *An Approach to Industrial Strategy*, Cmnd. 6315 (H.M.S.O., Nov. 1975).
The key current statement of long-term national industry policy.
[9] WORSWICK, G. D. N., and BLACKABY, F. *The Medium Term* (Heinemann, 1974).
Conference papers enable approaches of Treasury, two groups in the Dept. of Applied Economics in Cambridge, and N.E.D.O. to medium-term appraisal to be compared.
[10] YOUNG, S. and LOWE, A. V. *Intervention in the Mixed Economy* (Croom Helm, 1974).
Includes a detailed chronicle of the rise and fall of the I.R.C.

SECTION B

[11] BALL, J. and BURNS, T. *Nat. West. Bank QR* (Nov. 1968).
[12] BARKER, T. and LECOMBER, R. *Exploring 1972*, D.A.E. Programme for Growth, vol. ix (1972).
[13] BRITTAN, S. *Inquest on Planning* (P.E.P., 1968).
[14] CARTER, R. *Can we have an Economic Miracle?* (Manchester Stat. Soc., Dec. 1968).
[15] Confederation of British Industry *Industry and Government* (July 1974).
[16] Council on Prices, Productivity and Incomes *Fourth Report* (H.M.S.O., July 1961).
[17] DAY, A. 'The Myth of 4% Growth', *Economic Journal* (1965).
[18] D.E.A. *Industrial Reorganization Corporation*, Cmnd. 2889 (H.M.S.O., Jan. 1966).
[19] Dept. of Industry *The Regeneration of British Industry*, Cmnd. 5710 (H.M.S.O., Aug. 1974).
[20] HUTCHISON, T. W. *Economics and Economic Policy in Britain, 1946–66* (Allen and Unwin, 1968).
[21] KALDOR, N. *Causes of the Slow Rate of Growth of the UK Economy* (Cambridge University Press, 1966).
[22] KENNEDY, M. *Manual of Applied Economics*, 2nd edn. (ed. Prest) (Weidenfeld and Nicolson, 1968).
[23] KNAPP, J. 'Pragmatism and the British Malaise', *Lloyds Bank Review* (Oct. 1968).
[24] McFADZEAN, A. *Galbraith and the Planners* (Strathclyde University, 1968).
[25] MARRIS, R. (ed.) *The Corporate Society* (Macmillan, 1974) (particularly chapters by Marris, Olsen, and Schelling).
[26] MEADE, J. *Theory of Indicative Planning* (Manchester University Press, 1971).
[27] N.E.D.O. *Growth of the UK Economy to 1966* (H.M.S.O., Feb. 1963).
[28] N.E.D.O. *Growth of the Economy* (H.M.S.O., Mar. 1964).
[29] N.E.D.O. *Industrial Review to 1977* (H.M.S.O., Oct. 1973).
[30] N.E.D.O. *Industrial Performance in the Longer-Term: an Approach through Investment* (H.M.S.O., July 1974). (Technical Appendix by the author available on request from N.E.D.O.).
[31] *Nat. Inst. Ec. Rev.* (Feb. 1967).
[32] POLANYI, M. *Planning in Britain: Experience of the 1960s* (I.E.A., 1967).
[33] Political and Economic Planning, *Economic Planning and Policies in Britain, France and Germany* (Allen and Unwin, 1968).
[34] POSNER, M. in CAIRNCROSS, A. (ed.) *Britain's Economic Prospects Reconsidered* (Allen and Unwin, 1971).
[35] ROBINSON, E. A. G., *Economic Planning in the UK: Some Lessons* (Cambridge University Press, 1967).
[36] SARGENT, J. 'Recent Growth Experience in the Economy of the U.K.', *Economic Journal* (Mar. 1968).
(37) SHONE, R. 'Problem of Planning for Economic Growth in a Mixed Economy' *Economic Journal* (Mar. 1965).
[38] T.U.C. *The Chequers and Downing Street Talks, July to November 1972* (T.U.C., 1973).
[39] Treasury. *Economic Prospects to 1972: a Revised Assessment* (H.M.S.O., 1970).
[40] VERNON, R. (ed.) *Big Business and the State* (Macmillan, 1974) (particularly the chapter by Trevor Smith on U.K. experience).

18

The Nationalized Industries

D. L. BEVAN

1. The Background to Nationalization

1.1. Introduction

Quite apart from the over-all requirements of demand management, governments frequently wish to intervene in particular sectors of the economy. They may attempt this in a wide variety of ways, such as exhortation; or by setting up planning machinery; or by specific tax/subsidy arrangements (as in much of regional planning); or by policies designed to foster competition. It may seem obvious that the ultimate recourse is 'nationalization'; to bring the sector into 'public ownership and control'. But these familiar phrases convey a concreteness, a sense of precision, which is misleading. Is the acquisition of assets to be by expropriation, by compulsory purchase, or by free-market purchase? If purchase is to be compulsory, how are the assets to be valued? Are all the assets to be acquired, or just a controlling interest? Is ownership to be vested in the nation as a whole, or in some particularly affected group such as employees or users? What institutional structure is to be adopted? How is control to be exercised?

These are wide questions and have generated a large literature. In the present chapter we concentrate on the question of control in one particular type of public institution, the nationalized industry. Nationalized industries are public corporations created by statute and ultimately responsible to Parliament; powers and duties are delegated to both Ministers and Boards. The Boards are granted a considerable degree of independence, qualified by the powers of the relevant Ministers. There is, inevitably, confusion and sometimes conflict in the zone where these powers overlap. Parliament, through the Select Committee on the Nationalized Industries, has looked for ways of reducing day-by-day interference and confining Ministerial control to the 'strategic' level. This triangular relationship between Parliament, Minister, and Board, embedded in a hybrid social and commercial environment, is the distinguishing characteristic of the (British) nationalized industry.

At the time of writing there are nearly a score of nationalized undertakings, the most familiar being located in airways, rail, coal, gas, electricity, steel, and the post office. Collectively they contribute about 10 per cent of GDP, employ 7 to 8 per cent of the national labour force, and have annual investment programmes which are roughly equal to those of all private manufacturing put together. Their influence on the economy is perhaps understated even by these figures, given their strategic location in fuel, transport, and communication; hence the importance of ensuring that they perform efficiently and 'in the public interest'.

1.2. History of Government Control

Although there was some activity earlier, the main bulk of nationalization took place under the Attlee Government. While economic arguments had always bulked fairly large in the rationale for nationalization, the early discussions, including the Parliamentary debates of the late 1940s, paid very little attention to questions of financial or economic management. Typically, the industries were simply required to pay their way 'taking one year with another' while developing and maintaining an 'efficient, co-ordinated and economical' system of supply. Little clarification was provided of either a theoretical or practical nature as to how the industries should set about implementing these vague instructions. As a consequence, the 1950s were marked by poor and uneven performance and growing concern at the lack of proper co-ordination and control, particularly in their financial affairs.

The Select Committee, set up in the mid-1950s, became the leading critic of these arrangements and proponent of some attempt at clarification. The first response to this pressure was the 1961 White Paper, Cmnd. 1337, 'The Financial and Economic Obligations of the Nationalized Industries'. The main innovation was the Financial Objective; an over-all rate of return on assets which each industry would be obliged to earn. The particular rate would vary from one industry to another depending on differences in the extent of social (non-commercial) obligations and other circumstances.

Despite this provision for varying the required rate, the 1961 White Paper must be seen primarily as a piece of macroeconomic policy. Its central concern was to increase the extent of self-financing in the nationalized sector; to correct a macroeconomic imbalance in the national flow of funds (i.e. from private to public sector) caused by the previous lack of financial discipline. While this was a highly desirable step in itself, the 1961 White Paper still provided no guidance on pricing and investment procedure. In effect, it demanded an improvement in results without offering advice on how this improvement should be achieved; it discussed the end rather than the means.

This task was eventually undertaken in the 1967 White Paper, Cmnd. 3437, 'Nationalized Industries: A Review of Economic and Financial Objectives'. The key instruction is that prices should be 'reasonably related to costs at the margin'. This instruction is qualified in various ways, most notably by the (possibly contradictory) instruction that prices should recover accounting costs; it is nevertheless of major importance as an explicit recognition of the desirability of a marginalist approach to nationalized industry prices. The second major innovation was the introduction of the principle of discounted cash flow for investment appraisal (using a test discount rate originally set at 8 per cent but raised in 1969 to 10 per cent). Finally, 'social' services provided by the nationalized industries were to be separately costed and paid for directly by the Government.

The 1967 White Paper marked an impressive attempt to put the economic management of the nationalized industries on a sound footing. Despite a fair amount of bet-hedging and punch-pulling, the basic argument comes through reasonably clearly, and it is an argument to adopt what was considered to be the best practice in setting prices and determining investment. One apparent peculiarity should be noted at this point; the financial objectives of Cmnd. 1337 were to be retained. This is peculiar, at least superficially, because it leads to a possible contradiction. Once there is a fixed set of rules for pricing and investment, the industry's cash flow will be determined. As a result, the rate of return is also determined (unless one is prepared to make arbitrary changes in the book value of assets) and cannot be chosen independently. The financial objective, it seems, is either redundant (if fixed at the right level) or likely to lead to confusion and possibly misallocation (if not). The case for retaining it (at the 'right' level, of course) is that the world is dynamic and uncertain, and economic performance depends in large measure on managerial motivation and morale; on this argument managers will perform better if they can measure themselves against a required out-turn such as the financial objective.

There still remained a great deal of work to be done in finding ways of implementing the principles enunciated in Cmnd. 3437. Nevertheless, the way ahead seemed clear enough in the later 1960s. After two decades without a microeconomic compass, the nationalized industries had at last been provided with a complete set of allocative rules; a clear distinction had been made between social and commercial obligations; and the Select Committee had turned its formidable attention to the problem of ensuring that Boards were allowed to exercise 'tactical command' without undue Ministerial interference.

In the early 1970s this steady progress came to an abrupt halt. It began to seem that the 1967 White Paper had marked a high tide in the importance accorded to microeconomic questions. Since then the nationalized industries had been used repeatedly as blunt instruments of macroeconomic management to the complete eclipse of the allocative rules so painstakingly developed in the 1960s. They had been used in attempts to control the wage spiral, with the most notable consequence the miners' strike and settlement and the fall of the Conservative Government. They had been used in attempts to moderate the rate of inflation and to soften its impact on income distribution, the consequences being an annual deficit of a billion pounds, severe allocative distortion, increased inflationary pressure, and sagging management morale.

In the November Budget of 1974 the Government at last acknowledged the (bipartisan) error of its ways, and a firm commitment was made to allow the nationalized industries to return to a policy of economic pricing. At the time of writing (March 1976) several initiatives are afoot, some of which differ from previous practice. The Government proposes to nationalize the aerospace and shipbuilding industries, a major move into manufacturing industry. It is also intended to opt for a federal type of organization rather than the more centralized type that has become familiar. A National Enterprise Board has been established to act as a holding company for government shareholdings in private industry and as a channel of finance (via equity as well as loans). Finally, an organization called the Nationalized Industries' Chairmen's Group has been set up to 'present a unified voice to Government on matters of common interest'; one matter on which the voice will presumably be particularly unified will be an attempt to get agreement on reduced intervention in their affairs.

1.3. Performance of the Nationalized Industries

Before proceeding, mention should be made of the fact that there is considerable disagreement about the over-all record of performance of the nationalized industries. The conventional wisdom, much of it ill informed, is that the record of these industries compares very unfavourably with that of the private sector. If profitability is taken as the yardstick this is generally true, though this conceals very wide variations in the returns of different nationalized industries (losses were heavily concentrated in coal and rail). Given, however, that for most of the period considered the nationalized industries were not attempting to maximize profits, were for some of the period given allocative rules of behaviour which would explicitly prevent this, and were later used as vehicles of anti-inflationary price restraint, this is not surprising.

In these circumstances a measure of efficiency in terms of output per unit input is preferable. The one usually employed is labour productivity. The only proper investigation of this found that although performance in terms of the level and rate of increase of labour productivity was rather poor in the 1950s, the nationalized industries performed markedly better than the private sector in the 1960s. This remained true even when the figures were corrected for the fact that in the case of some nationalized industries, high capital intensity would itself tend to generate higher levels of labour productivity.

This is not of course the only measure of efficiency. The quality of the service provided may be higher or lower, but this will not be reflected in figures of output per man. Here the nationalized industries may suffer from their monopoly positions. This may reduce the incentive to maintain and improve service, etc. but also the lack of any available alternative may mean that the public notices their inefficiencies much more than it does when they occur in the private sector.

1.4. Reasons for Nationalization

This short summary serves to highlight the difficulties of controlling public enterprise. One part of the problem is to devise institutions and criteria which are well adapted to the objectives of the enterprise in question. But a logically prior aspect of the problem is the delineation of appropriate objectives. Nationalized industries were brought into being with a vast array of justifications, as vehicles for a wide variety of objectives. Let us divide these, rather arbitrarily, into groups; allocative, distributional, macroeconomic, and institutional.

Nationalized industries are clearly well suited to meeting allocative objectives. Where a market is distorted by monopoly, externalities, decreasing cost, inability to charge for services rendered, and so forth, public ownership will often be the best (sometimes the only) solution. The particular version involving the public corporation has the advantage that an efficient management structure can be set up at arm's length from Government and its other highly various activities and objectives.

Nationalized industry hardly seems an appropriate vehicle for redistributing income. A more appropriate instrument for this purpose is the tax system. It may well be that direct taxation does not go as far as the Government decides would be desirable; and in that case it may be optimal to distort prices, lowering those of goods most heavily consumed by the poor. Even so, the more sensible approach would be a general battery of indirect taxes and subsidies applied without discrimination *per se* between private and public production, and not a half-hearted intervention on public sector prices alone, which can have serious effects on their finance but little effect on the over-all rate of inflation.

We have already seen that the attempt to use the nationalized industries as instruments for suppressing inflation or as substitutes for incomes policy ended in failure. Experience has also shown that public expenditure is too sluggish, and the time-lags too great, for this to be a useful component of counter-cyclical policy. It is, of course, quite obvious from the figures given at the beginning of this chapter that the nationalized industries comprise an important part of the macro picture. The aggregate level of surplus, investment, self-financing, and so on is a legitimate matter of macroeconomic interest. But if the micro rules are properly chosen, these macro magnitudes should give no cause for concern; if they do, there is a strong prima facie case that the micro rules have been set at the wrong levels. Finally, we may mention an argument gaining increasing prominence, namely, that the nationalized industries have a duty to protect and preserve jobs. This is a dangerous argument as it fails to distinguish between the disappearance of jobs through structural change and growth on the one hand and that due to temporary insufficient effective demand on the other. In the latter situation it makes good sense for the nationalized industries to preserve jobs; in the former, not. Great difficulties arise when both causes are at work together.

Our last group was institutional, covering in the main non-economic objectives with a structural, organizational emphasis. All we can say here is that by and large the nationalized industries have not proved, and do not seem constituted, to be particularly effective vehicles. An example is provided by the largely unfulfilled hope that they would prove to be test-beds for worker participation and effective industrial democracy.

The conclusion of this discussion is that the function for which the nationalized industries are best suited is that of ensuring allocative efficiency in their domain; other objectives, broadly speaking, should be left to other institutions. The remainder of the chapter is therefore devoted to the question of allocative efficiency and how the principles of Cmnd. 3437 may be expanded upon and qualified.

2. Pricing Policy

2.1. Marginal Cost Pricing

The general argument for setting price equal to marginal cost was examined in an earlier chapter. It was also shown that this would be a natural consequence of perfect competition. In the realm of public enterprise there will be no natural consequence of this sort. Indeed, much of the rationale for nationalization has been that particular industries cannot by their nature be organized in a competitive way. An example is the distribution of electricity; it would be absurdly wasteful to have a 'large' number of suppliers laying cables in each and every street, so efficiency requires at least a local monopoly. If nationalized industry prices are to be related to marginal cost it will have to be as a result of deliberate policy. This very obvious proposition immediately leads us into difficulties. Specifically, we can no longer rely on the invisible hand of competition to identify which costs really are marginal; it is necessary to make explicit decisions in the matter.

Consider the additional costs incurred if one more unit of output is produced. In general, the extra output could be produced by working existing plant a little harder or by installing some new plant. The costs involved in these alternatives are quite different in nature. In the former case we are considering such items as increased wear and tear, fuel costs, and overtime payments; the components of *short-run* marignal cost. In the latter we are considering the price of new equipment, its operating cost characteristics, the level of the interest rate, and so on; the components of *long-run* marginal cost.

Which type of marginal cost is relevant to the pricing decision? Clearly, the relevant type of cost is the one which would actually be incurred, and ideally that should be the lower. Suppose for a moment that the plant of the industry is of one type only and that it is perfectly divisible (there is no minimum scale of operation, and small plant is as efficient as large plant); that it can be installed instantaneously (there are no gestation lags); that demand for output grows smoothly (there are no cyclical falls); and that there is no embodied technical progress (new vintages of plant are identical in design to old ones). In an industry of this highly artificial kind the capital stock would always be perfectly adjusted to demand; no plant would have to be installed until the demand for its output had materialized, and once installed it would not be made prematurely redundant. As a consequence, long- and short-run marginal cost would always be equated. New plant would never be installed if it were cheaper to run existing plant a little harder; and vice versa. Indeed, it is apparent that this is a consequence of optimal investment policy. The cost of investment (long-run marginal cost) should be equated with its benefit (short-run marginal cost saved) at the margin.

2.2. Plant Indivisibility

In practice, we cannot expect the assumptions of the previous paragraph to hold. Consider what happens if we relax the divisibility assumption. Suppose plant can be supplied only in whole multiples of output K units per period; that operating costs are constant at a rate of a per unit per period so long as output is less than capacity; and that average capacity costs per period of a fully utilized plant are b. This situation is represented in Figure 18.1.

Under these assumptions long-run marginal cost (LRMC) is constant at $P_1 = a + b$. When installed capacity is nK units the short-run marginal cost curve is the reverse L-shaped curve aGA; when the $n + 1$th plant is added,

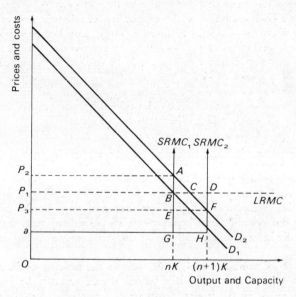

FIG. 18.1

it becomes aHD. The inclusion of these vertical segments as part of the short-run curves requires some justification. When spare capacity exists, the SRMC is clearly the operating cost, a. But how is marginal cost to be interpreted when no increment to output is possible, as at nK with n plant installed? Strictly, we might wish to say that at such a point marginal cost is only defined for reductions in output, but this would be to take too narrow a view. The question is best approached by returning to first principles. The origin of our interest in marginal cost is as a measure of opportunities forgone. If we expand production of a good, we absorb resources which have alternative uses. The value of these resources is then the benefit they would have yielded in the best of these alternatives—their opportunity cost. We may approach the question of marginal cost as a point like nK in exactly the same way. The opportunity cost of the marginal unit is the benefit it yields and this is measured by the price people are prepared to pay—P_1 with demand at D_1, P_2 with demand at D_2. Short-run marginal cost in these conditions is therefore the 'rationing' price which restricts demand to the available supply or the operating cost, whichever is the greater.

Suppose demand is at the level D_1; with n plants installed, SRMC = LRMC = P_1, and total revenue equals total cost. Now suppose that there is a once-for-all shift in demand to D_2. How large must this shift be to justify the installation of another plant? Clearly, if D_2 passed through or above D at least one more plant would be required. The interesting case is the intermediate one shown in Figure 18.1. With n plants, the price must be set at P_2, implying a surplus of revenue over cost for the producer, while with $n + 1$ it must be set at P_3, implying a loss. There is, however, the question of the possible gains to the consumer, and to determine whether over all the the new plant should be installed we utilize the concept of *consumer surplus*:

Consumer surplus is the difference between the total amount of money which consumers would be prepared to pay for some quantity of a good, and the amount they actually have to pay. It is therefore a part of the benefit of producing the good which is not reflected in the revenue of the producer. Changes in consumer surplus will not be considered by private producers, but should be taken into account by public owned ones.

The consumer surplus of any unit is, graphically, the distance between the price level (what he actually pays) and the demand curve at that output level (what he *would* pay—a measure of his benefit), e.g. JP_2 for the first unit when the price is P_2. Adding up the consumer surplus over all units of output gives the triangular area JP_2A. At price P_3 (with the new plant) consumer surplus is JP_3F. The gain in consumer surplus is therefore given by P_2AFP_3. Meanwhile the producer loses his surplus of P_2ABP_1 and incurs a loss of P_1DFP_3. Cancelling out the offsetting areas leaves a gain of the triangular area ACB offset by a loss of CDF. For investment to be justified, demand must shift enough for ACB > CDF.

In the case of indivisible plant, then, price should be set equal to short-run marginal cost and this may be above (P_2) or below (P_3) long-run marginal cost (P_1). In a dynamic setting, with demand growing continuously, this would imply a price oscillating about some trend level given by long-run marginal cost. Oscillations of this sort may be undesirable in themselves and it may be better to keep prices reasonably stable. For it must always be borne in mind that prices are essentially signalling devices. It only makes sense to have very sensitive pricing if customers are capable of responding rather quickly. For many purposes, particularly as regards domestic consumers, it is probably most important to convey steady information as to 'average' marginal costs; attempts to reflect short-term variations may simply lead to confusion. (But see Appendix 1 below for an important qualification to this argument.)

2.3. Economies of Scale

The classic worry about marginal cost pricing is that in the case of declining average cost industries (where MC is below AC—see p. 160) it will lead to deficits. These deficits would have to be financed by general taxation unless there were sufficient offsetting surpluses from increasing cost industries within the public domain. General taxation has distorting allocative effects and it makes little sense to increase distortion in one sector of the economy (for example, by raising an indirect tax on some privately produced good) to prevent it in another. This consideration naturally suggests the idea of minimizing distortion by 'spreading it around'. A consequence would be that prices should be set somewhat above marginal cost in the public sector. An alternative approach is the two-part tariff with a fixed standing charge and a running charge set equal to marginal cost. The intention here is to recover overheads without distorting choice at the margin. In fact, it may be doubted whether declining cost is a common feature of the nationalized industries, at least on the production side. (It is quite clear that there are economies of scale, of course; but it seems plausible that these are exhausted at the chosen scale of operation.) It is on the distribution side of the electricity and gas industries that there is the clearest evidence for declining cost; hence the popularity of two-part domestic tariffs in these industries.

The distortion argument raised in the previous paragraph is of rather general applicability, however. The optimality of setting price equal to marginal cost in any industry depends on the same rule being followed in all other industries. If it is not, whether because of taxation, monopoly, or externalities, then we are in the realm of the second best where no neat general conclusions are possible. For example, if the price of oil is much above its marginal cost, the result of setting the price of a substitute for it like electricity equal to marginal cost is that people will switch too much to electricity. Oil, the marginal cost of which is below the marginal benefit it would confer, is not bought because its price is way above that level. In this case it may well be better to price electricity above marginal cost to discourage people from switching away from oil. This could result in oil consumption reverting back towards what it would have been had all prices been equal to marginal cost (the 'optimum' consumption) but total expenditure will nevertheless of course be 'too high'. Otherwise each case must be examined in detail on its own merits. One rough and ready proposal is to set nationalized industry prices at some multiple of marginal cost to yield an over-all surplus determined by macroeconomic considerations; and to vary the factor of proportionality for a given product only if very strong evidence of unusual second best features is available.

3. Investment Criteria

3.1. Test Discount Rates

It was argued in an earlier chapter that investment proposals should be assessed using the technique of discounted cash flow. Public investment is no exception, but it presents two rather special features. One of these is that we are now concerned with the calculation of social benefit rather than private profit; hence it may be necessary to impute values to services that are not marketed, or marketed at the 'wrong' prices. The other special feature involves the choice of the discount rate.

For a private individual, or even a large company, the appropriate discount rate (or rates) is determined by the terms on which credit is available. Investment opportunities should be exploited, provided they yield a return which is in excess, after allowing for taxes, risk, and so forth, of the rate at which finance can be obtained. Superficially, it may seem that the Government could evolve a similar test using the government borrowing rate. But this rate is managed in accordance with the requirements of monetary policy and cannot be taken as a measure of the opportunity cost of funds to the Government. A different approach is required.

Consider briefly a world characterized by a static population of immortal individuals, a complete absence of risk, taxation or any type of externality, and a complete set of perfect markets including a perfect capital market. Since all individuals could borrow and lend freely at the same interest rate, they would all equate their *rates of time-preference* to that interest rate. The rate of time-preference is basically the rate of interest an individual needs to be paid in order that he feels as well off postponing consumption to a later date (when he can of course consume more) as he would feel if he spent his money on current consumption. If the market interest rate was higher, he could lend today, as a result consuming more tomorrow than was necessary to compensate him for the loss of consumption today. This increased lending would tend to bring the rate of interest down towards equality with the time-preference rate. Similarly, if the interest rate was lower he would reduce lending (the interest is not enough to compensate him for forgoing consumption) and this would drive the interest rate up as it became harder for people to borrow. In equilibrium and given our artificial picture, the market interest rate would equal the time-preference rate. Assuming also all individuals to be the same, this common rate of private time-preference would then constitute the social rate of time-preference, or 'consumption' rate of interest. Meanwhile, investment would be carried to the point at which its marginal yield or social opportunity cost would be everywhere the same and again equal to the common interest rate. In this world the going interest rate would in fact be the appropriate test rate of discount for all types of investment, public or private. Investment which deprives people of resources for current consumption would only be carried out if the gains were higher than consumers' time rate of preference. But this is just the investment that they would choose to have occur because the future gain more than outweighs the current loss.

The curious collection of assumptions is necessary if all ambiguity is to be removed from the choice of a public sector discount rate. Mortality alone means that the social rate of time-preference cannot necessarily be equated with the common rate of private time-preference because the latter adopts too short a time horizon. An imperfect capital market yields a spectrum of different private rates; and in conjunction with taxation, externalities, risk, and monopoly drive a wedge between the social opportunity cost of private investment and this spectrum of time-preference rates.

The upshot is that the appropriate discount procedure for public investment depends on how the necessary resources are to be released. If an increase in public investment will lead to an equivalent reduction in private investment, it is the social opportunity cost of the latter which is relevant. If the increase in public investment can be arranged purely at the expense of consumption, and if it is impossible for the Government to undertake activities similar to those of the private sector, then it is the social time-preference rate or consumption rate of interest which is relevant. In general, we might expect the truth to lie between these extremes, and some sort of weighted average[1] procedure would be called for.

This sort of recommendation raises severe practical problems. A proper compromise would require very extensive knowledge of interrelationships in the economy; it is far from clear how the social time-preference rate is to be estimated; and by no means easy to calculate a value for the social opportunity cost rate. In effect, the Treasury has opted for the relatively simple solution of instructing the nationalized industries to use a social opportunity cost rate (currently reckoned to be a real rate of 10 per cent per annum).

The Treasury rate is calculated with reference to low-risk projects in the private sector. The argument is not that public investments are inherently low risk in themselves, but rather that the Government should behave in a 'risk-neutral' way. That is to say, it should choose projects having the highest expected return regardless of how risky they are. Now, individuals are normally thought to be risk averse; they would pay a premium to get rid of uncertainty. Since the Government is making its decisions on behalf of risk-averse individuals, it is necessary to justify the argument that it should be risk neutral in its choices.

A traditional argument is that the Government is able to 'pool' risks, rather like an insurance company. The collective outcome is reasonably certain, even though the individual projects may be highly uncertain. The weakness with this argument is that the pooling may only be apparent. If the benefits are risky and accrue *to individuals*, the risks on a large number of government schemes do not really cancel out. They would do so only if the Government were able to provide insurance and pool the risks as suffered by the individuals themselves. An alternative and somewhat more robust argument is that the Government can 'spread' risks. Any one project that goes wrong has a negligible effect on any one taxpayer since the damage is spread over so many individuals.

3.2. Social versus Commercial Considerations

The other special feature of public investment decisions is the interrelationship between social and commercial considerations. This has proved to be one of the most vexed areas in the rather ill-defined division of responsibilities between Ministers and Boards. Within its limits the technique of cost-

---

[1] Ideally, the market price of a good would equate the marginal social cost (MSC) of producing one more unit of it with the marginal social benefit (MSB) of having or consuming the extra unit. It would not then matter whether a new (small) demand was met from extra production or by inducing an existing consumer to consume less. In either case the market price would measure the opportunity cost. If, however, markets are distorted so that MSB diverges from MSC, things become more difficult. We now have to estimate opportunity cost, and in two steps. First, we must estimate the values of MSB and MSC (typically by adding or subtracting known distortions from the market price); second, we must take a weighted average of the two (with the weights depending on the elasticities of supply and demand). An opportunity cost calculated in this way is often called a shadow or accounting price.

benefit analysis is well adapted to weighing these considerations against each other. Cost-benefit analysis involves the imputation of values where the market provides incomplete or misleading information or indeed none at all, so that *all* the benefits and costs, whether they command a market price or not, are included in the calculation of whether the benefits of a project exceed the costs. Formidable problems, both theoretical and practical, arise in trying to assess the value of non-marketed costs and benefits, and many of these imputations, for example putting a value on noise, congestion, time saved, and even human life, cannot easily be delegated to the Board of a nationalized industry. Other parameters in the cost-benefit calculus, such as the discount rate itself, are also essentially the responsibility of Central Government. It would therefore be inappropriate for a nationalized industry to attempt to carry out its own cost-benefit analysis. The proper discharge of social obligations by the nationalized industry requires that Central Government play a more active role. Either the industries must be given a general framework and set of approved parameter values and instructed to conduct their own cost-benefit studies in the same way as they are instructed to carry out financial and economic studies: or ministries must carry out cost-benefit studies to place values on social services so that these may be directly subsidized. In either case it is appropriate that nationalized industries be instructed to act as commercial undertakings with social obligations clearly identified, costed, and funded by Government through general taxation. There seems to be no good reason for requiring 'commercial' classes of consumer to cross-subsidize 'social' classes of consumer; and no sense at all in subsidizing 'social' services without regard to (or indeed knowledge of) the cost of doing so.

In respect of separating out these social and commercial considerations the post-war record of Government is very poor. However, the 1968 Transport Act marked a new recognition of the principles outlined above and notably in respect of the railways, which had suffered most markedly from this neglect. Unfortunately, British Rail does not appear to have benefited much from these changes, suffering a huge increase in its deficit during the 1970s despite massive fare increases. Solutions suggested by outside commentators all involve surgery ranging from the extreme to the merely drastic.

4. Conclusion

Lack of space has forced us to keep the preceding discussion brief. Rather than restrict attention to a few characteristics which could have been given more comprehensive (and perhaps more comprehensible) treatment, we have opted to introduce a variety of considerations, despite the inevitable compression that this has entailed. It seemed desirable in a text of this kind to indicate the flavour and range of questions discussed in the more specialized literature. Even so, it has been necessary to confine ourselves mainly to rather general questions of control: little or nothing has been said about innovation, finance, or management structure; nor about productivity, overmanning, and manpower reduction; and few distinctions have been drawn between the characteristics of the different industries. The select bibliography which follows the chapter is in part intended to help the interested reader repair these omissions.

Appendix 1: Peak Pricing

It is argued in Chapter 18 that prices should not always follow costs if these are very volatile. It must be stressed that this argument applies to variations of an unsystematic and unpredictable nature. There is another source of variation in marginal cost which is regular and should most certainly be reflected in price. This is the variation due to peakiness of demand coupled with difficulties of storing output. It is a peculiarity of the nationalized industries that they suffer from this combination of characteristics to an unusually marked degree. As a consequence, units of output produced at different times are very different economic commodities however homogeneous they may appear to be physically. Thus we cannot run commuter trains in the middle of the night and store the journeys for sale in the rush hour. Nor could it ever make sense to generate electricity in the summer for sale in the winter. Since the capacity of the system will be determined largely by the size of the peak load it is obviously sensible that peak-period consumers should pay the bulk of the capacity costs.

Imagine a situation like that depicted in Figure 18.1, except that the single type of plant is now divisible, and that there are two separate periods with different, independent demands, i.e. a peak period and an off-peak period. Two possibilities are depicted in Figure 18.2 (a) and (b). In case (a) peak demand D_2 is so high

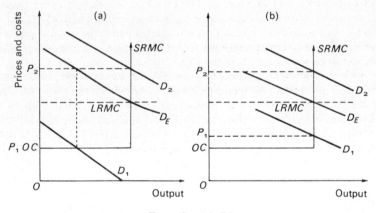

FIG. 18.2 (a) (b)

relative to the off-peak D_1 that it will bear the whole capital cost of the system. Even when off-peak users are charged only the operating cost of the plant they still do not purchase all the available output. In case (b) the off-peak users bear some part of the capital charges; if they paid only operating cost, they would demand a larger output than the peak users would be prepared to finance. In each case it is possible to construct an effective demand for capacity curve (D_E) by a weighted vertical summation of the parts of the two demand curves lying above the operating cost line. Given the divisibility assumption the intersection of the effective demand curve with the long-run marginal cost curve determines the optimum capacity and hence whether the system is in case (a) or (b). It is straightforward to extend this type of approach to allow for indivisibility in plant size, different types of plant, and several periods with different (independent) demands.

In practice, however, peak/off-peak prices have not been set in this way. The difficulty is that far too little is known about demand functions. It also seems likely that peak and off-peak demands will be related rather than independent in many cases. (For example, night storage heaters were designed specifically to shift demand from peak to off-peak.) The most developed example of peak pricing is provided by the electricity industry. The Central Electricity Generating Board sells electricity to the Area Boards at the Bulk Supply Tariff. This is quite complicated, with three running charges and two capacity charges. The capacity charges are divided between the Area Boards according to their contribution to specified levels of system demand. There are two to allow for the fact that the heavy costs are incurred to meet the winter 'shoulder' which accounts for about 90 per cent of the peak demand. The remainder is of very short duration—the so-called needle peak—and is met by plant of relatively low capital cost and high running cost. Apart from this explicit recognition of plant diversity, the Bulk Supply Tariff is rather arbitrarily constructed as if the system were in configuration (a). Even so, the BST is far too complicated for the average final consumer, and the Area Boards have tended to fix their tariffs in a much cruder way.

Appendix 2: System Interdependence

In this appendix we consider another aspect of investment in the public sector which, while not being a special feature like those discussed above, is still highly characteristic. Many of the nationalized industries can only be viewed as interrelated systems. We cannot appraise an investment project simply by calculating the time pattern of sales and the associated costs. We must instead attempt to embed each project into the system and assess what happens to the whole pattern of system sales and costs. The most highly developed example is again provided by the Central Electricity Generating Board. It is worth examining the problem in some detail, albeit in a highly simplified form.

There are several different types of plant which can be used to generate electricity and these have widely different cost characteristics. At one extreme nuclear and hydroelectric plant have high capital costs and low running costs. At the other extreme are gas turbines with low capital costs and high running costs. Conventional oil and coal-fired plant lie in between the two.

Demand varies through the year so that varying proportions of capacity are in use at different times. Once plant has been installed it evidently makes sense to operate the plant with the lowest running cost. This is the now well-tried merit order system whereby nuclear plant is in more or less continuous use while gas turbines are brought into operation only at times of peak demand when all other plant is already in action.

The question is, how are we to choose an optimal mix of plant when faced with a particular load duration curve, and a particular set of cost curves? A diagrammatic solution to the static case is sketched in Figure 18.3 where unit operating costs of the different types of plant are assumed to be constant.

While Figure 18.3 gives a clear picture of the requirements for static optimization, the real problem is of course a dynamic one. At any one time the system has a given collection of plant of different types inherited from the past. The ability to adjust plant mix as the load duration curve shifts is limited. The desirability of investing in any one type of plant to meet load growth will thus be qualified by the inherited plant mix and its suitability to the current load pattern.

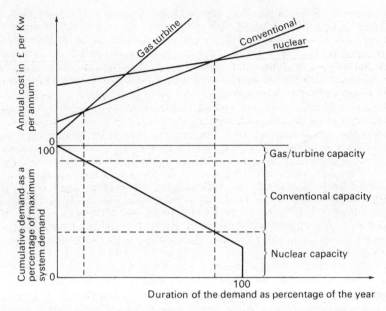

FIG. 18.3

The other complication in a dynamic world arises from the technical progress embodied in newer plant coupled with wear and tear raising operating costs in old plant. Together these mean that as plant ages, its position in the merit order will gradually shift, even when the over-all mix between different types of plant is constant. A changing mix may speed up or slow down this movement. The effect of this second complication on plant utilization is illustrated in Figures 18.4 and 18.5.

In Figure 18.4 the drift of a nuclear plant down the merit order as it ages is shown by the successive positions N_1, N_2, N_3; likewise for a conventional plant C_1, C_2, C_3. A static plant mix in the future is assumed. The solid lines in Figure 18.5 show the

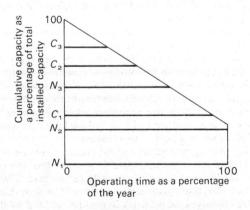

FIG. 18.4

consequential lifetime utilization patterns of the two plants. It is quite clear from Figure 18.5 that the decision whether to install a nuclear or a coal-fired plant (for example) can never be made simply in terms of the characteristics of the two plants. There is no way of ensuring that they provide the same services through their working lives; and the precise difference in what they would provide, as well as the value of this difference, depends on the characteristics of the rest of the supply system (and indeed on the structure of demand).

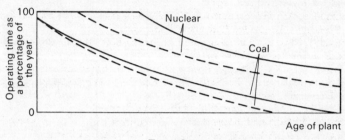

FIG. 18.5

To reinforce the point, suppose that in future plant mix is shifted in favour of nuclear plant. This will lead to a more rapid erosion of the merit order position of the two plants under consideration and hence, differentially, of their lifetime utilization (now represented by the broken lines). In brief, the choice between nuclear and conventional plant in the present depends in part on what choice between them will be made in the future. This is awkward, but not insoluble. The solution is a reiterative procedure; fairly crude calculations are made for plant mix into the future and used to make more precise calculations as to more immediate choices, the whole being checked for consistency.

Bibliography

SECTION A

[1] Webb, M. G. *The Economics of Nationalized Industries* (Nelson, 1973) offers a good theoretical treatment of allocative criteria aimed at the level of second- or third-year undergraduate courses. A more descriptive approach is well provided in [2] Reid, G. L., Allen, K. and Harris, D. J. *The Nationalized Fuel Industries*; and [3] Thomson, A. W. J. and Hunter, L. C. *The Nationalized Transport Industries* (both Heinemann Educational Books, 1973). A useful selection of readings, mainly extracts from official publications of the 1960s, is available in [4] Tivey, L. (ed.) *The Nationalized Industries since 1960* (Allen and Unwin, 1973). An interesting discussion of the institutional problem of control is offered by [5] Foster, C. D. *Politics, Finance and the Role of Economics; An Essay in the Control of Public Enterprise* (Allen and Unwin, 1971). [6] Pryke, R. *Public Enterprise in Practice* (MacGibbon and Kee), 1971 constitutes the major attempt to analyse productive efficiency.

The two White Papers on Economic and Financial Objectives, [7] Cmnd. 1337 of 1961, and [8] Cmnd. 3437 of 1967, are seminal; but there is a host of other White Papers directed at specific problems, sectors, and corporations. In addition, a wealth of important information and comment is contained in the various Reports of the Select Committee on Nationalized Industries.

SECTION B

The literature in this area is very extensive. The inevitably small sample that follows has been restricted in the main to full-length books, partly for reasons of space, but partly because many of the more important articles have now been collected into books of readings or absorbed into the more recent texts.

[9] BATES, R. and FRASER, N. *Investment Decisions in the Nationalized Fuel Industries* (Cambridge University Press, 1974).

[10] COCKERILL, A. (with SILBERSTON, A.) *The Steel Industry: International Comparisons* D.A.E. Paper 42 (Cambridge University Press, 1974).

[11] CURRIE, J. M. *et al.* 'The Concept of Economic Surplus and its Use in Economic Analysis, *Economic Journal* (Dec. 1971).

[12] FOSTER, C. D. *The Transport Problem* (Croom Helm, revised 1975).

[13] HALL, P. and SMITH, E. *Better Use of Rail Ways* (Department of Geography, Reading University, 1976).

[14] JOY, S. *The Train that Ran Away* (Ian Allen, 1973).

[15] LAYARD, R. (ed.) *Cost Benefit Analysis* (Penguin, 1972).

[16] MILLWARD, R. *Public Expenditure Economics* (McGraw-Hill, 1971).

[17] MISHAN, E. J. 'The Post-War Literature on Externalities: an Interpretative Essay', *Journal of Economic Literature* (Mar. 1971).

[18] MUNBY, D. (ed.) *Transport* (Penguin, 1968).

[19] NELSON, J. R. (ed.), *Marginal Cost Pricing in Practice* (Prentice-Hall, 1964).

[20] PESTON, M. *Public Goods and the Public Sector* (Macmillan, 1972).

[21] POLANYI, G. and P. *Failing the Nation: The Record of the Nationalised Industries* (Fraser Ansbacher Ltd., 1974).

[22] POSNER, M. V. *Fuel Policy: A Study in Applied Economics* (Macmillan, 1973).

[23] —— 'Energy Policy at the Centre of the Stage', *National Westminster Bank Review* (1974).

[24] PREST, A. R. and TURVEY, R. 'Cost Benefit Analysis: A Survey', *Economic Journal* (1965).

[25] PRYKE, R. and DODGSON, J. *The Rail Problem* (Martin Robertson, 1975).

[26] REID, G. L. and ALLEN, K. *Nationalized Industries* (Penguin, corrected 1973).

[27] STEINER, P. O. 'Public Expenditure Budgeting', in A. S. Blinder *et al. The Economics of Public Finance* (Brookings Institution, 1974).

[28] THOMSON, J. M. *Modern Transport Economics* (Penguin, 1974).

[29] TURVEY, R. (ed.) *Public Enterprise* (Penguin, 1968).

[30] —— *Optimal Pricing and Investment in Electricity Supply* (Allen and Unwin, 1968).

[31] —— *Economic Analysis and Public Enterprise* (Allen and Unwin, 1971).

19

Industrial Policy

D. J. MORRIS

1. Introduction: The Need for an Industrial Policy

1.1. Economic Performance in the U.K.

All the economic policies described in earlier chapters have direct and significant effect on Industry. Fiscal, monetary, and exchange rate policy are all main determinants of the level of demand that Industry faces, its ability to earn profits, its investment plans, and its ability to finance them. The stability of demand, with its implications for long-range financial and investment planning, is also partly a function of the degree to which these policies are successfully applied. Prices and Incomes policy can have a major effect on industrial labour costs, the availability of labour to particular firms, gross profit margins obtainable, and the continuity of production. Competition policy, planning, and nationalization all represent policies which are directly concerned with the structure, behaviour, and performance of different sectors of Industry.

With so many possible ways of influencing Industry, both short term and long term, at their disposal it may be asked why the Government should require a separate Industrial policy, and what that policy might involve. The first section of this chapter attempts to answer the first of these questions, while the remaining three examine the second question by looking at past industrial policy, the present options available, and the course chosen recently and currently being put into operation.

Policy towards Industry has many aims, relating to efficiency, conditions of employment, remuneration, safety, etc. Here we focus on the overriding economic objective of recent years, namely, productivity.

Output per head of the working population is, and has been at a low level relative to that in most other industrialized countries, and in addition has been growing at a slower rate as well. This is a serious problem for two reasons. Firstly, unless the proportion of the population working rises sufficiently to offset it, a slow rate of increase in labour productivity implies a low rate of increase of material living standards for the population as a whole—in other words, slow economic per capita growth. Secondly, it is very likely that most, if not all, the economic difficulties that have beset the U.K. in recent years can be attributed to this factor. In view of the significance of these statements it is appropriate to be slightly more specific about the economic relationships involved.

Low productivity must in nearly all circumstances result either in correspondingly low wages, or high prices, or low gross profits, or, more usually, some combination of these. This can be seen as follows: (Taxation is ignored in order to simplify the exposition) Total Revenue (TR) for a firm by definition equals Total Cost (TC) plus profit (Π). Total Revenue is also equal to the Average price level of the firm's products (P) times its output (Q). Therefore

$$TR = P \times Q = TC + \Pi$$

and

$$P = \frac{TC + \Pi}{Q}$$

The simplest way to see the implications of this is to multiply the right-hand side by W/W which does not change the equation, where W is the total wage bill of the firm, and then by L/L which again leaves the equation unchanged where L is the total labour force in the firm. This gives

$$P = \frac{TC + \Pi}{Q} \times \frac{W}{W} \times \frac{L}{L}$$

This can be rewritten as

$$P = \frac{TC + \Pi}{W} \times \frac{W}{L} \times \frac{L}{Q}$$

However, W/L is the average wage rate per man (w) and L/Q is the same as $1/k$ where k is Q/L, that is, output per man or labour productivity. It is therefore *definitionally* true that

$$P = \frac{TC + \Pi}{W} \times \frac{w}{k}$$

Thus if productivity (k) is low it follows that either wage rates (w) must be low, or the price level (P) must be high, or the term ($TC + \Pi)/W$ must be low. This in turn entails either that non-wage costs must be low, i.e. raw material costs, semi-manufactured input costs, fuel or rental costs, or gross profit must be low. But all these costs will generally be given for the firm, dependent on the prices charged and the firm's scale of operations and output levels. So in the absence of low wages or higher prices to compensate, low productivity will result in low gross profits.[1]

In practice, all three have occurred. Low wages are, of course, part of the means by which low productivity gets transmitted into low living standards, and many firms in the U.K. have only been able to remain internationally competitive despite significantly lower levels of productivity because they have paid much lower wages than abroad. Equally serious, low wages and low rates of increase in wages are thought by many to be one major cause of

[1] If industrial costs rise as a result of higher import prices, then to that extent wages have to rise less fast than productivity to avoid inflationary consequences. Or again, if profits are required to rise rapidly, for example from an inadequate level, the same conclusion holds.

inflation through the resulting attempts of the workforce to obtain higher wage increases than can be absorbed through higher productivity. Thus the pressure of low productivity has been partly switched to prices. This has meant an inability to compete adequately in international markets, with a consequent slow growth of export demand, a falling share of world trade, and a tendency to balance of payments deficit. Finally, to the extent that higher prices have not been able to take up all the pressure of wage increases in excess of productivity, gross profits (profits and interest payments) have fallen. This has tended to mean inadequate investment either because it curtails the supply of funds for investment or the incentive to invest, or both.

All this is not to say that other factors have not been important, but that low productivity has been a major and continuing factor in the generation of inflation, low investment, and balance of payments problems in the U.K. The problem did not stop there, however. A decline in export competitiveness meant that sterling became overvalued. To defend the exchange rate successive rounds of deflation of aggregate demand were required, and this further reduced investment by reducing the level of demand and increasing its instability. Low profitability led to an ever-growing incentive to invest abroad for both U.K. and foreign firms, thereby increasing the long-term outflow of capital from the U.K. The loss of foreign market share also directly operated to reduce investment in the U.K. The low rate of investment implies that the average age of the capital stock in the U.K. may tend to be higher than in most other industrialized countries and its productivity lower, further undermining export performance. In short, low productivity has caused or exacerbated almost all the economic problems faced in the U.K., and in addition tends to magnify itself. A very large improvement in productivity is therefore an essential prerequisite if the U.K. economy and living standards are to improve, and the central role of industrial policy is to bring this about. Table 19.1 charts the performance described.

TABLE 19.1

	Original 6 E.E.C. Countries	U.K.
Growth rate of industrial output per man-hour 1966–72	51%	26%
Growth rate of average hourly gross earnings 1966–72	114%	89%
Rise in wage cost per unit of output 1966–72	38%	52%
Rise in consumer price index 1966–72	27%	41%
Growth of export volume 1966–72	160%	66%
Net operating surplus (% of GDP) 1972	25·2%	17·3%
Investment (% of GDP) 1972	23·6%	19·8%

Sources: *Basic Statistics, Eurostat. Annual Digest of Statistics.*

1.2. Alternative Approaches to Industry

It is against this background that the need for an Industry policy over and above the policies already discussed can be seen, for none of them has made sufficient impact, if any, on productivity performance. As we have seen, monetary, fiscal, and exchange rate policy have been primarily directed towards managing the level of demand and improving the balance of payments with a *given* productivity level. Except for a relatively brief period when emphasis was placed on productivity bargaining, Prices and Incomes policy has been mainly concerned with direct control of inflation rather than with productivity improvements. The impact of these policies on productivity has therefore generally been a secondary concern or been ignored altogether because of the shorter-term problems to be dealt with. Longer-term growth and investment strategies of firms may have suffered as a result.

The same point cannot, however, be made with regard to the longer-term anti-trust, planning, and nationalization policies discussed. Each of these has been partly conceived of as a means by which productivity could be increased—anti-trust legislation by generating increased efficiency in the use of resources through the enhanced pressure of competition, planning through provision of a more stable background for investment and to advance identification of potential obstacles to faster growth of productivity, and nationalization by allowing rationalization of production and distribution facilities and the achievement of all the economies of scale inherent in the industries concerned. In practice, each has failed for different reasons to have the impact on productivity necessary to radically alter the performance of the U.K. economy. For reasons discussed in Chapter 17, planning has not had either the backing or the success necessary to contribute significantly to this aim as yet. The nationalized industries, despite having a rather better record of productivity than the private sector in recent years has not on average achieved comparable levels with these industries in other countries, and, equally important, cover very little of the manufacturing sector. Yet this sector is vital partly because it appears to be a main determinant of over-all productivity (see p. 229) and partly because it provides 80 per cent of the exports of the U.K., where, as we have seen, high productivity is a crucial factor in over-all performance.

The impact of the anti-trust legislation has been more complex. The Restrictive Trade Practices Act of 1956, augmented by the 1968 Act, together with the abolition of resale price maintenance, is generally thought to have stimulated more competition in the U.K. initially—an effect which was reinforced by entry into the European Economic Community with its own anti-trust laws and the progressive removal of protective trade barriers which this has entailed. Yet a concurrent phenomenon, almost certainly caused in part by the increase in competition, has been a wave of mergers. These in turn appear to have been the main cause of the increase in industrial concentration which has occurred in recent years (see Hannah [15]). In practice, this has meant an increase in the number and extent of dominant market positions, thus at least mitigating and perhaps reversing the trend towards greater competitive pressure. The largest 100 firms were responsible for approximately 50 per cent of net manufacturing output in 1975 (as compared to 25 per cent in 1950, only 15 per cent in 1910, and a figure of 66 per cent forecast by the N.I.E.S.R. for 1985), and virtually all more comprehensive measures of industrial concentration in the U.K. support this trend. It remains to be seen whether increased international competition both from the E.E.C. and from other countries currently industrializing will force higher productivity on U.K. industry, but it must be noted that there is no necessary reason why it should. The intensification of competition may lead to a further weakening of industry's ability to foresee and earn the profits necessary to increase investment in manpower and machines in the private sector, and an increasing relative rate of decline rather than a reversal of it. Finally, it is difficult to discern any significant effect of the Monopolies and Mergers Commission on the process of concentration or the over-all level of productivity, and the alterations in company behaviour which it has recommended should be made in specific cases have tended to be concerned with price, profit, and advertising levels rather than productivity (although it is difficult to see what such a body could do in this regard except ensure that anti-competitive strategies are halted).

Thus continuing poor productivity performance, together with the inappropriateness or inadequacy of the more well-established policies examined, have necessitated the development of other measures more directly aimed, if not exclusively so, at improving productivity. Before considering these alternative measures, which are far from representing a comprehensive approach to industrial performance, it is useful to review the fundamental problem, namely the causes of the low level and rate of growth of productivity in the U.K.

1.3. Productivity in the U.K.

Much has already been said about the causes of low productivity in Chapter 17. Here we simply draw together the main reasons, largely following the Government's own interpretation of poor manufacturing performance presented as recently as November 1975 in a White Paper on Industrial Strategy.

- (a) Investment—a low level, poor choice, and inadequate untilization.
- (b) Labour—inefficient management, inadequate consultation, restrictive practices, overmanning, disputes, regional and sectoral shortages of skilled labour, opposition to labour mobility, and opposition to changes in relative pay and the relation of pay to productivity.
- (c) Finance—inadequate provision to industry, especially over the medium and long term.
- (d) Government—sharp and frequent changes of policy, excessive priority to public expenditure and personal consumption at the expense of of resources for investment and exports, and intervention in the decisions of nationalized industries.

Most, if not all, can be seen as both the result as well as the cause of low productivity, thus exacerbating the problem, and it is tempting to believe that that there is either amongst or underneath these causes one basic reason for the U.K.'s poor record from which all the other difficulties spring. Certainly it would appear that reasons (c) and (d) require only their recognition and the will to deal with them in order to remove these causes. Even so, if there is one prime cause, there is still relatively little agreement about what it is, and it is of course quite possible that no such single cause exists, but rather a number of different reinforcing and self-amplifying factors, each of which has to be dealt with if performance is to be improved.

None the less, three not entirely unrelated factors have been cited in recent years as fundamental, and are worthy of mention. The first is the drying-up of the supply of labour in adequate amounts or with appropriate skills to the manufacturing sector. This has been examined in Chapter 8 and will not be elaborated upon further.

The second is the very substantial shift in the distribution of GNP from marketed products to non-marketed ones. Individuals' satisfaction from the resources available to a country can come from products and services which they buy in a market or from products and services provided by the Government, such as Health, Education, and Transport services which are financed out of taxation. Both are means by which increases in output are translated into increase in living standards, but more rapid increases in one must be at the expense of a slower rate of increase in the other. It has recently been argued that the Government in the U.K. has brought about a much more rapid growth in non-marketed goods and services than in output as a whole, with the inevitable result that the growth of resources available for the production of marketed ones has been very slow (see [8]). If people accept this then there need be no difficulty, but if they collectively do not recognize that non-marketed products represent the main form of improvement in living standards then they may well push for higher real post-tax wages to allow them to obtain the more rapid increase in *marketed* products that they believe themselves to be entitled to. If this happens then an extension of the public non-marketed sector which increases the demand for marketed products, but reduces the supply of them, will lead to excess demand, inflation, loss of competitiveness, and balance of payments problems. The low growth of GNP that this generates further exacerbates the problem of unacceptably low growth of marketed products.

This is by no means the end of the story. The pressure to maintain the rapid growth of post-tax wages despite the fact that the taxed part is providing the main component of the rise in living standards means that the tax burden falls on profits, which are squeezed heavily, reducing investment. Growth could still continue at a rapid rate, despite low growth of investment if the new equipment invested in were such that less capital was required per unit of putput and per worker. However, the wage inflation generated works in exactly the opposite direction, because it makes it more profitable for firms to use *more* capital-intensive methods in order to avoid the high cost of labour. Less output is generated from the investment that does occur therefore, further worsening the over-all rate of growth.

All this would be less serious if wage claims implicitly recognized the consequences of the expansion of the public sector. It is argued, however, that the role and objectives of organized labour prevent this. Though fragmented in structure and diverse in its mechanisms for determining pay, it is cohesive in the strength it exerts through free collective bargaining and in its deep-seated belief that its only concern is with the wages and working conditions of its members. If this is so, then it follows that no fundamental improvement can occur unless the Government takes action to reverse the expansion of the non-marketed sector.

The third view relates poor performance to the educational system in the U.K. Several aspects are involved here. Firstly, it has been suggested that a high degree of selectivity at an early age, whether it is based primarily on income as in the earlier decades of this centruy or more on intelligence as has mainly been the case recently, has created or exacerbated a substantial division between management and workers, reflected in inadequate communication and co-operation and failure to recognize their mutual interdependence. This may then have been worsened by the differences of wealth, income, and power that have frequently been associated with the differences in education. Secondly, that there exists a bias towards arts and pure science subjects, and away from the applied scientific, engineering, and business studies which are regarded as essential for a progressive and efficient industrial base. If valid, this appears to be less because of a deliberate channelling of educational resources into the arts and pure science side and rather because society or the educational system has generated a more prestigious image for these subjects, with the result that fewer very able people have been attracted to the other disciplines. Finally, this may have been matched by an inadequate emphasis on explicit managerial training and education, primarily at the adult level. In various ways, therefore, it is argued that the educational system in the U.K. has restrained the growth of productivity through its effect on management skills, the commercial application of technology, and the degree of co-operation between management and workforce.

All these suggestions—the sectoral disposition of labour, the growth of the public sector, and the educational system are all very controversial and to a great extent speculative. Few would disagree that improvements could be made in all three areas, but whether one or more of them is a major cause of the U.K.'s poor record of productivity remains uncertain. Although efforts have been made to improve all three, policy has been, and is likely to be, specifically directed at the more immediate causes given earlier.

2. Previous Policy towards Industry

2.1. Investment Incentives

One of the major instruments used by successive governments to improve the performance of Industry in the U.K. has been the use of Investment Incentives. As seen earlier (p. 52), firms are allowed to deduct from profit an amount to cover the depreciation of assets before taxable profits are arrived at. The most common method has been to deduct $1/n$th of the initial cost of the machine each year where n is the estimated number of years the machine will last. (Other methods exist, however, and are complicated by such things as scrap values, inflation, and technological obsolescence.) In 1945 the Government introduced a system of Initial Allowances. This permits firms to accelerate depreciation for tax purposes. For example, a 40 per cent initial allowance allows firms to deduct 40 per cent of the cost of a machine in its first year, independent of its normal annual allowance in that year. However, the annual allowances in subsequent years must be reduced so that, as before, the total depreciation over the life of the machine is equal to its net cost. The effect is to reduce *taxable* profits in the first year but correspondingly increase them over the remaining years of the machine's life. Taxation is therefore to a certain extent deferred.

In comparison with the previous system this therefore represented an automatic interest-free loan without security from the Inland Revenue. This entailed a net reduction in the cost to a firm of financing its operations and made more funds available than otherwise in the early stages of new equipment. This second effect was not immediate, however, because taxation is normally paid a year in arrears.

In 1954 Investment Allowances were introduced. These operated in the same manner except that no corresponding reduction in subsequent annual depreciation allowances was made. Thus if the Investment Allowance was 30 per cent, the total depreciation allowance for tax purposes over the life of the machine was 130 per cent. Taxation was not only deferred, therefore, but reduced in total because the reduction in the first year was not matched by any increase in later years. In that firms were then being credited with expenditures which they had not in fact incurred this system involved an effective subsidy, and increased the over-all expected post-tax profitability of investment.

One or other of these systems, and sometimes both together, have operated for much of the period since the war, the rates being, however, different in general on buildings as opposed to plant and machinery, and being varied over time (sometimes set at zero, thus effectively suspending operation). Increasingly, they were regarded as having several drawbacks. One, the delay in obtaining the benefit, has already been noted. In addition, firms had to make sufficient profit to have an initial tax bill larger than the value of the allowances before the full benefit could be obtained. Thirdly, the system or the rates were changed so frequently, on average more than once every three years, that it was both difficult and risky to take them into account in planning investment.

Partly as a result of these objections, and bearing in mind that the Investment Allowance system had involved an effective subsidy for some years, a new approach, the Investment Grant system was introduced in 1966. (Such grants had, however, already been employed on a regional basis as part of an incentive scheme to relocate firms; see below.) Investment Grants, generally equal to 20 per cent of the cost of plant and machinery (buildings continued to receive initial allowances), were paid in cash, thus making the subsidy explicit. The system was planned to be one on which firms could rely, with the cash payment being made within six months of the capital expenditure and being payable irrespective of whether the firm concerned was making profits. It was therefore hoped that, unlike the previous system, this would help firms making low profits or losses who were attempting to climb out of that situation by modernization, re-equipment, and expansion to obtain economies of scale.

The grants were tax-free, but their net effect is none the less only found by deducting the going company tax rate from them. This is because the total of annual allowances permitted is only the actual expenditure incurred by the firm—the remaining 80 per cent. In obtaining the grant, therefore, total depreciation is reduced by 20 per cent and tax is therefore now paid on this amount. With a tax rate of 40 per cent, a 20 per cent grant is then worth 12 per cent (the same as a 30 per cent Investment Allowance).

In practice, the payments were rarely as fast as had been intended, and the system itself only lasted four years (though payments agreed under it will not taper out completely until approximately 1980). Criticism focused on the payment of subsidies to loss-making firms, the need for confirmation that investment was eligible for a grant, and the large increase in both government taxation and expenditure figures that resulted. So in 1970 the Grant system was scrapped and a return was made to Initial Allowances at 35 per cent, but at 60 per cent for the first year as a short-term measure to accelerate investment, because of the high unemployment then existing. But in 1972 the rate was increased to 100 per cent (and from 15 to 40 per cent on buildings). In effect, capital costs are on a par with current costs, and there is the maximum deferment of tax liability in the first year consistent with no over-all subsidy (other than the zero interest charge on the deferment).

It is, of course, very hard to determine the over-all impact of these incentive schemes on the level of investment. Their impact on the supply of funds may only have effect if firms' investment is limited by financial constraints. Except for small fast-growing firms, and apart from a couple of relatively short periods, this generally appears not to have been the case in the U.K. Their incentive impact on the expected rate of return may be swamped by the changes to the expected return that relatively small adjustments in sales, cost, and price forecasts make; and their effect may be partly or totally negated if non-profitability criteria are used (explicitly or implicitly), if pre-tax calculations are done, or if the frequent changes in the incentives used have led to their exclusion from investment decision-taking. The majority of studies of the interview type at the microeconomic level support the view that they have not been very effective. More aggregative econometric analysis is inconclusive. Many studies indicate relatively little effect, but two or three more recent onces indicate the opposite. What cannot be disputed is that they have been unable to increase investment in the U.K. to a level comparable with other countries, and have therefore at best only served to mitigate what would otherwise have been an even worse record of investment and productivity.

The present system of 100 per cent Initial Allowances is thought to be appropriate because the generally poor and uncertain outlook for investment induces industry to adopt relatively short time horizons, and because the present system heavily concentrates its incentive in the first two years of an investment project. The absence of any effective subsidy nevertheless reduces its impact in comparison with other systems, and it is unlikely that a marked improvement will accrue as a result of it. In recent months discussions have started on a system whereby existing price controls would be eased and any profits obtained by companies as a result would be banked in an investment fund. These profits could then either be released only for investment purposes, and perhaps only at particular times determined by the Government, or taxed according to whether they were used for investment or not. Such an approach need not of course be tied to relaxation of price controls, and may in one form or another become an important element in the attempt to increase investment in the future.

2.2. Regional Policy

Regional policy in the U.K. has been primarily designed to halt and reverse the growing disparity between different regions in terms of income per head, unemployment, and economic growth. However, it has also been seen as a means of reducing inflationary pressures and increasing productivity; the first by preventing excess demand for labour and wage inflation in some areas when unemployment in others requires further reflation of the economy; the second by preventing under-utilization of resources, both public and private, capital and labour, in some areas when acute shortages exist elsewhere. The depressed regions, which tended to do less well on all the criteria used, were regarded as being depressed either because they were heavily dependent on one or more declining industries—mainly coal, textiles, shipbuilding, and agriculture—or because they were inherently less conducive to industrial expansion, through distance from supplies or from main markets or through geographical barriers to good communication and transport. Attempts to measure the relative importance of the two suggest on balance that the former is generally the more serious, especially when allowance is made for the fact that dependence on a declining industry, by reducing the rate of increase of incomes per head in the region, leads to less rapid advance in other local trades, services, and firms, and so in the region as a whole.

Conceived of purely in terms of differential rates of unemployment, it might be argued that policy could be designed to relocate the excess supply of labour in areas of excess demand, or relocate jobs through inducing firms to expand in the areas of high unemployment. While some gestures have been made towards the former approach, primarily through wider circulation of job opportunities, assistance for interview travel expenses and removal expenses, and through housing policy, it has never represented the main line of attack. Even in terms of unemployment alone it faces three disadvantages. Firstly, if the skilled and semi-skilled are generally more in demand and therefore potentially more mobile, schemes designed to increase migration from the depressed regions may well have their main impact on skilled workers, thus further reducing the attractiveness of the area to current and prospective employers, and so worsening unemployment among the unskilled. Secondly, movement of labour into the expanding areas not only increases the supply of labour but also the demand for goods, part of which will tend to be met by local traders, services, and manufacturers. Only part of the labour imbalance is therefore removed, and so the total migration required to remove the imbalance may be much larger than initially thought necessary. Thirdly, there is no guarantee that migration will be from among the unemployed or from jobs subsequently filled by someone previously unemployed. The rationale is further undermined if other objectives are brought in. Such migration may well increase the imbalance in congestion and in the demands placed upon various social services and resources such as schools, hospitals, etc. Over- and under-utilization of resources may continue to impair productivity, and the demands on local goods and services may exacerbate inflation. The main line of policy has therefore been to encourage firms to move to, or expand in, the depressed regions.

Here there have been two main types of instrument, the first being a system of control based on Industrial Development Certificates (I.D.C.s). Any industrial development over 5,000 square feet required one of these to be obtained before planning permission could be granted, and they were only readily issued for development in Development Areas, as the officially designated depressed regions became known in 1966 (I.D.C.s are in fact no longer required in these areas). The general policy elsewhere was only to issue an I.D.C. if it was likely that refusal would result in the loss of the development, either because it would not be embarked upon at all or because it would be relocated elsewhere in Europe. It is in fact very difficult to know how stringently this control was applied from the figures on applications and refusals because considerable informal discussion would normally occur first, during the course of which the unacceptability of a proposed development could be indicated.

The second instrument was to give incentives to firms to relocate. Initially these mainly took the form of higher investment incentives in the Development Areas. Cash grants were introduced in 1963 on both plant and machinery and buildings, in addition to 100 per cent initial allowances for the former. When Investment Grants were introduced throughout the country, the rate in the Development Areas at 40 per cent was twice that elsewhere. Buildings also received 25 per cent cash grants in both Development Areas and a new classification known as Intermediate Areas (generally 'fringe' areas suffering the symptoms of regional depression but not so acutely), and 35 per cent in the new Special Development Areas where the problems were most acute. Only the cash grants for buildings (at different rates) were retained after the abolition of Investment Grants in 1970, with 100 per cent initial allowances again becoming the main regional incentive. But this was subsequently regarded as a mistake, not only because it reduced the assistance given but also because it is especially in the depressed regions that firms may be potentially and actually efficient in their operations but still inadequately profitable, and therefore unable to take full advantage of allowances as opposed to grants. So in 1972 cash grants were reintroduced for buildings, plant, and machinery at 20 per cent in Development Areas, 22 per cent in Special Development Areas, and at 20 per cent on Buildings in Intermediate Areas. Unlike Investment Grants, these Regional Development Grants, as they were known, did not result in a corresponding reduction in the total annual depreciation permitted. The introduction of these grants provoked criticism on the grounds that they were a capital subsidy with the biggest attraction for capital-intensive firms, whereas the high unemployment in the Development Areas suggested that it would be more efficient to attract labour-intensive ones. Partly in response to this the Regional Employment Premium was introduced in 1967. This was a direct subsidy to all firms in Development Areas per employee per week, with different rates for men, women, and minors. Although they were originally to be phased out in 1974, and their future is still under review, they are none the less still being paid and are currently forecast to continue at least until 1980 (see [3]).

This too has been criticized on the ground that as it is paid in respect of all jobs in the depressed regions it is a relatively expensive way of stimulating *new* jobs. Against this it can be argued that the size of the problem is so large that job-creating policies could easily be undermined by simultaneous contractions of employment elsewhere in the depressed regions unless prevented through a general subsidy, quite apart from the fact that it would be administratively impossible to identify 'new' jobs for any appreciable period of time. On the relative merits of labour and capital subsidies there is a strong argument for continuing with both. Although labour subsidies may deal more directly with the problem of unemployment in the short term, if the over-all problem is to a great extent the dependence on declining industries then in the long term it will require the attraction of new, expanding industries which tend to be, though not exclusively, more capital intensive.

Many other regional instruments have been used, including the provision of infrastructure—roads, drainage, etc.—government-owned land and buildings at preferential rates, selective measures for land reclamation, clearance of derelict sites, removal grants, cheap loans, and grants to cover the cost of commercial loans. New Scottish and Welsh Development agencies will receive grants to establish and develop new industrial estates and purpose-built factories. In addition, there have been some efforts to polarize growth in particular areas by concentrating assistance, so that the expenditure there will have reinforcing 'regional multiplier' effects as the funds are spent on locally available goods and services rather than on ones 'imported' from outside the area. The size of these amplifying effects depends also on whether the subsidies are used to expand employment, increase wages, increase investment, lower prices, or pay out more dividends (the latter ones generally having smaller effects). There are, however, many unknowns in the process of growth geographically and to date little has been achieved in this direction.

Over all, regional policy has had mixed success. It is estimated that between 70,000 and 100,000 jobs have been created or maintained as a result, but this appears to have done little more than offset the decline in jobs that would otherwise have occurred. Recent changes in the prospects for the coal industry and the development of North Sea oil will both have some impact, as may the E.E.C.'s developing regional policy. Yet there is little sign that assistance at the present level will bring about over-all regional balance or make a very significant contribution to the improvement of industrial productivity in the U.K. through its effects on resource utilization and supply constraints.

2.3. Labour Mobility

The third element in previous policy has been the measures designed to increase the movement of labour from sectors of low productivity, over-manning, and long-term decline to those where the opposite conditions apply. The main instrument used was Selective Employment Tax, introduced in 1965. It was a levy per head on nearly all firms in the country, rebated back to some and rebated back with an additional premium in others. Thus employment in some sectors, primarily services and distribution, could be taxed, and in others, primarily manufacturing, subsidized in an effort to induce over time a reduction in employment in the former and an increase in the latter.

This measure suffered in two ways. The subsidy element was only main-tained for two years, after which the tax became a general revenue-raising tax no longer well suited for its redistributive function. In addition, its introduction coincided with a seven-year period of relatively high unemploy-ment in which labour shortages in key sectors, manifest in periods of low unemployment, were much less significant. The measure was then removed shortly before the next sharp upswing in demand, and it remains unclear whether it had an impact in the interim.

The effectiveness of such a measure also crucially depends on the extent to which the necessary retraining of those changing jobs is provided. Assis-tance for training has been a much-discussed policy, but the total expenditure on it by Government remains small in comparison with what many think necessary. Current plans do, however, envisage a doubling of the 1975 figure of £86m. in real terms and a further 25 per cent increase over the following four years. These funds go mainly on skill centres, colleges of further educa-tion, employers' establishments, etc. and on grants to Industrial Training Boards and to sectors not covered by them. In addition, there is the Employ-ment Services Agency responsible for placing people, and the Manpower Services Commission with, amongst others, the function of planning sectoral shifts of labour, and the retraining it requires.

The planned doubling of the total of all these 'redeployment' expenditures in real terms by Government over a five-year period is an indication of the greatly increased priority this area is receiving. It is not at present combined with any measure explicitly designed to encourage sectoral mobility such as S.E.T. originally was, and it remains to be seen whether the Government can bring about a substantial improvement in productivity through its retraining and job placement assistance.

2.4. Other Measures

Of the many other items of assistance given by the Government with implications for industrial productivity, two should be mentioned. An amount generally in excess of £300m. per annum (1975 prices) has been spent under the heading of support to Industrial Innovation. In fact, nearly all of this went on the Space and Aircraft Industries or Nuclear Power. Only about 10 per cent goes on general industrial research and development and technological and industrial sponsorship. The over-all effect may be larger than this implies because much of it is on a cost-sharing basis with industry. None the less, it appears that in general the amount of industrial innovation carried out is very largely determined by private industry's willingness and ability to finance it, and current Government plans involving relatively small increases in this support and very large cut-backs in its support to the aircraft industry, appear unlikely to alter this.

The second is direct aid for private industry. The main recipients have been or will be the shipbuilding industry, International Computers (Holdings) Ltd., Chrysler (U.K.) Ltd., and British Leyland Ltd., the last of which it is planned will receive £200m. in addition to the £247m. spent in purchasing the shares of the company and the £300m. earmarked for it from the National Enterprise Board (see below). In the case of both car companies, aid has been provided partly because of the consequences for unemployment if either failed and for balance of payments reasons. The collapse of either would have led to increasing dependence on imported cars, particularly in the case of British Leyland Ltd., which is also a major U.K. exporter. The bulk of the funds is designed for investment expenditure on re-equipment, modernization and expansion to make the firms profitable, self-financing, and internationally competitive on the basis of high levels of productivity. The aid to British Leyland is of particular importance. It represents one of the largest sums ever provided to a largely autonomous, if now nationalized, undertaking to enable it to escape the self-amplifying effects of low productivity and low or negative profits. If successful, this approach might easily become the basis for radical improvements in performance in many other industries in the U.K., but if not, then unless it is for reasons peculiar to the car industry or the firm concerned, it would indicate that the problem of productivity in the U.K. is too deep rooted for the provision of finance and investment alone to overcome.

Part of a successful strategy will be to identify in advance the firms that it will be productive to assist. A recent White Paper (H.M.S.O., 6315), gave some preliminary indications of how this might be done. Firstly, data will be collected on the past performance of the different sectors of the economy, and in particular their size, rate of growth, trading performance, import content, their competitiveness, importance to other sectors, and the growth of world demand for the products concerned. Secondly, the implications for the sectors of the Government's own medium-term projections will be analysed, together with the expected impact of different possible future rates of growth of the U.K. economy. Thirdly, the possibility of new developments leading to improvements in performance will be examined. This would focus on such factors as the possibility of import substitution, the development of new technologies, the minimum economically viable size of firms, the security of raw materials, the progress of the E.E.C., and the growth of new competition from overseas.

All this is designed to allow some industries and even individual firms to be classified as either:

  (a) intrinsically successful;
  (b) having the potential for success if action is taken;
  (c) vital for other sectors of the economy.

In general, only firms coming under one of these headings would qualify for assistance, especially if its actual or potential success was based on comparative advantage. It would then be necessary to examine the disaggregated implications of this for particular firms, and in addition there would need to be criteria for deciding which firms in a qualifying industry would receive any aid requested. Again, past performance, potential for the future, and special factors would be the main ones. In all this the role of N.E.D.C. would be vital, both in disaggregating the implications and in providing the vehicle for general agreement on the strategy as between Government, Management, and Unions.

3. Policy Options in the Current Situation

3.1. The Market Mechanism

Two main conclusions can be drawn from an examination of past government Industrial policy. Firstly, the range and level of assistance has been considerable, being not less than £1,000m. excluding the nationalized industries and including only those measures likely to have some effect on productivity.[2] Secondly, it has either been inappropriate or inadequate in the sense that the problem of relatively low productivity still remains in an acute form. As a result, it has in recent years been questioned whether a more radical approach to the problem is required. Here we briefly describe two proposals, each representative of a type of programme actively discussed in the last three or four years.

The first is based on a substantial withdrawal of intervention or support by Government and very much increased reliance on the operation of a free market mechanism. Very briefly, the main elements in such a programme would be the removal of most incentives or aid, with a corresponding reduction in company taxation (at least on retained profits); letting companies that fail collapse, thus allowing resources to go to other companies where the management and/or the workforce is more efficient, where funds are more readily available, where market prospects are stronger, etc. Dominant market positions would be removed where possible, if necessary by splitting up large companies, and anti-trust policy would be maintained or strengthened. Just as there would be restraints on firms utilizing dominant positions

---

[2] Regional Support and Regeneration £441m.; Industrial R & D £36m.; Selective Assistance £408m.; labour training and mobility £143m., all for 1974–5.

so the activities of unions would also be circumscribed to prevent them from exercising a monopolistic influence on wage levels. Instead, wage bargaining would be at plant level, based on productivity, profits, working conditions, and other economic aspects of the *plant*. Given such an environment it is argued that firms would have to be efficient to survive, and real wages, profits, and employment would all depend directly on improving plant productivity through co-operation, innovation, and effort. The explicit dependence of the firm on both management and workforce might then lead to, and gain from, substantially increased representation of the workforce in the decisions of the company.

Such an approach is controversial and its feasibility has been called into question. The existence of rapid inflation and of an incomes policy have tended to remove wage bargaining further from purely plant-level factors, and reversal of this trend might be difficult. Efforts to reduce union members' bargaining power through the Industrial Relations Act were largely unsuccessful, and a policy of not intervening to assist ailing companies introduced in 1970–1 was fairly rapidly reversed, with the Industry Act of 1972 considerably extending the potential scope for government assistance. Unless substantial import competition exists it is generally difficult to envisage the removal of dominant market positions because of the managerial and physical problems involved, and the possible loss of valuable economies of scale, if not in manufacturing then in finance, marketing, and distribution. In addition, there would almost certainly be increases in localized unemployment at least for a period and changes in the distribution of income, both of which might have unfavourable repercussions on the over-all record of industrial disputes, productivity, and prices, and therefore on the balance of payments. Finally it should be reiterated that the market mechanism, if left to itself, may be just as likely to worsen firms' ability to compete internationally as to improve it, and the effect of low profits on investment and productivity is not the only aspect. It may be less profitable for any individual firm to expand in a depressed region, yet more profitable over all if a substantial number of firms expand there. It may be more profitable for firms to let others operate training schemes and then offer higher wages to attract the skilled men away, but over all, all firms will suffer through a shortage of skilled labour. Imitation rather than innovation may be safer, but against worsen industrial performance over all, and so on. For these sorts of reasons, attention has focused more recently on identifying an acceptable minimum level of post-tax profit for industry, and framing taxation and industrial policy so that this minimum can at least be achieved.

3.2. *Public Ownership*

Far removed from this is the proposal, increasingly made in the last few years, for a very substantial extension of public ownership of industry. A specific suggestion around which discussion has crystallized is that the Government should take over at least 25 of the largest 100 firms in the private sector covering approximately one-sixth of turnover and one-fifth of profits currently in the private sector. One hundred per cent control would remove the need to worry about minority private shareholders. This situation would give the Government a very powerful instrument to directly control prices, investment, trade, employment, training, export performance, and the development of technology. Cost-benefit criteria could be employed on a wide scale to ensure the inclusion of all social cost and benefits in major decisions. Subsidies would be tied to the needs of both employment and productivity, and increased co-operation between management and workforce could be generated through an extension of industrial democracy and worker representation. A series of agreements between the Government and other individual firms would ensure adequate information and supervision of them, with the possibility of nationalization for failure to agree or comply.

The approach outlined here also faces potentially big problems. There is very little experience in the U.K. of successful government control of manufacturing from which to learn, though the behaviour of the State holding company in Italy (I.R.I.) on which the proposal is partly based may give some guidance and indication of the scheme's potential. But the major problem is that change of ownership by itself does nothing to improve productivity. It may permit the allocation of funds for long-term investment which would not otherwise be forthcoming through the capital market but it is not clear that many of the 100 largest firms have experienced serious financial shortage. There is still little agreement over whether public ownership in the past has improved industrial relations significantly, and emphasis on the social costs of job relocation and unemployment are generally thought unlikely to improve productivity. Finally, there still remain serious and almost totally unexamined difficulties in maintaining efficiency in managerial planning, supervision, control, and decision-taking in publicly owned enterprise because of the multiplicity of objectives they are given, government intervention in management operations, or the lack of such stringent financial disciplines as exist in many private firms. Therefore, while this approach may make Industry more responsive to government intentions, and more responsible to many of the needs of society as reflected in government policy, it is more doubtful whether it can bring about the radical change in productivity necessary for a marked improvement in material living standards.

Out of this approach developed the proposal for a National Enterprise Board as the main vehicle for such intervention, primarily into the manufacturing sector of the U.K., backed up by a system of Planning Agreements with firms remaining in the private sector. In the course of further discussion and preparation for Parliamentary approval the character, rationale, and intended method of operation of both were very significantly altered. It is even possible to interpret the final form of the proposals as an adjunct to the normal forces of the market, extending on a more systematic basis the assistance previously given to overcome particular problems thrown up by the operation of the market mechanism. Partly because of this change, and partly because these proposals are only just being put into practice, it is not possible to say how the new initiative will operate or what its effect will be. It none the less marks a major stage in the development of a comprehensive industrial policy in the U.K. and it is to this that we now turn.

4. The New Approach to Industry in the U.K.

4.1. The National Enterprise Board

The 1975 Industry Act established a National Enterprise Board. This is now in operation and has £1,000m. at its disposal, although it is envisaged that the bulk of this will be spent in roughly equal annual amounts over the four financial years 1976–80. Its major functions are specified as the improvement of industrial efficiency and international competitiveness, assistance to firms who are short of necessary funds, the take-over of existing government share-holdings to ensure profitable public enterprise, and the promotion of indus-trial democracy. It is able to buy up the shares of private companies in the open market and provide funds to firms in return for a stake in their equity. Such public ownership is generally intended to be by mutual agreement with the company concerned, with compulsory nationalization being quite separ-ate and normally requiring, as previously, a Bill to Parliament. Approval by the Secretary for State for Trade and Industry is required if a stake in a com-pany is in excess of £10m. or 30 per cent of its total equity. He may give both general and specific directions to the N.E.B., against which there is no appeal, though it appears that this is primarily designed with over-all strategy con-siderations in mind as opposed to day-to-day operations, together with the need to ensure over-all Ministerial control of public funds. He also lays down the financial duties of the N.E.B. subject to the approval of the Treasury. The acquisition and operation of a loss-making concern for non-commercial reasons is to be separately accountable, emphasizing the commitment to profitability in its main operations. The first large provisional commitment of its funds so far—approximately £300m. over the initial four-year period— is to British Leyland Ltd., dependent on the current and expected perfor-mance of the company. Rolls-Royce is another Company likely to receive a large loan from the Board.

According to draft guidelines announced in March 1976 the N.E.B. will be subject to the same obligations and opportunities as companies in the private sector. In particular this includes: the City Code on Takeover and Merger operations; Prices legislation; Fair Trading Legislation; Industrial Development Certificates; Planning Controls; Regional Development Grants. In addition its subsidiary companies will not be able to obtain a competitive advantage by obtaining loans from the N.E.B. at lower than usual interest rates. Finally, the N.E.B. will not have access to information supplied by companies in confidence to the Government, for example in a Planning Agreement (see next section) even if a joint venture of some sort between the Company and the N.E.B. is being contemplated.

This brief description of its main characteristics illustrates clearly how different the N.E.B. will be from its original conception. Its scale of interven-tion at £1,000m. is very much smaller than originally planned, though it is of course quite possible that its scale will eventually be increased. Compul-sory acquisition is no longer possible, and earlier emphasis on a cost-benefit approach and the creation of intense competitive pressure on firms remaining in the private sector has been replaced by emphasis on the provision of long-term finance, reorganization of the firms acquired, and the need to ensure profitability of operations. In addition, any extension of industrial democracy under the N.E.B. umbrella is likely to be in the form of increased worker participation at the company level rather than at the level of the Board itself.

All this indicates that the N.E.B. could adopt one or more of a number of different roles. At one extreme it could operate purely as a Government holding company with over-all responsibility for, but little active intervention in, the conduct of its subsidiaries. Or it might be more like a public Merchant Bank, taking up non-controlling but sometimes significant shareholdings in companies, exerting influence over strategic decisions, and acting as an important channel of finance. Alternatively, it could take up the role of the abolished Industrial Reorganization Corporation, attempting to promote changes in industrial structure, perhaps accompanied by changes in management, which seem desirable on grounds of efficiency or export competitiveness but which are unlikely to occur through competitive pressures alone. Other roles which appear to have been rejected at least for the present, but which it might adopt at a later stage, are as a vehicle for providing various types of grant and subsidy for non-commercial reasons, in particular to avoid heavy local unemployment, though some have expressed concern that this could lead to the support of firms with no commercial future at all; as a type of nationalized industry, laying down price, investment, and financial rules in accordance with which its business should be conducted; and finally, as a vehicle for a cost-benefit approach, intensified competition, and industrial democracy. For the foreseeable future it is the first three, or possibly four, functions that will be paramount though, and section 4.4 below provides a framework for assessing their likely impact.

4.2. Planning Agreements

Here again the policy finally established is rather different from the intention which provided the initial impetus. Planning Agreements will not be enforceable civil contracts but the Government nevertheless intends they should be dependable from both sides. They are primarily designed for large firms but there will be no statutory requirement for any firm to enter one. If it does, however, it must provide the information required by the Government which is at the heart of the system. This covers existing and planned operations mainly with regard to investment, prices, product development, employment, exports, import requirements, industrial relations, consumer protection, and environmental aspects. It is envisaged that they would be three-year rolling agreements, but that existing company planning mechanisms and time horizons should be adopted if more convenient. In return the Government will make available its forecasts for the economy, its plans for the management of the economy, make grants under its existing powers where desirable, and guarantee these for the life of the Planning Agreement. Unions will have access to these agreements but will not be a party to them.

Although this is not unlike the process which has occurred in nationalized industries in the past, it is difficult without direct experience of Planning

Agreements to know what they will achieve. Probably their most important function will be in providing a means for direct discussion between Government and large firms, which will not only increase the ability of both to foresee the consequences of the other's actions but allow each to clearly present its own viewpoint and objectives. In particular, the Government may be able with sufficient warning and in conjunction with the Manpower Services Commission, local authorities, and the firm itself to deal with the employment consequences of commercially necessary closures, and discuss at an early stage before decisions become rigid such matters as the location of plant, changes in industrial relations, and other matters which have important social implications. In the other direction Planning Agreements offer a new and potentially powerful way by which firms can impress on Government its need for a stable economic environment, a period of perhaps five to ten years without major changes in incentive systems, company taxation, subsidies, etc. and the maximum information on how the Government would be likely to react to various possible developments such as a further deterioration in the balance of payments, further wage rises very much in excess of productivity growth, and so on.

The need for a co-operative approach from both sides is seen more clearly if one considers what would happen if a company radically departed from its Planning Agreement as a result of unforeseen changes in its economic position. No sanction exists to deal with this situation. The existence of the agreement would mean, firstly, that the Government would get maximum warning, and therefore maximum time to consult the people and institutions effected. Secondly, it would enable the Government to present its view of the problem, and attempt to come to an agreement with the company on the best way forward, bearing in mind *all* the consequences of the new course of action for the economic performance of other companies and for the pursuit of wider objectives such as the external position, inflation, and employment. Such discussions might reveal irreconcilable objectives, but even here the forewarning received by the Government would be of use to it. The more serious worry from some business quarters is that such a system will inevitably involve a lack of confidentiality of company plans with possibly quite serious consequences for companies' competitive strategy and profitability. It is possible, however, that this might be handled in a manner proposed in connection with Information Agreements, to which we now turn.

4.3. Information Agreements

The 1975 Industry Act also contains separate provision for company disclosure of information. Any firm may be required by the Secretary of State for Trade and Industry to provide information on its employment, output, capital, investment, sales, productivity, acquisitions, exports, industrial property, and other less important items, the main purpose being to make firms more generally accountable for their performance. Clearly, any firm with a Planning Agreement will already have provided information on many, if not all, of these, but the disclosure clauses can apply to any firm and are not voluntary. This information will again be available to the trade unions concerned, unless it is in the national interest that it be kept secret. A company can, however, appeal to a committee specially created for the purpose on the ground that the disclosure would be harmful to the company's interests. If this appeal is accepted, the only people with access to the information apart from the committee and the company itself will be the government department concerned and the Manpower Services Commission. Whether this potentially harmful effect occurs will therefore depend on the discretionary power of this committee and whether it interprets it in a manner essentially sympathetic or hostile to the companies concerned.

4.4. Prospects for Industrial Productivity

This is by no means an exhaustive list of recent proposals in the field of Industrial policy. In particular, it does not include recent changes of approach to pricing and finance in the nationalized industries, nor plans for an extension of public ownership in the Aircraft, Oil, and Ship-building industries and some financial activities. It nevertheless covers the core of a new approach, and it is useful to conclude by trying to evaluate its likely impact on the performance of industry in the U.K.

In so far as the N.E.B. will be able to provide long-term finance to enable firms to climb out of current difficulties, and in so far as Planning Agreements provide a more certain economic environment for firms, the new measures offer a basis for improvement. On the other hand, they so yet provide only a starting-point for dealing with the many problems of labour supply and skills, management performance, wage control, innovation, and foreign market penetration which will have to be overcome. But a more fundamental point may be made.

To simplify greatly, assume two major goals of government economic policy, namely full employment and rapid improvement in productivity (the latter to abate inflationary pressure and improve the balance of payments). In the short term these two objectives are frequently inconsistent with each other. Rapid increases in productivity generally require substantial reductions in manning levels, rapid switching to the newest and usually more capital-intensive methods of production, and the contraction of inefficient plant in declining industries in favour of more efficient ones in expanding industries. Each brings with it the prospect of local or more widespread unemployment which can only be absorbed later as total demand expands.

Faced with this dilemma we can identify, on the basis of what has been said, three different responses. The first places maximum emphasis on employment, tends to oppose closure, rapid de-manning, etc. and requires that improvements in productivity, whether via the private or public sector, occur against a full employment background. This implies a much slower rate of change in productivity levels, and the acceptance of either low profit or losses in a number of cases. The second is to renounce the commitment to full employment, emphasizing profitability criteria alone, as a means of obtaining better productivity performance. But we have already seen a number of reasons why such an approach might well fail to achieve this end, and so result in the non-attainment of either objective.

Between these one may discern a third response which has elements of both. This recognizes that the commitment to continuous full employment must be relaxed but that investment must be much increased in the short and medium term largely irrespective of the forecast profits for individual firms, in order to achieve the very rapid improvements in productivity necessary to be more competitively viable internationally, to reduce inflation, and to eventually improve living standards more quickly. This policy would then be coupled with greatly expanded assistance for the training and movement between jobs that the expansion will require.

If carried far enough this could entail some form of training or retraining for all those not employed or receiving other full-time education who wished it.

It is not inconceivable that such an approach could be provided by the new industrial strategy described, but initial impressions suggest that it might pursue an exactly opposite one—a re-emphasis on profitability as the criterion of the N.E.B.'s operations, coupled with stress being laid on the employment consequences of commercial decisions in the Planning Agreements system and the implication that this criterion may take precedence over that of productivity. If this interpretation is correct then there may be an essential contradiction in the proposed strategy, and a constraint on its ability to generate substantial improvements in industrial productivity.

This line of argument is again both speculative and controversial, and is mainly provided to draw out the main issues lying behind the new strategy. It may be that the increased range of instruments available, and the increased scale of government control will allow it to obtain rapid productivity growth against a background of full or near full employment. But the only certain conclusions are that neither the market mechanism nor previous intervention has been able to do this adequately, and that in the coming years the N.E.B. is likely to face in acute form twin pressures to be both profitable and responsive to many social objectives. To be able to meet these demands *and* achieve a very substantial improvement in productivity in the U.K. will be a very difficult task indeed.

Bibliography

In that the problems faced by Industry policy are low growth, inflation, and external deficit the further reading of Chapters 5, 7, and 8 are all relevant. For recent Government statements of its industrial strategy see:

[1] *The Regeneration of British Industry*, Cmnd. 5710 (H.M.S.O., Aug. 1974).
[2] *An Approach to Industrial Strategy*, Cmnd. 6315 (H.M.S.O., Nov. 1975).

Planned government expenditure in all areas is summarized in:
[3] *Public Expenditure to 1979–80*, Cmnd. 6393 (H.M.S.O., Feb. 1976).
For detailed analysis of Regional policy see:
[4] BROWN, A. J. *The Framework of Regional Economics in the United Kingdom* (Cambridge University Press, 1972).
[5] McCRONE, G. *Regional Policy in Britain* (Allen and Unwin, 1971).
[6] STILWELL, F. *Regional Economic Policy* (Macmillan, 1972).

The major statement of the case for much greater government intervention is to be found in:

[7] HOLLAND, S. *The Socialist Challenge* (Quartet Books, 1975).
while that arguing the opposite case is to be found in:
[8] BACON, R. and ELTIS, W. *Britain's Economic Problem: Too Few Producers?* (Macmillan, 1976).

A general discussion of many of the economic and political problems involved is to be found in:
[9] DELL, E. *Political Responsibility and Industry* (Allen and Unwin, 1973).
[10] KNIGHT, A. *Private Enterprise and Public Intervention* (Allen and Unwin, 1974).

The literature on the impact of Investment Incentives is generally more advanced. See:
[11] CORNER, A. J. and WILLIAMS, A. 'The Sensitivity of Business to Initial and Investment Allowances', *Economica*, 32 (1965).
[12] AGARWALA, R. and GOODSON, G. 'An Analysis of the Effects of Investment Incentives on Investment Behaviour', *Economica*, 36 (1969).
[13] FIELDSTEIN, M. and FLEMMING, J. 'Tax Policy, Corporate Saving and Investment Behaviour in Britain', *Review of Economic Studies*, 31 (3) (1971).
[14] HARCOURT, G. 'Investment Decision Criteria, Investment Incentives and the Choice of Technique', *Economic Journal*, 78 (1968).
The latest estimates of the role of mergers in industrial concentration is in:
[15] HANNAH, L. *The Rise of the Corporate Economy* (Methuen, 1976).

20

Postscript on Current Policy Options

D. J. MORRIS

The last eleven chapters have dealt with different government policies designed to influence and improve the working of the U.K. economy. Some were classified as short-term policies, primarily concerned with the management of aggregate demand and the objectives of full employment, stable demand growth, and balance of payments equilibirum. The others were classified as long term and were mainly concerned with industrial structure and performance and the objectives of improving efficiency and the rate of growth of productivity. In both cases there has been controversy and some changes in policy in the light of different economic situations, new priorities being attached to different objectives, and changing views about the way in which the economy operates. The policy options available for dealing with the long-term problems of the U.K. economy were reviewed in the last chapter, but it is appropriate to conclude by summarizing the options available over the shorter term for dealing with unemployment, inflation, and the balance of payments.

At the time of writing (March 1976) the U.K. economy may be described briefly as follows. Gross Domestic Product has fallen over 5 per cent from its 1974 peak, industrial production has fallen nearly 10 per cent, and unemployment has therefore risen from under 600,000 at the beginning of 1974 to approximately 1,200,000 at the beginning of 1976. Although output is now beginning to rise again, the rate of growth is unlikely to be sufficient to halt the rise in unemployment, particularly in the short term because of the lagged impact of output on employment. Investment in manufacturing has fallen 20 per cent although here too there are the first indications of an upturn in recent investment anticipations data. The current account of the balance of payments, though very erratic recently, is on an improving trend with a greatly improved non-oil deficit turned round into a surplus which, together with a roughly constant invisible surplus, has now offset over half of the visible deficit. The increase in average earnings (year on year) has fallen from a peak of over 30 per cent to nearly half that figure, and price inflation has dipped from a peak of 27 per cent to under 20 per cent with the prospect of further falls. These movements contributed to a reduction in real disposable income of nearly 4 per cent in the earlier part of 1975, but the second half of 1975 saw a halt to this and a partial reversal. On the policy side the expansion of the money supply through 1974 and 1975 first stopped partly maybe because of a reduced demand for money consequent upon the depressed state of the economy, but has since started to expand again. The public sector financial deficit is now running in the region of £10,000m., and the exchange rate has continued to fall, to over 34 per cent below its value against a weighted average of other currencies in August 1971. Internationally the expected increase in world activity has been slow to appear, but both the U.S. and West Germany are now moving into a strong growth phase. In the crucial matter of relative inflation rates the U.K. is still noticeably above all her major trading partners, especially the U.S. and West Germany, although the latter's has recently risen perhaps temporarily from 5 to 7 per cent.

This presents a gloomy picture when compared with the objectives of full employment, rising living standards, low inflation, both absolutely and relative to other countries, and balance of payments equilibrium. Despite a very large government deficit and substantial falls in the exchange rate neither full employment nor balance of payments surplus is being achieved, and inflation is still a major problem. While the part played by the oil crisis and the subsequent policy reactions to it have been examined earlier (Chapter 14) it is still necessary to identify the best way forward from the existing position. In turning to the policy options that have been discussed two factors are immediately clear. The first is that there are at least three quite distinct schools of thought as to the best demand management strategy, and second, that they all largely agree in rejecting the traditional emphasis on a one- to two-year time horizon. Not only has the concept of 'fine tuning' largely been rejected, but short-term demand management in all cases is seen only in the context of the much longer-term strategy of which it is part. This shift of emphasis has occurred because (i) the control of inflation has become the dominant objective and is more intractable than that of unemployment, (ii) the time-lags involved and the problems of forecasting have both become clearer, reducing the role of fine tuning, (iii) there is now widespread acceptance that short-term demand management, both fiscal and monetary, has longer-term consequences which are difficult or impossible to avoid and which have hitherto received less attention than they deserve, (iv) the increase in the proportion of GNP pre-empted by the public sector has increased, implying that the Government's long-term expenditure plans are a bigger constraint on demand management strategies, and (v) the long-term trends in U.K. economic performance are a major constraint on the success of demand management policies but appear relatively little affected by them, thus redirecting attention to the longer-term trends.

To see these points more clearly the three different approaches are briefly described below. The first on which current government policy is based we term the 'Treasury' Approach. The main strand in this is the continuation of a stringent incomes policy coupled with income tax relief. This is designed to have two effects. Firstly, to bring down the rate of increase of wages to a level much nearer to the long-term trend rate of growth of productivity, thus over a period removing much of the present inflation, and secondly, to permit only that growth of post-tax real incomes and hence of consumer expenditure consistent with the demand on resources of an improvement in the balance of payments, planned government expenditure, and demand-led investment. The less stringent the incomes policy the smaller the tax concessions in order to prevent an increase in the demand for consumer products increasing the balance of payments problem and pre-empting resources needed elsewhere. A major assumption of this approach is that the expected growth of world demand and trade will bring about a rapid improvement in U.K. exports, and that this will then be a major factor in improving the balance of payments and stimulating demand and investment at home. This, together with the fall in the rate of inflation, would mean that the exchange rate, already much lower than a year ago, could be retained at roughly its current level. The public sector's financial deficit would increase further initially as a result of the tax cuts, but would then start to fall quite quickly as the increase in employment increased tax revenue, both direct and indirect, (and reduced welfare benefits) against current plans for a very much smaller growth in government expenditure. The money supply growth would be controlled as far as possible to meet increases in demand for money to prevent deflationary rises in interest rates, but not expanded beyond this and possibly restrained a little below it to add to the restraining influence on prices. If successful this strategy would it is thought by 1978-9 bring the balance of payments into surplus, inflation down into single figures, and unemployment down to the target level of 650,000.

This approach is strikingly different from that traditionally pursued in the past. There is no commitment to reduce unemployment to its minimum over an eighteen-month to two-year period, but a three- to four-year one to achieve a level historically speaking still quite high. Recognition of an inconsistency between internal and external balance is not seen as a basis for further devaluation but for the postponement of full employment until reduction in the rate of inflation and external developments makes them consistent. Finally, despite heavy unemployment a semi-permanent and strict incomes policy is seen as the only way of reducing the rate of increase of wages.

Different as this is from previous economic policy in terms of strategy and time horizon it is less of a departure than the second approach—the latest developments in the New Cambridge school.[1] This focuses on the resources that will be available to 1980 for the private sector after the prior claim of current government expenditure plans and the need to channel resources in to the balance of payments to correct the current account deficit and repay at least some of the debts accumulated in the past. This includes an allowance for the expected deterioration in the terms of trade which implies that more needs to be produced for export to pay for a given volume of imports. After allowing for rebuilding of stocks, the payment of interest on public sector debt, and the forecast movement in profits (dependent on expected growth of output and capacity utilization), the amount left for increases in

[1] See *Economic Policy Review* No. 2 (Dept. of Applied Economics, Cambridge University, Mar. 1976).

real wages is calculated by the Cambridge Economic Policy Group (C.E.P.G.) to be at best a 7½ per cent increase *in total* over the next five years, and at worst a 2½ per cent *fall*, dependent on the change in unemployment and the trend of profits. This leads them to argue that on existing strategy incomes policy would have to be maintained over the whole of that period and be very much tougher than currently envisaged. Failure to bring the growth of real wages down to this at best very low figure would again result in an 'inflationary gap', that is, an excess claim on resources which could only be met (temporarily) by de-stocking and a balance of payments deficit in the course of which there would again be an inflationary pressure, a squeeze on profits, and reductions in investment.

The implication of the C.E.P.G. analysis is not only that the Treasury approach is undesirable but most unlikely to succeed. This argument is based on the view that wages are very largely unaffected (except temporarily perhaps) by either unemployment levels or incomes policy. Thus the problem, instead of being one of reducing the rate of increase in wages, becomes one of increasing the rate of increase in real output so that the largely autonomously determined rise in wages will not generate an excess claim on resources. A more rapid rate of growth of output would have unacceptable consequences for the balance of payments, unless exports could be increased sufficiently to offset this, but a central aspect of the analysis is that the U.K.'s export performance has in fact been marginally worse than even that determined by our relative decline in international competitiveness. They therefore conclude that only a massive devaluation (nearly 40 per cent) or the imposition of import controls could generate the increase in exports and import substitutes necessary both to stimulate the required growth of output and achieve the required balance of payments surplus. Of the two it is argued that import controls are preferable because a large devaluation would push up import prices directly, generate severe inflationary pressures at a time when wage settlements were being held down, and would result in real post-tax wages in 1980 about 5 per cent below those existing in 1975. Import controls, by contrast, would avoid these consequences, reduce unemployment by the same amount, generate the required balance of payments surplus, *and* permit an increase in real post-tax wages over the same period of between 3 and 8 per cent. A progressive reduction in the public sector's financial deficit would help by reducing the excess claim on resources. This is likely to happen anyway over the next four years, but it would be completely eliminated given the C.E.P.G. strategy.

This is again very obviously a four-year strategy. Unemployment would still be 900,000 in 1980 (in contrast to their forecast of 1,580,000 under existing policies and the Government's target of 650,000 by 1979). It implies that the Government's plans involve claims on real resources which are inconsistent unless very rapid growth of output occurs, or incomes policy is long term and very severe. It is based on the view that present policy offers no hope of the former, despite the forecast upturn in world trade, and no hope of the latter because it would be unacceptable and unworkable if attempted. While incomes policy may be of some assistance, therefore, they believe that import controls are essential if the U.K.'s problems are to be overcome.

The third approach is the monetarist one discussed earlier (Chapter 12). This argues that free collective bargaining will tend to generate excessive wage settlements, that this would tend to price labour out of the market with a consequent rise in unemployment, but that commitment to full employment results in this being avoided through budget deficits and expansion of the money supply. The combination of free collective bargaining and the commitment to full employment are then only compatible at the cost of accelerating inflation (see Chapter 7), which undermines export competitiveness, generates low growth of demand and productivity, and in any case cannot ultimately prevent the appearance of the 'natural' rate of unemployment. The main policy implications of this are, first, to set the public sector deficit (or surplus) so that at full employment with the same tax rates, etc. it would be zero (the New Cambridge approach also focuses on the need to determine the public sector financial balance in this way). Actual deficits or surpluses then only result from cyclical swings in the economy itself and are inherently stabilizing. Second, to control the growth of the money supply strictly in line with the maximum sustainable growth of real output. On the monetarist model this ensures maximum growth, full ('natural') employment, and the elimination of inflation. The balance of payments could then be brought into balance by movements in the exchange rate, made fully flexible apart from government intervention to stabilize large short-term flows. Again a short-term focus is abandoned, and as we have seen it is the monetarist school which has been the strongest critic of the view that short-term demand management can achieve employment levels for very long above these which would be generated by the market mechanism. It is recognized that the short-term consequences would in fact be to substantially increase unemployment but it is argued that this is the inevitable cost of avoiding high unemployment in the longer term. Incomes policy on this approach is seen as unnecessary if the money supply is controlled and inevitably unsuccessful if it is not.

The difference between the three schools is very great. The Treasury approach places main emphasis on incomes policy which the New Cambridge school regards as inadequate and the Monetarist school regards as irrelevant. The New Cambridge school places its emphasis on import controls which the Treasury (so far) and the Monetarists reject as leading to protection of and further decline in the U.K.'s poor industrial performance instead of a reversal of it. The Monetarist school relies on control of the money supply, which the Treasury approach sees as a subsidiary aspect of the Government's deficit and the New Cambridge school largely ignores.

Not only their main policy instruments but their method of dealing with specific problems is quite different. To control inflation the three respectively advocate an incomes policy to control wages, an increase in real output to match wage increases, and control of the money supply. The balance of payments is primarily brought into equilibrium respectively by the control of U.K. costs coupled with an upturn in world demand, by import controls, and by price and exchange rate flexibility. Finally, the reduction of unemployment respectively depends on export demand and budgetary policy, on import substitution, and on the workings of supply and demand in the labour market.

These glaring differences can all be related back to one fundamental conflict of view, namely, how wages are determined. Monetarists believe in supply and demand functions for labour, a market-clearing price, and equilibrium levels of employment. Interference in this process when unemployment rises can only result in the inflationary pressures that are central in the explanation of the U.K.'s poor performance. The other two approaches are both explicitly Keynesian in their belief that no such labour market exists, and that wages are determined (except possibly in the short term) largely independent of the state of the labour market. Where the latter two differ is over whether incomes policy can make a significant impact on the process of wage setting. The present Treasury view is that it can; the New Cambridge school view is that it cannot.

Thus any view about the appropriate economic policy to be pursued in the U.K. in the next four years requires or implies a view about the determination of wages. Yet this is one of the areas where uncertainty is greatest. Chapter 10 described the many factors, economic, social, moral, and psychological that are involved and about many of which there is still much ignorance. Nor is historical evidence all that much help. The absence of a prolonged tight monetary squeeze in the U.K. makes it difficult to infer whether this would bring down inflation. A continuous tight incomes policy has never been tried either, and the relatively small gains from previous rather short-lived incomes policies may reflect inevitable lack of success as the New Cambridge school implies, or just that their form was wrong or that there was insufficient preliminary bargaining beforehand on their terms and on other government policies then in operation to ensure their acceptance. Even the rather rapid decline in inflation in the later part of 1975 may be attributed to the £6 a week incomes policy, to the record levels of unemployment, to the previously tighter control of the money supply, or to the reduction in the rate of inflation of import (especially raw material) prices.

Perhaps the nearest to a generally agreed conclusion would be as follows. The present strategy can *only* succeed if three conditions are met: (i) the Government continues to adhere to a four-year time horizon for achieving internal and external balance, (ii) a tight incomes policy is maintained and adhered to, (iii) investment and exports grow as fast as current Government forecasts indicate they will. In this case the public sector deficit would be largely removed, with the 'full employment' financial balance in surplus, inflation would be largely eliminated also, and in these circumstances the growth of the money supply would on all three approaches come into line in broad terms with the real rate of growth of output. The failure of the conditions to be met would result in either the need for import controls or in continuing high unemployment and inflation in proportions dependent on the monetary and fiscal policy adopted by the Government, and a continuation of the balance of payments problems, falling exchange rate, and low growth, which have characterized the recent performance of the economic system in the U.K.

Index